Beauty, Health, and Permanence

STUDIES IN ENVIRONMENT AND HISTORY

EDITORS
Donald Worster   *Brandeis University*
Alfred Crosby   *University of Texas at Austin*

ADVISORY BOARD
Reid Bryson   *Institute for Environmental Studies, University of Wisconsin*
Raymond Dasmann   *College Eight, University of California, Santa Cruz*
E. Le Roy Ladurie   *Collège de France*
William McNeill   *Department of History, Chicago*
Carolyn Merchant   *College of Natural Resources, University of California, Berkeley*
Thad Tate   *Institute of Early American History and Culture, College of William and Mary*

Beauty, Health, and Permanence

Environmental Politics in
the United States, 1955–1985

Samuel P. Hays

University of Pittsburgh

in collaboration with
Barbara D. Hays

The right of the
University of Cambridge
to print and sell
all manner of books
was granted by
Henry VIII in 1534.
The University has printed
and published continuously
since 1584.

Cambridge University Press

Cambridge
New York   New Rochelle
Melbourne   Sydney

Published by the Press Syndicate of the University of Cambridge
The Pitt Building, Trumpington Street, Cambridge CB2 1RP
32 East 57th Street, New York, NY 10022, USA
10 Stamford Road, Oakleigh, Melbourne 3166, Australia

First published 1987

Printed in the United States of America

Library of Congress Cataloging-in-Publication Data
Hays, Samuel P.
Beauty, health, and permanence.
(Studies in environment and history)
Bibliography: p.
Includes index.
1. Environmental policy – United States – History.
2. Environmental protection – United States – History.
I. Hays, Barbara D. II. Title. III. Series.
HC110.E5H39   1987   363.7'0525'0973   86–18784

British Library Cataloguing in Publication Data
Hays, Samuel P.
Beauty, health, and permanence: environmental politics in the United States,
1955–1985. – (Studies in environment
and history)
1. Environmental policy – United States
– History – 20th century
I. Title II. Hays, Barbara D.   III. Series
333.7'0973   HC110.E5

ISBN 0 521 32428 9

Illustrations by Michael Hays

FOR PETER, POLLY, MIKE, AND BECKY

Contents

Preface

This book is intended for a variety of audiences. The largest is composed of those who maintain an active interest in environmental affairs. They number in the millions. But usually they are preoccupied with a limited environmental task and find it difficult to grasp the wider range of environmental matters that are extensive, diffuse, and beyond immediate experience. For this group of readers I hope the book will provide some insight into the wider social, economic, and political ramifications of environmental affairs, and give meaning to smaller and more limited actions. With no little presumption, I assume that the integrative predispositions of a historian can be of some value in thinking about the meaning of piecemeal ideas and action.

I hope this sense of perspective will be of special value to those engaged in political confrontation over environmental issues. Most such participants, both advocates of environmental objectives and those who oppose them, become preoccupied with the crises of the moment, which usually precludes time and energy for reflection. For those who can enjoy the luxury of observing rather than only participating, the meaning of the events in such close encounters often is quite different. While antagonists have been engaging in highly charged combat, they also have been creating a new society, a new economy, and a new polity, which a historian, at greater distance, might be able to observe and understand more clearly. If such larger meaning could influence, even slightly, the quality of contemporary debate, this book will have served its purpose.

There is a special message here for decision makers and associated professionals – scientists, economists, and planners. They are actors, too, for whom a major task is to formulate a rationale and justification for making pressing decisions. After their tours of duty such experts often write about their experiences as public servants. But invariably they merely transfer the way they saw the world as administrators into retrospective reflection. As a historian I have been struck by the degree to which such records, used as historical materials, must be modified drastically in the light of a larger perspective beyond the decision maker and divorced from the imperatives of decision making.

This book is an attempt to make such modifications closer to the time decisions take place and before they distort the historical record. I do not expect much agreement from the managerial and technical experts at the center of decision making with my attempt to place their behavior in the context of circumstance, for this is a challenge to their self-images as searchers for "truth" and the "best policy." Such views sustain their ability to act effectively. Yet the observer, in contrast with the actor, must attempt to view such decision makers in a wider frame, and I do so here. That strategy is a major part of the historical perspective for which this book makes a claim.

To historians there is a still different message. Many will be tempted to view this book as an example of "environmental history," just as my earlier book on the history of conservation between 1890 and 1920 was thought of as a part of "conservation history." For me, however, the contribution of the following pages lies far more in an attempt to understand the broader relationship between society and politics than in environmental history as such. I make a special effort to chronicle social change since World War II and to identify environmental affairs as a part of that. I seek also to chart changes in how the United States is governed. Hence the book is about much more than simply environmental affairs. It is about social change and governance in America as analyzed through the role of these emerging public values and objectives. The relationship between society and politics in the American past has become an important preoccupation of American historians. Although much of their debate arises out of concern for the nineteenth century, it is hoped that this treatment of very recent history will extend the range of that debate and provide some clues as to how social and political change interact.

This larger historical perspective can also further an emerging public debate about the differences between environmental regulation in Western Europe and in the United States. Comparative works have demonstrated that the American governing system is more open, with higher levels of citizen participation, more vigorous scientific enterprise and debate, and administration and courts in which the public plays a far more extensive role than it does in Western Europe. This book sustains that description of the American governing system as it pertains to environmental affairs.

Yet these works have two peculiar twists. One is skepticism, even hostility, toward the more open and participatory political system in the United States and a greater admiration for the more closed and "efficient" modes of decision making in Europe. The penchant among many writers for normative analysis greatly reduces the effectiveness and accuracy of their observations, to which I hope this book provides a corrective. Even more significantly, however, these works make clear the limitations of contemporary policy analysis that is not informed by an understanding of the deep roots of institutional development that underlie the divergence in the relationships between citizens and the state in Western Europe and the United States. There is a significant problem in historical analysis here: Why is it that two regions of the world, which at one level of analysis are similar in their governing systems, at a deeper level are very different? The contemporary policy analyses can only state the problem; a historical perspective is required to understand its ramifications and its origin.

Finally, I hope this example of contemporary history will provide for Americans generally an example of the way in which historical perspective can provide insight into current events that goes beyond the coercive effect of sensational day-to-day accounts. Some larger context, with an appropriate degree of firmness, is required through which to filter episodes so as to escape their emotional power to dominate our lives. History cannot play this role simply by providing past examples of present events, which convey the sense that what happens today merely continues the past. On the contrary, as I argue in later pages with respect to the discontinuity between the earlier conservation and the later environmental stages of history, often the greatest insight of the historian lies in providing a sensible account of how one period of time differs from another.

The key to understanding the contemporary world is the ability to sort out the persistent from the changing. The sense of the persistent enables one to withstand the oft repeated argument that the drama of the moment hides vast and revolutionary meaning in events, which every massager of episodes and ideas seeks to convey. The sense of change enables one to understand the constant tendency in America of social, economic, and political forces to sweep away the past and create the new. Such a historical perspective has shaped this book. Perhaps a different mode of observing the present through sensitivity to the long-run balance between continuity and change can spill over from the case of environmental issues to larger realms of public affairs.

These thoughts rightly convey to the reader the notion that a brief set of acknowledgments cannot do justice to all those who have played a part in formulating the larger ideas that have gone into the following pages. I can only give passing reference to students, colleagues, and friends who have sparked ideas for more than three decades and influenced the historical perspective implicit in what I have said here. More specific acknowledgment is in order for those who have helped shape the content of the book.

Especially important was a group at the Woodrow Wilson International Center for Scholars, where I held a fellowship during the 1978–9 academic year as one of four fellows and two staff members with environmental interests: Dan Botkin, Mike Lacey, Denton Morrison, Walter Rosenbaum, and Al Runte. A considerable amount of the research on the 1960s was done during that year, but even more useful was the constant conversation among this group from a variety of academic fields but with a focused interest in environmental affairs. Equally important were the discussions with speakers the group invited to the center to talk about common interests. Terry Davies, Jerry Franklin, Tom Jorling, and Robert Mitchell were among them; I am sure I have left out others who should be included. I am grateful to the Wilson Center for making all this possible.

A number of people have contributed much through interviews and discussions. Among them I note here William Eichbaum, Brock

Evans, Carl Holcomb, Leon Minckler, Herbert Needleman, and Joel Tarr. I am especially grateful to J. Michael McCloskey for reading the entire manuscript and making valuable contributions from his long tenure as executive director of the Sierra Club. Few people besides him span in their personal experience in environmental affairs the entire range of years covered by this book. During a year in England in 1982–3 I was able to discuss at some length the American environmental scene, in comparison with the British, with several knowledgeable about both: Philip Lowe, Ann and Malcolm MacEwen, and Timothy O'Riordan.

Even more of the course of the argument in the book has been shaped by conversations with Barbara Hays. Some of the research, especially that dealing with pesticide policy and acid rain, was hers. Much of the material relating to biology, ecology, and wastewater treatment was informed by her knowledge, which is far greater than mine. Continual discussions throughout the fifteen years in which the chapters were developing made it difficult to sort out what is mine and what is hers. On backpacking trips in the Bridger-Teton National Forest and on Isle Royale; on visits to national parks and nature centers in Western Europe and England, as well as the United States; in conferences jointly attended in both the United States and Europe; and in reviewing a wide range of magazines, journals, newspapers, and newsletters, we debated from all angles the meaning of what we heard, saw, and read. Barbara read and reread the manuscript more times than either of us cares to recall and each time added new facts, ideas, and perspectives. The word "collaboration" on the title page means far more than meets the eye.

Several noteworthy academic and professional experiences have been helpful. One was a week-long visit to Oberlin College, where I taught a short course in recent environmental history to about thirty alert and exciting students; I am grateful to Clayton Koppes for that opportunity. Another was a conference on environmental history, sparked by Kendall Bailes, at the University of California at Irvine, in January 1982, at which the first statement of the argument in this book was presented and debated. Still another was a conference on environmental history in June 1984 organized by Mike Lacey at the Wilson Center, at which a more extended version was presented. Finally, much of the book was shaped through a course in environmental politics I taught for ten years at the University of Pittsburgh.

A considerable proportion of the book also comes from being a participant observer of current environmental affairs. This has several dimensions. One is my penchant for acquiring material as it is produced and thereby collecting documentary sources that tend to disappear quickly. I began this in 1970. The range of such materials is readily apparent in the notes. On several occasions I asked participants in critical meetings or events to write their accounts of what went on. I recount all this with the notion that the current vogue of creating historical records in the form of oral history could well be expanded by historians to acquire contemporary documents for their own work and make them available for future historical research.

I have also recorded my own experiences in environmental decision making in state and national legislative and administrative arenas. Administrative politics constitutes a major part of this book primarily because of my direct participant and observer's role in it as a commentator on policy on some fifty occasions. Each session provided evidence to observe as well as an opportunity to shape decisions. My fascination with administrative politics is informed by both academic treatment as reflected in my earlier book on conservation history and by personal involvement in such matters since 1970, mostly as a representative of the Pennsylvania chapter of the Sierra Club.

Such experiences have been especially helpful in identifying the meaning and significance of seemingly mundane administrative issues that are rarely reported in the media and hence often escape observers. To most, the debates over cost-benefit analysis, the level of blood lead concentrations considered potentially harmful, and the comparative net present value of recreation and wood production in the national forests are esoteric and remote; to participants in administrative politics, they are the critical points of political debate and choice. To observe while participating has been especially helpful in identifying the significance of these environmental controversies.

As a participant in environmental conferences in Pennsylvania and Wisconsin; Alabama, Virginia, and Wyoming; Washington

State and Washington, D.C.; England and Germany – on such diverse subjects as management of state and national forests, the policies of the Bureau of Land Management, water quality and air quality, workplace "right to know," water-development projects, and national-park affairs – I have had opportunities to discuss many environmental subjects with a great number of people. The contribution of each to my thinking has often been small, but cumulatively it has been significant. Because they have been so many, and because I have forgotten to record them all, they will remain anonymous. I would like, however, to mention discussions with Paul Pritchard and the staff and board members of the National Parks and Conservation Association, where I have served on the board of directors for several years; they have sharpened considerably my knowledge about the problems of the national parks.

I am especially grateful for the keen and sympathetic eye of editor Frank Smith of Cambridge University Press, and for the review of the manuscript by Donald Worster.

Finally, I am extremely pleased with the contribution of Michael Hays to the book in the form of the line drawings. They add a much appreciated personal as well as a substantive dimension.

SAMUEL P. HAYS

Introduction: Environmental Politics – the New and the Old

During the past two decades environmental affairs have sparked a wealth of political and governmental action. The ensuing debate has produced a massive historical record – books and articles, polemical arguments and scholarly accounts, day-by-day reports and intensive investigative journalism, newsletters and governmental records. Environmental science has generated new knowledge in fields ranging from human health to ecology, biogeochemistry to landscape architecture, the sociology and psychology of public values to the behavior of scientists and environmental managers. It is the task of this book to bring all these matters together in an integrative context in which the diverse pieces of environmental affairs might be understood as a whole.

What I encourage in the following chapters is some reflection on environmental events to understand them, even with fascination and excitement, as part of the process of history. Here is a panorama of human energy and effort, of aspiration and achievement, of deep controversy as values, policies, and programs clash. One cannot probe far into these events without confronting deeply rooted human values at work and conflicts that go far beyond merely casual matters of public affairs. My aim here is to observe environmental objectives and the resulting controversies in which they became entwined as a significant part of post–World War II America.

For the majority of readers, accustomed to environmental writings that work out policy alternatives, it seems appropriate to give more than passing emphasis to the book's focus on politics rather than policy. Most people involved in environmental affairs are deeply absorbed with decision making. Some are active environmentalists seeking new directions; others are equally active opponents seeking to hold back the tide. Legislators, administrators, and judges are also decision makers, preoccupied with the task of resolving differing demands. All of these people are concerned with policy options. They organize the ideas and details of environmental affairs around the task of defining problems and shaping policies to cope with them.

Here I have chosen not to follow the lines of organization in ideas and action growing out of such a policy perspective. My object is not to aid those who make policy choices but rather to understand the entire realm of environmental affairs including citizens and policy makers as people who also must be subjected to careful scrutiny. Each thinks and works within a limited realm of experience; the scientist and the manager, the economist and the planner, as well as the citizen interested in wilderness or toxic-waste dumps – each has a peculiar experience and way of looking at the world. Each must be captured in his or her own situation in order to observe and understand ideas and choices, strategies and action. Some might get from this book a sense of the sociology of history. For my focus is on people amid circumstance who think and act out of the particular world they perceive and seek to shape.

Hence the emphasis on politics. Whereas policy seeks to shape options for choice, politics seeks to understand all those who shape options and choices. In history we can examine that political setting as it evolves and changes over long periods of time. Environmental affairs energized distinctive personal and public values that differed markedly from those of an earlier time, even from the years of the New Deal a half century ago. As they work themselves from society into politics, social changes become political changes. New public demands arise, new scientific knowledge and new technologies, new modes of political involvement and expression.

The historian comes onto this scene to observe the interplay among those varied factors as older ones yield to newer ones, as some succeed in shaping the larger world of public affairs and others fail, as the way some who try to define the nation's fate win out and others fall by the wayside.

The Transformation of Values

Environmental concerns were rooted in the vast social changes that took place in the United States after World War II. Although some beginnings can be identified in earlier years, only after the war did they become widely shared social phenomena. Although there is some interest in the following chapters in those past events, there is more emphasis on environmental affairs as a part of more recent social change. The expansion of this interest brought it to the forefront of public life. This began with a rapid growth in outdoor recreation in the 1950s, extended into the wider field of the protection of natural environments, then became infused with attempts to cope with air and water pollution and still later with toxic chemical pollutants. Such activity was hardly extensive prior to World War II; afterward it was a major public concern.

Two observations help to identify the historical timing of the environmental concern. One is the transition from an older stress on efficient development and use of material resources such as water, forests, and soils known as the conservation movement, which took place in the first four decades of the twentieth century. Conservation gave way to environment after World War II amid a rising interest in the quality of life beyond efficiency in production. The two tendencies often came into conflict as resources long thought of as important for their material commodities came to be prized for their aesthetic and amenity uses. Rivers, forests, wetlands, and deserts were seen as valuable in their natural state as part of a modern standard of living; it was maintained that some such areas should be left undeveloped and undisturbed. This preposterous notion was difficult if not impossible to accept to those whose preferences were rooted in an older time. Many clashes between older commodity and newer environmental values occurred in the Environmental Era. World War II is a convenient dividing line between the old and the new values.

Evolving environmental values were closely associated with rising standards of living and levels of education. These changed markedly after the war. Personal real income grew and the percentage of Americans with college education increased. The social context within which environmental values flourished was twofold: younger people and the more educated. With each level of age from younger to older, environmental interest fell; and with each level of education from elementary school to college degree, it rose. The advancing edge of demographic change included an advancing interest in environmental objectives. Quality of life as an idea and a focus of public action lay at the heart of what was new in American society and politics; environmental affairs were an integral element.

Several aspects of these changes are worth keeping in mind throughout the following chapters. One is that they can be thought of as part of a history of consumption rather than of the history of production. They arose not out of the way in which people carried out an occupation and earned income, but out of the kind of life that income made possible and the ways in which people chose to express their new standards of living.

At one time income was spent largely to purchase necessities, and in the third decade of the twentieth century that was extended to the capacity to acquire conveniences that lightened the tasks of normal living. But with rising incomes something beyond necessities and conveniences now lay within the reach of many; they can be called amenities. Associated with home and leisure, with recreation and the "good life," these came to involve considerable choice because spending was not dictated by necessity or convenience. A general direction to the new opportunities emerged that came to be described as quality of life. Sales analysts in private business were particularly attuned to such changes as they identified diverse markets to be supplied with new goods and services. Environmental quality was an integral part of this new search for a higher standard of living.

These changes did not come to all sectors of American society in the same degree or at the same time. There were the older and the newer, those adhering to previously dominant values and those searching out more recently emerging ones. Although age was often the dividing line, there were also geographical variations. New England and the Pacific Coast were among the leading sectors of change, whereas the South moved much more slowly. In between were the Mountain West and the Midwest. These regional differences could be identified in many realms of new cultural values from the changing role of women to self-expression to environmental interests.

Several writers have attempted to analyze the social roots of environmental affairs in a more limited fashion. They emphasize factors on the periphery of American society rather than central to it, or the capacity of a few leaders of environmental organizations to manipulate the attitudes of their members or the public so as to create imaginary problems.

All this seems rather complex and contrived; public interest in environmental affairs is far simpler. It stems from a desire to improve personal, family, and community life. The desires are neither ephemeral nor erratic; they are evident in many nations, first in the advanced industrial and consumer societies and then in more recent years in those of middle and even earlier stages of development. They express human wants and needs as surely as do demands for better housing, more satisfying leisure and recreation, improved household furnishings, better health, and a greater sense of well-being. We customarily associate these with human "progress," which normally is accepted as a fundamental concern unnecessary to explain away in other terms. An interest in the environmental quality of life is to be understood simply as an integral part of the drives inherent in persistent human aspiration and achievement.

The Environmental Experts

We shall also deal with another set of actors in environmental politics: the experts, the professionally trained scientists, engineers, planners, and economists, and the equally highly trained managers and administrators who play important roles in public decisions. The distinctive values and objectives, the peculiar social and political roles of these people are also part of the environmental drama.

Experts are normally thought of as standing apart from the realm of politics. Empirical professionals and managers differ markedly in their roles from those who either make laws or mobilize public calls for legislative action. They seek only to determine the facts about an objective world and then to apply them. Often public controversy tends to place the demands of politics against the demands of apolitical scientific and technical knowledge. We reserve a different mode of analysis for the role of the technical professional and the manager than for the public leader who pursues the profession of politics.

Study of environmental controversy, however, soon shows that this formula is far from adequate. For if environmental politics has revealed anything, it is the politics of controversy within science, within economics, within planning, and within management. Technical matters are laden with dispute over what problems are to be chosen for attention, how they will be examined, and how to assess the available knowledge.

Every decision maker in government – the legislature, the agencies, the executive, and the courts – is faced with disagreement among the experts. Testifying for one side is an expert who argues that low-level exposures to lead have a detrimental effect on the intelligence test scores of children. Another, equally well qualified, argues that they do not. Whose judgment to accept? The world of environmental controversy is rife with such disagreements among the experts. They are as basic to environmental politics as the controversies between those who look on forests as a source of wood and those who view them as a place for aesthetic enjoyment.

It is tempting to approach the disputes among technical professionals by trying to determine who is closer to "the truth." I shall try to steer clear of such a task. For, as indicated earlier, this is not a book about policy options with a conclusion about which policy is best but, rather, a study of disagreement as a matter to be observed and understood. Environmental politics includes the politics of science, planning, economic analysis, and management, each with its own internal dynamic. We shall avoid attempts to determine who has the "truth" but instead shall seek to understand the peculiar values, experiences, objectives, and political roles of each of these groups of technical and professional experts.

Controversies among experts in environmental affairs focus on management. Environmental policy becomes incorporated into management of land and water resources on the one hand and pollution on the other. Such activities are often thought of simply as the means by which legislative decisions are implemented. Legislators enact laws; managers as administrators carry them out. Hence lawmaking is often thought of as political; administration, as apolitical.

But close scrutiny of administration reveals quite another set of circumstances. For choices are made here that are as fundamental as those made in the legislature. As soon as a law is passed the political actors shift their focus of attention from Congress to the agency. In this new arena they seek to fight through the controversies all over again. Those who sought to achieve a social objective through the law hope that administration will maintain and advance that goal. But their opponents hope that through administration the impact of the law can be reduced. In this way administration becomes the focal point of fierce controversy. To those in contention decisions here are considered to be more vital because they are more final. Although Congress and the courts set some limits to administrative action, within those limits enormous consequences are at stake. Administration in the United States is the primary governmental institution of political choice.

In this process the technical experts – the scientists, engineers, planners, and economists – become major participants in political controversy. Managers gather such experts around them to provide advice. That advice underpins administrative choice. One economic or scientific assessment or prediction of the future undergirds one option; another set of conclusions supports another. The actors in the wider political scene, the proenvironmentalists and the antienvironmentalists, fashion their weapons through their own experts. The manager then becomes the focal point of choice of the technical analysis that underpins the policy choice. In this way the internal politics of science, economics, and planning becomes closely entwined with public choice. The two are intimately related in environmental politics, and in the pages to follow I subject that relationship to considerable scrutiny.

The Environmental Experience

These two social contexts, that of widely shared environmental values on the one hand and professional experts on the other, engender two quite different modes of organizing the subject of environmental politics. Policy debate, the world of the professional expert, involves an emphasis on topical specialization along lines of separate problems, each of which requires detailed knowledge. The pattern is most obvious in the specialities in which technical professionals are organized, such as in air or water pollution, energy, endangered species, or landscape design.

Administration takes on a similar pattern of distinctive expertise. Legislative bodies develop their own specialized subcommittees, each entailing specialization of experts. And environmental organizations tend to work along similar lines, in some cases giving rise to groups emphasizing a given area of policy, in others bringing together several different specialists with different concerns. As political analysts have often observed, much of the political world is organized in "iron triangles," in which experts of similar specialization in the legislature, the agencies, and the interest groups develop close relationships with one another and through their own interaction heavily influence policy.

But environmental affairs in society at large take on quite a different character. They stem from the circumstances of daily life, not from those shaped by technical specialization. People live and work in given places, and the character of those places defines whether an environment is attractive or degraded, healthful or dangerous, acceptable or unacceptable. What are defined as problems arise from those settings and are solved or not in terms of changes in those environments of personal meaning. These contexts of human experience are the beginning point in understanding what environmental affairs are all about.

We can identify the city, the wildlands, and the countryside as three distinct environments of perception and experience, from which distinct ideas and action flow. What the "environment" means to people in one setting differs considerably from what it means in another. The experience of air quality in the urban context differs markedly from experience of it in the wildlands or countryside. Hence the attempt to root environmental ideas and action in circumstance starts out with a strategy to distinguish systematically between circumstances. City, wildlands, and countryside are important organizing principles for examining the political sociology of environmental ideas and action; they will be used extensively in the chapters to come.

Environmental experience and perception in some cases went beyond these limited contexts to more extensive ones. The experience of chemical hazard, while arising often in particular places, generated the perception of a chemical universe surrounding human life. A set of general perceptions about chemicals emerged: They persist through time; they are transported through air and water over vast areas; they change in concentration as they move through the food chain; they remain undetected until they unexpectedly crop up in one's immediate environment. And infusing this broad understanding was the perception that the entire process was not under effective human control. Even the first step in control – knowledge – was so limited that intelligent action was often impossible.

Whereas the world of environmental experience and action amid the general public was shaped by the geographical context in which people live, the world of environmental expertise was shaped by thought and professional organizations dominated by the specialization of knowledge. That experience was derived not from where one lived and worked but from specialized training and ability that tended to establish personal ties with others of similar specialized knowledge to create many but different and separate worlds of expertise. These varied worlds were often divorced from one another, generating differences in perception and action, and coordinated only through management.

Here was a fractured world of specialized endeavor, relatively cut off from public experience, deeply rooted in the experience and culture of expertise. This perspective imposed on environmental affairs a distinctive analysis shared by the environmental experts rather than by the public at large. In our own day environmental affairs have evolved so that the expert thinks of the political context as one of "us" and "them," of the knowledgeable and rational experts and the uninformed and emotional public.

In many cases the organization of the ensuing political struggle took the form of one set of perspectives based on the occurrences of daily life in distinctive geographical settings in contest with another set of perspectives arising out of professional expertise. That is the focus of much of the drama described in this book.

But in a number of realms the course of environmental politics has been dominated more by professionals than by the public. This is especially true of those large problems concerning the balance between population and resources. On only a few occasions have these issues aroused the wider public. Only when such broadly conceived problems have some immediate personal connection to daily life, such as the cost of energy to the consumer or decisions about family size, do these questions stir personal emotion. In most such issues the lead was taken by technical professionals who imposed their specialized organization of expertise with little challenge from the larger public.

The Ramifications of Environmental Politics

Beyond the growth of environmental concern in the society at large and the different ways in which the environmental world was organized, viewed, and expressed by the public and by technical specialists, I emphasize four dimensions of environmental politics.

One pertains to the thought and ideology implicit, often half expressed but rarely fully developed, in the drive for environmental objectives. Environmental affairs have provoked much action but little focused reflection. The most extensive was the rationale for decentralization in the organization of institutions. Yet this notion was quite limited in the degree to which it expressed the range of ideas implicit in environmental values and action.

Those ideas mirror: deep commitments to scientific and technological endeavor but equally strong notions about the direction these activities should take; preference for modes of economic analysis that bring end-use consumption more in balance with production and reflect the realities of the advanced consumer society; ideas about the course of history that identify innovation and response to innovation as integral to the social, economic, and demographic changes in the United States since World War II; and alternatives in ways of living and new modes of social equity that evolve from older ones. I shall attempt to make explicit these ideas and ideologies that are usually implicit in action.

A second theme is the development of a coherent antienvironmental movement that sought to restrain environmental action. Opposition to environmental objectives has been continuous and intense. It evolved from separate and at times sporadic reactions into a more integrated and coherent opposition. That opposition was persistent, profound, and effective. It succeeded in turning back, muting, restraining many an environmental effort. Its general strategy was that of maximum feasible opposition and minimum feasible retreat. Its fortunes ebbed and flowed over the years, depending on circumstances. I am as interested in identifying its various ingredients, its successes and failures, as I am in environmental concern itself.

Third, I shall examine this drama of change and response within two broad contexts. The first is the varying circumstance of scale in human affairs, from national to state to local. Environmental politics, like so much of our public life and history, is most often thought about in terms of national affairs of state. The national media and the national documents in the historical record often persuade the observer to focus on national affairs simply because it is the easiest path. Fifty different realms of action in fifty different states, and more at the local level, are much more difficult to pursue than is one in the nation's capital, which is in itself a mighty subject to examine.

But there are many realms of human affairs, of issues and action, of government and politics at the local and state as well as the national level. Happenings in one cannot be taken as a reflection of happenings in another. Effective analysis requires that each level be examined separately and then brought together in some manner faithful to the way that interaction works out in practice. I do not profess to have a firm grasp on the environmental affairs of all fifty states. But I have sought out detailed knowledge of a sufficient number to provide some sense of the different levels of environmental politics and their interaction. These patterns will constitute the subject of several chapters.

At the same time there are the formal governmental institutions in which environmental action and antienvironmental response is played out. These include the legislature, the agencies, and the courts, described by the phrase "separation of powers," and the levels of government from federal to state to local, described at least partially by the word "federalism." Although it is customary to sort these by their different functions in an integrated system, here I shall treat each as a distinct focus for political controversy. Advocates and opponents of environmental objectives formed around each point of decision making. Some players in the political drama sought to have decisions made by one body rather than another, at one level in the hierarchy of government than at another. Where a decision was made in this range of institutions strongly affected that decision. Several chapters of the book are devoted to this comparative analysis.

Finally, this study of recent environmental politics seeks to identify long-term changes in the United States and responses to them. History subsumes the evolution of values and institutions, in the ways in which people think, behave, and make choices, in organized efforts to express common concerns. Historians seek to identify what emerges as new over the course of time, as well as the way in which the old either is transformed or is not changed by the new. Through stages of the past a series of such changes takes place with transitions from one pattern to another.

American society since World War II has been marked by such a new period of change and response. In most previous eras of American history, sequences in the mode of production have been dominant, whereas the postmanufacturing society of recent times has involved an equally significant change in modes of consumption. New human values associated with what people want mark the advanced consumer society that now shares a role equal with the advanced society of information production. How this emerged in the field of environmental politics, with the full complex tension between the new and the old, is the theme of this book.

1 From Conservation to Environment

Accounts of the rise of environmentalism frequently have empha-sized its roots in the conservation movement of the early twen-tieth century. But environmental differed markedly from conser-vation affairs. The conservation movement was an effort on the part of leaders in science, technology, and government to bring about more efficient development of physical resources. The en-vironmental movement, on the other hand, was far more wide-spread and popular, involving public values that stressed the quality of human experience and hence of the human environment. Conservation was an aspect of the history of production that stressed efficiency, whereas environment was a part of the his-tory of consumption that stressed new aspects of the American standard of living.[1]

Environmental objectives arose out of deep-seated changes in preferences and values associated with the massive social and economic transformation in the decades after 1945. Conserva-tion had stirred technical and political leaders and then worked its way down from the top of the political order, but environmental concerns arose later from a broader base and worked their way from the middle levels of society outward, constantly to press upon a reluctant leadership. Many of the tendencies in efficient management of material resources originating in the conserva-

13

tion era came into sharp conflict with newer environmental objectives. The two sets of values were continually at loggerheads.

At the outset we explore this discontinuity between conservation and environment, this transformation of aim from efficient production to better quality of life, in order to define the historical distinctiveness of environmental affairs.

River Development

The first clear notion about conservation as more efficient resource use developed in connection with water in the West. As settlement proceeded, water limited farming and urban development. It was not so much that water was scarce as that rainfall came unevenly throughout the year and winter snow melted quickly in the spring. Such patterns did not conform to the seasonal uses of agriculture on the more sustained needs of city dwellers.

How to conserve water? The initial thought was to construct reservoirs to hold rain and snowmelt for use later in the year. Cities began to build storage for urban water supply much as in the East. But for irrigated farmland larger engineering works were needed. The Newlands Act, which Congress passed in 1902, provided for a reclamation fund from the proceeds of the sale of western public lands that would finance irrigation works. By World War II vast projects included plans for a series of dams on the Missouri and the Colorado as well as other western rivers.[2]

Schemes to conserve water for irrigation soon came to encompass more extensive notions about the construction of large engineering works to control the flow of entire river basins. Hydroelectric power was built into irrigation dams, fulfilling two purposes at once. In the East the idea arose that floods could be controlled by means of reservoirs to hold back the flow of snowmelt or excessive rainfall; the water could then be released later when river levels had subsided. The flow could also facilitate navigation. By 1926 Congress had granted the U.S. Army Corps of Engineers, which had long been responsible for navigation works, authority to conduct full-scale studies for flood-control projects throughout the nation, and by the 1930s that agency was ready to proceed with construction. The most ambitious example of "multipurpose" river development was the Tennessee Valley Authority, established in 1933, which constructed engineering works to control the entire flow of the Tennessee and Cumberland rivers.[3]

The spirit of intensive management, born in these projects, was extended to rivers in other sections of the nation. As projects of lesser cost and scale were completed, the agencies moved on to those of greater and more extensive water transfer. Although the initial projects emphasized the main stems of the larger rivers, the drive to control water expanded steadily into the headwaters to include the flow of entire river basins. By the end of World War II, multipurpose river development was extending its influence to wider and wider realms of action. And it ran headlong into conflict with newer environmental interests that began to emphasize the importance of free-flowing streams unmodified by large engineering structures.[4]

Sustained-Yield Forestry

The spirit of large-scale management for efficient resource development also pervaded the early forestry movement. Concern for the depletion of the nation's wood supplies grew steadily in the last quarter of the nineteenth century. Cutover lands in the East, which took on the appearance of wastelands, deeply influenced public opinion. And their social impact was massive. Towns, jobs, and governments based on the lumber industry boomed, but when the supply of timber was gone they collapsed. Local governments found their tax base depleted as lands were abandoned and became tax delinquent. All this provided fertile ground for the concept of a balance between cutting and growth that would provide a continuous supply of timber and a reliable foundation for local economies.[5]

Far less dramatic in its impact on the general public, but more persuasive to scientists, was the marked decline in forested areas resulting from land clearing as settlers moved west. This could be measured in the growing proportion of land that was classified as improved or cleared farmland. For the nation as a whole this stood at 5.8 percent in 1850 but rose to 14.7 percent in 1880 and 21.4 percent in 1900. But nationwide statistics did not reflect changes in specific regions. In the North Central states the corresponding figures for the three dates for Ohio were 37.3, 68.5, and 73.0 percent; for Illinois, 14, 72.3, and 76.7 percent; and for Iowa, 2.3, 29.89, and 69.5 percent. The best account of this change was recorded in Ohio, which became so concerned with its declining forestland that it conducted an extensive survey of the problem. Scientists of the American Association for the Advancement of Science drew on this study for their recommendations from the 1870s onward that public action be taken to establish public forest reserves.[6]

Amid experiences such as these a number of individuals and organizations pressed for innovations in forestland management. Foremost among these was Gifford Pinchot, who in 1905 became the first chief forester of the U.S. Forest Service. Congress in 1891 had enacted legislation that permitted the president by executive order to establish national forest reserves that would be retained permanently in public ownership as protected forestlands rather than be sold to private individuals. By 1907 Presidents Harrison, Cleveland, McKinley, and Roosevelt had established 150 million acres of timberland in the West as national forests.[7]

The western demand for national forests came primarily from those who wished to protect water supplies for agricultural irrigation and urban use. Reserves were often demanded to restrict cattle and sheep grazing, which was thought to cause severe soil erosion and to endanger water supplies. Accustomed to extensive use of rangelands within the forests, livestock owners fought to keep them open. In the ensuing battle, Pinchot permitted controlled grazing to protect himself from the political wrath of the grazers. Irrigators and cities, on the other hand, supported restricted grazing to conserve water supplies; they provided the key support that kept the national forests from being transferred to the states.[8]

The first national forests were established in the West on federal lands. Demand arose for similar forests in the East, where most land was privately owned and public forests would have to be purchased rather than simply reserved from sale. Federal action came with the Weeks Act of 1911, which authorized federal acquisition. The opportunity for purchase became real in the 1920s and 1930s as formerly cutover lands proved marginal for farming and were abandoned. The private forest industry supported federal acquisition in order to remove these lands from competition with its own enterprise. By the 1970s 25 million acres had been incorporated into thirty-four eastern national forests.[9]

The major theme of forest management was "scientific forestry." This involved reforestation of cutover lands, protection from fire, and a balance of annual cut with annual growth, to produce a continuous supply of wood – known as sustained-yield forest management. Over the years foresters improved techniques for measuring yield and cut and for controlling both through a regulatory process that shaped more precisely the flow of growth and harvest.

The economic value of wood production was emphasized above all else. Pinchot was firm in his view that forestry could be promoted in the United States only if it could be profitable through the sale of wood. This spirit continued over the years through the more intensive application of science, technology, and capital to the production of more wood per acre. But this direction also ran counter to new values that were emerging in the American public as the meaning of forestland began to change. Forests were increasingly viewed as environments, aesthetic resources that provided amenities and enhanced daily life, rather than as simply sources of commodities.

Soil Conservation

Water and forest conservation emerged in the late nineteenth century and evolved steadily throughout the first half of the twentieth, but interest in soil conservation developed at a later time. In the 1920s a number of writers warned of the severe long-term problems confronting the nation because of the persistent erosion of productive croplands. Soil that had taken thousands of years to build up now was being lost by destructive farming practices. The future food supply was seriously threatened.[10]

These claims could be documented impressively. The amount of soil loss from the nation's croplands reached millions of tons a year. During the 1930s examples of soil erosion by water were augmented by the even more dramatic case of wind erosion in the "Dust Bowl" of the Great Plains. Crops withered and died. The dust swirled high into the air, creating huge clouds of airborne soil that blackened the sky and generated dust storms that traveled hundreds of miles, mute testimony to the rest of the nation as to the effects of farming practices.[11]

Hugh Hammond Bennett played the role of prophet and politician for soil conservation as Gifford Pinchot had for forestry. He advocated a program to educate farmers and persuade them to change their practices, a strategy akin to the long-standing emphasis in the agricultural extension service. Led by the Soil Conservation Service (SCS), established in 1935, farmers organized soil-conservation districts to fight erosion under the guidance of agency experts. SCS officials mapped farm soils, suggested crops and cultivation patterns appropriate for each portion of a farm, and provided continual guidance. Farmers were paid to take up approved soil-conserving practices.[12]

The results were dramatic. Crops formerly planted up and down the hillside without regard for the terrain were now planted to contour, around the slope, to reduce the force of erosion. Over the years the soil conservation program was seen as a successful example of federal action to cope with a major economic problem.[13]

In the 1950s soil conservation took a new twist and emphasized the enhancement of land for greater productivity. Cooperating farm districts were given funds to construct reservoirs on smaller upland streams to provide benefits similar to those of large reservoirs built by the Corps of Engineers. Channelization was promoted: the straightening of streams either to enhance flow through flood-prone areas or to drain swampland so as to make it available for sustained farming.

These new turns in policy shifted the SCS program from preventing soil erosion to developing farmland and related water resources, and helped to identify the spirit of the SCS as part of earlier water and forest conservation – efficiency in resource production. The new policies also triggered extensive conflicts with emerging environmental concerns. Those who considered streams valuable for their biological merits and the aesthetic experience they offered, rather than for development, found the SCS watershed program as much a threat to their objectives as were the projects of the Corps of Engineers. The new departure set the stage for a series of new confrontations between the older conservation movement and newer environmental objectives.

Fish and Game Management

By the 1930s, fish and game management came to have a role in conservation affairs equal to that of the management of waters, forests, and soils. All of these dealt with closely related resources that were thought of as renewable. And in political affairs they tended to work closely together. Yet the concern for wild animals prompted fish and game advocates to consider water, forests, and land as habitats for wildlife rather than as commodities; this established compatibility with newer environmental interests and led to conflict with earlier conservation ideas.[14]

Wildlife conservation arose among Americans concerned with the disappearance of species. Game hunters were instrumental in shaping Yellowstone National Park in the 1890s as a refuge for buffalo and elk and in inaugurating a policy of prohibiting hunting in the national parks. Duck hunters became incensed by the excessive taking of game birds and the loss of habitat and nesting grounds; after World War I they sought to protect breeding areas in Canada and the northern United States and to establish refuges along the flyways. Others became worried about the destruction of birds and animals for ornamental purposes such as plumes worn in women's hats; in the late nineteenth century, they took up their interest through the Audubon societies.[15]

Interest in wildlife matters expanded markedly in the twentieth century as hunting and fishing became more popular. Increased access to wildlands by means of the automobile transformed interest in game from a preoccupation of a relatively affluent few to a mass recreational activity. And as the interest in hunting extended throughout the society so did the concern for more effective wildlife management. The major objective of management was to reduce and then control hunting pressure. Through a variety of state laws one could hunt only by license, only a limited number of animals could be taken, and hunting was permitted only for a few weeks during the year. This regulatory system restricted use sharply by closely regulating the right to kill wild animals, a right policed by a special system of game wardens. It constituted one of the most highly controlled systems of resource use then developed. Yet it was widely accepted because hunters came to believe that only through such restrictions could hunting continue.[16]

Two aspects of this system should be noted. First, wildlife in the United States customarily was treated as a public resource, not as the private possession of individuals. Hence the problem of determining relative rights between private ownership and public use was never as severe with wildlife as with other resources. Second, the movement for restricted hunting came at the same time as the vast extension of the opportunity. Earlier hunting had been a sport of the affluent; there were numerous private hunting clubs to which one could belong for a fee and enjoy the privilege of hunting. Now came a demand for public hunting lands so that more could enjoy the sport. The drive for public ownership and control of wildlands, especially in the states, often came from those who wished to use them for hunting. Especially important in the democratization of hunting was the inexpensive license.

Fishing was even more popular than hunting and by the 1970s had attracted 49 million license holders. Here also there were restrictions, including required licenses, a limited catch, and closed and open fishing seasons. Fishing was influenced heavily by the public ownership of the waters of rivers and lakes, as well as the fish themselves. Moreover, whereas game animals did not thrive in the midst of human habitation and seemed to require special lands, fish inhabited rivers in heavily populated cities as well as in the countryside and the wildlands, and hence fishing areas were more accessible to urban people.

If game and fish management was a matter of maintaining a balance between supply and demand, the growing demand for recreational opportunities would make the prime objective an increase in supply. Populations of wild animals such as the white-tailed deer and the wild turkey were restored above their former numbers. These drives to expand populations led to two federal laws, the Pittman-Robertson Act of 1937 and the Dingell-Johnson Act of 1950, which established funds derived from federal taxes on hunting and fishing equipment. The funds, in turn, were granted to states to finance their fish and wildlife programs.[17]

In these programs wildlife was seen as a commodity. This view brought the wildlife conservation movement into close harmony with water-, forest-, and soil-conservation efforts in a common interest to use science and technology under centralized direction for natural resource management. Yet the concern for game and fish habitat also led to conflicts with water, forest, and soil conservation. Dam construction and channelization destroyed habitat; many forest practices that placed primary emphasis on wood production reduced the extent and quality of habitat; intensive farming destroyed areas available for wildlife. The stress on habitat also brought those interested in fish and game into closer cooperation with a new breed of wildlife enthusiasts who emphasized appreciation of wildlife rather than hunting and fishing. Hence the wildlife movement arose out of a conservation background but also played an integral role in newer environmental affairs.[18]

From Conservation to Environment

In conservation, forests and waters were closely linked. As soil conservation and game management developed they became allied with both water and forest conservation in a shared set of attitudes. Together they emphasized the scientific management of physical commodities and brought together technical specialists for a common purpose. Departments of state government dealing with such affairs were commonly called departments of natural resources. And professional training at academic institutions evolved from an initial interest in forestry to a larger set of natural resource or conservation matters.[19]

The management of natural resources often displayed a close kinship with the entire movement for scientific management that evolved in the twentieth century and pervaded both industry and government. It emphasized large-scale systems of organization and control and increasing output through more intensive input. Professional expertise played an important role in all four facets of conservation, with strong links among them and a sense of kinship with the wider community of technical professions as a whole. Their self-respect came to be firmly connected to the desire to maintain high professional standards in resource management.[20]

Equally important was the evolution of a common political out-look among resource specialists that professionals should be left free from "political influence" to determine how resources should be managed and for what purpose. This shared sense of profes-sionalism was itself a political stance, an assertion that those with special training and expertise should determine the course of affairs. From the management of commodity resources in water, forests, soils, and wildlife emerged not just a sense of direction that stressed maximum output of physical resources but also a view about who should make decisions and how they should be made.

The coming conflicts between conservation and environment were rooted in different objectives: efficiency in the development of material commodities on amenities to enhance the quality of life. In these earlier years the national-parks movement and lead-ers such as John Muir had provided important beginnings for the latter. After World War II extensive changes in human values gave these intangible natural values far greater influence. To them now was added the growing view that air and water, as well as land, constituted a valuable human environment.[21]

The early conservation movement had generated the first stages in shaping a "commons," a public domain of public ownership for public use and the public ownership of fish and wildlife as re-sources not subject to private appropriation. This sense of jointly held resources became extended in the later years to the con-cept of air, land, and water as an environment. Their significance as common resources shifted from a primary focus on commod-ities to become also meaningful as amenities that could enhance the quality of life.

The Search for Environmental Amenities

The most widespread source of emerging environmental interest was the search for a better life associated with home, commu-nity, and leisure. A new emphasis on smaller families developed, allowing parents to invest their limited time and income in fewer children. Child rearing was now oriented toward a more extended period of childhood in order to nurture abilities. Parents sought to provide creative-arts instructions, summer camps, and family vacations so as to foster self-development. Within this context the phrase "environmental quality" would have considerable personal meaning.[22]

It also had meaning for place of residence. Millions of urban Americans desired to live on the fringe of the city where life was less congested, the air cleaner, noise reduced, and there was less concentrated waste from manifold human activities. In the nineteenth century only the well-to-do could afford to live some distance from work. Although streetcars enabled white-collar workers to live in the suburbs and work downtown, blue-collar employees still could not pay the cost of daily transportation. But the automobile largely lifted this limitation, and after World War II blue-collar workers were able to escape the industrial community as a place of residence. Still, by the 1970s as many as one-third of urban Americans wished they could live farther out in the countryside.

The search for a higher quality of living involved a desire for more space both inside and outside the home. Life in the city had been intensely crowded for urban dwellers. Often the street in front of the house had constituted the only available open space. Moving to the suburbs reflected a desire to enjoy a more natural setting, but it also evidenced the search for nature beyond the metropolitan area in the parks and woodlands of the countryside. This desire increased with the ease of access to rural areas by means of the automobile. The state-parks movement of the 1920s expressed the demand by city dwellers for places in which to enjoy the countryside on the weekend or during summer vacations.[23]

There was also the desire to obtain private lands in the countryside so as to enjoy nature not found in the city. In the 1960s and 1970s the market for vacation homesites boomed. Newspaper advertisements abounded with phrases that signaled the important values: "by a sparkling stream," "abundant wildlife," "near the edge of a forest road," "200 feet of lakefront," "on the edge of a state forest."[24]

This pursuit of natural values by city dwellers led to a remarkable turnabout in the attitudes of Americans toward natural environments. These had long been thought of as unused wastelands that could be made valuable only if developed. But after

World War II many such areas came to be thought of as valuable only if left in their natural condition. Forested land, once thought of by many as dark, forbidding, and sinister, a place to be avoided because of the dangers lurking within, now was highly esteemed.[25]

Wetlands, formerly known as swamplands, fit only for draining so that they could become productive agricultural land, were valued as natural systems, undisturbed and undeveloped. Similar positive attitudes were expressed for the prairies of the Midwest, the swamps of the South, and the pine barrens of the East. For many years wild animals had been seen as a threat to farmers and others. Little concern had been shown for the sharp decline even in the deer population, let alone among the bear and bobcat. Yet by the 1960s and 1970s predators, as well as deer, small mammals, and wild turkey, had assumed a positive image for many Americans, and special measures were adopted to protect them and increase their numbers.[26]

Close on the heels of these changes in attitude were new views about western deserts. The desert had long been thought of as a forbidding land where human habitation was impossible and travel was dangerous. The desert hardly figured in the debate over the Wilderness Act of 1964. But by the late 1970s this had changed. The increased popularity of nature photography had brought home the desert to the American people as a place of wonder and beauty. By 1976 western deserts had been explored and identified by many Americans as lands that should be protected in their natural condition.[27]

Environmental Health and Well-being

The search for greater health and well-being constituted an equally significant element of the drive for environmental quality. Such concerns had firm roots in the earlier public-health movement, which emphasized the social conditions that gave rise to health problems. Improvements in water quality all but eliminated typhoid fever and other waterborne bacterial ailments while parasitic and viral diseases such as malaria and yellow fever were brought under control by sanitary measures. The discovery and widespread use of antibiotics after World War II limited the adverse effects of secondary infections. Such measures greatly reduced human suffering and prolonged life. But they also emphasized new causes of illness, many of them environmental.[28]

As tuberculosis declined, other lung problems such as emphysema and cancer received more attention. The Tuberculosis Association changed its name to the American Lung Association to reflect the new emphasis; it became especially concerned with smoking as a cause of lung cancer and air pollution as a cause of pulmonary problems. Exposures formerly associated with infectious diseases now were found to be responsible for more deep-seated problems. Asbestos, for example, once had been thought of primarily as a cause of asbestosis, a pulmonary condition. Many lung problems arising from exposure to asbestos could not be treated with antibiotics and were found to be cancer.[29]

Cancer received particular attention, as its incidence seemed to increase. By the late 1970s one-fourth of all living Americans would contract cancer during their lifetime, and two-thirds of these would die from it. The long latency period between exposure and the appearance of cancer created a sense of peril that made the disease more dramatic. At the same time, cancer was identified with either personal habits, such as smoking and diet, or environmental pollutants in air and water.

The new concerns for environmental health also focused on the workplace. Occupational dangers to workers had long been thought of mainly as posed by physical factors such as machinery. Increasingly the workplace was seen as an environment in which the air itself could transmit harmful substances to cause diseases in workers. Recognition of this danger came only slowly. Much of it awaited evidence accumulated from long-term studies of the relationship between occupational exposure and disease.[30]

The concern for environmental health was primarily an urban phenomenon. The incidence of cancer was twice as high in cities as in the rural countryside, a difference attributed to the impact of urban pollution. The chemical products involved in manufacturing, increasing with each passing year after World War II, seemed especially to affect urban people adversely. The exten-

sive use of the automobile in cities also posed continuing pollution threats. And studies of indoor air identified health hazards in
offices and households.[31]

Although older waterborne diseases had been controlled through
chlorination and disinfection of drinking-water supplies, the rapid
accumulation of newer chemical pollutants in the nation's rivers
and its underground water generated new health concerns. Synthetic organic compounds, as well as heavy metals from industry,
were discovered in many drinking-water sources. The disposal
of industrial toxic wastes constituted an even more pervasive
concern; they were often injected underground, but just as frequently they were disposed of in landfills from which they leaked
into water supplies.[32]

The increasing emphasis on environmental health arose from
a rising level of expectations about health and well-being. As life
expectancy increased, the average American could look forward
to a decade or more of active life after retirement. As the threat
of infectious disease decreased, fear of sudden death or disability from polio, secondary infections from simple surgical procedures such as appendectomies, or other dangers declined sharply.
All this led to a new focus in health associated more with expectations of well-being than with fear of death. There was a special
interest in the quality of life of elderly people. An increasing portion of the population became concerned about preventive health
care, showing interest in physical fitness, food and diet, and protection from exposure to environmental pollutants. This marked
innovation in ideas about personal health was an important element in the expanding concern for one's environment as a critical
element in well-being.[33]

The Ecological Perspective

Ecological objectives – an emphasis on the workings of natural
biological and geological systems and the pressures human actions placed on them – were a third element of environmental
concern. Whereas amenities involved an aesthetic response to
the environment, and environmental health concerned a choice
between cleaner and dirtier technologies within the built-up environment, ecological matters dealt with imbalances between de-

veloped and natural systems that had both current and long-term implications. These questions, therefore, involved ideas about permanence.[34]

The term "ecology" had long referred to a branch of biology that emphasized study of the interaction of living organisms with their physical and biological environment. Popular ecology in the 1960s and 1970s went beyond that scientific meaning. One heard of the impact of people on "the ecology." Professional ecologists disdained this corruption of the word as they had used it. Popular use involved both a broad meaning, the functioning of the biological and geological world, and a narrower one, the disruption of natural processes by human action, as well as the notion that the two, natural systems and human stress, needed to be brought into a better balance.

The popular ecological perspective was reflected in the ecology centers that arose in urban areas. Initially these grew out of the recycling movement – the collection of paper, glass, and tin cans for reprocessing. These centers drew together people who wished to help solve the litter problem and thus to enhance the aesthetic quality of their communities. But soon the concept of recycling seemed to spill over into larger ideas about natural cycles, a traditional ecological theme, and to human action to foster such processes. Ecology centers often expanded their activities into community organic gardens, nutrition and food for better health, and changing life-styles to reduce the human load on natural resources and natural systems.[35]

An ecological perspective grew from the popularization of knowledge about natural processes. These were ideas significant to the study of ecology, but selected and modified by popular experience rather than as a result of formal study. An increasing number of personal or media encounters with the natural world gave rise to widely shared ideas about the functioning of biological and geological systems and the relationship of human beings to them.[36]

Even before World War II, the problem of deer overpopulation on the north rim of the Grand Canyon, or imbalances between the numbers of deer and food in the cutover forestlands of Pennsylvania, Michigan, Wisconsin, and Minnesota, had popularized knowledge about predator-prey and food-population relationships. Overgrazing by cattle and sheep on the western range sparked discussions in the media of the problem of stress in plant communities in which, through overuse, the more vulnerable plants gave way to the hardier, reducing the variety of species. This conveyed the ideas that species diversity had evolved in the process of natural succession, that the number and diversity of species were reduced under population pressures, and that the capacity of ecological systems to sustain human use without major changes were limited.

The threat of toxic chemicals diffused throughout the biological world led to the spread of knowledge in the 1960s about biological and chemical cycles. Transported through the atmosphere, falling into water and on land, chemicals were absorbed by plants, eaten by animals and then by humans. With each step in that food chain they increased in concentration. Media coverage in the late 1950s and early 1960s of radioactive fallout from atomic testing increased awareness of these processes. The most dramatic example was radioactive cesium, which was absorbed by lichens in the Arctic, eaten by reindeer and in turn by Alaskan Eskimos and Laplanders, at each step increasing in concentration in fatty tissues.[37]

The public encounter with pesticides drove home ideas about the accumulation of toxic materials in the food chain. These persistent pesticides found their way into water to be taken up by small fish that were eaten by larger fish, and then by birds to produce weakened eggshells and reduced hatching. Rachel Carson's book *Silent Spring,* published in 1962, spread the word about the problem; even more influential was a widely reported administrative proceeding about DDT in Wisconsin in 1968 and 1969.[38]

Experience with water pollution conveyed still further notions about ecological processes. If one lived in a coal-mining area one soon became aware that acid, formed from sulfur in coal, was toxic to aquatic life, leaving only those organisms that were adapted to stress. At a lake one learned of eutrophication, the way in which phosphates and nitrates from fertilizer and sewage provided nutrients that greatly increased the production of algae; these, in turn, decayed and used up the available oxygen required by fish. Eutrophic lakes with reduced fish life were widely known as dying lakes.

Water brought both geological and biological phenomena closer together in the ecological perspective. The water cycle was pervasive; the natural cycle of rainfall, runoff, and percolation, flow to oceans and lakes, evaporation, and rainfall was readily understood. So also were malfunctions of this cycle as human activities diverted it into new physical channels, and these in turn generated adverse human consequences. In the nation's suburbs, for example, upstream construction of roads and shopping centers reduced land available for normal percolation of rainfall into soil and groundwater, increased runoff and caused flooding in downstream basements. Stream channelization deepened channels, destroyed the use of low-lying streamside areas as natural floodwater reservoirs, diverted water downstream to cause more flooding there, and lowered the water table. Near the seacoast it led to the intrusion of salt water in water supplies.[39]

Such experiences as these led to an image of a web of life in which "everything was hitched to everything else." If human beings modified one part of that chain it could well have detrimental effects for them. And this realization led to the conviction that human action in relationship to the ecological world would have to be closely monitored and in many cases modified.

Ecological Life-Styles

The interest in natural processes led to criticism of life-styles that placed heavy loads on ecological systems. Many sought deliberately to change the houses in which they lived, the sources of their food, the approach to personal health, and their mode of work and leisure in order to "live more lightly on the earth."[40]

These tendencies had some earlier roots. During the 1930s there were proposals for a more decentralized society, a technology of smaller scale, organic gardening and farming, and personal health care that emphasized preventive medicine. A few decades later the organic gardening and farming activities established by J. I. Rodale at Emmaus, Pennsylvania, became a creative center for such ventures. Its publication *Organic Gardening* was widely read; and its newsletter, the *Environmental Action Bulletin,* was an important source of information about environmental and ecological affairs. In the 1970s a magazine from quite a different source, *Mother Earth News,* played a similar role; by 1977 its circulation had reached 550,000.[41]

Ideas about ecological life-styles emphasized a personal responsibility for the impact of daily living on the wider natural world. Ways of working, living, and recreating should be changed so as to lower that pressure. This required individual commitment that brought into play a moral task: to conduct one's personal life so as to be consistent with the larger scheme of things.

Attention was focused on the enormous amounts of waste that people produced in their daily lives, the most dramatic example of which was the profusion of solid waste generated by advanced industrial societies. Was such elaborate packaging necessary? Another issue was wasteful use of energy – cars with low mileage per gallon, the use of mechanical gadgets powered with fossil fuel such as lawn mowers and off-road motorized vehicles, and more common energy-using household appliances. Ever changing styles, moreover, seemed to be altogether unnecessary. Such examples underlined the degree to which the American economy rested on excessive consumption that placed undue pressure on scarce resources.

These new life-styles revolved around three aspects of daily living: food, health, and shelter. The production and preparation of food could be carried out with far less input from intensive chemistry and technology and far more direct involvement with biological processes. Organic gardening, biological farming, and natural foods became increasingly popular. Natural-food stores arose first through mail-order houses that produced and sold organically grown food, then in cooperative retail outlets, and finally, as the demand grew, through franchise stores and natural food sections of supermarkets.[42]

Health care seemed entirely too intensive in its scientific and technical context, too removed from personal relationships between individual and physician, too dependent on drugs and quick fixes. Increasing emphasis came to be placed on prevention, on habits of eating and exercise that could promote better health, rather than on cures. An intense debate, for example, persisted between those who sought to treat cancer after it was detected and those who stressed its prevention. The ecological approach was to remove the environmental cause and thus to attack illness at its origin. *Prevention,* published by the Rodale press, stressed these themes; it reached more than 2.5 million subscribers by the end of 1984.[43]

The design and construction of houses, a part of the do-it-yourself movement, came to incorporate ecological perspectives. One could use natural materials, integrate internal and external space, and blend natural processes outside the building with internal arrangements. Building design had long insulated interior living from the elements, emphasizing protection from wind and rain, from cold in winter and heat in summer. Could houses not be designed to fit in with the slope of the land, perhaps be underground as well as aboveground, let in sunlight instead of keeping it out, bring the production of plants for both food and enjoyment into closer harmony with living quarters, and, through composting, for example, integrate waste disposal with the production of living things?

These emphases on food, health, and shelter were associated with themes of autonomy and self-help. The ecological perspective involved an affirmation of the capacity of individuals to take personal responsibility for their lives by designing with nature rather than with larger, remoter, and more centralized human institutions. There was a focus on natural materials, as contrasted with plastics, and especially those that were biologically generated, such as natural fibers. And there was interest in eliminating waste through reducing demands on one's environment, recycling, and natural processes. All these came to be summed up in the phrase the "conserver society."[44]

These varied tendencies in thought and action that constituted the strands of environmental quality and ecology often came together. The most pervasive factor in this was the emphasis on the importance of a larger role for the natural world in the advanced industrial society. Aesthetic appreciation of nature often was closely connected with intellectual understanding as many people sought both to enjoy and to comprehend the natural settings around them. The adverse impacts of pollutants on human health and one's environment emphasized that the natural world was fragile and had to be cared for. Personal responsibility in life-style identified the natural world as a vantage point from which one tested appropriate human behavior. It was no wonder that ideas associated with biology, ecology, and geology came to be integral parts of popular thinking about the quality and permanence of life in modern society.

The Social Roots of Environmental Values

Public-opinion analysts began to measure attitudes toward environmental issues as early as 1965. At first their questions were confined to issues of air and water pollution. The studies demonstrated a strong and continuing concern for these matters. In a Harris poll in 1976, for example, 66 percent of Americans believed that air pollution was a "very serious problem" and 67 percent held the same view about water pollution – the highest levels of concern yet recorded. The most extensive study of environmental attitudes was made in 1978 by sociologist Robert Mitchell, who identified environmental concerns in all population groups; a significant majority of respondents preferred improvement in environmental conditions at the cost of growth in other sectors of the economy or higher personal taxes.[45]

A 1977 study underlined attitudes toward the natural environment. While 7 percent of the sample believed that there was too much land in the federal wilderness system, 32 percent believed that there was too little. Although 28 percent felt that the yield and sales of timber should be increased, 62 percent felt that trees should "continue to be preserved in their natural state." Natural-environment values were especially striking among those who purchased woodlands for the amenities they offered rather than for their wood products; the attitudes of these owners were studied extensively by foresters who hoped to change those values so as to increase the supply of wood. And urban dwellers placed a very high value on the presence of wildlife around their homes.[46]

The acceptance of ecological concepts, as reflected in attitude surveys, underscored the degree to which the American people had adopted natural values. One study in 1973 examined such attitudes in the Pacific Northwest. With the statement that "humans must live in harmony with nature in order to survive," 95.6

percent of a general population sample agreed. And with the argument that "humans need not adapt to the natural environment because they can remake it to suit their needs," 84.7 percent disagreed. With the statement that "there are limits to growth beyond which our industrialized society cannot expand," 75.3 percent of those surveyed agreed.[47]

These changes occurred more rapidly in some segments of the population than in others. Attitudes did not vary significantly, for example, with occupation and income, but did with age and education. Value changes associated with younger generations and with education were the key elements. This suggests a historical evolution in which environmental values associated with broad social changes came to be expressed as one generation succeeded another.[48]

The study of attitudes toward wilderness, cited earlier, and conducted by the Opinion Research Corporation under the auspices of the American Forest Institute, provides a more complete picture of the roots of both widely shared values and variations among sectors of the population. The study contrasted those who thought there was too little wilderness with those who believed there was too much. Whereas only 19% of those over sixty years of age felt that there was too little wilderness, 46% of those between eighteen and twenty-nine did so. There were differences in education: 21% and 10% for those with some high school education and 43% and 5% for those with some college. Those with incomes below $7,500, a high proportion of them older people, divided 27%–9%, and those with incomes over $25,000 did so by 42–4%. The views among whites were 33% versus 7% and those among blacks were 20% versus 11%. And although those in nonurban areas voted 28% and 12%, respectively, on the two alternatives, those in the twenty-five largest metropolitan areas did so by 35% and 6%. Age and education, then, were especially important in determining environmental values.[49]

Environmental values were associated with distinctive psychological as well as sociological factors, as indicated in a 1982 study sponsored by the Continental Group, a business conglomerate. Those with a "resource preservation" preference tended to have a higher level of personal drive in their work and a greater sense of personal challenge and responsibility than did those with a "resource utilization bent." Moreover, the first group tended to place more emphasis on a "scientific approach" to problems they encountered in contrast with a "spiritual approach," which was more characteristic of resource utilizers. This limited foray into the psychological dimension of environmental values confirms the notion that they were associated with factors that were increasing in American society in contrast with those that were declining.[50]

The Historical Evolution of Environmental Values

Those who struck back against environmentalists variously described them as radical and conservative, radical in that they represented both new and undesirable tendencies in American society and conservative in that they objected to material progress and preferred an earlier, more primitive society. Both descriptions are far from the mark. Environmental and ecological values were an integral part of the continuous search for a better standard of living. They reflected changing attitudes about what constitutes a better life. The natural and the developed became intermingled as coordinated, mutually reinforcing aspects of the quality of living.

We could place these ideas about quality of life in a historical sequence of evolving levels of consumption. A century ago most consumption involved necessities, elementary needs in the areas of food, clothing, and shelter. As real incomes rose, so did standards of living, giving rise to a new stage of consumption in the form of conveniences, those material possessions, such as the automobile and indoor plumbing, that reduced the time and energy required for daily chores. After World War II, for an increasing share of the American people, these wants had been filled; discretionary income could now be spent for other goods and services beyond necessities and conveniences.

The search for environmental quality was an integral part of this rising standard of living. Environmental values were based not on one's role as a producer of goods and services but on consumption, the quality of home and leisure. Such environmental concerns were not prevalent at earlier times. But after World

War II, rising levels of living led more people to desire qualitative experiences as well as material goods in their lives. In earlier times only the well-to-do could afford a summer at the seashore or a home in the suburbs, away from daily exposure to urban air pollution and congestion. By the mid-twentieth century similar desires were expressed by an increasing number of people so that the search for amenities became a normal expectation on the part of most Americans.[51]

In the past rarely had changes in standards of living come to the entire population at once. The telephone, the wringer washing machine, the gas stove, indoor plumbing, the automobile, and electric household appliances all first came only to the small minority of Americans who could afford them. Telephone directories of the late nineteenth century bear witness to what then was a luxury enjoyed by only a few. The first automobiles were "touring cars," and the first automobile clubs were composed of the affluent. So it was with still another aspect of the rising standard of living, environmental amenities. Enjoyed in the nineteenth and early twentieth centuries by only a few, after World War II they were an integral part of the desires of the many.

Often these new qualitative consumer demands could be provided by the private market. One could buy a house in more pleasant surroundings, in the suburban fringe or the countryside. But many such amenities could not be purchased. The air surrounding the city was common property, incapable of being carved into pieces that could be bought and sold. The same was true for the water environment. Since the private economy could not supply these environmental amenities, there was increasing demand that public and private nonprofit institutions do so.[52]

Changes in consumer preference were not confined to the United States; they appeared also in the industrialized nations of Western Europe, Australia, New Zealand, Canada, and Japan. Ronald Ingelhart has described the underlying change in values as a "silent revolution." "The values of Western publics have been shifting from an overwhelming emphasis on material well-being and physical security toward greater emphasis on quality of life." The focus was on changing life-styles, those qualitative concerns associated with increased leisure time and a greater ability to use leisure time creatively and enjoyably.[53]

The Context of Environmental Perception

Environmental and ecological concerns were not abstract matters; they involved specific circumstances that people knew personally. They were about places where one worked and lived, physical settings that one valued and that often were endangered. The environmental movement grew out of concern for the quality of such places, and often it was organized and drew its strength from a shared sense of what was at stake on the part of many people in a given place.

The physical character of the American landscape has been a significant force in shaping human environmental perceptions and a sense of belonging, a mechanism for focusing a feeling of shared responsibility for one's surroundings and in crystallizing action. The Adirondacks, for example, played a powerful role in defining for the people of New York the quality of their environment and in galvanizing their attention and action. To protect this land, declared "forever wild" by the state legislature in 1885 and by the 1894 state constitution, was to protect a statewide sense of belonging.[54]

In many regions of the nation land forms played a similar role. In California such meaning was generated by the Sierra Nevada Mountains, personified in the historic figure of John Muir and in one of the most vigorous of all environmental organizations, the Sierra Club. In New England there were the White Mountains; in the Southeast, the southern Appalachians and the Blue Ridge; in Colorado, the central Rockies; in Washington, the Cascades; and in Montana and Idaho, the Bitterroots and the Sawtooths. Throughout the nation historic concern for natural values has long been associated with the appreciation and exploration of these mountain forms with which entire regions have identified.[55]

The same can be said of bodies of water. The Chesapeake Bay exerted a powerful force on the imagination of those people in intimate contact with it, leading to organized action, such as through the Chesapeake Bay Foundation, to protect its environmental quality. Long Island Sound drew together people from both sides as if it constituted a common property and a common experience for those who lived and worked on its periphery. Appreciation of the waters of the Great Lakes, vaster and more difficult to experience as a whole, generated the Lake Michigan Federation and then the Great Lakes Federation; furthered by an increasing number of opportunities for common thought and action, these diverse systems gradually took on a perceptual quality as a whole. On the West Coast two powerful centers of water-oriented perception, San Francisco Bay and Puget Sound, also were central to common action to protect and enhance the quality of a common environmental resource.[56]

Grand vistas of perception, thought, and action were enhanced after World War II by the growth of color photography. Pictures aroused in many the memories of personal visits and in others conveyed an initial experience of the beauty of the physical landscape. The Sierra Nevadas and the Adirondacks have long been the subjects of photographic books in many households. More recently portrayals appeared of Chesapeake Bay and the Great Lakes. Large-format books that convey the immense splendor of natural places were published, most notably by the Sierra Club and Friends of the Earth, to spread the visual images and sense of belonging more widely. A host of photographers, among whom the best known was Ansel Adams, helped shape the environmental perception of the American landscape for millions of people.[57]

Visual images stirred the imagination of many Americans who had not visited natural places in person, and these images were important in the political drive to establish national wilderness areas and especially the campaign to manage significant areas in Alaska as natural environments. One came to distinguish between direct and vicarious experience and direct and indirect use of wilderness and wildlands. To most Americans dramatic natural environments were national monuments, so closely intertwined with the self-image of nation and region that they were considered an indispensable aspect of civic life.[58]

In the 1960s and 1970s lesser natural formations acquired environmental significance at the regional level. Amid the search for environmental quality, they became prized as more Americans explored the countryside and found new special places. Thus it was that the pine barrens of Long Island and New Jersey, the prairie lands of the western Midwest, the swamps of the Southeast, and the Big Thicket of Texas and the Congaree of South

Carolina came into prominence. Whole regions took on new significance for being relatively undisturbed: the Maine woods, the
northwest coast of California, the lake country of northern Michigan, Wisconsin, and Minnesota, the West Virginia Highlands, the
Missouri Ozarks, the Knob and Valley country of southern Ohio,
Indiana, and Illinois, and the ridges and plateaus of Kentucky and
Tennessee.[59]

Perceptions of high-quality environmental areas in region and
nation constantly served as reminders of an environmental quality that might be achievable, in part, in urban surroundings. Cities
seemed to be encumbered with lower levels of environmental
quality that were difficult to change. Yet there was a constant
attempt to bring to the city those natural values found beyond its
borders. The striking land and water forms of the region that constituted the larger urban environment, the "urban field" as it was
often called, served as a constant source of inspiration for enhancement of the city.

Much interest arose in the perceptual quality of the city. Kevin
Lynch wrote of the "images of the city," the way in which its physical features and especially its landscape, its hills and rivers, provided perceptual meaning for those who lived there. Whereas
cities endowed with such natural features had a higher order of
such form and meaning, those occupying flatlands were far less
structured. Appreciative works of urban photography drew the
attention of readers to natural spaces that might easily be forgotten in the daily routine of travel along the built-up corridors of
urban thoroughfares. The perceptual quality of the city could
generate a heightened sense of environmental belonging.[60]

Regional variations within the United States in land and water
forms, and therefore regional variations in environmental perception, played a significant role in regional differences in environmental attitudes and organized activity. That activity was strongest in such places as New England, Florida, the West Coast, and
the upper Great Lakes, where people had become attached to
nearby natural features. In the Gulf Coast and prairie states, on
the other hand, environmental affairs received far weaker support. The same could be said of the factory belt, which includes
Illinois, Indiana, and Ohio. Here there were few striking land and
water formations; the region's inhabitants were far more aware

of the North Country amid the Great Lakes than of their own terrain.

One could also distinguish between areas of environmental concern of long standing and those of more recent interest that contained less striking, and more recently discovered, natural features. New environmental interests developed in Maine, northern Michigan, northwest California, the Ozarks, and southern Illinois and Indiana – reflected in part in new regional newspapers such as the *Maine Times,* the *New Hampshire Times,* the *North Woods Call,* the *Illinois Times,* and *Econews* of northwest California. Their readers tended to be recent migrants to those areas.

These varied perceptions of the physical environment played no little role in shaping a common sense of environmental belonging and in translating values into action. Around the protection of such areas many battles were waged in the Environmental Era.

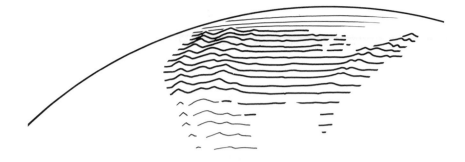

2 Variation and Pattern in the Environmental Impulse

Changes in society and values that underlay environmental action did not come to all areas of America at the same time or in the same way. Moreover, some aspects of environmental affairs made their mark early in the 1960s, but others came later. These variations and the patterns they spawned provide further insight into the nature and meaning of the social roots of environmental politics.

Congressional Voting Patterns

The most comprehensive view of variations in environmental values across the nation can be obtained by analyzing voting patterns in Congress. Beginning in 1971 the League of Conservation Voters (LCV) compiled an annual record of congressional environmental votes. Individual legislators were given a score from 0 to 100. Because they reflect the views of relatively small geographical areas, the records of members of the House of Representatives provide an especially useful portrayal of regional variations.[1]

I have selected for analysis here the data for the Congresses of 1971, 1977, and 1983. The highest level of regional support in 1977, to take the midpoint between the first and last of these

40

years, was in New England with a score of 71.0, followed in turn by the Middle Atlantic states with 62.9, the North Central with 52.0, and the Pacific Coast with 51.5. The lowest-level regions were the South Atlantic with 37.3, the Mountain states with 32.9, the Plains with 25.1, and the Gulf states with 20.5.

Those areas with a long history of urbanization where urban demands had influenced the course of politics for many years provided the strongest environmental support, and those where rural and raw-material-producing influences persisted well into the twentieth century had the lowest. The regions of greatest environmental activity, the Northeast and the Pacific Coast, were heavily urban. The urbanized areas of relatively low support were those that were more newly populated, such as Texas, New Mexico, and Arizona. The other most visible centers of low environmental strength were the Great Plains and the South, long sections of strong rural tradition in which the more cosmopolitan values arising from urbanization had not yet had more dominant effects on politics. Yet even in these sections there were important distinctions in that urban areas within them displayed greater environmental interest than did those that were more rural.

Equally significant were the patterns of change over the twelve-year period. Environmental voting strength increased in all regions except the Mountain states. But the gains were greatest in the South Atlantic and Gulf states, which in 1971 had recorded the lowest environmental scores. Whereas the earlier environmentally strong regions such as New England and the Middle Atlantic states increased their voting scores, the more dramatic change was the sharp rise in these formerly low areas to become more like other regions.

Variations within each region help to sharpen the analysis. Vermont, Maine, Massachusetts, Connecticut, and Rhode Island had scores of 60 and above, but New Hampshire scored much lower at 43, a figure that confirms the impression from other evidence that New Hampshire lagged behind other New England states in environmental support. In the Middle Atlantic states Pennsylvania's score of 50 was much lower than that of New York (68) or New Jersey (70); other evidence supports the view that the environmental movement was generally weaker in Pennsylvania than in either of the other two Middle Atlantic states. In the eastern Midwest, scores for Michigan (60) and Wisconsin (67) were well above those for Indiana (55), Illinois (45), and Ohio (45), indicating a marked difference between the northern and southern parts of that region. Yet even if some states within the North and East were lower than others, the area ranked relatively high in the nation as a whole.

In the Mountain states, while Montana had a score of 55 and was recognized as having the strongest environmental movement in the region, Idaho's two representatives received a score of only 7. With the exception of Idaho the entire northern area of the region was stronger in environmental support than were the more southerly states of Arizona, New Mexico, Utah, and Nevada. One might also contrast Hawaii and Alaska; the tension between population and resources on the islands gave rise to a drive to limit and control growth, whereas in rapidly growing Alaska the state's leaders objected strenuously to federal programs to protect wildlands from development. Within the South there were also important distinctions as the states ringing the Gulf, from Texas through Louisiana to Mississippi and Alabama, had the lowest scores for the entire South while the upper South and the Atlantic coast ranged somewhat higher.

Voting patterns in Congress were shaped by party loyalties and ideologies as well as by constituencies. In 1977 the average environmental voting score for Democrats was 56 and for Republicans 28.5. But the two parties also differed markedly within themselves. The variations within the Democratic party reflected circumstances in different regions. Democratic scores in New England, the Upper Midwest, and the Pacific Coast were high, whereas those in the Gulf South and the Plains states were low; those in the northern "factory belt" from Pennsylvania through Illinois were in between. Within the Republican party sectional variations were less marked. There was only one clear distinction: Republican scores in New England were far higher than in the rest of the nation. Most Republican legislators' environmental views stemmed more from ideological than from constituency influences; their negative environmental votes were shaped by responses to more generalized, nationwide institutions and ideologies.

Internal Democratic party variations were especially note-worthy in the South, where rapid social change was creating new urban views within a more traditional rural climate. Here environmental support among Democrats ranged from scores of 95 in two districts in northern Virginia adjacent to the District of Columbia to those of 0 in four rural districts in Texas, Louisiana, and Alabama. Between these extremes was a range of environmental voting that varied with the degree of urbanization. Over the course of the 1970s the East Coast states from Virginia to Florida improved their environmental support steadily, reflecting the rising levels of urbanization there. Among the varied groups of Democrats in the House of Representatives, the highest environmental support came from black members. And in the South marked increases in environmental voting often came when urban districts became represented by blacks.[2]

The two parties differed especially in internal regional changes between 1971 and 1983. The Democrats became much more unified, narrowing the gap between the high and low of the nine regions by 15.7 percentage points; the regional gap among Republicans widened by 12.2 points. In other words, between 1971 and 1983 the regions in which the Democrats as a whole scored 50 points or more rose from four to eight out of nine, but for the Republicans this number stayed at only two. Democrats in all regions improved their environmental voting scores, but among Republicans scores increased only in New England, the Middle Atlantic and North Central states, and the Central Plateau. In the rest of the nation scores declined. Republicans in different regions were reacting quite differently to the environmental movement, and their responses to it were becoming increasingly divided.

Regions of Environmental Strength

These regional patterns based on variations in voting can be confirmed and elaborated by using a wider range of evidence about citizen organizations and activities, state governmental agencies and their policies, the activities of state legislatures, public-opinion polls in the states, and newspaper accounts of environmental issues. Although in most respects this evidence confirms congressional voting patterns, it also provides a more detailed look at variations among the states.[3]

The environmental movement derived special impetus from three areas: California, New England, and Florida. In each, innovations took place in the 1960s that influenced the nation as a whole. California was often the lead state, originating policies in coastal-zone management, environmental-impact analysis, state parks, forest-management practices, open-space planning, energy alternatives, air-pollution control, and hazardous-waste disposal. Often environmentalists sought to apply California's innovations to the rest of the nation.[4]

Initiatives in New England were not far behind. Here was born the conservation commission, an instrument of local government to identify and manage open space. The Massachusetts Audubon Society, the nation's strongest state Audubon organization, had over the years built a distinctive network of nature centers and nature-education facilities. The *Maine Times,* a weekly published in Topsham, Maine, produced some of the best environmental reporting in the nation. Connecticut was distinctive for its land trusts formed to manage lands as natural environments in the midst of heavily urban areas. In southern New England were located two of the "new age" magazines, *New Age* and *New Roots,* each of which circulated far beyond the region's borders. Here were some of the first state laws to restrict billboards to enhance the region's aesthetic quality, early initiatives in solar energy, and strong antinuclear action.[5]

The evolution of environmental activities in Florida was no less significant. Here also was one of the strongest Audubon chapters in the nation. Whereas in other regions the protection of mountain or forest areas or particular problems of air pollution shaped the course of environmental affairs, in Florida the primary focus was on water. Change in the state's coastal wetlands, which destroyed wildlife habitat, gave rise to protest against dredge-and-fill operations and one of the first requirements that environmental-impact analyses be conducted before development. Diversions of water in central Florida threatened the habitat of the Everglades and led to protective action. The aesthetic quality of the coral reefs off the state's southern coast and their endangerment by both pollution and the declining food supply from the destruction of coastal mangrove swamps added to the state's environmental perspective.[6]

Other regions were not far behind as environmental pacemakers. New York had its own distinctive environmental experience. The Adirondacks, from the mid-nineteenth century on, had long played a special role in the environmental perception of people in New York and on several occasions had led to significant protective action. The Hudson River became a setting in the 1960s for one of the nation's first environmental legal battles, the Scenic Hudson court case, which was fought to protect the aesthetic quality of that river from the Storm King pumped-storage project. And around Long Island Sound controversies took place over attempts to build bridges from the island to the southern New England mainland. The bridges were not built and new highways eventually were routed away from high-quality environmental areas and wetlands.[7]

In Michigan, Wisconsin, and Minnesota, a historic pattern had developed much as in New England and New York, in which the southern urban populations reached out to the more natural northern environments for recreation and leisure. In Detroit and Chicago, in Milwaukee, Madison, and Minneapolis, concern arose for the "north country" as a special place. The term was encountered repeatedly: the *North Woods Call,* one of the most widely read outdoor papers in Michigan, Northland College in Ashland, Wisconsin, which houses the Sigurd Olsen Institute of Environmental Studies, and the Northern Environmental Council located at Duluth, Minnesota. Such natural areas as Isle Royale National Park and the Porcupine Mountains of the upper peninsula of Michigan, Sleeping Bear Dunes, and the Boundary Waters Canoe Area in northern Minnesota aroused regional interest and, when threatened, calls to action.[8]

New Jersey, Delaware, and Maryland generated their own particular brand of environmental initiative, focused primarily on the coast. Development pressures here generated an awareness of the coast as a special asset much as in California. Those states took the lead in protecting valuable wetlands, barrier islands, and sand dunes, which remained largely untouched. The rush to the ocean for both permanent and vacation homes and for weekend tourist travel was even more intense than in the Lake States because of the much nearer metropolitan areas. Delaware's decision in 1967 to prohibit any further industrial development on its coastal lands was a remarkable action. The episode started one of the nation's foremost environmental leaders, Russell Peterson, on a career from governor of Delaware to chair of the Council on Environmental Quality and the presidency of the National Audubon Society.[9]

The Pacific Northwest became a center of environmental initiative in which Seattle played a leading role. In 1965 the Sierra Club moved its first regional office outside of California, established in Eugene in 1961, to Seattle. The Olympic Mountains to the west, the Cascades to the east, and nearby Puget Sound provided a distinctive setting of high environmental quality that soon led an increasing number of citizens to become involved in environmental affairs. The interest spread to nearby states. In Idaho action focused on the protection of Hell's Canyon on the Snake River from dams and the establishment of the central Idaho "River of No Return Wilderness," the nation's largest. Oregon became a pioneer in a host of environmental measures under the leadership of Governor Tom McCall. The Oregon Environmental Council and the Washington Environmental Council were formed in 1970 to give expression to these emerging citizen interests. Oregon led in the adoption of a returnable-container law and state land-use regulation; both states, along with California, were the first to complete plans and qualify for federal funding under the coastal-zone management program.[10]

The northern Rockies was an especially visible area of environmental interest. Here were state groups such as the Colorado Open Space Council, the Montana Wilderness Association, the Northern Plains Resource Council, the Idaho Environmental Council, and the Idaho Conservation Council. Environmental interest here coincided with worries about the combined effects of population growth – the Rocky Mountain West was the fastest growing region in the nation during the 1970s – and the adverse impact of development, which seemed to threaten the environmental quality that had attracted migrants in the first place. The most significant environmental paper in the nation, *High Country News,* was published in Lander, Wyoming. In Montana and Wyoming opposition among ranchers to strip mining provided a critical addition to the more urban wilderness movement, the environmental orientation of state wildlife agencies, and college and university environmental centers. Montana's Senator Lee Metcalf became one of Congress's foremost environmental leaders. And the University of Montana at Missoula produced one of the nation's few environmental forestry periodicals, *Western Wildlands.*[11]

Finally one should mention the environmental intiatives from the two newest states, Hawaii and Alaska, each in marked contrast to the other. In Hawaii the tension between population pressures and a finite environment was particularly acute, giving rise to advanced measures to control land use, to maintain air quality at levels higher than federal standards, and to bring about some of the few innovations in water-quality standards. Hawaiian congresswoman Patsy Mink played a major role in shaping the federal Surface Mining Control and Reclamation Act of 1977.[12]

The setting was quite different in Alaska, a state of vast lands and few people, with the aura of unlimited opportunity for resource development. Yet Alaska also had a vigorous environmental movement, which might well have been the strongest in the nation in proportion to population. The Southeast Alaska Conservation Council took the lead in promoting wilderness designations on the Tongass National Forest in the southeast panhandle; the council represented a significant wilderness movement indigenous to the state. While the battle over the Alaskan lands in Congress and in the media of the lower 48, culminating in the Alaskan Lands Act of 1980, tended to identify the controversy as one between Alaska and the rest of the nation, it was, in fact, a controversy within the state, and the struggle was shaped more by Alaskans than by those in distant states.[13]

Regions of Weakness in Environmental Interest

One can also identify areas of peculiar weakness where voting support was more limited, the level of citizen action lower, and state agency programs less vigorous.

In the Plains states of North and South Dakota, Nebraska, and Kansas, for example, farming, because of its many adverse environmental effects, provided a rather infertile ground for environmental action. The most pervasive critical issue was water supply, which led to opposition to such environmental uses of water as wild and scenic river designations or wetlands. The massive Garrison project in North Dakota, drawn up by the Bureau of Reclamation to divert water from some areas to irrigate others, and debated persistently in the 1970s and 1980s, would destroy wetlands. A host of regional and national environmental groups took the lead in opposing it on the grounds of cost, limited benefit, and environmental harm. Such action provoked the state government to retaliate against several long-established programs to protect waterfowl nesting areas. The distinctive environmental setting of the northern plains led to the formation of regional organizations known as "natural resource councils," which focused on the adverse impact of energy and water development on farming. "Environmental" was deliberately avoided in organizational titles because its wider connotations made it unacceptable to farmers.[14]

Similar water problems also underlay an extensive skepticism about environmental objectives in Oklahoma, Texas, New Mexico, Arizona, Utah, and Nevada. In the first two states energy firms were established and dominant factors in both the economy and politics. Many of the region's newer residents were older and hence less prone to express emerging values. The entire area was undergoing a spurt of economic development during the environmental years. Uranium mining and milling and atomic research and development in New Mexico, and copper mining in Arizona and Utah, reflected dominant institutions committed to environmentally hazardous types of development. Public-land management here under both state and federal auspices tended to be dominated far more by mining and grazing interests than by environmental concerns. The southern Mountain states were centers of the "Sagebrush Rebellion," in which ranchers sought to transfer federal lands to the states. The dryland and mineral region of the Southwest was not fertile ground for environmental enterprise.[15]

The South had its own variations. One might well attribute limited environmental concern there to the region's agricultural roots, the persistence of rural attitudes and institutions, and the slower growth of urban populations with newer interests and values. There was a marked distinction between the Gulf states and the mid- and upper South. In the former, offshore oil production and the chemical industry dominated much of the economy and the political climate; hence the lower level of environmental activities. In the mid- and upper South, however, concern was greater. Growing urban centers such as Nashville and Memphis, Louisville and Frankfort, cities in North Carolina around Raleigh-Durham and Chapel Hill, Charleston and Greenville in South Carolina, and Arlington and Alexandria in Virginia all provided sources of new points of view including those pertaining to the environment.[16]

Some of the most important targets of southern environmental concern were wetlands and natural areas. The region had extensive wetlands along the lower reaches of rivers, in the bayous of the Gulf states, and around the coastal areas of Florida, Georgia, North and South Carolina, and Virginia. Both hunters and appreciative wildlife users sought to protect these wetlands. The drive helped to shape the region's growing environmental movement. In the later 1970s the Nature Conservancy found that the South was quite receptive to its program to survey the region for representative natural areas. Here, the natural-areas program provided an especially significant opportunity for environmental action.

The southern Appalachians played a distinctive role in the South's environmental history. The region dominated by the Shenandoah Mountains and the Great Smokies had long displayed concern for the special quality of the mountains of the Southeast. West Virginia's mountains and rivers played an influential part in the evolution of a vital and active group, the West Virginia Highlands Conservancy, which had an impact on state and federal policies far beyond what would be expected of its eight hundred members. Environmental affairs in this region were influenced heavily by coal mining and the construction of dams. A special target was the Tennessee Valley Authority, which in its drive for regional development with a special emphasis on expanded energy facilities, not merely opposed but defied the environmental movement. Its actions provoked a vigorous counterattack that helped to promote the steady growth of environmental action in the region.[17]

The distinctive character of forestry in the South after World War II also influenced the course of the region's environmental affairs. Here, in the Gulf Coast states and in Tennessee, forestry was more fully committed to wood production than elsewhere, industrial land holdings dominated, and there were few public forest lands that could serve as examples of, and opportunities for, environmental forest practices. Intensive management led to the conversion of natural stands from hardwoods to softwoods for pulp, short-term rotations that could be harvested in forty years or less, and monocultures that precluded diversity of species as well as of age. All of these trends in southern forestry alienated those who viewed forests as natural environments for wildlife and human appreciation.[18]

The northern industrial states of Pennsylvania, Ohio, Indiana, and Illinois displayed relatively low levels of citizen and state environmental activity in view of their relatively high degree of urbanization. In these states heavy industry had long played a major role in the economy and in politics; it was a primary source of pollution that was especially difficult to control, and many plants were old and inefficient. Ohio was distinctive for its constant defiance of the national environmental-protection program. These states had a legacy deeply rooted in manufacturing that prompted them to retain a commitment to older values as well as modes of production while other regions moved more rapidly to an advanced industrial and consumer age.[19]

Idaho and Pennsylvania might be singled out for the degree to which they displayed distinctively low levels of environmental interest in contrast with other states in their regions. Although public-attitude studies in Idaho indicated a high level of environmental concern and strong support for wilderness and wild rivers equal to that of most other states, the legislative and executive response was far weaker. With the exception of a few leaders such as Senator Frank Church and Governor Cecil Andrus, political leadership in Idaho seemed to be out of balance with its popular sentiment. This was especially true with regard to water use, where repeated expressions of public opinion on behalf of environmental values were ignored in legislative decisions until a massive environmental-initiative campaign in 1977 caused the legislature, which usually responded to organizations of farm water users rather than to environmentalists, to modify its stand – but only slightly and only temporarily.[20]

Pennsylvania was even more distinctive. The state had large areas of undeveloped and relatively mountainous land that constituted a great environmental asset. But in Pittsburgh and Philadelphia, near opposite southern corners of the state, this land was almost unknown territory because residents of both cities looked outside the state for their natural-environment interests. Historically, the state was strongly proconservation; it contained more than 4 million acres of publicly owned forestland, more than 80 percent of which was in state ownership. And it had a history of concern for the protection of streams. Its fish and game program was unusual, and its sportsmen had played a major role in early surface-mining and water-quality programs.

Yet the state participated in only average fashion in the newer environmental activities of the 1970s. The strong role of mining and manufacturing institutions, coal, iron, and steel, continued to shape thinking about the state's economy and to exercise considerable restraint on environmental objectives. By the end of the 1970s newer, urban-based environmental concerns were still far overshadowed by groups interested primarily in efficient commodity development. Pennsylvania was an extreme example of a region rooted in the values and institutions of an older, manufacturing, past and slow to move into an economic future.[21]

These patterns of environmental activity across the nation were distinctive in several ways. First, there was a close connection between levels of environmental interest and levels of urbanization, emphasizing that the environmental movement arose from demographic changes originating from the cities and the values of an advanced industrial and consumer society. Second, there were differences in values and attitudes between older and newer demographic groups, older and newer cities, older and newer regions. The cities of the "old factory belt" in the Middle Atlantic and midwestern states displayed less environmental interest than did the newer ones of the West – and even the South – that were attracting younger people with newer values. Finally, there was a close connection between the positive expression of environmental values and the proximity of natural landscape features that served as reference points for action, baselines from which environmentalists sought to spread environmental values to the wider urban society that now dominated the nation.

Trends in the Evolution of Environmental Action

Environmental concern did not emerge full blown but evolved slowly and steadily at much the same pace as its underlying social roots. Several stages in its development can be charted, one succeeding another and each giving rise to distinctive substantive issues, organized environmental action, governmental response, and balance of power between environmental advocates and their opponents. This sequence of historical development provides as much insight into environmental politics as part of a new social order as does a knowledge of its geographical variation.

Some date the beginnings of environmental politics from the publication in 1962 of Rachel Carson's *Silent Spring,* which alerted the nation to the dangers of pesticides. Others emphasize the oil-well blowout in the Santa Barbara Channel off the coast of California in 1969. There is also the theme, taken up by one vocal critic of environmental objectives, that it began with the controversy over the proposal to construct the Storm King pumped-storage power plant on the Hudson River in the mid-1960s. The most common interpretation is that it started with Earth Day 1970, when an outpouring of student interest on college campuses set things in motion.[22]

These varied views depend heavily on the selection of a particular dramatic event or personality as the key factor in recent environmental history. Here we are more impressed with the larger context of social change within which events occurred. And this leads to quite different interpretations.[23]

Earth Day was as much a result as a cause. That event came after a decade or more of evolution in attitudes and programs without which it would not have been possible. One can focus on the extensive legislation of the early 1970s to emphasize the creative role of Earth Day and its immediate aftermath. But there were also the Clean Air acts of 1963 and 1967, which established the basic approach of the 1970 act, and the Clean Water acts of 1960 and 1965, on which the 1972 statute built. The endangered-species laws of 1964 and 1968 were important steps in the development of the 1974 act. A host of wildlands measures were adopted in the 1960s, including the Wilderness Act of 1964, the 1968 laws authorizing wild and scenic rivers and national hiking trails, and the establishment of both the Redwood and North Cascades national parks.[24]

The 1960s were remarkable for the rapid growth of organizations concerned with the amenity values of wildlands. The Sierra Club, Wilderness Society, National Parks Association, and National Wildlife Federation had long been derided as "preservationist" for their efforts to establish natural-environment programs in the nation's wildlands. These organizations were instrumental in the development of the national-park system, the wilderness movement, and the growing interest in nature and wildlife. For them the 1960s were stirring and expansive years.[25]

John F. Kennedy and Lyndon B. Johnson responded to this expanded interest with a level of concern far higher than that displayed by the Eisenhower administration. The new legislation of the decade – the Wilderness Act of 1964, the Land and Water Conservation Fund Act of 1965, the National Wild and Scenic Rivers Act of 1968, and the National Trails Act of 1968 – reflected interest in the aesthetic qualities of nature and wildlands. The President's Commission on Natural Beauty, strongly endorsed by Lady Bird Johnson, wife of the president, was a source of ideas and inspiration concerning the nation's aesthetic values. From this arose a drive to reduce the number of billboards on highways, to eliminate junkyards, and to impress people with the unsightliness of air, water, and solid-waste pollution.

President Johnson's annual messages in 1964 and 1965 were vigorous statements about environmental issues, which might well surprise the reader accustomed to dating environmental action from 1970. And the highly significant role of Secretary of the Interior Stewart Udall should also be underscored.[26]

The events of the 1960s have been given too little emphasis. They show the importance of seeking the roots and meaning of environmental affairs not in 1970 but in evolutionary social changes that had begun much earlier.[27]

The Evolution of Issues

The initial environmental issues of the 1960s involved natural-environment values in outdoor recreation, wildlands, and open space. These shaped debate between 1957 and 1965. Outdoor recreation grew rapidly after World War II as Americans sought out the nation's forests and parks, its wildlife refuges, and its state and federal public lands for recreation and enjoyment. In response, Congress in 1958 established the Outdoor Recreation Resources Review Commission. Its report, completed in 1962, heavily influenced public policy during the Johnson administration and led directly to legislation already described.[28]

These federal laws reflected a widespread interest in natural environments that affected local and state as well as federal policy. Many in urban areas had become concerned about "overdevelopment" and the need for open spaces in their own communities. In 1961 Congress provided for federal financial aid to purchase such lands. The concern for open space extended to a wide range of proposals pertaining to pine barrens, wetlands, swamps, creeks and larger streams, and remnants of the original prairies. Throughout the decade there were also attempts to add new units to the national park system such as Canyonlands in Utah, national lakeshores and seashores, and national recreation areas.

These issues, which set the dominant tone of the initial phase of environmental concern, continued over the years to shape administrative and legislative action. Proposals for specific wilderness, scenic rivers, or other natural areas emerged regularly. Such general legislation as the Eastern Wilderness Act of 1974, the Federal Land Policy and Management Act of 1976, and the Alaskan Lands Act of 1980 testified to the strength of the perennial public concern for natural-environment areas. This was the more enduring and fundamental environmental issue of the two decades. Other concerns might ebb and flow, but interest in natural-environment areas persisted.[29]

Amid this initial stage in environmental policies, a new and different concern arose about the adverse impact of industrial development, with a special focus on air and water pollution. Interest in these matters had evolved slowly on a local and piecemeal basis but had obtained national prominence only in the early 1960s. The first national public-opinion poll on pollution was conducted in 1965. Throughout the remainder of the decade and on into the 1970s these issues evolved with considerable force. The years from 1965 to 1972 constituted the second phase in environmental politics, when concern for pollution took its place alongside the earlier-arisen interest in natural-environment areas.

Public concern about air and water pollution was reflected in extensive media coverage after the mid-1960s and new laws in 1970 and 1972. Growing worries about pesticides gave rise to public demands for their control, which resulted in the new pesticide law of 1972. Interest in the coastal zones, and threats posed by dredging and filling, industrial siting, and offshore oil development led to the Coastal Zone Management Act of 1972. Earth Day in the spring of 1970 fell in the middle of this phase of historical development and was both a result of the previous decade of activity and a new call to action. The years between 1965 and 1972 were a well-defined phase of environmental history in terms of issues that emphasized the reaction against the adverse effects of industrial growth as distinct from the earlier emphasis on natural-environment objectives.

The initial interest in pollution was shaped by the older concern for the natural environment in that it stressed harmful effects on ecological systems. In the years between 1965 and 1972, "ecology" had emerged to reflect the intense public interest in the protection of natural environments from disruption. The impacts of highway construction, electric-power plants, and industrial siting on wildlife, on aquatic ecosystems, and on natural environments in general significantly affected the resulting issues. This was reflected in the enhanced role of the U.S. Fish and Wildlife Service in challenging decisions by development agencies and seeking to reduce their adverse environmental effects. Pesticides were thought of in terms of their impact on wildlife and ecological food chains rather than on human health. The major concern over harm from nuclear power plants in the late 1960s involved the potential disruption of aquatic ecosystems from thermal pollution rather than the effect of radiation on people.[30]

Beginning in the early 1970s a third phase of environmental politics brought three other issues to the fore: toxic chemicals, energy, and the possibilities for social, economic, and political decentralization.

Concern about toxic chemicals was influenced heavily by the seemingly endless series of well-publicized episodes involving polybrominated biphenyls (PBBs) in Michigan, kepone in Virginia to polychlorinated biphenyls (PCBs) in the Hudson River, and the discovery of chemical junkyards along the Love Canal in Erie County, New York, and the Valley of Drums near Louisville, Kentucky. These events, however, were only the more sensational aspects of a deep-seated new twist in ideas about human health. Interest in personal health and especially in preventive medicine leapt forward in the 1970s. Debate about the harmful effects of pollutants now seemed to emphasize human health far more than ecological effects. Whereas proceedings against DDT in the late 1960s had centered on adverse ecological consequences, similar proceedings in the 1970s focused primarily on human health.

The energy crisis of the winter of 1973–4 sharpened a new issue. Energy problems had not gone unnoticed earlier, but their salience now became more central. Oil shortages, rising prices, and the emphasis on energy conservation all helped to etch into the experience and thinking of Americans the limits to potential consumption. Demands for the development of new energy sources increased significantly the political influence of the energy industries, which had long chafed under both natural-environment and pollution-control programs. Now environmental leaders often could scarcely be heard. They formulated their own energy program and it met with some success in acts passed in 1975, 1976, and 1979 that established fuel-economy standards, a 55-mile-per-hour speed limit, appliance efficiency standards, the solar bank, and other innovations in energy policy.[31]

Life-style issues also brought a new element into environmental politics in the 1970s. Behind them lay the growth of new ways of organizing daily living, one's home, community, leisure activities, and even work. These promoted more personal, family, and community autonomy in the face of expanded social, economic, and political organization. The impact and role of this change were not always clear, but it emerged in the energy debate as decentralized solar systems and conservation seemed to be appropriate to decisions made personally and locally, contrasting markedly with the high-technology systems preferred by government and corporate leaders. Issues pertaining to the centralization of political control assumed greater importance in environmental politics as the 1970s came to a close.

The Presidential Response

Successive presidential administrations displayed changing responses to changing patterns of environmental issues. The conservation congress President John F. Kennedy called in 1961 indicated that earlier resource issues, with their perennial debate over whether development should proceed under private or public auspices, were giving way to newer environmental concerns.[32]

President Lyndon B. Johnson and his secretary of the interior, Stewart Udall, responded positively to emerging natural-environment issues. They took up the proposals of the Outdoor Recreational Resources Review Commission, supported the proposed Land and Water Conservation Fund, and pushed forward with national parks, monuments, seashores, and lakeshores. They gave strong support to wilderness, wild and scenic river, and national trails proposals. Johnson's annual message in 1964, a strong statement of environmental advocacy, compared favorably with that of President Jimmy Carter in 1977 and constituted an especially eloquent plea for the creative role of aesthetic values in American society.[33]

By 1965 new issues gave an equally elaborate and forceful presidential message a far different tone. Now the president vigorously supported legislation for air- and water-pollution control and urged that cleanup of the Potomac River and the air of the nation's capital be promoted as models for the entire country. During the latter part of the decade preoccupation with the Vietnam War undercut Johnson's environmental leadership. But environmentalists could point to congressional sessions in 1964, 1965, and 1968 as high points in legislative achievement.[34]

The full force of the growing drive to control the waste products of modern industry was felt by the new Nixon administration. During the 1968 campaign, Nixon's advisers sought to capitalize on environment issues so as to counteract the unpopularity of the

Vietnam War. The strategy reflected political expediency rather than agreement with environmental objectives. To counter the environmental drive Nixon enhanced the role of industry within the administration by appointing a National Industrial Pollution Control Council, composed of the nation's top corporate executives, which was housed in the Department of Commerce and financed with public funds. He also sought to tone down important environmental legislation and refused to approve such measures as the Clean Water Act of 1972, which was passed over his veto.[35]

The political drive toward environmental goals gave rise to significant action by President Nixon, however. The administration supported the Clean Air Act of 1970 and delivered an environmental message in 1971 that was remarkable, in view of the president's lack of sympathy for the environmental movement. Much of this positive response came from several key appointees, most notably Russell Train, undersecretary of the interior, who became chairman of the Council on Environmental Quality in 1970.[36]

During the campaign of 1976 environmentalists found Jimmy Carter's a highly sympathetic ear. Citizen leaders in Georgia had discovered that Carter as governor was especially interested in the protection of wild rivers, wetlands, and natural areas. A strong critic of the dam-building activities of the Army Corps of Engineers, Carter vowed during his campaign that he would "do something" about the corps. Nationwide environmentalists rallied to his side during the primary and the ensuing campaign.[37]

This close relationship continued during the early days of the new administration through the middle of 1977. It was reflected in appointments in key departments and agencies, which gave environmental views a strong voice. The breadth and substance of Carter's environmental message in July 1977 also pleased environmentalists immensely. During that year a number of legislative proposals received his support, such as the Surface Mining Act and revision of both the Clean Air Act and the Clean Water Act. Added to all this was Carter's advocacy of action to protect Alaskan lands. By the fall of 1978 environmental leaders could look with great approval on the Carter administration.[38]

A counterthrust had also appeared, however. During 1977 a

group of advisers had come into the administration who were concerned with expanding economic development more than environmental benefits. The focal point for these views was the Council of Economic Advisers, its Council on Wage and Price Stability, economic advisers in the White House, and officials in the Departments of Energy and Commerce. This resulted in two sets of advisers, one environmental and the other economic, who served as advocates for the two large and contending political forces. By the fall of 1977 those concerned with development had begun to get the upper hand and to call into question regulatory proposals that agencies initiated to carry out legislative enactments. They constituted a formidable force in opposition to environmental objectives.[39]

By the time of the energy crisis in the spring and summer of 1979 this group had obtained a commanding influence. During the transition of 1976 and the early months of the new administration in 1977 environmental energy analyses seemed to sway the president considerably; they were reflected in his first energy message in May 1977. But now those views came to be submerged as energy advisers with an overriding development focus came to dominate. By the crisis of the summer of 1979 they had become the major source of advice to the president; environmental energy experts were relegated to the periphery. Relationships between Carter and environmentalists were almost completely ruptured when the White House in late 1979 proposed an Energy Mobilization Board that would have authority to override environmental laws, a proposal environmentalists united to defeat. The 1979 annual environmental message paled in force and meaning next to that of 1977. Only Carter's firm support for Alaskan lands protection maintained environmental loyalties to the administration.[40]

But if environmentalists were discouraged by trends within the Carter administration, they were appalled by the victory of Ronald Reagan in 1980. The new president launched a massive assault on two decades of environmental programs. His appointees were confirmed opponents of environmental policies; many came form the very corporate firms that had taken the lead in opposing past governmental action. The Reagan environmental program involved drastic and radical action, under executive power and discretion, to make across-the-board changes in almost every environmental program and to turn them over to the direction of their opponents.[41]

The Ebb and Flow of Political Forces

Among institutional leaders in government, in business, and in the scientific and technical professions environmental values never took deep root. Those leaders were far more preoccupied with more traditional forms of economic growth. They emphasized production rather than newer forms of consumption, the creation of jobs rather than the protection of environmental quality, and scientific and technical strategies to bring about more intensive development rather than the enhancement of intangible environmental values. Many of these institutional leaders perceived the environmental movement as emotional rather than rational, a phenomenon of national hysteria rather than of sound action. The more sober ones felt that although the environmental movement reflected legitimate public desires, it also expressed demands the economy could not afford to meet.[42]

The strategies institutional leaders used to bring this drive under control were reactive rather than expressive. During the first two periods of environmental politics, 1957–65 and 1965–72, they could do little but try to hold back the tide. By 1972 they began to launch counterattacks, and by the mid-1970s the political climate shifted in their favor. Energy issues provided a major opportunity to check environmentalists. By 1980, two-thirds of the public expressed positive environmental concerns, whereas only one-third of the nation's leaders did.[43]

Among environmental groups themselves the years after 1970 saw the establishment of a number of organizations that were increasingly effective in the give-and-take of politics. New organizations in Washington, D.C., such as the Environmental Policy Center, Environmental Action, the Environmental Defense Fund, and the Natural Resources Defense Council, became knowledgeable about the technical aspects of substantive issues such as air-pollution control and equally adept at political strategy. These organizations enabled environmental affairs to be advocated with considerable effectiveness in judicial and administrative as well as legislative decision making.[44]

During the 1970s, however, environmental action changed. This change stemmed not so much from a shift in public attitudes as from alterations in the character of environmental politics. One problem was that the range of environmental issues had become so extensive that organized environmental groups were unable to act effectively in all areas. Even more important, many issues had become matters not for public debate and legislative action but for administrative choice, an area in which politics was dominated by technical issues that placed a premium on the financial resources necessary to command expertise. This gave considerable political advantage to administrators and private corporate institutions that employed far more technical personnel than did environmentalists; the weight of influence moved toward the developmental side. Yet legislative issues continued (and with considerable environmental success) through wilderness bills, Alaska legislation, and in 1980, Superfund.[45]

Environmental efforts came to be neutralized by the constant interaction of the regulated industries with administrative agencies in the context of technical-scientific, economic, and planning choices. The environmental opposition was able to limit greatly the scope of policies adopted by Congress, reduce the level of enforcement, and restrict the availability of information to citizen groups and hence their political effectiveness. The control of information was perhaps the most crucial weapon used by environmental opponents. They also succeeded in making regulatory action far more complex, time-consuming, and costly by demanding that general policies give way to detailed actions, tailored to individual industrial circumstances. And they stymied effective control by demanding high levels of precise proof of adverse effects of pollution and minimal margins of safety.

The Reagan antienvironmental revolution stimulated and renewed citizen environmental activity. The vigor and determination with which the administration sought to reverse a host of policies, and its open antienvironmental pronouncements, galvanized the environmental movement into renewed action. Citizen activists had become somewhat lethargic during the Carter administration under the impression that the White House would effectively implement environmental objectives. But interest revived when it now appeared that the gains of two decades were threatened. Organizational membership and financial contributions grew. Although the administration argued that the environmental movement was no longer of political consequence, its actions led to a new period of institution building that strengthened environmental affairs on the American political scene.

The Organized Environmental Movement

Patterns of environmental concern can also be seen in the evolution of organized action. To the casual observer the most striking examples were the national organizations such as the Sierra Club, the Audubon Society, the Wilderness Society, the litigation groups such as the Natural Resources Defense Council and the Environmental Defense Fund, the Environmental Policy Center, Environmental Action, the National Wildlife Federation, and Defenders of Wildlife. But most environmental groups were organized locally to deal with community problems and disappeared almost as rapidly as they surfaced. In each episode a few people looked beyond their immediate circumstances to the wider world of politics and thereby became involved in larger spheres of environmental organization. Over the years such people grew in numbers and swelled the ranks of national groups.[46]

Environmental organization began with a desire to control one's immediate surroundings. Action was prompted if one's special place of home or recreation were threatened by some intrusion such as large-scale development or pollution. Often it was difficult to comprehend subtle long-term changes that might drastically modify such places over the years. But dramatic threats roused people to action. Individuals had little ability to influence the wider world of corporate enterprise and government, but joint efforts might be more effective.

Public agencies were less responsive to individual complaints than to those coming from an organization. The agency could well placate one individual with a perfunctory response, but it felt constrained to give greater attention to a group. If the inquiry or protest could be lodged through an organization known for its sustained capabilities to act through litigation or legislation, it would be more likely to receive attention.

Citizens also found that public authorities often provided only limited assistance. They had to be constantly prodded, watched, stimulated to act. A temporizing, slowly activated, limited response to environmental concerns on the part of governmental agencies was common; often it led to as much cynicism and lack of confidence in governmental institutions as in private corporations. Governmental agencies were hampered by their technical and professional limitations, by their lack of time and funds, and by constant efforts by those responsible for environmental harm to neutralize administrators into inaction so that their own activities could proceed.[47]

To environmentalists it seemed especially difficult to cope with the larger technical world with which each environmental problem was entwined. Some taught themselves the details of complex subjects such as forestry, water pollution, or radiation. In each environmental episode there were usually a number of people who had learned skills of investigative research in college. Many citizen groups could enlist the aid of technical expertise outside their ranks. And often some within their organizations were biologists, chemists, engineers, epidemiologists, economists, and lawyers.[48]

Those who faced a problem in one place established ties with those dealing with a similar problem elsewhere. Knowledge and skills could be shared. Such cooperation usually took place within a single state where a common concern with the same governmental agency added another unifying factor. There were state organizations such as the Wisconsin Wetlands Association, the Montana Wilderness Association, and in Pennsylvania, the Environmental Coalition Against Nuclear Power. In other cases information and ideas were shared through networks rather than formal coalitions. The Nuclear Information and Research Service, located in Washington, D.C., grew out of a joint effort on the part of antinuclear alliances throughout the nation to obtain and share the latest scientific and technical information.

Many national groups did not have state and local branches, but the Audubon Society, Trout Unlimited, the National Wildlife Federation, and the Sierra Club did. These and independent local and state groups often collaborated, especially in the formation of state environmental councils such as the Ohio Environmental Council and the Oregon Environmental Council. Usually they lobbied during legislative sessions, compiled records of votes on key issues, and urged members of their organizations to contact legislators. They issued newsletters to their members and published reports on legislative sessions to maintain citizen interest and action.

The national organizations were most successful in mobilizing people in periods of environmental crisis. But they were well aware that effectiveness required sustained, not intermittent, influence. This alone would enable them to cope successfully with the much more continuous political presence of development advocates. Members of outdoor organizations such as those mentioned earlier were quick to act when the environmental setting of their recreational activities was threatened, for instance, by logging or water pollution. But they were slower to sustain the quieter, persistent political role that was far less visible and dramatic.

Among many environmentalists tendencies toward decentralization gave rise to attempts to free oneself and one's community from dependence on the larger political world and to have greater autonomy. Environmental concerns often led to decentralist political strategies emphasizing personal and local rather than national action. Preoccupation with personal life-styles often resulted in relative indifference to efforts to influence larger centers of power. It was far easier to organize a cooperative food store or manage a homestead than it was to seek to change policies in high places.[49]

Most environmental organizations, however, believed that undesirable public policies could be countered only through larger public action. For over a decade in the 1960s and 1970s they concentrated on increasing their ability to influence national decisions through litigation, lobbying of Congress, and pressure on administrative agencies. Toward the end of the 1970s they began to broaden their base. In 1978 the National Wildlife Federation expanded its national staff to include experts in fund raising, organizational strategies, and political action to increase the capabilities of its state affiliates. National and state organizations began to employ more professional experts in scientific and economic analysis and developed publications that would have an appeal beyond their members. The League of Conservation Voters began in 1978 to canvass door-to-door with trained organizers in order to carry the environmental message to the voters and hence to the polls.[50]

Among only a few environmentalists did action come from general ideologies, larger managerial motives, or more detached analyses of national and international problems. Most became aroused through personal circumstances and immediate needs, shared with others through common experiences. Many people took for granted their own daily preferences for quality in their environment, and it was the threat of loss that prompted action. In the Environmental Era threats came thick and fast. These were the occasions for organization. But more fundamental than the threats were the aspirations themselves for a more satisfying life within the context of family, home, community, and place of leisure and recreation.

The Conservation Response

Older conservation organizations found the new environmental strategies disturbing. They wanted to share credit for much of the emerging environmental enterprise, but they drew back because it was in the hands of new people who seemed to be leading policy in a different direction. There was far greater emphasis on the appreciative relationship of people with natural resources than they felt appropriate, and the emphasis on environmental pollution was vastly different from their traditional concerns. They could find some common ground with the theme of resource limits, but this seemed to play a subordinate role in the face of larger environmental objectives.

Yet these older conservation organizations did not wish to seem too vigorous in their opposition. Although they continued to press for the development of water resources, forests, and agriculture, they sought to convey the image of being "environmentalists, too." They thought of themselves as more moderate and, therefore, more reliable in finding solutions to environmental problems. Their strategies rarely dovetailed with those of environmentalists. The response of conservation organizations to these new ventures highlights the tension between the old and the new.

Older conservation organizations concerned with water resources found the greatest difficulty in sharing the new values. To assert that rivers and streams should remain in their natural condition was hardly reconcilable with the view that they were more valuable as developed waters controlled by engineering works. Groups formed to promote reclamation, flood control, hydroelectric power, or navigation could not accept environmental efforts to restrict water development. They made some political concessions to the environmental interest in free-flowing rivers simply to smooth the way for their own projects, but there was little thought of modifying their objectives to accommodate the new goals. Environmentalists, in turn, formed their own groups to foster their objectives, many of them at the state and local levels, which came together in 1972 in the American Rivers Conservation Council.[51]

The impact of the new view of the forest as environment on older organizations devoted to wood production created greater tension. Industrial-forest organizations, like those concerned with water development, made few overtures to environmental groups. The American Forestry Association, the Society of American Foresters, and state forest organizations, all long representing forest-conservation interests, however, sought to establish an ideological connection with the environmental movement while remaining skeptical of it. They frequently opposed natural-environment values in wildlands management as "unwise preservation." They joined more with game rather than appreciative wildlife groups, often expressed concern about the adverse impact of hiking trails and wild and scenic rivers on private timberlands, and resisted efforts to develop effective state forest acts to control erosion as well as federal nonpoint water pollution programs.

In its magazine the American Forestry Association maintained the image of an appreciative rather than a commodity view of forests. Yet its leadership had deep roots in commodity forestry and was especially fearful of the implications of environment use of forestlands. It opposed the movement to establish formally designated wilderness that led to the 1964 Wilderness Act, and with each evolving stage of wilderness activity it served as a restraining rather than an advancing influence. In its organizational strategies the association sought members among owners of smaller woodlands who were committed to timber as a crop and who participated in the Tree Farm Program of the American Forest Institute, rather than among those who advocated the view of the "forest as environment."[52]

State forest organizations reflected these tendencies in sharper form. Most tended to speak for wood-production objectives, and industry played a significant role in shaping their policies. This had not always been the case. Two of the oldest such groups, the Society for the Protection of New Hampshire Forests, established in 1895, and the Pennsylvania Forestry Association, formed in 1883, had been closely associated with the movement to establish eastern state and national forests. The New Hampshire organization, unique among state forest groups, continued in this vein in the Environmental Era, combining and balancing in its own distinctive way tendencies toward the restoration and management of forests both as sources of wood production and as attractive environments.[53]

The Pennsylvania Forestry Association took a different turn. After World War II, industrial holdings of Pennsylvania forestlands increased, and industrial forestland owners became influential within the association. When environmental concerns began to surface within it they were challenged by industry representatives and were overcome. The organization aligned itself with the forest industry and with farm forest owners and came into sharp conflict with environmental groups in the state on questions concerning wilderness and forest management.

Environmentalists found little that was attractive in the purposes of these older forestry organizations. Those groups seemed to be among their opponents, at times seeking to hew a middle course but strikingly friendly to wood-production interests. They were prone to temporize if not oppose environmentalists during the heat of a forest-management controversy and then to seek identification with the environmental side once the dispute had been resolved. Environmental forest views were expressed more adequately through organizations with firmer environmental roots, such as the Sierra Club, the Wilderness Society, Trout Unlimited, the Audubon Society, and the Natural Resources Defense Council. Older forest-conservation groups remained apart from these activities and left to them the field of environmental forestry advocacy.[54]

The soil-conservation movement resulted in an extensive set of local soil-conservation districts, which the federal program had required for the distribution of technical and financial aid. These organizations and their county associations were shaped by farmers and influenced by a predominant interest in agricultural production. The view that natural environments had inherent value found little acceptance in soil-conservation circles; farmers saw little harm in draining wetlands, channeling streams, or inundating habitat with reservoirs.[55]

Still another difference between soil conservationists and environmentalists became clear. The new concern for water pollution emphasized the adverse impact of sedimentation on downstream areas caused by upstream practices. All this seemed to bring soil-conservation activities more firmly into the orbit of environmental affairs. Yet this was not so. Environmentalists were already at odds with farmers over water pollution from fertilizers and pesticides. Hence soil-conservation organizations sought to control the administration of the new sedimentation program by placing it under the jurisdiction of soil-conservation districts; as a result, its effectiveness was greatly limited.

Conflict arose as newcomers moved into rural areas within the jurisdiction of the soil-conservation districts and sought to direct their policies more toward environmental objectives. At times disputes arose over the composition of the district boards of directors. Historically the boards had represented only farmers and others directly associated with farm production. But new nonfarm rural people now demanded representation, which the districts were reluctant to grant. Hence environmentalists sought new types of organizations that would advance their objectives more wholeheartedly.

The old and the new in these affairs could be observed in the older and newer types of watershed associations that formed especially in the North and East. The older ones had been organized by soil-conservation districts to develop water resources through small-scale dams that would protect farmlands, increase flat-water reservoir recreation, and reduce downstream flood damage. But a new type of watershed association now was created that emphasized water quality and the scenic surroundings of free-flowing rivers and undeveloped streamsides. Often they became mechanisms whereby land along streams could be acquired and maintained as natural environments. These newer associations were formed by residents who looked on their watershed as an environment rather than as an area to be developed. They found little compatibility with the soil-conservation watershed associations.

Of similar significance were commissions sponsored by local municipalities to foster open-space activities. When this "conservation commission" idea first surfaced in New England, New York, and New Jersey, it found little opposition from soil-conservation districts. But in other places the districts viewed them as competitors and sought either to restrain or control them. In Pennsylvania the state Association of Soil Conservation Districts opposed an enabling act that would have permitted local municipalities to establish conservation commissions; the association relented only when provisions were added that would require statewide coordination among the commissions to be carried out through the soil-conservation associations.

The Response of Fish and Wildlife Organizations

Wildlife organizations had long been joined with water, forest, and soil organizations in a common conservation enterprise. But wildlife concerns promoted the view that water, forests, and soils were not just resources in themselves but habitats, environments that could be enhanced or degraded in their ability to sustain fish, animals, and birds. This approach established a common ground between the older conservation and the newer environmental wildlife interests.

By the time of the Environmental Era wildlife organizations were well established. State organizations were federations of local hunting and fishing clubs; the National Wildlife Federation, in turn, was a national coalition of state federations. Strong ties existed between the hunting and fishing public and professional managers in state agencies. As newer environmental wildlife interests began to take shape, this complex of institutions felt threatened and sought to protect its programs from the demands of environmental interests.[56]

Between older and newer interests in fish and wildlife affairs stood the National Wildlife Federation, which melded the two tendencies with considerable finesse. First organized in 1936 as a cooperative venture among state sportsmen's organizations, the federation sought their financial support. But little emerged and the national organization remained weak and limited. After World War II it established a more independent base with a new group of "associate" members who were individuals from the general public not connected with the local and state organizations of sportsmen. Two new magazines, *National Wildlife* and *International Wildlife,* strongly appreciative in tone, enhanced that support, as did a magazine for young people, *Ranger Rick,* which reached more than 2 million subscribers by the end of the 1970s.[57]

These two sets of constituents had quite different wildlife concerns. Associate members expressed great interest in appreciative and nonconsumptive uses of wildlife. They were drawn by the aesthetic qualities the federation's publications displayed in their color photographs and in their articles. When the organization at times openly defended hunting, some of the associate members felt betrayed. The federation, in turn, spoke out for endangered-species programs that environmental wildlife groups advanced; it broadened its concerns to include air and water pollution and toxic wastes; it supported the movement for wilderness and the protection of natural environments.[58]

These responses of conservation organizations to environmental objectives constituted a spectrum, ranging from those concerned with water supply at one end, through soil and forest groups, to wildlife organizations at the other. That spectrum reflected the degree to which older organizations felt they could or could not accommodate newer environmental objectives and, in turn, the degree to which environmentalists felt they shared a common ground with conservation organizations. Few of the older organizations could speak directly and fully to environmental concerns. They did not start from the same personal and social experience – quality of life in the environment of home, work, and leisure – as did environmentalists. To express these newer values many Americans sought new organizational vehicles.

3 The Urban Environment

Cities were the major source of the environmental movement. Here was the largest membership in environmental organizations and the greatest expression of environmental values. Almost every foray into the dynamics of environmental affairs takes one back to the urban experience.

Since the mid-nineteenth century the city had been mainly a manufacturing center in which the needs of industry were uppermost, and its environmental effect on the urban community was considered to be an essential price to pay for material progress. There were few public efforts to reduce that impact. Some sought to work in factories and live elsewhere, but the cost of transportation confined most industrial workers to homes "in the shadow of the mills." The more affluent found residences upwind from factory smoke or lived outside the city and commuted to and from their jobs by rail.

Opportunities to escape the city grew with the electric trolley and the automobile. By the close of World War II a majority of urbanites could establish home and community in truly residential areas, often in the suburbs. It was even possible to travel to still more attractive natural environments for weekends of recreation. The resulting experience of contrast between the city and

71

the land beyond it lay behind much of the environmental movement.

There were also attempts to improve the urban environment from within. These were often limited to ideas and plans drawn up by landscape architects and fostered by civic leaders rather than the public. There were few tangible results, but the plans did serve as focal points for hope and aspiration as to how the city could be made different.

There seemed to be agreement that the varied types of urban pollution made life more than unpleasant, especially in the summer, when heat forced people to seek relief in the streets and to keep their windows open at night, exposing themselves to din and odors. In some cities "quiet zones" were established around schools and hospitals; there were some smoke-control ordinances with little results; and the most offending sources of odors such as slaughterhouses were restricted. But these were exceptions, and on the whole, environmental civic action was limited.

Urban Pollution

The experience of pollution did much to shape the urban environmental awakening. Cities had formed sanitary departments in the nineteenth century to deal with solid waste and had developed programs to make water supplies safer; by the mid-twentieth century new forms of pollution seemed to call for further action.[1]

Several options were debated. Sources responsible for air and water pollution as well as solid waste had long since dumped their waste on the most readily available land, into nearby streams, or into the air. Most of these argued that this strategy of dispersion should continue. An alternative stressed treatment before disposal to reduce the total amount of pollution and hence its impact. Thus, sewage could be treated before discharge into a river, and particles and gases from coal combustion could be removed by fabric filters or scrubbers and concentrated for continued disposal.

But environmentalists advocated a third alternative, source reduction, which would reduce the amount of waste in the first place. Only this option would limit the load on the receiving environment. Much environmental strategy was intended to promote new technologies that would shift action from dispersion to containment and eventually to source reduction.[2]

These alternatives lay at the root of most controversy over pollution. They could be thought of as a struggle over the appropriate role of the urban commons. How should the larger realm of air, water, and land be used? Those responsible for pollution thought it should be reserved for the waste they produced. But those adversely affected sought to reclaim the commons for public use as an amenity, to improve the quality of urban life in terms of aesthetic values and human health.

Community Air Quality

Improvement in air quality became one of the first of the new urban environmental concerns. In the North and East one talked of smoke, but in the newer cities of the West, where the motor vehicle rather than the factory was the main offender, one heard of smog. Doctors, city councils, and mayors joined with private citizens to reduce pollution.[3]

The smoke-control movement met resistance from industries, whose leaders were willing to undertake some cleanup but were worried about the extent of the demands. Current levels of air pollution, they argued, were not unhealthy, and to support their argument they presented scientific data to city councils and local magistrates. In the face of this expertise local governments felt helpless and for counterarguments turned to the U.S. Public Health Service (PHS). After the Clean Air Act of 1963 that agency had begun to develop assessments of health effects of air pollution known as criteria documents. These were used by local governments and citizens to bolster their case.[4]

Even in these early years the political lines were drawn between industry and the public. To offset the growing demands for action, business groups sought to develop state pollution-control programs through which they might exercise restraint on local governments. In response, those who favored stricter controls turned to the federal government to establish federal standards and to provide funds to enhance local and state technical and management capabilities. This led to the Clean Air Acts of 1967 and 1970, which shaped a program incorporating both federal and state roles.[5]

Several sources of pollution were readily reduced. Open burning of trash in backyards or in city dumps was ended with little difficulty. Smoke from household heating and locomotives ceased with the advent of natural gas in the North and East as a result of the pipelines built from the Texas fields and with the expanded use of diesel fuel for trains. But industrial sources vigorously opposed regulatory efforts to reduce their emissions. There was some success in persuading automakers to manufacture cleaner engines, but regular inspection and maintenance of automobiles by car owners met stiff opposition.[6]

The clean-air program involved both setting standards and implementing them. Primary standards safeguarded public health, and secondary standards protected crops and forests, visibility, aquatic life, and materials. A rationale for establishing standards was also developed. Criteria documents were to serve as the bases for defining acceptable levels of contamination, "thresholds" above which exposures would not be permitted. Because the entire control program rested on these scientific assessments, they became a subject of intense controversy. Those who resisted controls usually interpreted the evidence to justify higher exposures, and those who sought greater protection interpreted it to mandate lower levels. Such debates became a staple of environmental dispute.[7]

Another question remained before a standard could be set, the "margin of safety," which would take into account those effects that were suspected but not as yet well established. Of special concern were the effects of persistent low-level exposures, in contrast with short-term high-level ones, and the synergistic effects of several interacting pollutants. Little such knowledge was available. Even among those who agreed on the principle of the margin of safety, the precise level was a matter of continuing debate.[8]

This general air-pollution strategy was applied to few pollutants. Six, known as the criteria pollutants, were identified in the 1970 act: particulates, sulfur dioxide, hydrocarbons, carbon monoxide, nitrogen oxides, and photochemical oxidants. Although it was expected that more would be added to the list, in subsequent years only one more, lead, came under regulation, and this only after considerable citizen litigation by the Natural Resources Defense Council. A few more in the special category of toxic pollutants were regulated, but the number of these also remained small.[9]

Health protection under the program was confined for the most part to mortality and irreversible illnesses. Usually it did not include temporary sickness that interfered with normal daily work and leisure. And although there were some promising steps in the 1960s toward protection against physiological and behavioral effects, such action did not materialize. This seemed to run counter to changing popular values. The public increasingly defined health objectives in terms of physical fitness, feeling well, and the ability to perform up to one's capacity, rather than the simple absence of serious illness. But these aspirations rarely were reflected in the strategies of those in control of environmental administration.[10]

The health bases of air-pollution control were debated continually. The draft of the first assessment of the health effects of sulfur oxides, drawn up by the Public Health Service in the spring of 1967, was vigorously denounced by the coal industry. Congress, in turn, approved legislation that year requiring revision of the document under the guidance of a committee that included representatives of the coal, oil, and steel industries. Throughout the 1970s the criteria documents continued to provoke bitter dispute. At times industry succeeded in revising them to raise the thresholds of adverse health effects or to prevent new evidence from lowering them. Environmentalists resisted these efforts. Because they were highly technical these all-important political battles were carried out far from public scrutiny or knowledge.[11]

Steps were also taken to implement the standards. How would a shift take place toward more desirable, cleaner technology? The pollution-control program contemplated a strategy of "forcing" such innovation by requiring pollution reduction to a given level by a set compliance date. This would create a guaranteed market for pollution-control equipment, thus stimulating third-party innovation. The strategy worked, even though slowly, as it gave rise to a new pollution-control industry and steady replacement of environmentally obsolete technology.[12]

Resistance to implementation was as vigorous as resistance to the standards. Polluters sought to postpone compliance dates and thus to put off the cost of installing controls, a strategy the automobile industry used with some success. Although considerable progress was made in reducing some pollutants – the most success was achieved with lead – for others, efforts resulted in more of a holding action. The sharp increase in air pollution of earlier years was halted; in the face of rising levels of fuel combustion, this was a major accomplishment. Toward the end of the 1970s progress slowed; the ability of industry to use loopholes in the law to retard cleanup, in addition to the predicted increase in the use of energy, made clear that emissions would rise in the future.[13]

By 1980 knowledge about air quality had advanced sufficiently to lead to demands for action to deal with newly identified types of harm: fine respirable particles that were most damaging to human health; mutagenicity; reduced lung function among school children; acid precipitation; lowered visibility and damaged crops and forests. These problems defined a new stage of controversy as environmentalists sought new legislative and administrative action that industry resisted. Struggles begun in the 1960s continued with unabated vigor, leading often to stalemate but sometimes to persistent, even though slow, environmental progress.

Water Pollution

Concern for water quality was closely related to human health. Urban water supplies initially were drawn from wells, and human wastes ended up either in nearby outhouses or in "dry wells." This endangered the quality of the water and led to steps to obtain it from cleaner and more distant sources. By the early twentieth century water use and waste production had risen considerably. But cities were reluctant to incur expenses to deal with both problems. Usually they chose to improve the quality of the water supply through filtration and chemical treatment and to continue to discharge raw sewage into nearby rivers.[14]

State public-health agencies sought to encourage municipal sewage treatment, but because they had few powers beyond persuasion they were ineffective. Cities frequently argued that states could not require them to act until they proved that raw-sewage discharge into streams was harmful. To overcome this resistance state legislatures declared that the discharge of raw sewage itself was illegal. Sewage treatment lagged far behind water supply purification, did not receive much attention until the New Deal public-works programs in the 1930s, and was not taken up by most cities until massive federal funding became available beginning in the 1960s.

After World War II, industrial discharges began to arouse as much interest as did municipal sewage, and the effect of pollution on aquatic life became as much a public concern as was human health. Biological decay of organic matter used up oxygen, making streams uninhabitable for fish. Fish kills increased, were reported frequently by fishermen, and reached newspaper headlines. Usually they were attributable to industrial discharges. In 1961 the Public Health Service began to record information about fish kills and to issue annual reports about them.[15]

Industrial discharges gave rise to several new problems. One was the task of acquiring information about their extent. Details about municipal sewage were fairly well known. But little information had been collected about industrial wastes. Efforts by federal authorities to rectify this in the 1960s met stiff resistance from industry. For eight years a form for collecting discharge data was delayed by the federal Bureau of the Budget because its industry-dominated committee on report forms objected to it. Not until the Clean Water Act of 1972 did the federal government have the legal authority to require the disclosure of such information.[16]

Another problem was the organization of federal administration. Those concerned with the aquatic effects of pollution became highly critical of the limited view of the health scientists and demanded that the program be removed from the Public Health Service. In 1965 water pollution was placed under the jurisdiction of an assistant secretary in the Department of Health, Education, and Welfare, and then in 1966 was transferred to the Department of the Interior.[17]

Underlying these changes was a new interest in in-stream uses and quality, not just streams as sources of water. Swimming and fishing took on as much emphasis as did health. Protection of the aquatic environment, and hence fishing, required high water-quality standards and measures far beyond chlorination.

In the 1920s it commonly had been argued that although some streams could be set aside for their recreational and aesthetic value, most were important for waste disposal. By the 1960s this view had changed radically; the prevailing sentiment now was that waste disposal was not a legitimate use of a stream, and the 1972 Clean Water Act reflected that opinion. It affirmed that all discharges of pollutants into the nation's waters were illegal and that permits to be granted to industrial sources would be only a temporary permission to pollute pending the end of all discharges into receiving waters. The act proclaimed that the new goal was to "restore and maintain the chemical, biological and physical integrity of the nation's waters."

Rising public interest in water pollution led to new federal legislation in 1965, 1970, and 1972 that contained elements similar to those of the air-pollution laws: standards and implementation. There were important differences, however. The beginning point was to define the various categories of usage, such as domestic drinking, cooking, and bathing, swimming and fishing, and industry and agriculture, and then to set standards for each. Maximum concentration levels were established for specific chemicals and for specific stream segments.[18]

The most distinctive aspect of the water-quality program was in its implementation. The lengthy court battles of earlier years led to an innovation in the 1972 act to bypass proof of cause and effect and require each discharger to install a given level of technology per se. These were known as technology standards.

The 1972 act had stipulated that the "average of the best" treatment facility should be chosen as the exemplary plant and others would be required to adopt it. To implement this approach the Environmental Protection Agency (EPA) studied each category of industry to determine the effectiveness of its water-treatment technology. But what was the "average of the best"? The EPA decided that it meant the average of the top 5–10 percent of existing technology. Industry argued that it meant the median plant in the entire industry, which would compel only 50 percent rather than at least 90 percent of the plants to modernize. The courts favored the EPA's interpretation.[19]

This "technology forcing" aspect of the 1972 act stimulated innovation in the wastewater-treatment industry and changes in production processes to a far greater extent than had occurred in air-quality control. There was great potential for redesign of processes both to reduce the amount of water used and the level of discharge and to recover products for reuse. From the industry side the most eloquent advocate of this strategy of "profits from pollution prevention" was Dr. Joseph Ling of the 3M Corporation, who avowed that process-oriented changes in his firm had both reduced effluent and paid for themselves.[20]

The 1972 act set the stage for much political controversy between polluters and environmentalists. Some segments of industry had not yet agreed that waste disposal was not a legitimate use of the nation's waters. Of particular concern to environmentalists was the mixing zone near the point of discharge within which ambient standards would not apply. This came to be allowed because it was argued that the natural capacity of the stream to biodegrade pollutants should be allowed to work at least within the immediate vicinity of the outfall and that standards should not be applied until after some of that process had taken place. The mixing zone was circumscribed for each outfall in terms of depth, width, and length. If plants were limited in number, the effect on streams was minimal. But on a heavily industrialized river a series of mixing zones might well increase significantly the allowable pollution for the entire stream segment.

As the federal water-quality program unfolded, environmentalists increasingly stressed source reduction, water recycling, and reuse of materials. The 1972 act had emphasized municipal and industrial discharges. But it was also clear that runoff from city streets, from agriculture and forestry, and from mining and construction was a significant cause of water pollution. As the control of point sources improved, attention turned to these nonpoint sources. Through litigation by citizen environmental groups, the EPA was forced to pay more attention to this problem, but by the end of the decade the agency had taken only limited action. In this case treatment after the fact was virtually impossible. Only better management practices at the source would be effective.

Even more hopeful to environmentalists was the possibility of a different approach to municipal sewage. For years the sludge resulting from sewage treatment had been either discarded in a landfill, incinerated, or dumped into the ocean. To environmentalists sewage sludge was valuable as fertilizer. But it was often unusable because it contained toxic chemicals that came from industrial discharges into municipal sewage-treatment plants. The EPA was pressed to require industry to pretreat these discharges so that the sludge could be safely used. But a decade after passage of the 1972 act a pretreatment program had not yet been implemented.

Solid Waste

Over the years refuse had been one of the most visible and immediate environmental problems. Garbage mounted up around homes and businesses and in the streets. In the late nineteenth century, refuse disposal became the first major urban environmental program. It included regular sweepings and collections and strategies to recycle, create landfills, and incinerate.[21]

After World War II household waste increased as a result of the frequent discarding of old belongings – the consumer economy emphasized rapid product obsolescence – and the rise in packaging. One of the ways in which solid waste was understood by the general public was through the problem of litter, which had long given rise to cleanup campaigns. This was a major emphasis of the Commission on Natural Beauty established by President Johnson in 1965; state groups formed through the inspiration of the national commission, such as the Arizona Commission on Natural Beauty, promoted litter removal for community beautification.[22]

Concern for the urban solid-waste problem mounted. Firms that manufactured throwaway products such as cans, bottles, and paper containers sought to place responsibility for action on the general public. They formed Keep America Beautiful (KAB) to launch a public-education program to persuade people to dispose of trash in litter barrels. But this seemed to have only limited results.

Volunteer efforts in many communities, often involving high school or college students, led to the establishment of centers to which newspapers, glass bottles, and tin cans were brought. These ecology centers then sold the materials for reuse in new products. Recycling was taken up by industries such as the Aluminum Company of America and bottle manufacturers who found that recycling centers provided raw materials as well as an additional weapon in their antilitter educational campaign. Many environmental groups insisted on using recycled paper even though it was more expensive, and many public institutions did so to identify themselves with this attempt to further a more ecological approach to resource use.

Environmentalists pressed beyond recycling, however, to stress the reuse of containers and a reduction in packaging. In 1972 Oregon enacted a law to encourage the use of returnable glass bottles for beer and soft drinks. Mandatory deposits on containers would encourage consumers to return them to reclaim their deposit. The Oregon program greatly reduced the amount of highway litter and the public cost of trash removal. It was copied by a number of states such as Vermont, Michigan, Maine, Connecticut, and Iowa. National legislation was proposed but was not passed.[23]

In the years after the Oregon law was passed, proposals to extend it sparked intense political controversy. Container manufacturers bitterly resisted the drive for returnables, arguing that the Oregon law had not worked and that the KAB antilitter campaign was preferable. Organized labor in steel, aluminum, and glass also protested. Environmentalists argued that the program had worked well, that it had in fact increased jobs and had saved a considerable amount of energy that otherwise would be used for recycling. After the energy crisis of the winter of 1973–4, the Department of Energy supported a national returnables bill. All this kept the KAB campaign on the defensive. To recoup its prestige it sought unsuccessfully to rename the annual Earth Day as Keep America Beautiful Day.

There were other attempts to foster source reduction in paper and cardboard packaging. Studies were made to devise a packaging tax that would cover the cost of waste disposal. But industry and labor opposed these also. In 1978 the Minnesota legislature required that new packaging proposals be filed with a state agency that would evaluate them in terms of state solid-waste reduction goals. The agency would then transmit its findings to the legislature for possible action. But even this approach failed because of industry's insistence that such information was a trade secret that, if transmitted to a public agency, might give competitors an unfair advantage.

Political controversies over returnables and packaging reflected alternatives in dispersion, recycling, and source reduction. Producers of materials preferred the first two; and environmentalists, the last two. Manufacturers viewed packaging as a consumer convenience that should be encouraged, but to environmentalists the main objective was to remove materials from the waste stream before they presented a disposal problem, and the best such strategy was source reduction.

The alternatives were sharply divided in the debate over the new proposals for municipal solid-waste management that stressed the centralized collection of waste, recovery of metals and other "usable" materials by mechanical and magnetic means, use of the remainder as fuel to produce electricity, and disposal of the residue in landfills. Promoted by both cities and equipment manufacturers, this approach became an integral part of federal policy stemming from the Resource Conservation and Recovery Act of 1976.[24]

Environmentalists emphasized source separation and recycling at an early stage in the waste and stream rather than incineration. Households could be persuaded to sort their waste into different types that then could be transported to recycling centers. Promoters of centralized systems argued that households would be reluctant to take up source separation. More vital was the degree to which centralized systems, in order to be economically viable, would require all waste to be channeled to them and prohibit removal for other purposes such as selective recycling earlier in the waste stream. Municipal contracts with central-system managers provided for penalties if a given amount of waste were not delivered to the waste-processing facility. Hence, so environmentalists argued, centralized systems would both encourage higher levels of waste and prevent experiments in more environmentally sound alternatives.

Household and community responsibility for recycling solid wastes reflected an ecological approach. Garbage was useful organic material that could be recycled in the home garden. In January 1980, Seattle developed a program to promote composting as one method of reducing waste disposal. Ecologists were also drawn toward use of the compost toilet, which would decompose both household and human waste. But into the 1980s this was still only an experimental venture, important because it exemplified ecological notions about small-scale biological rather than large-scale engineered recycling.

The Use of Urban Land

Environmental pollution in the city became intimately connected with choices about land use. That use could be either environmentally degrading or environmentally enhancing. At times the impact of past use could be mitigated; junkyards, for example, could be screened from view. But urban residents knew well that it was easier to prevent environmentally undesirable land use than to control it once established.[25]

Early American cities often included plans for open space. Many cities laid out along streams included a common on the flood plain or waterfront that was described in parklike terms. But in the rush to development, these lands were devoted to other uses. Toward the end of the nineteenth century there were attempts to capture land for city parks. At first these parks tended to be appendages of more affluent residential areas, but as time passed open space became an amenity for the entire population.

A major focus for these matters came in the defense of the environment of the urban neighborhood. City dwellers sought to move away from factories and, once having done so, to protect themselves against further intrusion. But urban communities found that their residential aspirations were constantly undermined by the free market in land, which promoted change to uses of higher value. How could the urban community foster stability so as to establish a sense of place and geographical belonging?[26]

The most widely used technique was zoning, a public policy to allocate land for defined uses, which became legally acceptable and increasingly popular in the 1920s. Land was customarily divided into industrial, commercial, and residential categories. Community residents hoped to limit industrial and commercial use to specific areas and to prevent intrusion into their domain. Industry, on the other hand, fearful of efforts by residential owners to restrict their operations, also wanted zoning to guarantee land for plant expansion.[27]

A different aspect of community environmental quality was the role of urban streets. In many areas of the built-up city developers had packed houses close together and left little land around them. The more affluent could afford houses on the urban periphery with land and trees, but to the majority of the city's population the street was the most accessible outdoor space where one could walk or sit and relax on the doorstep and children could play. The affluent could go to their vacation homes during the summer, but most urban dwellers could only escape to the streets.

As the city grew, traffic began to "take over" the streets. First there were horse-drawn wagons, made with heavier wheels and wider tires to haul heavier loads. Because these cut more deeply into the dirt streets, wagoners demanded harder surfaces. Community residents fought back; to prevent heavier traffic they argued against paving streets. Since abutting property owners paid for improvements, they could easily influence street development. By the early twentieth century motorized traffic had become the primary intrusion; this time protests were in vain. Transportation engineers pressed relentlessly for traffic patterns that, so they argued, required increased flow through residential neighborhoods. Community legal defenses were torn down by urban traffic experts in their search for citywide systems.

These historic struggles were repeated in the 1950s and 1960s in the response to new highways. The federal Highway Trust Fund, established in 1956, financed a massive new phase of transportation development. Initially the system was intended to bypass cities in order to provide faster nationwide traffic. But urban pressures shifted the plans to make the city center more accessible to the periphery and to construct beltways around them. Appropriation of land for this purpose destroyed many residential communities. Community reaction was intense as both the more and the less affluent fought to protect themselves.[28]

Urban highway issues introduced many citizens to administrative politics. They used the environmental-impact statement to focus on undesirable consequences of highway construction. They mobilized communities for political action and took part in hearings held by state and federal transportation agencies. Often they were successful in stopping construction. They also became involved in devising strategies to protect their communities against existing traffic. Barriers could be erected against through traffic. Yet this only reorganized the flow of motorized vehicles toward some streets and away from others and did not reduce it. But in some cities such actions led to increased community influence in transportation planning.[29]

The use of urban land for airports constituted another disturbance to urban communities. Air traffic grew rapidly after World War II, and the shift from propeller to jet engines increased the noise to which urban residents were exposed. Especially affected were those who lived near airports and within the flight patterns. Many people had purchased homes when planes had been less noisy only now to be faced with jets. The prospect of the supersonic transport and the British version, the Concorde, with even higher noise levels, was especially feared. Many communities sought to restrict use, shift flight patterns, prohibit nighttime flights, and bring liability suits for personal and property damage.[30]

In the late 1970s a new phase of environmental history in the urban community began as a significant number of people invested resources in the renovation of inner-city housing. This was stimulated by the relatively low value of such real estate and also by federal policies that stressed rehabilitation of older structures rather than redevelopment. The new drive for historic preservation also played an important role. Community efforts in rehabilitation were aided by federal programs that identified buildings and entire urban communities as worthy of preservation.[31]

These drives to renovate the central city, in contrast with the flight to the suburbs, heightened emphasis on the city as a place to live; they were one of many tendencies over the years that cumulatively revitalized the city. But the popularity of such efforts increased dramatically the cost of urban housing and limited the number of people who could afford to participate.

In the competition between residential land use and commercial and industrial uses, these tendencies toward urban renovation helped to undergird the former and restrain the invasion of urban neighborhoods by other enterprises. Despite all this the heightened residential role of the city brought with it more people and more intensive human activity, which were major sources of environmental degradation. Movement to the suburbs, in fact, continued at a more rapid pace than did commitment to the city proper.

Land and Water as Urban Amenities

Urban citizens also sought to enhance the use of land and water as environmental amenities. In the face of overriding development pressures this was more than difficult. But in the redevelopment push after World War II some opportunities arose to modify land use. Cities cleared away decaying buildings, including factories, commercial establishments, and housing, to make way for rebuilding. Through federal programs cities bought land, demolished structures, and revised urban land uses. Considerable land was given over to intensive development, but some opportunity also arose for environmental uses.[32]

The interest in urban open spaces led to one of the first federal environmental ventures, the open-space program of the Department of Housing and Urban Development (HUD). In 1961 Congress approved a purchase program of which many cities took advantage, and a decade and a half of activity on behalf of open space ensued. Much of the initial vision, however, failed to be realized because of the high cost of city land. To obtain results public agencies, including HUD, turned to cheaper land on the urban fringe. This helped to establish parks, but they were not readily accessible to central-city residents.[33]

Tracts bypassed in the course of urban development because they were too difficult to build on presented prime opportunities for action. Such was the case, for example, in Cincinnati and Pittsburgh, both built on hills. But the most persistent opportunities for urban open space were presented by bodies of water. In the earlier stages of urban growth rivers and lakes had been used primarily for navigation and sewage disposal and had been lined with many businesses. Now they came to be used in a different way.

Underlying these changes were new views of the meaning and importance of rivers to urban people. Citizens desired to increase their use for fishing, swimming, and boating. Rivers, lakes, and harbors came to be seen as providing environmental amenities just as did the attractive terrain of steep and wooded hills. Cities with varied land- and waterscapes fostered a much sharper sense of environmental image and hence of urban identity.

These new roles for rivers were enhanced by changes in the use of the waterfront, a shift in the location of water-transport facilities, and a relative decline in inland navigation in contrast with trucking – all of which hastened a lowering of waterfront property values. Urban flooding contributed to these trends. For many years cities had tried to protect flood-prone lands by levees or through upstream reservoirs. But these only stimulated intensive development on flood plains and increased future flood damage. When floods destroyed buildings, a chance arose to revise land-use patterns, and this often was facilitated by federal redevelopment financing.

The Carter administration developed plans for a major program to facilitate these tendencies. Its efforts were aided by the growing cost of energy and the attempt to encourage recreation closer to home. Waterfront development could make recreation more available to lower income groups. Federal action was limited to plans, but it stimulated local governments to act, and over the years these efforts added up.[34]

Urban national parks also might provide open space. This was a relatively new idea for the National Park Service, which had traditionally thought in terms of parks in wildlands. In 1972 two national urban parks were established: Gateway National Recreation Area in New York City and Golden Gate National Recreation Area in San Francisco. But the high cost of such a program prompted several presidential administrations, notably those of Nixon and Carter, to back away from their initial support. The Reagan administration replaced skepticism with outright opposition. It sought, though unsuccessfully, to eliminate the entire program and to transfer existing urban national parks to the states and cities for management.[35]

The search for enhanced urban environmental amenities gave rise to new emphases on urban forestry and wildlife. In the early 1970s urban forestry became popular with the U.S. Forest Service, which established a research program concerning the benefits of trees in cities. *American Forests* magazine popularized urban forestry programs. This was one of the few instances in which foresters defined forests as human environments rather than as sources of commodities. But the results of their efforts were limited.[36]

More extensive was the emphasis on urban wildlife. Bird-watching came to be increasingly popular, to which rising memberships in wildlife organizations testified. Nature centers grew in numbers and popularity to make nature education more accessible to urban residents. This education, in turn, stimulated efforts to attract birds to urban backyards. Many families purchased bird feeders and followed the seasonal course of bird migrations. In 1975 the Urban Wildlife Institute was organized to promote the enhancement and enjoyment of urban wildlife.[37]

Amid these efforts standards of environmental quality displayed in the wildlands and the countryside served as examples to be emulated. Although results were limited, some successes demonstrated what the city could be. One such reality-as-symbol was a designated wilderness area on the Fire Island National Seashore on western Long Island in the New York City metropolitan area. But still it was far easier to protect existing natural environments in developing cities than to recapture natural amenities from the city once they had been destroyed. No wonder that much environmental effort among urbanites lay in attempts to retain elsewhere in the nation's wildlands what was so difficult to create closer to home.[38]

Environmental Possibilities in the New Urban Economy

Shifts in the national economy from manufacturing to service and information functions seemed to heighten the possibilities of creating more livable cities. These shifts generated new occupations and rising levels of education, which created a large new middle class with expanded desires and concerns. New values associated with home, family, and leisure rather than physical work gave rise to efforts to make cities more attractive places in which to live.

In the nineteenth century the most dominant aspects of urban land use had been the factories, whereas in the twentieth century the main features were office buildings, structures integral to leisure and recreation, and shopping centers. These incorporated many elements of environmental design.

Many businesses knew well the negative impact of their appearance and as a result sought the services of landscape architects to make them more attractive. These ventures were especially evident in office buildings, which housed white-collar and managerial workers, and research centers, which employed technically trained professionals. In Pittsburgh, for example, the Equitable Life Insurance Company agreed to invest in Gateway Center, part of an extensive redevelopment program, on the condition that the area beyond it at the junction of the Allegheny and Monongahela rivers be changed from a conglomeration of old factories and railroad yards into a park.[39]

Industrial parks, established by industrial development authorities, exemplified these new ideas. These housed commercial and managerial enterprises with white-collar workers. More significant, however, were the environmental values reflected in the terms under which they were leased. Research Triangle Park, established in 1953 in North Carolina, set the pace. Each lessee was required to adhere to specific performance standards, limiting emissions of air and water pollution, noise, odors, and vibrations; moreover, each property was to be landscaped in accordance with open-space, drainage, and slope standards. These provisions were quite similar to community environmental standards developed later in state and federal pollution-control programs.[40]

Environmental values were also incorporated into interior design. Hardly a new office building was without its natural decor, and specialized firms were created to care for it. New hotels were designed around massive interior spaces with hanging plants and other greenery and flowers.

All these efforts to improve the environmental quality of the cities, however, could well be frustrated by larger populations and more intensive human activities. This was illustrated most markedly by the greater use of the city's streets. Higher levels of traffic created higher levels of air pollution, noise, and congestion; the amount and speed of intrusion into human-scale activities grew.

The car and truck came to be looked on as major problems of urban life.[41]

In the early 1970s, the urban environmental movement became convinced that the only sensible solution was mass transit. The critical problem, so it was argued, was the degree to which transportation options were so heavily skewed toward the street and highway. It could all be traced to the federal Highway Trust Fund, which provided a guaranteed source of money, and behind it were the manifold business enterprises that benefited from its expenditures. A movement developed to "bust the trust" and allocate some of its funds to alternatives.[42]

Some inroads were made. Congress first permitted states to use a portion of their grants from the fund for mass transit. As some expensive urban beltway projects were halted because of public opposition, cities were permitted to reallocate their highway funds to mass transit. Federal funds were made available to purchase buses and even build subways. The new metro in the nation's capital received considerable attention and symbolized a new era in urban mass transportation.

The growing concern for long-term energy supplies beginning with the winter of 1973–4 brought a new dimension to these debates. Environmentalists began to emphasize the high energy cost of motorized transport. The urban automobile was used mainly for short-distance travel between home and work. This state of affairs, they argued, was encouraged by public policies that made living on the urban periphery relatively attractive. Those policies should be reversed to encourage people to live near their place of work. But all this made little dent in the continuing tendency of urbanites to work in one place and live in another, to seek a more environmentally attractive setting on the urban periphery and hence to remain dependent on the personal motor vehicle.[43]

Amenities on the Urban Fringe

The urban fringe provided precisely the environmental quality that was not available in the center. Hence it served constantly as a magnet for urban residents as a place to live. The shift to the suburb often came when younger generations sought surroundings that were more pleasant than those in which they had grown up. Often they wanted more space within the home as higher living standards came to emphasize more personal and individ- ualized rooms; but they also prized outside space in yards and streets not continually disturbed by traffic.[44]

Entrepreneurs found that they could profitably sell environ- mental quality on the urban fringe. Many environmental ameni- ties such as cleaner air and water could not be packaged and sold; they involved a jointly experienced environment that could be enhanced only through public action. But natural amenities associated with one's home could be purchased privately in the form of specific tracts of land with attractive surroundings. Home builders and real estate dealers marketed housing to respond to new values.

But there was a paradox in suburbanization. Amenities pur- chased there often soon became threatened by the increase in people, traffic, and pollution. The world seemed to close in and destroy what one had sought to secure. This experience shaped much environmental concern. One spoke of the problems of growth. How to approach the problem was another matter. The confrontation with environmental degradation in the city now was augmented by a confrontation with threatened degradation in the suburbs.[45]

A natural succession seemed to be taking place in which land owners, home builders, money lenders, and utility companies persistently fostered more intensive use of land. Local govern- ments joined in with the hope of securing more tax revenues from higher land values. Could this natural succession not be brought under control? A series of factors defined the problem: shopping centers, airports, and highways; utility lines and billboards; the allowable size of lots; the use of parklands for solid-waste trans- fer stations; the use of trails for off-road vehicles. There was a pattern to the contending forces: Some sought the economic ad- vantage of more intensive development, and others wished to provide greater environmental amenities.

Suburban environmentalists also went on the offensive to se- cure undeveloped land as open space. There were hillsides or stream valleys not yet built on and remnants of former farms that owners might still value as undeveloped land and would coop- erate to work out some kind of permanent protection for. In New

England a new approach to this problem appeared in the 1960s: the conservation commission, a citizen body appointed by a municipal governing board that was given the responsibility to identify ways and means of protecting such land. In the West, regional park and open-space districts played a similar role.[46]

Land was expensive. Yet monies were gathered by a judicious combination of tax revenue, municipal bond issues, private land donations, and private fund raising. Often those who owned undeveloped lands were residents of middle age or older who had formed an attachment to the community, whose memories of a more natural setting remained strong, and who were inclined to keep their land undeveloped if at all possible. Income tax laws that made such gifts deductible helped them to achieve their goals.[47]

An alternative to outright acquisition, and often a transition to that end, was the conservation easement. One could separate control of the use of the surface from its fee ownership, retain the property but at the same time convey the right of use, with limitations, to others. Often such conveyance involved the transfer of development rights to an agency such as a municipality or a private land conservancy with restrictions as to what development might take place. Through devices such as these some lands on the urban fringe were protected as permanent open space.[48]

These strategies reflected personal involvement in the creation of public assets in which individuals could dovetail their own deep attachment to open lands as users and as owners with the wider interest in their public value. It also represented one of the environmental movement's most significant motives, namely, the desire to ensure that future generations would be able to enjoy an environment of high quality.

Open-Land Strategies

Amid these efforts one of the overriding environmental experiences was the inexorable development of farmland. Lands on the urban fringe that had been devoted for years to agriculture now were prime sites for houses, shopping centers, stores, and even factories. Real estate developers kept a sharp lookout for such possibilities as they predicted the course of urban expansion. And municipalities, looking ahead, extended water and sewer lines, as well as streets and roads, into undeveloped areas precisely to attract developers.

These pressures fell with special impact on farmers in the shape of higher taxes. Tax authorities customarily assessed land in terms of its anticipated potential rather than its current use. Thus, farmers might well find their assessments increased even though the actual use of their land had not changed. The increased financial burden only encouraged them to sell to developers and speeded up conversion.

In the mid-1970s this problem assumed greater proportions because of concern over a decline in the nation's productive agricultural land. This, in turn, led to proposals to permit farmland assessment on the basis of actual rather than potential use. But such proposals could become simply a tax subsidy for farmers, since many were now prone just to postpone the decision to quit farming rather than to keep their lands permanently in agriculture. Hence new strategies were called for. In New York State an agricultural district system was devised. Farmers could vote to establish such a district, which would then be subject to land-use restrictions as well as use-value assessments. Municipalities were prohibited from incorporating nearby farmlands into utility districts. This reduced the freedom of the farmer to sell in return for immediate tax advantages.

Municipalities often used indirect methods to restrain development pressures by not extending public services. This approach seemed called for as evidence came to light that much development actually was costly to local governments because it required more expenditures for streets, sewers, water, schools, fire and police protection, and welfare than it returned in higher taxes. Now municipal governments often held developers at arm's length. Their wariness had little to do with environmental values but much to do with municipal finances. But it did lead to some cooperation with farmers and environmentalists to deal with the pace of development on the urban fringe.

Similar tendencies affected forestlands, since suburban sprawl spread into woodlands as well. Rising land values made many forestlands uneconomical to manage for wood production; they were more valuable as environmental forests. This also led to tax-abatement measures for forestlands, and some farmland reassessment plans actually benefited industrial timberland owners.

In the late 1970s commercial timberland owners advanced another strategy. They feared the inroads of environmental forest uses for both homes and woodland recreation, and they began to experiment with a new approach called "prime timberland identification," first launched in the upper peninsula of Michigan. Lands were classified as to their potential for wood production, and the best or prime ones were identified. Planning agencies and zoning bodies, it was hoped, would act to limit uses of such lands to commercial wood production and discourage their use for building, highway development, or outdoor recreation.

The search for open space in metropolitan areas often singled out stream valleys. These laced the heavily settled conurbations and because of periodic flooding and steep slopes often had been bypassed. Cities recaptured flood plains for open space and thereby avoided flood-damage costs and at the same time enhanced natural amenities. Developers were always tempted to encroach on flood plains and steep slopes, both of which held out potential for later harm.

Environmentalists emphasized the positive values of the flood plain and the small stream valleys. Both provided a relatively inexpensive source of permanent open space, especially when the price of uplands purchased for parks rose steadily. Planners began to argue that flood plains and valley slopes should be reserved for these purposes. Environmentalists, in turn, argued that human occupancy of these areas should be strictly controlled.[49]

The federal Flood Disaster Protection Act of 1973 contributed to these initiatives. It required property owners in flood plains to purchase insurance against flood damage, thereby reducing federal outlays for disaster relief. As a condition of participation local governments would map and control occupancy of the flood plain. But insurance often only reinforced development by reducing the economic risk of floods. Only sporadically did it result in effective controls.

These efforts encountered much opposition. Private-property owners objected that their lands were being "taken" from them unlawfully by such restrictions. This harked back to the legal doctrine that no person should be deprived of life, liberty, or property without due process of law. Courts had long interpreted this in a substantive manner; that is, they had ruled that private property could not be taken by the public without just compensation for the loss in value. The issue often revolved around the amount of taking involved. Owners claimed compensation for the full potential future value of the property, if new growth might make more intensive development likely. But courts often did not recognize such speculative values and argued that at times the public interest in limiting flood-plain development outweighed the private-property interest.

An equally important perspective was the attempt to modify development so that it would be more environmentally sensitive. Thus the admonition of landscape architect Ian McHarg to "design with nature": Developmental design should be adjusted to the natural terrain. Building should not take place on flood plains, steep slopes, sand dunes, or land subject to subsidence. Housing designs could provide for blocks of open space and closer integration of buildings with their natural settings.[50]

The urban fringe continued to be a major battleground in the conflict between environmental and developmental objectives. Out of this experience came many ideas about environmental quality, support for environmental organizations, and political action.

Urban Dynamics and the Urban Environment

Demands for improvement of the city as a place to live had implications for the traditional manner in which cities had grown. Formerly cities had attracted new industries without much thought about their contribution to increased pollution loads, but this was no longer possible. As environmental-control programs evolved, the implications of that connection became clearer.

Tension between the city's previous and possible economies was faced directly in the air- and water-quality programs. Each of these required cities to clean up pollution but also not to "backslide," that is, not to permit an increase in pollution from new sources to nullify reductions in older ones. In air quality this resulted in the nonattainment problem: Would new sources be permitted in areas that had not yet attained minimal goals? In water quality it took the form of the "water-quality limited stream": How could new plants be allowed on a stream if current discharges were at the maximum allowable level for that stream?

Would environmental goals be met by requiring new industries to meet more stringent standards or by requiring existing industries to clean up further and hence create a larger cushion of allowable pollution for new sources? Controls built into new plants were less expensive than those added onto old ones. But for cities the political problem was one of balancing the ever present demands of existing industry with the less pressing demands of future firms. The burden was usually shifted to new industry because of the political demands from that already in place.

From the EPA came pressures to facilitate new growth by requiring existing industry to provide pollution increments for it. New sources of air pollution were to pay older sources to clean up so as to accommodate the new amounts of pollution; the trade-offs would bring about some improvement in air quality in the bargain. For water the EPA sought to require that discharges be tightened in order to give new plants a cushion. Cities faced great difficulties in freeing themselves from pressures from existing industries to stimulate new economic activities; those industries often saw their pollution as a protection against new competitors. Few of these proposals worked out in practice.

Cities also displayed contradictory tendencies when they both encouraged greater population and sought a higher level of environmental quality. We have already dealt with this in the case of automobile traffic; equally difficult was noise. Urban residents placed noise high on their list of environmental problems. There were many urban noise ordinances, but the noise levels did not abate. The cities seemed unable to extricate themselves from the twin tendencies of increasing population levels and increasing environmental degradation.[51]

In a number of cities these problems led to efforts to control urban growth under the assumption that there were limits to desirable expansion. In a few cases environmentalists were able to persuade the community to control its rate of growth by limiting annual building construction. Analyses indicated that above a population of 100,000 the cost of city services per capita increased sharply; smaller cities, it was argued, were more efficient. Such efforts contributed to the discussion of the larger question of the limits to growth.[52]

Cities also displayed marked tendencies toward the export of their environmental problems. In earlier years they had dumped raw sewage into rivers without serious concern for the impact on people downstream. In air-pollution matters cities were prone to encourage industrial sources to build tall smokestacks to disperse polluted air up and away from nearby communities; the air was then blown downwind. To dispose of solid waste cities sought places farther out in the countryside for landfills. Hazardous-waste dumpers found convenient sites in less densely inhabited places where they would be less noticed. And those responsible for radioactive waste sought "isolated sites" that would be far removed from human habitation.

The export of pollution by the city had its counterpart in the export of people. The number of people in a city tended to grow beyond the city's capacity to absorb them, creating a constant pressure to expand residential areas into the countryside. Urban dwellers placed an increasing burden on outlying lands, bringing new problems to the less settled areas. Those living there who prized the environmental quality of their communities sought to ward off these intrusions but were often unsuccessful. Urbanites who sought to move into the countryside saw such protective strategies only as selfish attempts by those already there to discourage newer settlement.

The environmental movement attempted to persuade urban Americans to extend their mental horizons from a search for environmental quality in their immediate circumstances to the larger problem of expanding human loads on a finite physical and biological environment beyond their borders. These were efforts by a segment of urban America to protect the lands beyond the cities from suffering the same kind of environmental degradation that had already taken place in the cities themselves.

Early in the 1980s a new strategy was developed to sensitize urban dwellers to their environment. A Boston television reporter, Jack Borden, came to believe that it might be possible to make people more aware of the sky and hence to enhance their desire to improve air quality. Inspired by artist Eric Sloane and his book

For Spacious Skies, Borden organized a venture by that name to promote urban "sky awareness." As if to echo this wider interest, a *Field Guide to the Atmosphere* was published in 1981 as part of the well-known Peterson naturalist guides. This combined scientific information about the atmosphere, details about air pollution, and aesthetic appreciation. Sky awareness might well acquaint urban people with the higher environmental quality of the countryside as a model of what they might be able to enjoy more often at home.[53]

4 The Nation's Wildlands

Well beyond the cities and their surrounding farmlands lay regions of almost no settlement, which remained wild. Earlier these lands had been used primarily for their raw materials such as wood and minerals. Often after these had been extracted the lands were abandoned. But new values transformed them into environmental assets that interested an increasing portion of the American public. They came to be prized both for the experience of their environmental values and because they symbolized what America was and ought to be.[1]

Here in their nation's wildlands Americans found it possible to express their environmental values more fully than they could in cities. Organized efforts to ensure that forests, parks, wildlife refuges, and the western public domain did not fall prey to pressures for development were the most consistently successful of environmental activities.

Americans often took their wildlands for granted. They were public lands, not the private preserves of an aristocracy, as in Europe, where the public had been excluded from using them. During the nineteenth century these lands were disposed of to individuals and corporations to promote economic development. In the late nineteenth century this practice began to give way to permanent public management as the lands were looked on as clothed with a public interest and no longer subject to private alienation. By the 1950s public ownership had become a firmly rooted American political tradition.[2]

These were lands that had been "left over," that had not been taken up for private ownership. They were too distant from human settlement to appeal to more than a few; they were in rugged mountain areas; or they were too arid for farming. But as America changed and wildness came to have positive environmental value they became available for new environmental uses. The proper use of the American wildlands came to be one of the most dramatic issues of the Environmental Era.

Federal Land Systems

An act passed by Congress in 1891 led to the establishment of the first major federal land-management system – the national forests. Under it forest reserves were established by presidential executive order; in 1905 these became known as national forests. At that time it was not at all clear what public purposes this implied, and that question became central to ensuing issues about their management. In 1911 the Weeks Act provided that national forests be established in the East, to be acquired by purchase from private owners. National forests constituted an increasingly important public environmental asset in the urbanized East, even though their acreage, 25 million by 1980, never approached the size of the public domain in the West.[3]

The national forests were established initially to protect watersheds and to guarantee a future supply of wood. A similar type of specialized reservation was represented by the national parks. The first was Yellowstone, established in 1872 and followed in the late nineteenth and early twentieth centuries by Yosemite, General Grant, and Sequoia, all in 1890, Crater Lake in 1902, Glacier in 1910, Rocky Mountain in 1915, and Grand Canyon in 1919. These were lands of spectacular geological phenomena such as mountains, waterfalls, geysers, hot springs, and canyons. Proposals for protection came not from the public at large but from small groups such as explorers, big game hunters, archaeologists, and naturalists who had ventured westward for purposes other than settlement. Private ownership and development, they felt, would deprive the nation of assets that would be increasingly prized over the years.[4]

The National Park Service was organized in 1916 to manage these lands. The U.S. Forest Service, which managed the national forests, was in the Department of Agriculture, and the Park Service was in the Department of the Interior. After World War I travel in the West grew, and with the rapid increase in park visitation environmentalists became alarmed in later years that overuse might well destroy the natural values the parks were intended to protect.[5]

Later national parks were established in the East; the earliest ones were Acadia in 1929 and the Great Smoky Mountains, Shenandoah, and Mammoth Cave, authorized in 1926. These were obtained not through federal purchase but through private or state acquisition that led to donations to the federal government. In the West additions were often made by the transfer of lands from the national forests. These involved bitter quarrels with the Forest Service, which fought to retain its lands. But park advocates felt that the Forest Service was far too oriented toward wood harvest. In 1903 Gifford Pinchot, the first head of the Forest Service, had sought to obtain jurisdiction over the national parks to cut their trees for lumber. He failed to do so, and soon the different objectives of national-forest and national-park administration became clearly defined. As the Forest Service failed to respond to the interests of park advocates it lost control over lands that became Olympic, Kings Canyon, and North Cascades national parks in 1938, 1940, and 1968, respectively.[6]

The national wildlife refuges, established to protect fish and game habitat, had their beginnings in 1903, when Theodore Roosevelt, by executive order, established Pelican Island on the Florida east coast as a reserve for brown pelicans. Many more refuges were to come, usually on the remaining public domain not reserved for other purposes. In later years much wetland acreage was added to the system through funds raised from the purchase of duck stamps by hunters.[7]

These refuges were under the jurisdiction of the Fish and Wildlife Service in the Department of the Interior. Only slowly did a management system for the refuges arise, and even by the 1980s it remained far less developed than those for the forests and parks.

From the earliest years one of the major objectives of the refuge system was to sustain habitat for waterfowl. Birds nested at one latitude and migrated over distinct flyway routes to lower ones for the winter. Duck hunters in particular sought to protect both the nesting grounds in the north and habitat along the flyways to the south. Through Ducks Unlimited, an organization of duck hunters, private funds were raised to acquire and protect nesting waterholes in the upper plains of the Dakotas and Canada. Over the years refuges were acquired along all the major flyways in the United States, along the Atlantic and Pacific coasts, through the Great Basin, and in the Mississippi Valley.

The refuges attracted an increasing number of outdoor enthusiasts. Here were areas important not only for hunters but also for naturalists and nature photographers. As the interest in wildlife grew, so did the numbers of nonconsumptive users. During the 1970s appreciative users in organizations such as Defenders of Wildlife, the National Wildlife Federation, and the Audubon Society became the most ardent supporters of the refuges.

By the 1930s steps were taken toward permanent public management of the remaining public domain. The Taylor Grazing Act of 1934 led to the formation of the U.S. Grazing Service to supervise grazing so that it would not result in overuse and deterioration of the range. In 1946 the Bureau of Land Management (BLM) was formed to provide a more permanent management framework.[8]

After World War II many new users discovered these lands. Environmentalists were attracted by their beauty and wildlife. At the same time, hard rock, oil and gas, and coal mine enterprises began to exploit them more intensively. Added to these two groups were users of off-road motorized vehicles. These increasing demands brought a veritable revolution to the BLM. Now it was forced to supervise a wide range of conflicting activities that could generate considerable resource damage and were difficult to control. Environmentalists sought to shape BLM policies; they feared the environmental repercussions from a massive disturbance of fragile western lands. The Federal Land Policy and Management Act of 1976 affirmed more definitively that these lands would remain under federal ownership and established a management system more receptive to environmental uses.[9]

State Lands

State-owned lands – almost 100 million acres – were equally important as a focus for environmental issues. These came initially from federal grants to states when they were admitted to the Union to provide endowments to finance education. In earlier years such grants had been given with few strings attached, but those given to states in the mountain West in the late nineteenth century included "trust" obligations that the states manage the lands so as to maintain their value. This changed considerably the earlier tendency to sell the lands to private owners and gave rise to state trust or endowment lands in the West, totaling more than 35 million acres. In these states, then, there were two systems of public wildlands, one federal and the other state. While environmental uses became increasingly important for federal lands, the income-producing obligations required of state trust lands made commodity uses for them far more important.[10]

State lands in the East reverted from or were purchased from private owners. Lands abandoned after their timber was cut provided an opportunity for acquisition, and in fact the timber industry encouraged public purchase to shift ownership burdens to public hands. Lands that proved only marginal for farming also were available. Rural depopulation in the East was extensive; it undermined the economy and society of many areas and led to demands that state and federal governments purchase the lands that had become a burden on local governments. The New Deal provided the opportunity, as it purchased marginal farmlands as a device to cope with the agricultural depression. These lands were incorporated into national forests, but considerable federal monies were granted to states for their own purchases as well.[11]

The northern states – primarily New York, Pennsylvania, Michigan, Wisconsin, and Minnesota – embarked on extensive public-lands programs. In 1885 New York halted sales of public lands in the Adirondacks and in 1894 declared in its constitution that they should remain "forever wild." Acquisition of state forestland in Pennsylvania, inaugurated under the impetus of the Pennsylvania Forestry Association, reached over 2 million acres. In the northern Lake States, acquisition came after the failure to establish agriculture on cutover pine lands. Similar lands were added to state forests in Washington, Oregon, and California.

State forests did not develop in the South. Much of the South's "Third Forest" was in small, private holdings, but most of the large tracts outside of those owned by the federal government were industrial forests whose managers emphasized short-rotation softwood plantation forestry for pulpwood. Southern interest in environmental forest values came after World War II; the environmental movement there did not enjoy the use of state wildlands as was the case in the North. As a further variant the vast forested lands of Maine were owned primarily by private timber companies.[12]

Other state patterns are worth noting. In the West, the trust obligations attached to the state lands severely limited their use for recreation, parks, fishing, and hunting. These were not income-producing uses, and the state land boards in such states as Idaho, Utah, and New Mexico argued that on state lands such uses were illegal. Users looking for recreation and sport therefore turned to the federal lands in their states to engage in their outdoor activities. In the East new devices arose to finance land acquisition. In 1977, for example, Michigan established the Kammer Fund, a trust fund into which income from oil, gas, and mineral leasing was deposited, to be used to purchase park and recreation land.

As the 1976 Federal Land and Management Policy Act was implemented demands arose, as they had in times past, that federal lands be transferred to the western states. This drive was known as the Sagebrush Rebellion. The demand was instigated by a new BLM program, the result of a successful environmental lawsuit, to develop plans for each grazing district, including an environmental-impact statement, which would describe the condition of the range and suggest changes in use so as to protect land from overgrazing. Throughout the West, cattle and sheep grazers protested vigorously. They also objected to the provision in the 1976 act that the BLM review its lands for potential wilderness, an objective that also drew fire from mining interests and users of off-road vehicles.

After an initial burst of enthusiasm in 1979, the Sagebrush Rebellion began to subside in the face of opposition in the West. If federal lands were to be transferred to the states, management objectives that prevailed for state-owned trust lands also would be applied to them. This meant that many users would be excluded from state lands as unlawful trespassers. Federal lands, now open to recreation, fish, and wildlife uses, might well be closed to them. Recognition of this potential limitation on access severely dampened enthusiasm for transfer within the West.

It is useful to ask why there arose separate forest, park, and wildlife management systems at both state and federal levels. In New York, for example, whereas the state forests and game lands were administered by the Department of Environmental Conservation, the state parks were managed by a separate agency. In Pennsylvania, the parks and forests were under one agency, but the game lands were managed by a different one. In Michigan all three were under a "superagency."

These separate administrations, as well as those described earlier for federal lands, reflected different goals. Hence those who advocated federal parks in 1903 succeeded in preventing the Forest Service from acquiring the national parks and then in 1916 persuaded Congress to establish a separate National Park Service. At the same time, state and federal foresters in the first third of the twentieth century were long hostile to recreation, fishing, and hunting as legitimate uses of the public forestlands; they felt they should be used primarily for wood production. In response, wildlife clienteles after World War I shaped their own, often separate land systems. These comparative observations about management agencies therefore provide clues as to the varied evolution of environmental values.[13]

Public-Land Struggles

Some of the most intense dramas of environmental politics involved efforts to bring new land into public ownership for permanent environmental management. But the setting for such action now was much different. Lands that once were unwanted now had come to be valued by private owners.

One debate took place over the Redwood National Park in northwestern California. From the mid-nineteenth century that state had protected some giant sequoias from cutting. More extensive was the activity of the Save the Redwoods League, which, beginning in 1918, purchased tract after tract of the taller coastal red-woods and transferred them to the state for inclusion in its park system. To many, however, special action was needed to protect more of the tall trees of the California northwest coast from the persistent threat of logging. Redwood National Park was established in 1968. But logging continued on the headwaters of the eastern fringe of the park and threatened park streams with sedimentation. Environmentalists emphasized the need to establish watershed lines as boundaries and by the mid-1970s had formulated a proposition for park expansion partially to do this. Despite vigorous opposition from the lumber industry and lumber workers the bill to expand the park passed in 1978.[14]

Many such issues had a more regional import. A forested area in Texas, the Big Thicket, and a river bottom of huge pines and hardwoods in South Carolina, the Congaree Swamp, became subjects of successful public campaigns in the late 1970s to incorporate them into the national park system. There was also interest in protecting wild rivers, the most publicized successful efforts involving Hell's Canyon on the Snake River in Idaho and the New River Gorge in southern West Virginia and western North Carolina. Both efforts halted attempts to construct dams for hydroelectric power, which would have destroyed spectacular scenic stretches of the rivers. In both cases local support for protection was combined with national campaigns organized by environmental groups.[15]

In the East the Appalachian Trail had become over the years a significant part of the public consciousness. Running more than two thousand miles from Mount Katahdin in Maine to Springer Mountain in Georgia, this trail had been laid out and maintained through private action by organizations of hikers. But the expansion of settlement now led to encroachments on the trail. And this, in turn, led to action to protect it further. The Appalachian Trail had been one of a number of national trails established by the National Trails Act of 1968. In 1978 Congress took further action by authorizing acquisition by eminent domain of a strip an average of a quarter of a mile wide on each side to protect the trail's scenic quality.[16]

The most spectacular public-land issue of the 1970s involved Alaska. At the time of statehood in 1958, all but a fraction of this vast expanse of some 360 million acres was owned by the federal government. The statehood act provided for transfer of land to both the state and native Alaskans; it also specified that the secretary of the interior would identify "national interest" lands that would be incorporated into the various federal land systems. As these provisions were carried out, major controversies ensued over the degree to which lands to be in federal ownership would be open for development.

Alaska's environmentalists, working in alliance with those in the lower 48, pressed for considerable acreage to be allocated to those federal agencies for uses that stressed environmental objectives. The Alaska Coalition, which was formed by these groups, called for 116 million acres to be added to national parks, wildlife refuges, and scenic rivers, with little allocated to national forests. Alaskan officials sought to reduce this figure to 25 million acres and to leave the rest to future decision. They would also allocate most national-interest lands to the national forests.

For environmentalists the Alaska decision symbolized the "last chance." No more large tracts of public lands remained for environmental purposes. Millions of Americans became caught up in the issue; an outpouring of activity led to extensive citizen participation in the form of letters, petitions, and attendance at hearings. Several decades' political action to protect Alaskan lands was finally successful when Congress passed the Alaskan Lands Act in December 1980 and placed 104 million acres in national park or wildlife refuge units.

The New Era of Acquisition

During the 1960s and 1970s it became apparent that wildlands could be added to public ownership only with increasing difficulty. Prime undeveloped areas were scarcer and smaller. At the same time, remaining wildlands had become more valuable to private owners with each passing year. All this gave rise to considerable innovation in acquisition techniques.

Environmentalists sought sources of funding independent of legislative appropriations. Acquisition of game lands through the proceeds from hunting license fees served as an example. But legislatures were as reluctant to earmark revenues for selected

public expenditures as they were to provide regular appropriations.

Missouri enacted a small sales tax on soft drinks to provide a
sustained source of revenue for conservation programs; that drive
was led by sportsmen. Michigan established the Kammer Fund,
previously mentioned, in 1977 under the leadership of the Michigan United Conservation Clubs. Steadier revenues came from
the federal Land and Water Conservation Fund in which certain
federal revenues were allocated for both state and federal use in
acquiring wildlands. The states were required to match these funds
and to prepare an outdoor-recreation plan every five years on
the basis of which proposals for funding would be approved.

The Nature Conservancy became the most successful private
venture in land acquisition. It was able to attract gifts and sales
of privately owned lands for permanent preservation. Many of
these tracts were small, and they would be more appropriately
called natural areas, but the Conservancy was able to acquire
some consisting of several thousands of acres. Often it provided
crucial assistance to public-land agencies because it could act
quickly when a private owner wished to sell without waiting for
approval from officials in Washington or congressional appropriations; it could then hold the land while repurchasing arrangements were worked out.[17]

A thorny problem for many public-land agencies was private
inholdings, smaller tracts of private land within the boundaries of
public areas. These created problems of use that were incompatible with agency objectives. Within Yosemite National Park,
for example, were 242 privately owned acres out of a total of
761,000. But a new policy during the Carter administration to acquire these park inholdings caused a storm of protest. Led by
Yosemite inholder Charles Cushman, these landowners organized a national association of inholders, often supported by others who objected to national-park policies; by the time of the
Reagan administration, this group had become one of the most
vocal sources of political opposition to the National Park Service.

For the national forests, especially in the East, the problem
was even more serious. Few forests had acquired more than 65
percent of the acreage within their purchase boundaries. Some
in the Forest Service even proposed that the eastern forests be

sold and that the proceeds be used to advance ownership in the West. An even greater problem involved private ownership of subsurface mineral rights where the Forest Service owned the surface. Subsurface owners had the right to extract minerals without the consent of the surface owner, and often the Forest Service was not informed of pending extractions. Moreover, oil and gas drilling and mining created serious pollution problems that plagued managers of both state and federal lands.[18]

The close intermixture of private and public values in the nation's wildlands led to increasing attention to the possibility of a combination of public and private action in land management for environmental objectives. This did not seem possible in the case of subsurface mineral inholdings where mineral and surface environmental values were incompatible. Nor did it seem feasible in the case of clear-cutting, which conflicted with the objectives of nearby property owners who had purchased their lands for the environmental value of the full canopied forest. Yet if both private owners and public agencies would agree to surface-use restrictions, some joint approach might be feasible that would make full public ownership unnecessary.

Several proposals of this kind were initiated. One involved the Adirondack Park Agency in New York, devised to control development on private land that was intermingled with public. The policy caused continuing controversy between the agency and private owners, but it also received considerable support from those who shared the agency's environmental objectives. In 1977 Congress approved a similar approach for the New Jersey pine barrens that included improved management of public lands, public acquisition of selected private tracts, and retention of most land in private ownership under land-use controls. Referred to as "greenline parks," the concept seemed to hold some promise at a time when the possibilities of public acquisition were increasingly limited.

From time to time opposition arose to the policy of expanding the nation's public lands for parks and outdoor recreation. Timber and mining companies and livestock grazers had long looked on such expansion as unwarranted. But the public seemed to desire otherwise, and in the 1960s and 1970s plans to expand national recreation lands accelerated. The Reagan administration, however, undertook a major effort to bring all this to a halt. It called for an end to parkland acquisition and suggested that authorization for newly approved areas be rescinded. Although environmentalists were able to deflect these moves, they were able to sustain only a modest level of acquisition.

Wildland Environmental Issues

As long as use was limited, public-land managers were able to apply their own ideas about management relatively freely. But as the public interest in public lands grew after World War II a host of controversies developed that aroused intense debate and subjected agencies to many conflicting demands.

Traditional commodity uses were now augmented by proposals to develop ski slopes and resorts, overland routes for motorized recreation, and other recreational facilities. But the public lands increasingly came to be thought of as environments for an urbanized society, a qualitative setting for living and leisure. They were a natural world that provided a larger setting for the built society of urban America.[19]

Some observers have described this as the expansion of the "urban field," a world of human experience that, although centered in the daily life of the city, extended far beyond. An increasing number of Americans came to know wildlands as they traveled to the parks and forests, to the West and northern New England, to Florida and the Appalachians. Color photography expanded this experience in informal slide presentations and in large-format books. These extended public knowledge of the world beyond the city.[20]

Many had actually been in the wildlands. By 1977 fully 19 percent of all Americans and 26 percent of those twenty-four to thirty-five years old had been in a national wilderness area. In the Rocky Mountain West the proportion reached 60 percent of the population. Many more had enjoyed the national parks. Still more knew wildlands closer to home. Experience of wildlands was often vicarious rather than direct, and close observers were constrained to identify both indirect and direct wilderness users. In varied ways the nation's wildlands had become an extension of the urban world.[21]

Wildlife and Wildlife Habitat

For many years hunting had constituted the predominant wildlife concern. Duck hunting, for example, had shaped much of the early state and federal wildlife programs. The terms "game" and "game management" figured heavily in discussions of wildlife issues. Sportsmen and wildlife managers stressed policies to increase the amount of game available for hunting. In 1937 the Pittman-Robertson Act provided funds for the development of wildlife habitat, raised through a tax on firearms and distributed to the states. A number of organizations were formed in the 1930s to support these activities: the National Wildlife Federation, the Wildlife Management Institute, the Wildlife Society, and the annual North American Wildlife and Natural Resources Conference. The recovery of some game populations to numbers far beyond their historic levels testified to the success of these efforts.[22]

Newer wildlife interests soon came into play. One followed from increased observation of wildlife rather than taking it through hunting. The National Audubon Society, reorganized in the 1940s and long interested in problems of endangered species, gathered increasing support and brought together local groups into a national force. By the 1970s it had become one of the nation's largest environmental groups. The interest of its members expanded from the traditional annual migratory bird counts into a concern for wildlife habitat. In the 1950s and 1960s it became especially concerned about the adverse effects of pesticides on bird life and played a major role in pesticide litigation and regulation.[23]

In 1964, 50 million Americans reported that they were wildlife observers; by 1975 there were 15 million wildlife photographers in contrast with 17 million hunters. It was no wonder that the publications of both the National Audubon Society and the National Wildlife Federation contained spectacular color photographs. By 1973 even the traditional wildlife leaders had recognized the change; they republished a major document in wildlife affairs and retitled it from "American Game Policy, 1930" to "The North American Wildlife Policy, 1973."[24]

Still a third view emerged that emphasized the humane treat-

ment of wildlife. This grew out of the humane societies that originally had been concerned with the mistreatment of children and
over the years had come to emphasize cruelty to animals. Much
of this interest arose from the mistreatment of household pets,
as well as animals in laboratories and zoos. It focused less on
animals in the wild and their habitat and more on suffering caused
by hunting and trapping. It developed a sharp "antihunting" attitude that questioned almost every facet of traditional game management.

This three-pronged set of attitudes in wildlife management inevitably resulted in conflict. Both hunters and game managers,
on the one hand, and humane organizations, on the other, tended
to define issues in terms of hunters versus antihunters. Those
who expressed the appreciative habitat-ecological complex of
ideas occupied the middle ground. The Audubon Society, the
Sierra Club, and Friends of the Earth stressed not animals per
se but wildlife in its habitat.

One major wildlife issue was the protection of endangered
species. Development threatened to endanger and even destroy
many animals and plants by eliminating their habitat. These species might be important for many reasons: as sources of plants
critical for food production, medicines, and drugs; for the enhancement of diversity and variety in the genetic pool; for the
acquisition of knowledge about, or increased enjoyment of, the
natural world. A program to protect them evolved through a series of federal acts in 1966, 1969, and 1972.[25]

Under these statutes the Office of Endangered Species in the
Fish and Wildlife Service worked with biologists across the nation
to identify species that were in immediate danger of extinction or
that could readily become endangered. The objective of the program was to provide habitat for such species sufficient to guarantee their survival, and to take steps to avoid federal actions
that might disturb that habitat. The preservation of habitat generated considerable controversy as it forced choices between
development and protection. In all but a few cases the issues
were resolved by modification, rather than cancellation, of development projects.

Environmentalists argued that the Office of Endangered Species hesitated to include certain species on the list, because it

would interfere with construction projects and thereby unleash opposition that might threaten protection. The program survived considerable stormy weather. In 1978, in response to the especially controversial case of the protection of the snail darter from the construction by the TVA of the Tellico Dam on the Little Tennessee River, Congress established a mechanism to resolve differences. But it remained little used. And in 1982 not only was the Endangered Species Act renewed but its procedures for identifying species for action were also strengthened.[26]

Two innovations of the early 1970s gave new twists to wildlife politics. One involved the Marine Mammal Protection Act of 1972 to protect the whale and the dolphin. The dolphin was endangered because of its close relationship with tuna, which were fished commercially. In the past, dolphins caught with tuna had been killed. Now policies were initiated to improve catch techniques so as to save the dolphins, and they were successful. The whale population, on the other hand, was slowly declining, owing to continued whaling by some nations. Through the International Whaling Commission, environmentalists sought a worldwide ban on whaling, but continued support for the whaling industry in some nations, such as Japan and Russia, thwarted these efforts.

The other innovation concerned wild horses and burros on the public domain that were protected by the Wild Free-Roaming Horses and Burros Act of 1971. Brought in by white settlers, these animals had turned wild and now competed with sheep and cattle for forage. Stockraisers often simply destroyed them. But now several organizations were formed to protect them. The new law permitted the BLM to round them up and ship them elsewhere.

These new programs modified the context of wildlife politics by stressing ecosystems rather than target species. Both the hunting and endangered-species programs had emphasized particular species for game and for observation. But the intensifying focus on habitat led to an interest in the larger ecosystem of which the species was only one part, and this in turn yielded a greater number of factors to be considered in wildlife management. A single-species approach had concentrated on food, water, and shelter, and the balance between these and population numbers. Now a broader ecological view extended the relevant ecosystem factors to sex balance within species, age distributions, and the balance between weak and healthy animals. This view was promoted by several ecologists, notably Lee Talbot of the Council on Environmental Quality. But it was not well received by wildlife managers of the older school because it required broader ecological training and perspective. More important, it led to new mathematical formulas to establish the proper balance between populations and habitat that would raise the total population above which harvest should be permitted and thus reduce hunting quotas.[27]

Wildlife debates involved controversies over the relative roles of the state and federal governments. Wildlife policy over the years had resulted in almost exclusive state jurisdiction. Even on federal lands, federal managers did not control the regulation of wildlife populations; they had to defer to state agencies. New nongame policies found greater support at the federal level, and this was especially true of endangered-species programs and those stressing an ecosystem approach. In an issue involving the wild horse and burro program, the courts argued that although the regulation of animal numbers rested with the state, the federal government had the authority to protect the land over which it had jurisdiction. This seemed to give the federal government authority to manage the ecosystem, including animals. Wildlife leaders were alarmed by this decision, which might well threaten state power, and the Carter administration assured them the decision meant no change in policy.[28]

These issues made clear that wildlife policies and politics were in a state of transition. One aspect of this was the drive to secure special programs and funding for nongame species. Whereas wildlife managers insisted that game management provided considerable habitat for nongame species and that, in fact, hunters were only a small portion of game-land users, appreciative users pointed out that with a different viewpoint policies might well shift in a different direction. In some states they were able to secure funds from special licenses or stamps to finance programs for nongame species. A more popular system was the income-tax checkoff whereby taxpayers could earmark some of their state income tax refund or increase their payment for that purpose. By 1984, thirty-three states had adopted such a provision, which in that year raised almost $10 million for state nongame wildlife programs.[29]

Public interest in these issues, no doubt, was related to a humane concern for the suffering of wild animals through hunting, trapping, and fishing. The annual harvest of seal pups off Newfoundland, for example, brought such concerns to public attention regularly in the 1970s. While the humane interest provided added support to some wildlife issues, it led to an emphasis markedly different from that of the more ecological approach, which stressed the relationship between animals and their natural habitat as part of an ecosystem. Hence the interest in the suffering of wildlife did not carry over to these larger issues.

Recreation in the Natural Environment

Growing interest in outdoor recreation in a natural setting also shaped the new environmental approach to the nation's wildlands. An increasing number of Americans began to enjoy leisure activities – hiking and backpacking, canoeing and rafting, fishing, and nature study and photography – in nearby woods and in more remote wildlands. Once in the woods and on the rivers, many urban Americans broadened their involvement from the simple desire for recreation to a larger set of concerns for their environmental and ecological management.

Outdoor activities reflected a desire to interact with rather than to overcome nature. Stephen Kellert's study of attitudes toward wildlife, conducted in the late 1970s, distinguished between the values of hunters who both feared and wished to dominate wildlife and those of appreciative users who sought to understand wildlife in its natural setting. Similar distinctions could be applied to many types of outdoor recreation in which there arose an attitude of enjoyment of the outdoors for its own sake. This search for values in nature did not symbolize a desire to return to a more primitive level of civilization, as critics often argued. On the contrary, it was a facet of leisure that people desired to complement their lives in the built-up city.[30]

Guidebooks for hikers reflected changing values. The earliest ones in the West had stressed mountain climbing; they took the reader rapidly through the terrain from the starting point to the base of the mountain, and then provided detailed directions for climbing. As the outdoor-recreation movement broadened, the guidebooks began to stress the hiking trail itself, providing details as to the various stretches and landmarks to guide the way. Still later, an appreciation of the surrounding biological life came into stronger focus, and guidebooks included material on trees and plants in the area through which one journeyed and information about natural history and ecology.[31]

Newer values brought about changes in the interests and activities of outdoor recreationists. Among fishermen the traditional pattern of management had involved raising fingerlings in hatcheries and then planting them in streams to grow and be caught later; this was known as "put and take" fishing. Other fishermen sought the experience of the natural setting and involvement with the natural cycle of the fishing habitat. Trout fishermen formed their own organization, Trout Unlimited, which took a strongly environmental stance.

Hiking groups had shifted from a heavily social to a more environmental interest. Previously groups had been content simply to clear trails, build overnight cabins, and organize hiking expeditions. A few organizations, the Sierra Club being the most notable, went beyond this to add to their outing programs a well-developed strategy of conservation action. Members were admonished to "protect" as well as to "explore and enjoy" the nation's wildlands.

A spectrum of preferences for different recreational settings evolved. Many wished to encounter few people in their experience with nature. Others wanted more developed facilities. A 1964 study of the values sought in the Boundary Waters Canoe Area distinguished between those who thought of themselves as entering wilderness as soon as they set out on their canoe trip and those who felt they had not reached that point until they had met no one else for several days. Administrators began to classify values in outdoor recreation in terms of experience levels. The Forest Service devised the most elaborate system with categories ranging from Experience Level I, the most natural, to Experience Level V, the most developed.[32]

Those who sought to overcome nature with motorized vehicles

seemed to engage in activities incompatible with environmentally oriented recreation. When hikers encountered snowmobiles or motorbikes, they recoiled in anger. These intruders into the natural setting destroyed the experience they sought and disrupted natural processes. The machines' speed, noise, and exhaust, and their users' seeming lack of appreciation of nature, had little place in the natural setting. Users of off-road motorized vehicles found themselves to be the most unpopular of all wildlands users in public-opinion polls and came to rely heavily on the political influence of vehicle manufacturers to secure opportunities for their activities.[33]

A marked increase in outdoor recreation could be observed in the 1930s and after World War II, but it was some time before federal and state agencies understood the magnitude of the change under way and developed new programs to respond to it. In 1956 the National Park Service announced Mission 66, a plan to greatly expand the parks and their services by 1966. Shortly thereafter the Forest Service announced a similar program to provide recreational facilities in the national forests. During the 1950s a major push was led by Joseph Penfold of the Isaak Walton League to establish federal leadership in outdoor recreation; this resulted in the establishment of the Outdoor Recreational Resources Review Commission in 1958. Its report in 1962 set the agenda for the expansion of federal action in the 1960s.[34]

Under the National Trails Act of 1968 both scenic and recreational trails were established, the first in the more remote wildlands and the second nearer the cities. From this came designated national trails such as the Appalachian and Pacific Crest trails, which had already been worked out, and newer ones such as the North Country Trail from Vermont to Missouri and the Potomac Trail from Washington, D.C., to Pennsylvania, linking with the North Country Trail. States also took up the development of hiking trails. In Michigan a lakes-to-lakes trail was established across the northern lower peninsula as well as shorter pathways. In Pennsylvania hiking trails were an important aspect of the new forest plans formulated in the 1970s. Many of these trails were revivals of those established for fire fighting by the Civilian Conservation Corps during the 1930s.

Wilderness

The most powerful expression of environmental values in wildlands management was the wilderness movement. Wilderness advocates believed that some wildlands should be set aside to undergo natural biological and geological succession in which human beings would come and go as visitors and not as permanent occupants. To those committed to the intensive development of material resources, such objectives were incomprehensible and reflected a desire to return to some more primitive past. Wilderness advocates, however, saw them as a major step forward.[35]

Although the idea of wilderness had important historical roots, the first action in the twentieth century came from two employees of the Forest Service. Aldo Leopold, then a forest ranger in New Mexico, proposed that a portion of the Gila National Forest be set aside as a permanently unroaded and undeveloped area. This was done in 1923. Yet just five years later the same official who had accepted Leopold's proposal built a road through the area for wildlife management, which indicates the tenuousness of this first wilderness venture.[36]

Another Forest Service employee, Arthur Carhart, a landscape architect in the Denver regional office, urged that similar protection be given to Trappers Lake in the Colorado Rockies, and then in 1924 proposed similar action for the much larger Boundary Waters Canoe Area in northern Minnesota. His plans for the latter were turned down by the Forest Service. But the ideas persisted, and in the late 1920s the agency officially designated several million acres as "primitive areas" but without permanent protection. Firmer steps were taken in 1939 when some 15 million acres were designated temporarily as wilderness with the thought that they would be reviewed in greater depth for permanent decision.[37]

These reviews began in earnest after World War II, but debate over a number of specific cases convinced wilderness advocates that the Forest Service would take only minimal action, include no heavily forested areas, and confine protection to land above the tree line. Hence the Wilderness Society, which had been organized in 1935 to further citizen action on the question, devised a plan whereby Congress would remove wilderness areas from nonwilderness use. This led to the Wilderness Act of 1964, which established a system of congressionally designated areas. Several such areas were included in the act, and it specified that the Forest Service study others and propose them to Congress for action.[38]

Throughout the West citizen groups argued that the initial 15 million acres chosen by the Forest Service in the 1930s and comprising the areas of study and action provided for in the 1964 act were insufficient. They began to formulate their own proposals and persuaded their representatives in Congress to introduce bills requiring the Forest Service to study these as well. These "de facto" wilderness proposals began to make their way through Congress. The first area to go the entire route and become officially a part of the National Wilderness Preservation System was the Lincoln-Scapegoat area in western Montana, which was approved in 1975.[39]

The Forest Service soon realized the implications of these new citizen ventures; they might well lead to far more wilderness than it thought best. As early as 1967 it took steps to conduct its own reviews of these areas, a process that led to the Roadless Area Review and Evaluation (RARE I), which was completed in 1973 and became a focal point of intense dispute. To wilderness advocates the additional 15 million acres recommended for study was too little and to opponents it was too much. In 1977 a second such study, RARE II, which recommended a similar amount, was carried out.

In the 1960s little attention had been paid to the possibility of wilderness in eastern national forests, but citizens soon began to make their own proposals to Congress. The Forest Service objected that these were not appropriate areas. Wilderness, it argued, should consist of "virgin" areas in which human activity such as logging or settlement had never taken place. But wilderness advocates argued that the 1964 act defined candidate areas as those in which "human influences were relatively unnoticeable," irrespective of how they came to be that way. They affirmed the validity of "restored" as well as "virgin" wilderness. And their views were accepted by Congress in the Eastern Wilderness Act of 1974.[40]

The wilderness movement was the most successful organized citizen effort in the Environmental Era. Over the years it grew steadily and expanded both its ranks and the range of its activities. In the 1950s the Wilderness Society, headquartered in Washington with a predominantly eastern leadership, was the major source of action. By the late 1970s citizen groups had been formed in every western state, independent of national organizations, each with an indigenous leadership that desired to protect areas in its own state. The key to the success of wilderness action lay in mobilizing people who knew first hand and enjoyed areas of potential wilderness designation and became committed to political action to protect them.[41]

There were wilderness areas on federal lands other than the national forests. The 1964 act had provided that both the National Park Service and the Fish and Wildlife Service should identify candidate areas on their lands and propose them to Congress for inclusion in the system. This went forward without serious controversy, though rather slowly. The lands of the Bureau of Land Management were another matter. Under the 1976 Federal Lands Policy and Management Act the agency was directed to undertake full-scale wilderness reviews on its lands. In the debates leading up to the 1964 act there had been little talk about dryland areas, such as those administered by the BLM, as wilderness. But by 1976 the public concept of wilderness had been extended from spectacular alpine meadows, lakes, peaks, and forested areas to include desert lands and especially the canyons and gorges of the Southwest.[42]

The BLM reviews came to be as controversial as those of the Forest Service. Mining companies, cattle and sheep grazers, and users of off-road vehicles were as hostile to wilderness on public-domain lands as in the national forests. At first the BLM vowed to be less controversial in its reviews than the Forest Service had been. But at an early stage pressures from commodity groups to keep the acreage as small as possible came into sharp conflict with the desire of environmentalists to expand it. The environmental drive was limited because it had not yet become as organized around the dryland areas as in the case of the national forests.[43]

Toward the end of the 1970s the drive for protection of lands in Alaska tended to overshadow other wilderness action. The Alaska Coalition sought to include in the Alaska bill provisions that would designate areas in the Tongass and Chugach National Forests as wilderness. These had become sources of intense dispute between Alaskan environmentalists such as the Southeast Alaskan Conservation Council on the one hand and lumber and mining companies on the other. While the coalition fought to include 144 million acres in the Alaska wilderness system, state officials tried to limit it to 25 million. The final act in 1980 added 50 million acres to the National Wilderness Preservation System.

Much of the environmental movement was shaped by the ideals and inspiration embodied in the drive for wilderness. Citizens aroused in behalf of wilderness extended their interest and action to other segments of the American landscape, to the countryside, the wildlands, and the cities themselves. Wilderness areas were the base from which thought and action were launched into wider environmental realms.[44]

Wildlands as Areas of High-Quality Air and Water

For many Americans the nation's wildlands were also areas of the highest quality air and water. They served as reminders of environmental changes that had come about with the growth of urban-industrial society. In matters of air and water pollution, environmental interest soon included the task of protecting these areas of higher quality. And these innovations were closely associated with the management of the nation's wildlands.[45]

Two factors entered into this. One was the way in which visibility was a part of the wildlands experience. One sought out such areas to enjoy the vistas of clear space and skies; if visibility were lowered by air pollution, the value of wildland use was sorely compromised. The other was the enjoyment of natural waters for their pleasing appearance and smell, as well as for their high-quality fishing for species such as trout and salmon, which require well-oxygenated silt-free waters.[46]

Public concern about the degradation of clean air surfaced just after the passage of the Clean Air Act of 1970. The Sierra Club argued that the act required programs not only to improve air quality but also to prevent its degradation. The EPA held back, but the club took legal action, and the court agreed with its interpretation. This judicial decision sharpened public debate, and the 1977 Clean Air Act included a full-scale policy for the "prevention of significant deterioration" of air quality, thereafter referred to as the PSD program.[47]

The act established three classes of air quality, I, II, and III. Class I, the cleanest, provided for the least deterioration, Class II somewhat more, and Class III even more. But even Class III air was not to deteriorate as much as was allowed under the secondary standards. Class II standards were applied to the entire nation, and national parks and wilderness were designated as Class I areas. States could take up action to reclassify Class II areas into either Class I or III, but the process by which this was to be done was specified and required full public participation.[48]

The connection between wildlands and high-quality air was given particular emphasis by a provision in the 1977 act that required that attention be given to visibility in the national parks. Special concern had arisen over declining visibility at the Grand Canyon due to the construction of nearby power plants at the Four Corners where Arizona, New Mexico, Utah, and Colorado join. Some argued that threats to visibility might limit the tourist trade attracted by the parks. The 1977 amendments to the Clean Air Act required the EPA, with the advice of the National Park Service, to define visibility standards and the areas to which they would be applied.[49]

A similar policy was established for water quality that was known as an "antidegradation" program. Leaders in the federal water quality program argued that it did not make sense to allow some streams to become more polluted while large sums of money were being spent to clean up others. They required that states adopt an antidegradation policy. But for the most part it was rather perfunctorily applied, depending on political forces within each state. The political role of fishermen was often crucial, especially those who sought to protect high-quality streams for trout fishing. In Pennsylvania and Michigan, for example, Trout Unlimited sought to secure a classification of such waters for special protection. In Pennsylvania they were known as "wilderness trout streams."

By the end of the 1970s the impact of urban-generated air pollution in the wildlands took a new turn with the growing concern about acid rain. This was a result of the long-distance transport of air pollution such as sulfur dioxide and nitrogen oxides, their chemical transformation into acids during transport, and their dry and wet deposition downwind. But initial expressions of concern about the effects of acid rain pertained to the wildlands, especially those where there was a direct interest in the water quality of streams. Similar concern later was expressed about the effects of acid deposition on forests.[50]

This newly emerging phenomenon prompted many concerned with maintaining a healthy biological life in the wildlands to come together to take action. Fishermen and their professional allies took the lead. They were joined by those who were more interested in forests. Wildlife experts feared the adverse effects on habitat, and the tourist industry became worried about the effect of acid rain on its business. Acid rain was a widely shared problem that galvanized cleaner-air advocates across many interests, providing a potential base for extending the concern for air quality far beyond urban centers.[51]

Strategies to protect high-quality air and waters in the nation's wildlands came under continual attack from industrial sources of pollution. High-quality waters were confined primarily to publicly owned lands. But air quality was a different matter, for downwind wildlands could be threatened by sources in urban-industrial areas far upwind. Hence attempts by environmentalists to require stricter controls on the emissions of acid-forming pollutants were vigorously opposed by fossil-fuel-burning sources. They argued that acid rain was a relatively minor matter and that no connections could be established between their emissions and specific downwind effects. They were equally adamant that visibility standards be confined to only a few wildlands in the national parks and not be extended to larger areas.[52]

Environmental Values and Wildlands Management

Environmental values brought a series of stresses and strains to public-land management that frequently led to eruptions of vigorous political debate. The manner in which this worked out varied with each agency and its previous history. With both the Forest Service and the Bureau of Land Management the primary impact of environmental influence was to modify the dominant role within them of commodity objectives and commodity users to shape policy more toward environmental purposes. With the National Park Service and the Fish and Wildlife Service, environmentalists worked more to protect their more explicit statutory objectives from developmental inroads. The different responses of these agencies to environmental objectives provide an opportunity to compare them and pinpoint more precisely the nature of environmental politics in public-land administration.

The U.S. Forest Service. Over the course of the twentieth century the Forest Service developed a strong emphasis on reconciling competing forest users, in an approach based on the concept of multiple use. The concept was embodied in law in the Multiple Use – Sustained Yield Act of 1960, which specified five major uses of the national forests (wood production, water, forage, recreation, and fish and wildlife) and stipulated that wilderness use was not incompatible with them. Decisions were to be made by balancing competing uses in some calculus of maximum benefit.[53]

Before 1960 the Forest Service had admitted one use after another as legitimate, but on a selective basis. The 1897 Organic Act had specified two uses, wood production and water-supply protection. In the West, water supply was more important; in the rest of the nation, future wood supply was uppermost. Those in the West concerned with water supply saw grazing as detrimental to their interests, but as policies began to be developed that placed special emphasis on water and seemed to provide only a secondary role for grazing, sheep and cattle growers protested so strongly that the Forest Service approved grazing as a legitimate use of the forest. At the same time the Forest Service accepted mining under the Mining Act of 1872, which gave miners a privileged position on public lands and continues to do so to this day.

As forest wildlands became accessible through motorized travel, their use for fishing and hunting increased. To Forest Service administrators these were not high priorities. They thought they interfered with more important forest uses and should be accommodated by state rather than federal land programs. So also with hiking, driving for pleasure, and skiing. But these activities became more widespread and were recognized as legitimate uses in the Multiple Use – Sustained Yield Act.[54]

The central controversies over forest management pitted those who sought to continue the past focus on wood production against those who wished to emphasize the forests as an environment. To the Forest Service the bottom line in management was wood production. The training of foresters played a major role in this view as it also stressed that primary objective. Those dominant in the profession (represented, for example, by the leadership of the Society of American Foresters) were more than skeptical about the notion of environmental forestry as a distinctive viewpoint. In 1972 an effort by 151 members of the society to establish a specialized working group devoted to "ecological" or "environmental" forestry was sharply rejected on the grounds that forestry was already environmental, and hence no distinctive emphasis was needed.[55]

The new environmental forestry attitudes held by the public kept bursting in on both the profession and the Forest Service with persistent regularity. In a public-attitude study in 1977 only 28 percent of the American people agreed that the Forest Service should "try to increase the yield and sales of timber" from the national forests, whereas 62 percent agreed that "it should continue to preserve these trees in their natural state." That view was shared by fifty-six population subgroups in the poll, categorized by age and sex, income, occupation and education, degree of urbanization, and race. Even in rural communities, which customarily gave the least support to environmental values, 35 percent opted for increasing yield and sales and 52 percent for continuing to preserve trees. Two years later a poll sponsored by the American Forest Institute, an industry group, found that 65 percent of the public believed that the main purpose of the national forests was to maintain wildlife habitat.[56]

In the 1970s public concern grew over the way in which forests were managed. In the 1960s the Forest Service dropped its long-standing practice of selection cutting (harvesting individual trees) in favor of clear-cutting (cutting an entire area uniformly). Lower management costs lay behind the change. Clear-cutting aroused considerable debate with especially well-publicized opposition in West Virginia and Montana. It led to the National Forest Management Act of 1976, which required that forest plans consider a wider range of factors than in previous years and that the Forest Service draw up standards for the maximum size of clear-cut, cutting along streams, removal of low-yield lands from the commercial timber schedule, and enhancement of diversity of timber species rather than monoculture.[57]

Forest professionals, the Forest Service, and the forest industry all defended clear-cutting and the wisdom of permitting the Forest Service to retain discretion in managing its lands. But environmentalists argued that the Forest Service was dominated by wood-production objectives to such an extent that environmental objectives were sorely neglected. The meaning of multiple use had been distorted so that to professional foresters uses could not be "multiple" unless they included wood production; in such a view wood production was the indispensable factor. The new act of 1976 resolved few of these differences; it only set the context for continued debate. By the end of the 1970s it appeared that environmentalists were primed to enter a new round of controversy with the Forest Service over these issues in the context of forest planning. To facilitate this a new periodical, *Forest Planning,* appeared in 1980, which was of major help to environmentalists seeking to shape national-forest policy.[58]

The Bureau of Land Management. Lands administered by the Bureau of Land Management were also subject to multiple-use demands. Before 1950 cattle and sheep grazing predominated, but recreational uses and energy ventures brought many new pressures to bear on BLM policies. These new uses came upon the bureau with far greater suddenness than was the case with the Forest Service, and the Federal Land Policy and Management Act of 1976 legitimated them.[59]

The early BLM was shaped by grazing administration. Cattle and sheep raisers were the agency's major client group, and through "grazing advisory boards" they developed an entrenched position in BLM affairs that was jealously guarded and firmly supported by western congressmen. Wildlife was the major competitor of livestock in range management. Wildlife organizations in the West argued that they should have a greater role on the advisory boards, where usually they were given only one out of a dozen places. Only during the Carter administration was there more balanced advisory board membership, and this caused such a storm of reaction from livestock interests that a complete reversal took place during the Reagan administration when non-commodity users were excluded from the boards.[60]

But new demands on BLM lands changed policy and practice, even though slowly and with great controversy. The public domain contained both coal and oil that the federal government leased under the Mineral Leasing Act of 1920. As the price of energy rose, so did the pressure for exploration. Energy companies sought to ease the terms, while environmentalists worked to ensure that regulations would protect other uses. Court suits favorable to environmentalists led to a new leasing program in the late 1970s, but this gave way to more relaxed regulation under the Reagan administration. Amid this debate energy companies assumed a BLM client position of importance equal to stockmen.[61]

Environmentalists also became more interested in the public domain. They began to speak and write about the natural beauty of the western drylands and to insist that some areas be protected from development. The new appreciative interest in wildlife reinforced more traditional concerns of hunters that more range be allocated to wildlife. Citizen environmental organizations were formed in the western states and began to constitute a major political force in the region. A regional newspaper, *High Country News,* started in 1970 and published in Lander, Wyoming, brought a new environmental awareness to public-land questions that helped to underpin environmental objectives on the public domain.[62]

New public-domain activities sharpened use conflicts. One derived from the discovery by users of off-road motorized vehicles of the recreational potential of BLM lands. Four-wheel drive vehicles reached farther into these lands, which previously had been too distant for travel. The drylands and especially the southern California deserts were now used for off-road motorcycle travel. The situation was dramatized by the annual 150-mile Barstow to

Las Vegas motorcycle race, which attracted as many as five thousand participants. Environmentalists were appalled by the extent to which these vehicles disturbed the soil and meager plant life and destroyed desert relics, historical artifacts, and archaeological remains.

These new uses of public lands rapidly transformed the BLM into a comprehensive land-management agency. Steps in this direction came initially during the 1960s when Stewart Udall was secretary of the interior. Lands were described and classified in greater detail, and distinctions were made as to the most appropriate use of different types of land. These measures were influenced by environmental groups that obtained court decisions to require that grazing management and coal leasing be preceded by more thorough analyses of environmental consequences. These new processes became codified in the Federal Land Policy and Management Act of 1976, which was the BLM's organic act.[63]

The Bureau of Land Management became subject to multiple-use demands as extensive as those the Forest Service had experienced. Would their impact on the bureau be similar? In the Forest Service the overlay of multiple demands and the ideology of multiple use had shaped the agency as a broker among conflicting demands, which had reduced its capacity for clearly defined leadership. Although the emergence of many new demands on the BLM modified its dependence on stockmen and generated a more complex decision-making system, its development seemed quite similar to that of the Forest Service. It also became a broker among many competing users and had great difficulty in defining for itself a role of leadership in public-land affairs.[64]

The National Park Service and the Fish and Wildlife Service. Both the National Park Service and the Fish and Wildlife Service had more specific missions than did either the Forest Service or the Bureau of Land Management. The Park Service was mandated to give primary consideration to scenic and historic resources, and this gave the agency a clear sense of direction. The objectives of the Fish and Wildlife Service did the same for that agency. Statutory authorization for both agencies established a dominant use, which precluded the multiple-use context to which the other two agencies were subject. This did not mean that they were free from controversy, but it did mean that both the Park Service and the Fish and Wildlife Service could avoid the broker role the Forest Service and the Bureau of Land Management continually played and could generate a clearer sense of stewardship as trustees for the protection of particular public values.[65]

Environmentalists found the National Park Service congenial. Yet although the Park Service was required by law to protect valuable scenic and historic resources, it was also required to provide for their use. These two purposes often conflicted. As park visitation climbed steadily after World War II, it appeared that overuse would destroy the very resources the agency was mandated to protect. In the 1950s it seemed the service was succumbing to the temptation to promote greater use; its Mission 66 was geared to attracting more visitors. Environmentalists believed that ways and means should be devised to reduce visitor pressure by shifting intensive-use activities such as overnight accommodations and visitors' services outside the parks. A review of park policy published by the Conservation Foundation in 1972 detailed these proposals.[66]

Pressures for expansion of park facilities came continually from concessionaires who ran visitors' facilities within the parks and from business promoters in nearby communities. The concessionaires demanded long-term leases, which then generated pressures for renewal because of their monetary value. In the 1960s such leases were bought up by diversified corporations, replacing smaller, often family, concerns that had taken a more personal interest in the parks. This brought to the parks a more intensive set of commercial market pressures.

In Yosemite National Park, for example, the Music Corporation of America replaced the Curry Company as concessionaire and developed plans for a convention center in the valley. This generated angry protest from environmentalists, who forced the Park Service to back down temporarily. The service produced a second plan that scaled down the proposals and called for removal of many facilities from the valley to the park's periphery. Public meetings on the issue were held across the nation and more than sixty thousand individuals obtained copies of the proposal; a large fraction of these submitted comments. The episode revealed the existence of a major environmental clientele which the Park Service could at times rely. Yet the final plan issued in 1980 scaled down the removal proposals markedly, and one could observe only modest results from the environmental protest.

In the late 1970s environmentalists began to focus on threats to the parks from outside park boundaries. As settlement and development advanced in the West many such adverse impacts could be found in parks throughout the nation. In 1977 the National Parks and Conservation Association, a citizen organization, urged the National Park Service to identify and catalog such threats, and the following year Congress required it to do so. The result was a report, "State of the Parks," issued in 1980.[67]

These threats came in varied ways. Biological life in the Everglades National Park, for example, had long been subject to fluctuations in water levels brought about by water development "upstream." The numbers and movements of birds and water animals such as alligators varied with that level. In 1974 the Big Cypress National Reserve was created north of the park to protect the water supply. The California redwoods were affected by logging on the headwaters of park streams that created massive siltation, destroyed fish habitat, and increased downstream flooding. Almost every park in the nation had some such external threat; Glacier National Park had the greatest number.

The mandate under which the Fish and Wildlife Service managed the refuges was less formal; there was no organic act to provide specific guidelines. Yet various laws had identified the agency's objectives as the enhancement of fish and wildlife and their habitat. Other uses were subordinate, acceptable only as long as they did not interfere with those purposes. Despite this the service faced constant pressures to allow incompatible uses.[68]

Mineral development and motorized vehicles were special threats. Western refuges had been carved out of the public domain under which there were hard-rock and fossil-fuel minerals. Each refuge had been established individually with tailored management. In some instances where there were known minerals joint administration had been established under both the Fish and Wildlife Service and the Bureau of Land Management. This provided an opening wedge for mineral exploitation to the detriment of wildlife. During 1975 three such cases on upland game ranges came to be the subject of intense dispute when Secretary of the Interior Rogers C. Morton sought to remove their mineral component from the jurisdiction of the service and give it exclusively to the BLM. Environmentalists fought back; Congress prohibited the move and gave full control to the Fish and Wildlife Service.

The wildlife refuge program was shaped also by efforts from appreciative users and humane protectionists to bring their concerns to bear on refuge management. These constituted a new clientele to which the service sought to respond. In 1976 it produced an environmental analysis of its program for the coming years that included 352 pages of letters it had received as comment. These reflected the entire spectrum of wildlife interests and made clear that game management had receded in relative importance in the face of newer wildlife concerns. At times it appeared that the divisions between older and newer wildlife users would have greater priority in agency politics than would the impact of development pressures on the refuges.[69]

Comparative Agency Responses

Each of the four public-land agencies was affected by the new environmental interests and modified its policies accordingly, but this took place in quite different ways and at various paces because of the distinctive history and institutional framework of each land system.

For appreciative wildlife users the National Park Service was the model agency. Since the late nineteenth century park policy had permitted fishing but not hunting. This no-hunting policy had evolved initially at Yellowstone National Park, where big-game hunters had sought to define the park as a refuge for buffalo and elk, which were endangered by overextensive hunting. This policy came to prevail in most national parks.

But increases in animal populations often either depleted food supplies or had an adverse impact on other species or park resources. Hence the Park Service at times authorized controlled hunting so as to reduce numbers. This was practiced especially with feral animals, those formerly domesticated species that now roamed the West and often in their biological aggressiveness threatened the forage of other, more highly prized, animals. Environmentalists with an ecological perspective accepted these strategies, but those with a more exclusively humane bent did not. Such conflicting views led to many controversies over wildlife management in the national parks.

A different kind of wildlife issue confronted the Forest Service in several eastern national forests where heavy deer browsing due to overpopulation stunted and killed young trees and threatened regeneration. Foresters called for a reduction in the numbers of deer. Environmentalists were inclined to agree, especially since the Forest Service had long argued that the size of the deer herd justified clear-cutting so as to protect seedlings from browsing. In the upper Great Lakes area aspen had succeeded earlier pine and maple forests, and these provided excellent deer browse as well as pulpwood for the paper industry. But in the 1970s federal and state forest managers in Michigan sought to shift forest species to pine for future lumber production. Because this would greatly reduce the amount of browse for deer and grouse, it encountered strong opposition from hunters and game managers.

Natural-environment recreation gave rise to several new policy directions in public-land management, but the most controversial was the effort to restrict the use of motorized off-road vehicles. User organizations sprang up throughout the nation to press their case. Environmental groups, on the other hand, sought to protect areas from noise and traffic. Each land-management agency found itself involved in volatile debate.

Motorized-vehicle users argued that they had a right to use public lands for recreation; they fought for the freedom to go anywhere. But wildlife advocates argued that such vehicles unduly disturbed wildlife, and hikers and backpackers agreed that their presence disturbed their recreation. In 1972 the problem came to a head, and President Nixon on May 5 of that year issued an executive order requiring each agency to adopt a system to control off-road vehicles to protect both natural resources and the enjoyment of the outdoors for environmental use. In carrying out the order, each agency tended to permit motorized vehicles in designated areas and exclude them from all others.

Wilderness policy influenced each of the four agencies differently. The first to confront it, the Forest Service, was reluctant to share the growing popular interest in wilderness. As the movement evolved the service found it difficult to turn its negative responses into innovative leadership. To each new turn of activity, from the initial ideas in the 1920s through the new study areas of the 1970s and the drive for eastern wilderness, the service reacted with misgivings and opposition; only the persistent political force of the wilderness movement prompted it to modify its views.

In contrast, the Fish and Wildlife Service moved ahead rapidly with the reviews mandated by the 1964 Wilderness Act. Often it proposed as wilderness islands that were far smaller than the minimal 5,000 acres contemplated by the act, thereby initiating a new turn of events concerning the appropriate size for wilderness. The National Park Service was also more congenial to wilderness. But it was fearful that designations could restrict future choices to expand visitor accommodation and administrative facilities. It sought to exclude such areas. These tendencies were countermanded successfully during the Nixon administration by Assistant Secretary of the Interior Nathaniel Reed. Although there were some misgivings within the National Park Service on this question, on the whole, much as was the case with the Fish and Wildlife Service, the agency found wilderness to be compatible with its objectives.

After passage of its organic act in 1976, the Bureau of Land Management played a far more active role in wilderness affairs. The new BLM during the Carter administration took up wilderness reviews with considerable enthusiasm. But soon it began to limit what it thought appropriate as candidate areas. Areas already roaded were excluded even when these were little used rights-of-way. Human artifacts that were miles away and not readily observable disqualified areas. The BLM was especially reluctant to include areas with broad vistas because such lands were too extensive. As the BLM review proceeded, developmental demands tended to transform positive agency commitment into neutral mediating between the contending parties and to reduce the agency's capacity for leadership.

Innovation in Management Procedures

Environmental concerns also led to changes in the methods by which agencies made decisions and in particular the extent of public participation in the process.

The Forest Service took up land-use planning early in the 1970s and solicited public views both before planning began and along the way. Although the agency was not always happy with the result and found some public sessions to be tense confrontations, the procedure helped it to identify more accurately the political world within which it now had to operate. Environmentalists were able to express their views about agency policy far more than in years past, but the Forest Service also learned how to discipline the process so as to minimize their effect.[70]

Public participation in BLM planning came more slowly and with far more controversy. In this case much of the tension over agency procedures focused on who should be represented in decision making. Livestock operators still insisted on a dominant role, and hence, although the agency made some overtures to environmentalists, many issues centered on environmental legitimacy. Thus, whereas much environmental litigation involving the BLM concerned resource use, as was the case with the Forest Service, it also concerned issues of the adequacy of public participation. Many BLM controversies during the Reagan administration were generated by the attempt to give the livestock operators a more exclusive role in decision making and the resulting effort of environmentalists to retain influence in it.

Environmentalists scored some of their most effective planning victories with the National Park Service and in a number of instances succeeded in forcing marked changes in proposals. Especially important as cases in point were plans for seashores and lakeshores such as those for Assateague National Seashore and Sleeping Bear Dunes National Lakeshore. In contrast with those involving the Forest Service and the BLM, these changes came about not so much as a result of litigation and court order as through the direct response of the agency to the interested public. In the give-and-take between the Park Service and environmentalists, it appeared, significant changes in policy were being forged in such a way as to bring public environmental values and agency policy into closer harmony.

Fish and Wildlife Service planning, though far less extensive than in the other agencies, also changed direction with new public attitudes. Alone among the four federal land agencies, the service undertook a comprehensive study of the public values of its clientele, not limited to specific management problems, such as the provision of recreational facilities, but extending to the entire spectrum of public attitudes toward wildlife.

Agency differences were reflected in the varied devices each established to maintain close relationships with the public. The Park Service was the most effective through its interpretive program, which provided continuous contacts with visitors, and its insistence that its personnel be able to communicate with the public. In the 1970s the Fish and Wildlife Service took up similar types of activities; it developed visitors' facilities and established interpretive programs. Similar Forest Service activities were restricted to areas that catered to outdoor recreationists. And the BLM displayed little interest in establishing effective contact with the environmental or recreational public; in fact, during the Reagan administration it sought to reduce its recreational facilities.

The Forest Service came to define its role as a broker among competing interests. Personnel viewed themselves as being in the middle, resisting developmental demands on the one side and environmental demands on the other. They thought of environmentalists as only one among many competing "special interest" groups, as special pleaders no different from off-road vehicle advocates or lumber companies. The more the service came to be known as a broker and mediator, the less it came to be thought of as exercising leadership in public-land matters.

Foresters identified themselves as professionals who should be given the freedom and authority to make resource decisions by themselves. Efforts to define agency objectives more precisely through legislation were looked on as political interference with more "objective" judgments. Their own choices were described in general terms as "wise use," implying that the service knew what was best, and they complained that in being forced by legislation to accept environmental values they were being prevented from managing. These views only tended to define the Forest Service as a political agency that sought freedom to continue its broker's role on its own terms and to divorce itself as far as was feasible from external political influence.[71]

The National Park Service and the Fish and Wildlife Service responded to the emerging environmental movement by seeking to identify a bit more closely with its values. Their more clearly defined mandates enhanced their legitimacy to govern the parks and refuges as leaders rather than as mediators. Both were known as environmental agencies in which personnel were inclined to foster environmental values to a far greater extent than either the Forest Service or the Bureau of Land Management had.

5 The Countryside: A Land Rediscovered, yet Threatened

Between the city and the distant wildlands was the settled countryside, containing varied lands and land uses: farms and woodlands, rivers and floodplains, wetlands, lakes and ocean shores, mines and "unproductive wastelands." In the Environmental Era the countryside was a vast area in transition. Its fate was yet to be determined.

Until World War II the American countryside was land nobody wanted. Decade after decade rural people fled their farms and towns. As agricultural production per farm worker rose, fewer hands were needed, and those who were superfluous moved to the cities. The more productive agricultural areas came to be preferred, and the less productive, the so-called marginal lands, declined – in numbers of people, homes, and villages, and in property values. The relocation of American agriculture created vast areas of countryside to which few wished to lay claim. In the 1930s the rural population became somewhat stable as during the Depression the return of some to the countryside served as a safety value against economic privation, but by the 1940s the decline resumed at a rapid pace.[1]

After World War II this was dramatically reversed. Lands that nobody had wanted were increasingly in demand. Some people financed farming for a livelihood with savings earned from urban occupations. More found in rural communities the kind of environment they sought for work, home, and play, which they had not found in the cities. They came to visit on weekends and vacations, to enjoy the more relaxed atmosphere away from crowds, where the air was cleaner and the water more sparkling. Here were restful open spaces and wildlife to observe with interest and appreciation. Such visits to the countryside often led to the purchase of land for weekend and vacation homes, ranging from modest trailers to more substantial dwellings, where environmental amenities could be enjoyed on a regular basis.[2]

Real estate values began to rise. Land that in the 1930s had sold for $25 an acre now moved up to $400 or $500. The price often depended on proximity to environmental amenities. Property along a river or shoreline or borderline public land in parks or with mature forest was more prized. But such lands were of varied environmental value, and what the buyer sought was usually in finite supply. Little land lay along or near natural streams or lakes, or on mountainsides with spectacular views.

But others in the cities also reached out to use the countryside. Urban areas had long drawn on the lands beyond them for much that was essential to their growth. They sought food, lumber, and minerals. They constructed reservoirs in the hinterland and purchased timberlands to protect the watersheds above. They used the countryside for communications between cities in the form of railroads, highways, and telegraph lines. In the mid-twentieth century they sought energy supplies, coal, oil, uranium, and shale, which led to the further use of the countryside for pipelines, electrical transmission lines, and coal slurry lines, each with its own right-of-way.

The city also tried to export its waste and pollution to the countryside. Facing a shortage of sites within their borders, cities sought new landfills in rural areas. Sewage was dumped into rivers and was carried downstream, and air pollution released by tall stacks was blown downwind. Industries sought rural sites for their hazardous wastes, as well as their own manufacturing establishments, which urban dwellers thought of as undesirable neighbors.

These demands on the countryside grew at the same time as it was discovered by urban residents for its environmental qualities. The two sets of forces collided, exacerbating the drama of the struggle for control of the land, air, and water beyond the city limits. The circumstances of the resulting issues appeared to be many, varied, and often complex, but they were, in fact, rather simple. What was the desirable and appropriate balance between a more natural environment and a more developed one? As episode piled upon episode the general character of the issues became clear. The future of the countryside was now at stake.[3]

River Development

Some early events in this series of controversies centered on plans by federal agencies to construct dams on the nation's rivers. These were a threat to alternative uses of the sites – to the aesthetic and recreational use of free-flowing streams, to agricultural production, farmsteads, villages, and cemeteries that reservoirs would inundate, and to aquatic life that would be markedly altered.

At first opponents of such projects worked in isolation, especially farming communities about to be wiped out by reservoirs. Each protested individually against threatened destruction, but with little success. Urban-industrial demands for flood protection, water supplies, and navigation proved politically more powerful than the claims of rural communities. But over the years other people felt threatened by river-development projects and joined with farmers to constitute a formidable opposition.[4]

In the two decades after World War II several spectacular issues riveted the nation's attention on the growing objections to the construction of these large engineering works. One involved a proposed dam at Echo Park near the Utah-Colorado border, which would flood portions of Dinosaur National Monument. A coalition of national conservation groups, led by the Sierra Club and the Wilderness Society, fought the proposal in the 1950s and successfully prevented construction. A decade later came another proposal by the Bureau of Reclamation to build on the Colorado two dams that would flood portions of the lower Grand Canyon. Under the leadership of the Sierra Club, this effort was also defeated in the late 1960s.

Then arose the issue of dams in Hell's Canyon on the lower Snake River in Idaho. In this case the Supreme Court ruled that federal authorities had to consider among their alternatives for the river one of "no dam at all," a decision that set in motion action in Congress, successful in 1976, to protect the area permanently. Such episodes as these communicated dramatically to the nation's leaders that the new environmental interest was a force to be reckoned with.[5]

These conflicts were soon followed by a more widespread movement to halt dam building on many of the nation's rivers. Because of such opposition the Tennessee Valley Authority (TVA) abandoned plans to construct a series of dams on the upper French Broad River in eastern Tennessee. In addition, in 1978 Congress accepted the environmental alternative of a national scenic river instead of a proposed Corps of Engineers dam at Tocks Island on the Middle Delaware. The corps also planned a series of dams to control the Wabash River in Indiana and Illinois, which was frustrated by environmental opposition and led finally to a decision by the Indiana legislature to withdraw support.[6]

In the 1950s the Soil Conservation Service (SCS) entered the river-development business, which extended the opposition to tributary as well as main-stem rivers. In 1955 Congress approved a small watershed program that gave the SCS authority to construct dams and to dredge rivers in order to reclaim nearby farmland. The resulting projects were not as spectacular as those of the Bureau of Reclamation or the Corps of Engineers, but they aroused considerable local opposition.[7]

Channelization projects, promoted by the corps as well as the SCS, were especially controversial. These were intended to straighten meandering streams, usually through low-lying wetlands, to speed the flow of water, and to lower its level in order to reclaim lands for crop production and other development. Wildlife groups protested that this destroyed valuable habitat. Court action undertaken by environmental groups led to some changes and slowed down the practice. The channelization issue added an ecological dimension to the protests, namely, the concept of a stream as a natural biological system that engineering works would destroy.[8]

These issues generated considerable personal involvement with streams and rivers much as was the case with wilderness. As people canoed or floated on specific streams, hiked along their banks and observed wildlife, fished and hunted in and by them, or photographed their natural settings, they developed an attachment to them. And this prompted them to rise to their defense when dams and other modifications were proposed. Watershed and river associations united those who shared an interest in the same stream, and formulated alternative plans that could be used to counter the proposals of developmental agencies.[9]

From such beginnings arose a drive to make national water policy more environmentally acceptable. Under the leadership of Brent Blackwelder, the Environmental Policy Center sought to coordinate opposition to dams nationwide so as to bring cooperative effort to bear on national water policy. The task was formidable. Case by case, environmentalists exposed the high cost of projects, the environmental damage they caused, and agency efforts to manipulate cost-benefit analyses in order to justify them.[10]

The opponents perfected their lobbying skills to bring together a wide variety of interests, including the National Taxpayers Union, to their side. And they made full use of the efforts of both the Carter and Reagan administrations to reduce the federal budget by urging that Congress disapprove authorizations of new projects and appropriations for old. They played a major role in preventing the passage of any omnibus water-development act for almost a decade after 1977.[11]

Large-Scale Facilities

River-engineering works were only the first of a number of environmental intrusions into the countryside. Attempts to site large-scale facilities there were equally controversial. These included lead, copper, and zinc smelters, iron and steel mills, oil refineries, pulp and paper mills, and petrochemical plants, as well as highways, oil and gas pipelines, and electric-power lines. A number of communities in the nation were involved in a confrontation with a proposed industrial development.[12]

The vast majority of incidents in the 1970s concerned energy facilities. Projects ranged from oil-transfer stations in San Diego to convey Alaskan oil to the lower 48, to refineries at Hampton Roads, Virginia, liquefied natural gas installations at Point Conception, California, offshore oil drilling in the Santa Barbara Channel and on Georges Bank off the coast of Massachusetts, and shale-oil recovery and synthetic-fuel plants. They included pipeline ventures such as that in Alaska from the north coast to the port of Valdez in the south, the gas pipeline across Canada, the Northern Tier pipeline across the Northwest, and the Caltex line from southern California to Texas.[13]

Industrial entrepreneurs found it increasingly undesirable to locate new facilities in or near metropolitan areas because land was limited and public opinion adverse. They chose to shift sites to the countryside. Often these new locations were thought to be in "remote" areas and hence not likely to generate public opposition. But to significant numbers of people few areas were remote. Those who had long called these places home now developed a new awareness of their capacity to resist, and they were aided by more recently arrived neighbors.

Siting issues were fought out case by case. Although such battles occurred across the nation, they did not give rise to joint efforts to exercise national leverage. In some states protests led to proposals for land-use planning, but these were promoted just as frequently by industrial-siting advocates who wished to counteract local resistance to their plans. Communities often used local zoning or referenda to protect themselves. In doing so they reflected a general public hostility to large-scale enterprise in the countryside whether promoted by private or public agencies. Accumulated sentiment of this kind prompted state governments to exercise control over facility siting. In response, industrial promoters often turned to the federal government for authority to override state as well as local objections.[14]

These public reactions were a response to the enormous size and scale of new development. When electricity plants or transmission lines were small, they aroused relatively little opposition. But after the war, plant output grew from 100 to 400 and then more than 1,000 megawatts, and transmission-line capacity from 85 to 320 and then 765 kilovolts. Such increases led to greater amounts of fuel, residue, water for cooling, waste heat and air pollution, and width and length of transmission-line corridors. The gap between the size of these proposed changes and the smaller scale of daily personal experience and community institutions constituted the measure of the human response to these projects.[15]

After passage of the National Environmental Policy Act of 1969, energy facilities involving federal action required environmental-impact analyses before construction, and a formal Environmental Impact Statement (EIS) became the focus of opposition. It provided an opportunity to debate publicly the environmental impact of projects. These efforts brought together diverse people concerned with the varied impacts: fishermen worried about the destruction of aquatic habitat from waste heat, local officials concerned about the disruption of community life from a massive influx of people, farmers and ranchers who feared the loss of water, and native Americans who worried about the disruption of their traditional ways of life by mineral and energy development on their lands.

Energy facilities aroused special opposition when proposed for areas long valued for their natural environment qualities. One of the first proposed nuclear plants in California sparked objections because it was to be located on a site on Bodega Bay that the state had acquired for a public park and that it now agreed to release for the plant. Pumped-storage reservoirs were often proposed for areas in spectacular rugged hills and valleys such as St. Anthony's Wilderness near Harrisburg, Pennsylvania, the Canaan Valley in eastern West Virginia, or the lower Hudson River Valley. All of these plans brought celebrated environmental controversies.[16]

At times reaction to facility siting was mobilized statewide. Maine and Vermont, for example, insisted that siting decisions be approved by the state legislature. This approach resulted from several rather dramatic incidents such as an attempt to build an oil refinery on the New Hampshire coast. All along the Atlantic and Pacific coasts local protest concerning energy facilities generated demands that states be given major authority in siting decisions. Struggles continued, in turn, between state and federal energy authorities in which the energy companies sought to enhance federal control to overcome opposition from the states.

The adverse effect of energy-facility siting played an important role in shaping the environmental experience after World War II. The issues were pervasive; they shaped concerns and perspectives in almost every region and state. They also provoked considerable thought about a national energy policy and about the possibilities of alternative approaches to energy that might be environmentally less destructive. Was it not possible either to limit the nation's insatiable appetite for energy or to supply it in a less damaging manner?

Mining

Mining had been carried on in the countryside for decades. It affected only the wildlands themselves and did not disturb communities other than those of the miners. But the rediscovery of the countryside led to new confrontations between people and mining. Industries began mining in established residential areas, and reoccupation of the countryside brought people into more intimate contact with mining.[17]

Objections arose to the many adverse effects of mining: contaminated water supplies, acid mine drainage, unstable piles of mine spoil, disturbances from trucks hauling coal and from air pollution during mining, the interference with daily and seasonal wildlife routes, and the permanent scars at abandoned mines. Demands for higher standards produced a series of controversies between mining companies and the affected communities.

In the 1970s surface mining became a major issue. Surface mining had become more widespread after World War II because of the rapid increase in the size of earth-moving equipment and in the scale of its use. It uncovered large expanses of land to reach relatively thin seams of coal lying near the surface, removed the layer of soil above the coal called "overburden" or "spoil," and then extracted the coal. In many communities vast areas were scraped clean of all vegetation and topsoil, overburden was piled nearby, and permanent pits were left to gather water, all of which resulted in an extremely unattractive landscape.[18]

Surface mining had widespread adverse effects on water quality that could not always be clearly anticipated. Coal contained considerable amounts of sulfur that, when exposed to the air, became oxidized into sulfuric acid. These chemical reactions continued even after the coal, once exposed, was recovered. The large piles of exposed spoil continually produced more acid as rain fell, creating runoff into streams, raising their acid content, and destroying both fish and the aquatic life on which fish depended.[19]

Fishermen became a major influence in bringing surface mining under control. In Pennsylvania, the first state to act with any degree of effectiveness, the Pennsylvania Federation of Sportsmen was instrumental in securing the enactment and enforcement of surface-mining laws. These had a twofold purpose: the limitation of pollution and the reclamation of disturbed land. Both were intended to reduce the damage to stream water quality. The erosion of disturbed soil increased the amount of suspended solids in streams, making them turbid.

Concern over the effects of surface mining grew steadily during the 1960s. This concern arose first in the Appalachians, then spread to the newer mining areas of the upper Plains States and still later to the Illinois coalfields, where mining threatened to reduce the natural fertility of some of the nation's best agricultural lands. After the sharp rise in energy prices in the winter of 1973–4, a new surge in surface mining brought miners into more intense conflict with rural communities. Amid this drive, even the Pennsylvania program seemed to become less effective and to require a stronger federal presence to bolster it.[20]

The move to secure federal regulation began early in the 1970s under the leadership of Louise Dunlap, a self-taught surface mine expert and legislative strategist with the Environmental Policy Center. Support in Congress came rapidly; twice it passed legislation that was vetoed, first by President Nixon and later by President Ford. During the presidential campaign of 1976 Jimmy Carter committed himself to the measure, and when Congress again passed it in 1977 it became law as the Surface Mining Control and Reclamation Act.

Surface-mining regulation met stubborn and relentless resistance from the coal industry. Although it could not prevent final passage of the act, it set to work to reduce the force of its application. In this drive it had the full support of coal-state governors such as Jay Rockefeller of West Virginia. Objections were made to the regulations the Office of Surface Mining adopted to implement the act, and when the industry could not influence that agency directly it worked through the White House to modify the regulations. In this it had some success. It was able to secure the dismissal of the two officials in the Department of the Interior who were most directly responsible for supervising the Office of Surface Mining in the hierarchy above the director. The industry also worked in Congress, though unsuccessfully, for a new law to reduce the effectiveness of regulation.[21]

Upon becoming president, Ronald Reagan fully supported efforts to limit the surface-mining program. The federal courts upheld the law in the face of industry challenges. Nonetheless, the Office of Surface Mining revised the initial regulations so as to reduce their effectiveness. Environmentalists, in turn, brought lawsuits to halt implementation of the revised regulations. These were successful, and the regulations underwent still another revision.[22]

River development, industrial siting, and mining were persistent intrusions in the countryside. To those who had sought out such lands as attractive places to work, live, and play, it appeared as if forces far beyond their daily activities constantly disturbed their way of life. Their most compelling experience was of the vast contrast between the smaller and more human context of their own affairs and the enormous size and complexity of the new demands.[23]

Although such large-scale ventures might make sense in some view from the top in private and public life, where the manipulation of massive and far-reaching affairs was a matter of course, they seemed vastly out of phase with the more human scale of those affected in communities throughout the nation. This countryside confrontation gradually generated community self-confidence and resources to resist. The sometimes faltering steps undertaken in these circumstances were one of the major sources of the environmental movement.

The Search for Areas of Ecological Significance

Equally as important as the resistance to large-scale development in the environmental struggle in the countryside were efforts to enhance objectives by identifying and protecting land, air, and water with special environmental and ecological value. These efforts reflected the more positive attitudes people sought to express in opposing development projects, and the underlying personal and social values that had long since changed in barely noticed ways, now to become manifest in more overt action.[24]

A variety of areas served as rallying points: coastal and inland wetlands; natural streams and rivers; lake and ocean shorelands; sand dunes and barrier islands; estuaries of rivers; flood plains; pine barrens, which took on a peculiar fascination as remnants of once more extensive natural lands; and smaller areas that represented biological systems on the point of extinction. All these assumed high public importance as places where ecological, hydrological, and geological forces could be experienced, carefully observed, and retained for human enrichment in the midst of a more dominant drive for development.

The methods in this search differed markedly from the strategies of protest. They involved, first of all, attempts to identify and inventory examples of each type of area. Environmentalists scoured the countryside to determine the precise locations of wetlands, wild and scenic rivers, high-quality streams, undeveloped barrier islands and dunes, and other natural areas. What began as individual forays were aided frequently by scientists from colleges and universities and often expanded into larger efforts organized and financed by public agencies. The inventories became both a warning signal to potential developers to steer clear of the listed areas and a basis on which environmentalists developed protection strategies.[25]

These came to be referred to collectively as "areas of critical environmental concern" because they were examples of a natural world now threatened with eradication. They also constituted a natural baseline from which the changes brought about by development could be observed and judged. The drive took on a special urgency in the countryside because development here was proceeding rapidly, and it was still possible to strike a different balance between natural and developed lands than had occurred in the city.

This search for critical environmental areas involved a close relationship between the aesthetic and the ecological. Bird-

watching often led to an interest in habitats, food-chain relationships, and the wider environment of bird life. Outdoor recreationists developed an appreciation of biological succession and the
varieties of plants and animals one encountered. Nature photography, which stressed aesthetic appreciation, developed into nature study, which emphasized ecological understanding. An increasing number of people sought to think about and justify their
activities in terms of ecological analysis and language.

Two types of personal involvement exemplified these approaches. One was the nature center where informal study by
adults and schoolchildren took place. The Audubon Society
had long taken a special interest in establishing nature centers;
these grew from 356 in 1969 to 558 in 1975 and were sponsored
by schools, colleges and universities, and city, county, state, and
federal governments. Another was the organized effort to inventory, study, and protect particular places. There were the watershed associations with a distinctly environmental flavor, in
contrast with the more traditional watershed associations fostered by the Soil Conservation Service. Those concerned with
the barrier islands along the East Coast formed the Barrier Islands Watch in 1976 to monitor specific islands and sound the
alarm when they appeared to be threatened by development. As
with wilderness, this personal interest in identified natural systems shaped significant elements of environmental action.[26]

These activities emphasized the need to acquire baseline information about less disturbed ecosystems so as to understand
more precisely the ecological effects of development. The search
was often frustrating because of the difficulty in finding places
where human influence had not penetrated. And unless action
was taken immediately even the remaining few would be lost forever. By identifying and studying such areas, by associating them
with larger scientific enterprise, and taking action to protect them,
environmentalists attempted to establish footholds for natural
systems in urban-industrial society.[27]

Wetlands

Wetlands had long been thought of simply as wastelands waiting
to be drained, filled, and developed. As land became scarce,

wetlands that earlier had been bypassed came to be prime choices for industrial and residential sites. Coastal marshlands were attractive for large-scale housing projects because the incorporation of bodies of water into residential areas appealed to home buyers. These pressures drew increased attention to wetlands as prime natural areas that should be protected from further development.[28]

The East Coast and Florida were areas of special controversy. In Florida the U.S. Army Corps of Engineers dredged shallow lands for commercial navigation and for use by pleasure craft. Spoil from dredging was deposited in other shallow lands, building them up above the waterline and making them available for development. The corps became involved in massive modifications of the marshes and wetlands along the coast. But as environmental interest grew in the 1960s the corps refused to consider the ecological effects of dredging in its review of permits on the ground that its statutory authority was confined to the effects on navigation.[29]

In 1966 Congressman John Dingell of Michigan pressed the corps to change its views. He introduced a bill to require that all permits issued by the corps be approved by the Fish and Wildlife Service, which had a direct interest in environmental values. Because Dingell's proposal gathered considerable political support, the corps relented and signed a memorandum of agreement giving the service far more influence in approving permits; it was not given veto power over them, however. In subsequent legal action the National Environmental Policy Act of 1969 also gave considerable leverage to those who argued that environmental effects should play a role in such decisions.[30]

The rising public interest in the value of wetlands was a rather remarkable turn of events that had gone on almost unrecorded. When researchers began to conduct attitude studies in the 1970s about how coastal wetlands should be managed, they were struck by the high degree to which the public thought of wetlands in terms of natural values and the extent to which they were willing to protect them from development.[31]

Along the northeast coast, from Massachusetts to Delaware, widespread public interest led to state programs. Delaware took the strongest stand in 1967 by prohibiting entirely any large-scale development on its coastal wetlands. A separate movement grew up on the West Coast out of concern for the aesthetic qualities of the natural coastline. In the Gulf States the influential oil and gas industry, which used wetlands for navigation channels and pipelines, prevented significant action from proceeding.

The wetlands inventory became one of the major instruments of action. Delaware developed an inventory – complete with mapping and biological details – of its coastal wetlands. Similar action was undertaken by Rhode Island. The crucial policy, however, was to require that coastal development, including that on low-lying marshlands, be allowed only by specific permit. Permitting agencies were established, complete with judicial review of administrative decisions. The crucial environmental feature of these programs was the degree to which decisions reflected a balance of uses that recognized and protected the natural values of wetlands.[32]

The concern for coastal wetlands expanded to a similar interest in inland wetlands. Often this arose as part of a more general concern for open space near settled communities or in wildlife habitat on the part of bird-watchers and hunters. Inland wetlands were prime targets for dredging and filling for development or drainage for crops. Inland wetlands often served as major areas for disposal of mine tailings or industrial and municipal wastes. Many hazardous-waste sites were also located on wetlands. As interest in wetlands increased, reaction against these uses grew.[33]

Environmentalists sought to enhance federal authority to protect wetlands. They argued that the 1972 Clean Water Act required such action. But the Corps of Engineers, to whom earlier legislation had given jurisdiction over such matters, resisted. It argued that its constitutional authority was confined to navigable waters and did not extend to the headwaters where many wetlands were located. Section 404 of the Clean Water Act, which was the specific part in question, was extensively debated, leading to congressional action in 1977 to confirm the interpretation of environmentalists. Under certain conditions, administration could be delegated to the states. And this, in turn, stimulated passage of some new state wetland laws.[34]

Environmental action with respect to wetlands seemed to be closely associated with their identification as locations of significant biological activity. Here one could observe wildlife, a type of recreation that combined both aesthetic and intellectual interests. At the same time, professional ecologists argued that wetlands performed important functions such as fish production, natural treatment of polluted waters, reservoirs for temporary retention of floodwaters, and buffers to protect land against the forces of ocean winds and tides. These came to be identified as quantifiable economic benefits. But economic analysis seemed to be far less important in the political struggle over wetlands than the simple and direct value people placed on them as natural systems prized both for their aesthetic quality and their ecological processes.

Natural Rivers

Environmentalists were also engaged in identifying streams of high natural quality in order to protect them from engineering works. Emphasis on the first process often led directly to the second, for example, the drive in West Virginia and North Carolina to protect the New River from construction of a dam by the American Electric Power Company, in New Jersey and Pennsylvania to protect the Middle Delaware from inundation by the proposed Tocks Island dam, and the long-lived but successful attempt to sidetrack attempts by the corps to build a series of dams on the Potomac River not far from the nation's capital. Such incidents only prompted environmentalists to identify valuable natural streams ahead of time to avoid proposals for dams in the first place.[35]

To carry out these objectives scenic river associations were formed in the 1970s in Oklahoma, Tennessee, Ohio, and other states. Beyond these were organizations to protect specific streams, such as the Ozark Society in Missouri or the West Virginia Highlands Conservancy, which then expanded their range of interest. Several states established programs to identify streams of high natural quality; they were categorized as wild, scenic, pastoral, and recreational, distinguished by the existing level of development and desired future policy. These were not the more spectacular wild streams, which were more likely to be covered by the national program, but streams in the more settled countryside with varying degrees of naturalness.[36]

State laws to protect streams caused controversy between property owners along them and state agencies and environmentalists who wanted a more protective program. Riparian owners feared the influx of recreationists classification might bring. Yet they also desired protection against large-scale development, which might threaten the environmental quality of the streams on which they lived. When faced with an active proposal for a dam, riparian owners tended to support stream protection.

A major objective of the natural-stream program was to maintain the scenic quality of the land along it. Full public ownership could achieve this objective most readily. But the countryside involved a mixture of authority. Streams were public waters, but the bordering lands were usually privately owned. Those who desired to protect rivers sought to establish streamside land-use controls. In Michigan, for example, the law required that building be prohibited within 300 feet of the stream bank. But localities often declined to establish such controls, and the state did not enforce them. Hence riparian land protection moved forward only slowly.

Environmentalists became interested in natural streams for their periodic flooding action as well as their amenities. The flooding river and its streamside lands came to be thought of as an ecological system of interacting land and water relationships. They described the adjacent lands as "belonging to the river," a part of its ebb and flow through the course of hydrological cycles and seasons. They argued that human occupancy of the flood plain should be reduced in contrast with the prevailing tendency to use upstream reservoirs to protect it from development.[37]

One implication of this approach was that the flood plain should be used as a natural storage reservoir for floodwaters, and the Corps of Engineers was urged to use this "nonstructural" approach. In a few cases the agency did so. Persistent opposition to proposed levees in Colorado Springs, Colorado, and Prairie du Chien, Wisconsin, led the corps to drop these projects and use the land already acquired for open parkland. This would be subject to periodic flooding with relatively little monetary damage. The Massachusetts Audubon Society cooperated with the corps to develop for the Charles River a plan that involved the purchase of adjacent wetlands to serve multiple uses as natural reservoirs, open space, and wildlife habitat. These innovations drew ardent support from environmentalists; in policy, however, they remained the exception rather than the rule.

These efforts to combine the varied functions of wetlands with flood management were reflected in environmental alternatives to channelization. One could identify many ways in which river channeling interfered with natural hydrological cycles, such as the lowered water table in Florida that, in turn, led to the intrusion of salt water in Miami water supplies. Channelization often destroyed wetlands in one place upstream only to create more floods downstream. When the corps proposed a project for the Cache River in Arkansas, downstream owners, with environmental support, objected to the threats to their farms and forestland because upstream channelization would cause greater flooding. The protest brought forth more than the usual amount of opposition from other governmental agencies that supported an alternative approach that would greatly reduce the amount of river modification.[38]

High-Quality Waters

Closely related to these efforts to protect natural streams were strategies to protect higher-quality waters from degradation. This was an implicit element of EPA regulations under the Clean Water Act of 1972, which called for special attention to streams of high quality. No degradation would be permitted in such streams save for "necessary and justifiable" economic and social development. The response of states to this requirement varied. Few wished to implement a full-scale antidegradation program, but some established a special class of streams of exceptional waters to protect. Pennsylvania, for example, maintained a category of "conservation stream."

Local and regional action on this matter was often associated with heightened citizen interest in water-quality protection. Analysis of water quality became one of the most readily available methods of introducing students to environmental science. Teachers encouraged students to measure conditions of in-stream water quality such as pH, turbidity, temperature, and bacterial counts. With more time and effort one could count numbers of species and the populations of each (diversity counts) for both benthic (bottom-dwelling) and in-stream organisms, as well as insect populations above the streams. Such studies encouraged appreciation of the intricate relationships of plants and animals within the stream ecosystem, and identification of "indicators" of larger relationships. Many elementary and secondary school pupils were introduced to ecological concepts through the study of nearby streams.[39]

Several types of citizen action focused this concern on the protection of water quality. One was the new form of watershed association, in contrast with the older ones that had grown out of the soil-conservation movement, in which water quality was a more central issue. These often focused on some stream that citizens sought to protect from erosion caused by upstream construction, mining, lumbering, or farming. They organized stream monitoring and measurement as a guideline against which to measure change, but they also emphasized streamside land protection. At times these associations acquired lands so as to control future use.

Lakes were also significant as centers of citizen action to protect high-quality waters. Lakeside property had long been sought out for home sites. Soon residents organized to protect the quality of the lake in which they had a common interest. Each lake could readily become a "sink" for pollutants from the surrounding lands. Lake associations were formed to monitor water quality. A special threat was the construction of high-rise apartments. Another was agricultural activity on water that drained into the lakes and overloaded them with nutrients. In 1966 Congress appropriated funds to assist in restoring lake water quality; this promoted widespread citizen activity and in 1980 led to the organization of a national lake-management association.[40]

The nation's fishermen were among the most vigorous defenders of high-quality waters. Many had developed a personal identification with favorite fishing locations; threats to them triggered defensive action. The effectiveness of state water-quality programs, in fact, often depended on the level of political activism on the part of its fishermen. In Pennsylvania, for example, the list of streams classified for special protection as conservation streams depended heavily on proposals from fishermen. And from that quarter came pressure to upgrade streams further and protect others from degradation.

Because of these concerns the nation's fishermen developed a high level of understanding of aquatic biology, especially of the relationships between fish and the aquatic life on which they depended. Trout fishermen were well known for this interest. They were inclined to be far more interested in enjoying the outdoors than in merely taking fish for food. Their search for natural amenities in fishing seemed to carry with it a greater desire to understand streams as ecosystems. This view was displayed in a motion picture produced in 1978 by Trout Unlimited (TU) called *The Way of the Trout,* which depicts the animal's life cycle. TU's perspective often allied it with the newer environmental groups, and it insisted that it was not a conservation but an environmental organization.[41]

Barrier Islands and Sand Dunes

The nation's coastal shorelands aroused interest also as areas for protection; they gave rise to quite a different ecological perspective based on the natural forces of winds and waves. Such forces caused sand dunes and barrier islands constantly to change their form and shape. Those who wanted to build homes on them also wanted to erect breakwaters, dikes, and walls to prevent the constant shifting of sand and encroachment of waves. But to environmentalists who stressed the need to "live with nature" these seemed to be self-defeating attempts to challenge natural forces in ways that could only lead to disaster.[42]

As one after another of these coastal areas came to be subject to residential and even industrial development, concern for the environmental consequences grew. Barrier islands were given special attention; environmentalists argued that they should be left to shift and change with the wind and tides rather than be subject to stabilization by engineered works such as seawalls and jetties. The Conservation Foundation was a major center of interest where John Clark, a geologist, took the initiative in fostering study and policy. His books on the subject provided both general principles and case studies to aid others to act.[43]

The Army Corps of Engineers was often called on to stabilize the shoreline. Property owners along the coast banded together to secure federal funds for this purpose. After each hurricane or in the face of the cumulative effects of continuous wave and wind erosion, the political demands intensified in Congress to take further action. Environmentalists opposed such measures. Often they drew on the ideas of Ian McHarg for inspiration; in his book *Design with Nature,* published in 1969, McHarg argues that in such areas one should build so as to dovetail human design with natural forces.

In 1980 Congressman Philip Burton of California introduced a bill to establish a program for federal acquisition and management under the National Park Service. Although this proposal failed, it led to more limited but persistent protection efforts in which the Nature Conservancy was a leader. Along the coasts of Maryland and Virginia, it had acquired a string of barrier islands more than seventy miles long, the largest such system under environmental management. It continued to manage this privately as the Virginia Coast Reserve, which became a major center for barrier island study and an inspiration for action.[44]

One of the more dramatic confrontations over the use of dunes and barrier islands concerned Assateague Island off the coast of Maryland, managed by the National Park Service. In the prodevelopment atmosphere of the Nixon administration, plans for Assateague had included an asphalt road the entire length of the island, a major tourist hotel, eating facilities, and parking lots. To protect the island's natural qualities, a Committee to Preserve Assateague, headed by Judy Johnson of Laurel, Maryland, was formed in 1971. Under considerable citizen pressure the Park Service revised its plans, designs for the road and motel were abandoned, and a far lower level of use was proposed. The committee continued to serve as "friends of Assateague" to cope with continual developmental threats.[45]

Natural Areas

The most extensive program pertaining to areas of "critical environmental concern" dealt with "natural areas." This term had a far more precise meaning than just the naturalness of undeveloped lands. One had to distinguish especially between the larger tract of wildlands and the smaller natural area, identified more by its biological and geological characteristics than its aesthetic environment. Such areas might include unusual geological formations such as rocks or waterfalls; botanical species such as virgin trees, unusual flowers, or species of shrubs; bogs with uncommon plant or animal types; or areas of particular ecological limitation and stress such as the barrens of the Midwest.[46]

The initial concern for natural areas, which extended back to the early 1920s, had emphasized the preservation of geological and biological remnants so rare that they were thought of as museum pieces. They were leftovers from the past, most examples of which had been destroyed. Much concern for these natural areas arose from the view of biologists that scientific inquiry required baseline examples with which to compare the transformed world of modern urban-industrial society. There were long discussions of what was natural and what was not, but usually the determining factor was the degree to which the area was unusual or distinctive. Often such an interest arose from the botanical surveys states such as Illinois and Ohio had developed over the years to map the distribution of plants and animals. Although such efforts had been carried out with extremely limited funds and at a snail's pace, the emerging natural-areas movement gave them new life.[47]

These activities were stimulated by organizations that came to be known as conservancies. The Western Pennsylvania Conservancy, for example, became interested in land preservation in the late 1950s and a few years later inaugurated a program to identify and protect natural areas. The best known, however, was the Nature Conservancy, a national organization that grew rapidly in the 1970s and formed regional offices and state chapters. It sought to identify, acquire, and protect natural areas, stimulated other private organizations and state agencies to do the same, and brought to the effort a solid ecological perspective.

By the mid-1970s the natural-areas movement emphasized natural diversity as a major theme of action. Ecologists ascribed great importance to the way in which natural selection had resulted in species diversity. They feared that monoculture – the replacement of diverse species with a single one – would destroy these natural processes and deprive human society of the benefits of diversity. Environmentalists found these ideas congenial and supported them.[48]

In the last half of the 1970s, the Nature Conservancy approached state governments to establish cooperative programs to identify and classify lands in terms of the degree to which their plants and animals represented important examples of natural diversity. The conservancy developed an elaborate scheme of classification that included several hundred biological types and set out to search for them in cooperating states. The information was stored in computer, readily available to use in natural-areas strategies. Inaugurated in 1976, it was called the Natural Heritage Program.[49]

The natural-areas movement was taken up with special enthusiasm in those states that had not previously protected their wildlands and that had only small holdings of state forests, gamelands, or parks. This was the situation in Ohio, Indiana, and Illinois, where vigorous and popular natural-area programs developed. It was also true in the South, where larger forested areas were in industrial rather than public ownership. In many states the public search for natural values found expression in the forested wildlands, but in others it took on the tone of a more desperate search for the remnants of natural systems rendered unique and hence more valuable by the rapid pace of development. In the South especially, the search for biological diversity provided a contrast with the forest industry's intense drive toward monoculture.[50]

The environmental search for remnants of natural systems in the developing countryside led to the continuing discovery of newer types of leftover areas with special ecological significance. In Kansas the remaining tallgrass prairie attracted particular attention. In the East it was the pine barrens, which had long been bypassed as worthless and which now, from Long Island to Georgia, became an object of aesthetic appreciative interest, as well as ecological analysis.

Cumulative Environmental Change in the Countryside

A third arena of action in the countryside involved slow, cumulative changes in the use of land, air, and water. These attracted less attention because of their low visibility and hence did not take on the crisis atmosphere that surrounded other types of environmental issues. Incremental development led to incremental change, and this, over the long run, could modify the balance between natural and developed environments as fully and as irreversibly as changes caused by more dramatic intrusions.

There were individual choices leading to temporary recreational activities in the countryside, a summer cottage or permanent residence, and efforts to promote tourism for the rural economy, which led first to seasonal facilities to serve summer visitors and then to year-round activities. State and federal governments also devised strategies to attract environmentally acceptable light industry. Each of these developments, though small initially, often led to extensive environmental degradation.[51]

Such change could take place with little notice because there was little environmental monitoring in the countryside. Monitoring had arisen mainly in the cities where measurements were directly related to campaigns to clean up the dirtiest spots. More than likely, rural inhabitants would be assured that the changes about which they might be concerned were "within the standards," but this often served more to justify incremental degradation than to understand and cope with it.

Despite the lack of such data, there was considerable personal awareness of the declining quality of air and water and a more congested landscape. As had been the case in the suburbs, this generated two reactions. One was a sense of betrayal, that the very aspects of environmental quality one had sought in either moving to or remaining in the countryside were now threatened by too many others deciding to do likewise. The second reaction was the attempt to implement a rising sense of the limits to growth by restricting the number and kinds of developmental activities. It was no wonder that some of the most vigorous action came from people newly arrived in the countryside.

Air Quality

State and national air-quality programs were overwhelmingly biased toward urban problems and gave only secondary attention to the countryside. In rural areas programs focused primarily on isolated industries such as power plants and smelters, pulp mills, and cement plants, which were dramatic cases of excessive local pollution. While the effects of these sources were known, few monitors existed to provide information about levels of rural air quality.

The manner of organizing air-quality management at times reflected this bias. In the Pennsylvania program, long established but revised in 1970, control regions were divided into three classes: the "critical air basins," which consisted of the two largest metropolitan centers, Pittsburgh and Philadelphia; the "other air basins," which included the twelve smaller cities such as Erie, Johnstown, Harrisburg, Reading, and Scranton; and all the rest of the state, which was described as the "nonair basins." In most states public reports concerning rural air quality were usually cast in terms not of changes within the area itself but of whether it met the established standards. These particular twists of air-quality management were closely associated with the long-standing tendency to think that cleaner rural air provided a safety valve for urban pollution problems. If one considered ill health to be the major consequence of urban air pollution, it seemed especially logical to argue that it could be avoided by moving industry. This was often encouraged by allowing higher levels of emissions in rural than in urban areas. In the face of these tendencies it was difficult to gain a perspective about rural air quality as such and to view it as a problem created by the impact of the city on the countryside.

New scientific observations in the 1970s indicated that levels of some pollutants in the countryside were higher than had been assumed. Although levels of sulfur dioxide had declined in the cities, the chemicals to which it was transformed in the air, sulfates, had not declined in rural areas. Ozone, which was formed largely from nitrogen oxide emissions from automobiles and coal-burning power plants and which came primarily from urban areas, remained at high levels in the countryside. Observations such as these began to link urban causes of air pollution with rural effects.[52]

The antidegradation provisions of the Clean Air Act of 1977 provided an initial focus for action, since it established a framework for measuring changes and formulating controls. But few state air-quality agencies took up these opportunities for preventing the decline of rural air quality, and most sought instead to change the law; moreover, the program came under increasing fire from industries. These groups now recruited allies from among the many air-quality professionals who were not convinced that cleaner air needed much protection.[53]

Acid precipitation gave a new emphasis to these problems. In its initial phase the issue stressed long-distance transport of air pollutants and their transformation to produce acid rain in areas far downwind. The phenomenon tended to link sources and effects that were far apart, especially those in urban and rural areas. Atmospheric currents respected no political boundaries or demographic patterns. Hence as the debate over acid rain heated up it tended to undermine the notion that the countryside could be given less attention. The problem was increasingly described as an interstate and international, or "transboundary," problem.[54]

The ensuing controversies emphasized two kinds of effects that reflected incremental environmental change in the countryside. One concerned reduced yields of farm crops. Farmers had long complained about the slow but persistent effect of air pollution on production. Protests from California farmers east of Los Angeles, in fact, had played an important role in the development of the state's air-pollution control program in the late 1950s. Research on such problems had persisted over the years and in the late 1970s took on new momentum as a result of the growing interest in acid rain. The possibility that air pollution harmed forest growth became an even livelier issue. Tree-ring analysis of forest growth identified lower annual increments and higher metal content of trees up and down the Appalachians beginning in the early 1950s.[55]

Visibility also attracted increasing attention. The earliest urban concern for air pollution had arisen from the adverse reaction to smoky skies. As health effects had become the more central issue in air pollution, the interest in visibility had declined. But now new measurements, especially of visibility at airports since the 1930s, identified considerable change in the smaller cities of the countryside and in the entire South. Elevated levels of sulfate, associated with acid rain, were found to be the major factor in lowered visibility. By the early 1980s one began to read of improved visibility as an important benefit from air-pollution control.[56]

The expanded focus on air-quality problems to include wide-ranging atmospheric contamination was as much a result of scientific studies as of popular demands in the countryside itself. Relentlessly air pollution was thought about, researched, understood, and debated as an extensive atmospheric phenomenon, linking sources and effects over long distances, resulting in slow and cumulative buildup of contaminants that required special action to control. One of the major results of the use by industry of tall stacks to disperse air pollution rather than to reduce it at the source was to increase the concern for atmospheric contamination and to build up evidence about the wide extent of the problem those stacks had created.

Water Quality

Potential water-quality degradation posed similar types of options for the countryside. In this case the pressures on rural areas were not carried directly from the cities, as with air, but were more in the form of indirect impacts from development. These came from both larger-scale projects and smaller, more cumulative, activities. Each placed an additional load on streams and groundwater in rural areas. One could either ignore the potential degradation, assuming that in some fashion the development from which it came was beneficial, or face its impact directly and seek to mitigate it. By the end of the 1970s even the definition of the problem, as was the case with air, had advanced only to the point of limited recognition rather than serious action.

We have already described briefly the emergence of a federal antidegradation policy in the 1960s. Most states complied with it only perfunctorily by including in their regulations, verbatim, the antidegradation statement formulated by the federal agency. Only a few states took up the challenge to translate these words into action. After the 1972 Clean Water Act was passed, environmentalists sought to strengthen these federal provisions in order to counteract state lethargy. Some states were willing to compromise water quality by relaxing the standards for cleaner streams, but a state-backed effort during the first Reagan administration to change the EPA's regulations to permit this downgrading met resistance from environmentalists and Congress and was abandoned.

The antidegradation program for water was not as elaborate as that for air. By dividing high-quality air into three classes, each one with allowable pollution below both primary and secondary standards, air quality was measured and controlled at five different levels. But for water, although the initial idea of antidegradation was somewhat similar, the federal regulation always allowed lowered water quality in these streams for "reasonable and necessary social and economic development." The major effect of this approach was to require an explicit justification for lowered water quality, and this did tend to retard such changes.

Water-quality programs involved special types of antidegradation action. One was the Clean Lakes Program, adopted in 1968, which provided federal funds for lake improvement. This led to an EPA classification system that identified three levels of eutrophication and categorized lakes in terms of one level or another. Some lakes were identified as cleaner and others were judged as deviations from those of higher quality. A more extensive system involved water quality in the Great Lakes. Each was rated in terms of nine parameters, and a background value was determined for each in order to measure the degree of deviation from natural conditions that had occurred or might occur. Approaches such as these tended to identify bench marks of high quality and build into thinking the assumption that degradation should not be permitted.

Several problems highlighted the incremental degradation of water quality in the countryside. I have already mentioned acid precipitation. The issue emphasized incremental change, which in the earlier stages of acidification was difficult to detect and often had proceeded so far that it was all but impossible to reverse. The most significant observation was the changing level of alkalinity. If the water in a lake or stream was sufficiently alkaline, increasing levels of acid would be neutralized and rendered relatively harmless. One could identify the danger point or threshold of alkalinity and classify waters as endangered. If one did not reverse slow, persistent change early, one might well create an irreversible balance between acidity and alkalinity.

Another persistent change in rural water quality was the buildup of toxic metals and synthetic organic chemicals in groundwater. Sewage disposal through septic tanks provided the initial concern for groundwater degradation. The underground accumulation and flow of metals and synthetic organics gave it sharper focus. Although some monitoring of surface water had taken place over the years, to describe changes in quality, there had been far less assessment of groundwater. Toxic pollutants often were discovered almost by accident rather than by systematic measurement. Environmentalists began to argue that a nondegradation policy should be adopted for groundwater. But when the EPA suggested such a strategy as part of a proposed groundwater policy, it met resistance much like that in the case of air and surface water nondegradation measures.[57]

Land and Land Use

These environmental issues inevitably involved the use of land. I have already described the land-use effects of large-scale development. But smaller changes seemed to be far more in harmony with the smaller scale of personal and family endeavor and hence to fit into, rather than to contrast sharply with, community institutions. Minor changes in the size and number of buildings or the layout of roads could well be accepted as consistent with daily life instead of as a threat to it. Over the years, therefore, major changes in land use and its consequences could take place without opposition if they occurred incrementally.[58]

Incremental development was closely associated with population growth and the facilities needed to accommodate it. Between 1970 and 1980 the most rapid population changes took place in "areas of recreational and scenic amenities." The fastest growing counties were ones with "seashores, inlets, lakes, rivers, mountainsides, ski resorts, hunting preserves and other such places . . . of outdoor recreation and natural scenery." These newcomers were permanent residents, not just seasonal vacationers, and hence produced incremental development beyond the level of temporary visits. Once the 1980 census had identified these changes it was also found that they had begun even in the 1950s.

Rising population levels led to new uses of land for private and public services: grocery stores and gasoline stations; retail shops; utility lines for telephone, electrical, and heating services; fire and police protection; schools, churches, and town halls; and landfills. There were demands that roads be upgraded to carry cars at higher speeds and that bridges be widened. One kind or level of development led to another in cumulative and interactive fashion.

The tourist industry was one of the more significant aspects of these changes. Tourism was looked on by leaders in the countryside as the main way in which their jobs and incomes, as well as the value of their property, could be readily increased. After the 1950s states established tourist agencies to develop public-relations campaigns to boost the number of visitors. Departments of commerce worked with countryside leaders to provide the overnight accommodations, restaurants, and commercial facilities that would swell income there. The theme of these ventures was invariably "more," to increase the number of visitors and opportunities for them to spend their vacation money in the region.

Within the countryside these tendencies resulted in divergent attitudes. Many had been attracted there because of the high level of environmental quality, and they sought to emphasize and retain those values as community and regional assets. But others were more interested in the profitable activities that might result from the exploitation of natural surroundings and hence were ardent supporters of development. The two clashed continually. Those who preferred a more natural environment were constantly in search of "less commercialized" tourist areas. Others sought to increase commercial activity, though within the context of tourism, and this heightened incremental development with its subsequent environmental degradation.

Developmental pressures in the countryside seemed relentless, and environmentalists could fight only a rearguard defensive action. Although they could counteract large-scale development with some degree of success and identify and protect tracts of land that were of high environmental quality, it was far more difficult to cope with these smaller changes that came from daily decisions by individuals and institutions. Could the public exercise control over the environmental quality it had come to prize?

Land-Use Planning

These confrontations between environmentalists and developmentalists in the countryside led many to look to land-use planning as a means to resolve conflicts with less controversy. To developers it appeared that special action had to be taken to guarantee sites for future industry, mining, and energy facilities. The drive for environmental quality seemed to preclude many projects. To environmentalists, on the other hand, the major fact of life was the constant threat of development to the environmental quality of the community. Action was required to check the persistent tendencies of large-scale development to expand. Through planning, each side thought its objectives would be given greater consideration. Those not directly involved saw planning as a means of reducing the intensity of the debates.[59]

Planning might enable one to identify the more important uses and to assign particular uses to particular lands. If land was more important for agricultural production, it could be reserved for that use. Areas more valuable as open space in settled communities could be so specified. Sites particularly appropriate for industry could be reserved for that purpose. And on and on. Every land-use issue seemed to imply special allocation for special uses; it was tempting to believe that planning could fit land potential and land use together more precisely and, at the same time, cause less controversy.

Initial action came at the state level in the late 1960s and early 1970s. Both environmentalists and state officials in Vermont became concerned about the effects of uncontrolled residential development on the upper slopes of the Green Mountains, which were prized as one of the state's most valuable natural assets. Through action to determine where and how much development should take place, the state hoped to establish some protection. Hawaii, which experienced intense population pressure and competition for use of land, formulated a far more comprehensive program that served as a model for those who advocated land-use planning on a larger scale. In Oregon the state Land Use Development Commission was given the task of requiring counties to take up detailed land-use planning under statewide guidelines.

In the early 1970s an unsuccessful drive was undertaken to formulate a federal program to encourage other states to take similar action. The long debate over this proposal revealed the variety of land-use objectives in dispute and the difficulty of persuading the contending parties to support a procedure – planning – in which one side was bound to lose. Although environmentalists initially supported land-use planning, they came to view it as a device by which large-scale industry could use federal authority to restrain environmental action that at times had greater clout at lower levels.

Land-use planning was often another version of zoning. Over the years there had been little thought of extending this practice from the city to the countryside. Often in the countryside zoning was a "dirty word" that was bitterly resisted by property owners. But when the community objected to proposed land uses zoning became more popular as a defensive measure. Agricultural and residential zoning could protect communities from industrial and commercial development.

Facing continual difficulties in securing community support for their projects, advocates of large-scale development sought to establish state authority to guarantee siting. When that could not be secured, they sought to enhance federal authority to override that of the state, and this was a major source of their support for the proposed federal land-use law debated in the early 1970s. But environmentalists' misgivings about the proposal increased for that very reason. They turned to state and specialized federal planning opportunities as more advantageous to their objectives.

Coastal-Zone Management

In 1972 Congress established a special planning program for the coastal zone under the Coastal Zone Management Act. Here were opportunities for land-use planning to be worked out before it was applied more generally to the countryside. Coastal environmental protection had considerable public support and was well advanced in California and states along the North Atlantic coast.[60]

The act had a distinctive environmental history. Initial interest in the coastal zone arose out of public concern for wetlands protection; it involved a proposal drawn up by Congressman John Dingell of Michigan in 1967 to establish a national estuarine system, much akin to the national seashores and lakeshores, to be subject to protective management by the National Park Service. Opposition from those who sought to keep the coastal wetlands open to development blocked this. But it was sidetracked more permanently by a growing interest in the potential development of coastal resources. In 1968 President Johnson appointed the Stratton Commission to formulate ideas for the management of coastal-zone resources. Composed overwhelmingly of scientists and engineers concerned with development, it included no member with a primary commitment to environmental objectives. The commission's report strongly emphasized the intensive application of science and technology to development of coastal land and water resources and displayed only minor interest in aesthetic, appreciative, or natural values.[61]

While the 1972 act had a significant overlay of environmental language, befitting the tenor of the times, it also contained a major element conducive to intensive coastal development. The resulting program, which provided federal funds to the states for coastal-zone planning, displayed this blend of forces, as over the course of the 1970s it slowly shifted toward development. Only in a few states such as California did environmental objectives remain strong. Federal involvement in coastal-zone matters, moreover, often strengthened the position of developmental advocates. The Department of Energy, for example, continually sought to blunt the role of the states in coastal planning, which might restrict the construction of large-scale energy facilities.

Each state had to specify the coastal-zone boundary within which it would exercise jurisdiction, establish a system by which it could make specific decisions about land use within that area, and identify geographical areas of particular concern that would include those of value for both environmental and facility-siting purposes. Three issues became central: identification of areas of high environmental quality for protection; controls over general patterns of development; and siting of large-scale facilities.[62]

The first of these revolved around the processes of identifying the environmental component of "geographical areas of particular concern." To environmentalists this provided an opportunity to designate areas of high environmental quality; in fact, it was the key element of the program. But developers sought to restrict it; even to identify such areas would give environmental objectives too much leverage. By 1980 when the 1972 act was up for renewal, environmentalists sought to strengthen the federal mandate that states determine areas of special environmental concern. But they obtained no more than a permissive authorization without required action.[63]

Somewhat more successful from an environmental point of view was the way in which controls were established over developmental activities. In states with the most advanced programs major proposals for development had to be approved by a siting agency. Appeals were heard by quasi-judicial boards. Often there were pressures to postpone granting a permit until planning was completed, but environmentalists were able to forestall this in a number of states. Siting agencies analyzed the impact of proposals with a sensitivity to their environmental effects and in some cases in terms of the cumulative impact of successive actions.

These strategies reduced markedly the pace of destruction of coastal wetlands. The mere existence of the program prompted many developers to modify plans before submitting them; others were changed through negotiations between the agencies and the permittee prior to approval. The most striking success involved San Francisco Bay, where the Bay Area Development Commission, established in 1965, sharply reversed the historic tendency to fill the bay for development. In the three decades before it was established the total area filled each decade had risen from 500 to 1,000 to 2,000 acres; the first year after its authority was established this dropped to 75 acres and the next to 25.

Siting of large-scale facilities was the third type of action under the coastal-zone management program. Energy companies were adamant in insisting on the need to construct oil-transfer stations, refineries, petrochemical complexes, and liquefied natural gas terminals on the coast. Because of environmental opposition a number of projects had been abandoned in the 1960s, and state laws had been enacted to set the conditions for siting and to require state approval of specific projects.[64]

In response, the energy companies sought to enhance federal authority in the belief that because of the nation's energy needs they would receive a more sympathetic ear in that quarter. But the states were unwilling to accept that authority. In the Coastal Zone Management Act they had secured a "consistency clause," which provided that decisions on the siting of large-scale facilities had to be consistent with state plans. But what was consistency? The intense debate over that question continued to involve issues of relative state and federal authority, court battles, and congressional action.[65]

The coastal zone was a particular setting for the larger struggles under way over the future of the countryside. Here were opportunities to establish protection for areas of high environmental quality; here also were opportunities for future intensive development. Coastal-zone management sought to channel these contending influences into a more disciplined context, but in doing so did not diminish their force markedly. It also demonstrated the almost insuperable odds environmentalists faced. The growth of a developmental spirit on the coast was reflected in the way public and private agencies were often able to establish the ideology of "multiple use" as the context within which coastal-zone matters were discussed. This had long been an important ideology used by those who wished to combat environmental efforts focused on the nation's forests. Now on the coasts it came to play a similar role.[66]

6 The Toxic Environment

In the preceding chapters I analyzed environmental issues in three different settings: the city, the wildlands, and the countryside. Another perspective of much greater scope exercised an equally formative influence in environmental affairs – an experience of a world of radiation and chemicals that pervaded almost every facet of human life. It reflected a concern about human health rather than about amenities and the permanence of natural ecosystems. This toxic "sea around us" became a preoccupation of many Americans. The air, water, and land were media through which threats affected a wide range of human experience.

This world was largely shaped by new developments in science and technology. Since the mid-nineteenth century, modern industry had brought together many of the earth's minerals such as lead, cadmium, asbestos, and beryllium from widely dispersed natural sources, concentrating them into both usable products and harmful by-products and wastes. Atomic fission and the use of X rays exposed humans to radiation considerably higher than background levels. Modern science generated new chemicals, the synthetic organics, not before known in nature. They were created precisely because they differed markedly from natural products, could withstand biological decay, and were more resilient.

171

The new chemical environment appeared to be both beneficial and harmful. The benefits were conveyed by innumerable products useful in daily life; the potential harm was made apparent by incidents in which human health and the functioning of biological life were impaired. Some of these involved acute effects in which a dramatic chemical release caused immediate damage. More significant were the subtle results that worked more slowly and gave rise to long-term human health problems such as cancer, neurological disorders, reproductive defects, lowered resistance to bacterial infections, genetic change, and premature aging.[1]

The Toxic Experience

A distinctive element of the emerging awareness of toxicity was the realization that radiation and many synthetic chemicals persisted in the environment because they were not readily biodegradable. The decay of radioactive elements was often slow, lasting tens of thousands of years. Synthetic chemicals were created precisely because they resisted biological deterioration. They would be in the environment far beyond the lifetimes of individuals and coming generations. Being ever present, their potential harm was also ever present. They thus differed markedly from bacterial infections, which could be cured if properly treated.[2]

These toxic agents were also ubiquitous. They were to be found in the air, water, and land. They might be released at one place and affect human and other biological life at another. Lead from distant urban centers was found to have accumulated in the ice of Greenland and the Antarctic. Radioactive iodine from the atomic bomb explosions at Hiroshima and Nagasaki was found in lichens in Alaska and Lapland. Polybrominated biphenyls manufactured in only one plant in St. Louis, Michigan, were found in ever wider circles beyond that state in animals, produce, and breast milk. Toxic threats seemed to be as widely dispersed as the environment itself.[3]

To this evidence was added in the 1960s a knowledge of bioaccumulation, the concentration of radiation and chemicals in living organisms. Accumulation became magnification as one animal absorbed into its tissue increasing amounts of chemicals from the foods it ate. The concentration in animals higher in the food chain was many times greater than in those lower down. Such processes became commonly recognized. The very term "bioaccumulation" conveyed a sense of the way in which a danger not only would not go away but could increase with time.[4]

Finally, these toxic threats were surrounded by mystery; because their effects were not easily observable, laypersons could not know their extent. And neither could those in positions of authority. For their capabilities for monitoring and measuring were so limited that only a small portion of the larger toxic environment was known to them. Toxic perception often included the notion of a chemical "time bomb," that a sequence of events begun at one time could remain undetected only to work their effects later. One could suddenly discover cancer caused by much earlier exposures, now coming to light when preventive action would be pointless. Or a lake that appeared unchanged over the years could be found to be losing its buffering capacity and on the verge of creating virtually irreversible effects.[5]

These observations tended to bring the various elements of the human environment together in a single set of relationships. Many harmful chemicals migrated through air, water, and land, joining localities so that one could not remain aloof from what happened elsewhere. These were widely shared media, which extended far beyond a given place or a striking landform. Just as the problem of acid rain linked pollution in many places with its origin in distant areas, so the world of toxic transmission extended that sense of a common fate and interest to a wide range of people and places.[6]

The ubiquity of the toxic environment also generated the perception that modern institutions were unable to bring these threats under control. This was illustrated by the Three Mile Island incident in the spring of 1979. The central political context was twofold: the profound sense of the need to control a diffuse problem, on the one hand, and the equally profound sense of the limited capabilities for control by the prevailing private and public institutions, on the other. In response, the public sought to work out control strategies, to determine and set acceptable exposure limits, and to devise methods of containment when the social institutions could not.[7]

The Beginnings of Concern with Toxicity

The initial public concern about the toxic environment was shaped by knowledge about radioactive fallout from atomic testing after World War II. In 1958 a group of scientists at Washington University in St. Louis, of whom Professor Barry Commoner, a biologist, was the most widely known, formed a committee to publicize information about fallout from atomic testing in Nevada. The Greater St. Louis Committee for Nuclear Information soon published a small magazine, *Nuclear Information,* which in 1964 became *Science and the Citizen,* and which emphasized the need to relay to the general public information about testing that was not being disseminated by the Atomic Energy Commission. The committee argued that the public needed more nearly complete information about fallout so as to make sound decisions.[8]

An international agreement in 1963 to restrict aboveground testing reduced public interest in fallout and atomic radiation; the St. Louis Committee likewise reduced its coverage of the problem. But even before this it had become interested in pesticides. The newer pesticides were synthetic chemicals, chlorinated hydrocarbons, which were long-lived. Previous pesticides such as arsenic and mercury had been acutely toxic to the applicator, while newer organics were far less so. The latter were safer in their immediate effect on the user, but they had potential long-term effects. They did not degrade in soil and water and could be carried long distances (they were even detected in the Antarctic); they were absorbed by plants and were taken up by fish and birds and spread through the food chain.[9]

Early governmental concern with pesticides had been confined to their efficiency, that is, whether they killed pests as effectively as manufacturers claimed. Not until the 1960s did concern extend to their effects on people and on the environment. That interest originated with biologists who began to suspect that the new pesticides, especially DDT, were extremely harmful to wildlife. In 1957 scientists persuaded Congress to provide funds for research, which was then conducted at the Fish and Wildlife Service research station at Patuxent, Maryland. In 1962 the situation received wide public attention when Rachel Carson, a researcher at Patuxent, published *Silent Spring,* which detailed the dangers posed by pesticides to wildlife. They were a special threat to birds because they led to thinner shells so that eggs broke before hatching.[10]

Public concern rose rapidly during the 1960s as residents of Long Island and then of Michigan and Wisconsin sought to restrict the use of DDT. Encouraged by the Audubon Society, scientists and naturalists concerned with birds pushed the issue forward. In 1967 they organized the Environmental Defense Fund to pursue litigation on wider fronts, and in 1969 that organization petitioned the Department of Agriculture to restrict sharply the use of DDT.[11]

The public debate over pesticides was accompanied by a parallel scientific debate. The petition to the Department of Agriculture led to a request from the department to the National Academy of Sciences to investigate the effects of pesticides. This resulted in public disagreement among scientists about the interpretation of the scientific evidence and led to yet another report, this time sponsored by the Department of Health, Education, and Welfare (HEW). This study was carried out by a more diverse group of scientists and was far more skeptical about the safety of pesticides.[12]

Those who tried to raise questions about the wisdom of the use of pesticides felt they were severely hindered by the predominant influence in such matters of the Department of Agriculture, the agriculture committees in the House and Senate, and scientists who were attached to the agricultural colleges and universities. To advance their point of view, environmentalists sought other channels of influence. They turned to scientists more concerned with the effects of chemicals on human health, tried to shift regulatory policy out of agriculture departments and into agencies concerned with environmental effects, and urged that new congressional committees be established that would take more seriously the potential adverse effects. In 1970 federal pesticide regulation was transferred to the newly formed Environmental Protection Agency (EPA).[13]

The U.S. Food and Drug Administration (FDA) had also been concerned about pesticides as a food contaminant. In 1957 Congress had passed the Delaney Amendment, which prohibited the use in food of any substance that had been demonstrated to cause cancer in laboratory animals. Chemists long had argued that substances became harmful only above a certain minimal or threshold level. The Delaney Amendment now said that there was no safe exposure to carcinogens and that data from animal experiments could be used for regulatory action; hence any substance that in any manner caused cancer in experimental animals was prohibited.[14]

The major focus of FDA action was to set standards for the level of pesticides permitted in food. In 1959, for example, the agency found that cranberries grown in New Jersey had residues of aminotriazole, a weed killer applied in the field, higher than allowed. The berries were recalled and destroyed. This was one of the first public episodes involving the regulation of pesticides. It called forth angry complaints from growers who referred to the incident then and thereafter as the "cranberry scare" and used it as an example of what later both agriculture and industry constantly referred to as overregulation. It sharpened issues such as what levels of residue were harmful and actionable, how such levels should be determined, and how claims for compensation were to be handled.

Toxic chemicals could also reach food through the broader environment. Fish became a special bellwether of toxic chemicals in the aquatic environment because, through bioaccumulation and biomagnification, they became contaminated as food. Early in the 1950s the U.S. Public Health Service began to keep statistics on the incidence of fish kills and the number of fish involved. DDT and, later, polychlorinated biphenyls (PCBs) were carefully charted to indicate their presence in water and in fish eaten as human food. In 1964 a massive fish kill in the lower Mississippi River was traced to the discharge of the pesticide endrin from a Velsicol Chemical Company plant at Memphis, Tennessee. The episode led to the first major attempt, though unsuccessful, to establish a system of chemical control for pesticides.

In years past, the effect of chemicals on fish had been assessed in terms of readily observable effects such as death or physical abnormalities. But as concern grew for the impact of pesticides on wildlife, especially animals used directly for food, chemical concentrations in fish began to be more closely monitored. When high levels of DDT were found in Lake Michigan trout, officials warned against eating too many fish caught there, and pregnant women were advised to avoid them entirely. Such monitoring and warnings were one of the major ways in which the pervasiveness of toxic chemicals came to be known by the population at large. Commercial and sport fishermen complained against warnings not to eat contaminated fish. They supported cleanup efforts, but they also pressured state and federal agencies to forgo such warnings in the future.

By the early 1970s the American people had experienced the toxic environment in a variety of ways – radiation from nuclear-testing fallout, pesticides in wildlife, chemicals in food, and fish kills. These were only the beginnings of confrontations with toxic chemicals that later were to emerge with greater force. New ways in which toxic chemicals could become dangerous, such as in the workplace or in industrial wastes, came into prominence. Running through these episodes and reinforced by them was the perception of a wider toxic environment surrounding daily life that was both dangerous and difficult to bring under control. Events in the 1960s had begun to shape that perspective; in the 1970s it was to become a major political influence.

Nuclear Radiation

In the latter part of the 1960s the outputs of proposed nuclear plants leapt from several hundred to almost a thousand megawatts. This greatly increased their environmental impact and, in turn, generated a drive to restrict the development of nuclear power.[15]

The initial response to this scale-up of nuclear energy stressed not radiation, accidents, or waste, which later became central issues, but thermal pollution. The larger plants produced far more waste heat, which was discharged to the environment, than did the smaller ones. Fishermen and aquatic biologists were especially concerned about the cumulative effect of waste heat on particular lakes, streams, or bays. In 1969 opposition arose to proposals by the Atomic Safety and Licensing Board to approve several new plants. In each case thermal pollution was the central environmental issue, and the major citizen complaint was the unwillingness of the board to consider the adverse effect of waste heat on aquatic life in its licensing decision.[16]

The first radiation problem to emerge in these debates was radionuclides in water. The issue arose when states were required by the 1965 Water Quality Act to establish water-quality standards. The Atomic Energy Commission (AEC) had set effluent limitations for proposed plants as they pertained to radionuclides. But the states wanted lower standards. The technology was available to control releases at much lower levels than the AEC required, and in fact the Westinghouse Corporation announced that it could guarantee zero emissions. The AEC resisted efforts to lower allowable levels, claiming that it alone, not the states, had the authority to establish such standards.

In the mid-1960s Dr. John Gofman and Dr. Arthur Tamplin of the Lawrence Livermore Laboratory at Berkeley, California, were asked by the AEC to review the potential health effects of the radiation standards then in force. That standard limited the average public exposure to 170 millirems per year from human sources, which was double the amount that could be expected over a thirty-year period from natural radiation sources. Reviewing recent studies on the effects of radiation, Gofman and Tamplin first argued that the 170-millirem standard would produce 16,000 excess deaths; they later revised that estimate to 32,000 and then to 74,000.[17]

Gofman and Tamplin advocated that the allowable exposure be reduced to one-tenth the existing standard, but atomic energy advocates, including industry leaders, atomic physicists, and the AEC, rejected their arguments. A series of intense debates ensued in the professional and popular media. Gofman and Tamplin presented their arguments before a Senate committee chaired by Senator Edmund Muskie. Although the AEC refused to accept them as credible scientists, an increasing number took them seriously. Robert Finch, secretary of HEW in the Nixon administration, urged that the National Academy of Sciences reevaluate the health effects of the 170-millirem exposure limit. Even before that report was completed responsibility for setting allowable exposure levels was transferred from the AEC to the newly formed EPA, which in subsequent years lowered it to 25 millirems per year.

This debate served as the opening wedge in a growing series of critiques of nuclear energy on the ground that it produced too much radiation from a variety of sources: normal power-plant emissions, extraordinary releases from nuclear incidents, exposures in uranium mines and generating and reprocessing plants, releases from waste disposal or from plants no longer in operation. As investigators probed into nuclear energy, more ways in which it might affect people, both now and in the future, came to light.[18]

In the early 1970s concern for potential nuclear accidents began to be expressed by the public and by nuclear physicists and engineers, a few of whom questioned the safety of nuclear reactors. They argued that the AEC was far too friendly to the industry and gave insufficient attention to public safety. In 1971 a group of nuclear scientists and engineers at the Massachusetts Institute of Technology formed the Union of Concerned Scientists to take up the issue of nuclear safety. Some engineers who had been employed in nuclear facilities, both private and public, resigned their posts to join citizen groups to help press these concerns; three of these engineers were from the General Electric Corporation and two from the AEC. Their technical expertise enabled the citizen antinuclear movement to participate effectively in the varied administrative proceedings pertaining to the safety of nuclear energy.[19]

From these groups came technical estimates of the likelihood of a nuclear accident, with its accompanying meltdown and release of radioactive particles, that differed markedly from those published by the AEC. In response to these concerns the AEC in 1975 required that each new plant – existing ones were exempt – have an emergency core-cooling system (ECCS) to help keep nuclear reactors under control. Even after that, however, technical experts in the antinuclear movement were able to identify many plant safety problems and warned about possible dangers. Almost at the time that the decision to require the emergency cooling systems had quieted concern, the nuclear accident at Three Mile Island in 1979 reopened the issue.[20]

Although nuclear advocates yielded somewhat to critics on issues of nuclear safety, they were far less willing to compromise on low-level radiation from normal plant operations. They did not take seriously those who argued that neither the amount of these releases nor their cumulative health effects were accurately known. From time to time several scientists maintained that there were higher rates of infant deaths and deformities in areas surrounding or downwind of nuclear plants. Such arguments usually became entangled in the problem of scarce reliable data. But the AEC and its successor, the Nuclear Regulatory Commission (NRC), were convinced that the matter was of such limited consequence that more effective monitoring was not needed. Antinuclear critics, in turn, doubted almost every statement by nuclear authorities about releases and their health effects.[21]

Other stages of the nuclear fuel cycle were emphasized as well. One was the "back end" of uranium mining – ore processing and tailings – which took place primarily in the West. They first became public issues as a result of studies that revealed the high rate of lung cancer among uranium miners. Mine unions and HEW argued that allowable exposure levels for miners should be reduced. Mining companies, in turn, replied that the health information was faulty and that added protection would be too expensive.[22]

Western mining communities were also threatened by the tailings or waste left after mining and deposited near the mines. Firms sometimes constructed ponds by using the mine tailings as fill for retention dams. Such a dam broke in New Mexico in October 1979 and discharged millions of gallons of water into the Rio Puerco, resulting in far greater human exposure to radiation than had occurred even at Three Mile Island. In Grand Junction, Colorado, tailings were used as landfill in constructing homes that were later found to contain high levels of radioactivity. In other communities tailings were left exposed to wind and rain; subsequent erosion leaked radioactive materials into groundwater used for domestic supplies.

By the end of the 1970s concern over uranium mining had reached far beyond the West. When mining firms began to explore for uranium in Vermont, all but two of the thirty-nine towns that held referenda on the issue in 1980 voted to ban it; the legislature, in response, required that it approve any future uranium mining. One month later a South Dakota county voted to ban uranium mining there. And in 1981 the New Jersey state legislature enacted a seven-year moratorium in that state.

Until the last half of the 1970s little thought had been given by either industry or the AEC to the disposal of radioactive waste. When nuclear fission had been confined primarily to medical and military uses, waste disposal had been limited to a few sites. The nuclear-power industry stored its own wastes at reactor sites; but as the amount of waste grew, this storage appeared insufficient. Pressures for permanent disposal of nuclear wastes grew and with them the debate over the feasibility of various proposals.[23]

The problem was quite simple. These materials would remain harmful for thousands of years. How could they be disposed of so as to isolate their effects for that length of time? Nuclear enthusiasts tried to assure the public that there was no serious problem in storage; it could be accomplished readily. But at stage after stage in the debate a solution that had seemed feasible at one time – for example, ocean dumping or deep-well injection – was eventually considered insecure. Originally it was thought that highly radioactive wastes could be disposed of in liquid form in concrete-lined pits deep in the earth, but this idea soon gave way to the more expensive alternative of solidifying them and burying them in salt deposits also deep below the surface. The first such site, selected below Lyons, Kansas, was found to be vulnerable to intrusion from ground water.

The long-term consequences of nuclear energy seemed to press in on Americans in new and different ways as the decade wore on. There was, for example, the problem of decommissioning. How would plants be made safe to communities after their useful life of thirty to forty years was over? Would they merely be protected as mausoleums or would they be torn down and decontaminated? The possibility that the disabled reactor at Three Mile Island might be cheaper to decommission than to refurbish accentuated the question of what would be done with such plants. Who would pay to make sites permanently safe? Ultimately, of course, consumers would pay, and hence by the end of the 1970s this issue became more salient to state public-utility commissions as they were prompted to include such costs in their rate proceedings.

In the background of all these issues was the debate over the subsidy that had been granted to the nuclear industry by limiting its liability in cases of nuclear accidents. Industry had demanded this before it would take up nuclear power. The Price-Anderson Act of 1957 limited total liability to $560 million per accident, of which the federal government, as of 1975, would provide $435 million and private insurers $125 million. Nuclear critics sought to repeal the act and to require the industry to assume full liability. The costs of the Three Mile Island accident in 1979 highlighted this problem; subsequent legal action made clear the size of the liability claims an accident might entail and the relatively small degree to which insurance would cover them.

As increasing numbers of citizens recognized the threats nuclear power posed, they developed local organizations to combat its spread. By the mid-1970s, for example, the Clamshell Alliance in New England, the Abalone Alliance in California, and the Headwaters Alliance in western Montana had formed to take up issues such as the safety of particular plants and seek local and state referenda on various steps of the nuclear fuel cycle. Local groups became linked through the *Critical Mass Journal* published by Ralph Nader's Critical Mass Project in Washington, D.C., and the Nuclear Information and Research Service. The accident at Three Mile Island galvanized these groups even further and gave people hope that there would be a new turn in national nuclear policy.[24]

But such was not to be the case. In the year after Three Mile Island the nuclear industry and its allies in the federal government not only deflected every major effort to restrict it, but even recovered initiative among the nation's institutional leadership. While the American people, as charted in several years of public-opinion polling, had become increasingly antinuclear and were opposed to siting plants near their own communities, industry and government leaders took up the nuclear commitment after Three Mile Island as strongly as before. The Carter administration reaffirmed its support of nuclear energy, refused to modify significantly the role and authority of the Nuclear Regulatory Commission, and considered it a major frontline source of future energy supply instead of the last resort, as Carter had emphasized in 1977.[25]

The Chemical Workplace

Chemical hazards in the workplace were an equally significant aspect of the growing concern about toxicity. Safety and health authorities had long worked to prevent accidents in the workplace, but modern manufacturing substituted chemical hazards for mechanical ones. It took some time for both trade unions and workers to recognize the dangers fully. But gradually they did. And liability suits often brought to light information about such problems. All this led to passage of the Occupational Health and Safety Act of 1970, which created the Occupational Safety and Health Administration (OSHA) to protect workers.[26]

To many industrial workers much of the new concern involved the right to know, that is, the right to have information about the environmental hazards to which they were exposed and the resulting effects on health. One might be able to understand a mechanical hazard because it could be seen and comprehended directly, but airborne chemicals and their effects were a different matter. The results of physical examinations by company doctors were not made known to those affected on the grounds that it was company information and therefore privileged. Employers posted some information about chemicals that workers used, but it was insufficient to enable employees to take action on their own. Medical examinations, geared to detecting traditional medical problems, did not seem capable of providing early warning signals about newer chemical effects. Hence workers insisted on more extensive examinations and the right to choose their own examining physicians.

To deal with exposures in the workplace workers had two types of political leverage. One was the unions themselves, through which they could bargain collectively for both information and action. In 1973 the Oil, Chemical, and Atomic Workers Union (OCAW) sought from refinery employers several new health provisions in its collective bargaining contract: The firm should share with workers information about health hazards to which they were exposed and medical information the company had gathered about them; it should finance more intensive medical tests to detect subclinical health problems. Most employers accepted these terms but the Shell Oil Company did not. In a strike in which the union secured extensive support from environmentalists and health professionals, Shell finally came to terms.[27]

Even greater leverage came from liability suits brought by workers against employers for health problems due to exposures at work. The most dramatic of these involved asbestos workers. Once asbestosis, a treatable disease caused by asbestos, had been brought under control, scientific data made clear that asbestos caused cancer as well. Workers had firm grounds for liability suits, which they often won. The proceedings brought to light records from the asbestos companies that indicated that they had known about the carcinogenic effects of asbestos for many years but had tried to prevent the information from reaching either the public or workers. Liability awards from courts often persuaded firms to clean up the workplace more rapidly and effectively than did public regulation.[28]

The new occupational-health program inaugurated in 1970 reflected the shift from accidents and infectious disease to chemically induced health problems. But it took some time for health professionals to emphasize the change. Those who had developed their views about occupational health earlier, when more acute and short-term infectious diseases were emphasized, were often slow to turn their interest to long-term, low-level chronic problems. Industry was extremely leery of the extensive implications of the new approach. In the face of political influence from industry it took several years for OSHA to carve out an effective program of action.[29]

The program was bolstered by the general accumulation of scientific data. The Occupational Health and Safety Act of 1970 had also established the National Institute of Occupational Safety and Health (NIOSH) in the National Institutes of Health to develop criteria documents similar to those created in the community air-quality program. These assessed scientific information and recommended acceptable levels of exposure. Because NIOSH was not part of the regulatory agency but was located within a scientific body, it was freer to undertake studies to identify hazardous pollutants. NIOSH served as a vehicle to bring scientific data to bear on public policy more quickly and more effectively than had the EPA. On the basis of NIOSH documents, OSHA then was to set standards and require employers to implement them. But whereas NIOSH moved ahead with a number of criteria documents, OSHA was far slower in acting.

The initial administrator of OSHA, George Guenther, appointed by President Richard Nixon, followed the older school of occupational health. His most controversial step was the review of the asbestos standard. New information seemed to call for a reduction in exposure from the old standard of 5 fibers per cubic centimeter, but Guenther kept it at the older level. Succeeding OSHA administrations created a new standard of 2 fibers and, at the urging of NIOSH, considered reducing it still further. Guenther's successor, Morton Corn, an occupational-health engineer, brought more vigorous direction to the agency but also some reluctance to move rapidly in the direction indicated by emerging scientific evidence. President Carter's appointee, Eula Bingham of the University of Cincinnati Medical School, was a public-health professional who pursued a vigorous application of the law during her tenure between 1977 and 1981.[30]

In a series of actions pertaining to the control of occupational exposures from cotton dust, lead, benzene, and other substances, the major points of contrast between occupational-health advocates and industry became clearly defined. There were arguments over the scientific evidence and the criteria documents: Did a particular chemical substance present a health hazard, and were the methods used in making the determination sound? There were arguments over techniques of control: Were workers to be required to wear protective clothing or employers to redesign equipment to reduce exposures? In almost every case employers contested both the grounds for action and the methods of control. Regulation, they argued, would be economically disastrous. They fought proposal after proposal in both administrative and legal arenas.

The most comprehensive OSHA action involved an effort to formulate a generic cancer policy that would establish an accepted process for determining the carcinogenicity of exposures. In each proceeding involving a carcinogen, the agency had gone over similar ground to confirm the legitimacy of its methods for determining health effects. Hence it decided to promulgate a regulation that would set up a more generally applicable method. The resulting controversy with industry joined the issues firmly.

Was animal data a legitimate basis for predicting the effects of human exposures to chemicals? Should one assume that there was no threshold below which a carcinogen was safe? Were benign tumors sufficiently prone to become malignant that they should be counted in assessing the results of animal experiments?[31]

Industry answered all three of these questions with an emphatic no. In 1978 chemical and related industries organized the American Industrial Health Council (AIHC) to oppose the generic cancer regulation. It was the most powerful agglomeration of corporations and trade associations yet formed in the realm of environmental politics. OSHA adopted the regulation, but the AIHC challenged it in the courts, and the Reagan administration withdrew it. Once energized on this score, the AIHC began to oppose occupational-health initiatives on a variety of fronts.

In the face of growing demands to regulate occupational exposures, industry promoted other options. Workers, it argued, should wear protective devices such as respirators to prevent exposures from affecting them. Or they should be removed from the source of pollution and perform some other job that involved less exposure. Workers exposed to lead should undergo periodic chelation therapy in which their excessive blood lead levels would be reduced by chemically induced excretion; they then could return to their former jobs until lead levels rose once again. The burden of control was placed on the worker rather than on industry.

The debate over occupational health highlighted two issues. One was the use of medical records by scientists in order to carry out epidemiological studies on the relation between exposures and health effects and hence to justify regulation. It was precisely this kind of knowledge that would make possible a firm scientific basis for action. Yet employers considered such information proprietary and argued that they were not legally required to divulge it. When OSHA proposed regulations that would require releasing such data to qualified researchers, employers objected and contended that they were protecting the workers' right to confidentiality. The trade unions rejected this defense because they well understood the critical role of scientific knowledge about occupational exposures in the effort to enhance worker protection.[32]

Even more controversial was the debate over the proportion of all cancers caused by industrial exposures. In 1979 Joseph Califano, secretary of health, education, and welfare, publicized data developed by the National Cancer Institute indicating that up to 35 percent of cancer cases were related to industrial exposures. To this the chemical industry, and especially the American Industrial Health Council, responded that the level was closer to 1 percent, or 5 percent at the most. Many chemicals that had caused problems were now under control, they argued; hence future adverse health effects would be much reduced. But, argued some occupational-health experts, thousands of new chemicals, whose effects were not yet known, were manufactured yearly, and these would cause new exposures and future cases of cancer.[33]

Toward the end of the 1970s the long-term effects of radiation exposure among several types of workers began to link nuclear environmental hazards to the workplace. This emerged partly from studies indicating that workers exposed to radiation at the Hanford, Washington, nuclear facility and the nuclear shipyard at Portsmouth, New Hampshire, had higher than average cancer rates. This scientific data was hotly disputed, for it indicated that there were adverse effects at lower levels of exposure than formerly had been assumed.[34]

Claims were also made of elevated rates of cancer suffered by military personnel exposed during the atomic tests in Nevada in the 1950s, which had only begun to appear as a health problem in the 1970s. Victims brought suits for liability, thereby forcing courts to come to terms with the disputed scientific information. Early in 1980 a number of individuals who had suffered from radiation exposure, many of them occupationally but also as victims of radiation drift from atomic testing, joined to demand both compensation and a reduction in the allowable exposure limits for workers.[35]

The most significant political aspect of the drive to protect workers from occupational hazards was the support by organized labor for the scientific and regulatory program developed by OSHA. Here was a well-organized constituency that had learned to exercise leverage on labor issues over the years and could readily transfer that leverage to the new problems of occupational health. Few environmental organizations had such financial resources or staying power. Environmental groups had not been involved in the legislative battle leading up to the 1970 Occupational Health and Safety Act. But they soon found common ground with labor in a combined strategy to advance both occupational health and community air quality. This political strength provided some protection for programs when they came under attack from the Reagan administration.[36]

Can the Toxic Environment Be Brought under Control?

During the 1970s a series of dramatic episodes sharpened for the American people the experience of their toxic environment. Incidents involving kepone at Hopewell, Virginia; PCBs from the General Electric plant on the upper Hudson River; polybrominated biphenyls dispersed into food in Michigan; contaminated drinking water in New Orleans; hazardous wastes at Love Canal – all creating widely used buzz words.[37]

A general climate of distrust developed toward private and public institutions for being unable to prevent and even to know about conditions that might lead to such events. To public authorities such as the Environmental Protection Agency the task appeared so enormous and resources so limited that only sporadic and cosmetic action could be taken. To the chemical industry the dangers were grossly exaggerated and proposed actions were unwarranted; it sought to minimize efforts to control toxic chemicals. Even many public authorities shared the view of private industry that the problems were far less than many thought; some were prone to belittle citizen concern as involving "housewives' data" or "political pollutants."

Among many of the nation's leaders there seemed to be a growing conviction that the toxic burden would have to be accepted as a normal condition and that science should be used to protect humans only against its worst effects. Yet greater knowledge about the effects of even "normal" exposures rendered this approach unacceptable to the public. Research on the health effects of lead on children, for example, pointed to lowered IQ scores and reading comprehension for those with exposures within the normal range for urban dwellers. Could one expect society to become resigned to lifelong IQ deficiencies in young children? The toxic world was gradually increasing the disparity between what sources of pollution wished to justify and what society would accept.[38]

Preventive Strategy in Pesticide Control

Because of the impossibility of cleaning up a harmful chemical once dispersed in the environment, the most logical course was to shape its manufacture and use in the first place. The first major effort to deal with pesticides came in 1965 in response to the lower Mississippi River fish kill. During investigation of that incident it became apparent that the problem lay in the way in which the Velsicol Company, which was responsible for the discharge, operated its plant near Memphis, Tennessee. Senator Abraham Ribicoff, who conducted the investigation, wanted to restrict discharge of effluent from pesticide plants and provide regulatory officials with the authority to inspect manufacturing processes and require changes. But industry quickly rebuffed this strategy. Attempts to control pesticides would come by restricting allowable uses rather than by controlling production.

But how to determine allowable uses? Early strategies with DDT had led to plans for regulations that emphasized harm to wildlife. But in succeeding action on pesticides the EPA changed its emphasis to effects on human health and especially cancer. To work out its strategy on this score the agency established a set of guidelines, or "principles," on the basis of which it would determine whether a pesticide was carcinogenic. Three items in this set of principles were especially controversial: Positive animal tests indicated that a chemical was probably also carcinogenic in humans; there was no threshold below which a suspected carcinogen was safe; and benign as well as malignant tumors should be counted in experiments on toxic exposures because they could become malignant.[39]

The guidelines caused an intense debate between those who argued that regulatory action should proceed once tendencies in evidence indicated "reasonable anticipation of harm" and those who argued that it should wait until "conclusive proof of harm" had been established. Critics of the new policy argued that it was a case of law triumphing over science. But it was more a matter of a debate between pioneering scientists who were willing to recommend protective action on the basis of emerging tendencies in scientific data and scientists who preferred to confine conclusions to that about which more was known. Those who demanded high levels of proof before action were prone to describe the debate as one of "good science" versus "bad science," but it was more accurately a controversy between those who took emerging evidence seriously and those who required absolute proof as a basis for action.[40]

The critical importance of scientific proof in regulatory action was emphasized by an innovation in the 1978 amendments to the pesticide regulatory law. Who would assume the burden of proof? Until 1978, the agency proposing the regulatory action (the EPA) had done so; if it claimed that a pesticide was harmful, it had to demonstrate that to the court. Now the EPA proposed a new procedure known as rebuttable presumption against registration (RPAR). If the EPA felt there was reasonable doubt in the evidence about safety – not conclusive proof but reasonable doubt – then it could issue a presumption that a pesticide should be withdrawn from registration and invite others to rebut it. The manufacturer was required to prove that the chemical was not harmful.

Pesticide regulation was carried out amid continual controversy between environmentalists and representatives of agricultural industry and science. In 1972 the Federal Insecticide, Fungicide, and Rodenticide Act (FIFRA) was revised for the first time since 1947. Environmentalists were able to secure some changes, in particular a provision that pesticides previously registered solely for their effectiveness in killing pests should now be assessed with regard to their environmental effects. Because it knew that actions unacceptable to the agricultural community would generate intense counterpressures, the agency was extremely cautious in its strategy. Proposed registrations were often perfunctorily approved, and reregistrations went very slowly. The procedure proved to be a mechanism for inaction.

The herbicide issue was especially thorny. This burst onto the political scene in the late 1960s as a result of the use of 2,4,5-T and 2,4-D in a mixture known as Agent Orange to defoliate forests during the Vietnam War. Herbicide chemicals stimulated such rapid cell production that they "grew plants to death." Concern soon arose about the health effects of herbicides used in the United States, which included a special interest in dioxin, a contaminant manufactured along with the herbicides that also was released into the environment. Within the United States herbicides became popular in forest management to suppress the growth of competing hardwood species in commercial southern pine and western Douglas fir. Herbicides also became increasingly popular in "no-till" agriculture in which fields were prepared for planting without disturbing the surface, and weeds were controlled by herbicides rather than by plowing.[41]

Applying herbicides and pesticides from airplanes presented special problems because of the difficulty in controlling spray drift. Often fields, homes and gardens, water supplies, and forest workers were sprayed. Aerial applicators became sloppy and even deliberately sprayed the property of those who complained. During the 1970s many people moved into forested areas, creating homes, gardens, and communities amid woodlands, making it difficult for broad-brush pesticide application to avoid them. An organic garden or farm was especially at risk because the presence of very low levels of pesticide residues in organically grown food made them commercially unacceptable and led to economic loss. On occasion individuals and local doctors noted unusual medical problems such as excessive miscarriages in northwestern Montana and birth defects in Lincoln County, Oregon, which they argued might well have been caused by herbicides.

The initial scientific experiments that indicated that 2,4,5-T produced birth defects in laboratory animals were challenged on the grounds that the problem was not the herbicide but the dioxin contaminant. Levels of dioxin then being measured were in concentrations of parts per million and the issue was the degree to which reduction from 20–30 to 1–5 ppm would resolve the problem. The political debate prompted researchers seeking to protect human health and manufacturers seeking to prove that their herbicide was harmless to measure more precisely at even lower levels. Use of new methods of chemical analysis such as gas chromatography and mass spectrometry, or both in conjunction with each other, enabled scientists to push the analysis to even lower levels. By the end of the 1970s the concentrations at issue had been reduced to parts per trillion, or one-millionth of that of a decade before.

Even at this lower level of detection evidence indicated adverse effects from dioxin; some research suggested that the herbicide itself was harmful. Regulation rested on the interpretation of scientific evidence. Some felt the evidence warranted a presumption that even at levels of 1–5 parts per trillion dioxin was harmful, but others argued that there was no conclusive proof of harm at these lower levels. Amid advances in chemical analysis and data, the EPA at first chose to postpone a decision. But as some scientists made new assessments of the evidence that suggested a reasonable prediction of risk, the EPA undertook action to respond to the original environmental petition by instituting an RPAR process established by the 1978 amendments to FIFRA. This now required the manufacturers to prove that 2,4,5-T was not harmful.[42]

This action not only triggered a vigorous defense of herbicides by the manufacturers but also provoked in 1980 a full-scale assault on the EPA led by the Dow Chemical Company on the grounds that the agency's scientific and technical capabilities were inferior and that it relied on bad scientific evidence for its regulatory proposals. Dow took up the RPAR hearings with such vigor and determination that one could rightly describe it as religious zeal. Although it derived little income from herbicide sales, Dow maintained, it would press the case because "good science" was at issue.[43]

This contest between the EPA and Dow reflected symbolic as well as practical aspects of the politics of toxic chemicals. Dow's vigorous attack on the EPA was viewed by industry as reflecting accurately its profound objections to the entire range of environmental regulatory activity. While frontal assaults were difficult to justify, objections to the agency's scientific and technical competence might well enable the private sector to recoup its public reputation, which had fallen to a low point.[44]

A significant aspect of this political drama was the degree to which laboratory capabilities in technical analysis had come to constitute a major factor in political power. The more issues came to turn on technical data, the more they came to hinge on the most advanced and costly analytical capabilities. By 1980 only five laboratories in the United States could measure dioxin at the level of parts per trillion, one of which was maintained by Dow. It was inevitable that scientific conclusions emanating from such laboratories would carry unusual weight.

By the autumn of 1980 the outcome of the herbicide proceedings was still very much in doubt; they promised to be the longest and most extensive such hearings yet held, with a documentation that overshadowed any previous one. The hearings had already sharply etched the dimensions of the problem: Could society through its public agencies bring toxic chemicals under control in the face of the massive political influence of those who defended their use? The new administration of Ronald Reagan, however, soon erased any doubt about the proceedings themselves. New administrators in the EPA came from those sectors of the business and scientific community who believed that the potential harm of chemicals had been greatly exaggerated. They worked out a settlement with Dow that ended the entire affair.[45]

New Strategies for Chemical Control

As the toxic episodes of the 1970s unfolded, support grew for a more general program that would control all toxic chemicals – not just biocides – and substitute prevention for cleanup after the fact. In 1976 Congress approved such a measure, the Toxic Substances Control Act (TOSCA). The key idea in the debate on this law was premarket testing, the notion that new chemicals should be tested before marketing in order to determine their harm ahead of time. The general public, so the argument went, should no longer be used as "guinea pigs." The introduction of chemicals before their full effects were generally known should stop.

Industry adamantly objected to premarket testing, and as a result the law created only a limited approach known as premarket notification (PMN). A manufacturer would be required to notify the EPA if it wished to market a chemical, and the EPA, in turn, would evaluate the substance's potential harm, approve it for use, require further information to prove lack of harm, or restrict or ban its manufacture. Thus, a prescreening by the EPA and a burden of proof on industry were substituted for a comprehensive premarket testing program.

By 1980 the regulations under which the act would be administered had become clear, issues had become sharp, and industry had taken vigorous steps to challenge it. The most critical issue was that of confidentiality, that is, the degree to which information about chemicals to be manufactured would be made available to the public. Environmental groups argued that the public as well as the EPA should be able to judge the potential harm of a proposed chemical; unless information in the premarket notification were made available, such scrutiny would be impossible. But industry refused to modify its stance. The first firm to submit a PMN to the EPA required that its name, the name of the proposed chemical, and the amount it proposed to manufacture not be divulged. Most subsequent submissions included similar stipulations.

These issues of confidentiality seemed to portend a rough road ahead for chemical control. When effective regulation involved crucial information, control over it became not only an issue of confidentiality and proprietary rights but also an instrument of political power. Industry, for example, often avoided court proceedings because in that forum it was far more difficult to prevent disclosure of critical information. This role of the courts became evident in the first case in which the EPA returned a PMN to a firm in 1980 on the grounds that it had submitted insufficient information as to the proposed substance's safety. Rather than pursue the issue, which might well have led to litigation, the firm withdrew the application.

Polychlorinated biphenyls (PCBs) received particular attention during the 1970s and indicated the political tightrope the EPA walked on these matters. PCBs had been so thoroughly investigated, their occurrence in the environment was so extensive, their health effects were so clearly known, and incidents involving them were so widely publicized that the 1976 act singled them out for attention. To environmentalists, however, the resulting rules were a massive disappointment. While prohibiting further manufacture of PCBs, which the law also did, they would phase out fewer than 1 percent of all PCBs then currently in use. Smaller sources would be exempt. Equipment such as electric transformers and capacitors that contained PCB fluids would not be subject to disposal regulations on the grounds that PCBs in them were sufficiently contained. Environmentalists argued, however, that a long-term source of PCBs was landfills where such equipment was frequently dumped and from which leakage and volatilization created a continuous hazard.[46]

The most striking implication of the PCB experience for successful toxic chemical control came in 1979 in a report on that chemical by the National Academy of Sciences. The study used PCBs as an example of the degree to which the Toxic Substances Control Act would be effective in coping with chemical hazards. Because the EPA's strategies emphasized the analysis and control of only acute environmental effects and not their chronic, long-term cumulative impact, the report concluded that the TOSCA program would have been unable to prevent the introduction of PCBs into the environment. This made clear that even though the 1976 act had aroused considerable opposition, it was markedly deficient in providing the necessary action to bring the toxic environment under control.[47]

Toxins in the Ambient Environment

Chemicals already in the environment also presented a hazard, and these came to be dealt with under the existing air- and water-quality program.

The Clean Air Act of 1970 provided in section 108 that hazardous air pollutants should be subject to special federal control. Three that had been of interest in the 1960s – asbestos, mercury, and beryllium – were placed under regulation early in the 1970s. In the ensuing years a group of air pollutants came to be identified as presenting special hazards to the public, and these were politically as difficult to cope with as were pesticides and toxic substances generally.[48]

Early in the 1970s the EPA added vinyl chloride to its list of regulated hazardous air pollutants. This involved attacks on the chemical as both an occupational and a community air problem by OSHA and the EPA after it was discovered that it produced angiosarcoma, a liver cancer, among some groups of workers.

New manufacturing technologies enabled industry to meet the regulation with little difficulty. But once again the agency seemed able to take action only as a response to a media crisis once the pollutant had already done its damage.[49]

Lead was especially dangerous to humans, causing brain and central nervous system damage in children and kidney disorders in adults leading to continuous blood-dialysis treatment. Communities around copper and lead smelters such as Kellogg, Idaho, and El Paso, Texas, in highly publicized cases were found to be especially subject to adverse effects from lead inhalation and ingestion. Lead levels were high in old housing where children ate lead paint, where levels of automobile exhaust were high, or where lead from water pipes had entered drinking-water supplies. The most pervasive sources of lead were leaded gasoline and automobile exhaust. Along heavily traveled streets and roads lead contamination was found to be much higher in plants, soil, and the ambient air than it was elsewhere.[50]

The EPA drew up a schedule to phase out the use of lead in gasoline, and the petroleum and automobile companies and their scientists, in turn, took up the defense of lead by arguing that the causal relationship between ambient air lead and adverse health effects had not been proved. After a series of legal maneuvers the Supreme Court in 1976 upheld the EPA's strategy, and the agency moved to a gradual phaseout of lead in gasoline. Lead in the ambient air was a larger issue. Environmentalists argued that the EPA should regulate it as another ambient-air-criteria pollutant so that a broad-based attack on this threat to human health could be inaugurated. Yet only after persistent legal initiative from the Natural Resources Defense Council, a citizen litigation group, and court orders over a period of six years, did the EPA develop a criteria assessment and standard for lead.[51]

This action sharpened the classic problem of debate over levels of scientific proof that seemed to run through almost every problem of toxic control. The EPA's initial draft called for a standard of 5 micrograms per cubic meter of air as the maximum allowable limit. Under review by its scientific advisory committee, the document went through two further revisions, leading finally to a standard of 1.5 micrograms. In the 1960s industry had identified 10 micrograms as perfectly safe, but in the face of new scientific knowledge it took a stand on a level of 5. Now additional information indicated that adverse health effects occurred at even lower levels, hence the 1.5 microgram standard.[52]

Another issue concerning lead was the degree of protection that should be provided against chronic effects. Several researchers had discovered that higher lead levels in children were associated not just with readily observable brain damage but also with subtler effects such as lowered IQ scores and limited attention span. The lead industry reacted sharply against the new evidence. Issues such as these reflected the way in which new scientific research was continually pushing back the frontiers about the health effects of pollutants. At each stage sharply different political positions were maintained between those scientists associated with industry who demanded high levels of proof before action and those who argued that reasonable inferences based on new knowledge provided a sound basis for a regulation.[53]

The concept of reasonable anticipation of harm rather than conclusive proof as a standard of judgment in setting air-quality standards resulted in proposals by the Environmental Defense Fund (EDF) in 1978 that the EPA establish a general policy on carcinogenic air pollutants similar to that which OSHA had undertaken. The EDF's proposal called for a three-tiered system whereby immediate regulatory action would be required for pollutants whose carcinogenicity had been confirmed by two separate animal experiments involving different species; in the case of only one such experiment precautionary action would be called for in conjunction with further experiments; where evidence had given rise only to general suspicions of carcinogenicity, experimental research rather than action would be required.[54]

The regulatory proposals that emerged from this petition were modest. In 1979 the EPA proposed that chemicals identified by federal health agencies as carcinogenic would be placed on a list of suspected cancer-causing agents and made subject only to housecleaning regulations concerning storage and handling. There would be no limitations on manufacture or sale. Industry objected even to this listing procedure, however, on grounds that it unfairly implicated a chemical and provided a mechanism whereby those who sought to regulate hazardous air pollutants more fully could target chemicals for action.[55]

The potential hazards of toxic chemicals were dramatized in the mid-1970s when carcinogens were found in drinking-water supplies. This discovery posed a new problem because conventional antibacterial treatment of drinking water did not affect toxins. But measurement of toxins in drinking water was infrequent, and information about where and when they occurred lagged far behind the use of the chemicals themselves. And although one might isolate a given chemical and learn more about it, the consequences of the simultaneous presence of many such chemicals were not known.[56]

For a number of years Congress had been pressed without results to enact safe drinking-water legislation on the grounds that states did not deal adequately with toxic chemical hazards. Then late in 1974 the Environmental Defense Fund released information about the presence of toxic chemicals in the drinking water of New Orleans and associated them with above-average levels of cancer in that city. In response Congress passed the Safe Drinking Water Act of 1974, and the EPA began to investigate the presence of toxins in the nation's drinking-water supply. Its studies revealed a wide range of such substances, among them chloroform, which seemed to be associated with the extensive use of chlorine (which reacted with organic material to produce chloroform). In the fall of 1977 the EPA proposed regulations that would require large water-supply systems to adopt activated-carbon filtration in place of chlorination in water treatment. The process adsorbed synthetic organics on carbon that then could be purified and used again.

The proposal was roundly opposed by the nation's private and public water-supply systems. The problem, they argued, had been vastly exaggerated. Activated-carbon filtration would be far more expensive than the EPA had estimated. The EPA, in turn, argued that some water companies had already established a minimal level of activated-carbon filtration to control taste and smell and that the technique provided a treatment method that would deal with many chemicals at once. But the opposition of water suppliers through their organization, the American Water Works Association, prevented the adoption of the EPA's proposal.

The role of toxic chemicals as water pollutants went far beyond drinking water. There was the larger problem of toxic chemicals in rivers, lakes, and the ocean; hence concern also developed for action under the 1972 Clean Water Act. The EPA had full authority to institute such a program, but despite prodding from environmentalists it refused to do so until court orders forced the issue. Toxic chemicals required new methods of control. Conventional pollutants could be dealt with through traditional techniques of biodegradation. But toxins did not undergo such biological changes, and hence control at the source seemed necessary. This, in turn, heightened confrontation with industry. Environmental agencies often sought to avoid such conflicts by permitting either pollution dispersion or contained disposal. But toxic chemicals required them to face sources and their political power more directly.

The Natural Resources Defense Council took up court action to force the EPA to control toxic water pollutants. In 1975 the courts required the EPA to control a set list of toxic pollutants on a specific time schedule. Composed largely of synthetic organics, the list was incorporated into the Clean Water Act when it was revised in 1977. The law distinguished between the older conventional pollutants, which were subject to biodegradation, and the newer toxic pollutants, which were not. Although it relaxed the time schedule to clean up the former, it tightened the program for the latter. Variances were permitted for industries to reach goals for treating conventional pollutants, but not for toxic chemicals.[57]

Waterborne toxic pollutants also included heavy metals such as lead and cadmium. These came from both point and nonpoint sources. The major nonpoint source was storm runoff from city streets, which contained significant amounts of metals from automobiles and trucks. In most older eastern cities storm runoff was combined with household wastes in the same sewers to produce a sludge with undesirable levels of metals. But toxic metals also entered municipal treatment works as a result of joint construction by cities and industry of "combined treatment works."[58]

Municipal authorities were most concerned about metals because they could disrupt sewage treatment by poisoning bacteria. But toxic metals in sludge were a growing problem. Environmentalists had long argued that municipal sewage sludge should be recycled as a soil nutrient for agricultural production. As secondary sewage treatment became the norm it produced greater quantities of sludge, and disposal through recycling became more popular. The presence of toxic metals greatly restricted this option. When sludge was used as fertilizer the concentration of lead and cadmium in the soil increased; they were taken up by plants and if consumed by humans could constitute a significant health hazard. This served as a roadblock to recycling of sewage sludge.

To resolve this problem the EPA required industries to pretreat their effluent to remove a considerable portion of toxins from discharges. But pretreatment was easier to conceive of than to put into practice. Industries resisted it as an undue burden or, if they relented, sought to increase the allowable toxic content. As with so many environmental issues, the argument centered on the technical data. There was especially the need to know the nature and amount of discharges in the first place. Often the EPA sought to require that municipal treatment plants, as a condition of securing discharge permits, obtain information about the industrial effluent. But industries claimed that this would reveal data of value to competitors and hence was a matter of trade confidentiality. Municipal authorities had neither the personnel nor the political clout to force disclosure and sought to limit their information requests to what was required to protect their treatment processes rather than to make effluent safe for recycling.

Hazardous Wastes

Toward the end of the 1970s the safe disposal of hazardous wastes became the dominant toxic-chemical issue. In community after community toxic-waste dumps were discovered from which chemicals leaked into water or volatilized. At some dumps there were dramatic fires and explosions. But more frequently such sites came to public attention as a result of a more limited human encounter with chemical wastes in drinking water, the air, and the places where children played. In the 1960s the few encounters with hazardous wastes came from fish kills. But in the 1970s they seemed to come from almost every sector of the environment as hazardous wastes were discovered escaping from innumerable sites nationwide. They confirmed the overriding toxic experience of an environmental threat that was out of control.[59]

Knowledge about hazardous-waste disposal, the location of sites, and their impact on individuals and communities usually came to light through public initiative rather than through business or governmental agencies. The typical case involved citizens who found that their drinking water smelled or tasted strange, discovered dark water in streams near their homes or oozing out of their yards and into their basements, or smelled foul air in their homes. Citizens associated these experiences with illnesses of various kinds. Often they observed unusual patterns or incidences of sickness that they attributed to toxic chemicals.

Complaints to public authorities often met mixed and even negative responses. Citizens would be rebuffed as having inconsequential concerns. When health authorities measured the chemical content of water in drinking wells or in nearby sources, they often reported that although some toxins were detectable the levels were insignificant and harmless. But citizen protest continued. Frequently these concerns were taken up by journalists who interviewed residents and reported their statements. And at times there were elementary epidemiological investigations in which citizens and reporters canvassed neighborhoods and identified unusual numbers of health problems to compare them with their normal or average incidence. The data was often rejected as "anecdotal" or "scientifically unsound," or belittled as the complaints of "housewives." Experts were often inclined to assert authoritatively that no problem existed and to argue that further studies were not needed.[60]

These issues occasionally erupted with considerable force. The most dramatic case occurred in 1975 at the Hooker Chemical Company's disposal site at Love Canal in Niagara Falls, New York. Three years later at Montague, Michigan, another Hooker landfill led to a series of controversies between the firm, on the one hand, and citizens and the state of Michigan, on the other. Hooker finally agreed to develop a new landfill and transfer its wastes there. Other cases became newsworthy in quick succession. In Hardeman County, Tennessee, the Velsicol Chemical Company was implicated in a leaking landfill where it had stored wastes from its Memphis plant. Midnight haulers drained wastes from their tank trucks along North Carolina roads; a hazardous-waste site in Elizabeth, New Jersey, caught fire and exploded early in 1980; in Louisville, Kentucky, a waste disposer was found to have dumped hazardous wastes into the city sewers, an action that caused an explosion in the municipal sewage plant.[61]

Chemical companies received considerable criticism as the concern over hazardous waste grew. They had produced the chemicals in the first place and often had been responsible for their disposal. Hooker and Velsicol had been implicated in a wide range of chemical hazard problems, and the entire industry came under attack. By 1980, according to its own opinion polls, public esteem for the chemical industry was at an extremely low level. But the industry argued that it should not be blamed, that for the most part hazardous-waste disposal had been conducted using the best state of the art at the time. The industry had not known then the degree to which chemicals were hazardous, and it should not bear the blame for what had been due to its lack of knowledge rather than an effort to escape responsibility.[62]

Industry was interested mainly in the cost of cleanup of older sites and the possibility of liability claims for damage to human health. The abandoned sites that needed attention presented a massive financial problem. At Love Canal both state and federal authorities sought to recover the costs of cleanup and removal of families, but the Hooker Company disclaimed responsibility because it had transferred the site to a local school district in 1955. In Montague, Michigan, Hooker received a low-interest loan – that is, a public subsidy – from the state industrial-development authority to build its new landfill. In 1979 and 1980 Congress considered a more general superfund bill to finance cleanup of abandoned sites, but industry argued that the entire cost should be paid from general taxes rather than from industry.

Even more ominous to industry were the liability claims for health problems that citizens might allege were the result of environmental contamination from landfills. Court awards could well reach sums far greater than the cost of making landfills more secure. Studies already made on those most affected indicated the possibility of a wide range of health problems, including cancer, reproductive and genetic damage, and subtler consequences such as neurological effects and reduced immune capabilities. If such problems became the subject of liability claims the financial consequences would be enormous. Liability became a major element of the debate over the Superfund bill. What firms could be sued? The original chemical manufacturers, the processors, the users of chemicals as raw materials, the haulers, the landfill operators? Industry wished to limit these. Who could sue? Public agencies for cleanup costs or citizens whose health was affected? Industry sought to prevent the general public from bringing lawsuits to collect damages for health problems.

As the battles over hazardous wastes evolved, the EPA developed a regulatory control program under the 1976 Resource Conservation and Recovery Act. Its proposals constituted not a preventive policy on the cutting edge of hazardous-waste problems but a more conventional one largely dependent on major known hazards. The strategy essentially was determined by the agency's limited finances and political leverage against larger industries.[63]

The regulations, proposed in 1980, dealt primarily with transport and disposal. A manifest system was to be required to track hazardous wastes from the point of origin to the point of disposal. This would help to get rid of the haulers who dumped wastes along roads and in out-of-the-way places rather than at designated sites. Equally uncontroversial was the notion that landfills should be made more secure. They should be lined with impervious clay, covered firmly, monitored so as to track their performance, and include a system to collect, treat, and dispose of leachate so that it would not penetrate groundwater.[64]

More controversial issues brought regulatory agencies into direct confrontation with industry in the late 1970s so that the initial proposals were scaled down considerably. Who would be covered? The EPA exempted farmers, retailers, and any firm that produced less than 220 pounds of hazardous waste per month. How long would landfills be monitored? The EPA reduced its initial proposal of forty years to twenty after protests from industry. What would constitute a hazardous waste? Instead of an openended set of categories that would cover future as well as present cases, a specified list of pollutants, processes, and types of industries was compiled and specific chemicals excluded from regulation. A number of industries such as oil and gas drilling and electric power production were exempted.

Central to the problem of determining the hazards against which the regulations should provide protection were the kinds of tests required to determine whether a chemical was hazardous and subject to control. For industry this was an important way to limit the scope of the program. The number of chemicals already tested was small, and the time and cost of testing more would put a brake on expansion of the control program. What health effects should implicate a chemical and hence be part of the test protocols? Cancer, mutagenicity, reproductive disorders, or depressed immune systems? The initial proposal to test for mutagenicity was dropped, and the program was limited to those dealing with carcinogens. Because of the burdens of cost and time extensive testing would place on it, the EPA accepted the limited approach industry advocated.[65]

In some states these issues had evolved to suggest more advanced approaches. A prolonged dispute over a hazardous-waste site at Wilsonville, Illinois, had created considerable skepticism about landfills and led to provisions there that landfills be monitored much longer than forty years, even one hundred. The waste disposer should be required to demonstrate that alternative disposal methods such as chemical neutralization, recycling, or incineration had been considered and that landfill disposal was the only feasible option. And local communities should be given a veto over siting. A New York State commission argued that landfills were unacceptable long-term methods of disposal and recommended incineration as the alternative. The New York debate was infused with the idea that landfills required perpetual care, not just short-term supervision, and hence in the long run would be far more costly than other methods of disposal.

Disposal of hazardous chemicals sharpened the role of underground water as a major aspect of the toxic environment. In the past it had been argued that chemicals could be stored effectively in the ground because they could be isolated from waters that served as human supplies. Thus, deep-well injection in which wastes were forced deep into the earth was widely used. But many well-publicized incidents emphasized the widespread contamination by hazardous wastes of wells, a source from which one-third of the nation drew its drinking water.[66]

The political debate over hazardous waste seemed to confirm the perceptions that had been evolving for two decades. There was a marked lack of knowledge about both the presence of hazardous wastes in the environment and their effect on human health. The chemical industry seemed unable to control them, as well as unwilling to be responsible for their ultimate effects. The response from federal and state agencies was marked by hesitation and inaction, limited time and resources, and minimal strategies for coping with major incidents that would reduce the cost of regulation. They offered only minimal challenges to industry. All this contributed to a profound sense that society's dominant institutions were unable to solve a problem they had created.

By the end of the 1970s radiation and toxic chemicals had assumed a central place in the environmental experience of the American people and in so doing had brought about a marked shift in perspective in environmental affairs. During the years from 1965 to 1972 threats of pollution had been thought of primarily in terms of their impact on the larger biological world rather than on human health. The Fish and Wildlife Service was the major agency to protest against such matters as thermal pollution from power plants, water pollution from dredge-and-fill operations, the destruction of wetlands, and the impact of pesticides on wildlife. The extensive and varied controversies about development in the city, the wildlands, and the countryside had shaped a widespread ecological perspective.

The experience of the toxic environment in the 1970s created alongside this view one that focused more on human health. Both nuclear and pesticide affairs shifted emphasis away from ecological effects. Increasingly the EPA became a health-protection agency. Environmental affairs had come full circle from the time when the water-pollution control program had been forced out of the hands of the Public Health Service in 1964 because of its narrow emphasis on the threat to humans of waterborne bacterial infection.[67]

Much of the debate over the threat of radiation and toxic chemicals came to emphasize risk. Attitude studies highlighted the vast differences of opinion about the degree of risk chemicals entailed. Whereas corporate leaders believed the public was oversensitive to risks from radiation and chemicals, the public believed it was more aware of risk. Whereas only 38 percent of corporate leaders believed that risks in 1980 were greater than they had been twenty years before, 78 percent of the public believed so; moreover, 24 percent of corporate leaders believed risks would be greater in the future, in contrast to 55 percent of the public.[68]

These different perceptions of risk underlay much of the intensity of the debate over the toxic environment. The cumulative experiences of the American people generated a widely shared perception of harm that episode after episode justified. But public agencies seemed unable to control the threats, and the persistent opposition of industry to tighter regulation helped to create the widespread public conviction that only through citizen action could the problem receive adequate attention.[69]

The experience of toxic hazards gave rise to attempts by citizens to take matters into their own hands to control them when private and public institutions could not. Attitude studies indicated that only 14 percent of the public felt that industry would take effective action to deal with the problem; 35 percent believed that government should be relied upon, but 42 percent thought that only action by individual citizens would work. Citizens could make their own studies of health effects so as to force agencies to act; file liability suits for damages to pinpoint responsibility and protect themselves against economic loss; demand more effective monitoring and develop citizen monitoring so that they could identify threats; and demand that communities have a right to veto the location of sources of toxic hazards such as landfills, radioactive-waste disposal sites, and chemical industries.[70]

Toxic control was a highly technical subject, and the degree to which regulation would be required and be effective depended on agreement about the scientific data. Controversy over such issues made clear the importance of the ability to generate information and apply it to public decisions. Those who controlled technical skills, laboratories, and resources had far more leverage over the issues than those who did not. Information – its development, acquisition, dissemination, and application – became the crucial facet of environmental political power; inequality in information capabilities between citizens and corporate and governmental institutions played a central role in shaping the political structure of environmental affairs.

7 Population, Resources, and the Limits to Growth

Beyond the city, the wildlands, the countryside, and the toxic environment loomed even larger environmental affairs involving the balance between population and resources. Limited resources, so the argument went, could not long sustain the ever-growing population and consumption of material goods. The problem was worsened by the new burden of pollution, of which air, land, and water could absorb only limited amounts. The assimilative capacity of natural systems had been reached and often exceeded, producing ecological disruption. Such issues gave many a sense of global limits, of the finite character of Spaceship Earth.[1]

The Limited Personal Encounter with Limits

Although the idea of limits as a general notion seemed to have considerable appeal, only in selected circumstances did it involve people intimately. They could agree that the "earth is like a spaceship with only limited room and resources," but they could also agree, though a bit less firmly, that "my community ought to continue to grow." Personal involvement in strategies to limit growth was far less than personal concern for quality of life. The more intimate context in the city, the wildlands, the countryside, and the toxic environment provided the setting for most human environmental response. But personal links with population-resource questions were more tenuous. People experienced few direct connections between their lives and global problems.[2]

Initiative in these issues was taken by leaders more often than by the public at large. The impetus lay with professionals, scientists, technical experts, and those "thought leaders" who observed universal problems and studied and wrote about them. They were joined by leaders of environmental organizations whose work seemed to bridge a gap between their program strategies in response to the public and a view of the larger resource world. Such matters became the subject of debate and action, especially on the part of those in higher education, students and faculty, whose activities were shaped often by detached study rather than the personal circumstances of daily life.

On occasion this role of thought leaders dovetailed with more immediate human concerns. When a couple became worried about the size of their family and sought to minimize it to limit economic and psychological burdens, they could associate their own population problem with the global one. Often they thought about limits to growth in terms of people, buildings, and traffic in their own community. Sometimes growth was associated with greater tax burdens for current residents that would accompany more buildings and people. Hunters often spoke of the need to limit growth when they found their favorite hunting grounds, frequented in earlier years, now being closed off by the advance of people and housing. And for many the problem of growth came home most sharply through the indirect impact of reduced supply, in relationship to demand, on prices.[3]

Nor did the larger idea of limits in the Environmental Era fall on a vacuum of previous thought and concern. Whereas one branch of Protestantism, for example, historically had justified resource development for human benefit, an even more powerful strain had expressed the notion of stewardship. God's creations were given to humans to be cared for, not squandered. Hence significant sectors of organized religion struck close connections with environmental concerns in the post–World War II years. Often a larger context of thought came to be enhanced as people focused on the world of their children. *Chemical Week,* an industry publication, reported that 3.5 million couples, for whatever reason, were unable to have children; others predicted that the "deadly winter" following nuclear war would have disastrous consequences. Such views enhanced public awareness of the larger effects of environmental degradation.[4]

The interest of thought leaders in these matters was often shaped by a desire for efficiency in the use of material resources in the face of the declining availability of productive farmland for escalating food demands, the limited supply of energy and minerals, the finite ability of the oceans to produce fish. Rapid cutting of tropical forests was reducing future supplies of wood and at the same time resulting in massive erosion and sedimentation, which impaired productive resources. One heard, thus, of the problem of sustainable production.[5]

But most of the concerns that provided strong bonds between individuals and larger environmental issues were closely related to the quality of daily life. And this provided little firm base among the American people for the larger and often global problems of resource scarcity. Even by the mid-1980s it was relatively rare for Americans to become aroused about shortages in other areas of the world. Their own lives were surrounded by such abundance that they could hardly imagine, except occasionally or in some remote way, scarcities elsewhere. Whereas environmental leaders could well identify these global limits as the crucial problem for the future, few members of their organizations, let alone the general public, could feel as great a sense of urgency.[6]

The links that did develop between these two levels of environmental interest and action often were mediated through biological and ecological concerns, emphasizing not so much material as biological resources. Ecology was the major context of thought through which environmentalists viewed the larger world. Hence they could be most readily aroused to larger ideas and action through problems in the functioning of ecological systems, such as the reduction of the genetic pool of grains by monoculture or the destruction of tropical forests. These raised issues of larger genetic survival. But even these often depended on symbolic features with great emotional appeal. Most interest in endangered species came about through the desire to protect the large and dramatic animals such as the whale and the rhinoceros, rather than the invertebrates and more obscure plants as critical factors in the genetic future.[7]

Population and Resources

Debate over the relationship between population and resources grew in the early 1970s, died down for a few years, and then revived in the early 1980s. Could current levels of resource use and predictable increases in them be sustained over the long run? Predictions became the stock-in-trade of many who thought about population and resources; they depended on a combination of projections of past rates of change and speculation about whether those projections could be modified by anticipated changes in institutions and personal behavior. These, then, were placed beside estimates of resources, both known and plausibly subject to discovery, and estimates of resources required to control pollution or restrictions on supplies rendered unfit by contamination.[8]

The simplest projections applied to population; relevant data was readily available. Moreover, population change was a simple matter to think about; it depended largely upon two factors, births and deaths. But population predictions were subject to considerable dispute since the birth rate was rather unpredictable. What one could say with safety, however, was that if the current birth rate were to continue, population would reach a given level at a given time in the future. Such predictions pointed to a future U.S. population of 300 million by the year 2000 and a world future of 8.2 billion by 2025.[9]

Population growth was exponential rather than incremental; the increase was always added into the base from which further increase took off. If population grew by 3 percent each year it would take not $33\frac{1}{3}$ years but only 23 years to double. Each year new female births added to the number of potential mothers. At any one point such growth built in preconditions for population increase that persisted for years. In the United States an increase in births between 1946 and 1957 produced female children who, by the time they reached childbearing age, beginning in 1966, would constitute a larger group of potential mothers who would produce even more children. If one hoped to reduce the population, it was essential to reduce considerably the number of births in the years 1966–2000 in order to offset the long-term demographic results of the earlier increase.[10]

By the same token, one could project not just the numbers of people but their use of resources. Pressure on resources involved both people and their consumption levels. This was particularly important in the modern, affluent society in which increased standards of living placed greater demands on resources. Implications of projections of consumption were extensive. In the decade before 1975, electrical-energy use grew in the United States at the rate of 7 percent a year. What if this continued exponentially? One could estimate the implications for the number of generating plants, the space they would occupy, the land needed for transmission lines, the cooling water required, and the pollution generated. And in the debate over plans by the electrical-utility industry for growth it could easily be estimated that one hundred years of such growth would use up all the space and water resources of a given state.[11]

One striking aspect of these projections was the idea that the crunch between resource pressure and resource availability could evolve quietly without awareness of what was happening, only to burst forth suddenly in its full reality. Such a rude awakening, expressed in the phrase "population bomb," was implied in exponential growth. Rates of change could proceed without direct recognition of the long-run implications, and when those implications materialized they were far more difficult to mitigate than if they had been dealt with earlier. A favorite symbol of the analysis came to be the lily pond, in which one lily produced two lilies and then four the next day. The question was posed: If in twenty-eight days the pond was half filled, how many days would it take for it to be completely filled. Another twenty-eight? No, just once more, for on the twenty-ninth day, the doubling rate of growth would fill the entire pond. Hence the title of a book, *The Twenty-ninth Day,* by Lester Brown of The Worldwatch Institute.[12]

To these somewhat traditional perspectives on the simple balance between population and consumption, on the one hand, and resources, on the other, was added the human load of pollution. The urban-industrial society was faced with balancing its consumption with its resources, and also with coping with the wastes it produced. This confronted modern society with as serious a problem of limits as did levels of population and consumption. One of the most convincing experiences of the limits to growth involved the exponential increase of pollution and the limited space in which to store wastes. While for most in the environmental movement space was thought of as essential to improve the quality of life, for resource analysts space often was thought of in terms of the disposal of the by-products of modern production.[13]

It was relatively easy for those dealing with physical and chemical materials to understand spatial limitations in the disposal of waste that was itself physical and chemical. But to this was now added a biological dimension. The problem was not just permanent physical disposal but recycling through the ecological system. Natural cycles became overloaded and natural processes became modified so drastically that they created major problems for human life. Barry Commoner, as director of the Center for the Study of Natural Systems at Washington University in St. Louis, was especially eloquent in outlining these circumstances for the general public. Commoner's writings helped to etch into the minds of many Americans ideas about how biological systems worked and could be overloaded and disrupted to the detriment of human life.[14]

Commoner gave special emphasis to the course of modern technology. New technologies had become more materials-intensive and had created greater loads of pollution. By substituting aluminum throwaways for bottles, synthetic fibers for natural ones, and plastics for paper and wood, and by vastly expanding packaging, modern production and distribution had become increasingly energy intensive. Rising levels of horsepower in the internal combustion engine raised levels of pollution. Commoner focused on the role of technological choice as a critical element in the population-pollution-resources balance. What needed to be changed, he argued, was the kind of technology used. Society needed to shift to those technologies that were environmentally and ecologically less demanding.[15]

Many swept aside predictions concerning the limits to growth as stemming from irrational fears or, at best, misguided calculations. Physical resources were not exhaustible; it was merely a matter of economics. As less expensive resources were depleted, costlier ones would be substituted. There was ample space and materials for higher levels of consumption both for the already developed and the developing world.

This argument was revived in response to *The Global 2000 Report,* sponsored by the Carter administration, which sought to predict population and resource conditions in order to make plans for coping with them. Herman Kahn of the Hudson Institute had long criticized those who warned of future population-resource problems. He was now joined by an economist, Julian Simon, who argued that additional population in fact led to improvements in economic well-being. Simon's ideas appeared first in 1977 in technical writings and then were revived in 1980 in *The Ultimate Resource.* In 1984 he and Kahn brought together twenty-eight writers to contribute to *The Resourceful Earth,* which presented the same argument. These ideas also had limited impact and stirred the media only momentarily. Among thought leaders population-resource problems continued to shape ideas and policies.[16]

For the general public the crucial aspects of the debate were not the broad concepts and ideologies, but the persistent changes in circumstance within which people made daily choices. As they faced the rising cost of raising children and buying energy, or the destruction of the air, water, and land resources they prized, or pollution that brought sickness and adversely affected their physical and mental capabilities as well as their living conditions, they made choices that more eloquently addressed the limits of growth than did the arguments of high-level debate.

The Population Controversy

In 1970 President Nixon appointed the Commission on Population Growth and the American Future to study the relationship of population to the American society and economy. Its report in 1972 was widely publicized, issued in paperback, and available at low cost; its conclusions were given extensive television coverage. No sooner had it been issued, however, than it became highly controversial. Upon receiving the report, the president announced that he would neither accept its recommendations nor act on them. During the publicity surrounding the report there was a flurry of public interest and debate about population, but interest declined almost as quickly as it had arisen. What does this course of events reveal about this aspect of environmental affairs?[17]

First, a brief look at the report's conclusions. Was there a population problem in the United States? Yes. By the year 2000 we could expect population to reach 300 million and from there go further upward. The birthrate had reached 25.3 per thousand in 1957 and despite some decline stood at 17.6 per thousand in 1970. A more important factor, however, was the fertility rate, the number of births as a ratio not of total population but of that portion of the female population of childbearing age, fourteen to forty-five. The main fact to observe was the number of children born per woman capable of giving birth. In 1970 the fertility ratio stood at 2.5, enough to push population continually upward.[18]

What was the solution? Population stabilization, popularly known as zero population growth. Births should not exceed deaths and in-migration should not exceed out-migration. The emphasis was on the number of births each 1,000 women would be expected to have during their childbearing years to replace people who died. This was calculated at 2,110 children per 1,000 childbearing women, or 2.11 per potential mother. Throughout the 1960s this figure had stood at around 2.5, since the postwar baby boom had set in motion a desire for larger families. Hence, the commission argued, the fertility ratio should be reduced to reach the replacement rate of 2.11.[19]

How should this goal be reached? Because a considerable number of children were unplanned for and unwanted, family planning and contraception should be the major approach. Conversely, the value placed on large families was another major roadblock impeding population reduction, and population education thus was needed to encourage couples to want fewer children. Most controversial, abortions should be permitted and abortion services provided free of charge. The commission's report contemplated a rather comprehensive public program of education tnat would change values and birthrates and bring about population stabilization.[20]

Environmentalists widely approved the objectives and the strategies of the Population Commission as a major attack on a significant problem. One of the environmental organizations to grow out of the activities of Earth Day in 1970 was Zero Population Growth (ZPG), which over the years sought to highlight the population problem and to shape public policies for education and action. A major focus of attention was the role of women. The number of children women wanted was influenced heavily by the degree to which they chose careers other than child rearing. Hence much of the impetus behind ZPG came from the affirmation of new roles for women among those of college age. If women's values could be changed, the larger social objective of population stabilization could be reached through changing personal choices.[21]

After 1972 the interest in population questions rapidly declined, and this seemed to stem from the persistent downward trends in population growth. Year after year the statistics reported reduced birthrates until they fell below 14 per thousand in 1976 and the replacement ratio fell to 2.1, then to 1.8, and finally in 1976 to 1.6. This was especially surprising because the decline took place at the same time as the number of women of childbearing age increased. Some argued that women were merely postponing marriage and children rather than reducing the eventual number; they predicted a reversal of the ratio in the near future.[22]

In the mid-1970s a new factor in population stabilization occupied the attention of environmentalists — immigration. As the relative contribution of births to population expansion began to decline, it became apparent that a balance between births and deaths could well be prevented by immigration. The precise figures were difficult to determine. There were some 400,000 legal immigrants each year, but there were also many illegal immigrants, estimated at 600,000 to 1 million a year. One could well predict that this share would increase as births continued to drop. Environmentalists concerned with the population problem therefore became increasingly interested in immigration, advocated that the annual quota be lowered to 150,000, and joined in efforts to bring illegal immigration under control.[23]

Food Production

To most Americans the population problem was not closely linked with their own food supply; famine and food shortages were not part of their personal experience. Nor did they know obvious malnutrition. Hence they did not personally encounter conditions that might substantiate arguments about world food problems. Throughout its history the United States had enjoyed ample productive land and had been able to supply not only its own needs but many of those of other countries as well. Surplus production was sent abroad to make up for limited crops. Such abundance was hardly conducive to public interest in the possibility of shortages.[24]

Famines in Africa and Southeast Asia on occasion turned the attention of Americans to such problems. In the developing countries it appeared that each new level of agricultural production reached after World War II was more than consumed by each new level of population growth. Nation after nation had made marked inroads into its dependence on foreign supplies, only to find that this margin had been eroded by new mouths to feed. During the Environmental Era this relationship was etched in "limits to growth" terms, as many analyses emphasized the imbalance between population and food resources. Productive agricultural land was finite, and if restraints were not placed upon population, famine and starvation would continue.[25]

The World Food Congress in Rome in 1974 helped to instill the problem in American thinking. Shortages and famines of that year in such countries as India emphasized the degree to which the supplies of the green revolution, which had led to spectacular increases in rice production in Asia and enabled grain-short nations to catch up, were now spoken for by hungry mouths. Population pressures already in place because of high birthrates would lead to demands upon food far beyond those already experienced. The American grain surplus, which once had been extensive and from which supplies had been shipped abroad, had declined. The world's food reserve had dwindled to seventeen days' stored supply for use in emergencies. In such ways the role of food production in the United States was brought into the issue and with it the role of American food consumption.[26]

From the production side there were warnings by such specialists as Georg Borgstrom of Michigan State University and Lester Brown of the Worldwatch Institute that world food production was reaching a plateau. Between 1950 and 1970, for example, fish had supplied an increasing share of the human diet, but this had now reached an end. The catch exceeded the ability of the fisheries to re-stock, thus leading to declining productivity and endangering a sustained supply. All over the world productive land was declining through encroachment by urbanization and conversion to nonagricultural uses. Overgrazing on the world's grasslands was leading to a decline in carrying capacity.[27]

Productive land seemed to be limited. The best growing areas were those with a fortunate combination of rainfall, temperature, and daylight. Without intensive care it was difficult to carry on sustained agriculture in the tropics, where heavy rains and high temperatures accelerated biological processes. Only in the temperate regions was easily cultivated, productive land to be found, and most such areas had long been farmed. One might think in terms of investment in new forms of production, such as aquaculture, but these were increasingly costly.

It also appeared, so the argument went, that diminishing returns had set in with agricultural science and technology, and although productivity could still be enhanced in this fashion, it would also entail rising costs. For many years fertilizer had been relied on to increase production; yet over the years each additional amount of fertilizer applied to grain produced a smaller increase in harvest. Each million tons of fertilizer had yielded an additional 10 million tons of grain in the 1950s, 8.2 million in the early 1960s, 7.2 million in the late 1960s, and 5.8 million in the early 1970s. At the same time genetic innovations in grain production, which had increased yields in the 1950s and 1960s, had by the 1970s run their course. Increasing production per acre would require major breakthroughs in science and technology that had not yet materialized.[28]

Of special interest was the nutritional content of crops, particularly protein in fish, soybeans, meat, dairy products, and grains. The implications of the decline in fish yields for protein intake were considered serious; and the increasing diversion of fish from human to animal food, equally so. Whereas hybridization had augmented the weight of corn grown per acre, its protein content had declined, rendering it less valuable as food despite the improved yields. Although soybean production had increased rapidly in America, it did not lend itself as easily to hybridization and had apparently reached its limit in production per acre. Food experts were inclined to focus on the declining availability of protein, an important factor not just for the hungry abroad but also for nutrition at home.[29]

Environmentalists were concerned about several aspects of modern agricultural production beyond the sheer availability of food. One was the degree to which life-styles of urban-industrial society appeared conducive to wasting basic food products. Rising living standards placed increasing emphasis on more meat and less grain. In Southeast Asia the per capita consumption of meat per year was seven pounds; in the United States it was two hundred pounds and in the 1970s was still rising. Industrializing nations were experiencing the same change in diet. These patterns entailed a massive increase in grain consumption, for the grain required to produce meat was far greater than needed if eaten directly. Hence, environmentalists argued, American life-styles led to very high consumption levels of grain that could better go to hungry people abroad.[30]

Changes in farmland use in the United States brought a new twist to these concerns in the late 1970s. Much was being converted to intensive uses such as residential building. Many now argued that the nation's real problem was not farm surpluses but the reduction of land available for agricultural production. This led to the organization of the American Land Forum, which in 1982 published *The American Cropland Crisis,* and the American Farmland Trust, which took a lead in farmland-protection legislation. These concerns included a renewed interest in soil erosion. Although one could hardly argue that this venture attracted much popular support or even had significant strength in the organized environmental movement, it constituted a small and vocal center of activity at the level of policy leadership that tended to revive the older theme of conservation as efficiency in resource use and to steer the environmentally concerned public in that direction.[31]

Consumption

Food and agriculture productivity issues aroused the environmental movement only occasionally and in limited ways. They developed not out of personal circumstances but from the impact of knowledge about deprivation abroad on human sensitivities at home. At times more personal connections were drawn, for example, in asserting that the high consumption of meat used far more grain resources than were needed for an adequate diet while people in other countries had insufficient supplies. There were many such implications of the nation's high level of consumption. And if consumption, as well as population, was responsible for the imbalance between population and resources, such matters would continue to nag consciences, if not prompt serious change in styles of living.

One heard many critiques of the high standard of living of the American people, who, as a small percentage of the world's population, used a great portion of its resources. This circumstance had two roots. One was the way in which rising real income led to the purchase of more and more material goods and services. But there was also the commitment of the private economy to ever higher levels of production and sales. The American economy seemed to thrive on promoting consumption by creating new consumer wants. Although this had prompted critical observation over the years, it now assumed special meanings for environmentalists.

Controversies over questions of life-style often took place. Among those above median income levels consumption increased markedly. While differences between those in upper and lower levels were relatively small with respect to food consumption, on the order of 3 to 1, in the areas of household furnishings and leisure activities the gap widened to 12 to 1 and 15 to 1, respectively. Much of this increased per capita consumption was in amenities rather than necessities and conveniences. Greater demands on material resources such as energy, as well as increased production of pollution per capita, stemmed from afflu-ence; the middle and upper-middle strata were the main sources of the problem.

In the 1960s much youth unrest stemmed from a revulsion against such "excessive" consumption, and to some degree such attitudes shaped in early life continued into later newly formed households. The popularity of recycling centers was often a re-sult of a self-conscious concern with the undesirability, even im-morality, of throwing things away. They could become useful ma-terials. Such centers were supported by the more rather than the less affluent. During the energy crisis conservation came to be a major theme for action as there were many ways to reduce the use of energy. And this move also was associated with the more affluent, who used far more energy per capita than did those with less income.

Choices to reduce consumption were most attributable, how-ever, to the increasing cost of products and services. As the price of gasoline rose so did the number of individuals who chose to purchase smaller cars that would travel more miles per gallon. Such economy cars had been pioneered by manufacturers in Germany and Japan, where the cost of energy had long been much higher than in the United States; in the 1970s they were able to capture a large share of the American market. American manufacturers held back because of the greater profitability of larger and heavier cars. By the late 1970s, however, they began to respond with smaller models, partly because of the require-ments in federal legislation but even more because of the in-creasing share of foreign cars on the market.

In the 1970s one could observe the impact of the rising cost of living on life-styles and sense the beginnings of more. For ex-ample, there was the choice to have fewer children. Although for many couples that choice was the result of the changing roles of women and their desire to have an occupation outside the home, it also stemmed from the desire to reorganize family expendi-tures so that fewer children could receive the benefits of more intensive upbringing. Scarce family resources were reallocated from quantity to quality. The anticipated higher cost of education greatly influenced choices as to family size.

The increasing cost of goods and services to the consumer

had its larger counterpart in the economic analysis about the constraints on resource use that arose from cost. In many cases increasing inputs of technology, capital, and energy no longer resulted in decreasing costs of production. In the late 1960s the decline in the real cost of energy per unit of production, which had proceeded for decades, came to an end. From that point on, each increment in the use of energy increased rather than decreased its real cost. This could present an entirely new situation for personal consumption in view of the large role energy played in a wide range of consumer items. If using more meant paying more, one might well be prompted within the context of personal family choices to consume less.

Limitations in the amount of available land, translated into rising costs, constituted another way in which the consumer confronted limits to growth. Land was finite. In the decades prior to World War II the interest in owning land in the countryside, where it was most available, had steadily declined. Land values there dropped, creating a sense of unlimited supply. The rediscovery of the American countryside and the increasing popularity of land ownership after World War II reversed this trend, leading to continually rising prices. Rapidly growing desires to use and own finite lands were translated into prices every consumer could understand. Within a few decades land had become scarce, not because of changes in the supply of land itself but because of sharply rising demand.

In these ways rising real prices shaped Americans' environmental perspective. They sharpened the notion that resources were finite and that by making new choices in response to higher costs one was, in fact, making choices of environmental and ecological relevance.

The Social Context of the Limits to Growth

Most projections of the long-term impact of population, consumption, and resources were based on rather abstract calculations. Each factor was worked into a computerized model in terms of quantitative numbers of people, resources used, levels of pollution, and available resources. From such calculations predictions were made that projected levels of use could not be sustained and that a collapse would occur. Others argued that there were no such limits in sight.

The most widely debated of these computer models was presented in *The Limits to Growth,* written by four researchers at the Massachusetts Institute of Technology. It was based on a model called World 3, an adaptation of an earlier model, World 2, which had been described a year earlier by Jay W. Forrester in *World Dynamics.* These authors sought to forecast population growth, resource depletion, food supply, capital investment, and pollution and to point out the coming limitations to conventional "growth." These, in turn, led to vigorous critiques based on other models, which were said to be more accurate. One, *Models of Doom,* was prepared in 1973 by a team of specialists at the University of Sussex in England. Such arguments were popularized by Cy Adler in *Ecological Fantasies* and by J. Peter Vajk in *Doomsday Has Been Cancelled.*[32]

Other kinds of thought and action on limits to growth came more from the daily environmental choices of people and had a far more profound effect on public policy than did the systematic calculations of the experts. There was the concern for space, for more natural and fewer developed areas in one's community. Zoning laws to restrict the amount of permissible development in a city limited growth. So also did protests against the location of industrial facilities in particular communities. Some argued that such decisions only determined where rather than whether more intensive development might take place. But such choices placed restraints on land use and, taken as a whole, imposed incremental limits.[33]

The identification of natural environments as critical environmental areas served in a more direct way to restrict intensive development. If one could protect a wetland, a barrier island, or a natural area, a free-flowing stream or a wilderness, this explicitly prohibited more intensive development. Such actions reflected consumer choices much as such choices were expressed in the private market. And like private market decisions, they had broader implications for the larger arrangement of supply and demand. In a cumulative fashion they both generated and reflected a climate of opinion attuned to less intensive development.

Pollution-control programs had similar implications. There were the conditions attached to the development of new industry in nonattainment areas, that is, cities that had not yet attained their primary air-quality standards. Although such requirements did not prohibit new development entirely, they placed it under greater restraint. Such industries either had to be cleaner or, through a trade-off strategy, had to be responsible for cleaning up other sources. These were added restraints on new development and were so intended. And although implementation of the prevention of significant deterioration provisions of the Clean Air Act would not restrict development as much as the utility industries maintained, they would restrict the conditions, and hence increase the costs, under which such development could occur.

Ambient water-quality standards, as did those pertaining to air quality, restricted the amount of pollution that could be discharged into a stream. If too many industries discharging too much effluent were located on a given reach, either they would be required to clean up further or new industries would not be permitted. In addition, to carry out an antidegradation policy on streams of quality higher than the universally applied minimal standard for all streams would either prevent new development entirely or limit it to those cases where effluent could be treated in ways other than direct discharge.

The most significant aspects of the politics of the limits to growth were not the long-term and ultimate implications of projected rates of resource use but current decisions to limit growth in specific places. Although larger-scale analyses came and went in the media and the public consciousness, the drive to limit growth went forward steadily in the form of countless decisions to restrict more intensive development. And it was precisely because of these implications that most state environmental agencies stoutly resisted the implementation of both the prevention of significant deterioration and the antidegradation provisions of the air- and water-quality laws.

Almost all environmental issues raised the possibility of limiting development and had some implication for limits to growth. The most pervasive environmental debate was over the balance between more intensive and more natural alternatives. Often it was possible to reformulate issues into terms of either where development would occur or the conditions under which it would take place. There were alternative locations; the more sensitive environmental areas could be avoided. And there were technological innovations that would make possible development under more environmentally acceptable terms.

Although almost every environmental issue involved questions of limits, few in fact presented absolute choices between environmental quality and development. During the environmental decades there were few cases in which alternatives were not available that would make possible both material development and the enhancement of environmental quality. Much of the push and shove of environmental politics was, in fact, the painful process of determining just what those alternatives were and how they could be worked out.

It was rather widely agreed that population growth should be limited. In 1976 Gallup conducted a public-opinion poll on this question in a number of countries. The strongest opinions came from North America, where 84 percent said that they did not want more people in their country and 82 percent not in their community. In Western Europe the same opinion was expressed by 74 percent and 65 percent of the respondents, and in Japan by 87 percent and 52 percent. Such findings seemed to reflect a belief that desirable population levels had been reached. The poll indicated an even more striking distinction. Attitudes against further growth were strongest in those nations where population was growing more slowly. Respondents in countries where population was growing more rapidly, such as those in Latin America and Africa, were the most strongly in favor of larger populations.

One might pinpoint more precisely the social context that sustained such views in the United States. Positive environmental values seemed to rise with urbanization; the more crowded an area, the greater the desire for natural space. Some hints can be obtained from several state organizations formed at the height of the concern for population growth in 1972. In Michigan the state's population coalition included, among others, the sportsmen's organization, the Michigan United Conservation Clubs. Hunters were well aware of the relentless pace of development that had led to the closing of lands formerly opened to hunting. As settlement proceeded, restrictions on hunting followed. Similar experiences were described by those in cities who had moved to the suburbs to enjoy more open lands.

The most focused expression of these tendencies to limit growth came when smaller cities sought to restrict population through limiting building construction. Boulder, Colorado, Petaluma, California, and Boca Raton, Florida, were notable pioneers in this effort. Zero Population Growth became an important environmental center of interest in such matters, associating in its strategy and thinking the larger problem of population growth and the specific problem of growth in particular communities. Often such concerns received considerable support, not because of the environmental values involved but because of the increasing costs of public services. City governments found that with growth the tax base increased, but so did the cost of municipal services.

These efforts to restrict urban growth went through intense and persistent controversy. Those with a direct interest in development, such as real estate promoters and builders, opposed them strongly and argued that they were unconstitutional restraints on both the freedom of enterprise and the freedom of individual movement. But courts tended to accept such restraints. Initially they gave their assent in cases where development outstripped public services and forced the extension of water and sewer lines in unplanned ways. They also accepted more direct limitations on development if they were part of a well-thought-out plan that incorporated broadly accepted community values. Size and intensity of development were aspects of public welfare for which municipal authority could legitimately be used.

In years past, the emphasis on social benefits from the use of resources had underscored the value of turning undeveloped into developed land. Now, in the mid-twentieth century, a different view was emerging that stressed the positive value of more natural undeveloped areas. The implication was not that all development should cease, as many sought to claim, but rather that positive benefits from natural environments should be guaranteed alongside those from the use of material resources. What the appropriate balance between developed and natural environments should be remained to be seen. The political struggles of the environmental years were attempts to define that balance, not in a fixed and final way, but in response to the changing expression of values in different regions and communities. In this way the environmental movement shaped a balance between population and resources that was far more real to the public at large than were the more abstract calculations about ultimate limits to growth.

The Great Energy Debate

During the 1970s the issues involved in the relationships between population, consumption, and resources and the larger context of the limits to growth were focused sharply on energy. The ensuing debate tended to crystallize thought for environmentalists and to shape more explicit ideas about both energy and resources. It also tended to link the larger questions of resource limits with personal circumstances in more fundamental ways than did population and food. Energy issues activated environmentalists to develop new ideas and new strategies far more than did other aspects of the balance between resources and human demands on them.[34]

Environmentalists were primed to think in larger ways about energy as a result of the innumerable controversies in which they had engaged over energy-facility siting. Once mobilized on these issues many began to explore energy as a general problem, especially after the energy "crisis" in the winter of 1973–4. What were the alternatives? Were the energy needs projected by energy companies well founded? Could these needs be met only through the large-scale conversion systems proposed by the energy companies and their governmental allies, or were there other means that would have less adverse impact? Who should bear the brunt of that impact, those in less settled areas where facilities were sited, or those who used the energy in the high-consumption centers? How should the energy-supply system be organized, in highly centralized units or in more decentralized fashion?[35]

Such questions focused particularly on the continuous struggles over nuclear energy, which were the most intensely fought of all. Environmentalists were concerned not just with the problem of siting per se but also with the larger questions of nuclear energy that continually prompted thought about alternatives. While opposition to many siting proposals had been local and sporadic, proposals concerning nuclear energy produced a more wide-spread environmental network of organized activity. These groups were brought together in 1974 in the Critical Mass Project, which instituted a monthly journal to provide communication links among them.[36]

New circumstances predisposed many toward emerging alternative-energy analyses and proposals. Some were concerned with the quality of their environment. They sought a form of energy that would produce less air or water pollution, use less land, and cause less visual and aesthetic degradation. Others were preoccupied more with new life-style preferences. They sought a form and source of energy that would be more closely associated with natural processes and cycles, more decentrally organized and controlled, more human in scale, and less remote from the daily context of understanding and living. The search for both environmental quality and ecologically compatible life-styles provided fertile ground for emerging environmental energy ideas and served to bring these different segments of the environmental movement more firmly together.[37]

Some alternatives already were being pursued. The more they were explored, the more it appeared that the problem was not so much the lack of acceptable alternatives but the reluctance of those dominant in energy decision making to take up innovations already under way. By the last half of the 1970s, therefore, the debate over energy policy had developed into a larger political controversy over who should influence it, whether the leading voices in private industry and government were capable of thinking flexibly about such matters or whether their commitments to older ways of thinking restricted the options too narrowly. All this set the stage for a major confrontation between environmental and developmental forces that involved not just value choices as such but the larger political question as to what technologies should prevail and who should make decisions about them.[38]

Conservation Supplies

The evolving environmental energy policy of the 1970s entailed several different but interrelated elements: slower energy growth, conservation and energy efficiency, alternative supplies, a reduction in the schedule for the development of nuclear power, and a shift from oil and gas to coal until new sources of energy could be brought into play. Environmentalists increasingly integrated these varied elements into comprehensive analyses. One of the earliest was a chapter in a book on environmental strategies, *The Unfinished Agenda,* published in 1977. The new ideas achieved forceful expression in the public media, beginning in 1976, as a result of the ideas of Amory Lovins, a physicist who wrote and spoke eloquently about new ways of thinking about energy.[39]

Central to environmental energy strategy was a program of energy efficiency, to make less do more. An enormous amount of energy, so it was argued, was wasted, and much of the work of American society could be accomplished with far less. On this score environmentalists took their cue from a study undertaken by the Ford Foundation, *A Time to Choose,* which worked out several scenarios at different rates of energy growth. One involved a "no growth" alternative, which, it was argued, would not preclude economic growth because of the possibility of capturing the vast amount of energy now wasted.[40]

Sweden, it was argued, which had an industrial mix similar to that of the United States, used only two-thirds the amount of energy per capita. A different approach was to draw up regional alternative-energy plans that emphasized conservation supplies similar to that developed in the Ford study. One was prepared for the Pacific Northwest. Here, the Bonneville Power Administration proposed to build several new coal-fired plants, and Congress approved this in 1980. But as a result of the regional alternative-energy study prepared by the Natural Resources Defense Council, Congress required the Bonneville Power Administration to explore alternative sources of supply, including efficiency, before it took up additional electrical generation.[41]

In converting fossil fuel to electricity, well over 60 percent of the energy in the fuel was lost through waste heat; in the case of nuclear plants it was 66 percent. Steam generation of electricity required water to cool waste heat to lower the temperature of discharge into waters of lakes and streams. If waste heat could be captured, so the argument went, it could serve as a major source of new energy supply. But the peculiar organization of the electrical industry, in which generating plants were located far from potential users of waste heat, made its dissipation into water or air more feasible. To environmentalists this simple problem of using what was customarily wasted emphasized the need to decentralize the location and reduce the size of electrical generating plants.

The use of waste heat had many possibilities. One was "total energy systems" in which, within one building, electricity generated on site could supply not only power and light in the form of electrical current, but through the use of waste heat in the form of hot air or water could supply heating and cooling within the same building. A variant on this approach was the district system, said to be common in Europe, in which a central urban electric-power plant provided hot air or water for nearby buildings. Finally, considerable heat was wasted in industrial processing. If it could be used for generating electric power prior to use for processing, then two kinds of work could be performed by the same energy. This was called cogeneration.

Energy conservation could also be furthered in a variety of less dramatic ways. One of the most important was home insulation. This was a relatively simple solution that required only financial incentives for installation. A far more controversial way of saving energy was to shift to more fuel-efficient automobiles. After the first "energy crisis," in the winter of 1973–4, environmentalists sought legislation to impose a tax on automobiles with low gasoline mileage. But industry vigorously opposed it. Congress enacted legislation that required automobile manufacturers to attain an increasingly higher mileage per gallon for their entire fleet with each passing year, but it declined to target high-mileage cars with disincentives. Higher gasoline prices and changing consumer preferences brought changes in fuel efficiency more rapidly than did legislation.

Environmentalists also argued that licensing agencies should require utilities to consider alternative approaches for each new proposed plant, for example, conservation as a source of future energy needs. They also questioned utility calculations of those needs. The standard approach in the 1970s was to calculate projected need on the basis of recent population and use patterns. But, argued environmentalists, these would not continue at the same pace. The rate of population growth had slowed down and rising energy prices would lead to declining per capita use.

In the late 1970s energy conservation – now called energy efficiency – came to be almost a religion. To the energy industry, conservation was only a minor part of a larger energy program that stressed the need to develop new sources. It publicly supported energy conservation more to capture and limit it than to extend it. For environmentalists conservation was an integral part of a permanent and expanding program. Consumer goods that were highly energy-intensive in their manufacture, that is, products that embodied high levels of energy, should be discouraged in favor of less energy-intensive products. Throwaway steel, aluminum, and glass containers, for example, consumed far more energy and should be replaced with returnables.[42]

The central role of conservation in the energy strategy of environmentalists prompted them not to object to the rising price of energy. In their minds one of the preeminent reasons for energy waste was that energy's low cost did not encourage consumers to use it frugally. The energy debate of the 1970s took place within the context of a rising real cost of energy that inevitably pushed consumer prices up. Although consumer groups objected to these increases during proceedings before public-utility commissions, environmental organizations did not always join them. For they expected that rising consumer prices would lead to more efficient use.[43]

They argued especially that energy should be priced at its replacement cost. New energy supplies were far more expensive than old. Consumers of these new supplies wished the two to be averaged in order to blunt the force of rising prices. But this would lessen the impact of price on conservation. If consumers of new energy were forced to face directly the full amount of its higher cost, pressures for efficiency would be greater.

New Sources

Environmental energy policy emphasized new sources of supply as well as conservation. Supplies of oil and gas, extremely low, could be relied on only during the short run. Each year the amount of domestic oil and gas consumed exceeded the newly discovered reserves, and recoverable supplies declined. The nation's energy leaders turned to coal and nuclear power as alternatives. The United States had an abundant supply of coal, which would last for several hundred years at current rates of use. Since uranium from which atomic energy was produced was not abundant, they also supported development of the breeder reactor, which created new supplies of usable fuel as it consumed existing ones.[44]

To this program environmentalists gave little support and much opposition. Skepticism about nuclear energy turned into hostility during the 1970s when an increasing number of environmental organizations urged a nuclear moratorium. Plants currently in use or under construction should continue, but no new ones should be started. As the energy establishment came to favor the breeder reactor, so environmentalists increasingly opposed it. By the time of the Carter administration the breeder reactor had become a major focus of controversy. Environmentalists were also skeptical about many of the ventures to develop new energy supplies such as synthetic oil and gas from coal, shale oil, or liquefied natural gas because of both their tremendous cost and their environmental impact. Because these alternatives required extensive public subsidies, including price guarantees as well as capital funds, and because costs continued to favor imported oil, the proposal to produce synthetic fuel faded from the scene in the early 1980s.

To those who opposed nuclear energy, coal appeared to be the most available immediate alternative; it could provide a domestic source of energy to substitute for foreign oil. But environmentalists were also wary of the high potential for environmental degradation from the use of coal. So they encouraged coal only if the environmental hazards could be reduced significantly to make it "clean."[45]

Environmentalists were especially hopeful about solar energy's many advantages. There were few adverse environmental consequences so long as its application was direct and decentralized rather than by means of central generating stations. And it could be applied and controlled by individual users, thus bypassing centrally organized energy systems. Innovations in solar-energy technology proceeded apace, but environmentalists believed that failure to move faster was attributable to the lack of interest of those dominant in energy affairs. Energy companies argued that solar energy was "exotic" because it could supply less than 1 percent of energy needs by the year 2000 and hence deserved low priority. Environmentalists countered that it was already in place and growing in commercial importance; with a promotional program on a scale similar to that for the breeder reactor, as the Carter administration projected, solar energy could supply 20 percent of the nation's energy needs by the year 2000.[46]

The expansion of solar energy benefited from the ready availability of solar technology. For heating and cooling in buildings much solar energy could be captured simply by more appropriate design; this was "passive solar energy." It could also be collected and then transferred by water or air throughout buildings for heating and cooling. Even greater possibilities lay in the solar cell, which converted solar radiation into electricity. A relatively simple technology, it had been developed initially for spacecraft. The major task in its application was not research and development but engineering, that is, the mass production of solar cells. New methods of manufacturing were reducing the cost steadily. Whereas the space program cells cost twenty dollars a peak watt installed capacity, by 1973 this had fallen to fifteen dollars, by 1977 to seven, and in 1982 one manufacturer filled an order for three dollars. Given the rising cost of electrical conversion from conventional fuels, this made it reasonable to look forward in the near term to the time when solar cells would be competitive with other forms of electrical energy.[47]

For many energy markets in the late 1970s solar cells were already competitive. This was especially the case in areas remote from conventional energy supplies where fuels had to be transported long distances in order to generate energy locally. The photovoltaic strategy was to tap markets that were already competitive and to expand the scale of production to fill them; this would lower unit costs, which, in turn, would lower prices and enable manufacturers to enter new markets. Solar advocates argued that within a decade these cost reductions would make photovoltaic cells cheaper than conventional sources for home electrical supplies within the United States.[48]

The steadily declining cost of the solar cell made it unique among energy sources. Almost every other frontier source of energy was predictably inflationary – real costs would continue to rise as they were developed – whereas the trend for photovoltaic cells was downward and cost-reducing. In the midst of long-term energy trends, then, in which the dominant note was the persistently rising real cost of energy, photovoltaics were one exception that seemed to lean toward lower real cost. The aura of possibility was enhanced because the solar cell's was a semiconductor technology, and the success of the semiconductor industry in reducing the cost of pocket calculators transferred confidence to solar-cell technology. Whereas leaders in the conventional electrical industry committed to fossil fuel and nuclear energy were skeptical about the possibility of photovoltaics, firms experienced in semiconductor technology were optimistic.

The appeal of solar energy had distinctive psychological and sociological roots. It was a form of energy individual consumers could comprehend and relate to directly. This accounted for much of its popularity. At the same time it could be integrated into the organization and management of one's home and daily activities and hence could elicit personal initiative. Heavy technology depended on specialized research in physics or chemistry, and its development and application could be undertaken only at specialized research centers and in large-scale demonstration projects; by contrast, solar energy depended more on elementary innovations in design and smaller-scale organization. It could be understood through visual perception and did not require abstract and mathematical abilities. The challenge of solar energy called forth human endeavor more reminiscent of the early nineteenth-century Yankee tinkerer than the highly centralized and collective initiative of mid-twentieth-century corporate management.[49]

By the early 1980s energy issues had become firmly entwined with issues of cost. Conventional energy appeared to be highly inflationary. New technologies seemed to be so expensive that they could be fostered only through massive public subsidies and future guaranteed prices. The high cost of nuclear power led the TVA, other public power agencies, and many private electricity firms to cancel projects already under construction. Increasingly known as energy efficiency, conservation was taken up on many fronts, not the least of which was manufacturing industry, which consumed large amounts of energy and came to constitute one of the major influences to counter inflationary energy tendencies.[50]

Reflecting these trends, the Center for Energy Analysis, led by Roger Sant, took up the terminology of "least cost supplies," thereby giving the older conservation option emphasized by environmentalists a new twist. After his stint as head of the Solar Energy Research Institute during the Carter administration, Denis Hayes, who was highly critical of the new Reagan policies, began to categorize options as those of "smart energy" and "dumb energy," with a central emphasis on the inflationary alternatives the conventional industry advocated. By the early 1980s it appeared that the economics of the photovoltaic industry might enable it to grow steadily despite opposition from the new administration. An annual review of energy trends early in 1982 indicated that solar energy was growing so much faster than atomic energy that foreign entrepreneurs might well wrest leadership of the photovoltaic industry from American firms.[51]

The Organization of the Energy System

Environmentalists also saw major problems in the way the energy system was organized. On every side one witnessed larger and larger generating plants, reaching 1,000 and more megawatts and higher and higher voltage transmission lines that required wider and wider swaths of land. The increasing scale of both generating and transmission was closely associated with the tendency to site facilities farther and farther from the point of use, and hence the user was less than dimly aware of the human stakes in the areas asked to bear the brunt of the impact. Environmentalists began to formulate ideas about the scale under which the electrical energy system should be organized and managed.

Was this centralization economically efficient? Were there not diseconomies of scale? There were the added costs of the transmission lines, land, the towers, and the lines, which increased the ultimate cost of energy to the consumer; and there were the line losses of electricity during transmission, which grew as lines became longer. Centralization also aggravated interruptions in the flow of electricity. If a city were dependent on a single 1,000-megawatt plant and if it went down, the entire city would be without electricity, whereas if the same source were in the form of ten 100-megawatt plants and one malfunctioned, far fewer customers would be inconvenienced. Such alternatives became especially salient in those few cases of citywide blackouts that gave rise to more serious thoughts about decentralization of conversion facilities.[52]

Energy analysts began to examine the varying sizes of plants to determine the degree to which they actually produced energy up to their rated capacity, as well as the cost per unit of energy produced. These figures were difficult to secure because most data dealt with the rated capacity and not actual production. One set of studies by Philip Comey of Businessmen for the Public Interest in Chicago argued that the production of electricity from nuclear plants continued to be far less than the rated capacity and that the gap was greater for larger than for smaller units. Another set of studies led to the conclusion that although there were economies of generation up to about 500 megawatts, diseconomies set in above that level. The energy companies hotly disputed the conclusions, but environmentalists became convinced that increasing scale did not always mean decreasing unit costs and that after a certain point the reverse was true.

These economic analyses of scale were supplemented by political analyses. Almost every siting issue seemed to involve a decision by management in highly centralized private energy institutions that, in turn, entailed considerable authority to carry out their objectives. The private firm had a concentration of expertise that could help it outmaneuver objections on technical grounds; it enjoyed a scale of economic resources that enabled it to engage in massive efforts to influence public opinion; it often had agents who could purchase lands for siting long before opposition could crystallize; and it seemed able to establish close relationships with governmental officials, especially in administrative agencies, which enhanced its ability to control and influence. The persistent experience with such power led to the conclusion that there was a close connection between centralized technology and centralized political power.

One series of events that helped to confirm that view was the persistent use by private energy companies of authority at a higher level of government to combat resistance to their proposals at a lower level. If a community tried to use local zoning ordinances to protect its lands from massive energy facilities, the energy companies sought support from state governments to counteract that local influence. If at the state level they found sympathy for those who objected to energy siting, they turned to federal authority to restrain the states. Energy companies were willing to use political leverage at any level in government to reach their objectives.

Concern with tendencies toward centralization of political authority played a major role in predisposing many environmentalists to a decentralized technology in matters of energy conversion and distribution. Solar energy provided that opportunity. Here was a source of energy that could flow directly to the site of use rather than through large-scale systems. With solar energy homes could be designed to be less and less dependent on the larger network of energy institutions. In the past architecture had stressed the protection of those inside buildings from outside elements. This now could be rethought so as to integrate interior design with the sun as well as the topography of the site. To design with nature had long caught the imagination of ecologists; that now seemed possible through solar energy.[53]

New Energy Analyses

The emergence of energy issues to a central place in American public life generated a host of new analyses. In the past most thought about energy had been devoted to new needs and new sources. Many economists, physicists, political scientists, biologists, and a new breed of energy specialists looked at energy questions in new ways. Studies were financed by the National Science Foundation or the Energy Research and Development Administration, which was incorporated into the new Department of Energy in 1977. These analyses revealed the degree to which many aspects of energy had gone unexplored in the past. Environmentalists felt that new perspectives on energy questions were needed in order to break out of the traditional preoccupation with greater supply in response to greater demand.

One such concept was net energy, the comparison of the amount of energy generated by a given technology with the amount consumed in its production. Shale oil production pilot plants in Colorado showed that the energy cost of producing shale was greater than the energy return. As the search for oil and gas went deeper into the earth and as surface mining required the removal of more overburden and as lower-quality sources of supply required more technology for extraction and refining, the energy required in tapping energy resources increased. To drill deeper required more energy and less return of energy per unit of energy expended. Net-energy analysis now required that the relationship between energy cost and energy return be identified.[54]

Net-energy analysis brought into play the need to make calculations about the entire energy stream, not just the conversion system such as the electricity-generating plant. One had to determine the energy cost of extracting raw materials such as uranium, their processing, their transport, and the disposal of waste. Such calculations, it was argued, often revealed a cost far beyond that generally assumed and, in fact, a net energy loss. New technologies of electrical generation or oil production and refining had customarily lowered energy costs; hence there had been little effort to examine the entire energy stream. Rising real energy costs now seemed to make such analysis essential.

Other modes of accounting followed. There was the analysis of energy productivity. Was the energy cost of a given product, such as an automobile or a typewriter, increasing or decreasing? Or, conversely, was a given unit of energy more or less productive in creating goods and services? Historically energy cost had steadily declined per unit of production, but beginning in the late 1960s both the energy cost of production and the energy component of goods and services began to rise, thereby reversing the past trend.

Amory Lovins was especially influential in these debates. In his initial writings, which appeared in 1976 in *Foreign Affairs,* he contrasted two energy paths. The first, the hard path, consisted of the increasing reliance on "high technology," large-scale systems of electrical generation, fossil and nuclear fuels, and centralized organization and management. To this prevailing mode he contrasted the "soft energy path," which stressed smaller scale and decentralized modes of energy supply, conversion, and distribution, with a heavy but not exclusive emphasis on solar energy.[55]

In his analyses Lovins addressed many factors such as energy waste, the environmental cost of large-scale systems, the diseconomies of scale, the unfavorable net energy balance in much of the nation's energy program, and the rising real cost of energy. To these he added his own analyses of such factors as the quality of energy needed for ultimate uses and the capital implications of energy-supply programs. His ideas provided a worldview that brought perspectives together. Lovins constructed a "paradigm" of diverse strands of emerging thought.

Much of Lovins's contribution to the energy debate consisted in his observation that the use of high-quality heat for low-quality needs wasted much energy. Energy experts were fond of insisting to the general public that energy, unlike many consumer items, could not be used up; it could only be changed from a form of higher heat quality that produced more work to one of lower quality that produced less. The technology of energy involved processes by which the heat potential in fuel was concentrated for higher levels of work such as steam or electrical energy.[56]

But, so Lovins argued, to produce steam from coal and convert it into electricity in order to heat a house to 68 degrees Fahrenheit was extremely wasteful. Only 8 percent of all energy needs in America, he maintained, actually required electricity; some 55 percent of all uses called for some form of space heating or cooling, which could be accomplished with lower-quality energy. In the United States, he concluded, there was an oversupply, not a shortage, of electricity, and no additional facilities would be needed for some time to come.

Lovins's analysis emphasized end uses. Energy observers, he argued, stressed the cost of production rather than consumer uses. The first step in energy policy should be to inventory actual needs so that the quality of supply could be adapted to the quality of use. Such an approach made sense to those concerned with conservation who had already given considerable emphasis to the waste heat generated by centralized electricity production. Environmentalists readily took up the end-use fit analysis as a central aspect of their arguments.[57]

Lovins also brought to the economic analysis of energy the capital-investment implications of conventional plans for expansion of the energy supply. These, he argued, had been severely underestimated and were beyond the capabilities of the economy. The Ford administration proposed a massive federal energy-development corporation with a capital of $100 billion. This, Lovins argued, would increase the capital diverted to energy production so that it would absorb 75 percent of the nation's available savings. In the face of other capital demands, it would result in shortages and marked inflation in capital costs in the form of higher interest rates.[58]

Lovins's arguments gave rise to relatively clear-cut alternatives in supply strategies, the soft in contrast with the hard path. In some cases large-scale generation seemed feasible, especially in those cases in which end use was equally large in size and scale. But for the most part he urged a shift to soft energy paths. His calculations of the feasibility of this were often questioned by dominant energy leaders. But equally as often they were forced to accept them. The Federal Energy Administration was persuaded to take up his approach for the state of California. A team of analysts concluded that the state could rely henceforth on a soft energy path and by the year 2025 sustain an economy eight times as great as in 1977. The Department of Energy, after prodding from environmentalists, released the study, but it did so with the argument that the inflexibility of existing institutions made such changes extremely unlikely. This only seemed to underscore environmentalists' contention that the real problem was the scale of energy institutions, which made it difficult for them to change.[59]

Within the environmental movement Lovins stimulated a transition from an energy analysis based on siting issues to one of alternative-energy strategies. Henceforth environmental policy statements were heavily influenced by his arguments. In wider circles he became a forceful exponent of the environmental alternative. He appeared before state legislatures and his views were the subject of a congressional hearing. His ability to crystallize thought, in combination with a credibility based on extensive knowledge and clear presentation, helped to sharpen the thinking of many Americans concerned with energy affairs.[60]

The Course of Energy Policy

Environmentalists increased their participation in the national debate over energy after the oil crisis in the winter of 1973–4. But their role was quite modest. That debate activated a wide-ranging set of political forces, each clamoring for recognition. Every sector of society had an important stake in the outcome. Each group of energy producers wished policy to go in its direction; there were different interests between domestic and foreign producers, established and newer firms, the major and the independent oil producers.

Consumers, including manufacturers, public and private institutions, and less well organized residential users, sought to hold down energy prices in the face of producer demands to raise them. Such conflicts often were organized in sectional terms, pitting the gas- and oil-producing states of the South and near Southwest and the coal-producing states of the Upper Plains against consumers in the North and East.

During this debate each consuming group wanted to ensure that its share of energy was maintained. Automobile manufacturers opposed restrictions on the use of low-mileage cars. Owners of private airplanes fought to protect the use of fuel for recreational as well as business air travel; the tourist and recreation industry, heavily dependent on motorized transportation, sought to guarantee allocations for leisure travel. Truckers were adamant about their own supplies and their right to move goods at speeds higher than the legal 55 miles per hour.

Amid such political currents environmentalists sought to maintain a clear sense of direction for energy conservation and alternative sources. They opposed the massive energy-development corporation that was at the heart of President Ford's approach to energy supply. They persistently questioned the dominant role of the Atomic Energy Commission and the Joint House-Senate Committee on Atomic Energy in both the regulation and the promotion of nuclear energy. On the whole, they sought to modify the dominance of the energy establishment in energy matters in order to open up debate and to make room for alternative approaches.

When the Carter administration assumed office environmentalists hoped to exercise considerable influence in shaping both new energy policy and new administrative arrangements. In the election of 1976 they had given Carter strong support. During both the campaign and the ensuing transition in administration, Carter's staff had received environmentalists warmly and had given them an important role in suggesting both new administrative appointees and new policies. Environmentalists were particularly heartened by the president's receptivity to new ideas about energy and especially the role in energy matters being played by S. David Freeman, author of the Ford Energy Study on which environmentalists had drawn for inspiration and ideas.

The president's energy message, delivered to Congress in the spring of 1977, was encouraging, as was his fireside chat with the nation on the same subject. He emphasized the urgency of the energy crisis and heavily underscored conservation and the goal of reaching an annual energy growth rate of 2 percent. He focused on waste heat as a major future source of energy supply, stressed solar energy as a real possibility, urged that nuclear energy be a supply "of last resort," and gave special emphasis to coal as the most important near-term source. This followed closely the environmental energy program. A message was one thing, but action was another. Amid the push and shove in Congress much of this program fell by the wayside. A pessimist could have emphasized how little of the Carter energy program was taken up seriously.

As the administration's policy unfolded, environmentalists were most disappointed by the imbalance between nuclear and solar options. Although Carter sought to restrict funding for breeder reactors, he did little to restrain other forms of nuclear energy. Budget proposals to Congress in 1978 called not for continued increases in solar-energy funding but for reductions. Support for solar alternatives seemed to be rising in the nation at large and Congress responded. Hence environmentalists found themselves working with Congress to increase funding for solar energy and to pass the Energy Act of 1979, which incorporated

some of their ideas. They were especially disturbed that for advice on energy the president seemed to rely most heavily on nuclear advocate James Schlesinger, the new secretary of energy.
In this second half of Carter's administration, they found his energy policy to be the most disappointing aspect of his environmental record.

The one aspect of that policy they could look on with some
satisfaction was the president's firmness with respect to an environmentally acceptable use of coal. The industry argued persistently that surface-mining and air-quality regulations would
hamstring coal production. The president, however, signed the
Surface Mining Control and Reclamation Act of 1977 and firmly
supported amendments to the Clean Air Act that enhanced the
role of the EPA in tackling air-pollution problems caused by coal
use. A rough political bargain had been worked out; environmentalists would support expanded coal production if the administration would be firm with surface-mining and air-quality controls.

There were also state energy programs that tackled circumstances peculiar to each. Federal policy contemplated the promotion of state energy programs to further conservation or to
assist in new production. But many states took the initiative either
because of their own energy resources, over which they could
exercise some control, or because they depended on out-of-state
supplies. New England, for example, long energy-deficient, was
attracted to nuclear power as a regional source of supply. But
people in the region also placed high value on its natural environment and hence opposed large-scale energy installations. They
gave considerable support to alternatives such as wood and solar energy.

In some regions abundant energy supplies shaped policies.
The oil and gas states of Louisiana, Oklahoma, and Texas were
preoccupied with the development of those resources and their
sale to other parts of the nation. They gave little support to environmental objectives. From the central coal region of Pennsylvania west through Illinois, utility consumers of coal and railroad
coal carriers were very influential. Here was to be found some of
the most vigorous opposition to environmental proposals to mitigate the adverse effects of the use of coal. The coal-rich Upper
Plains states, which produced raw materials for other regions and

which were subject to external private and public policies in their coal development, demanded the right to set the terms of development. They established controls to protect surface owners from strip mining and severance taxes to finance energy-related public services.

Some states were pioneers in new energy ventures. In California there was considerable opposition to nuclear power; a 1976 law provided that no nuclear plant could be constructed in the state without a positive finding that facilities were available for effective disposal of nuclear waste. And the California Department of Energy took up alternative sources of supply, requiring utilities to explore such possibilities instead of simply expanding traditional courses of action. Washington, Montana, and Minnesota devoted a small but significant share of their funds, some raised from taxes on energy extraction, to experiments in new energy technologies proposed by citizens of the state. All these gave rise to considerable ferment to move in new directions; to mark some states as innovative while others continued in more conventional ways.

Energy and Resource Limits

For the general public, interest in the balance between population and resources ebbed and flowed in accordance with personal experience. In matters of population there was for a time a close connection between personal choices for smaller families and the larger thrust for a more stable population. The lack of immediate personal experience with food shortages removed this issue from the experience of most Americans, who expressed concern about it only sporadically. The most striking experience of the limits to growth arose from a different quarter, the search for environmental quality in living space, which many felt was becoming scarce. This conveyed directly a sense that there were "too many people" and fed a concern that the population could not continue to grow at its current pace.

Energy circumstances fixed such issues more sharply. After the winter of 1973–4 many Americans experienced energy shortages, although less in the form of deficient supplies and more in terms of higher prices. For several years the persistent pressures toward energy inflation and the continuing debate over energy policy kept the issue constantly before the public. After these pressures eased in the late 1970s as a result of the growing use of conservation supplies, which eased pressures on price, public interest declined, only to rise again later as consumers faced new rounds of energy inflation. Yet amid all this there was a reluctance to think about energy as a problem in the relationship between finite supplies and growing human wants. There was always the hope, fostered by the ideology of the Reagan administration, that future energy supplies depended more on the will to find them than on material limits.

Two alternative tendencies prevailed in the national debate. On the one hand, there was the temptation to argue that shortages and rising costs of energy were due to external circumstances, especially to the practices of the oil-exporting countries. This gave rise to the search for energy independence. But there was also the more persistent reality that shortages and inflation were more inherent in limited domestic supplies and the inflationary impact of prevailing energy technologies.

It seemed that the private energy firms and high-technology professionals often preferred inflationary energy, which could transfer the cost to the energy consumer. All this reinforced the least-cost supply ideology. Amid these contradictory tendencies were the continual realities that to foster domestic supplies required heavy public subsidies and that foreign oil, despite OPEC pricing, continued to be attractive to American consumers because it was cheaper.

The realities of energy circumstances kept shaping these alternatives in public debate. Conservation supplies or greater energy efficiency restricted the impact of inflationary price pressures. Persistent inflationary tendencies made the photovoltaic solar option increasingly feasible for extended use in existing markets. Public subsidies for nuclear and synthetic fuel exposed their inflationary role in the economy and prompted skepticism about programs to sustain and extend them. And an expanded end-use emphasis generated considerable public interest in personal and community efforts to organize energy use more effectively, which served as an alternative to a more highly centralized and less flexible corporate management.

These elements of the real world of energy had the potential of enlarging human perspectives to questions of limits. That they rarely did so testifies to the slight degree to which issues of the balance between population and resources had taken root in the minds of the American public.

8 Environmental Inquiry and Ideas

Environmental efforts and the environmental movement were forged not so much by general theory and preconceived thought as by day-to-day concern and action. They arose from the varied ways people confronted their surroundings and found them either helpful or harmful for the realization of their aspirations. Such action implied large ideas about human beings and nature, economics and politics, the social order, inequality and power. But daily environmental action and events were so demanding that only rarely were those active in environmental affairs able to think about the larger implications of what they did.

Yet the assumptions implicit in environmental argument and action comprised a set of ideas through which one could understand the American social and political order. If brought together, more modest strands of environmental inquiry added up to ideas about the changes that Americans experienced in the years after World War II and the directions in which these changes were leading.

The few expressions of formal ideas about the environment were narrow in scope. One involved the ethical relationship of human beings and nature, which stressed the "rights of nature" more than the role of nature in society. This was the recurrent theme of the journal *Environmental Ethics,* one of the few reflective rather than action-oriented environmental publications. Another approach, called "deep ecology," stressed the need for a nature- rather than human-centered environmental ethic. It was promulgated by several eloquent writers but had few followers. Neither of these viewpoints was widely expressed.[1]

Some writers affirmed the importance of personal and community autonomy, an idea that struck a chord among a larger number of people. Independence, self-reliance, and greater personal, family, and community freedom from the larger institutions of modern society were widely shared aspirations. And since they involved a do-it-yourself strategy many publications combined practical advice with general philosophy.

In academic circles the most compelling theme for inquiry was the balance between population and resources. Some stressed resource limits and others the sources of increasing environmental loads. In particular, they examined the institutional roots of the problem in the demands imposed by modern productive enterprise and inquired as to the failure of either the public or institutional leaders to deal adequately with it.[2]

The absence of systematic environmental inquiry stemmed largely from the degree to which the intellectual activities of environmentalists were influenced by their opponents, who dominated the definition of environmental issues. Hence, public environmental debate often was shaped by negative rather than positive assertions about environmental affairs: antitechnology, bad science, single-issue politics, adversary strategies, opposition of the environment and the economy, belief in a no-risk society, hostility to cost-benefit analyses, and elitism. The ideas these phrases conveyed structured the way in which the popular and professional media wrote and spoke about environmental affairs.[3]

Environmental inquiry did not lead to a single system of thought such as social theorists might prefer, and it would be difficult to reduce its varied strands to a single pattern. Although environmentalists called for greater governmental initiatives on behalf of their objectives, they were as skeptical of public as of private enterprise. Much environmental writing affirmed a decentralist view, but environmental action so frequently involved attempts to enhance the authority of the state that a comprehensive intellectual perspective on this score did not emerge. Environmental ideas, moreover, were difficult to relate to socialist traditions. The latter grew out of the struggle among producers for shares of the profits of production, but environmental values were more associated with consumption, which drew lines of demarcation between environmentalists and producers as a whole.

Nor did the more conventional language of American public debate, conservative versus liberal, seem to fit. Environmentalists could be described as liberals in that they expressed values associated with the advanced industrial society, were instruments of innovation and change, voiced the concerns of consumers and advocated intervention in the economy on behalf of the public. But they were also conservative in that they objected to the radical role of private and public developers in altering the face of the earth and disrupting more stable ways of life. Environmentalists tended to work out their values amid a sense of place that provided roots to life's meaning much in the spirit of traditional conservative ideology.[4]

The ideas that emerged among environmentalists were far more pragmatic, often a mixture of contradictory tendencies that precluded a commitment to a single system of thought or utopian vision. Environmentalists were keenly aware that people balanced views about work, on the one hand, and consumption and the quality of life, on the other. Although many roundly condemned major trends in modern science and technology, they also affirmed the value of new scientific inquiry and new technologies that were more appropriate to the social values they promoted. While the increasing concentration of population in metropolitan areas spawned increasingly intractable environmental problems, the dispersion of that population into the countryside only threatened the more natural environment that was prized. There were intricacies and contradictions galore in these strands of thought, but they only underlined the degree to which environmental inquiry itself penetrated into the complexities of modern life.[5]

The way in which the media shaped public controversies often made it appear that environmentalists simply objected to many recent technological innovations. But negative critiques resulted from a more fundamental affirmation of new values, of attempts to define an emerging personal and community life in the advanced industrial era. The impulses of environmentalists were firmly tied to the perennial tendency of Americans to view the future as improvement, as possibilities, as capable of providing a continually more abundant standard of living. This expression of positive values lay at the root of the sustained force of environmental politics.

Science and Technology

Science and technology were central in environmental inquiry. The range of new questions that environmentalists insisted be investigated, in fact, greatly strained limited resources and perspectives. They placed demands on the nation's scientific institutions far greater than they were capable of meeting.

There was little data about water or air quality or patterns of land use, and health monitoring was equally skimpy. Environmentalists urged that public funding help fill the gaps. They also sought experimental studies and statistical analyses to identify environmental hazards and to develop methods of reducing them; to increase knowledge about ecological systems; to develop cleaner – environmentally more efficient – technologies; to elaborate the role of biological organisms in soil building and decay through biogeochemical analysis; to understand transmission and transformation of chemicals in the atmosphere and the impact of ingested or inhaled particles on human behavior.[6]

In science and technology there was considerable controversy over what should be emphasized for study and research. And this often reflected fundamental differences in values. Much of science and technology was concerned with the use of knowledge to transform natural resources into more useful commodities. But environmental values were changing the meaning of natural resources and affirming their importance as undeveloped air, land, and water. And there was the question of the degree of allowable contamination of both people and the environment. Industrialists were skeptical about the alleged harm of chronic low-level exposures to pollutants. They considered such problems to be more imaginary than real, and hence they could readily dismiss many environmental health goals as unnecessary.

Scientists and engineers often thought that environmentalists rejected the validity of their enterprise itself. Yet running through much of environmental action was an instinctive affirmation of the need for greater scientific knowledge and better technologies and an argument for their redirection. To what new realms of understanding and what new technologies should scarce resources be devoted? What to pursue in science and technology rather than their usefulness was the question at issue.[7]

Toward Cleaner Production

The most immediate and direct demands of environmentalists involved alternative technologies that would make industrial production environmentally less burdensome. Existing technology, they argued, was more dirty than clean; it had dispersed pollution rather than contained it. They encouraged innovation to make technology environmentally less demanding and more efficient.[8]

Environmentalists urged, for example, that funds be shifted from personal to mass transportation so as to reduce pollution. Materials such as glass, tin, and steel should be reused; they worked to secure container deposit legislation as well as railroad rates that would encourage the use of recycled rather than virgin materials. They promoted energy and water efficiency as ways of dealing with resource shortages. And they favored policies to shift the manufacture of automobiles from low- to high-mileage cars to reduce gasoline consumption.

To environmentalists the issue was the pace and form of technological change. Much existing technology was environmentally inefficient; in the normal course of modernization one could expect it to become more efficient in both environmental and product output. But progress in this area seemed exceedingly slow. It did not appear that tendencies toward innovation from within the business community could be relied on to bring about the desired changes. How could society, through public action, take steps to bring about efficiency more quickly? It was one thing to argue, as industry did, that higher community environmental standards should wait for technology to advance so as to make them feasible to implement; it was another to ensure that progress would indeed take place.

Much current environmental technology was devoted to treating rather than preventing pollution. Consequently environmentalists pressed for changes in industrial processes so as to reduce pollution in the first place. This came about most rapidly in water quality. Environmental regulations sought to reduce the total amount of water consumed, to extract and reuse polluting materials, and to develop processes that would produce less waste. Their views were echoed in the "Pollution Prevention Pays" program of the 3M Company described in an earlier chapter. Four questions guided that program: (1) Can the product be formulated with substitute, nonpolluting raw materials? (2) Can the process be changed? (3) Can the equipment be redesigned? (4) Can materials be recycled and reused?[9]

Environmentalists favored policies to require sources of pollution to install improved technology – "technology forcing" it was called. A given level of innovation was identified as a public objective, and industry was required to meet that goal within a specific period of time. In some cases incentives were provided to speed up technologies already under way; in other cases new technologies required new research. Could industry be required to accelerate innovations on the verge of practical application or to undertake more research so as to reach that level? Environmentalists felt that both approaches were justifiable. But while the courts were inclined to accept the first, they were not so friendly to the second. It seemed appropriate for society to require industry to move ahead those technologies that were clearly in the offing, but carrying out more fundamental research was beyond the obligations of private enterprise.[10]

Should less advanced firms be required to adopt technologies more advanced companies already had in place? The more advanced were thought of as model cases, more socially desirable in both environmental and product efficiency. Their practices should be extended to other plants as well. In 1976 when the EPA sought to establish an emissions standard for polyvinyl chloride, which had been discovered to be a liver carcinogen, it was found that several firms had fashioned simple technological changes to reduce exposure to workers by recovering and reusing escaping polyvinyl chloride gas. Once the regulation was in place most firms readily applied the new technology and found that the cost was covered by the savings from reusing gas formerly wasted.[11]

One might think of these efforts to speed up technological change as a matter of relationships among firms within a given industry. Each line of manufacturing comprised a range of technologies, from the most obsolete to the most modern. In each case there was a close connection between product efficiency and environmental efficiency. In the normal course of economic change the more obsolete plants would be closed and newer ones built. But firms seemed too prone to keep older plants operating. To environmentalists all this constituted a roadblock to change. If private entrepreneurs could not bring about more rapid innovation, public action was called for.

The Clean Water Act of 1972 provided that the pollution-control technology of those firms designated as the "average of the best" in each line of production should be applied in all plants in that category. The EPA investigated several hundred industry groups, categorized the range of equipment then in place from the most obsolete to the most modern, and selected the highest 10 percent of the range as the best. These were then considered to be exemplary plants the remaining 90 percent would follow. A standard thus was brought to bear on industry from within its own ranks.[12]

Environmental strategies were part of a growing critique of American industry that emphasized a lag in its technical creativity. Innovations to improve traditional types of productivity seemed to go hand in hand with process innovations to reduce pollution. Pressures from environmental demands on industry often provided the impetus by means of which industrial processes as a whole could be examined and technical innovations that included product as well as environmental efficiencies could be brought about.

New Scientific Knowledge

Environmentalists sought to generate new scientific knowledge as well as new technologies. The overriding experience in environmental science was the degree to which much of what one wished to understand was not yet known. Each advance in knowledge seemed to expand what was not known more rapidly than it did what was known; society seemed to be faced with escalating ignorance, adding a constant frontier aspect to almost every facet of environmental science.

The resulting strain on scientific resources could be observed in the choices not to pursue inquiry. For example, few resources were allocated to the study of behavorial toxicology or the effects on the central nervous system of inhaling polluted air. Research on soil mycorrhizae and soil biogeochemical relationships was carried out more extensively in Europe than in the United States. Of funds available for research in forestry, water resources, and in the federal sea grant program, little was devoted to the study of aesthetic values and aesthetic resources.[13]

Data to describe more general environmental conditions and to chart changes were extremely limited. The most extensive descriptions of resources were those of minerals and water quantity that had been completed over the years through federal and state geological and hydrological surveys. Topographical mapping carried out by the U.S. Geological Survey was completed only in the 1960s, and the more detailed $7\frac{1}{2}$-minute maps took even longer. There were few organized programs to conduct biological surveys of plants and animals, most of which were carried out by the states – Ohio and Illinois were examples – rather than by the federal government. Although considerable resources had been put into forest surveys, they were confined almost solely to a few commercial species; by the late 1970s these surveys were revised not by direct observation but by extrapolations from earlier surveys on the ground or from aerial mapping.[14]

Water- and air-quality data was far from satisfactory. The federal air-quality program had promoted monitoring, but the limited number of stations produced at best only general trend data and failed to describe the quality of air in most communities. In the countryside there was almost no monitoring except of conditions immediately surrounding major sources. Here it was impossible to describe trends; the most that could be said from measurements was that air quality "met the standards."[15]

Water-quality information was more extensive. Yet even in this case state and federal agencies measured a small number of chemical, biological, and physical characteristics of streams at only a few sites. Because the water quality of a given stream varied along its course, measurement in one segment was inadequate to describe the characteristics in another. High-quality waters were monitored more effectively than high-quality air because of the long-standing interest of fishermen in cold-water streams of high oxygen content.

Public health long had been described in terms of death rates because of the nineteenth-century innovation that physicians be required to record the cause of death on death certificates. Because contagious diseases were a threat to the entire community, public-health departments came to require that these be reported. But facts were sparse on newer chronic health problems associated with environmental causes. Cancer registries that charted the incidence of cancer rather than deaths from that illness were not widely used. Health statistics other than those pertaining to contagious disease could be gathered through physicians and hospitals, but only when individuals had sought out their services.[16]

In the absence of direct data many devices were used to infer general conditions of public health, such as emergency admissions to hospitals or absences of pupils and workers during pollution episodes. But this provided only a minimum of desired information. When health authorities were asked to determine whether a community was endangered by a toxic chemical dump, little could be said because of the lack of information about the "normal" incidence of miscarriages, childhood abnormalities, chronic infections, immune system impairments, chronic headaches, or minor ailments. These effects were readily noticed by those who felt that their health had been adversely affected, but inadequate data made it difficult to verify their claims.

Environmental demands pushed forward the frontiers of scientific judgment as well as of research and monitoring. It was one thing to conduct an experiment effectively. But to assess the overall meaning of many experiments and statistical studies, often carried out with different methods, different subjects, and in different circumstances, required quite different skills. Such assessments gave rise to much disagreement. This was especially true at the forefront of science, where measurements were finer and not yet as reliable, the statistical analyses were suggestive rather than conclusive, and the pertinent factors had not been separated as precisely as one might want.

Some scientists were prone to state that a particular threat presented "absolutely no harm" and at the same time to belittle those who thought otherwise. Others were willing to make tentative judgments on the order of "reasonable anticipation of harm." A third group preferred to avoid making any assessments at all. These varied responses to the demands for scientific conclusions to undergird environmental policies often became the most crucial aspect of public environmental debate.

Categories of Empirical Analysis

The relationship between the new and the old in empirical inquiry often can be identified in terms of the different kinds and categories of data each emphasizes. The new factor is often a new reality one observes or a new way of organizing familiar information into new categories. Both the new data and the new mode of organization then enable one to pose new questions and employ new types of analysis. So it was with environmental affairs.

Past analytical categories in resource and environmental affairs had emerged around problems of material development and hence were not appropriate to newer environmental description and analysis. The challenge to the environmental scientist was how to advance new ways of thinking in the midst of old.

In years past, the usefulness of a technology had been determined primarily in terms of whether it reduced labor costs; the term "productivity" referred to production per worker. Environmentalists sought to stress efficiency in the use of resources other than labor; hence there was energy productivity, its output for each unit of input, or the productivity of water. Waste productivity could be measured as well. This new measure of technological usefulness was the degree to which it decreased the output of waste per unit of input as well as increased the output of commodities. If new technologies in steel production required more water per unit of production for cooling and hence produced more waste, they were less efficient.[17]

Environmentalists sought to analyze waste in relation to the receiving space of air, water, and land. These resources were seen not as some open-ended "out there" but as a finite system that could easily become saturated. Air-quality benefits from improved mileage and car performance could readily be nullified by an increasing number of cars and mileage because of the fixed space into which pollution was emitted. Pollution productivity should be thought of not in terms of the sources of emission but of the receiving environment.

Land-use classifications had evolved to describe different types of developed areas. Agricultural censuses described land as productive or unproductive. The Soil Conservation Service classified lands in terms of levels of soil productivity, leaving the remainder as "unproductive." To these production-oriented systems of classification environmentalists sought to add descriptive categories that reflected environmental land values: wilderness, wild areas, natural areas, open spaces, green spaces, pastoral rivers, scenic rivers.

Those who formulated descriptions of resources, such as statisticians and resource managers, had difficulty in thinking about resources in newer environmental ways. There was a tendency to use "noncategories," that is, terms that described what people and resources were not rather than what they were. Residents of the countryside who came not to farm but to enjoy an environment of higher quality were described in the census as a "nonfarm" population. Those who purchased woodlands for their environmental quality were referred to by professional foresters as "nonfarm, nonindustrial woodlot owners." Appreciative users of wildlife were described as "nongame" users. In the state of Washington, where state-owned forestlands were managed primarily for income-producing objectives, uses such as recreation and wildlife observation were described as "nonforest" uses. Those who used such terms found it so difficult to incorporate new facts into older ways of thinking that only a "noncategory" term seemed appropriate.

The Ecological Perspective

From the Mid-1960s on, ecology as a scientific discipline became central in environmental inquiry, and much of its perspective was adopted and adapted by environmentalists in their views as to what kinds of scientific knowledge and technologies should be advanced. Many were intrigued aesthetically and intellectually by nature and thus were drawn into larger ideas about biological communities and the relationships among the varied aspects of the natural world. Hence their support for ecology as a scientific discipline and their attempt to transfer ecological knowledge into a wider range of environmental issues.[18]

One such idea was that of natural cycles. There were chemical cycles, the flow of carbon dioxide or lead, geological cycles, the flow of water from rainfall to runoff to evaporation, nutrient cycles, the flow of nitrogen or potassium, or the more limited segments of cycles such as the food chain. Environmentalists argued that small-scale recycling techniques were much to be preferred to larger-scale ones. Household garbage, for example, should be recycled on the premises by means of composting rather than disposed of through large-scale incinerators or distant landfills. Large-scale transfers of water through channelization or sewage collector systems should be replaced by small-scale transfer technologies. Large-loop mechanical cycles depended on energy simply to transport materials over greater distances; as the price of energy rose, they became increasingly costly. To bring farm products closer to the consumer through local markets would be far cheaper than to transport them across the nation.[19]

Another popular ecological concept was the notion of carrying capacity, namely, that a biological system can continue to function in its "normal" state only when the loads on it are limited. One spoke of the way external influences on ecological systems, such as extremes of rainfall or temperature, limited their capacity or the way pollutants wiped out aquatic species and left only those that could tolerate the stress.[20]

Stressed ecosystems resulted in undesirable changes in environmental conditions. Pollution destroyed aquatic life and hence fishing; off-road vehicles and overuse of wilderness camp sites caused soil erosion; overgrazing changed plant life in dryland areas and reduced the quality of the forage. Indicator species such as lichens in the cities or birds reduced in population by pesticides often reflected the health of the larger ecosystem. Environmentalists argued that these were early warning signals that humans were seriously endangering the biological foundations on which sustained life depended.[21]

Environmentalists extended the concept of carrying capacity far beyond these ecological origins. Carrying capacity was psychological as well as biological; there was a limit to the number of people who could use a given area, and beyond that limit the area's appeal would be lost. One spoke of the carrying capacity of wilderness and of outdoor recreation generally or of the fact that motorized vehicles placed greater stress on an area by driving out nonmotorized users.

Biological diversity was a third ecological concept important in environmental inquiry. Variation in species was characteristic of the biological world. But intensive management in agriculture and forestry destroyed competing vegetation so as to maximize the growth of specific target species. Much intensive management eliminated diversity in favor of homogeneity. Environmentalists advocated methods that would favor diversity as an alternative.

The customary manner in which broad-based pesticides were used, for example, did not take into account the intricate biological relationships between predators and prey, the biological niches each occupied, and the biological vacuum that was left when both were destroyed, thereby enabling surviving species to proliferate. Integrated pest management, the alternative pest-control system favored by environmentalists, combined the use of natural predators with strategic application of pesticides.[22]

Biological diversity came to be emphasized in environmental forest policy. Foresters had long concentrated their attention on commercially valuable trees rather than diverse plant species and their interrelationships. Environmentalists observed far greater diversity in forests. They objected as foresters restricted competing vegetation in order to enhance the growth of commercial trees or sought to convert forests from native hardwoods to commercially more valuable softwoods. In the 1976 Forest Management Act they obtained a provision that species diversity should become an objective of forest planning and management.[23]

Environmentalists tended to view many issues as conflicts between an ecological and a mechanical view of resources. Many tendencies in science and technology seemed to emphasize concepts that entailed uniformities in ever larger systems. When used to describe or manage biological life, these concepts distorted and disrupted it. Ecological management highlighted the more intricate and diverse characteristics of the natural world. It called for more rather than less knowledge. Hence integrated pest management demanded more precise pinpointing of the use of pesticides, and this in turn required the use of trained scouts who went into the fields daily to measure pest populations and provided information to guide control.

Alternative Ways of Living

New life-styles deeply affected American society in the 1960s and 1970s. Many of these had environmental implications that were reflected in the outpouring of books and periodicals devoted to the subject. Bookstores from Washington, D.C., and Pittsburgh to Seattle, from Maine and the upper peninsula of Michigan to Atlanta and Los Angeles, had well-stocked paperback sections on preventive health care and well-being, on living in harmony with nature, on the appreciation of wild animals and wild places, on the desirability of living lightly on the earth, and on autonomy and self-help.

A number of periodicals also expressed these interests. *Prevention* emphasized prevention rather than cure in health matters and set the stage for the later stress on wellness and physical fitness. *Organic Gardening* led many Americans into new ways of growing produce. *Mother Earth News,* with almost 700,000 subscribers by 1985, became the main "how-to" magazine for those who had become interested in the self-help approach, and *Co-evolution Quarterly* expressed a philosophy of living in harmony with nature. New magazines such as *New Age* and *New Roots* gave these tendencies regional flavors. There were magazines about physical fitness and vegetarianism, windmills and solar power, and the spiritual relationships between human beings and nature.[24]

Such publications indicated the degree to which environmental values had permeated American society, as did their relevance for the private market economy. Hardly a new-age magazine failed to reflect, in its advertising, new profit-making ventures: health foods ranging from vitamins to whole wheat flour, solar and windmill hardware, materials for organic gardening, "how-to" books for homesteaders, and field guides to birds, plants, and animals. Stimulated by the interests of environmental consumers, all these new products helped to shape the environmental economy.

Health and Well-being

Many Americans had long argued that the nation's medical system was geared to making sick people well rather than to preventing sickness in the first place. On many occasions in the 1960s leaders of the medical profession had stressed the need for a preventive approach to health. This reflected changing public attitudes already expressed in more popular media. But it was not until 1979 that the U.S. surgeon general issued a comprehensive report on preventive medicine, *Healthy People: The Surgeon General's Report on Health Promotion and Disease Prevention.*[25]

By this time, however, the public interest in health matters had moved to still another stage, well-being rather than prevention, which marked the surgeon general's report as behind rather than in the forefront of changing attitudes. The 1979 report defined health goals exclusively in terms of reducing death rates. Exercise was recommended primarily as protection against fatal heart attacks, and warnings were issued against smoking, in order to prevent death from lung cancer. But to the general public the central issue that prompted day-to-day attention to health matters was wellness. Most Americans below the age of sixty-five were not faced with imminent death. More important was the ability to function daily at one's highest mental and physical potential on the job and in leisure activities.[26]

Many new books and periodicals on health reflected these concerns: books about vitamins; jogging, physical fitness, and daily exercise; vegetarian diets; purer drinking water; and cleaner air. Food and nutrition constituted a major element of the concern for wellness. In the 1950s Adelle Davis had written cookbooks with this slant: *Let's Have Healthy Children* and *Let's Eat Right to Keep Fit.* They were followed by others such as *Laurel's Kitchen,* a "guide to cooking . . . natural foods," published in 1976. Wellness advocates applauded as the Department of Agriculture, under Secretary Robert Berglund during the Carter administration, began to emphasize nutrition as well as food production. Among nutrition professionals a shift was under way from the traditional focus on minimum daily requirements to prevent sickness to what was required to sustain optimal daily fitness. The resulting tension between the old and the new in nutrition science generated considerable political controversy over food policy.[27]

The nutritional aspects of the wellness movement involved subtle but significant wider implications. Whereas one might feel that the world of political and economic institutions was far beyond one's power to influence, it was quite feasible to have considerable control over what one ate and drank. This was the larger meaning of self-discipline in controlling exercise and diet. There was also a connection between the natural-foods movement and the attack on food additives and other cancer-causing substances in food. One could avoid toxic pollutants by one's choices of food and drink. One could read about, understand, and put into practice changes in nutrition as an act of autonomy and personal political control when larger institutions could not respond.[28]

Alternative Technologies

Alternative environmental life-styles called for alternative technologies. The term "appropriate technology" referred to smaller and less complex machines in developing countries in contrast with the larger-scale technologies of the advanced industrial societies. In the United States the term "alternative technology" was also used to refer to technologies that were smaller, more human in scale, simpler, and more directly understandable, and more subject to individual organization and management. These were alternatives not just to machines of massive size and scale but also to massive techniques of mobilizing knowledge and organizing its application.[29]

Alternative technologies appeared in various forms and places. There was the attempt to organize household activities around solar energy, composting to utilize waste, and organic gardening. The Fallarones Institute in San Francisco developed an integral urban house to demonstrate varied household technologies that could be worked out in close connection with one another. In Connecticut the New Alchemy Institute experimented in integrated fashion with a variety of small homestead techniques ranging from windmills and solar energy to organic production and greenhouses. Many urban and rural homeowners used attached solar greenhouses as a source of warm air and of food and natural amenities.[30]

The most striking technological aspect of all this was not so much the mechanical devices themselves as the kinds of knowledge and management they implied. Alternative technologies involved attempts to shift the acquisition and application of knowledge away from large-scale systems to more individual human endeavors. They fostered the acquisition of knowledge not through professional specialists but through self-education and personal experience.[31]

For many people knowledge was becoming increasingly esoteric. Even though one knew elementary statistics and calculus, or could use computers, the inner life of increasingly refined mathematics seemed more and more remote. For most people the real world was more immediate, a matter of direct experience and perception, often visually comprehended. The simplicity of alternative technology was appealing for these reasons. One was reminded once again of the perception that lay behind the mechanical innovations of the Yankee tinkerers of the early nineteenth century.

Alternative technology also allowed for a more human scale in design and organization. The design of a home around new forms of energy or in new relationships with natural forces, such as underground houses, provided possibilities. It was challenging to use the imagination to put physical objects and natural forces together in new ways. To design an entire homestead called for knowledge about a wide range of biological and geological factors along with machines appropriate to the scale of a home-sized management system. It is no wonder that a considerable amount of alternative technology grew up around the design and organization of housing and the attempt to integrate work, home, and consumption.

Two themes ran through these ideas about alternative life and work. The first was autonomy, the search for personal and family independence to counteract the dependence that was integral to the large-scale systems in which much modern work was organized. Alternative technologies enabled individuals to search for knowledge independently and increased the freedom to organize one's work, home, and play on one's own terms. These ventures in autonomy in creativity contrasted sharply with trends in organization, which often subordinated the individual to the larger enterprise.

The other theme was flexibility. Individual creativity required circumstances that fostered variety and change. Many feared the modern system of corporate and governmental organization because one could not readily change one's mode of work or even what one thought and how one lived. If it was not easy to make new choices about work, there were far more options in recreation, leisure, home, and life-style. Autonomy and flexibility went hand in hand as major elements in the search for greater personal creativity on the consumer rather than the producer side of life.

Living Lightly on the Earth

A third aspect of alternative life-styles was the exploration of attempts to "live lightly on the earth," to maintain a simpler life with fewer material possessions. Modern society placed far too great a burden on the natural systems that sustained it, and only through changes in personal consumption could that load be lightened.[32]

Although individual responses to this concern varied considerably, the general notion of a "conserver society" as the wave of the future reflected widespread interest in personal habits of living. One could live more simply by purchasing cars and clothes that did not involve style changes. Especially significant to environmentalists were the reaction against the throwaway mentality and the attempt to use products longer, to recycle them and to reduce the amount of discarded household belongings. If carried out by enough people, so the argument went, there would be less pressure on limited resources.[33]

Living more lightly on the earth also involved consumer choices that were more natural. Ecologist consumers urged the use of natural products. This was implicit in the natural-foods movement as well as in the attempt to avoid toxic chemicals that did not exist in nature. There was an emphasis on natural cotton, woolen, and linen fabrics instead of synthetic cloth, on natural dyes, on organic rather than commercial fertilizer, on natural sources of fuel, and on houses of natural stone and earth materials.

Both of these themes of living more lightly on the earth and in a manner more compatible with it came together in outdoor recreation preferences for self-propelled activities such as hiking, backpacking, sailing, and cross-country skiing. These symbolized a more intimate and personal relationship with nature rather than an attempt to dominate it. Motorized vehicles on both water and land, on the other hand, typified human arrogance in attempting to overpower nature. The sound of motors in forests and on lakes seemed to defy nature with human contempt. Self-propelled activities were less burdensome on the environment. If one ranked various recreational activities in terms of their energy consumption, both direct and embodied, sailboats and cross-country skiing were less demanding than motorized boats and downhill skiing, respectively; hiking and backpacking were the least demanding of all.

These attempts to define alternatives in the form of a conserver life-style took varied forms. Some tried to carve out a set of principles that would shape daily life fully and consistently. But this was difficult to do. Wood as a source of household heat also was a major source of pollution, often more harmful to human health than coal; automobiles were needed in decentralized rural life, and motorized equipment was popular in organic gardening and farming. Lightweight materials such as aluminum and plastics, more energy intensive, made self-propelled recreation possible. Although one might not be able to attain perfect consistency, one could live in ways that were less environmentally demanding.

Some observers are inclined to argue that there was a close connection between these searches for alternative life-styles and the counterculture of the 1960s. But beyond a somewhat superficial similarity there were sharp differences. The counterculture emphasized personal expression in dress and speech, the use of drugs, and unconventional sexual behavior, whereas the search for alternative life-styles in the 1970s stressed self-discipline and the development of personal skills in order to organize life effectively. The former embodied a negative reaction; the latter was infused with a commitment to positive alternatives, the creation through personal learning and entrepreneurship of alternative institutions on a more human scale.

If the new life-style movement of the 1970s had any ideological affinity with larger streams of American culture, past or present, it was far more with the do-it-yourself style that ran from Yankee ingenuity of the early nineteenth century to the home-repair craftworkers of the twentieth.

Environmental Equity

Environmental ideas also involved matters of social equity. One issue was the distribution of environmental goods and services, which had long been confined to the more affluent but now were more widely available. More far reaching in implication was the distribution of goods and services amid resource limits and scarcity.

In years past, increases in consumer goods and services in American society had come initially at the upper levels of the income scale and then had been spread more widely. This was the case with the wringer washing machine, the gas range, the telephone, the automobile, the radio, and electric household appliances. Initially only the more affluent could afford such innovations, and they were often thought of as luxury items. So it was with environmental amenities. Enjoyment of the natural environment long was confined to the affluent few. Now in the Environmental Era an effort was made to extend these amenities more broadly.[34]

From its very beginning inequality had been prevalent in the United States. Despite vast increases in the average income and value of property owned, inequality persisted from decade to decade in about the same proportions. Economic growth within the private market seemed not to change the pattern, and neither did public policies that were developed from time to time to bring about a greater balance. Although the real income of all segments of society rose rapidly after World War II, the relative shares of each in the range from top to bottom changed hardly at all. It was argued often that environmental policies would restrict eco-

nomic growth and hence destroy the dream of economic equality. Yet over the course of American history the shares of the
increment always seemed to be distributed unequally. There was
no reason to believe that this pattern would not continue.[35]

Because growth would be hampered by increasingly limited
resources, traditional private-market pressures toward inequality
would be reinforced. One could well predict that infinitely growing
demand pressing upon limited supply would raise prices sharply
and make more limited goods and services available only to those
who could afford them. To let the private market run its course
with environmental goods and services amid the finite limits of
air, land, and water was to invite more inflation and transfer benefits from those who had less to those who had more.

Equity in amenities. Environmental amenities had long been distributed unequally. The more affluent had sought to live on the
fringes of the city away from the noise, polluted air, and congestion of the more densely settled parts. It was only in the mid-
twentieth century, with extensive ownership of automobiles, that
this separation of work and home became possible for a large
portion of the population. Similarly, the more affluent early searched
out areas of high natural amenities in the countryside and the
wildlands for summer homes, estates, hunting and fishing grounds,
and water recreation.[36]

In contrast to these private natural amenities were the public
lands, a massive resource legally accessible to all. The egalitarian character of these lands is so much assumed by the American people that it is often overlooked. By the mid-twentieth century these lands had had a long tradition as a public resource. In
the early decades of the country's history, sale had been the predominant policy, but as the nineteenth century progressed a new
view arose that they had value as public assets with permanent
public management. Again and again transfer to private ownership was rejected in favor of public management for public objectives. In each case the choice involved reassertions that public
ownership would provide opportunity for use by a far broader
sector of American society than would private ownership.[37]

Equality of access to the public lands, parks and forests, wildlife refuges, and the rest of the public domain came to be more

clearly defined as the contrast with privately owned natural amenities became clear. Private land along lakes and rivers with scenic views or in wooded and mountainous areas was purchased for its amenities; prices rose and ownership was increasingly confined to the more affluent. The public lands, however, remained widely accessible for outdoor activities. Fear that private acquisition would exclude the public from formerly accessible areas, in fact, was the primary reason why people of the western states during the Reagan administration rejected the transfer of federal public lands to either the states or private owners.[38]

Public lands increased the value of surrounding private lands. Around every national and state park, forest, and game refuge there came to be private lands whose value was enhanced by their location. Real estate dealers advertised such facts to attract purchasers, and buyers in turn readily accepted the higher prices. The public lands could be thought of as an oasis of common property that constituted an equally important oasis of equity in contrast to private ownership, which led to inequality in the distribution of amenities.

The cost of travel was the main factor in preventing greater use of the public lands by the less affluent. National forests and parks drew both nearby and distant users. Those who lived more closely represented a broader cross-section of income levels than did those from other parts of the nation. This inequality of access was difficult to correct, for whereas most public lands were in the West, the population was primarily in the East. This often stimulated a drive to increase the acreage of the eastern public lands.

Environmentalists also pressed other amenity equity issues. There was, for example, an effort to create greater access to coastal shorelines for the public in the face of continual pressure from private owners to exclude them. There also was the problem of private encroachment on the Appalachian Trail by new owners who bought land adjacent to it and sought to close it to public access; this led to the drive for federal purchase of a public right of way along the length of the trail.[39]

The most difficult access problem, however, involved the less affluent in the cities, for whom the cost of travel to the outdoors was often prohibitive. Environmentalists sought to provide opportunities for hiking and camping for inner-city youth, environmental education centers to bring urban children to the outdoors for several weeks, much akin to the earlier fresh-air funds, and programs to increase access to urban waterfront recreation.[40]

In thinking about these matters there was much confusion between issues of equity and those of consumer preference. The more deep-seated tension was between the older values involved in older forms of consumption and the newer values associated with the newer forms. Within each of these, in turn, there were problems of equity.

Forest policy reflected this confusion. Environmental opponents often referred to the desire to protect forests for their amenity values as elitist with the implication that only a few wished to use the forest for that purpose. Its use for wood represented a more equitable distribution. Yet many wood commodities were used by only a few. High-quality hardwoods, such as walnut and black cherry, were so labeled because they were used for high-priced veneered furniture. Lumber for home construction was used more extensively for more expensive dwellings in contrast with lower-cost housing, which tended to use more nonwood materials. Use of the public forest as an environment for recreation was far more egalitarian.[41]

Equity in pollution control. Among those who faced environmental pollution the more affluent could afford to live in a more environmentally acceptable area or spend vacations in more desirable locations. But the less well off could not. The cost of buying property elsewhere might persuade one to continue to live near the noise, heat, and smoke of a factory or a newly discovered waste dump. If one had purchased a home near an airport, the newer and noisier aircraft might lead to the desire to move, but the new environmental burden lowered the value of the house and made escape financially less possible. Residents of Love Canal who discovered that they were threatened by the nearby toxic-waste dump could not afford to move, because their houses could not be sold at any price.[42]

Since most people could not escape environmental pollution, equitable action required that the commons be shaped to be less harmful. Environmentalists sought to enable all in the city to enjoy a higher-quality environment where they were. Frequently the urban poor were most likely to bear the burden of air pollution because sinks of sulfur dioxide or carbon monoxide were worst in low-income housing areas; and it was the urban poor who were especially subject to harm from lead in paint or corrosion from older lead water pipes. Improving the health of people in these areas depended on improving the environment of the entire community.

Much of the historic drive to improve public health had involved such shared dangers. Infectious diseases knew no class or residential boundaries; epidemics were a threat to all. Hence both polluted water supplies and urban waste were considered public problems that required public rather than private action. Such views underlay much of the movement for environmental protection in the 1960s and 1970s.

Public action was often frustrated by the lethargy of the less affluent, who were often far less interested in the very environmental conditions others considered a threat. In the early 1970s student environmental enthusiasts affected by the Earth Day fervor in the colleges and universities had high hopes that they might bring environmental benefits to the urban poor. They developed the view that they should become advocates for the poor when the poor did not take action on their own. But such strategies were ineffective. Successful urban environmental action seemed to require affluence, interest, awareness, and knowledge that rested on values and skills not widely present in low-income urban areas.

In toxic-chemical issues collective protective action depended on a relatively high degree of awareness and knowledge about substances that might be almost anywhere. In such circumstances the most important factor in environmental equity was the ability to know what might be threatening so that one could act. Those who were adversely affected often considered that they had been deprived of the right to know. Equity was a matter not only of benefits but also of power and control. Environmentalists threw their weight heavily on the side of equity of access to information about potential environmental harm.

Those exposed to newly discovered toxic threats could readily feel that neither they nor their neighbors were responsible for it.

The threats were the results of actions not by members of the community at large but by a few people in industry. It seemed more than equitable to require offending sources both to clean up the problems they had created and to refrain from causing similar problems in the future. As the sense of injustice about being subjected to such threats grew, so did the frustration over both the unfairness of the circumstance and the inequity in the power to correct it.

Equity amid limits. Environmental equity also raised the question of who would benefit in the face of limited resources. Those who promoted rapid material growth avoided this problem by assuming that growth would automatically eliminate inequities. But at best, growth simply perpetuated past imbalances or, in the case of limited resources, created greater ones. Resource shortages translated into inflation. Would the brunt of higher prices be borne equitably?

The issue was sharply drawn in energy matters because environmentalists opposed policies that would hold energy prices below the "free market" value and favored those that would permit them to rise. Wasteful energy consumption, they argued, resulted from prices that were far too low. Only if the cost were raised would consumers use energy more efficiently.

The more affluent used more energy per capita, wasted more of it, and thus, it could be argued, should bear the main burden of higher prices. But higher prices would also burden the poor who used far less energy but for whom the energy component of necessities was a greater proportional drain on their income. Environmentalists proposed a ceiling on energy prices for necessities in household consumption. Beyond that level, the private-market price should be permitted to rise without restraint.

Rationing was another environmental approach to the distribution of scarce resources; this was applied mainly to goods and services on public lands and waters. Hunting and fishing had long been closely regulated by the state, which eliminated much of the private market in fish and game. Hunting and fishing required a license and were confined to designated times of the year and to limited numbers of certain species and sexes. These restrictions were enforced by fish and game wardens. Initially this system of rationing met serious objections from sportsmen, but over the years it became accepted as sound practice because of the discrepancy between growing demands and the limited supplies. It seemed an equitable way of dealing with the limits to growth.

Similar policies were applied to the use of wilderness areas. When heavy use damaged hiking trails or degraded the wilderness experience of solitude, forest and park agencies established a permit and rationing system. When canoeists became too numerous on streams so that they disturbed fishermen as well as other canoeists, their numbers, too, were restricted. When cattle and sheep placed too heavy a burden on western grazing lands, there were attempts to ration use by limiting numbers. Rationing in these cases, it was argued, accomplished environmental objectives far more effectively than did the free market.

To environmentalists equity also involved the impact of decisions about the use of air, land, and water on future generations. The private market did not seem to be an effective device for restricting current in favor of future use. If action taken today could never be reversed, it constituted too heavy a burden on generations to come. The conversion of undeveloped to developed lands would deny future generations the benefits of natural areas. Restraints should be placed on population growth to ensure the availability of limited resources to those in the future. Some environmental hazards threatened children and their children through genetic damage.[43]

Environmental ideas about alternative ways of living and equity in the distribution of goods and services challenged existing ways of thought. The large-scale private and public institutions of modern society had become so removed from the notion of individual and community autonomy, from the search for wellness rather than cure, and from the exploration of reduced consumption levels that they hardly knew how to respond. At the same time, the private economy had for so long generated and sustained persistent inequality through rapid economic growth that it was difficult to modify those patterns by public action. Large-scale centralized management was based on inequalities in benefits and political power; to its leaders this was the natural order of things – it had always been so and would continue to be so.

Individual and community autonomy and individual knowledge,

management, and enterprise were tendencies of long standing in the American past. It was the large-scale institution in twentieth-century American society that constituted the new, revolutionary, and transforming force. Almost every facet of this force tended to destroy the American past and to replace it with new technical systems of massive organization and centralized control. While environmentalists affirmed the importance of new consumer values in the advanced industrial society, they also promoted the older values of self-reliance and community autonomy. Such values and practices were now thought of as radical by many institutional leaders who had fashioned a new and different economic and political order.

The Environmental Economy

Environmentalists frequently dealt with matters that were central to the thinking of economists: human wants and needs and how to meet them when resources are scarce. Environmental analysis was economic analysis, but existing forms of economic analysis did not offer environmentalists readily available ideas for thinking through the economic implications of their views. Hence they set about fashioning their own ideas about the new environmental economy.[44]

Economics had been concerned primarily with production, what it involved, and how it came to be distributed in the form of goods and services. Most past economic critiques had formulated different theories as to who created the value in production and who should benefit from it. Environmental inquiry started more from the world of consumption, of the new needs and wants within the advanced economy. It stressed the demand for intangibles, the meaning of goods and services amid changing values, and the limits of physical resources. Environmental economic analysis thus had little direct connection with earlier critiques.[45]

Economists had long subdivided the economy into types of production to understand it in greater detail: the extractive, manufacturing, and service sectors. But to delve into the advanced economy of the late twentieth century required categories based on consumption. One could identify the health economy, the recreational economy, the leisure economy, the arts and crafts economy, and the environmental economy as distinct clusters of consuming activity that now drove the economic order. Market surveys conducted since the 1920s distinguished the different products and services consumed by people of different ages, occupations and incomes, ethnic and religious backgrounds, rural or urban places of residence, and regions of the nation. Here was a perspective on the economy that started from consumption rather than production. Yet these studies remained largely unused by those who sought to analyze the workings of the economy.[46]

Environmentalists were especially insistent that intangible experiences should be included in economic analysis: health, physical fitness, more pleasant air and water, the quiet of more natural surroundings. These were at the heart of environmental affairs, but economists did not give them adequate consideration unless they could be bought and sold in the market. Some economists even seemed to argue that such matters were less real, less useful, and therefore less legitimate than more conventional goods and services. They tended to distinguish between human needs and human wants, arguing that the more traditional commodities and services served needs, whereas environmental values were only wants, which were dispensable. The primary task of environmentalists was to establish the legitimacy in economic analysis of the consumer values they stressed.[47]

By the 1970s environmental wants and needs had become an integral part of the American economy. A considerable portion of jobs and shares in the gross national product were the results of environmental consumption. One could identify the amount that came from federal, state, and local environmental programs such as sewer construction or public-land management. But much of the new environmental demand was expressed in the private economy: expenditures for recreational equipment, facilities, transportation, and accommodation; private housing with pleasant surroundings and forested land; better food and cleaner water; equipment for new methods of organic gardening and farming; physical fitness and wellness services; and the environmental-quality component of necessities and conveniences.

New consumer factors in the economy altered the meaning of economic growth. That term had long been confined to price-and-market transactions to which a specific number could be attached. But increased environmental goods and services, such as wilderness, cleaner workplaces, and better health, were as much a part of economic growth as the more traditional goods and services and an important element of the gross national product. Some economists began to argue that the concept of national product should be scrapped in favor of one of national amenities so as to identify the full range of goods and services the public desired.[48]

Environmentalists also argued that the total value of national amenities should be calculated on a net rather than a gross basis. Conventional economic accounting included the cost of repairing damage as a benefit. Hence the greater the damage from automobile accidents and environmental pollution and the more extensive the repair of that damage, the higher the gross national product. A national accounting system that stressed total benefits would have to subtract these repair costs to give an accurate picture. Thus developed the concept of using net national amenities in national economic accounting rather than the more conventional gross national product. Such an approach would give even sharper focus to the idea that economic analysis should start from consumption rather than production and that the objectives of economic activity should be not just throughput but the enhancement of national benefits.

Costs and Benefits

The economic analysis of environmental policies factored in both costs and benefits. Decision makers demanded that methods be devised to identify those costs and benefits so as to facilitate choices. This approach was routine in economic analysis. Economists were fundamentally accountants, experts in adding up the income and the outgo, in drawing up the balance sheet. But they often omitted environmental values because they were intangible and difficult to measure. Environmentalists sought new modes of analysis that would more fully take into account the environmental sector of the nation's economy.

Conventional economists agreed with one major element of environmental cost-benefit analysis. Polluters, environmentalists argued, imposed on the large society damage that required others to assume the costs of repair. These were called external costs; that is, they were external to the firm that created the pollution. These social costs should be internalized; they should be borne by the source of the pollution and incorporated into products as a cost to those who purchased them. Much conventional economic analysis of environmental matters was devoted to devising ways and means of internalizing these social costs.

Beyond this, however, environmentalists found little conventional economic analysis that "accounted for" environmental values. Those values often were simply ignored as economic benefits, and environmental harm was minimized as an economic cost. Much of the problem was that economists could not work into their accounting systems factors to which numbers were not attached. But they were very slow in attempting to quantify such values so that they could be included. They were often inclined simply to dismiss environmental values as unimportant or to assert their importance in general and then ignore them in particular.[49]

The National Environmental Policy Act of 1969 (NEPA) attempted to cope with this difficulty by requiring each agency to devise methods of incorporating into its analyses nonquantifiable factors. But a decade later no agency had taken up the mandate. There was some effort to quantify previously nonquantified factors but none of consequence to devise methods of dealing with those that were nonquantifiable. And the Council on Environmental Quality, which supervised the implementation of NEPA, did not take steps to require the carrying out of that provision.[50]

During the 1960s many felt that environmental harm was readily ignored by agencies that sponsored development. Congress began to hear of cases in which federal agencies were destroying environmental assets associated with land and water without acknowledging it: wilderness areas, free-flowing streams, wildlife habitats purchased with federal funds, coastal wetlands. Agencies downplayed the alleged harm as minimal and argued that the proposed projects involved far greater benefit than they did possible environmental costs. But environmentalists insisted that these be brought fully into cost-benefit accounting.

Environmentalists believed, for example, that the cost-benefit analyses used by the Army Corps of Engineers favored water development to the detriment of environmental opportunities destroyed by dams. Although the corps was prone to increase the monetary value of recreational opportunities created by reservoirs ("flat-water recreation"), it was unwilling to identify the recreational value of free-flowing rivers that would be eliminated. There also was the case of flood-prone lands that were built on because they were supposedly protected by a reservoir. Even though they would be subject to future flooding and hence involve later costs, the corps considered the protected lands to be more valuable and contended that the increased value was, in their cost-benefit calculations, a project benefit.

Some economists who were sympathetic to environmental objectives attempted to quantify environmental amenities. At Resources for the Future, for example, John Krutilla undertook to quantify the economic value of wilderness. These analyses placed major emphasis on increasing scarcity of environmental amenities. Not many wild and scenic rivers or wilderness areas remained in the nation, and with each decade they would become even scarcer. At the same time, increased demand for them, in the face of limited supply, would increase their value.[51]

Environmentalists also sought to analyze costs and benefits in matters of health protection from pollution. They often spoke of the number of premature deaths that might be avoided. But they were not tempted, as were economists, to assign a dollar value to such lives. What seemed especially to be missing in such discussion were the costs of lowered levels of human performance, which might be caused by chronic exposures to low levels of pollutants.

What was the dollar value of children's IQs being lowered by three to five points apparently as a result of exposures to low levels of lead? It was estimated that for each lowered point of IQ performance there was a 1 percent reduction of lifetime earnings. From such low levels of exposure, not only to lead but to a variety of chemicals, the cost for each individual might be small, but it would be quite large for society as a whole. Such environmental implications for economic analysis emerged only slowly.[52]

The Burden of Risk

Closely related to the debate over costs and benefits was the issue of risk. A string of environmental episodes, some of small but others of large impact, identified the fact of risk. They also involved considerable controversy as to how risk should be dealt with.

Environmentalists argued that decisions that might entail risks should be postponed until more was known so that controls could be instituted to reduce them. The risk in nuclear energy required a moratorium on new plants until some of the effects were more fully determined. Toxic chemicals should not be marketed until their effects were more clearly understood. Those involved in development argued that they should be allowed to proceed pending further studies. Most presumed risk, they argued, was relatively small, and development thus could come first and protection based on more complete knowledge could come later. Nuclear power, for example, could readily go forward even when the details of nuclear-waste disposal had not yet been worked out.

The cost of risk, known or unknown, should be borne, according to environmentalists, not by the victim but by the source. Sources of risk were likely to urge that the burden of protection be transferred to those who were harmed. Workers should be required to wear protective clothing, such as respirators. Those who felt they were harmed should be required to bear the burden of proving harm rather than place responsibility on the source to prove lack of harm. In the case of hazardous-waste dumps the chemical companies argued that the general public should pay the cost of cleanup. It was society's problem, and the entire society should pay.

Environmentalists also applauded proposals to require those responsible for damage to carry the full economic burden of cleaning up or compensating victims. Thus arose the proposal to transfer the economic cost of flood damage from the general taxpayer, who was called upon to provide disaster relief, to the property owner through flood insurance. Also to be considered were potential damages from atomic energy accidents. The limited liability provisions of the Price-Anderson Act of 1957, renewed in 1966 and 1976, so environmentalists argued, should be removed.[53]

After-the-fact compensation for environmental damage came about through several major types of accidents. For example, public action was usually taken by governments to clean up oil spills from tanker accidents. But should the private tanker company not pay the cost? Liability suits might well be filed against the firm, but these were costly and often inconclusive. Hence there arose proposals for automatic liability in which the tanker company would be responsible for cleanup costs irrespective of proof of responsibility. Such a provision was included in the bill authorizing the Alaskan pipeline, which covered tankers transporting oil from Alaska to the West Coast through Canadian waters.

Each of the major toxic-chemical cases of the 1970s, such as those involving polychlorinated biphenyls (PCBs), polybrominated biphenyls (PBBs), and kepone, raised questions of considerable liability. The offending companies refused to bear the full cost of cleanup. In the Hudson River PCB case, for example, the General Electric Company agreed to pay part of the cost of scientific investigation into the problem but not the cost of reducing the long-term harm caused by exudation of the chemical from bottom sediments, a cost estimated to reach at least $200 million. Such issues demonstrated the continuing practice of transferring the costs of both unknown risk and actual harm to victims rather than to those responsible and the way in which the public rather than the source often ended up paying for the damage.

These controversies were often debated in terms of "false positives" and "false negatives." What if a given scientific study turned up no evidence of harm from a pollutant general knowledge held to be hazardous? Could one safely rely on that evidence to allow exposure? What if later studies demonstrated this negative evidence to be false? Or, to take the opposite case, what if positive evidence that the chemical was harmful later turned out to be false? What was the relative risk of taking action based on false negatives in contrast with false positives? The debate was lively because at low levels of concentration one study might turn out one way and later ones another.[54]

If one wished to be cautious in environmental strategy one could argue that such false negatives gave rise to an unwarranted confidence of safety and hence were risky. The social risk from making a mistake by regulating a chemical later found to be safe was far less than the mistake in not regulating one found to be harmful.

The Environmental-Impact Statement

Environmentalists sought to develop modes of accounting other than conventional cost-benefit methods. One of these, environmental-impact analysis (popularly known as an environmental-impact statement, or EIS), identified the environmental costs of development; the other, alternatives analysis, focused more precisely on positive environmental benefits. The impact statement highlighted environmental concerns in negative fashion as environmental costs. But alternatives analysis focused more on positive environmental objectives that might be enhanced.[55]

Environmental-impact analysis was fostered by the National Environmental Policy Act of 1969; each federal agency that proposed a project of major significance was required to draw up a statement assessing its environmental consequences. Which adverse effects could be avoided and which could not? What alternatives could be chosen that would lessen the harm? Through such analysis it was hoped the development agency would modify, perhaps abandon, the proposed project so as to make it more environmentally acceptable. The EIS emphasized factors that conventional economists did not usually try to incorporate into their calculations.

The EIS grew out of the widespread experience of many people with the adverse effects of large-scale development. In Florida, for example, the 1956 Bulkhead Act had stimulated considerable dredging and filling in coastal swamps and, in turn, had led to protests that valuable wetlands had been destroyed. In response the Florida legislature in 1967 passed the Randall Act, which required wetland developers to analyze the environmental impacts of their proposals before the state would approve them. Such an approach soon came to be called for at the federal level when some agencies, notably the U.S. Fish and Wildlife Service, felt that their programs were adversely affected by projects proposed by other agencies. They sought a device to register their objections within the inner circles of the administration. In its origin, the EIS involved a process of interagency review in which one agency could comment on the proposals of another. Often the process was already under way and the EIS merely extended and formalized it. The procedure was considered to be a device to smooth out interagency differences within the administration.[56]

The general climate of public environmental concern led to an expansion of the EIS from interagency review to public review. The U.S. Forest Service had taken up a more specialized procedure of public review in its wilderness decisions: a draft proposal, public comment, and a final proposal that supposedly took that comment into account. The Atomic Safety and Licensing Board had begun to include citizens as intervenors in hearings concerning construction and operating licenses for atomic power plants in 1969 and 1970 as the EIS process was being developed. And the courts were accepting the notion that members of the public could have standing to protect their environmental interest in court; citizens could sue an agency on the ground that its EIS did not fully consider environmental concerns.

Other options to check developmental agencies on behalf of environmental objectives were in the wind but not adopted. At times, for example, it was proposed that an environmental agency whose program was adversely affected by action taken by another would have the right to veto as well as to review and object. This was provided in a bill offered by Congressman John Dingell in which the Fish and Wildlife Service would be given authority to approve all dredge-and-fill permits issued by the Corps of Engineers. The proposal had so much support in Congress that the corps was prompted to accept a compromise "memorandum of agreement" in place of the legislation in which the Fish and Wildlife Service obtained more leverage in dredge-and-fill matters than mere review.

The EIS was given considerable support by the courts, which looked upon it as an aspect of administrative procedure. Such procedures should be open, fair, and not arbitrary. Although the courts were reluctant to become involved in substantive disputes between environmentalists and developmentalists, they were quite willing to supervise the EIS process by which trade-offs in objectives were made. Agencies, the courts held, would be required to consider all relevant factors in an interdisciplinary fashion and do so openly so that any reviewing body, whether legislatures, other agencies, the courts, or the public, could know fully the basis of choice. To do otherwise was arbitrary and a violation of procedural due process.

The EIS also had limitations for environmental economic analysis. The context in which the statement was presented seemed to reinforce a mode of thinking in which developmental considerations were dominant and environmental ones subordinate. This perspective made it relatively easy for the developmental agency to dismiss environmental factors as too difficult to identify, less worthy of systematic measurement, or impossible to quantify. NEPA had required agencies to devise ways and means of taking into account intangible or unquantifiable factors. But it would be difficult to identify a case in which this was done. Agencies were prone to deal with the problem, if at all, only by attempting to turn an unquantifiable factor into a quantifiable one by devising some scheme to attach numbers to it. But this only continued the practice of giving less importance to the unquantifiable.[57]

Environmental Goals

"Alternative objectives" analysis provided a way of thinking more precisely about environmental values in the first place, identifying them more clearly even though not quantitatively, and then devising schemes for enhancing them. A given action could enhance development or it could enhance environmental quality; to increase one might diminish the other. To give coordinate emphasis to both in one context would enable one to think in positive terms about each and to trade off goals rather than just lessen impacts.

The most systematic format of this kind was drawn up by the U.S. Water Resources Council in its "Principles and Standards" adopted in the early 1970s. These were to serve as guidelines for the formation of federal water policy. Two plans would be drawn up simultaneously, one to maximize economic development and the other to maximize environmental quality; neither would be subordinated to the other. Only after each plan was formulated would the impact of each one on the other be analyzed. Then came a third stage in which trade-offs were made between the objectives and final choices made.[58]

A similar approach was involved in "alternative environmental futures," a scheme in which decisions would be shaped by thinking not in terms of isolated current decisions that had impacts but in terms of futures one wished to bring into being. In this format environmental objectives could be given an emphasis more equal to developmental objectives. The approach usually involved the notion that the public as well as representatives of business firms and government would be given an opportunity to define the desired future. Though used at times by planners, this approach was rarely put into practice in formulating decisions. It seemed to provide far too great a role for environmental objectives to suit the environmental opposition.[59]

Environmentalists at times formulated alternatives of their own to development projects. In the case of the Tocks Island dam planned by the Corps of Engineers on the Middle Delaware River, they financed in 1975 an alternative proposal for a natural-environment park that played an important role in the decision by Congress to include the stretch in the nation's wild and scenic river system. The long controversy over construction of a dam on the Meramec River in Missouri during much of the 1960s and 1970s led local environmentalists to draw up an alternative plan, which helped to resolve the dispute.[60]

In these cases plans originating from outside the mission agency forced it to contend with alternatives it had not proposed. Some environmentalists suggested that the EIS process should provide regularly for such externally generated alternatives. But such a proposal was not taken up by the Council on Environmental Quality, which supervised the process.[61]

All these attempts to devise schemes to take environmental values into account met considerable resistance from developmental leaders. They objected to procedures that would highlight environmental factors and give them greater importance in economic analysis. Such salience, they feared, would stimulate public support for the values so identified and hence would generate and galvanize political forces that would be difficult to counteract. Developmental agencies wished to be free to make their own choices about where and how development would take place and not be hampered by environmental considerations formulated as either adverse effects or desirable objectives.

The Economy of the Future

Environmental economic analysis inevitably promoted views as to how the economy ought to operate, its goals and objectives, its role in identifying and filling human needs and wants. These did not take the form of well-defined theory but instead charted a rough direction from which existing economic activity was subject to evaluation. To environmentalists the prevailing economic order seemed to emphasize motion and throughput rather than usefulness, the short run rather than long-term sustainability, and financial objectives rather than technical efficiency in production.[62]

Utility was a conventional economic concept. But what were use and usefulness? This went to the heart of the conflict between environmental and developmental values. It was no wonder that the concept of "use" in multiple use aroused so much heated debate. Was a wilderness useful? Were recreational activities such as hunting, fishing, and hiking useful? To the environmentalist an undeveloped natural environment, a clear sky, a positive experience were major elements in utility. But those who organized production preferred the more traditional connotations. Antagonists in the environmental debate battled for control of the meaning of these terms.

Within the more traditional meaning of utility, moreover, environmentalists felt that the economy tolerated an enormous amount of waste. The objective seemed not to be usefulness but simply disposal in the market. If waste resulted, so be it. Environmentalists found water flowing through taps and drains to be reusable but not reused and thought this was fostered by pricing systems that encouraged waste; only one-third of the energy in most fuels was recaptured for use while the rest escaped as "waste heat"; high-quality energy was used for tasks that required only low quality; and residuals in household consumption and manufacturing were dumped into landfills rather than recycled and reused.[63]

To the conventional economist all this made sense because the economic system as economists understood it was working;

if such wasted resources were not recoverable for a profit then they were not economically wasted. But environmentalists refused to accept waste as an integral part of the economy. To the conventional economist the key lay in what made the system run as a system; price, capital, and profit were the main elements. But environmentalists emphasized the user and ultimate use. Seen from that vantage point the economy was found wanting.

A viable economy should be not only useful but sustainable. This implied a long-term vision. Although the time span of sustainability was not always specified in arguments, it was clear that it involved a multigenerational frame of mind. The needs of future generations had long been a staple in conservation as well as environmental thought. Long-term corporate strategy, on the other hand, was usually defined by the period over which capital investment would pay out. If investments returned a profit of 15 percent annually, the entire amount could be recouped in seven years. Some economic analysts reported that the thought time span for the contemporary corporate world was closer to three or four years. To environmentalists such an economy based on throughput and profitability was geared to concerns that differed markedly from the long-term sustainability of human needs.

Equally significant was the environmental emphasis on efficiency in resource production. Efficiency was as venerable a concept in economic affairs as was use, and it was subject to equally contentious interpretations. To the conventional economist, efficiency emphasized price considerations: Did the monetary value of output rise relative to the monetary value of input? But the environmentalist was more likely to be impressed with real rather than money efficiency – did real output rise in relation to real input? – and to emphasize productivity in terms of residuals as well as conventional commodities and services, that is, to ask whether the output of residuals fell relative to real input. Efficiency was a matter less of monetary costs and benefits than of the real value that came from production.

On such questions the environmentalist was far closer to the thinking of the engineer than that of the economist, for efficiency in resource use was more implicit in the engineering outlook than the money efficiency of conventional economic analysis. The engineer on the one hand and the financier and the marketing expert on the other had long been thought of as viewing the economy differently. Corporate entrepreneurs seemed simply to object to the costs of environmental controls, but engineers often looked upon residuals as an opportunity to redesign production systems to generate improvements in both commodity and environmental output. Process redesign to reduce and reuse industrial water, for example, was the direction in which production technology should move.

Environmental views about how the economy should perform in order to meet human needs were rarely expressed as well-ordered ideas. For the most part one must reconstruct them as inferences from argument and action. But researchers at the Solar Energy Research Institute attempted to outline them systematically and contrasted them with more conventional economic ideas. This analysis dealt primarily with views about energy but had more general implications. It contrasted the values of national energy policymakers for whom traditional economics was "a model within which . . . they wished to conceive all other values," and which, therefore, provided a more conventional economic view, with those of environmentalists who had written especially about energy policy.[64]

Energy policymakers, so the analysis went, emphasized growth, short-term results, employment, and cost effectiveness limited to quantifiable factors. Environmental analysts, on the other hand, stressed the appropriateness of economic activities to human ends, the long-term sustainability of resources, labor-intensive economic activities, and intergenerational equity. Policymakers stressed efficiency in the system as a whole as an end in itself, while solar-energy advocates thought of efficiency in terms of economic results for the individual. The solar-energy analysts emphasized personal independence, renewability of resources, smallness, informed participatory democracy, freedom, and independence. The study reinforced the notion that the environmental perspective of consumption and usefulness in filling varied human needs differed markedly from that of production associated with traditional activities of the larger economic system.

Ideas about the role of energy in the advanced industrial society constituted one of the more comprehensive ways in which environmentalists sought to give larger meaning and coherence to their concerns. Yet when the immediate energy crisis subsided in the early 1980s so did the role of energy in environmental ideas. Action rather than self-conscious thought was the dominant theme of environmental affairs. In this more pragmatic approach, in which larger meaning would remain implicit in daily affairs rather than be stated in formal ideas, environmentalists demonstrated the extent to which their concerns had moved to the center stage of American society and politics.

9　The Environmental Opposition

It would be surprising if such widespread changes in public policy did not generate opposition. And so they did – opposition that was continuous, increasingly vocal and determined, accelerating through the 1970s, and rising to a peak in the early 1980s. A coherent antienvironmental movement emerged with an overriding goal of restraining environmental political influence.[1]

In its simplest form this was a reaction by long-established commodity producers to a new consumer politics. Economic politics in America had long been dominated by controversies among organized producer groups in agriculture, labor, and business. Such struggles took place with little significant influence from the public in its role as buyers in the market. At times measures on behalf of consumers were taken, but in the face of opposition from producers these were short-lived.[2]

Environmental affairs reflected a new phase of consumer politics, one more extensive and successful than in previous years. It was part of the more general consumer activism that developed in the 1960s and 1970s. Environmentalists presented a serious challenge to agriculture, labor, and business, which turned on them with alarm. Although these groups made opportunistic adjustments to environmental objectives, their overall political

287

strategy was one of maximum feasible resistance and minimum feasible retreat.

Farmers and Environmental Issues

The farm response to urban recreationists. The search by urban people for outdoor recreation brought them into direct conflict with rural communities. The automobile enabled them to reach the countryside, to explore and enjoy its relatively natural environment. Their intrusion was resented. For almost two decades in its early history the automobile was looked on by those in the countryside as a "devil wagon in God's country." People who drove cars, primarily affluent urbanites who took weekend touring excursions away from the city, were thought of as effete intruders into a more peaceful and virtuous land. Not until the 1920s, when the Model T Ford brought the new contraption within the economic reach of rural people, did they make their peace with the automobile.

In increasing numbers town and city recreationists sought to hunt and fish, to boat, canoe, and hike in the countryside, all activities that clashed frequently with the customs, economic objectives, and pace of life of farm communities. To the visitor from the city the more open and natural lands served a special and fulfilling purpose. To the farmer that environment was commonplace and its natural values far less distinctive and impressive. The differences involved markedly divergent conceptions of the role and meaning of undeveloped lands. The nation's farms had been carved out of wildlands and the farming community had brought civilization to what formerly had been a wilderness. Yet environmentalists now emphasized the positive values of those very wild lands. It was difficult to reconcile such sharply divergent views.[3]

In rural communities there was much sympathy for public hunting programs. Many farmers were hunters; both as a source of food and as a symbol of personal independence, hunting fitted with rural needs and ideology. Farmers also looked on wild animals as pests to be exterminated. Yet, because wildlife was the common property of the general public through state ownership, no individuals, including farmers, could claim authority over it.

Wild animals prized for hunting roamed at will in private as well as public forests, and onto fields and farms.[4]

An especially serious conflict arose between farmers and environmentalists over attempts to protect wild animals. Some of these preyed on livestock or ate crops. In northern Minnesota attempts to protect gray wolves were opposed by farmers who maintained that they killed farm animals; on the western range sheep owners bitterly protested efforts to protect coyotes, which, they argued, were responsible for extensive destruction of lambs. In the East, rapid expansion of deer herds after the 1920s led to widespread complaints about crop damage by animals who left the forest to browse in fields.

Most states authorized farmers to kill marauding deer if they did, in fact, damage crops; such action had to be reported immediately and justified. Predation on farm animals was a different matter, since the farmer's response was either to hunt and destroy the predators or to use poisons to kill them. Environmentalists sought to restrict the first by, for example, prohibiting shooting from the air, and the second by banning the use of poisons, arguing that they destroyed not just the few target animals that might cause damage but other wildlife as well.[5]

Especially controversial were birds of prey, or raptors. Western ranchers looked on the eagle not as the nation's symbol but as a pest and sought to exterminate it by shooting. One major incident in the early 1970s in Wyoming led to arrests and a dramatic trial. Environmentalists saw the guilty as vicious and insensitive; ranchers considered them heroes.[6]

People in rural areas viewed the rapid increase in outdoor recreation with grave misgivings. Although they might like the economic benefits that accrued from those who purchased supplies and services in the countryside, they were not at all happy with some of the consequences of their presence. With such people came noise and congestion to disturb the peace and quiet of rural life, litter that was unsightly and increased the cost of solid-waste collection and disposal, intrusion on privacy, and persistent disregard of property rights. When use of the countryside was minimal, such impacts were limited, but the increase in numbers brought greatly increased conflict.[7]

The development of hiking trails through and near areas of

private property typified such problems. Initially the Appalachian Trail crossed much private land, and the hiking clubs that maintained it developed good working relationships with landowners. But as settlement pushed out toward the trail and as trail users became more numerous, conflicts arose. Users of off-road vehicles, though legally not permitted to use the trail, often did so. In the early 1970s some property owners, incensed by continued irritations, obstructed the trail and prevented passage.[8]

A variant on this type of conflict occurred in the late 1970s in the Midwest as recreationists sought state action to acquire former railroad rights-of-way for recreational trails. One such abandoned right-of-way was managed successfully by Wisconsin as a hiking trail in the early 1970s. But as recreational agencies in Minnesota, Iowa, and Illinois sought to take similar action they were met by rural demands that rights-of-way revert to the abutting property owners rather than be used for recreation. Rural leaders warned their constituencies about the problems recreationists would bring to their property and their community. The effort slowed down markedly.

Scenic-river proposals also generated controversy. Such programs were successful when the abutting lands were owned by public agencies, but they were often halted or modified significantly by rural people when streams flowed through private lands. Proposals to study a stream for possible designation frequently aroused local opposition as a result of fears that it would advertise the area and bring in larger numbers of recreationists who would interfere with the routine of rural life and be disrespectful of local property rights.

The use of inland wetlands came to be especially important in dividing farmers and environmentalists. Whereas a wide range of environmental groups valued wetlands as natural-environment areas, farmers considered them potentially productive farmland. Over the years farmers had established local drain commissions that supervised the digging of drainage ditches, acquired the needed land through the power of eminent domain, and financed it with local taxes. To farmers these were essential for the welfare of the farming community; their opposition to wetlands protection was uncompromising.[9]

Large-scale rural development. More cooperative relationships between environmentalists and rural communities came about on issues pertaining to the intrusion of large-scale development into the countryside. There were proposals for industrial plants, dams, electrical transmission lines, oil and gas pipelines, and surface mining that affected adjacent farm operations. As the scale of proposals and their potential impact increased, rural reaction intensified.

Reservoirs often submerged farmland and communities. Early protests against such projects had been ineffective because each area fought its battles alone. In the 1960s environmentalists interested in protecting the few remaining undammed rivers as free-flowing streams joined in these protests. Although cooperation was often tenuous because of differences in ultimate objectives, the common stake in preventing construction often brought the two together in effective working relationships. The most widely known case was the joint opposition to the proposed Meramec Dam in Missouri in the 1960s and 1970s, which led to an alternative proposal that balanced farmland, wildlife areas, hiking trails, free-flowing stream segments, and developed recreation.[10]

In the 1970s the controversy over surface mining brought about close and effective relationships between farmers and environmentalists. The initial drive for national regulation of surface mining arose because of its adverse impact on Appalachian communities. But support for control increased when coal mining started in the Montana-Wyoming-Dakota region. Surface mining there threatened to disrupt ranching operations and the communities on which they were based. In all four states rancher organizations formed with which environmentalists closely cooperated.[11]

Cooperation also took place on the question of the future productivity of farmland disturbed by surface mining. There was sufficient doubt as to the degree to which productivity could be restored to a premining condition so that many soil specialists felt it was unwise to mine in the first place. As a result of cooperative farm-environmental efforts the Surface Mining Control and Reclamation Act of 1977 included provisions to protect prime agricultural lands.[12]

The impact of energy transmission lines and pipelines was even more pervasive than that of dams and surface mining. Proposals in the 1970s to construct high-voltage electrical lines that traversed farms and farm communities led to intense rural reaction in Ohio, New York, and Minnesota. The problem was compounded by the power of eminent domain possessed by public-utility companies to acquire land, action that rural people could not prevent. Environmentalists supported rural communities that sought to defend themselves.[13]

Industrial siting generated similar protests. When this remained limited, the impact on rural communities was not so great, and in such cases benefits from higher tax returns or employment outweighed the potential environmental disruption. But as the scale of projects increased so also did the imbalance between benefits and harm. The proposal to establish an energy park in Pennsylvania, an issue of intense statewide debate in 1975 and 1976, united in opposition almost every segment of the ten rural communities targeted as potential sites. Each park would require fifteen square miles of land for a minimum of 10,000 megawatts of electrical production, and each community could well imagine disruptions of massive proportions. In such cases environmentalists and rural people found much in common.

The most dramatic example of rural-environmental cooperation came in response to the proposal to site the MX missile in the Nevada-Utah area. The potential impact of the proposal was immense, ranging from demands on scarce water resources to the disruption of rural and small-town life. Many of the communities that might be affected were Mormon, and their leaders were increasingly fearful of rapid urbanization in the heart of Mormon territory in the Wasatch Front in Utah. The roots of Mormon culture seemed to be at stake, and the church officially opposed the project. Environmentalists worked closely with community leaders to defeat the proposal, providing access to decision makers, help to analyzing impact statements, and testimony at hearings.[14]

These cooperative relationships were forged with considerable hesitation. Farmers and environmentalists differed markedly in their backgrounds and interests. Farmers were concerned primarily about the productivity of their lands and did not share the wider range of environmental objectives. Cooperation usually depended on the willingness of environmentalists to set aside their larger interests and concentrate on the immediate problem of farmland and farm-community protection. Farm- and ranch-based organizations declined to use the term "environmental" in their official titles; usually they were known as "resource councils," a term that stressed the limited concern with the protection of land for farming. Yet these ventures in joint action reflected a significant aspect of environmental politics, its role in seeking to protect the community's quality of life. That shared perspective brought environmentalists into working relationships with both rural and urban people for community self-defense.

The critique of farm operations. Environmental policies also affected farming operations, thus promoting considerable farm-environmental conflict. Those policies might restrict the availability of water, the use of pesticides and herbicides, and types of cultivation that resulted in erosion. Burning fields each year to clear them for new growth in New Jersey and Oregon produced significant air pollution; farmers objected to attempts to curtail this practice as an unjust interference with farm operations.

In the drylands of the West farming depended heavily on a continuous supply of water. Although the earlier issues of dam construction were still alive, by the mid- and late 1970s the issue of water rights had come to the fore. How would the limited amount of water not yet allocated be used? New environmental users were now making claims, and a complex of development forces, ranging from industry to urban water-supply agencies to farmers, opposed them.

Environmentalists insisted that recreational and aesthetic uses of water should be considered legitimate and beneficial uses on a par with residential, industrial, and agricultural uses. Minimum low flows should be required for each stream, below which appropriation for these commodity uses would not be permitted. Some states authorized agencies to acquire water rights for recreational and natural-environment purposes. But just as vigorously those with a stake in agriculture opposed such moves.

There were also continuing complaints about soil erosion. Runoff from farms now contained many pollutants, such as toxic chemicals from pesticides and herbicides and nutrients from fertilizer. Soil particles bore chemical pollutants downstream. Many argued that erosion had actually increased as a result of more intensive farm practices that put a premium on continuous crop production. Rotation of row and pasture crops, which, it was argued, checked the loss of soil, was now declining.[15]

The problem became highlighted as part of the growing concern with nonpoint sources of water pollution that came to the fore as point sources began to be controlled. These types of pollution included storm runoff in cities, sedimentation from excavation for highway and building construction, and erosion from farming, forestry, and mining. Although the EPA had been authorized to deal with these problems by the 1972 Clean Water Act, it had concentrated on the more manageable point sources. Litigation by the Sierra Club in the early 1970s, however, forced the EPA to take up the problem.

Nonpoint water pollution was a bit more sharply identified by the late 1970s, but little had been done to deal effectively with it. Both analyses and action were influenced heavily by representatives of the farm and forest constituencies responsible for creating much of the problem in the first place. They quietly exercised control over the program in order to reduce pressure for more vigorous measures.

Nonfarm people in farming communities were critical of many farming operations. Farmers were faced with an increasing number of complaints and lawsuits that came from people who had moved into rural communities and who did not like the noise of farm machinery, the odors from farm animals, or the drift of pesticide spray. To protect themselves from these complaints and the possibility of restrictive legislation, farmers formulated a farm "bill of rights" that, under the political leadership of the American Farm Bureau Federation, appeared in a number of state legislatures in 1980 and 1981. Most legislatures prohibited lawsuits for liability claims arising from "legitimate farm operations."

The most intense controversy over farm practices, however, involved the use of pesticides and herbicides. Environmentalists sought to restrict them, and farm political leaders, in turn, struck back in vigorous defense. Although operating farmers provided much of this political opposition, the manufacturers of farm chemicals in the form of the National Agricultural Chemical Association provided the financial, technical, and organizational strength. Cooperating closely with it, though with less public visibility, were a number of professional and business organizations such as the National Association of State Departments of Agriculture, the Association of American Plant Food, Pesticide, and Feed Control Officers, the National Association of County Agents, and the Christmas Tree Growers Association.[16]

Farm-producer and farm-industry groups had long maintained close relationships with the U.S. Department of Agriculture and had been able to exercise effective control over its policies. During the 1960s they had been somewhat worried about the environmental criticism of the use of pesticides and herbicides, but that concern was tempered by the knowledge that friends in the department were in charge and would not endanger the use of farm chemicals for agricultural production. But when the Nixon administration transferred the pesticide-control program to the EPA in 1970, these groups became alarmed because control over pesticide policy might now slip from their hands. They were critical of the department because it had not protested sufficiently against the transfer. But farm groups soon rallied. As the EPA took action to restrict the use of DDT, then aldrin/dieldrin, and then heptachlor and chlordane, farm-chemical interests shaped a vigorous counterattack.

On one front they sought to restore influence to the Department of Agriculture in pesticide affairs. They failed to return administration fully to that department, but they succeeded in restricting the EPA's freedom of action by requiring it to consult with an advisory committee in the formulation of pesticide regulations on which those allied with farm groups were heavily represented. Moreover, the EPA was required to obtain the secretary's opinion prior to taking regulatory action. Through the agricultural committees in the House and Senate that were friendly to their views, pesticide advocates were able to shape much of the new 1972 Federal Insecticide, Fungicide, and Rodenticide Act.

Farm antienvironmentalists sought to carve out a large role for state authority in pesticide matters. Here, in adversarial competition with environmentalists, farm groups were able to exercise far more control. In the early 1970s environmentalists sought to shift pesticide administration in the states to nonagriculture departments, as they had done at the federal level. But only in a few states, such as New York, did they succeed. At every turn they met stubborn resistance from the state farm organizations and the farm chemical industry. Throughout the 1970s pesticide advocates sought to shift policy steadily toward state administration in order to blunt the force of federal regulation. The new Federal Insecticide, Fungicide, and Rodenticide Act of 1978 constituted an important step in this direction.[17]

Patterns of farm opposition. Agricultural opposition to environmental policies was extensive and continuous. Although the two groups cooperated on specific types of issues, farm political leaders were fearful of environmental objectives and preoccupied with adversarial tactics of resistance and containment. Farm communities had much authority and power at the local and state level through which considerable influence could be applied in opposition to environmental objectives. This was especially the case in the less urbanized states.

On one issue in which environmental-farm cooperation might well have developed it did not: the adverse effect of air pollution on agricultural production. Often over the years farmers complained about damage to their crops caused by sulfur dioxide from TVA power plants, fluorides from Montana smelters, emissions from coal-fired power plants on Christmas tree plantations in Pennsylvania and West Virginia, to name a few examples. But these were usually isolated instances that did not lead to more general support for air-pollution control legislation by farm organizations. Little was heard in the 1970s about damage to agriculture from air pollution until late in the decade, when the issue was taken up not by farm organizations but by environmentalists.

Rural opposition to environmental programs could be observed in the voting patterns in Congress and the state legislatures. In both cases voting on environmental issues varied with the degree of urbanization: The more urbanized areas provided the stronger environmental support; and the more rural areas, the stronger opposition. Within the nation as a whole the more rural-based southern and western legislators provided the strongest opposition, and within the more urbanized states opposition came from the more rural sections. The only significant exception to this pattern involved instances in which large-scale industrial development and waste disposal threatened rural communities. In these cases rural legislators were prone to join with urban environmental leaders to combat mutual threats.[18]

The Response of Workers to Environmental Issues

Many environmental objectives directly benefited working people, whose income often forced them to live in environmentally less attractive circumstances; attitude surveys indicated that working-class people generally supported those aims. But the initiative in environmental matters usually came from more educated white-collar residents. Hence it was relatively easy for environmental politics to take the shape of conflict between white-collar consumers who sought environmental improvements and blue-collar workers when they looked on such ventures as a threat to their jobs.

At the level of organized national interest-group politics, however, closer cooperation emerged. Labor had long been a strong participant in producer-oriented political strategies and over the years had perfected unionization and collective bargaining techniques. In the past labor usually had sided with industry on issues that divided producers and consumers, and there were tendencies for such liaisons to continue in environmental affairs. But workers had a direct interest in the environmental condition of the workplace; on occupational-health issues it was easy to forge alliances with environmentalists. To reduce air pollution at work would reduce it in the community.[19]

Relationships between labor and environmentalists were shaped also by considerations of larger political strategy. Both constituencies were urban. Consequently conflicts between them presented urban legislators with especially difficult choices. Those who were sympathetic to environmentalists were also sympathetic to labor. They urged that the two groups work out their differences so that they would not be subject to continual "cross pressures." To facilitate achievement of that objective Senator Philip Hart of Michigan in 1971 took the lead in forming the Urban Environment Conference.

Labor's interest in environmental matters in the 1970s was not without precedent. In 1948 the United States Steelworkers of America had requested that the Public Health Service study air inversion in Donora, Pennsylvania, and twenty-one years later the steelworkers organized in Washington, D.C., the first nation-wide citizens' conference on air pollution. In the 1950s the United Auto Workers (UAW) had opposed the construction of a fast-breeder nuclear reactor by Detroit Edison.[20]

The attitudes of labor toward environmental issues varied with job circumstance, and that often led to varied reactions. Coal miners, for example, were sensitive to clean-air issues because of the implication for the use of coal. They joined with the industry in condemning action both to restrict sulfur dioxide emissions in the 1960s and later to prevent action to cope with acid rain. Yet because coal miners looked on atomic energy as a major source of competition they joined with antinuclear groups in opposing construction of nuclear plants.

Labor was wooed by both industry and environmentalists. In the case of agriculture few expected much cooperation with environmental objectives. But the direction in which labor would turn was less predictable because its interests were more mixed. In some cases industry succeeded in winning labor over; at other times environmentalists formed alliances with labor.

Labor as environmental opposition. The most divisive issues between labor and environmentalists concerned jobs. Particularly serious, for example, was returnable-container legislation. Unions representing workers in the steel and aluminum industries who manufactured throwaway containers consistently opposed state and national bottle bills. Also at issue were job gains that would come from construction projects opposed by environmentalists. This brought construction labor and industry leaders into close cooperation against environmental objectives. Both argued that long-term environmental harm was minimal and greatly out-weighed by job benefits.

Organized labor supported national policies to make energy-facility siting easier, such as streamlining the permit process and giving federal agencies more leverage against states in siting decisions. Often they urged that the environmental-impact statement be bypassed or minimized. Construction labor supported modifications in the endangered-species laws and opposed a federal nongame wildlife program on the grounds that they would slow up and even prevent needed construction.[21]

The most widely publicized issues of this kind, however, concerned the cleanup of air and water pollution at existing plants. Although in general pollution-control programs caused relatively few losses of jobs, the impact on particular industries was more severe. Many iron and steel plants, for example, were obsolete and inefficient as well as heavily polluting. Slowly the industry was undergoing both technological innovation and relocation.

In a number of communities industry was a major contributor to air and water pollution. In promoting cleanup control, agencies often faced opposition from labor and community leaders as well as industry. The issue became especially dramatic in 1976 and 1977 as the steel industry began major retrenchment and modernization. Labor was concerned that jobs be retained in the current locations and was hostile to industry's desire to move them. Hence it demanded postponements and exemptions to protect existing plants.

The automobile industry underwent changes similar to those experienced by the iron and steel industries. It had long been under attack for resisting more advanced technological innovations in the form of cleaner-burning engines. Yet the technology-forcing aspects of the clean-air laws seemed to produce results. Amid all this, however, imports of small cars grew steadily; after the oil crises of the 1970s they captured a growing share of the domestic market. American auto manufacturers responded only slowly to this competitive challenge and increasingly found themselves to be at a disadvantage.

The UAW supported the industry in its attempts to relax the nitrogen oxide standard for automobiles and to postpone compliance dates for mobile source standards. On these issues environmentalists and labor were on opposite sides of the fence. The controversy generated a major rift between environmentalists and one of the long-time stalwarts in environmental leadership, Congressman John Dingell of Michigan, who represented auto-worker constituents.

In these arguments over cleanup of existing and often outmoded plants and lagging technological improvement, management frequently sought to blame environmentalists for plant closings and reductions in employment. Labor knew that environmental requirements were only one, and often a less important, factor in plant closures. It was prone to label such industry efforts as blackmail, holding out the threat of job loss merely to avoid action. Hence management was not always successful in winning labor over to its strategies of keeping old equipment running by holding off environmental regulations.

Lumber workers and loggers were also drawn into environmental controversies over park and wilderness proposals that would reduce the amount of timberlands available for commercial wood production. Throughout the 1970s forest managers persuaded labor to support its opposition to measures such as the expansion of the Redwood National Park. The United Steel Workers, the United Automobile Workers, and the Oil, Chemical, and Atomic Workers Union (OCAW) supported the environmental Alaska Coalition in its efforts to protect Alaskan lands, but unions in the woodworking industries, responding to the interests of employees in Ketchikan and other Alaskan mill towns, did not. The timber industry undertook an even more vigorous effort to rally support of woodworkers for the Roadless Area Review and Evaluation (RARE) II wilderness study and in so doing played an important role in persuading the Forest Service to scale down its wilderness recommendations.

Cooperation on occupational health. Occupational hazards from exposure to airborne chemicals and noise provided an opportunity for sustained cooperation between workers and environmentalists. It was relatively easy to forge a common interest in workplace and community air quality. This lay behind the long-standing support of the national clean air program by the United Steelworkers of America. But there was also a common potential interest in toxic exposure that affected workers and communities alike.

Agricultural workers were concerned about exposures to pesticides. Organized farmworkers, especially in California, took up this issue early in the 1970s and participated extensively in hearings on the revision of the federal pesticide law in 1971. They demanded a variety of new practices such as a waiting period between the use of pesticides and the reentry of workers into the fields. These concerns had been a major factor in the initiative by Senator Philip Hart to establish a subcommittee on environmental affairs in the Senate Committee on Commerce that would be more sympathetic to workers' problems with pesticides than was the Committee on Agriculture.

A decade later the issue of harm from pesticides had shifted to forest workers in the Pacific Northwest, where the Northwest Coalition for Alternatives to Pesticides was formed to restrict aerial spraying to suppress vegetation that would compete with conifers. By 1981 farm- and forest-worker groups, with the aid of environmentalists, formed the National Coalition against the Misuse of Pesticides.[22]

The most vigorous occupational-health action among workers was taken by the OCAW, many of whose members were subject to chemical and radiation exposure. In 1972 it established an occupational-health program, and in 1973 its activity became well known during a strike against the Shell Oil Company over health issues. The wide support the union received from environmentalists and health and welfare professionals helped to bring the strike to a successful conclusion.[23]

Occupational exposure to radiation aroused increasing concern. Exposure to radiation in X-ray rooms affected the reproductive health of both women directly exposed and the wives of male hospital workers. Political cooperation with the utility industry had prompted blue-collar workers in atomic-energy plants to accept radiation exposure without criticism. But toward the end of the 1970s, as a result of new evidence concerning occupational hazards of radiation, managers had more difficulty persuading workers to accept some job assignments. They began to hire young people for short-term employment until they reached their allowable exposure limits, thereby avoiding controversy with permanent workers.[24]

The most widely known cases of organized worker concern for occupational hazards became the subjects of motion pictures. One involved Karen Silkwood, active in the OCAW local in the Kerr-McGee plutonium plant near Oklahoma City. For some months she attempted to obtain evidence about company practices that permitted harmful exposures to workers, and on the night she was to give such evidence to a national union representative and a *New York Times* reporter her car was run off the road and she was killed. A court awarded her survivors substantial damages on the grounds of company negligence in exposing her to plutonium. The episode became a cause célèbre with trade unions, women's rights organizations, and environmentalists and was the subject of the movie *Silkwood,* produced in 1983.[25]

Equally dramatic was brown lung disease, which affected workers in the textile industry exposed to small fibers of cotton dust. The Amalgamated Clothing and Textile Workers Union took up the issue as an organizing strategy. Their principal targets were the older, less efficient mills where workers faced higher levels of exposure. In 1975 the union tried to persuade the Occupational Safety and Health Administration (OSHA) to develop a new standard for cotton dust. Action came slowly, was controversial, and continued into the 1980s. It too resulted in a movie, *Norma Rae.*

Organized labor found that action depended on assessment of the scientific evidence, which could turn out one way if shaped by scientists associated with employers and another if made by those with a more immediate concern for public health. Labor thus attempted to develop technical expertise that would be independent of the established occupational health professionals who, it felt, were more closely associated with industry viewpoints. These scientists, as did many others, started from the vantage point of those exposed to hazards rather than those responsible for the exposure. This shared scientific approach was an important factor in fostering cooperation between environmentalists and labor.

Labor alliances. Labor was wooed by both industry and environmentalists. The most common argument used by industry to draw workers to its side was that environmental controls would prevent new construction or force existing firms to shut down. Labor and environmentalists labeled such tactics job blackmail. Legislation soon required the EPA to account closely for job loss due to environmental controls, and the resulting quarterly reports made it clear that most job losses allegedly due to environmental controls were the result of phasing out obsolete plants and equipment.

Labor and industry formed the National Environmental Development Association (NEDA) to lobby against environmental laws and regulations that might inhibit construction. They enlisted the services of John Quarles, former deputy administrator of the EPA in the Nixon administration, as chair of their Clean Air Act Project; through him they were able to maintain considerable credibility in the eyes of environmental managers and the political intelligentsia in the nation's capital. During the debates over revision of the Clean Air Act in the early 1980s, NEDA sought to seize the initiative by shaping a middle ground in which most elements of the Clean Air Act would be retained but the program for the prevention of significant deterioration, which construction labor and industry opposed, would be sharply modified.[26]

Industry also appealed to workers exposed to occupational hazards; they should think of themselves, so the argument went, as producers rather than as consumers. These strategies were not as successful. The common interest in jobs provided a bond, but the issue of occupational hazards brought labor's political interests far closer to its traditional concern for working conditions. Occupational-health problems became an integral part of the historic controversies between management and labor over the workplace and hence of the issues that long had been subjects of collective bargaining. There seemed little likelihood that cooperative relationships between labor and industry could be formed around issues of environmental health.

In the area of occupational health, cooperation between environmentalists and labor was close; national environmental organizations found that they easily could incorporate such issues into their own strategies. As cancer became more central in a wide range of environmental concerns, effective links could be forged among many groups for whom toxic chemicals and radiation were continuous threats. Through the leadership of the Sierra Club a coalition, including crucial segments from organized labor, fought for passage of the Toxic Substances Control Act in 1976. When OSHA proposed its generic cancer rule in 1978, environmental and labor organizations gave it strong support in the face of industry opposition.

The organizations formed by Ralph Nader were a major source of influence for cooperation between labor and environmentalists. These groups stressed the health effects of pollution and were well established by the time of the new wave of environmental enthusiasm in the early 1970s. Books sponsored by the Nader group on water and air pollution, as well as food additives and occupational health, played a major role in the evolution of environmental affairs at that time. The 1970 Occupational Health and Safety Act, supported by trade union leaders, was also backed by the Nader organizations, the newly formed Environmental Action, and, among the older wildlife and wilderness groups, the Sierra Club. Nader-led activities played an important, though not always direct, role in building bridges between environmentalists and labor.[27]

In the mid-1970s new initiatives for closer cooperation came about as a result of interest in the implications of large-scale development for employment. Claims about the number of jobs that large dams or industrial plants would create were vastly inflated, environmentalists argued, because such capital-intensive ventures actually eliminated rather than created jobs. Environmentalists for Full Employment was formed in 1975 to encourage a shift in public funds into alternatives, which would be more benign environmentally and create more jobs. Solar energy, one such option, led to cooperation between sheet-metal workers and environmentalists to increase funds for solar-energy research.[28]

From the labor side the initiative in cooperative ventures was taken especially by John Yolton, director of environmental affairs for the UAW. Yolton was friendly to environmental objectives and sought both to soften labor's innate suspicion of environmentalists and to secure wider support for full-employment legislation. With the encouragement of Senator Philip Hart of Michigan, Yolton took the lead in organizing the Black Lake Conference held in 1976 at Black Lake, Michigan, to bring together labor, environmentalists, and urban leaders from poor and, especially, black neighborhoods.

In the 1980s these cooperative ventures expanded. One twist involved the right-to-know issue. Labor pressed its case for national right-to-know regulation, and it also sought action at the city and state levels. In Philadelphia community leaders and environmentalists joined with labor in the Delaware Valley Toxics Coalition to secure a city ordinance that required industries to provide chemical-exposure information to both citizens and workers. Other cities and states soon adopted similar requirements.

An even more ambitious effort at labor-environmental cooperation began in 1981 in the OSHA/Environmental Network. Spearheaded by the Industrial Union Department of the AFL-CIO and the Sierra Club, the network took up a joint defense of both environmental and occupational health and safety programs from the threats to both from the Reagan administration. This cooperative program gave rise to statewide OSHA/Environment Networks in more than two dozen states.

The working-class community. The Black Lake Conference and the events that grew out of it brought a new political element to the relationship between labor and environmentalists – the urban working-class community. Neighborhood organizations and their citywide coalitions emphasized a far wider range of problems than did organized labor, extending to older people, youth unemployment, recreational facilities, police protection, and the community's physical environment. Although organized labor took up some of these problems, it did not consider them central to its concerns.

The origins of many environmental initiatives in white-collar, better educated, and middle-class sections of the city made lower-income groups suspicious. Much of the environmental interest in improving the urban quality of life carried little weight with community leaders faced with what they considered the more pressing problems of jobs, welfare, and the cost of living.

During the 1970s environmental and working-class community leaders reached out to develop more cooperative action. Some concerned with public health realized the particularly great hazard posed by air pollution to lower-income people. Some black leaders did not think it was advisable to ignore concerns such as the physical appearance of the neighborhood or readily available outdoor recreation. The Sierra Club developed outing programs for inner-city youth, dayhikes and weekend trips to outdoor natural environments, and found community leaders who would work with them on such projects.[29]

Some leaders became interested in urban gardening and solar energy as conducive to greater self-sufficiency; this brought them into the orbit of environmental affairs. Others agreed with environmentalists that conventional large-scale urban public works provided few jobs and were not very useful to the community's unemployed. Still others sought to cope with rising energy prices by advocating lifeline electricity rates or energy stamps for the poor.

In these efforts the Black Lake Conference constituted a major event. It brought urban community leaders into direct contact, and confrontation, with union leaders and environmentalists. In addition, the Urban Environment Conference held a series of meetings in 1976 and 1977 in ten cities across the nation to foster further cooperation. At these meetings environmentalists often came under attack from community leaders who argued that environmental programs should not be supported until there was full employment. They emphasized jobs even to the exclusion of environmental health.[30]

In the spring of 1979 the National Urban League and the Sierra Club cosponsored the City Care Conference in Detroit, which stressed policies on which cooperation could develop. It focused on such matters as the effects of air pollution, occupational health, community self-help programs, and community open space and recreation. Many forces divided environmentalists and lower-income urban communities. But on both sides there were leaders who worked to overcome these differences, and by the 1970s they had produced some results.

As in rural communities the most important factor that could generate strong coalitions between environmentalists and urban working-class communities was the threat of disruption from large-scale development projects. The role of urban highway projects in this has already been emphasized. A notable case was the proposal in the late 1960s to construct the Three Sisters Bridge across the Potomac River in Washington, D.C., tunnel the highway under the Lincoln Memorial, and route it over the Mall and through the black community of the northeastern section of the city. Black community leaders, as well as middle-class whites, organized to fight this shared threat.

In Hudson County, New Jersey, residents resisted half a dozen attempts in the decade after 1967 to site oil refineries and petrochemical plants in Hoboken, long known as a major industrial center. The issue united blue-collar workers and middle-class whites, Italian, Polish, black, and other ethnic leaders in defense of their community.

Toxic-waste dumps were another community threat. South Deering, Illinois, for example, an urban working-class community of roughly equal numbers of whites, blacks, and Hispanics, with 35 percent unemployment, in 1980 became concerned about a proposal to site a waste dump on the edge of their section of Chicago's southeast side. In the 1983 Chicago mayoral election, candidate Harold Washington took up their pleas, and the Illinois Environmental Protection Agency agreed to conduct extensive health studies before acting on the permit application. The effort was strongly supported by Citizens for a Better Environment.

The Response of Business and Industry

The most vigorous response to environmental objectives came from the business community. In the mass media, in legislative, administrative, and judicial action, in educational materials distributed in public-relations campaigns, in scientific and technical circles, its resistance to environmental and ecological concerns abounded. Each segment of business, whether raw-material production, manufacturing, commerce, transportation, or construction, had its own particular objection to environmental proposals and almost all business groups found common cause that produced a shared opposition. Only those firms with an economic stake in pollution-control technology remained apart from this massive onslaught against environmental policies and programs.[31]

To business leaders the environmental movement was hardly understandable. At first it was looked on with fascination, but as its influence increased in the late 1960s and early 1970s, this perception turned to incredulity and fright. Now the business community had become thoroughly aroused to develop strategies for more potent opposition. The timing of action was determined mainly by the political success of environmentalists. The steady increase of environmental political capabilities in the 1970s and 1980s generated, in turn, an equally effective opposition from industry that was quite successful in retarding environmental initiatives.

Environmental policies confronted the business community with a continual series of choices about how much initiative to take to comply. Its commitment to material production and its bottom line of profitability prompted it to take minimal acceptable action. In regulatory matters it argued that applicable standards were unnecessary and sought to push allowable levels of pollution as high as legally permissible. It objected to the protection of amenity values such as wilderness or visibility on the grounds that development was more important. Although many interpreted this opposition as disagreement over means, it was, in fact disagreement over ends. Only determined regulatory action was able to force business and industry to adopt public environmental objectives.

The give-and-take of environmental politics led to steady environmental gains to which industry, with varied mixtures of reluctance and acceptance, made major contributions. In making these changes, however, the business world was pulled along by forces in the nation at large, rather than prompted by its own initiative. By the mid-1980s its political strategies could still be described as marked not by agreement on values but by tactics of containment, by a working philosophy of maximum feasible resistance and minimum feasible retreat.[32]

At first, business leaders believed that environmental affairs were only temporary, a product of the short-lived excesses of the late 1960s that had swept through American college youth. But they persisted. A host of public-opinion polls sponsored by the business community in the 1970s revealed the permanence of environmental objectives, and the polling agencies warned their clients that public interest and support were here to stay and should be accepted rather than resisted.

As the energy shortages, unemployment, and inflation of the 1970s unfolded, the business community raised a cry that the nation could not afford the luxury of environmental and ecological progress. Regulation would destroy the business community; the economy would collapse; American production was being strait-jacketed in competing with other, more vigorous, national economies. Public funds spent for environmental programs were "unproductive."[33]

The pulp and paper industry was one of the first business sectors to take an active interest in environmental affairs. Its mills were especially offensive to many communities because of the intense odors as well as the air and water pollution they produced. As early as the 1950s it established industrywide committees to undertake research, influence public-health authorities, and ward off attacks. The wood-production industry became aware of the environmental movement in the late 1950s as demands for outdoor recreation grew, and it feared that the nation's timberlands would be called on to fill the needs. The National Lumber Manufacturers Association vigorously opposed proposals for wilderness, wild and scenic rivers, and new national parks.[34]

Amid the growing concern about air pollution in the 1960s, the coal, coal-using, and petroleum industries became aroused. The National Coal Association resisted limitations on the use of coal. In 1966 the American Petroleum Institute formed the Committee for Air and Water Conservation with a full-time staff; its aims were to "work out principles to help guide formulation of public policies; and disseminate information and research findings." These political activities came about primarily in response to efforts by the U.S. Public Health Service to establish standards for the sulfur content of fuel that could be used without treatment. In their attacks on the emerging air-quality program, these groups were joined by others such as the American Iron and Steel Institute who represented major sources of pollution.[35]

In the West the increasing opposition to the construction of dams brought the National Water Resources Association, representing irrigation interests, into the antienvironmental fray. In the East the challenge to water-development projects was dramatized in 1970 when President Nixon canceled the Cross-Florida Barge Canal; this action galvanized those interested in river and coastal navigation. In 1971 the National Rivers and Harbors Congress and the Mississippi Valley Association joined to press the attack more forcefully through the new Water Resources Congress. Attempts to restrict dredging and the disposal of dredge spoil and to allow the U.S. Fish and Wildlife Service greater authority in reviewing proposed Corps of Engineers permits brought the National Association of Harbor Authorities and the National Sand and Gravel Association into action. And joining these groups were the regional river-development organizations such as the Ohio River Improvement Association, the Gulf Intracoastal Canal Association, and the Upper Mississippi Waterway Association.[36]

In the late 1960s the atomic-energy industry went on the attack. Through the Atomic Industrial Forum it tried to fight off growing objections to atomic energy. It sought to preserve the independent authority of the Atomic Energy Commission and the Joint House-Senate Committee on Atomic Energy, to meet demands for the control of thermal pollution by constructing cooling towers, and to defend the entire complex of atomic-energy institutions against environmental claims of harm from radiation. As scientists took up the theme of danger from low-level radiation they were countered vigorously by industry-allied scientists.[37]

Other business and industry groups followed. As environmental efforts to restrict the use of motorized vehicles in the nation's wildlands increased, industry formed organizations to counter them. Outdoors Unlimited was started by recreational-vehicle manufacturers; later Robert Honke, sales manager for Ford's recreational-vehicle division, formed Outdoor Nation. Both groups took an active role in adding a new dimension to the antiwilderness coalition, which long had been led by timber and mining groups.

Chemical manufacturers played a far more extensive role in the environmental opposition than did any other segment of industry. In the 1950s the Manufacturing Chemists Association, the industry trade group, sought to prevent passage of the Delaney Amendment and in subsequent years worked to repeal it. The association developed public-relations programs to combat the "scares" about the effects of chemicals in food. By the mid-1960s it had become active in opposing the evolving air- and water-pollution-control program. Its publication *Chemecology* was one of the first industry environmental trade organs devoted exclusively to environmental affairs. In 1977, with the Dow Chemical Company taking the lead, the American Industrial Health Coun-

cil, composed of a number of trade associations and corporations, was formed to oppose the generic cancer policy proposed
by OSHA.[38]

Some of the most significant industry organizations in the antienvironmental drive were the nonprofit institutes, research and
educational bodies formed by trade associations or by cooperative action among business firms. These served as centers of
research and education on behalf of the industry as a whole.
Because of their nonprofit status they could dissociate themselves from profit-making activities. The Tobacco Institute, for
example, undertook the burden of arguing that there was no connection between smoking and lung cancer; the American Forest
Institute generated statistics demonstrating that future needs for
wood made further wilderness allocations unwise; the American
Petroleum Institute produced statistics about oil and gas reserves, production, and supplies on which the federal government relied. Such institutes were especially important in shaping
the course of debate by gathering and disseminating data that
justified a particular industry view.[39]

The antienvironmental ideology. The business community was
concerned primarily with the decline of its influence on environmental policy. Forces that had no legitimate role in affairs of such
large consequence to business were now far too powerful. How
to hold back the tide? Two strategies evolved. The first was a
series of public-relations campaigns to cope with what it considered irrational, extreme, and emotional public attitudes that
were responsible for the new political forces. The second was a
quieter campaign to increase control over public decisions.

The public-relations campaigns took many forms. Most industry groups took up the customary strategies of distributing literature to selected groups such as teachers and "thought leaders"
and financing advertising campaigns on TV and radio and in
newspapers and magazines. Others published special environmental magazines such as *Down to Earth* (Dow Chemical Company) and *The Tobacco Observer* (the Tobacco Institute). There
were continual attempts to discourage media reporting that was
friendly to environmental concerns, ranging from opportunities
for direct rebuttal to efforts to suppress presentations before they

appeared. In the early 1970s the Pacific Gas and Electric Company attempted to discredit the professional reputation of TV producer Donald Widener for his documentary "The Powers That Be," which was critical of nuclear energy. The long-drawn-out legal proceedings brought by Widener vindicated his claims and led to a $300,000 award.[40]

Repeated campaigns to defeat environmental initiatives subject to popular vote were usually organized through public-relations firms financed by major corporations that might be affected. The public-relations tactics were legion, continually alleged to include misrepresentation and downright falsification, described in great detail to trade association members in trade publications to demonstrate that their representatives were on the job, and frequently exposed by environmental groups in their publications.

These campaigns to shape the course of public thinking on environmental matters produced a set of arguments that evolved from one stage of controversy to another. Each new argument took its place alongside previous ones so that by the end of the 1970s a rather coherent antienvironmental ideology had emerged that served as industry's front line of attack.

One of the most widely used themes was that of backlash. The environmental movement, it was argued repeatedly, had finally gone too far. The sequence of argument usually acknowledged that several environmental problems had once existed and approved early actions to cope with them. But now that the most severe cases had been dealt with, little further action was required. To demand more was to exceed reason; it would be far too costly to clean up further. In fact, it was warned time and again, a backlash had now set in that would threaten gains already made. Such arguments served both to enhance the image of the business community as responsive and to define environmentalists as advocating excess.

Then there was the prediction of dire consequences for the American economy if environmental programs persisted. Early in the 1970s special emphasis was placed on jobs, and "jobs versus the environment" came to be a regular media theme. But when the EPA gathered data about job loss on a regular basis, it was found to be slight, and this phase of the ideological attack declined sharply. Rapid growth in employment in the economy as a whole in the 1970s, a gain of more than 10 million jobs, made the 26,000 jobs lost because of environmental regulations seem insignificant.

In the mid-1970s business began to place more emphasis on capital and operating costs of environmental controls. Investments for such purposes shifted capital from productive opportunities to nonproductive uses, thereby reducing productivity gains in the economy as a whole. Environmental costs were labeled "penalties" to convey the notion that they were punitive rather than useful expenditures for socially desirable benefits. Environmentalists suspected industry cost reporting, especially because it usually came from public-relations offices rather than from more credible sources of economic analysis. Many claims, they argued, were for costs devoted to technological innovation in production rather than in environmental controls.

Environmentalists were especially suspicious when predictions of severe economic hardship turned out to be false. During the episode in which vinyl chloride workers were found to suffer disproportionately from liver cancer, industry reacted strongly to the demand for a standard that would reduce exposure to the lowest feasible level, that is, the lowest level technologically possible. It warned that this would lead to a direct cost of $2 billion and 150,000 jobs, and indirect costs for the larger economy of $30 billion. When the standard was adopted the firms made rather simple process changes to meet it, which, in fact, reduced rather than increased costs because of the recovery of useful waste materials. Industry's credibility was damaged by its continually crying wolf when presented with proposed environmental regulations.[41]

In the late 1970s business took up the argument that inflation had come primarily from environmental regulations. The construction industry blamed the regulations for the rising cost of housing; energy companies blamed them for the increased cost of electricity and gasoline. The administrative cost of regulation was said to have increased costs to firms and, at the same time, was a major source of inflation in the overall economy. During the Carter administration in 1978 and 1979 the Council on Wage and Price Stability adopted the argument and attacked both the substance and the methods of regulation for their inflationary effect. A variety of studies indicated that environmental programs contributed less than one-half of 1 percent to inflation. Yet the broad popularity of the argument continued to encourage business to resort to it.

The ideology of business defense often included the argument that if environmental programs were carried out under business leadership they would accomplish far more. Business was the pioneer in environmental improvement and knew best how to do the job. Investments to control environmental pollution had been made voluntarily out of concern for the community at large and not under regulatory compulsion; hence public programs were not needed. In its public-relations activities business sought to associate itself with environmental symbols such as the aesthetic quality of natural environments. And it formed a variety of organizations such as the National Environmental Development Association in order to identify itself in the public eye with environmental objectives. But the public remained skeptical of these attempts to cast business in such a favorable light.

Business sought to emphasize the adverse environmental consequences of environmental laws. One type of environmental control, such as in air quality, only created another type of environmental problem. The use of scrubbers to remove sulfur dioxide from flue gas created sludge, which still had to be disposed of. An ad campaign by the American Electric Power Company warned that this would produce a neck-deep layer of sludge across the nation. Hence environmental controls, though well meant, did not do the job.

By the end of the 1970s the sequence of argument of backlash, unbearable costs, inflation, and the harmful effects of environmental programs had come to constitute a systematic ideology of attack. Now came a more conciliatory strategy: Environmental laws were here to stay, business accepted them, and there was no further need for debate. "We should sit down and reason together." Although environmentalists had been instrumental in bringing about needed programs, the business community and its associated technical experts had the know-how to implement programs and hence should play a greater role in that objective.

Such arguments were highlighted in the writings of the business community, but they were unconvincing to environmentalists because in day-to-day politics continued vigorous opposition to environmental policies seemed to speak more loudly.

Strategies of institutional control. Many observers are accustomed to looking on the new environmental legislation of the 1960s and 1970s as a demonstration of the strength and vitality of the environmental movement. But this is only part of the story. For politics begins in earnest only after a law is passed, when the political contenders mobilize to shape the course of administrative and judicial decisions. Once politics was shifted to the administrative arena, its character changed markedly. Decisions now became more technical, more removed from public view, less capable of being understood and described by the media. In this realm the cards were more fully in the hands of environmental opponents in business and industry, whose resources were more attuned to fighting the inside battles of technical politics.

To influence administrative decisions, however, was not as easy for the business community as it had been. Environmental organizations now had developed some of the capabilities for engaging in administrative politics. Business leaders complained about this change in the "normal relationships between the regulated and the regulator" and argued that environmentalists should not "inject themselves into the nuts and bolts" of regulatory decisions but, rather, "should observe and comment on the regulatory product."[42]

Industry threw itself into the maelstrom of administrative adversary politics, bringing volley after volley to bear in hearings on proposed rules, in personal contacts with key personnel, in litigation, and in challenging the details of specific permits. In so doing it had considerable success in neutralizing the force of positive administrative action. Despite the drama of events in which public agencies sought to convey the message of persistent victories over the regulated, those very regulated, by the continuous weight of their demands, were able to shape much of the world of environmental affairs.

One strategy was to limit positive environmental goals and protective environmental standards as closely as possible. Political choices to allocate public lands and streams to natural-environment uses, for example, were closely monitored so as to reduce them to the minimum. Industry continually complained about the expansion of these natural-environment systems. Yet it succeeded in slowing markedly the pace of decisions to establish both wilderness and natural-river designations by identifying potential development that would be desirable in candidate areas and insisting that options for such possibilities be left open.[43]

Business also insisted that environmental protection be trimmed to the margin of acceptability by calling for high levels of proof of harm to human health and biological systems. It constantly attacked the criteria documents as justifying thresholds of safety that were too low. Business and industry sided with scientists who demanded higher levels of proof of harm that would serve to limit regulation. And they attacked the notion of the margin of safety and sought to cut it to the bone on the grounds that it was not needed.[44]

A second strategy was to increase the detail and complexity of administrative regulation so as to minimize its effect. To simplify administration, the EPA sought to classify sources of industrial wastewater into general categories, some 530 of them, and to apply a general set of standards to each. Industry attacked this on the grounds that each plant, each source, was unique and required a separate set of standards. OSHA sought to adopt a generic policy on carcinogenic agents in the workplace so that if a substance was found to be carcinogenic in a prescribed number of animal experiments it would be subject to control. But industry tried to retain the freedom to debate the carcinogenicity of each substance in administrative proceedings and in court and, in so doing, to bring up again in each case the major controversial issues such as the existence of a threshold for cancer effects.

A third strategy was to press for a more closed rather than a more open system of administrative decision making that would involve only those parties with a direct interest and confine making complex technical choices to the experts. Environmentalists had advocated more open decisions. But it was precisely this process that business and industry felt had brought undesirable influences into public affairs. Over the years they had been forced to face major changes, for example, in the composition of administrative advisory committees that formerly they had been able to influence. Because these committees were a crucial link between agencies and their constituencies, the environmental agencies had attempted to make their personnel more balanced.[45]

Problems for industry became more severe in the early years of the Carter administration, which made extensive changes in agency personnel. A number of people previously active in, or friendly to, environmental objectives now came to occupy key positions in the Departments of the Interior and Agriculture, the EPA, OSHA, and the Office of the Attorney General. Initially the business community was appalled by these new appointments. It was also restrained by court decisions that prohibited administrators from having "ex parte" contacts, that is, private and personal communication, outside of the regular channels of administrative procedure, with those having an interest in regulatory programs.

But during 1977 and thereafter business found that much of this burden of openness could be avoided by concentrating attention on friendlier quarters within the Executive Office in the Council on Wage and Price Stability and the Office of Management and Budget. Through agencies such as these and the influence they exerted on administrators in environmental programs, antienvironmental activities could be kept off the record and unpublicized because they were matters of privileged communication among the president's own administrators.

Tactics of opposition. In its strategy of opposition the business community used a variety of tactics. Together they constituted an accumulating set of battle plans that by the end of the 1970s were widely used by many different industries separately and by business organizations as a whole.

One of the most popular tactics was the use of evidence that would demonstrate the lack of support for environmental policies among the general public. Corporate industry sought to create the impression that environmental objectives were desired by only a few. Evidence was needed to give flesh and blood to this argument, and towards this end industries financed public-opinion studies: the American Forest Institute on attitudes toward wilderness and forest management; chemical companies on attitudes toward their industry; Allied Chemical and others on attitudes toward energy; Marsh and McLennon, insurance brokers, on attitudes toward risk; AMAX on attitudes in the Rocky Mountain area toward mining in wilderness.[46]

Combined with these tactics were attempts to capitalize on public reactions to the way environmental programs restricted individual choice. It had long been apparent that environmental cleanup could come more quickly through controls on industrial sources than through manipulation of public behavior. But many programs required both, and this provided corporate tacticians with an opportunity to identify their problem with that of the public. There was, for example, the effort to require cars to be regularly inspected and maintained so that their pollution-control devices would continue to function effectively. The American Automobile Association took up the challenge and opposed these "I/M" programs on the grounds of defending individual choice. Automobile manufacturers joined in.[47]

Such themes were extended to other issues. Owners of off-road vehicles such as snowmobiles and motorcycles should be allowed to drive freely over the public lands; to confine them to specific trails was an infringement on personal freedom. Large cattle ranchers or mineral companies cast their arguments in defense of the small rancher or prospector with whom the reader could readily identify. The "right to choose" symbolized these arguments: for example, to purchase beer and soft drinks without having to pay a deposit for returnable containers and to smoke cigarettes in airplanes or other places where the practice might be restricted.

A special twist in the corporate defense of personal freedom surfaced in the argument over the use of workers' medical records for scientific research. These were held by employers to be privileged, available to others only at the firm's discretion. But they were essential for epidemiological research concerning statistical relationships between exposures and health effects. During the Carter administration OSHA promulgated a regulation that required employers to make these records available. Employers argued that workers had a right to have this information kept privileged. But workers and their union representatives rejected this defense of their own "right to privacy" because of the records' importance for medical research on their behalf.[48]

From the beginning of environmental programs in the 1960s a constant tussle had taken place between corporations and environmentalists over who would pay for the costs of air- and water-pollution equipment. Corporate strategy was to seek funds from public sources such as tax credits, more rapid depreciation and amortization of equipment, and the use of municipal bonds that carried lower rates of interest. Since in the 1960s most regulation was at the state level, this assistance came at first from state and local governments, but as federal regulation grew, industry sought similar types of federal aid as well. In the late 1970s, proposals to clean up hazardous-waste sites sharpened the issue: Would it be financed by industry or the general public? Many legislators argued for more of the first, but the chemical industry fought for more of the second.[49]

Should the cost of monitoring emissions be borne by industry or by the public through the general treasury? Environmentalists had mixed feelings about this issue. If industry financed its own monitoring, the public might lose control over the reliability and availability of the information. But public monitoring was so expensive that industries were often required to pay the cost.

Michigan had a variant on this approach in which industry was required to pay a pollution fee with which the Michigan Department of Natural Resources financed the cost of monitoring. But in 1981, when the agency sought to raise fees to cover increased costs, industry argued that the entire amount should be borne by the general treasury. "Michigan industry," a chemical company official argued, "has opposed paying surveillance fees since the inception of the program because the fees represent nothing more than a hidden and totally unjustified tax on companies doing business in Michigan."[50]

Industry's most fundamental tactic, however, was to control the acquisition, assessment, dissemination, and application of information. Every environmental issue was laced with technical information. Much of the strategy of the environmental movement and much of the drama and outcome of environmental controversy lay in the use of information and attempts to control it.

There was the issue of "trade secrets," information about the composition of products industry proposed to manufacture that might or might not be harmful. Citizen environmentalists sought to have this information made public so that they and independent scientists could evaluate it, but industry refused to release it and worked out agreements with the EPA to withhold it. There also was the issue of the "right to know" in the workplace, to know the results of medical examinations conducted on workers by employers, to learn more fully the effect of exposures to chemicals in the workplace by conducting more elaborate medical tests, and to know the composition of chemicals to which one was exposed. Industry fought for the right to control access to such information.[51]

The regulators as well as the regulated sought to limit information availability, but were hampered by the federal Freedom of Information Act, which played a major role in making available undisclosed information. Often this was done by investigative reporters rather than by environmentalists. The health effects of atomic testing in Nevada in the 1950s were a notable example. Often court cases provided an opportunity to ferret information out of both private and public sources. One could argue that the control of information was the crucial element in environmental politics.[52]

The business community exercised its influence in environmental affairs not primarily through opportunistic strategy and tactics but through the persistent presence of its institutional power. Governmental leaders were influenced heavily by their assessments of the relative institutional capabilities of various parties who sought to influence policy. Did a party at interest have the resources to pursue litigation? Did it command influence with key legislators? Could it overwhelm the agency with scientific and technical information that the agency did not have the resources to counter? Did it have the ability to discredit the agency with key sectors of the media?

Such capabilities were formidable givens in any public decision. They were conveyed more by the persistence of inquiry and communication and the number and skills of available personnel than by argument and threat. The enormous inequality between the institutional weight of environmental organizations and those of the business community was obvious to even the casual observer. Institutional power was the most significant weapon in the corporate arsenal with which to combat the environmental enterprise.

Organizational strategies. Efforts by the business community to restrain environmental activities took organizational forms beyond its own corporations. Sometimes it participated in organizations with environmentalists in order to shape their strategies in an acceptable way. There were only a few such cases, but they were instructive. Such interaction was fostered by some environmentalists who argued that "enlightened businessmen" should be involved to "work things out" within an organizational framework rather than engage in adversary action in the wider political world.

One such case involved the Pennsylvania Environmental Council (PEC), which, contrary to the form of most such state councils, was not a coalition of independent environmental groups shaped by the objectives of its various organizational members but instead was a membership organization in which both the board of directors and organizational policy were determined by its leadership. The board was kept balanced among developmental and environmental members with strong segments from such quarters as the environmental-control industry and environmental professionals. As a result the council's environmental positions were sharply diluted before they were announced. Although this strategy was justified on the grounds that it was better to hammer out differences among contending parties privately, it did not enable the PEC to take a front-line advocacy role in environmental affairs. PEC annual meetings provided opportunities for those who sought to contain environmental objectives to express their views.[53]

A similar joint venture evolved in the last half of the 1970s in the Upper Peninsula Environmental Coalition (UPEC), located in the state's upper peninsula. Unlike its counterparts in the southern two-thirds of the state (the East Michigan, the West Michigan, and the Northern Michigan Environmental Action Councils), the coalition opened its executive committee to representatives of mining and paper companies. In 1978 an employee of the Escanaba Paper Company became its president, and the newsletter was printed by the same firm. The UPEC was far more accommodating to industry than were its counterparts in the lower peninsula; it supported the wood-production industry's efforts to convert forestland to pine, was skeptical of wetlands and land-use legislation, and was extremely cautious with respect to proposals for wilderness in the upper peninsula.[54]

A third instance of this kind of business penetration of environmental organization was provided by the Alabama Environmental Quality Association. This was a state group, but a clientele beyond its borders also subscribed to its publication *Enviro South.* It secured funding from the state as well as from corporations; its association with business groups was reflected in the large number of advertisements in its magazine, which were considered by most environmental publications to be incompatible with their objectives. Association affairs stressed the appreciative quality of the outdoors such as in natural areas and hiking trails but expressed much milder opinions about environmental-protection problems and avoided publicity about, or advocacy of, returnable-container legislation. Advertisements from national steel-, aluminum-, and glass-container manufacturers indicated that these corporations considered *Enviro South* to provide a forum to convey their message that litter education and industry recycling were preferable to returnable-container legislation.[55]

Environmental groups were often tempted to participate in such joint activities because they needed the financial support and accepted the argument that environmental results could not be obtained without the cooperation of the business community. Most environmentalists had become accustomed to political compromise but within a context of initial adversary action that would yield to accommodation in the later rather than the earlier stages of decision making. The key question for both environmentalists and business was the degree to which one would compromise objectives at the start by entering into such joint arrangements in the initial stages of debate. Would clear objectives even surface to the level of options for action if accommodation took place so early?

Two corporate-sponsored organizational activities that were intended to preempt independent citizen action were especially noteworthy. One was Keep America Beautiful (KAB), financed by manufacturers of glass, steel, aluminum, and paper containers, which emphasized citizen education to control litter in order to improve the aesthetic quality of cities and the countryside. KAB included environmental groups on its board. But when it vigorously opposed deposit and returnable-container legislation, most of them resigned in protest. KAB continued to argue that industry and publicly financed education campaigns were the desirable alternative and in so doing was able to persuade many Americans that it was a broadly based civic environmental organization.[56]

A similar industry strategy was manifested after the first energy crisis in the winter of 1973–4, when corporate energy firms organized Americans for Energy Independence (AEI) to counter energy-conservation programs in favor of increasing energy supply. Early in 1977 the AEI became especially fearful when President Carter in his first energy message placed considerable emphasis on conservation. His objective of a 2 percent annual energy growth rate was described as "disastrous" for the nation's economy. The AEI set out to sidetrack all this with a program, initiated in Allegheny County, Pennsylvania, to stress a more limited conservation strategy under industry control and highlighting new sources of supply. Its elaborate public-relations campaign avoided mention of significant energy-conservation measures such as returnable containers, 55-mile-per-hour speed limits, and higher-mileage cars, while emphasizing the need to increase the use of coal and atomic energy.[57]

Corporations were most willing to work with environmentalists in activities devoted to nature appreciation that did not seem to threaten or compromise their immediate interests. Such activities were directed primarily to elementary and secondary school students rather than to adults who might be more immediately aroused to political action. The educational messages conveyed in nature centers, their exhibits, and their literature, as well as their activities, went little beyond the appreciative. Messages about pollution, for example, were usually confined to the unsightliness of litter and not to identification of political issues that might focus on the sources of pollution as targets for action.

One of the most successful ventures in corporate-environmental cooperation was in the acquisition of land for permanent protection as natural environments. Because considerable funds were required, those who promoted purchase sought ways to appeal to potential donors. Landowners could donate property for permanent protection and by so doing obtain a significant tax deduction. This was especially attractive to people in high income brackets and to those who wished to reduce their inheritance taxes. Corporate acreage no longer needed as timberlands, as power-plant sites, or for future agricultural production could be donated with considerable tax benefit.

A sense of accommodation pervaded these ventures. Although it was clear that many involved in conservancy matters had broader personal environmental commitments, it was easy to accept inaction in other realms as the price of success in land acquisition and to adopt the view that accommodation was beneficial in striving for larger environmental objectives.

The control of technological innovation. In environmental affairs the central concern of corporate leaders was the threat of scrutiny of, or interference with, their technologies and processes of production. They were willing to accept controls such as ambient air and water standards, but they were hostile to a more direct system of supervision such as limitations on emissions or direct evaluation of technologies. In the implementation of the Clean Air Act they were able to sidetrack the EPA's efforts to identify desirable control technologies. The Clean Water Act, however, required technological standards, and as a result the EPA developed strategies to evaluate technologies in every branch of production and to rank them by their environmental efficiency. This provided the agency with a comprehensive basis for scrutinizing the degree of modernization within industry and for evaluating the less advanced in terms of the more advanced. Performance in one segment of industry was used to judge another.[58]

Industry objected strenuously to this practice. The EPA argued that when the 1972 act required it to use the "average of the best" as the model for others to follow, this meant the average of the top 10 percent in efficiency. But industry argued that the agency should use the median in the scale from best to worst; this, of course, would require changes in only 50 percent rather than 90 percent of the industry. In a series of decisions in the mid-1970s, the courts rejected the industry's interpretation. The industry also objected to the EPA's practice of using examples of advanced control technologies in other countries as a standard for what could be applied in the United States. But the courts rejected this argument as well on the grounds that science and technology were universal and knew no national bounds.

Faced with pressures from the pollution-control laws to move forward more rapidly with technological innovation, industries were inclined to resist and temporize. The customary response was to ward off the regulatory demands by resorting to public-relations programs and legal or legislative action. Industrial leaders seldom advocated publicly that internal manufacturing processes be examined in order to improve them.[59]

Notable among those who did so was Joseph Ling, vice-president for environmental control of the 3M Corporation. Ling argued that "pollution control pays," that process changes to reduce the level of effluent, recovery of products normally wasted in emissions, and reuse of water could produce savings greater than the costs. He encouraged plant workers to devise innovations in production processes, which, he argued, was preferable to defensive legal and political programs. Ling became popular with environmentalists but was less so with fellow industrialists, who were more inclined to respond to his recommendations with skepticism.[60]

The responses from the business community to environmental regulation were sharpened in the late 1970s through the argument that it lowered productivity. This was difficult to substantiate. When business leaders were requested by the Carter administration to provide more precise evidence, they cited additional costs rather than impacts on production efficiency. The most extensive study of the problem was carried out by Nicholas Ashford of the Center for Policy Alternatives at the Massachusetts Institute of Technology. On the basis of interviews with chemical-firm executives, Ashford concluded that regulation had both inhibited and stimulated innovation to about the same degree. If the burden of regulation was relatively light, the firm tended to oppose it with political and legal action. But if it was heavier, the firm would be inclined to examine its production processes to create greater efficiency.

In order to define their own pace and direction of technological innovation rather than to accept those demanded by the environmental concerns of the larger society, major corporations undertook more positive strategies. They were intended to enable business to take the lead in environmental affairs rather than to be reactive, and hence to have greater control over the course of events.

One innovation was to direct the creation and assessment of scientific experiments. Corporations found that work done by scientists in government or in universities with government funding was inadequate for their purposes. Hence they developed their own research facilities. Private laboratories such as the Haskell Laboratory at the DuPont Corporation and the Dow Chemical lab at Midland, Michigan, served as examples. Their resources and experimental capabilities had long enabled them to exercise considerable influence in environmental science controversies. In 1977 the chemical industry sought to establish a more general authority in toxic chemical science by forming the Chemical Industry Institute of Toxicology at Research Triangle Park in North Carolina. Many trade associations contracted out research to private investigators, for example, in universities, rather than establish their own laboratories. Long active in the field of the health effects of lead, the International Lead-Zinc Industries Association in 1976 began research on cadmium because it believed efforts to regulate it were in the offing.[61]

A more extensive preemptive strategy involved the intensive analysis of a firm's environmental characteristics by outside consultants, ranging from its potential for emissions to the impact of its products. These consultants offered "environmental management" services through which the firm could gather sufficient knowledge about the environmental performance of its own production processes and thus "shape the rules from the start" rather than be on the defensive in its relationships with regulatory agencies.

Much of this was a wider application of previously developed environmental-health strategies. Occupational-health experts, especially in the larger firms, had routinely conducted medical examinations of employees so that they could defend against allegations that working conditions threatened workers' health. The vigorous initiative in occupational health and safety under the Carter administration gave rise to greatly augmented environmental-health divisions in many industries. Even these activities, however, depended on pressure from regulatory agencies. As the climate for regulatory relaxation increased in 1981 under the Reagan administration, environmental-management firms reported that their clients appeared to be far less interested in their services.

The business corporation and environmental change. The response of the business community to environmental action reflected continued disagreement with its objectives and a persistent strategy to contain and reduce its impact rather than to advance it. Much of this opposition came from the simple fact that business did not wish to incur the costs of meeting social objectives considered unnecessary. Other social goals were far preferable. The intangible environmental values of the advanced industrial society deserved a relatively small and circumscribed rather than an expansive role.

Two attitude studies, both conducted in 1982, identified the striking differences between environmentalists and business leaders. In a wide range of questions industry stood at one end of the opinion scale and environmentalists at the other. If we associate environmental values with leading sectors of social change, as is argued in this book, business leaders lagged behind in their acceptance of the policy implications.[62]

The alienation of the business community from these changes in American society was reflected in the types of distrust it aroused among the public. One of the studies found that among a dozen major institutions of American society, corporations were the least trusted of all. And in 1983 the DuPont Corporation found that among the various sources of environmental information on which the public relied environmental groups stood at the top and corporations at the bottom.[63]

The response of the business community to public demands for a higher-quality environment was reactive and negative. It objected to proposals rather than spearheaded them; it did not lead in the search for a better environmental life but instead emphasized the potential undesirable consequences of more vigorous action. As each call for environmental action was sounded, business drew back and, in so doing, removed itself even farther from these aspirations of the American people.

10 The Politics of Science

Farmers, workers, and business people constituted a segment of the environmental opposition that stemmed from direct economic interest. Each of these groups considered its material objectives to be threatened by the expansion of environmental policies. There was another part of that opposition, however, that arose from quite a different quarter, in the realms of science, economics, and planning.

Professionals in those fields were not as firmly hostile to environmental objectives as were those in agriculture, labor, and business; rather, they were prone to argue that although environmental values were quite legitimate social objectives, those objectives were often pushed to excess and expressed in emotional rather than calm and rational terms. Hence they did not tend to array themselves in the forefront of efforts to attain environmental objectives but sought to restrain such efforts. In so doing they became an important element in the environmental opposition.

Diverse fields such as air- and water-pollution control, health, economics, forestry, soil conservation, water resources, and wildlife management were intimately involved with environmental affairs. Each came to argue that its role in such matters was to be neutral rather than one of advocacy, to be professional rather than promotional. Yet within the day-to-day choices of environmental politics, in legislative, administrative, and judicial action, individuals assessed their own specialized knowledge in one way rather than another so as to identify themselves with a particular direction of political choice. Underlying the ideology of political neutrality was the preference for one side or the other in political controversy.[1]

These choices evidenced a consistency and a pattern that reflected hesitation to identify with citizen environmental advocates or with advanced stages of environmental benefits. Most seemed willing to accept existing policies but at the same time were skeptical of too vigorous expansion into new frontiers of environmental action. They might argue that existing national park and wilderness designations were acceptable, but they also hesitated to advocate further ones; they might believe that existing air- and water-pollution control programs were desirable, but they were wary about expanding them to new realms of protection. Such hesitation led to caution rather than vigorous progress and to its own brand of environmental opposition.

Each of these groups had its own concern for the implications of environmental excess. They tended to come together, however, in a general belief that environmental advocates were pushing forward their objectives farther and faster than the nation's resources would permit. Those resources would not sustain as much natural beauty, as high levels of health, as much independence and autonomy in behalf of future generations as environmentalists believed. Whereas producers staked their case on their own interests, professionals argued on behalf of the national interest, which they identified with their own perceptions and values. The link between environmental action and national capabilities defined their distinctive role in the environmental opposition.

Scientific Controversy

Environmental science played a significant role in this strategy of containment. Scientific leaders often accepted environmental action when it increased appropriations for their work, but they also argued that the public's involvement in the scientific aspects of environmental affairs got it into matters best left to the experts. They tended to draw a distinction between informed and rational science, on the one hand, and the far less informed and often emotional public, on the other. Environmental politics entailed a series of confrontations between science and society over the direction of scientific work and the assessment of its results.[2]

The customary image of the role of science in public affairs was that as disinterested and objective investigators scientists would gather knowledge that then could be applied by others for public benefit. Public issues were often technical, and scientists were called on to determine the facts on the grounds that they were not interested parties to the particular outcome of inquiry and hence would be above controversy. Because it was objective, science could unify contending sectors of society and politics. Science readily accepted this view that others often had of its special ability to bring order to political emotion and factionalism.

These conceptions about the function and role of science were shattered in the Environmental Era as a result of a series of controversies over scientific matters that revealed disagreements within the scientific community. Such, for example, were the disputes over the health effects of radiation, dioxin, and lead. They emphasized that something besides "objectivity" had come into play. Different scientists analyzed the same experimental results and saw different facts; they made different assessments of the overall meaning of the same scientific studies. Why these differences? Hardly a public decision maker, from legislator to administrator to judge, did not face in some critical decision a disagreement among scientists of apparently equal training and ability about the meaning of the facts in a specific issue. How were decision makers to resolve disputes that scientists themselves could not?[3]

In their scientific work and in their views about science policy scientists made a host of choices: the appropriate subjects for research, the descriptive categories to apply to the evidence, the skills appropriate to conduct inquiry, the assessment of diverse results. Why did some scientists choose one way and others another? These aspects of the real world of scientific choice gradually led some to think of scientists as a particular group of people, expressing particular values and views as a result of their training, experience, and personal predilections, rather than as neutral investigators, observers, and advisers. Simply to raise such questions was to destroy the image of science as the instrument of universal truth and change both scientific self-conceptions and public views about science.

Scientists were organized into professional societies, research centers, and umbrella institutions such as the National Academy of Sciences (NAS), the National Science Foundation (NSF), and the National Institutes of Health (NIH). Collectively these constituted the institutionalization of science into ongoing activities each with its own leaders and participants, customary modes of operation, and established and dissident influences. The choices made by these institutions also came to be understood as particular and selective rather than universal. Did the problems they chose to study or the scientists they chose to carry out a study represent one point of view or another, one set of scientific skills or another? Did they display commitments to traditional or emerging questions and analyses? One often heard of a scientific establishment, especially in describing the National Academy of Sciences, the nation's central scientific institution.[4]

As one probed into the facts of choice within the scientific community, it became clear that dispute rather than agreement characterized the relationships among members of that community. Precisely because of this high level of internal controversy scientific institutions had developed techniques of mediating and containing it. Some involved the give-and-take of open discussion in journals and meetings; others involved more private interchanges in "peer reviews" of research proposals and results. In its assessments of scientific work the National Academy of Sciences was prone to preserve the anonymity of its committee members and their individual views so as to maintain a public posture of agreement. Such institutional arrangements had served the scientific community well for many years. But the new frontiers of science that environmentalism pressed forward and the ensuing disputes to which they gave rise put intense pressures on these methods of fashioning agreement.[5]

Issues through which scientific controversies were transferred into public debate in the 1970s did not stem entirely from environmental affairs, but they were shaped heavily by them. A significant number of scientists, working often at the edge of knowledge that environmental concerns had helped to fashion, became disaffected. In doing so they challenged the values and preferences of more conventional scientific work. The leaders of scientific institutions were forced to engage in open dispute over issues they had customarily decided in private. They did so reluctantly. At the same time they sought to recapture control over scientific debate and disagreement so as to divorce the internal politics of science from the larger politics of society.[6]

The Allocation of Research Resources

Environmental affairs, outlined previously, engendered an increasing number of demands on limited resources for scientific inquiry into new problems. Here was a persistent realm of political choice. If funds were spent for research into one area, they became unavailable for another; if skills were diverted into one line of investigation, they could not be available elsewhere. The proposals prospective researchers submitted to funding agencies always required far more than the available resources. The politics of environmental science, in the first instance, involved choices as to how these scarce research funds were to be allocated.

These choices involved competing claims within the scientific community. One group of scientists who wished to further a particular line of research sought to demonstrate why its research, rather than another line, should be supported, and to make that case both within the orbit of research institutions and in public discussion. These competing claims were sharpened by the tendency of scientific investigation to become more specialized and fractured, to give rise to a wide range of particular and limited viewpoints, each reflecting claim for support. Few specialists did not believe that the nation would be better off if more funds were spent to expand their own area of knowledge.[7]

Such competition pitted old and established claims against the new. Environmental concerns were new and often were resisted by those accustomed to thinking in older ways. In nutrition, for example, the former emphasis on minimum nutritional protection against disease and "minimum daily allowances" clashed with the more recent stress on optimum nutrition to promote maximum health and fitness; those who underscored a preventive approach to cancer that included environmental causes felt they were bucking a cancer dollar heavily geared to curative results; those who sought to emphasize reproductive health problems felt that amid the overwhelming interest in cancer there was insufficient concern for the mutagenic effects of pollutants on male potency and female miscarriages. The overwhelming emphasis on the acute effects of single pollutants made it difficult to gather knowledge about the cumulative or synergistic effects of many.[8]

There were also claims and counterclaims for funds to emphasize one method over another. Those who favored toxicological experiments on animals, for example, considered statistical epidemiologists to be methodologically sloppy and the resulting data to be unreliable. Analytical chemists were closely aligned in viewpoint with animal researchers; both sought to work with controlled techniques of analysis within limited experimental circumstances. There were, on the other hand, epidemiologists who insisted on individualized data and disdained the attempt to establish exposure and effect relationships with aggregate statistical data about communities of people. And within the realm of individualized data there were those who were willing to compare an exposed group to an average or a norm, whereas others insisted on one-on-one matched controls.[9]

The federal government was involved in considerable research about land and water resources; the manner in which those resources were allocated impinged on environmental issues. The most widely known of these programs was the system of ten forest experiment stations scattered throughout the nation and administered by the U.S. Forest Service. Traditionally these had been devoted to research on commercial wood production: new wood products, threats by insects and other pests to trees of commercial value; inventory of forested land confined to the volume content of wood for commodity use; and the economic analysis of the cost of producing, marketing, and manufacturing wood and wood products. All this was geared primarily to the needs of the wood-production industry. New environmental forestry concerns might have brought about major shifts in experiment station work, in scientific experiments, in inventories, and in economic analysis because of their implications for revised management objectives. But little of this took place.

In the West some experiment stations began to examine the use and overuse of wilderness areas, the values users sought in undertaking wilderness travel, and the management of wildlife. Nationwide the stations developed recreational research about the objectives outdoor recreationists sought so that management could provide for them. In some cases there was research in "aesthetics" or "visual appeal" that emphasized scenic viewing at a distance; in 1978 the Forest Service held its first national conference on forest landscape values. Analysis of the allocation of research funds in the late 1970s indicated, however, that at least 50 percent was fully devoted to wood-production objectives and another 25 percent partially so.[10]

In 1965 the Water Resources Planning Act established a set of university-based research centers throughout the nation that were financed primarily with federal funds administered by the Office of Water Research and Technology (OWRT) in the Department of the Interior. These centers played much the same role in water research as the experiment stations did in forest research. They were shaped during the heyday of the initial enthusiasm for environmental affairs; hence an important portion of their funds was devoted to research pertaining to pollution control. But even this was limited to objectives that could be absorbed into the more overriding concern with commodity uses of water. Few centers took up environmental concerns beyond pollution. A few conducted research on the management of free-flowing rivers, but only one, in Idaho, took up the focus sufficiently to be identified as a major environmental water-research center.[11]

These centers were far more likely to draw into their orbit hydrologists and engineers concerned with the physical movement of water, rather than landscape architects concerned with the aesthetic appeal of recreation in streams and in streamside areas; economists who measured benefits of developed recreation in flatwater reservoirs rather than the enjoyment of free-flowing streams; engineers preoccupied with wastewater treatment rather than the redesign of production processes in industry and the household to reduce water use in the first place; chemical engineers who measured the in-stream chemical composition of water, rather than ecologists who measured benthic organisms, the diversity of in-stream biological life, and insects in the stream environment.

A new set of research centers came into the scene in the Environmental Era that were devoted to coastal-zone and ocean problems. They were part of a sea-grant-program that contemplated a role similar to that of the traditional land-grant institutions, combining research, training, and extension education. Sea-grant programs were financed partially by federal monies but usually required local matching funds. Many academic institutions were able to secure some sea-grant funds, but only a few became established as authorized centers for the full range of sea-grant programs. These new centers stimulated much research associated with coastal and ocean problems.[12]

Despite the development of this complex of marine-research activities in the Environmental Era, it was little influenced by environmental concerns. The range of objectives was quite similar to that of the water-research centers funded through the OWRT. Sea-grant programs were heavily geared to the development of marine-commodity resources, especially fisheries, aquaculture, and mariculture, and the exploitation of the sea's mineral resources. Closely associated with such ventures were concerns about pollution, the description and analysis of pollution effluents into particular bodies of water, their flow and pathways, their residence time, and their consequences for a variety of economic activities. But these often dealt with pollution as subordinate to commodity rather than environmental objectives.

The predominant commodity focus of research on forest, water, and coastal resources was reflected in the limited attention these research centers gave to identification and elaboration of amenity values. A number of attitude studies sponsored by other sources made clear the great degree to which Americans held and sought to express environmental values about land and water. But few of these research centers chose to describe these attitudes, values, and perceptions, to determine the kinds of people who expressed them and the circumstances of their expression, to compare and contrast different levels of balance between natural and developed environments, or to describe patterns of historical transformation from more natural to more developed systems.

This kind of research would have tended to undergird environmental objectives.

The choices made by research institutions could be observed in the composition of their advisory committees that served both as sources of ideas and sounding boards for proposals. They constituted the political links to those institutions that formed the ongoing social context within which research programs were formulated and sustained. The advisory committees reflected a variety of interests: private industry, which supplied some research funds or utilized the institutions' results; professionals who shared in their specialized work the dominant objectives of the research institution such as commercial fisheries or wood production; and representatives of land- and water-management agencies with related commodity-development objectives. In their personal and institutional connections the advisory committees reflected the complex of commodity-development goals that were interlinked in the politics of scientific research and that exercised persistent institutional influence in directing research resources toward commodity and away from environmental objectives.

These preferences could also be observed in the dissemination of knowledge. The most prominent educational component of resource-related research institutions was the Extension Service of the U.S. Department of Agriculture, closely linked to the agricultural experiment stations. It was conceived as an effort to diffuse knowledge gathered through station research. Extension forestry was taken up in the 1950s as a facet of this program to transmit knowledge about forestry to nonindustrial and farm woodlot owners. It was heavily geared to promoting wood production from such lands. Environmental forest values, often dominant in the minds of those who owned such lands, received far less emphasis, if any. Both research and extension foresters, in fact, had difficulty in describing these values in positive terms and continued to refer to "nonindustrial, nonfarm woodlot owners" instead of "environmental forest owners."[13]

Controversies over Levels of Proof of Harm

Marked differences of opinion arose among scientists over the interpretation of the results of scientific work. For any one scientific problem there could be many different studies and a wide

range of evidence. How should they be assessed? To what overall conclusion did available evidence lead, for example, concerning the effects of nonionizing radiation or lead on human health?
Or about the effects of PCBs on marine life? One could be either
very hard or very easy on the evidence, could demand high levels of proof or be willing to draw conclusions on the basis of lower
levels. These were issues between scientists over standards of
evidence and proof.[14]

Both the indeterminate nature of the relevant scientific questions and the action implications of assessments encouraged
strong disagreement. Environmental issues had pushed science
far beyond conventional knowledge on many questions about
which the evidence was either limited or mixed. This was especially the case on the long-term, chronic effects of low-level exposure, which required more sensitive measurements than had
yet been perfected and which often were so complex that the
myriad relationships they entailed were subject to various interpretations. At the same time, whereas knowledge was extensive
about some subjects, for example, cancer, there was less about
others, such as sperm defects; or it might be relatively extensive
about some people such as healthy, adult male workers but less
about others such as younger and older people. Scientific work
had expanded the realm of what was unknown far more rapidly
than it had that of what was known.[15]

These controversies were driven as much by the pressures
impending action placed on science as by the nature of scientific
knowledge itself. Academic science was often leisurely, advancing by interchange among scientists in journals and scientific
meetings, giving rise to occasional sharp dispute but carried out
without pressures to agree. This relatively relaxed system changed
drastically as environmental issues came onto center stage in
the 1960s.[16]

Environmentalists concerned with the adverse effects of development insisted that more knowledge should be accumulated
before potentially harmful action should be allowed to proceed,
and they tended to be skeptical about the arguments of those
promoting development that there was no evidence that harm
would result for humans or the biological world. Industries were
equally eager to defend themselves against regulations to con-

trol their emissions by arguing that the case for harm had not been proved. They took up scientific issues as a major strategy of environmental opposition by demanding far higher levels of proof before regulation.[17]

Debate over the scientific evidence that supported action to regulate emissions was the most widespread instance. Some scientists would argue that there was sufficient knowledge to draw reasonable conclusions that a given pollutant posed a threat. But other scientists would respond that the evidence was insufficient to provide a sound basis for action and that further research was necessary.

These differences would often be expressed in intensely emotional terms. "Conventional" scientists argued that there was "absolutely no proof" that a given pollutant was harmful and derided dissenting scientists as tainted by nonscientific and emotional tendencies. "Frontier" scientists, on the other hand, argued that those who demanded high levels of proof of harm had their own unscientific commitments either in their predispositions or in their institutional loyalties such as to the industries for which they worked or those who financed their research.

In reviewing the scientific literature it was quite possible for one group of scientists to be easy on the evidence and another to be hard. If one wished to discredit a given study, one could readily question the experimental or statistical methodology, and regardless of the study one could find other factors as possible causes of a given effect the study had not taken into account. The intervening or confounding variable was of special interest to those who wanted to "take the heat off" a potential source of contamination and place it on another. Studies of industrial exposures to toxic chemicals, for example, might ignore the differences among workers in their susceptibility to carcinogens and hence enable those who assessed scientific work to argue that this confounding variable should be fully identified before conclusions were drawn.

Scientists could highlight deficiencies in experiments that indicated positive results about the effects of toxic exposures but at the same time gloss over similar deficiencies in experiments that demonstrated negative results from the same exposures. A classical case of this differential judgment occurred in an analysis of the health effects of sulfur dioxide exposures that had been drawn up by a group of British medical experts headed by Dr. W. W. Holland at the request of the American Iron and Steel Institute. The Holland committee rejected all animal experiments as unreliable and found only two epidemiological studies that showed even a slight positive effect. Professor Carl Shy of the University of North Carolina compared the Holland assessment with those of others and pointed out the different ways the same studies had been evaluated and the way the Holland report had taken a markedly different evaluation of positive in contrast with negative evidence.[18]

There were varied types of disputes. There was, for example, the simple question of how the results of an experiment that was visually represented on a slide or an X-ray plate would be described. When scientists sought to distinguish between malignant and benign tumors they could disagree as to just which was which. Interpretation of the X-ray plates of workers exposed to asbestos could lead some to find fewer lesions and others more. Examination of the slides of chromosomes of those exposed to toxic chemicals at Love Canal to determine abnormalities led some scientists to describe them as more numerous and others as less so. When the reasons for such differences were probed it was not uncommon for scientists themselves to respond that the observations were often subjective.[19]

Some disagreements over assessments involved problems of reducing varied measurements to a common denominator. This was the case, for example, with the recurring debate over the health effects of ionizing radiation. It was relatively easy to obtain a common unit of physical measurement for radiation, but a similar common unit for its effect on human tissue was far more difficult to derive. The atomic explosion at Hiroshima generated far less radiation than that at Nagasaki, for example, but its human damage was much greater because of the higher proportion of neutrons. Or the impact of a given amount of radiation absorbed at one time differed from the impact of a similar total dose in a series of exposures over some length of time. How to describe, in a common measurement, these effects when they varied despite the same quantitative level of exposure? Much of the disagreement among scientists over the biological effects of ionizing radiation stemmed from uncertainty over how separate measurements of various types of exposure could be translated into a single common denominator of "relative biological effectiveness." These uncertainties provided considerable leeway for personal judgment.

Although studies tended to be confined to exposures to some people, scientists were under pressure to draw conclusions about their effects on others; this led to quite different scientific assessments. Until the 1960s most evidence about the human effects of pollutants were confined to exposures of adult male workers who were, by the nature of their selection as workers, healthier and hence more resistant to health threats than others. But scientists were asked to assess the implications of these studies for those in the community who were more susceptible, such as women, children, and the elderly. Such reasoning provided considerable opportunity for the exercise of personal judgment and hence led to great controversy.

Similar disagreements could arise from drawing implications about the effects of long-term, low-level exposures from high-level acute ones or the effects of exposures from several pollutants, either in additive or synergistic fashion, from evidence about single ones. Most experimental and statistical evidence dealt with the latter, but it became increasingly apparent that the former were central in health and ecological effects. The demand for knowledge was far greater than its availability, resulting in pressure to make judgments about the unknown from what was known. One could demand that action be postponed until the required scientific evidence was in. But one could also argue that some judgments could and should be made on the basis of the limited evidence.

A central focus in issues about unknowns was the margin of safety. As a result of the wide gap between what was known and what was unknown, some argued that it would be unwise to permit exposures to rise to the level of known effects; a cushion should be maintained between known effects and allowable exposures. This margin was justified also on the grounds that evolving knowledge demonstrated adverse effects at decreasing levels, that this trend could be expected to continue, and that it should be provided for in acceptable levels of exposure. But those who wished to justify higher levels of exposure sought to set the limits only in terms of the firmly known effects. Much of the pressure for action under which scientific assessment labored was directed toward the margin of safety, and its role became increasingly battered amid the controversies in the 1970s over environmental effects.[20]

Leaders in the scientific professions tended to describe these debates as controversies over the relative abilities of scientists and the relative validity of their studies. Although there was "good science" and "bad science," scientists of equal ability could disagree over the meaning of evidence and the implications of different levels of proof. Controversy seemed to involve not the quality of scientific work but the degree to which one scientist or another felt that conclusions could be reasonably drawn from varied kinds of evidence. The values and assumptions of individual scientists played a major role in the fact that they could observe the same evidence and come to different conclusions.[21]

Different abilities were called for to conduct individual scientific studies on the one hand and to assess the implications of many divergent studies on the other. The first required highly technical skills in designing experiments, collecting data, and statistical analysis, skills that involved high levels of ability in identifying, sorting out, and measuring variables so that they could be related precisely. But the assessments needed for public policy required skills more appropriate to making careful and balanced judgments of many factors, more synthetic than analytic, and in drawing conclusions from indeterminate rather than firm evidence. Scientists trained in the first did not necessarily possess the abilities required for the second.[22]

The role of scientists in assessment became especially controversial because in making judgments about the overall meaning of the evidence they were willing to assume the role of objective and disinterested observers when at the same time they displayed their own value judgments in the form of personal, professional, and institutional commitments. The process by which criteria documents were drawn up under the direction of the EPA highlights this. From the time the first one was issued, in 1967, the documents became a special target of industry, which tried to influence the selection of scientists to serve on the committees that drew them up. In order to offset that strategy the EPA, in turn, sought to bring a wider range of scientists into the assessment process. The resulting controversies over the composition of science advisory committees became some of the most fundamental of all environmental disputes.[23]

Frameworks of Empirical Analysis

Differences such as these were often shaped by the different types of "reality" with which different scientists worked. Professional specialization led to increasingly more fractured scientific disciplines as each group of specialists came to know more and more about less and less and hence became distinctive in outlook from other specialists. Training and experience in a particular branch of science took on the character of personal involvement in a particular piece of reality to which one became emotionally attached and which made it difficult to assign to other segments of reality a similar degree of importance.

Scientists often argued that even though they were specialized in one field they were perfectly capable of assessing research in another. A common dedication to the scientific method enabled them to bridge gaps between specialized branches of knowledge. Yet the disputes tended to reveal more fundamental disagreements. The intensity of training and practice in one specialty created an intellectual and personal commitment to what one knew best and about which one could speak most authoritatively. Professional standing depended on the ability to describe a particular piece of reality in such a way as to convince others that one was right, and their confidence only reinforced one's emotional commitment to that reality. Specialization thus created limited, not universal, perceptions, mind-sets that gave rise to fundamental differences in the way the world of scientific reality was understood and interpreted.

In the historical evolution of science new subjects were carved out, categorized, and described amid old. At times disagreement took place between the old and the new that was intensely personal because it was difficult for scientists long accustomed to looking at a subject a certain way to be challenged as having an approach that was either incorrect or out of date. The politics of science often was a clash between different ways in which observers sought to organize the empirical world to which they gave specialized attention.

Early in the 1970s the National Academy of Sciences assessed the health effects of lead. The committee was dominated by specialists on the ingestion of lead and did not include experts in lead inhalation, which, it was now being argued, was the main problem, owing to the use of lead in gasoline. In analyses of the effects of DDT a 1961 NAS committee included few experts on its impact on wildlife, which was of major environmental concern. In each case scientists were criticized for having limited views and seeing only part of the problem. Often they considered these objections a challenge to their personal integrity rather than reflecting limitations inherent in their training and experience.[24]

And so it was with various health matters. Scientists analyzing the chemical effects of lead exposure had difficulty accepting the notion that there were subtle behavioral effects as well. By the end of the 1970s nutritional issues had come to pit specialists who emphasized biochemical analysis against different ways of looking at health and nutrition. While the first claimed there was no chemical proof of a relationship between cholesterol and heart disease, the second contended that their type of evidence confirmed such a connection.

Consider the different perspectives of research toxicologists and medical clinicians. The professional standing of the first depended on their reliability in describing toxicological effects; hence they tended not to draw conclusions until they were quite sure of the facts. This supported a personal commitment to high levels of proof in scientific matters both in the assessment of research results and in more indeterminate issues of margins of safety. Medical clinicians, on the other hand, dealt more directly with the consequences of exposures; regular observation of cases made them prone to be impressed with knowledge gained from personal experience and to draw conclusions from it. Although one might combine these observations with experimental science, they underscored a willingness to act on the basis of tentative conclusions and lower levels of proof because the test of success was not proof but workability. From such different settings, one might argue, arose different kinds of knowledge, one true and the other workable.

The categories used in classifying air, water, and land resources also reflected a clash between the old and the new in
matters of environmental science. I have already described some
aspects of this problem. Environmentalists devised a set of new
categories such as wilderness, wild, and natural areas, or wild,
scenic, pastoral, and recreational rivers alongside older ones. But
it was difficult for older professionals to give these the same weight
as older commodity-based categories. Professional foresters still
used the term "general forest" to describe the most important
part of the forest in which wood production was the dominant
use; other uses were "special uses." They complained about the
degree to which the latter were diverting areas away from the
primary goal of forest management. One even sensed an underlying fear that some day the "general forest" might be thought of
as the "environmental forest" and wood production as a "special
use."[25]

In national-forest management the varied uses outlined in the
Multiple Use – Sustained Yield Act of 1960 were wood, water,
wildlife, recreation, and grazing. Management skills, budget items,
and scientific work were organized in those terms. Newer environmental demands, however, began to shape a new set of classifications in terms of levels of development. This appeared first
in the field of outdoor recreation with the "levels of experience"
categories, which reflected a shift from describing the inherent
quality of the resource to describing human experience in its use.
One might say that many forest controversies in the early 1980s
were results of an attempt to drive the entire forestland classification system from its earlier functional focus to a newer natural–
developed one.[26]

In air-quality issues there was the category of nondeterioration
whereby greater positive emphasis was placed on cleaner air
areas. In water quality a similar term, "antidegradation," conveyed the same general idea of water areas whose quality would
not be permitted to decline; however, it did not lead to as comprehensive a system of classification. The term "conservation
stream" used in Pennsylvania reflected the newer approach.
Merely to establish such classifications constituted a marked innovation for scientific work in air and water quality.

The coastal-zone management program represented a new
realm of description in which it was easier for categories of levels

of development to come into more rapid use. Each state was required to identify permissible uses in the coastal zone, which, in turn, gave rise to resource classification systems to undergird categories of permissible uses. Some states formulated a full natural–developed spectrum of categories, ranging from "preservation areas" through "conservation areas" to "development areas." Use of this approach varied, but the main tendency was to establish some form of it as a basis for classifying data as well as for organizing management.

Water quality had traditionally been classified in terms of human uses: domestic consumption, industrial supply, fishing, swimming, and boating. None of these categories reflected directly the characteristics of aquatic ecosystems. Measurements setting forth the acceptable levels of water quality emphasized specific chemical constituents of particular importance to each use, for example, dissolved oxygen, coliform bacteria, and pH. Moreover, most description and measurement was at the point of outtake from which water was put to human use rather than within the body of water as an ecosystem.

Only slowly did an ecological approach begin to modify this pattern. The 1972 Clean Water Act affirmed an overall perspective by establishing that the goal of the nation's water-quality program should be to "restore and maintain the integrity" of the nation's waters, a concept based on ecological relationships inherent in water. Some biological indicators such as species-diversity indexes were added to earlier chemical and physical ones. But new water-classification systems to reflect ecosystem approaches were developed only slowly; Hawaii was the first to do this in 1978, when it began to assess bottom as well as surface in-stream water quality.

Forest vegetation had long been measured in terms of cover types, that is, the trees of commercial value on given sites. Wildlife specialists, however, were dissatisfied with this classification system and preferred one more attuned to the forest as a wildlife habitat rather than as a source of wood. New proposals first came about in the West, where wildlife biologists began to develop a system of "habitat types" that emphasized not so much the current forest stand and its commercial value as the future potential climax forest on the site.[27]

Problems in habitat classification stemmed also from the need to identify the characteristics of a particular habitat on the verge of being destroyed by a dam in order to replace it with land of similar habitat value elsewhere. The Corps of Engineers, supposedly responsible for providing such mitigation lands, insisted on identifying them in terms of their ability to supply a given number of hunter days of recreation rather than in terms of their inherent habitat characteristics. In this scheme of classification wildlife habitat always seemed to lose out. In response, wildlife biologists developed a classification that categorized habitat directly, thereby identifying more precisely the relevant plant-animal relationships.[28]

The difficulties of incorporating new ecological categories into old patterns of descriptions were illustrated by the tendency of the U.S. Forest Service to tack ecological language onto older categories rather than to change the categories themselves. A multivolume description of the Alaskan national forests entitled *Ecosystems of the National Forests in Alaska* merely categorized resources in traditional multiple-use terms such as wood, water, wildlife, and recreation but labeled each use as an ecosystem. A description of soils in a national-forest plan in Wyoming spoke of "ecological soil types" when, in fact, it simply renamed older categories of physical soils.[29]

The "real world" of scientists often could be found in the categories by which they classified the data they gathered, and the political role of those classifications could be understood through the intensity with which specialists clung to them in the face of change. When one had become immersed in a particular way of looking at the world through long-familiar descriptive categories, one responded only with great reluctance to demands that they be revised. Such challenges and the reaction to them lay at the root of many disputes in environmental science.

Patterns of Scientific Controversy

Two decades or more of controversy over environmental science produced a sufficient number of historical cases – involving lead, radiation, acid rain, and chemical carcinogens, for example – to permit comparative analysis. Were there similarities and differences in the patterns in which these controversies developed? With this question in mind we shall explore several of these cases.

Debate over the health effects of lead, and especially the role of lead in gasoline, arose in the 1920s, when tetraethyl lead was first used as an antiknock additive. After a flurry of disputes about its effects, primarily on workers in the industry, the U.S. Public Health Service assured the nation that no harm would come from its use. The issue died down and did not resurface until the 1950s, when the industry sought to increase the amount of lead in gasoline. During the new debate and on into the 1960s the principal sources of scientific data about lead were Dupont's Haskell Laboratory and the Kettering Laboratory at the University of Cincinnati; at both, research was financed primarily by industry. Two scientists, Robert Kehoe of Kettering and Gordon Stopps of Haskell, were considered the main authorities on lead science in the United States. They dominated the debate over lead.[30]

During the 1960s new researchers published new studies about the effects of lead on the environment and on humans. The work of Clair Patterson at the California Institute of Technology provided more accurate measurements because of his contamination-free laboratory. He was able to demonstrate that lead concentrations in humans in industrial societies were much higher than among preindustrial peoples. Randall Byers of Harvard University found that patients with acute lead poisoning who had been considered cured had permanent neurological disabilities. These new researchers obtained most of their funding from sources other than the lead industry, usually from public-health agencies. They represented a more diverse group of experts who were not constrained by industry needs. Soon, therefore, the debate over the health effects of lead was opened to public scrutiny and decision.[31]

Because of these changes, industry was no longer able to control the flow of data. The lead industry financed a study carried out in the 1960s under the auspices of the Public Health Service but prohibited the agency from releasing the results without its permission. Participants in a lead-regulation proceeding in California, however, released the data in what marked the first failure by the industry to shape public policy by controlling information. An even greater setback came in 1972, when the proceedings of the Lead Liaison Committee, which the Public Health Service had formed to carry out negotiations with industry, were opened by the EPA to public scrutiny. By the mid-1970s, therefore, the lead industry could no longer control knowledge about the health effects of lead by maintaining close relationships with government. The larger public debate now shifted against it.[32]

This shift became clear as a result of the EPA's decision to reduce the amount of lead in gasoline. But an even more dramatic episode was the development of the EPA's lead criteria document in the late 1970s that provided the basis for ambient air regulation. This document went through three versions; in each the new lead scientists were able to revise the assessment toward public-health protection and away from industry's view-point. The key issue was the level of lead in blood at which an "adverse health effect" was identified. The industry took its stand at 40 micrograms per deciliter of blood, but scientists at the Centers for Disease Control and the American Academy of Pediatrics had already accepted a standard of 30 micrograms. The EPA did so as well.

In the first flush of Ronald Reagan's victory in 1984, the industry sought to persuade the EPA to increase, rather than reduce further, the lead content of gasoline. Its initial efforts restored the close private negotiations between government and industry that had prevailed before 1972. But revision of the standard now had to be carried out with full opportunity for public review and comment. In the ensuing public proceedings the force of new scientific opinion was brought to bear on the EPA. The agency reversed its strategy and took steps to tighten lead regulation. By March 1983, when the new EPA administrator William Ruckelshaus took up his post, the agency was well on its way to reducing lead in gasoline from 1.1 grams per gallon on January 1, 1985, to 0.1 gram per gallon on January 1, 1986.[33]

Debate over the health effects of ionizing radiation took quite a different course. The context of the discussion was similar to that for lead; for many years, increased knowledge about the chronic effects of low-level exposures had steadily lowered the exposure level assumed to cause harm. But in this case the nuclear industry had a firmer relationship with government through the Atomic Energy Commission, its successor, the Nuclear Regulatory Commission, and the Department of Defense. Hence the debate did not shift, as had that on lead, to a more open arena but remained within close industry-government private relationships. As a result, a more independent group of scientists concerned with the health effects of radiation did not evolve in health agencies and academic circles, and those who sought to challenge the prevailing industry-government wisdom had to work from a more vulnerable position. The relevant data were more subject to control by others, they and their work were under more frequent attack, and the health-protection agency – the EPA in this case – was far less capable of taking a leading position in health protection.

Data on radiation were especially difficult to obtain. When veterans of the atomic tests in Nevada in the 1950s and early 1960s tried to get exposure data to relate their ailments to radiation, they found that their records had been destroyed or were otherwise unavailable. Measurements of radioactivity around atomic-power plants, which led some to question official statements about such releases, were curtailed. Debate over the health effects of low-level radiation exposure was continually disrupted by the suspicion that civilian and military agencies that had a stake in nuclear matters were able to prevent researchers from obtaining firm data for their work.[34]

Scientists who argued that there were greater health effects at lower exposure levels than conventionally accepted often found major roadblocks in their paths. John Gofman, Arthur Tamplin, and Thomas Mancuso, whose work was financed by federal nuclear agencies, discovered that when they came to such conclusions their funding was not renewed and their scientific credibility was questioned. When Gerald and Martha Drake and Ernest Sternglass undertook studies to identify adverse health effects on those in the path of radioactive fallout, in contrast with those who were not, their work was subjected to intense scrutiny from researchers close to the nuclear industry and government, and their competence was attacked. And there were cases, such as the debate over the effects of radioactive releases from the Shippingport, Pennsylvania, atomic-energy plant, in which the evidence appeared to have been tampered with in order to demolish arguments as to the possible adverse effects of low-level radiation.[35]

The entire debate over this question remained, to say the least, more than messy. Hardly an effort to establish adverse health effects at lower levels of exposure went without vigorous challenge. Several scientists survived relatively unscathed. One was Dr. Karl Morgan, one of the founders of health physics as a discipline. His standing had been so well established before these disputes that he was able to maintain it despite his view that studies indicating effects at lower levels of exposure should be taken seriously. Alice Stewart, a British scientist, had been one of the first to add scientific knowledge to the Japanese survival data when she demonstrated that the children of mothers who had been X-rayed during early pregnancy developed leukemia in a dose-response relationship. She was vigorously attacked for her support of Mancuso's work, but her reputation remained relatively strong. Most radiation scientists who challenged the established wisdom met a different fate.

The lead industry had attempted similar strategies, but without success. It tried to undermine the credibility of Dr. Herbert Needleman and Dr. Sergio Piomelli, for example, as being in a fringe minority of scientists on the question of the health effects of lead. But it also found that their work was taken seriously and helped to underpin public decisions that lowered the acceptable blood lead levels. Whereas these scientists, and others such as Dr. Irving Selikoff in the asbestos controversy, were able to hold their own, the radiation scientists could not. The difference seemed to lie not in the quality of scientific work but in the political context within which they had to obtain data, funds for research, and favorable assessment of their results. Because that political context differed for radiation and lead, the outcome in public policy also differed.

Acid Rain and Chemical Carcinogens

Controversy over acid rain involved the analysis of biogeochemical cycles, from sources to long-distance atmospheric transport and transmission, to deposition and wide-ranging effects. Because the problem provided many points at which scientific questions could be disputed, the debate tended to shift from one point to another in a mélange of arguments. Yet, among scientists directly involved in the relevant fields of specialization, the issue produced a high degree of agreement. A Swedish scientist, Svante Oden, first elaborated in 1968 the hypothesis involving relationships among sources, transmission, and effects. It obtained scientific acceptance rather rapidly, and new research over the following decade and a half bolstered rather than weakened that strong agreement.[36]

The main challenge to this scientific consensus came from outside the scientific community in the coal and coal-using industries. Their opposition to the restriction of sulfur dioxide emissions, first taken up in the 1960s, continued over the ensuing years. Their initial objections in 1967 had succeeded in increasing the allowable level of SO_2 from 0.02 ppm, initially proposed by the Public Health Service, to 0.03 ppm. When the National Air Pollution Control Administration and its successor, the Environmental Protection Agency, sought to bolster its data about the health effects of sulfur oxides in the so-called CHESS studies, industry attacked the scientific integrity of the study's leader, Dr. John Finklea, and created sufficient doubt in Congress to discredit the work politically. Thereafter, the agency did not seriously pursue research on the health effects of sulfur oxides.[37]

Before the concentration on health in air-pollution matters in the late 1960s and early 1970s, the main concern had been the effects of air pollution on crops, forests, materials, and visiblility, which secondary standards were to protect. But early in the 1970s the Kennecott Copper Company undermined the secondary sulfur dioxide program when it persuaded the federal courts to strike down the secondary annual average standard. Interest in each of these secondary effects revived in the 1970s and came to be focused on the issue of acid precipitation. New data were added to old to create a single set of concepts much on the order of Oden's ideas. These adverse effects occurred at lower concentrations than those threatening human health; hence, protection would call for restrictions on coal burning that would be more stringent than primary standards.

The fossil-fuel industry vigorously strove to control the direction of this expanding scientific inquiry and the assessment of its results. But the cumulative impact of the discoveries made this difficult. Industry sought to stall action by calling for more research and information before conclusions were drawn, and beginning in 1978, this led to increased federal funds for research. The electric-power industry and several states that felt adversely affected by acid rain also sponsored research. The accumulation of knowledge from all quarters solidified the consensus in the scientific community at large beyond the smaller confines of industry. New research confirmed older, established views and elaborated the interconnections in the biogeochemical cycle.[38]

Despite this consensus amid the rapid advance of knowledge, industry was able to extend the scientific debate because of its close relationship with the federal government. It had long enjoyed support from the Departments of Energy and Commerce on the issue of sulfur dioxide pollution. During the Reagan administration it obtained even more crucial support within the Executive Office of the President. That close relationship was underlined soon after the new administration came to office in 1981, when it sought to halt negotiations inaugurated by the Carter administration with Canada on acid-rain control.

The scientific committee in these proceedings, composed jointly of scientists from both Canada and the United States, was on the point of agreeing that the threshold of harm stood at 20 kilograms of sulfate deposition per hectare per year. If accepted, such a view would require considerable additional control of sulfur dioxide emissions. That figure, therefore, and the American scientists who agreed with it, came under attack. The administration replaced them with new personnel – not scientific specialists in the biogeochemistry of chemical cycles, but technical professionals in other fields who disagreed with the emerging scientific consensus more on policy than on scientific grounds.

The committee now faced a permanent deadlock, its work came to an end, and each country proceeded to make its own scientific assessments about acid rain. But the subsequent U.S. review carried out by the Office of Science and Technology Policy confirmed the prevailing scientific views rather than those in the administration. Industry's isolation was reflected in its relative lack of support in the scientific community. As scientists spoke out in favor of controls to protect against acid rain, they were countered not by fellow scientists but by industry public-relations experts.[39]

The role of chemical carcinogens gave rise to another pattern of controversy. Health scientists considered epidemiology useful primarily when relatively high levels of exposure could be related statistically to acute health effects; it was far less powerful in its investigation of chronic effects of persistent low-level exposures. For this type of problem, which was emerging as a central concern with respect to chemical carcinogens, experiments on animals had greater possibilities. Hence the increasing importance of animal toxicology.

The chemical industry was extremely wary of toxicological research because of its potential for identifying a large number of chemicals as carcinogens. The agricultural-chemical industry had objected to its use by the EPA as a basis for its "cancer principles" to regulate pesticides. When OSHA sought in 1979 to establish a general regulatory policy based on animal toxicology, as related in Chapter 6, the industry rebelled and, through the newly organized American Industrial Health Council, succeeded in thwarting it. But animal toxicology had considerable support among health scientists as the most useful way to expand knowledge about chemical carcinogens. If one rejected it because of the acknowledged weakness of epidemiology, little scientific progress on the matter seemed possible.

In the medical community, in Congress, and in the general public there was a great interest in discovering a "cure" for cancer, which led to the "war on cancer" launched in 1971. For several years thereafter the National Cancer Institute had concentrated its resources on virus cancer research. But this aroused the objections of specialists who sought to use other approaches, and their criticisms became more convincing as a cure for cancer was not quickly found.

By the late 1970s an alternative route, that of identifying environmental carcinogens to which exposure might be avoided, had attracted much support. As a result of this debate, Joseph Califano, secretary of health, education, and welfare, in 1978 established the National Toxicology Program, which served as the main governmental body to conduct toxicology studies and, thereby, to develop a list of hazardous chemicals. The program was promoted vigorously by David Rall of the National Institute of Environmental Health Sciences, who became its director. The National Toxicology Program led to a continually expanding list of chemical carcinogens that was used in making public policy; its experimental work enjoyed increasing credibility.[40]

The chemical industry sought to deflect this strategy on the grounds that the lists would unduly alarm the public, but, in contrast with the success of the coal and utility industries in the acid-rain debate, it failed to do so. In the first two years of the Reagan administration, during the tenure of Dr. John Todhunter as assistant administrator for the EPA's toxic-materials programs, the industry met some success. The regulation of formaldehyde was the key issue. The Chemical Industry Institute of Toxicology had found that formaldehyde caused cancer in animal experiments. Yet the chemical industry and the institute itself argued that such evidence was not a sufficient basis for implicating a chemical as a human carcinogen. The EPA, therefore, declined to regulate formaldehyde.[41]

But the new EPA under William Ruckelshaus took a different view. Whereas representatives of the chemical industry continued to question the use of animal data in environmental regulation, the EPA and other federal agencies looked to toxicology as the method by which they could make regulatory choices. At the same time, an EPA committee working under the auspices of the Office of Science and Technology Policy drew up a set of "cancer principles" for administrative policy-making. These principles did not differ much from those the EPA had prepared a decade earlier or those an interagency policy-making group during the Carter administration had favored. Increasingly the debate revolved not around the principle of animal toxicology but around research methods and the way the results were interpreted.[42]

In these varied cases of scientific debate in public policy the most significant element was the relationship among independent scientists, industry, and governmental agencies. When industry had a firm foothold in the agencies, as in matters involving radiation, it was able to undermine the credibility of both science and scientists among its adversaries. But when that connection was weaker, as in matters involving lead, the full weight of independent scientific opinion could be brought to bear on policy-making. Acid rain and cancer toxicology provided equally important contrasting cases. In both there was considerable consensus in scientific opinion. In the area of acid rain, industry had strong allies in government and succeeded in thwarting that opinion, but in the debate over animal toxicology its standing was weak, and it could not prevent the advance of toxicological testing as the basis of thought and action on chemical carcinogens.

The Roots of Scientific Dispute

To what do these controversies among scientists add up? Is there any pattern that runs through all of them? The initial temptation is to argue that scientific views depended heavily on the sources of funds that sponsored the work. There is much truth in this observation. The identification of problems for research, the selection of scientists to conduct it, and the construction of research designs stemmed from choices made by those in private industry and government who had funds to finance research. If one wished to advance a particular interest or public policy, one did not want to risk defeat by calling on an expert who did not share one's point of view.[43]

The institutional influences in scientific choice were often thought of as directly monetary. Scientists had a financial stake in the acceptance of their advice, and this stake helped to shape that advice. In accordance with this view, for example, the National Academy of Sciences excluded from its review committees scientists who were stockholders in either the companies for which they worked or those that financed activities the committee was asked to review. In the 1960s and 1970s, however, the idea of "conflict of interest," was broadened to include one's role as an employee. It was difficult for scientists not to express the points of view of their employers. Hence scientists employed by business and industry or by developmental agencies in government should not be relied on for scientific judgments about matters in which their employers had an interest.

The relationship in sponsored research was subtler. To some scientists the main question raised by sponsorship involved their right as independent investigators to publish freely the results of their research. Many private corporations would not permit this.

Several cases in which negotiations between industry sponsors and scientists had been broken off because of such disagreements were publicized among scientists as warnings of what could happen. But in the 1970s conflict of interest in funding went beyond even this. Some came to question the independence of scientists financed by those with an obvious political stake in the outcome. One could not conduct and report research without bias knowing that continued funding depended on results acceptable to the sponsor. Both scientists and corporations sought to mute this relationship by "laundering" funds through research institutes, but this seemed to modify neither corporate expectations nor the understanding of these implications by scientists.[44]

These observations about the relationship between scientists and their sources of funding were limited to the notion that the problem was one of independent scientists' being compromised by external political forces. But the compatibility of shared values played as significant a role. Scientific controversies often involved differences in values that went far beyond the immediate interests at stake. The close relationship between the sponsors of research and the views of those whose research they funded was rooted in shared personal values that transcended mere contractual relationships between employer and employee. They came together through reinforcement of sympathetic and symbiotic perspectives.[45]

Professional training involved the acquisition of specialized skills and led to strong commitments to particular branches of knowledge and investigative techniques. This evolved both in the course of formal training in higher education and in on-the-job training. Value commitments were initiated in the first and reinforced in the second. Some left employment because of conflicting personal and institutional values. This happened frequently in the forestry profession as young people trained in forestry schools found that employment with either industry or the U.S. Forest Service entailed unacceptable obligations.

Even subtler were the value commitments stemming from predispositions brought to training in the first place. On questions of the adverse effects of pollutants, one could separate those individuals who as students were prone to play it safe with evidence and require high levels of proof before drawing conclusions from those who were comfortable working in more indeterminate circumstances on the frontiers of knowledge. Such differences led one early in one's career to choose courses of study that were compatible with one set of values or the other.

Professionalization led to the reinforcement of personal preferences by institutional commitment. Some were comfortable with this, but others were not. Pressures toward intense specialization were found by some to be incompatible with their desire to synthesize divergent pieces of hard knowledge in order to make sense out of science. Pressures to confine their conclusions to what was established and conventional knowledge did not sit well with those who wished to work on the frontiers of health-effects inquiry.

These institutional, professional, and personal factors in scientific dispute tended to become organized around the value questions that lay at the heart of environmental politics. There were those with strong commitments to more traditional types of material development. They were friendly to the notion that developmental institutions in both private and public affairs should be given considerable leeway to pursue their objectives. Hence they tended to object to the claims of potential harm made either by those who wanted to investigate more fully the environmental impacts of development or by those who wished to regulate more closely sources of pollution. They viewed the nation's institutions as constituting a unified system of production that should be impeded only occasionally and in a limited fashion. They were sympathetic, therefore, to business and industry and their allies in the governmental agencies.

But there were others who tended to associate themselves with environmental objectives and who spoke more fully for those who were subject to harm. Often these were the scientists in fields such as public health and ecology, whose professional training and occupations attuned them to those aspirations and the threats to them. They sought to associate themselves with institutions such as Public Health Service, the EPA, and the Fish and Wildlife Service, which worked on behalf of environmental objectives, or to work in an academic setting in which they would be freer. Although some found private corporate business tempting; others believed that employment there would be far too restrictive of their freedom to express their values in their professional work.

In the scientific debates of the Environmental Era the private and public institutions that exercised considerable authority over the discovery, dissemination, and application of scientific knowledge also had considerable influence over the expression of the professional and personal values of the scientific community. The corporate world tended to establish close links with scientists who shared a hostility toward environmental objectives. At times scientists who early in their careers had expressed skepticism about working for industry later stated that they had come to appreciate the viewpoints of their employers and to agree with them. More often corporate leaders sought out scientists with views compatible with their objectives. Corporations institutionalized these shared values into a political force to influence the distribution of scientific resources, the scientific bases of public policy, and public scientific opinion.

The relationships between scientists and government were more varied and were formed in the first instance by the respective developmental or environmental missions of the agencies. Scientists associated with the Departments of Agriculture, Commerce, and Energy tended to share their objectives and to shape research and assessments toward those ends. But scientists associated with environmental agencies such as the Fish and Wildlife Service, the National Park Service, and the EPA took a more environmental turn. Especially significant was the role played by scientists in the Public Health Service who considered that their mission was to enhance rather than limit the quality of the nation's health.[46]

Trends in the Politics of Science

From the late 1960s onward the corporate world was increasingly influential in environmental science as a basis for public policy. The vigorous objection by industry to the sulfur oxides criteria document in the spring of 1967 and the scientific assessments by the Public Health Service on which it was based led to a successful action to force revision of the document under the advice of scientists outside the service, including those in the coal, steel, petroleum, and automobile industries. From that time on environmental agencies and scientists in general became more cautious in their scientific judgments.

Industry leaders continued to press their case. They sought to reinforce those scientists who in their own professional and personal commitments insisted on high levels of proof of harm. They brought to legislative and administrative hearings and court testimony scientists who argued that more proof was needed. They attacked the margins of safety as requiring an inordinate degree of protection, representing unreasonable notions about plausible but yet to be fully discovered unknowns. At times they played a major role in discrediting opposing scientists. In these strategies they played on deep-seated self-images. There was a constant tendency for scientists to think of themselves as reliable only if they refrained from drawing conclusions short of firm proof. Hence they were susceptible to these challenges from industry.

Especially through its lawyers corporate industry brought such pressures to bear on scientists in courts, administrative agencies, and legislatures. It was one thing for scientists to be willing to express views in the more leisurely setting of a scholarly journal or a professional meeting. It was quite another thing to be subjected to relentless cross-examination on a witness stand. These political pressures strengthened tendencies toward firmer positions concerning levels of proof. In the late 1960s a number of scientists had been willing to argue in favor of protective action against air pollution, for example, even though there was inconclusive proof of adverse health effects, because suggestive evidence seemed to make such action reasonable. By the early 1980s fewer scientists were willing to take a similar public position.[47]

Corporate political strategies took up the views of the leaders of scientific institutions who described these controversies as "good science versus bad science." Neither accepted the notion that the issues involved legitimate differences within the scientific world. Both sought to describe them in terms of the quality of the scientific work itself. To leaders of scientific institutions this separated them from scientists associated with environmental efforts; to corporate leaders it also reinforced their objectives of requiring high levels of proof before action.

As the issues over levels of proof became sharper some corporate leaders took up a more vigorous attack. Officials of the Dow Chemical Company especially displayed almost religious zeal. Governmental scientists and those on whom governmental agencies relied, they argued, were simply bad scientists, and the scientific assessments on which environmental regulation was based, in turn, were flawed. In its effort to challenge the EPA's proposal to restrict the use of the herbicide 2,4,5-T, Dow argued vigorously that the future of science itself was at stake. It would fight the case as a matter of principle regardless of cost because the quality of American science was involved.[48]

Many scientific leaders had been unhappy with the degree to which differences within the scientific world had become public disputes. They searched for methods by which scientific controversies could be resolved by scientific leaders themselves within the confines of their own institutions. The most widely discussed proposal was the "science court." Scientific disputes associated with regulatory activity, so the argument went, were resolved ultimately by judges in the courts or in administrative law proceedings who had little competence in scientific and technical matters. This should be replaced by an institution in which scientists should serve as judges and the parties to the dispute would present evidence under strict rules of procedure and cross-examination much like those governing judicial proceedings. Judges of the science court would resolve the differences on the basis of the resulting evidence. In the late 1970s an attempt was made to test this proposal experimentally; but it was not implemented, because of the belief that truly impartial scientists could not be found to serve as judges.[49]

Could a science court substitute the unifying power of truth for the divergent tendencies within science? The source of disagreement lay not in the formal mechanisms of decision making but in specialization within science and the personal predispositions of scientists on the one hand and the objectives of corporate and governmental institutions on the other. The science court was primarily an attempt on the part of leaders of scientific institutions to substitute scientist control over disputes among scientists for control by governmental decision makers. Scientific disagreements should be resolved within the realm of science alone and not in the wider public area. The political power to make choices amid disagreement should rest in institutions under the control of self-selected scientific experts rather than with the public at large. But it was precisely the breakdown in the ability of such institutions, notably the National Academy of Sciences, to serve as authoritative sources of agreement that led to open political debate on scientific issues in the first place.[50]

These events highlighted the degree to which scientific institutions were, in fact, political institutions. Acceptable scientific knowledge was acceptable precisely because it was agreed on. What was truth in scientific matters often was as much a question of what those influential within the scientific community took to be widely shared conclusions. If there was little dispute over the facts, the knowledge was conventional precisely because it was a matter of consensus. It was this consensus that environmental science had helped to fracture, and by doing so it had reduced the authority of established scientific institutions and expanded participation in the debate from the wider public.[51]

Both the scientific establishment and the corporate world now sought to reduce the range of that input and to gain control over the process of fashioning scientific consensus in order to shape public policy. Although their objectives differed markedly, the two sectors reinforced each other in attempting to recapture control over the political process in order to further their own version of agreement about the nature of environmental scientific knowledge.

11   The Politics of Economic Analysis and Planning

In the debates over the importance of environmental values amid many competing social and political objectives, decision makers insisted that some device be found by which one set of proposals could be balanced against another. Over the years two strategies were devised to do this, one in economics and the other in planning. Economics sought to weigh values as current costs and benefits in an accounting arrangement; planning attempted to identify future needs and the resources required to fill them.

There was a persistent temptation to believe that both economic analysis and planning were more objective and rational than the give-and-take of "politics." Each discipline was assumed to deal with a world "out there" independent of the vagaries of personal and institutional choices. Quantitative data tended to cloak their activities in a mantle of objectivity. Since they were value-free, they were associated with a larger public purpose than the objectives of more limited interests. Hence both economists and planners shared the reputation for disinterestedness that was enjoyed by scientists. Many looked on them as advisers who could play a major role in bringing order out of a political world of myriad contending objectives.[1]

Yet economic analysis and planning were prone to reflect personal, professional, and institutional value commitments much

363

as science was. The overlay of quantitative data often obscured those value choices. In environmental debate both economists and planners aligned themselves with one position or another and thereby brought their values to the fore. As in science, these personal values, professional commitments, and institutional affiliations tended to associate them with institutions of social order and management. And those associations reinforced developmental far more than environmental objectives.[2]

The initial response of these two professions to environmental objectives differed. Among economists there was considerable hesitation from the start about the wisdom of environmental aims. They sided with those who warned environmentalists about going too far rather than with advocates of innovation in advancing environmental objectives. They counseled restraint.[3]

Planning was far more receptive to environmental objectives. Both in the schools in which they were trained and in their organizations, planning professionals sought to encourage the acceptance of those goals. But in the web of both private and public institutions that constituted the daily political context of planning, thought and action were weighted toward developmental rather than environmental objectives. Hence, as environmental planning was put into practice, its environmental predispositions were sharply curtailed.

By the 1980s both economists and planners had begun to urge restraint in environmental affairs, economists enthusiastically and planners reluctantly. Although in both areas there were dissident elements that sought to advance environmental objectives more vigorously, leaders in both professions tended to join in with those who argued that rapid advance of environmental objectives would burden the nation's resources. They became associated with the advocacy not of steady environmental progress but of caution and a more restricted environmental agenda.

The Politics of Economic Analysis

Environmental accounting. Economists were able to give only a limited response to the new methods of environmental accounting that I outlined earlier. They often began their analyses with an affirmation of the importance of environmental wants and needs and ended by giving little weight to them. A major difficulty was the inability to attach numbers to consumer demands that could not be represented by prices. Some economists tried to do so with nonmarket environmental amenities, but their results were cumbersome and more useful as an academic exercise than as an aid in decision making.[4]

Economists found it far easier to focus on environmental costs to which numbers could be assigned in the form of the cost of repairing damage. Dirty air required housecleaning, necessitated medical care, and in the form of acid rain reduced fish populations and threatened the tourist trade. Strip mining led to disfigured landscapes that had to be reclaimed and polluted water that had to be treated. Economists could readily take into account such costs and then balance them against the costs of preventing the damage with the use of pollution controls. This type of accounting system was often described as an exercise in balancing costs and benefits, but it was more a matter of balancing costs to some against costs to others.[5]

Economists were especially intrigued with the idea of internalizing the cost of pollution damage, in which the firm would be forced to incorporate that cost into its own calculations rather than simply impose it on others. Costs should be shifted to those who purchased products made by polluting industries. One proposal was a pollution tax to be levied against the polluter to a sum equal to the amount of damage the pollution caused. Such a tax, it was argued, would lead to action to prevent pollution in order to avoid the tax. But attempts to work out the idea in detail, such as the Nixon administration proposed in 1970, led to the conclusion that it would be impossible to fix the amount of the tax in such a way as to avoid prolonged litigation by industrial sources that would argue that the amount they were required to pay was too high.[6]

A variant on this proposal, the "noncompliance penalty" approved in the Clean Air Act of 1977, was to be imposed on a polluter in the amount that had been saved by noncompliance. The formula for the precise amount was as complicated as the pollution tax. Only slowly did the EPA take steps to implement it; industry objected to the severity of the proposed penalty, and few economists defended the device their own analyses had helped to create. The noncompliance penalty gave the EPA greater leverage in establishing the level of fines it sought in civil suits against polluters, and settlements were sweetened by the EPA's concessions that the firms could use the money paid in penalties to install pollution-control equipment.[7]

Economists were better able to accept the environmental analysis of the public costs of development and the argument that those costs were frequently unjustified. The debate over water-development projects, described in Chapter 5, provided the main opportunity to refine these ideas. Economists as well as environmentalists were convinced that many such projects did not provide public benefits commensurate with their costs. Environmentalists stressed the failure of agencies to include in their cost calculations environmental damage such as the loss of a free-flowing stream, whereas economists were more likely to emphasize the inflated benefits that agencies such as the Corps of Engineers claimed for their projects.[8]

The item of accounting that came to be a special bone of contention in water-project analysis was the discount rate. An investment made at the time of construction was a current cost, but benefits would be realized over the life of the project. Some device was needed to estimate those future benefits, in much the same way as the return of any capital investment could be calculated. The key figure was the discount rate, which one might think of as similar to an interest rate. A lower discount rate would enhance estimated benefits for it would cover a longer period of time over which the investment would be fully returned, and hence total benefits could be increased. A higher rate would shorten that period and reduce benefits.

In order to maximize calculated benefits, federal agencies used a discount rate that was often lower than the going rate of interest earned by private investment. To economists the investment of public funds should be thought of as "opportunity costs," the relative returns of money in different investment opportunities. If public funds would bring returns of only $5\frac{1}{2}$ percent in public-works investments when those same funds invested in the private market would bring 8 to 10 percent, then public money was being invested unwisely. Environmentalists took up the same argument, widely publicized the low discount rates used in calculations of public-works projects, and pointed out that rates closer to the interest earned by current capital investment would render many projects economically unsound.

Similar arguments began to emerge in the late 1970s concerning the management of the national forests. Much land in those forests, so some economists and most environmentalists argued, was marginal in productivity. Although it might be profitable to remove timber already there (since one would be tempted to balance only the cost of harvest against the proceeds from the sale), investments in reforestation would not return profits commensurate with alternative uses of public funds.

Environmentalists began to develop data demonstrating that on much national forestland devoted to commercial wood harvest the cost of production exceeded the returns. They secured a provision in the 1976 Forest Management Act to the effect that the marginality of national forestland for timber production should become a major element in management decisions. The ensuing debate also involved the discount rate. The Forest Service sought to justify a low rate on the grounds that its operations were not intended to be profitable. But some forest economists not associated with the Forest Service began to accept the environmental argument that efficient expenditures of public funds required that marginality be taken into account.[9]

In these cases of public expenditures for water and land development economists could accept some aspects of environmental economic analysis, but there was far less agreement on the benefits of regulation to human health. Economists began to argue that one ought to place a monetary value on human life so as to balance the benefit of avoiding premature death with its cost. The suggested amounts varied widely from $100,000 to well over $1 million, and the proposed accounting usually suggested a range of possibilities. Often it was left to the courts to determine such amounts in liability cases, and these also varied considerably. Especially interesting were the differences placed on the value of human life in the case of liability claims brought in different countries as a result of international air crashes.[10]

This attempt to place monetary value on human life held out a special appeal to scientists. As the debate over environmental science revealed its limitations in coming to firm conclusions about health effects of pollutants, there was a tendency to argue that economic analysis provided the kinds of objectivity and rationality science no longer seemed able to claim. Hence scientists who could not make a judgment stick as firmly as their pretensions would indicate turned at times to economic analysis for the "hard data" that presumably provided more clear-cut and value-free judgments.[11]

The difficulties encountered by economists in accounting for environmental factors in a traditional cost-benefit mode led them to devise new strategies. One that became rather popular in the late 1970s was known as cost-effectiveness analysis. In this approach the economic analyst disavowed any attempt to question objectives, took them as given, and focused entirely on the least costly method of reaching those objectives. With this approach the thorny problem of quantifying benefits could be avoided. They could simply be taken as given, decided by other public decision makers, and presumably, therefore, reflecting public objectives. Cost-effective analysis had considerable difficulty remaining confined to its assumptions. In suggesting alternative means of achieving established ends it was quite easy to modify the ends themselves.[12]

By the end of the 1970s the analysis of risk had come to dominate economic analysis of environmental-health regulation. The main purpose of this approach was to classify different types of hazards in terms of their relative degree of risk and to focus on those that involved more risk in contrast with those that involved less. Risk was thought of primarily in terms of avoiding death or even incapacitating injury. One could determine the chances of death from cancer due to the operation of nuclear power plants, from driving an automobile, or from crossing the street. One environmental threat could thereby be compared with another. This approach was attractive to economists because of its potential for focusing on hard data; rates of risk were relatively easy to quantify.[13]

But this world of economic analysts was at odds with the experience of most people. To economists it was obvious that one should think of risk in terms of statistical probability. From this point of view both driving an automobile and living in one's home were relatively risky. But most people were not especially concerned about such activities, because they believed they could control them. These risks were distinguished from those over which one had no control, such as toxic chemicals in drinking water. It was not that either the public or economists were correct or incorrect; it was more that they lived in quite different worlds. Economists continually asked the public to accept "objective numbers," and the public asked economists to accept personal experience, choice, and control.

The success of economists in shaping the methods of environmental accounting was reflected in the fate of environmental-impact analysis. Although that format served to underscore environmental factors and forced developmental agencies to take them into account, the manner in which they did so often provided a forum for highlighting the adverse effects of such objectives on conventional production. As economists were brought into the group of interdisciplinary professionals who wrote environmental-impact statements (EIS's), they began to focus on the effect of environmental action on agency developmental missions. The analyses, therefore, often gave attention not to environmental goals but to trade-offs that stressed the adverse economic effects of environmental policies. They became economic-impact as well as environmental-impact statements, and the balancing format gave the authors of the statements considerable freedom to adjust the factors as they chose.

The politics of production costs. Throughout the 1970s the analysis of the cost of environmental programs to business and government came to exercise an influential role. It was not that cost considerations had been absent in the early stages of environmental programs but, rather, that the environmental opposition sought, with time, to increase their role. The economic-cost analysis of environmental affairs began to shift from an attempt to identify and balance factors from both sides to an instrument devoted more to reducing regulatory pressures on production. By the end of the decade production-cost analysis had become a major political tactic on the part of industry to delay and obstruct environmental policies.[14]

The clean-air and -water laws distinguished between standards and implementation, between environmental goals on the one hand and their achievement on the other. There was little disagreement about the wisdom of granting industries variances (extended time beyond the deadlines) to achieve standards in order to pace progress with the particular economic circumstances of each industry. Many firms, notably in the automobile and steel industries, regularly asked for such extensions. Sometimes these were the subject of legislative revision, but usually they involved administrative adjustments in the rate of cleanup; in some localities variance boards were established to decide on such requests. In these deadline extensions cost factors played an important role.

Industries, however, sought to incorporate costs into decisions to set standards as well. Environmentalists argued that standards should be based solely on judgments about society's desired levels of environmental quality, such as those relating to health, water supply, visibility and aesthetics, aquatic and terrestrial ecology, and forest management. But industry maintained that this procedure led to excessive and costly goals. To bring social goals under control, so the argument went, costs should be incorporated into the decision to set standards in the first place. Over the years their arguments bore fruit.[15]

Acutely aware of the political context within which it worked, the EPA continually modified its proposals so as to minimize reactions from industry on the grounds of cost. Business groups complained about additional costs; they used their own economic analyses and those of their consultants to demonstrate that proposed regulatory actions would have severe economic consequences. Such analyses often persuaded the EPA to modify both the level of standards and the rate of implementation. Hence there arose a contest between the EPA and the regulated industry as to whose economic analyses would prevail.[16]

Over the course of the 1970s, there were two general trends in this contest. First, the EPA was required increasingly by pressure from industry, the law, and the Executive Office of the President to undertake more extensive and intensive analyses of its proposed actions. Second, by the quality of its economic analyses the EPA persuaded many, although not its industry opponents, that it had taken cost factors into account and that the adverse economic impact of its actions were sufficiently minimal to be acceptable in the light of environmental goals.

In the early 1970s, production costs focused on the loss of jobs, but the EPA's statistical analyses on this score, discussed in an earlier chapter, demonstrated that its programs created far more jobs than they eliminated. When industry complained of the more general cost burden, the EPA was able to demonstrate that it had analyzed costs in each industry group thoroughly and was able to define the varying degree of burden on different plants. The courts accepted its argument that the test of the cost burden should not be its impact on individual, often obsolete, plants but the health of the entire industry.[17]

The EPA was sufficiently sensitive to the costs of implementing its programs that at times it softened its regulations even though the law was explicit that economic factors were not to be the basis of decisions. This happened with the control of hazardous air pollutants such as asbestos, beryllium, mercury, and vinyl chloride. In the last case the EPA's standards were loosened because of cost impacts in spite of the clear directive in the law that costs should not be taken into account in cases of hazardous, in this case carcinogenic, air pollutants. In the latter part of the decade a study of the relative accuracy of the EPA's and industry's predictions of costs concluded that studies sponsored by both had overestimated the amount – the EPA's by 50 percent and industry's by 100 percent.[18]

Despite these efforts at cost analysis the pressures for more extensive and elaborate calculations increased. Provisions of the Clean Air Act in 1977, for example, were more explicit about required cost-benefit and risk-benefit studies than were earlier statutes. At the same time, the National Air Quality Commission, established by the 1977 act to examine the air-quality program, was required to conduct studies of both economic and environmental consequences. More important, presidential aides during the Ford and Carter administrations placed considerable pressure on regulatory agencies to undertake more elaborate cost analyses of their actions. As each new level of intensity of analysis was taken up, industry demanded more. By the 1980s the Executive Office of the President had become the focal point of political leverage for industry in its drive to emphasize the production costs of environmental regulations.[19]

In the Carter years the Council on Wage and Price Stability (CWPS) brought the issue of economic analysis to a head. That body was established under the Council of Economic Advisers to undertake cost-benefit assessments of proposed regulatory actions. At the same time, in an executive order of March 23, 1978, President Carter required all federal agencies to perform such analyses on their own. The CWPS, as the supervising body, reviewed proposed regulations from that time on, constantly challenging agency actions. There was hardly a new regulation of importance to which the CWPS did not object as being too costly. As a result the interplay between the CWPS and regulatory agencies became a primary point of political debate and choice. Out of that controversy emerged several new lines of debate.[20]

First was the argument that in its analysis the CWPS did not confine itself to its alleged goal of guaranteeing "cost effectiveness," that is, the most efficient way of achieving congressionally mandated policy goals, but in fact sought to revise those goals and hence to reduce benefits. Thus, with regard to the photochemical-oxidant standard set in 1979, the CWPS argued that it was not necessary to provide health protection for older, susceptible people, and hence a higher level of pollution could be accepted even though Congress had made it clear in the air-quality laws that such individuals should be protected. And, concerning the cotton-dust standard designed to protect workers in cotton mills, the CWPS argued that workers should wear respirators to protect themselves, which provided less protection than engineering controls to prevent dust in the first place, an approach that industry opposed. Hence the CWPS was substituting a concern for costs for a concern for effectiveness in reaching a goal. In such cases it seemed the CWPS was challenging action mandated by Congress.[21]

A second set of issues arose from the problem of understaffing, which reduced the capabilities of the CWPS for economic analysis. Hence it was often dependent on others for data to support its inquiries. Because it challenged federal agencies it was frequently tempted to use data gathered by their opponents, usually from the business community. The CWPS's criticism of the proposed surface-mining regulations in 1978–9 rested on facts, as well as ideas, supplied by the coal industry. This tendency was facilitated by a common desire on the part of both the CWPS and industry to challenge the regulations as well as the need to rely on external sources because of limited in-house expertise.

The vigorous role of the CWPS in these matters raised questions about its unofficial role in administrative decision making. Under the requirements of the Administrative Procedures Act, evidence used in decision making was to be placed on the record and be subject to open scrutiny by interested parties. Now, however, through the initiative of the CWPS new evidence was being brought to bear on administrative decisions after the record had been closed, and decisions were often modified without the possibility of public review.

Throughout the 1970s economists had great difficulty in specifying benefits precisely so as to bring them into a conventional cost-benefit formula. But toward the end of the decade it became equally clear that cost estimates were also imprecise. A review of such estimates over the preceding decade and their comparison with actual costs revealed wide variations. In the case of beryllium dust and fume control, the estimate was 32 times the actual cost figure; in that of vinyl chloride, 200 times. One regulatory official concluded, "Whether by honest error, simple inability to compute, or outright chicanery, such exaggerations would play havoc with any cost-benefit balancing."[22]

Demands from both industry and economists for more elaborate cost-benefit analyses continued to be a major issue. On the side of the regulators, Douglas Costle, head of the EPA during the Carter administration, argued that "cost-benefit analysis is useful as a decision tool, but don't use it as a decision rule." On the opposing side, Lewis J. Perl of National Economic Research Associates, which spoke for industry, argued that cost-benefit analysis was the only viable method for evaluating environmental regulations and developing intelligent alternatives.[23]

The debate over productivity. Toward the end of the 1970s the response of economists to environmental policies was shaped increasingly by the analysis of productivity, which had become a general concern in national economic policy. Comparisons with other industrialized nations, such as Japan and those of Western Europe, did not turn out favorably for the United States. In the ensuing debate many identified environmental regulations as the culprit. The argument was frequently associated with the observation that in other nations there was closer cooperation between industry and government in economic affairs and that the public there was not permitted to exercise as much influence as was the case in the United States. Hence the environmental opposition in which economists played an important role wrote with admiration of the highly centralized methods of decision making in Britain, Western European nations, and Japan.[24]

The attempt to draw a close connection between environmental programs and productivity had its roots in the argument that these programs diverted capital to unproductive uses. Areas maintained as natural environments such as wilderness and open space were unproductive – so contended the timber, oil, gas, and mineral industries. Funds used to control pollution could be used to increase productivity, and this was especially a problem in industries, such as iron and steel, that had difficulty attracting capital. Hence much of the economist's problem with environmental objectives in productivity analysis went back to the difficulty in identifying environmental wants and needs in the first place. How could one compare open space in the United States as an element in the American standard of living with the relative lack of it in more congested Europe and Japan?

A variant on the productivity theme was the problem of innovation. The United States, the argument went, had fallen behind in the economic race because of its presumably lower rate of scientific and technological innovation. In some fashion environmental policies had diverted resources away from such desired innovations. It was difficult to determine where this problem lay. The automobile industry was under constant siege by environmentalists for its failure to produce a more energy-efficient and pollution-reducing automobile. William J. Abernathy's analysis of the industry, *The Productivity Dilemma,* supported that argument by emphasizing the "roadblock to innovation in the automobile industry." Abernathy and his colleague at the Harvard School of Business William J. Hayes argued that the financial leadership of conglomerate firms emphasized marketing and profit centers rather than technological innovation and production efficiency.[25]

The argument from economists that environmental controls stifled both productivity and innovation was adopted by the business community. But when business leaders were asked to make the argument specific, the resulting reports stressed the added costs of environmental controls and did not provide data about either productivity or technological innovation. One systematic study of the problem for the chemical industry was carried out in 1978 by Nicholas Ashford of the Center for Policy Alternatives at the Massachusetts Institute of Technology. Ashford interviewed chemical-firm executives and concluded that, although in some cases regulation had stifled innovation, in others it had stimulated it. If regulations were too light, he argued, they merely prompted "add on" tactics to lessen the impact, but if they were heavy they tended to prompt more fundamental rethinking of production processes and often led to innovations that both met environmental controls and increased productivity.[26]

In the late 1970s the Department of Commerce undertook a study of innovation. Determining the study's direction, the business community argued that lighter regulatory cost burdens would free it to innovate. Environmentalists were not included in the deliberations but were permitted to participate in the committee's final public session. They stressed the need to focus on technological innovation. Their views received little attention, however. Industry was unwilling to permit claims about the adverse effect of regulation on innovation to be openly and directly analyzed, and it did not allow its own deployment of scientific and technical expertise to be publicly scrutinized. To permit open review of such questions would disclose trade secrets to competitors.[27]

The role of economists in environmental debate. Over the course of the 1960s and 1970s the nation's interest in environmental economics shifted from the environmental costs of development to the production costs of environmental policies. In this shift economists were considered the experts who could describe the intricate realities of demand and supply, of costs and benefits. They were called on to explain what was happening on the economic side of environmental policy and hence were influential in establishing the context of argument and debate. That influence came from the common perception of their work: As disinterested professionals, they could objectively describe the "rational" world of economic facts. But this obscured the way those descriptions reflected particular rather than universal notions of what that world was like and how it worked.

In deciding how economic affairs were to be described and explained, economists were influenced by their own professional traditions and commitments. Customary modes of thinking made them prefer traditional production and cost analyses. They were unable to cope with many of the intangible and nonmarket goods and services of the advanced consumer society. They thought in terms of costs that involved repairs, which could be added up in terms of prices. And they could identify production costs more readily than environmental costs, which were harder to quantify. These predispositions were shaped in the course of professional training and experience in such a way that economists' values emphasized developmental rather than environmental considerations when they approached economic analysis. Although it was acknowledged by some economists that the concept of net national amenities reflected more accurately the real world of economic affairs than did that of gross national product, the idea made little dent on the economics profession.

These issues of economic analysis were, in fact, political choices; alternatives in economic accounting were alternatives in political strategy. Political choices were shaped by the details of economic facts, which made the choices complex and hence more difficult to identify. Within that overload of detail, however, there were political trends. Most important was the focus on production costs, which gave the economists who thought in these terms considerable influence in public environmental choices. These tendencies did not spring from the unfolding of knowledge per se but, rather, from the belief of many institutional leaders that environmental objectives played an important role in the new economic problems of the late 1970s.

The primary factor in developing this climate was the emphasis by members of the business community on the cost to them of environmental programs. Business leaders brought one economic analysis after another to the debate, each more detailed than the one before, and all emphasizing the unacceptable costs business and the economy were required to bear. These studies were often countered by competing governmental analyses, for example, from the EPA or the Council on Environmental Quality (CEQ). The give-and-take itself produced little progress in establishing "objective facts," but it did help in shaping the political context of cost itself and in shifting the attention of institutional leaders from environmental costs and benefits to developmental costs. By the beginning of the 1980s the claim that production-cost analysis should precede action on behalf of the human environment and human health came to compete effectively with and overwhelm the claim that careful environmental cost analysis should precede action on behalf of development.[28]

In the face of these trends the ability of environmental organizations to conduct their own economic studies was extremely weak. The field was left to corporate and governmental institutions that could provide the necessary funds for research. Economic inquiry had come to be extremely detailed, based on extensive amounts of hard data that became more elaborate over the years as computers enabled investigators to digest and manipulate expanding knowledge. Unless one either maintained such models directly or had access to them, one's contribution to the debate over economic alternatives was minimal. As long as public agencies had those resources they could counter the economic analyses of the business community, and during the Carter administration the EPA and the CEQ battled head to head with such corporate research centers as the National Economic Research Associates. Environmentalists, and the public at large, could only stand on the sidelines, watch the contest of computer models, and hope that in some way their own concerns would be identified and expressed.[29]

But such hopes failed to be realized. A gap developed between the economy of the economic analysts and the economy as understood by the general public. Whereas the former had developed a systems approach that saw the national economy as a single entity that could be manipulated by national policy and action, the public thought of the economy in the more personal terms of their own daily lives. New wants and needs in the advanced consumer economy had grown more rapidly than economists could factor them into their analyses. In response, economists became removed from these new realities and worked more closely within the context of national perspectives, models and data, and national institutions of authority. They contributed not only to professional and managerial skepticism about the wisdom of environmental objectives but also to the enhancement of national executive power to contain them.[30]

The Politics of Planning

Environmental affairs were as involved with planning as with economics. Much of the impetus for this came from federal agencies. Programs involving federal grants to states or municipalities required planning prior to the distribution of funds. Public monies were to be allocated according to a plan that projected needs and specified actions to meet them. Monies distributed from the Land and Water Conservation Fund required recreational planning; sewage-facility grants required water-quality planning; funds to promote local development required land-use planning; regulatory action on the coastal zone required coastal-zone planning.[31]

Planning also was a result of industry's attempts to secure sites for plants and offices. Often such searches were carried out by industry alone, but as competition for land increased industrial promoters encouraged public planning in order to guarantee future sites. The increasing scale of factories meant that in many areas level land of the required acreage was not easy to obtain. Equally important was the need to find sites where the construction and operation of facilities would not create negative public reaction. Industrial firms and their allies in public agencies encouraged planning to identify and reserve such sites.

Planning was also taken up to focus on environmental objectives. Much of the environmental effort was future-oriented. How could one control current development so as to ensure an environmentally acceptable future? A multitude of uncoordinated decisions cumulatively could modify the quality of the environment. Hence forethought had to be exercised in order to take current action consistent with long-range consequences. The planning spirit environmentalists promoted to identify and protect high-quality land, air, and water was similar to that advocated by industry, but the objectives differed markedly. On a variety of fronts, therefore, planning became a major context of political choice.[32]

Planning, like science and economic analysis, was considered by its practitioners to be a detached and neutral process of decision making. But, in fact, it was more significant as a setting for struggle over control of the future. In that future, what would be the role of environmental objectives and their balance with developmental ones? Planning merely transferred controversy over such questions from the present to future possibilities. It did not eliminate the conflict in the first place. Hence political controversy became an integral aspect of planning.[33]

In facing an environmental problem, many concluded that planning provided an opportunity to obtain better recognition of the values they sought to enhance. Often it could emphasize a more comprehensive range of desired social objectives when immediate action limited attention to only a few; at the same time one could stress steps needed to prevent future harm instead of the frequent case of working to avoid the harm of a current proposal. Planning enabled environmentalists to stress positive goals to be achieved rather than aspects of harm to be avoided.[34]

Environmentalists also found, however, that participation in planning led to confrontation with developmentalists, and the resulting controversy was as intense and uncompromising as in the case of current political choices. Planners seemed friendly to environmental objectives; often they had become interested in them in their professional training. But planning also was often influenced more by the larger institutions of government and corporate business, which were committed to development and sought to reduce the influence of environmental demands. Hence planning became the arena for persistent struggle between environmental and developmental forces as each sought to control it to further their own ends.[35]

Planning issues – values and scale. The traditional planning document predicted the future in terms of growth such as in population or numbers of employable people and then determined the number of highways, hospitals, jobs, and sewage-treatment plants that would be needed to provide for employment, social services, and public facilities.

Environmental planning brought new questions to the process. For what purpose should space be used? For intensive development alone or for the amenities of natural lands? Should the air, water, and land be used for waste disposal, or should it be used to raise the standard of living? It was an issue no longer of whether growth should be more efficient, as was the case with earlier planning, but of whether environmental values should be maximized in balance with material development.[36]

In the 1960s and 1970s a change in mood came over planning agencies as they became involved in controversies between developmental and environmental objectives. Planning reflected the gradual influence of matters of environmental quality. Land-use plans financed in the mid-1970s with federal funds differed from earlier ones, which had emphasized the location of sites for transportation and industry. Later plans provided for recreation and open lands, which sometimes resulted in separate documents for these objectives. Some of the most effective environmental land-use plans were produced by private agencies, for example, the School of Landscape Architecture and Regional Planning at the University of Pennsylvania.[37]

The principles and standards for water-resources planning developed by the Water Resources Council (referred to in Chapter 8) gave rise to one of the most comprehensive attempts to consider environmental goals in equal balance with developmental goals in planning. Two separate streams of planning would be used to maximize the two sets of purposes, with no attempt to trade off one against the other until farther along in the decision-making process. Translating this strategy into the plans of specific agencies was another matter. Only the Army Corps of Engineers did so in its general planning guidelines, and only a few of its specific plans were attempts to put the principles and standards into practice. At the state level there was no such two-stream planning; state water planning continued to be dominated by development.[38]

Plans usually implied that action on a wide variety of fronts required larger systems of administration and control. As the city replaced the ward as the context of action, the focus of change moved to the larger metropolitan area and a drive arose for countywide and later multicounty or regional planning. Planning was not associated with the push to decentralize public affairs. On the contrary, it fostered the political drive to overcome resistance of smaller-scale institutions to larger-scale organization and action. Planning was considered rational and implicitly valid, whereas opposition to it was viewed as irrational and emotional.[39]

Developmental values were associated in planning with larger-scale systems of management, whereas environmental values called for a varied and mixed approach. Many environmental objectives required the enhancement of authority and power at a higher level of political organization in order to influence decisions at a lower one. In environmental-protection programs for air, water, and solid waste, federal power was sought to secure leverage against the developmental opposition, which often worked through local and state agencies. Environmentalists also found more political support for the protection and management of natural-environment areas in federal than in state and local authorities. Federal programs favored planning for the public lands and water-quality planning in order to restrain developmental tendencies; they thus provided an opportunity for environmentalists to secure recognition of their objectives in ways that earlier had not been possible.

At the same time, however, environmentalists were confronted with the political reality that large-scale developers also sought assistance at a higher level of government in order to impose their demands on society at large. Energy companies tried to shift authority to site energy facilities from local governments to states and from state governments to federal agencies. In response, environmentalists tried to work through local and state governments. In coastal-zone planning, energy companies sought to guarantee that proposals by federal agencies and energy corporations would not be restricted by demands for ultimate state authority; environmentalists, on the other hand, supported state influence and power. Or, in matters of power-plant siting, whereas utilities sought state programs to override the authority of townships and counties to prevent the building of power plants, environmentalists often sided with the locality in asserting its right to prevent the installation.

These alternatives in political authority also produced marked changes in the attitudes of people in less settled areas toward planning and especially zoning. They were confronted with the adverse impacts of large-scale development, and they now demanded community authority to prevent it. When the issues had been confined primarily to smaller-scale development these areas had resisted planning and zoning to provide more leeway for landowners to make decisions about their own property. They continued to espouse that freedom. At the same time they recognized that external political authority was associated with new threats from large-scale development. Hence they became friendly to planning and zoning to prevent such intrusions.

Planning for environmental protection. Waste and pollution problems gave rise to a series of planning efforts with similar elements. Solid-waste planning grew out of the attempt to switch from incineration to sanitary landfills, on the one hand, and from many smaller rural dumps to fewer managed landfills, on the other. Water-quality management engendered efforts to plan for municipal sewage facilities that received large amounts of federal and state funding, as well as to deal with nonpoint sources. Air-quality planning emphasized the need to reduce overall pollution loads, to allocate those to individual sources, and to provide a margin for growth.

In each case the approach of planning agencies was similar. There was, first, an assessment of long-term generation of pollution through projecting population growth and use and, second, an effort to calculate action to cope with that waste. Planning assumed waste production as a given, calculated in terms of projected population and economic growth, and then called for strategies to accommodate it. Environmentalists, however, viewed this approach with considerable skepticism. For although it provided a means to mitigate the worst impacts of waste on environmental quality, it failed to address the problem of preventing waste. To environmentalists pollution-control planning was based on the wrong assumptions.[40]

Water-quality planning was shaped by the problem of allocating federal funds to construct sewage works. Who would get how much money first? And who would go further down the list? Amid jockeying for the benefits of federal allocations, little thought was given to the possibilities of wastewater treatment systems that were environmentally preferable. A provision of the 1977 Clean Water Act set aside a greater share of federal funds for such innovations, but few states availed themselves of it. Those advocating recycling sludge as a fertilizer, requiring treatment of industrial effluent before discharge into municipal sewage systems, or recycling water and reducing discharges in the first place obtained little support for their strategies. Population growth, pollution production, and wastewater management as a complex of attitudes dominated water-quality planning.

Similar disagreements developed among environmentalists and planners over solid-waste management that emphasized the calculation of future amounts of waste for which a given amount of landfill space would be needed. Environmentalists insisted on an approach that stressed source reduction and recycling. Often they would agree to landfill planning only if plans were also made to experiment in methods such as source separation and recycling. Planners, however, were prone to reject approaches that involved changing waste-disposal practices.

The overwhelming emphasis in planning on waste treatment rather than waste reduction stemmed from the acceptance by planners of the need for growth as a given in their calculations. Only when pressures from regulation to limit growth emerged did they begin to reverse their field. In both air- and water-quality programs, the limited space in which to dispose of pollutants restricted increases in emissions. In both cases this led to the idea of allocating waste among the industrial sources and then providing a growth factor for new or expanded industry by reducing the allocation further. Would planning respond to this new reality by redirecting its calculation of "needs" to the "given" of a fixed amount of allowable pollution in the future? This was implied by the air- and water-quality programs, but by the 1970s it had rarely been incorporated into planning.

Starting out in planning with the need to reduce pollution rather than merely accommodate it would require massive changes in perspectives. In the past planning had emphasized the cost requirements of providing for growth needs. Concentrating on waste reduction rather than waste growth would bring technological innovation squarely into the planning process as the critical element in meeting future needs. But this was a field of inquiry with which planning agencies could not cope, and they resisted it.

The projection of population trends came to be a key factor in environmental planning. The level of future environmental services depended heavily on future population. Because federal financial support was often tied to estimated future needs, every planning agency was tempted to inflate population projections in order to secure more funds. Environmentalists argued that only lower projections were justified. The issue became important in the mid-1970s as rates of population growth declined and the use of older projections based on higher rates seemed to be inaccurate. The U.S. Bureau of the Census sought to curtail the practice by creating alternative projections, each with different assumptions about birthrates, from which local governments could choose. But those governments continued to opt for the higher rates and with much encouragement by those with an interest in land development. The EPA had some leverage in this matter for with the shortage of funds it did not seem fair to overallocate to one community only to deprive another of needed resources.[41]

The one field of environmental protection in which there seemed to be some receptiveness among planners for technological innovation was domestic sewage treatment. For some years sewage-facility planning had sought to centralize so as to guarantee effective management. But the high cost of centralized treatment and interceptor lines turned planning agencies toward smaller-scale systems, and the tendencies in both clean-water legislation and the EPA's administration underscored the need for innovative systems. This drift toward decentralized technology, however, had little connection with the environmental proposal for waste-reducing technologies. On the contrary, it was geared toward effective methods of disposing of larger amounts of waste. It was, therefore, an innovation in planning for waste treatment rather than waste reduction.

Wildlands planning. Wildlands planning grew in the 1970s as a result of more intensive land use. In the face of such pressures agencies began to plan to control use more effectively and to make sure that short-term demands would not compromise long-term agency objectives. At the same time, however, environmentalists found that planning enabled them to secure consideration for their objectives because it opened up for long-term management a wider range of alternatives.[42]

Early in the 1970s the Forest Service began to develop plans for each national forest. The public was to be involved in the preparation of these plans. While environmentalists found this to be an improvement on past decision making, they also found themselves confronted with firm limits to agency willingness to consider environmental values. To what extent were future needs to include environmental as well as developmental objectives? Environmentalists were convinced that the definition of needs was heavily weighted toward commodity development and wood production and that these played a major role in planning.[43]

Public ideas about the role of the forest as an environment brought new values to the definition of needs. But forest administrators, who dominated planning, were oriented, by training and experience, toward wood production. They distinguished between needs and wants, arguing that wood production was a need but environmental quality only a want. They believed that demands for wood must be met, whereas pressures for wilderness had only to be placated. In still other cases, while wood was thought of as a national need and the market area for wood in terms of national supply and demand, the need for wilderness was thought of as a local matter and relegated to a parochial and secondary level.[44]

Planning for forest use as a context for decision making was enhanced by the Forest Resource and Planning Act of 1974 and the Forest Management Act of 1976. These required that a wide range of values be incorporated into the plans and that the public participate in planning. What effect this would have remained to be seen. The crucial question was the degree to which those responsible for planning in the Forest Service and their allies in the forestry profession would be willing to modify their preferences in the choice of subjects for scientific research, in forest economics, and in the definition of needs to which planning would be tied. One could not be confident that a change in the law would bring about a change in practice. There was a strong tendency among foresters to emphasize the need for political independence as professionals to decide in these matters. The claim became more insistent almost in direct proportion to the equally strong demand by environmentalists that those in the general public expressing new values should play a greater role in defining management objectives.[45]

The National Park Service also embarked on planning in the early 1970s. Because the agency was directly involved in serving people as well as managing physical resources it was far more open to influence from changing public values. One aspect of this was the long-standing emphasis on its interpretive programs. One of its major missions, so the service believed, was to enable the public to understand and appreciate the environmental resources it managed. At the same time the National Park Service was obligated by its enabling act in 1916 both to protect scenic resources under its jurisdiction and to provide for human enjoyment of those resources. This forced the service to be receptive to warnings that excessive development and use would threaten the permanence of the very resources it was obligated to protect.[46]

As planning evolved in the 1970s the Park Service was still in the throes of a development phase that had begun in the 1950s and that had been expressed in the "Mission 66" program. Planning, therefore, often consisted of predicting visitation and accommodating it by providing highways and parking lots, motels and eating places, shops and campgrounds – the entire range of tourist facilities. One such example was the proposal, mentioned earlier, to build a blacktop road the length of Assateague Island National Seashore off the coast of Maryland and Virginia, complete with parking places, overnight lodges, and restaurant.

Sometimes environmental groups insisted that plans be changed. The Committee to Preserve Assateague, for example, organized a successful campaign for a counterplan that abandoned the proposed road and moved visitor facilities to the mainland. Such drives on the part of environmentalists were supplemented by a review of national-park policy and planning sponsored by the Conservation Foundation, which warned against overuse of the parks and urged that planning and management protect natural and scenic resources. The report contributed to a new direction in planning.[47]

The Park Service faced opposition on such cases from business groups that held franchises within the parks and those outside them that looked to more profitable enterprise from increasing numbers of tourists. They sought to influence planning to accommodate more people. Environmentalists constituted a counterclientele that was at times able to offset their influence. At the same time, values internal to the Park Service provided some fertile ground within the agency to adopt environmental concerns for resource protection. The change in direction in planning was not always consistent but did reflect some impact of the new environmental values on planning.

Both the Bureau of Land Management (BLM) and the Fish and Wildlife Service developed planning later than did the Forest Service and the National Park Service. BLM planning evolved slowly within its own administrative context, largely in response to the same kind of growing user demands that impinged on the national forests. Environmentalists saw this change as an opportunity for environmental and ecological values to play a larger role in the agency's future. Even before the Federal Land Policy and Management Act of 1976 was passed, a court case won by the Natural Resources Defense Council required each BLM management unit to draw up a plan with an environmental-impact statement. This inaugurated a far more intensive round of planning in the BLM than had been seen previously. Throughout the West environmental groups began to participate in BLM planning in order to influence its outcome.[48]

The Fish and Wildlife Service, on the other hand, was much like the National Park Service in its planning orientation; its statutory obligations were closely connected with environmental values. Planning on wildlife refuges proceeded at a steady and less complicated pace. The service moved forward with wilderness proposals more rapidly than did either the Forest Service or the Park Service as it found fewer roadblocks from established modes of administrative thought and action. There were some developmental pressures, but it was not difficult to see them as incompatible with the agency's major mandates. The agency was freer to think in terms of resource protection in ideas about the future.[49]

The Comparative Response

It is useful to compare and contrast science, economics, and planning in terms of the degree to which they incorporated environmental and ecological values into their ways of thinking. Both scientific and economic analysis were tightly interwoven and relatively immune to environmental values, whereas planning was more open and receptive. Planners had absorbed environmental values in their training more than had scientists and economists, and the profession in action was also more receptive to those values when expressed by the general public. Some planning such as that conducted by the Forest Service seemed to be relatively inflexible and to respond more to the interests of the agencies to which it was attached. But other planning was more loosely formulated so as to establish a less rigid set of boundaries and to permit citizen influence and hence the entry of environmental and ecological concerns.

For the coastal zone Congress had required that planning include specific topics as a condition of receiving planning grants. Each state had to establish the geographical boundaries within which management would be carried out; identify "geographical areas of particular concern," which, it was widely understood, were primarily natural-environment areas of special value; develop a process for considering large-scale development with which federal action in siting decisions had to be consistent; and establish a set of permissible uses, implying that there were nonpermissible ones as well. These requirements set in motion a highly varied group of plans in which the most significant factor was the balance among the active political sectors of each state. Coastal-zone planning established a framework in which the particular definition of future state needs would emerge from the give-and-take of politics. In this case planning constituted a relatively open system of value choice that permitted social changes represented by environmental and ecological values to find some expression in decision making.

The planning strategy of "alternative environmental futures" described earlier gave rise to a variant that also provided a forum for environmental values in an even looser context. Several commissions sought to chart a course for their state's future. The lead in this format was taken by a private group in California called California Tomorrow, which sought to bring ideas to the general public under the rubric, "What do you wish this state to be like tomorrow?" This approach was used particularly in the East where state commissions were formed on "Maine's Future," "Vermont Tomorrow," and "Delaware's Future."

These commissions drew extensively on public-opinion studies, as well as on public meetings to elicit broader ideas about the kind of future the people of the state wanted. In each case environmental and developmental futures were juxtaposed freely and far more in balance than in the more formal planning process. A similar device was used in Idaho in connection with water-resources planning; the planning agency conducted three extensive public-opinion polls and held a number of public meetings to define the future uses of the state's limited but not yet claimed supplies of water. These meetings and polls revealed a sharp conflict between developmental uses, largely for agriculture, and environmental "quality of life" objectives that the public heavily supported.[50]

The choices made by science were much less susceptible to popular influence and far less directly modified by environmental and ecological values. Scientists were extremely wary of the idea that the public should participate in defining problems for scientific investigation. Such involvement, they felt, would undermine the rigor of scientific measurement and method. To scientists the acceptable relationship with the public was a one-way process in which the informed scientist had an obligation to educate the uninformed public. During the Environmental Era, in fact, the executive offices of two of the most prestigious scientific organizations in the nation, the National Academy of Sciences and the American Association for the Advancement of Science, served as pulpits for the frequent expression of skepticism concerning environmental objectives.[51]

Many in environmental and ecological affairs, however, as well as in the wider public, were convinced that the particular preferences of science for developmental rather than environmental objectives and the domination of science by the physical and chemical in contrast with the biological and ecological sciences led to undesirable choices in the allocation of public funds for research. Some device should be fashioned, so they argued, to permit a flow of influence from the general public to the scientist. Senator Edward Kennedy of Massachusetts became the champion of this view; through his influence Congress in 1975 directed the National Science Foundation to undertake a program to foster such activity. But the foundation resisted this innovation, formulated a program only slowly and in limited fashion, and modified it to concentrate heavily on the traditional pattern in which scientists educated the public in the ways of science.[52]

These predispositions among scientists gave rise to working relationships between environmentalists and a number of individual scientists who shared environmental and ecological values. Hardly an environmental issue emerged in which citizens did not turn to scientific and technical professionals for help in understanding the problems they faced. They found scientists who were willing and anxious to work with them and whom they helped to bring more fully into public decision making much in the same way as industry recruited scientists who preferred to stress the values for which industry contended. These ties had no small effect on the gradual evolution of EPA policy to rely on a wider range of scientific opinion for assessments of scientific studies.

Much of the influence of environmental objectives on science, however, came through the broader political process as public demands for action generated pressures for more scientific knowledge about that action. These demands redirected priorities for research beyond the prevailing patterns. Concern about the biological effects of pesticides and herbicides in the 1960s and about acid precipitation in the 1970s, for example, led to demands for more information, which, in turn, diverted funds in these directions. Similarly, the rising interest in increasing the nation's energy supply fostered significant advances in research on the environmental impact of energy proposals. In ways such as these, rather than through the internal evolution of priorities among scientists or the direct influence of the public on the working ways of scientists, science was forced to respond to new public environmental interests.

The economics profession presented a more complicated case of response in which attempts to incorporate environmental values into more traditional modes of thought failed for the most part. Environmental values prompted a number of economists to try to integrate them into existing practices of quantitative balancing of costs and benefits. These few efforts were interesting academic exercises but had little impact on public policy. The mandate in the 1969 National Environmental Policy Act that decision makers find some way of working into their assessments devices for dealing with nonquantifiable factors was not put into practice. The larger attempt to shift the focus in economic accounting from the gross national product to net national amenities did not have significant results. Economics emerged to a commanding position in environmental affairs, not by absorbing environmental and ecological values but by excluding them.[53]

Science, economics, and planning professed to undertake a search for universal truth that was disinterested, that would establish objective and rational relationships among conflicting motivations and thereby serve as a medium for resolving differences. Yet they were professions in which particular groups of people with particular values exercised considerable influence in defining their work. The values inherent in those choices were far more closely associated with material development than with environmental quality or ecological stability, and each tended to divorce itself from the "environmental advocacy" of the general public. They augmented political forces that sought to restrain and limit rather than to advance environmental objectives in American society and politics.

12 The Middle Ground: Management of Environmental Restraint

Technical professionals in science, economics, and planning became closely involved in environmental affairs and hence with citizen environmental groups that expressed widely shared public demands. But they were uneasy in this relationship. They tended to believe that environmentalists pressed their case too far and too urgently. They were more comfortable with strategies to implement a more modest set of goals and objected to advancement to new levels of environmental progress. They tended to organize their ideas and activities around environmental management, both private and public; management, in turn, reached out to bring technical experts into administration. As citizens demanded further progress, both technical experts and management urged restraint and argued that the nation could not afford a greater commitment to environmental goals.[1]

With these attitudes were closely allied the opinions of a wide range of the nation's leaders – officials of public and private institutions, including the media, and writers for influential newspapers and journals. These I refer to as "thought leaders." Between the 1960s and the 1980s these idea makers shifted from support to skepticism about enlarged environmental programs. They came to believe that environmental progress might well exceed the nation's resources. They began to urge restraint, saying that the main task was not to facilitate the advance of environmental goals as one might advocate the advance of standards of living, education, and technology but, rather, to moderate them.[2]

These two groups, management and the nation's thought leaders, represented a distinct force in environmental politics. They differed from leaders in agriculture, labor, and industry, most of whom displayed little sympathy for environmental goals and used strategies of direct opposition. Their involvement in environmental management and thinking reflected a strong and positive interest in such questions. Yet over the course of the give-and-take of environmental politics they came to dissociate themselves from public environmental efforts, argued that there was too much environmental advocacy, came to stress the difficulties of implementation, and avoided attempts to develop a rationale and support for continued environmental progress.[3]

The Politics of Environmental Management

Environmental politics shifted in the 1970s from legislation to administration, from broader public debate to management. Increasingly one heard of air-quality management, water-quality management, forest management, range management, coastal-zone management, risk management, river management, and wilderness management. Hardly an environmental problem could be dealt with outside the terminology and conceptual focus of management, and management, in turn, played a powerful role in shaping environmental choice.[4]

Like science, economics, and planning, management was often thought of as politically neutral. Its role was technical, that of implementing policy in the most efficient manner. Yet this presumed role was sharply contradicted by the innumerable controversies over alternative courses of action in which managerial agencies were involved and the high stakes the various parties in dispute found in those options. The shift from legislation to administration merely transferred the location where the choices were made and substituted administrative for legislative politics.[5]

This shift in context transformed environmental debate into a vast array of technical issues: allowable cut and nondeclining even flow, visual corridors and residual pricing, animal unit months, discount rates, mixing zones and lethal concentrations, acentric chromozome fragments and erythrocyte protoporphyrin, case-control epidemiology and levels of significance, benign and malignant tumors, minimum low flows, integral vistas, oxygen depletion, buffering capacity and aluminum mobilization, Class I, II, and III prevention of significant deterioration areas, and testing protocols. Such issues hardly modified the intensity of debate and disagreement; they only specified and structured it more precisely.

The overriding political assumption implicit in management was that centralized direction by technical experts was the appropriate way to make alternative choices and was far superior to the world of legislative and party politics. At the same time environmental management constituted a decision-making system many public leaders considered superior in resolving disputes with the public to the more open one of legislation, participatory citizen action, and litigation.

Management played an influential role in shaping environmental choice. Not only did it have the authority to coordinate discordant elements in the system on its own terms; it also comprised a set of institutions with ongoing capabilities for communication and action. Institutional power was the stuff of political power. Its continuous presence and potential for action forced others to reckon with it day in and day out. As a result it set the bounds, if not the agenda, of action. The larger ideological debates in environmental and ecological affairs came and went, but management established the context of daily political choice.

Forest Management

By the Environmental Era the principles and practices of forest management had become well developed. Its own brand of integration of science, economic analysis, and planning and the symbiotic relationship it had fostered between private and public management had gone through several decades of institutional growth. Precisely because of the richness of that institutional evolution the newer environmental and ecological values presented it with a severe challenge. Forest professionals had considerable difficulty in accepting them.[6]

The spirit of scientific management had been instilled into the forestry profession and the U.S. Forest Service from the late nineteenth century; the task of balancing cut and growth – sustained yield – established its framework. This involved the measurement of standing volume, annual growth, and allowable cut; increasingly intensive inputs of better seed and fertilizer; and control of pests and competing vegetation to increase yields. By the 1960s the elements of this technical system had been worked out in great detail.

The crucial factor was "regulation," the method by which the flow of wood through the biological system was controlled so as to balance cut and yield. Traditionally that had been achieved through fieldwork by foresters who observed sample plots, totaled up the existing volume, and selected trees of merchantable size for harvest. Shortly after World War II this began to be replaced with even-age management, a mode of organizing the forest area in terms of subunits, each with trees of uniform age. The number of such units would depend on the desired length of the rotation cycle: If trees were cut every one hundred years, the management unit would be divided into one hundred units.[7]

This system reduced the number of data points about which information had to be gathered – from a large number of individual trees to a smaller number of areas; it made possible management in gross terms, for example, by the use of aerial photography to calculate volume, and precluded the need for on-the-spot observation; more variables could be taken into account by simple quantitative data that could be computerized to provide complex manipulations to determine allowable cuts; and it could be done with lower levels of technical skills.

Even-age regulation was to be carried out through clear-cutting, a process of harvesting the entire stand with massive machinery that would permit a uniform age pattern of regeneration to replace it. Such clear-cutting, in both the East and the West, prompted enormous public outcry because it destroyed the amenity values of the "forest as environment" and was incompatible with ecological and geological conditions, which were far more varied and complex than uniform management assumed. Even-age management received considerable support from industry because it used large-scale machinery and hence lowered labor costs. The close relationship between larger clear cuts and lower costs stimulated a tendency toward larger areas for even-age treatment.[8]

These predispositions in forest management resulted in a view of the forest that differed markedly from the view held by the environmental forest user. To foresters, a forest was confined to those trees that were valuable for commercial purposes. As early as the 1920s the dendrology textbooks and courses in forestry schools that described forest species and their distribution became restricted to commercial types. The texts explained that foresters need not know all forest species – foresters were not botanists – but only those that were useful for wood production. This narrowed their conception of a forest considerably.[9]

Environmentalists and ecologists, on the other hand, developed a view of the forest based on direct experience and use. They hiked and backpacked, observed natural processes and studied them, and photographed and appreciated the natural world in ways that involved both intensive study and enjoyment. Among them were specialists in botany and ecology who brought to forestry affairs precisely those skills that had been separated from the central training and experience of professional foresters. Their vantage point was both appreciative and intellectual. They accepted the world of nature as a value to be absorbed emotionally and defined the forest as an environment of natural phenomena that was to be appreciated and interacted with rather than dominated. Environmentalists reflected not just a different interest in management choices but a separate world of experience.[10]

Environmentalists also emphasized the value of biological diversity, the forest as an ecosystem of varied plant and animal life, and this brought them also into conflict with forest managers. The goal of management, according to environmentalists, should be to maintain and even encourage that diversity through processes of natural selection specific to given sites. In many cases natural forces gave rise to uniformity of species, but in others diversity was more predominant and this was especially so in the mixed mesophytic forests of the temperate zones of the eastern United States.

Scientific management, however, emphasized uniformity. Foresters thought of a forest as a monoculture because all of the merchantable trees were of the same species. They sought to shift the composition of a given stand from variety to a single or dominant, commercially desirable, species. Thus, in the southern Appalachians they wished to convert natural stands of mixed hardwoods to uniform stands of pine. Environmentalists objected to this conversion as inconsistent with natural diversity.

The worlds of those who managed large-scale forest systems and those who used them as environmental and ecological resources differed markedly. Environmentalists sought to work out both scientific understanding and affective appreciation within the smaller context of immediate circumstance and to exercise control over that context, whereas systems managers wanted to manipulate forests over a larger scale with an alternative vision of increasingly intensive investments for greater material output.

The Management of Environmental Pollution

New efforts to control pollution created new management systems. Environmentalists sought to play a role in forming them, but on the whole they were outsiders. The drama of institution building in this field lay far more in the direct relationship between public managers and those who created pollution. Together they shaped a common ground that constituted the system of environmental control.

This interplay between government and industry was carried out in highly detailed, complex, and technical circumstances. There were arguments over the devices used to measure pollution and their location, how samples should be processed for measurement, the precise relationship between emissions and ambient quality. Would one control in terms of averages over a period of time or ceilings that could not be exceeded? The implementation of pollution-control legislation turned quickly to technical detail in which general citizens, even environmental organizations, played only a limited role because of their inability to enter into continuous technical negotiation. Although environmentalists occasionally penetrated this system, it was shaped largely by the more direct encounters between the technical agents of the agencies and those of the pollution sources.

Several specific aspects of environmental management illustrate these choices: the units of management, the factors to be controlled, the dilution potential of measurement and control, and averaging. Each of these involved a way sources of pollution could escape more effective control and in which public managers could tighten that control. They came to be important points of struggle within the management system.

Selection of the unit to be managed often affected the level of control since the degree of allowable emissions varied by unit. Those considered to have the most serious problems would be controlled more stringently than those with less serious ones. If a plant were located just inside an air-quality control area it would be subject to far greater control than if it were outside even though emissions might well affect the more distant area. Public management agencies usually defined units in terms of existing political boundaries such as counties, but sources sought exemptions from this when it would enable them to reduce the level of control.

One strategy was to exempt from stricter controls cleaner areas within management units when the larger unit, averaged as a whole, had not yet met the standards. Another was to confine monitoring to ground level and direct emissions into the air above the unit onto some management area nearby that would bear the brunt of the fallout. Or one might restrict the monitoring of mobile sources within a given distance from roads or streets to reduce the measured level of pollution. Management agencies sought to tighten up this type of escape hatch by requiring sources in one unit to be evaluated in terms of their effects on an adjacent unit. Emissions sources, on the other hand, sought higher levels of allowable emissions in cleaner management units. In Pennsylvania, for example, the cleaner areas were permitted to burn coal with more than six times the sulfur content allowed in the more urbanized areas.

Units of control in water-quality management presented similar choices. The primary unit was a stream or stream segment. Ambient water-quality standards referred to in-stream quality measured in the upper layers of the water. The regulatory system had to relate the effluent discharge to the larger ambient quality. Dischargers argued, however, that environmental residuals were biodegradable and became relatively harmless after some oxidation time; hence the area immediately surrounding the outfall should be excluded from water-quality standards. Thus arose the concept of the mixing zone, a stream area of given width and length near the outfall within which the standards would not apply. The strategy became firmly entrenched in EPA regulations, giving rise to a management system that related effluent with more distant water quality rather than established control at the source.[11]

A second problem in pollution management was to define precisely which pollutants should be controlled. On the surface this seemed clear enough. But emissions were complexes of chemicals whose ingredients were relatively unknown. Such was the case, for example, with particulates in air pollution. Regulators had two choices: They could control separately each chemical, such as sulfates or benzo (a) pyrene, or they could argue that it was far easier to regulate them as a whole through single indicator pollutants and use these as convenient handles through which to control the entire complex. Emission sources often objected that an aggregate approach to pollution control with indicator pollutants required them to control chemicals that were not harmful. Why, for example, should utilities be required to control sulfur dioxide when it was thought not to be harmful by itself as a gas, but only in association with particulates or as a precursor for sulfates that were harmful?

Air and water pollution presented peculiar forms of managerial control because they were gaseous or liquid rather than solid and hence were measured in terms of proportions in a given amount of air and water. Effective regulation required a precise and agreed measurement of dilution. If regulation was in terms of degree of concentration, the pollution source could emit any total amount of effluent simply by increasing the amount of water, for example, in the discharge. By the same token, an air-pollution source could dilute the emission by diffusing it into larger quantities of air. Effective action required emissions to be measured in terms of the total amount of pollutant such as pounds of phenol or sulfur in coal per unit of heat value (million BTUs). The classic case of dilution was the use of tall stacks in coal combustion to diffuse pollution into the wider atmosphere, a strategy that undermined effective control.[12]

Averaging was equally problematic. Amounts of pollution from the same source varied over time. There was variation even in the potential of a raw material, such as coal, for emitting pollutants because of the variability of its sulfur content. What level should be chosen as the basis of regulation? Should one select a central tendency or average, or should one establish a firm limit that should never be exceeded. The initial approach was to fix maximum allowables that bore some relationship to the damage one wished to prevent. But the regulated sources sought to absorb higher levels of pollutants at some times into lower levels at others so as to average them and thus permit greater total overall emissions. The longer the averaging time, the more higher emissions at one time could be averaged against lower ones at other times and thus be made acceptable.[13]

A similar opportunity for balancing higher emissions against lower ones lay in the fact that among sources in the same plant or between different plants some polluted more and others less. Industry sought to average these so that lowered emissions in one case would balance out higher emissions in another. This became known as the bubble approach; it placed a cap or bubble over the plant and limited the total emission from the entire area rather than prescribed maximums from each source. Environmentalists objected that this simply permitted greater emissions and especially should not be applied in areas that had not yet attained the standards. The issue finally became one of the firmness of the data to make sure that the trade-off was equal: Was the amount of pollution below the maximum at one source equal to the amount above it at another? Although environmentalists insisted that firm numbers be made available to determine this, the EPA proceeded with the approach without making clear that such numbers were at hand.[14]

The politics of averaging became a major issue in the water-quality program. EPA regulations required that effluent not exceed a given set of numbers of amounts for given pollutants from a given source and mandated technology that would accomplish this. Industries, however, argued against it, maintaining that the EPA should provide a range of numbers within which allowable discharges could fluctuate. The main thrust of the argument, however, was not against variation, for discharges could well have varied over a range below the allowable numbers. What industry wished was to raise that allowable limit by turning the maximum into an average, thereby relaxing controls. As a result of litigation on this question the Supreme Court approved the maximum numbers required by the EPA and rejected the variable approach.

Management choices such as these became central points of dispute. To resolve them involved a process of political accommodation and compromise between public environmental managers and industry representatives. Often in the course of constant interaction each side tended to wear the other down until much of the resulting working arrangement was attributable to the attractiveness of a more peaceable managerial climate. There was a persistent tendency to establish a relatively stable political and governing context. Environmentalists often contributed significant elements to the larger scope of these arrangements, but they were shaped in crucial detail by the ongoing interactions between public and private representatives. By the 1980s these mutually supportive accommodations had come to be far more fundamental in environmental affairs than the recurring tensions of public argument and debate.

Variations in Management Contexts

Each type of environmental-management program gave rise to its own peculiar form of management issues and management politics. Water management long had been preoccupied with commodity supply; to this set of uses it was relatively easy to add a concern with water quality. Both quantity and quality could be incorporated into a scheme of things that was confined to the management of engineering works to divert and regulate the flow of water. But when concern for water shifted to in-stream quality to maintain fishing or swimming the focus changed to the stream itself and away from diversions from it. This transition did not come easily.

The growing interest in the recreational and aesthetic uses of free-flowing streams through relatively undeveloped land corridors presented a problem for managers accustomed to thinking in terms of water as a commodity. Those managers tended to consider the public interest in free-flowing streams more as a political force to be placated than an integral objective of regulation and management. Yet they were forced to bend somewhat. In a few cases the Corps of Engineers was given responsibility for managing natural streams, instances environmentalists viewed favorably as providing an opportunity for new views to become more established within the corps. In other cases water-development agencies were willing to formulate management schemes in which one part of a stream was allocated primarily for natural-environment purposes and another for commodity development.

In the West water had long been allocated according to beneficial uses that were identified as property rights, recognized by law, and precisely distributed. Aethestic use had not been thought of as a part of this scheme of things. Would such a use now be recognized by allocations? The first step was taken in the new California water law of 1970, which specifically acknowledged aesthetic use as beneficial. In the first action under this law the California Water Resources Board allocated water to maintain a minimum flow in the Sacramento River. Such aesthetic uses were rarely recognized elsewhere. Minimum low flow was brought into river management more fully, when at all, in order to maintain biological life and especially fisheries.

On what basis would minimum flow be established? During the 1960s and 1970s a method for determining this (known as 7Q10) was devised by river-basin managers: The minimum flow would be maintained no lower than the lowest average for any seven consecutive days during the preceding ten years. Such a formula was based entirely on historic supplies rather than on current in-stream conditions. If it led to low-flow levels that destroyed the inherent quality of the stream, aesthetic and aquatic values would suffer. Fishery biologists took the initiative in proposing an alternative formula based on minimum daily flows, a procedure that set a basic minimum flow required for the biological needs of aquatic life. The biological system of the river itself, rather than external consumptive users, so the argument went, should determine the amount of low flow. By the 1970s, however, the 7Q10 system had become so firmly entrenched in management that states could and did argue that interstate flow of streams required a uniform policy, and hence no state could afford to deviate from that formula to a minimum daily-flow approach.

The legislative and administrative framework that evolved from the clean-air laws implied as complete a management system as did water and with the potential of incorporating environmental and ecological values from the start. But this was not done. Most air-quality management was confined to single cities under general state supervision and rarely included the countryside or the air between the cities. Urban-oriented air-quality managers continued to think of the countryside as a place that did not require lower emission levels and where urban industry could migrate to help improve urban air quality. While environmentalists were able to obtain provision for standards in cleaner areas that would prevent significant deterioration there, air-quality managers, preoccupied with trying to make urban air cleaner, considered this peripheral and expendable. In 1980 the organization of State and Territorial Air Pollution Program Administrators joined industry in urging that standards for Class II and Class III areas be dropped.

Somewhat more acceptable to air-quality managers was the notion that the transmission of air pollution over long distances required a larger geographical management framework. Pollution from one city could be transported to distant areas. The initial concern with this problem came when New England cities argued that they could not meet their air-quality standards for photochemical oxidants, because they were formed in their region from precursors that originated in New York, New Jersey, and farther west. They sued the EPA, unsuccessfully, to require those states to lower their emissions. The problem of interstate transport was also faced in the case of sulfates and nitrates as New York and northern New England began to stress the dangers to their lakes from acid rain attributable to states to the west, especially Pennsylvania, West Virginia, Ohio, Indiana, Illinois, and Kentucky, which generated higher sulfur dioxide emissions. By the end of the 1970s, however, only limited recognition of the need for a larger management context had emerged, and it was confined primarily to those states in the Northeast that bore the brunt of the problem.

The attempt to manage more closely flood plains and unstable geological areas such as steep slopes so as to reduce the threat of natural hazards constituted another type of management setting. This often led to public acquisition of such areas for parks and open space. In addition there was the problem of surface mining and the management of land restoration and reclamation; effective postmining land management was required to ensure permanent and self-sustained vegetation that, in turn, would reduce erosion potential. New large-scale facilities, such as power plants, suggested "siting management" rather than ad hoc decisions by industries, but was taken up by few states.

Endangered-species programs involved strategies to manage habitat, and open-space objectives required density management like that contemplated in the regulation of private lands in the Adirondacks or in the scheme for transferable development rights. Natural areas were managed also by private agencies such as the Nature Conservancy, colleges, and universities, as well as by public agencies; in 1979 an organization of natural-area managers was formed complete with annual meetings and a quarterly journal.[15]

The Integrative Role of Management

Each of the different disciplines involved in environmental affairs – science, economics, and planning – tended to proceed in different directions. But those professions came to be influenced heavily by the interest in applied knowledge of managerial institutions on which they were dependent for resources. Because management was vitally interested in all three sets of technical skills, moreover, it served as a mechanism for linking them into coordinate action for a common purpose.

Among environmental-management agencies the Forest Service perfected these arrangements most fully. Its experiment stations, established early in the twentieth century, served as major centers of forestry research. Forest economics came to be an integral part of the training of professional foresters and also of the professional skills in the Forest Service. In 1976 the first forester trained as an economist was appointed as a supervisor of a national forest. When the agency took up forest planning in the 1960s it hired both its own planners and the supporting resource specialists. Whereas other agencies might well have relied on external expertise, the Forest Service incorporated that expertise into its own management system. In doing so it fashioned an integrative system of considerable internal cohesion and power that was able to fend off attempts to modify its workings from both the assistant secretaries of agriculture under whose jurisdiction it fell and from the public as well.[16]

The EPA, with an even wider range of environmental-management tasks, made much use of science, economics, and planning – all three shaped by the immediate task at hand. Research at the EPA was devoted primarily to current regulatory problems. Only during the Carter administration were there moves toward long-term research associated with specialized centers at academic institutions, but this was cut back by the Reagan administration. Water-quality planning funded through the "208 program" was intended to deal with a broad scope of water-quality matters on a regional level, but often it was influenced by the pressing need to establish a rank-order list for federally funded, publicly owned treatment plants. The agency developed its own capabilities for economic analysis to justify regulatory actions but often also called on outside experts to assess the costs and benefits of its policies.

Environmental management linked private and public agencies in reinforcing and supportive relationships of common perception, purpose, and choice. Such relationships were influenced heavily by tendencies from all sides toward stability and predictability in system management. Both stability and predictability, in turn, were affected by a shared desire for an agreed base of information that described the real world with which the contending parties dealt jointly. Inherent in these circumstances was a persistent desire for agreement with respect to the real world with which both grappled.

The focal points of these political accommodations were defined in precise and quantitative terms, invoking the politics of numbers. There were, of course, intense controversies over the numbers, but there were also tendencies toward agreement in order to make action predictable and mutually understood. Particularly significant was the tendency for numbers, once described, to become inflexible articles of faith in which both sides had a powerful stake in their continuous use as a basis for action.

Hence both resisted external pressure to change them. The numbers context of management, in this fashion, constituted both a set of political accommodations and a bulwark against competing political challenges from those who argued either that important social values were excluded or that the numbers were inaccurate.

If one wished to balance cut and yield in the growth of wood in forests, both were quantified to know just what cut and what yield were in order to bring them into the desired relationship. If one wished to prevent deterioration of air or degradation of water, one had to know the numerical levels in specific places in order to know how much degradation had taken place or would take place under given actions. If one wished to establish and maintain open space in residential areas, then one needed to know how many people or dwellings per acre of land were to be guidelines for action.

In each case the key to management was the number agreed on to constitute the context of choice, and the selection of numbers was the result of intense debate. In forest management nondeclining even flow, a guideline for allowable-cut calculations, grew out of years of bargaining among the Forest Service, the timber industry, and the communities dependent on wood production. The specific allowable pollutant levels in water-quality measurements were often a result of agreements between public and private managers, and there were specific accommodations in the definition of mixing zones, their width, length, and depth, and in the standards to be required within them. In surface-mining reclamation there were agreements over what constituted satisfactory revegetation. Numbers such as these were at the heart of the day-to-day regulatory process.

Linkages among specialists in environmental management were reinforced by contacts established within professional associations. Insofar as managers, scientists, planners, or economists, private and public, developed in their relationships a common perspective, so would the institutions in which they worked be brought into harmony. The tendencies toward institutional accommodation, in turn, often shaped common professional perspectives. The National Air Pollution Control Association and the Water Pollution Control Federation, for example, brought together specialists from private corporations, public management agencies, and the academic world. In each there was strong emphasis on the application of knowledge to achieve practical results through management. They brought into their activities the engineers who designed machinery and equipment, as well as systems managers. And they enlisted relevant corporate trade associations such as the Electric Power Research Institute and the Industrial Gas Cleaning Institute.[17]

Those concerned with renewable biological resources also had their own integrative professional organizations. The Society of American Foresters contained within its ranks a balance between public- and private-forest managers. The Society for Range Management and the Wildlife Society brought together related professionals in those fields as did the Sport Fishing Institute. The precise mix in these groups was often influenced by the degree to which their activities were confined to publicly owned lands and waters. In the face of the growing movement for environmental amenities and especially the emphasis on natural systems these groups banded together into the Council on Renewable Resources, which emphasized the desirability of harvesting biological resources rather than their management as natural systems. This continued in more formal fashion shared viewpoints of earlier years that now were finding new common ground in their opposition to wilderness and other forms of natural-environment action.[18]

Occupational health had developed professional associations before the Environmental Era. The American Industrial Hygiene Association, which brought together specialists in the field of industrial medicine, was formed in 1939. Much like its counterpart in air-pollution control, it linked professionals in private industry and government with some academic participation. A more specialized segment of this set of professional ties was the American Conference of Governmental Industrial Hygienists, formed in 1942 specifically to develop standards to be applied in occupational health. This direct interface between industry and government constituted a powerful and controlling influence in the politics of occupational health by establishing the standards that represented public policy. Similarly, the National Council on Radiation Protection brought together professionals from industry and government to establish the standards of allowable radiation exposure. It was against such institutions as these and the choices they made that much of the force of the new environmental effort was directed.[19]

In these integrative activities environmental management tended to reinforce the developmental predispositions in each of its professional sectors, provided little room for significant initiatives in attaching science, economics, and planning to the enhancement of environmental objectives, and often blunted those aims. In the experiment stations of the Forest Service some researchers chafed under the agency's dominant wood-production aims. Because the stations were not under the direct control of the management side of the agency, they had some degree of freedom to explore the implications of environmental values, but their personnel felt frustrated that the agency seemed to lean in the other direction. In reaction they often established working ties with environmentalists to aid them in increasing their technical knowledge of forestry.

Economic analysis served especially as an integrative underpinning that directed attention away from the intangible to the concrete values, from less intensive natural processes to more intensive development, from enhancing the quality of physical well-being and aesthetic enjoyment to the benefits of "saving lives." Management tended to be concerned primarily with active uses of physical resources rather than passive enjoyment of amenities. Both economists and managers were committed to greater levels of management as a vehicle for more intensive resource manipulation through greater input of skills and capital rather than the maintenance of natural systems.

Ideology and the Politics of Restraint

In these strategies management played a political role in restraining environmental efforts. Managers and the professionals in science, economics, and planning whom they brought together for integrated action tended to be suspicious of the advocates of greater environmental progress. They viewed such advocacy with personal distaste and some degree of alarm. Their ideas and actions served primarily as a bulwark against the tendency of environmentalists to go "too far." Hence, in the drama of politics, environmental management was a force to neutralize and restrain the demand to advance environmental objectives.

In implementing existing environmental laws management was more inclined to interpret its authority in limited terms, to hesitate to act for fear of incurring the opposition of the regulated rather than to formulate a basis for carrying out the full intent of the law. Environmental groups continually pushed management to undertake action beyond what it was willing to do; management, in turn, continually complained about the excessive pressures those groups placed on it.[20]

This was reinforced by a persistent tendency among agencies to be more sympathetic to the argument that the nation needed increased production and development more than it needed further environmental progress. From the public came demands for new standards of environmental quality, the more rapid introduction of new scientific knowledge into policy making, and economic analysis more supportive of such advances. Hence by the 1980s, the managerial systems that had been developed in previous years to implement environmental programs often had become roadblocks impeding further innovation. It was hard enough just to keep going the system already constructed.

In this strategy of restraint managers were joined by others in political and intellectual leadership who formerly had been actively sympathetic to environmental change but now came to be more cautious about it. Two distinct groups are of interest. One comprised the political idea makers, the political intelligentsia who formulated notions about the broader significance of environmental affairs and who wrote in the major newspapers and journals of opinion. The other included the leaders of several environmental organizations such as Resources for the Future, the American Forestry Association, the Conservation Foundation, and the Environmental Law Institute who looked on themselves as the more specialized idea makers of the environmental world.[21]

Individuals in these groups took pains to dissociate themselves from what they called "environmental advocacy," which they criticized as confrontational and undesirable; they emphasized the practical tasks of management and efficiency in implementation with which the demands of citizen environmental groups interfered and urged that those groups limit their ambitions. These strategies led to activities apart from the mainstream of environmental action, a focus on the use of professional expertise that would be more restrained than citizen activists in guiding environmental affairs, and the economic limitations on the possibilities of environmental achievement.

We should think of these elements in the environmental political puzzle as constituting a middle ground between the antagonists on both the environmental and developmental sides. Their organizations and their leaders occupied a more neutral position in the spectrum of environmental controversy. They dissociated themselves from many citizen environmental groups (their choices depending on time and circumstance), and at the same time they sought to distinguish between the more and less responsible sectors of the business community and align themselves with the former. As a result they were suspected by both sides. Environmentalists considered them unreliable allies who would rarely join with them in advancing environmental objectives, whereas business groups felt that they were much too cautious in opposing environmental policies.[22]

Both of these groups, however, were influenced markedly by the ideas business disseminated to the wider public. During the 1970s the business community put forward a battery of ideas its superior resources enabled it to bring forcefully to the minds of American "thought leaders." In doing this it took the advice of its public-opinion analysts that this political intelligentsia was far more receptive to business arguments than was the general public. Business was thus able to shape the thinking of a wide range of leaders in government, in foundations, in colleges and universities, and in the press, as well as idea makers in influential conservation research and study groups.

This ideology of environmental skepticism began to extend beyond the more limited realm of the business community to the larger realm of the political intelligentsia during the last half of the 1970s and played an important role in blunting much of the receptivity of the Carter administration to environmental objectives. Prominent among these were the ideas that past policies had led to a nationwide stalemate, that environmental controversy was one of its major elements, and that executive leadership, unencumbered by popular influence, was the solution. The skeptics were receptive to the view that developmentalists rightly defined the nation's future and that environmentalists now formed a road-block impeding efforts to reach it.

The Social Analysis of Neutralization

In the 1960s and early 1970s the nation's thought leaders had been receptive to environmental analyses of public affairs and had provided a substantial intellectual legitimacy to environmental action in high places. This stood in sharp contrast to the managerial elite, which had been far more skeptical, and to the business community, which was overtly hostile. By the end of the 1970s, however, the idea makers themselves also had become more skeptical.

The most striking aspect of this change was the way environmental interpretations of events lost out in competition with those offered by business and managerial leaders. That influence was nurtured by the growing sense of crisis created by the rising price and anticipated decline in energy supply. This atmosphere enabled the business community to persuade others to accept its views of the nation's problems, how they should be understood, and how future alternatives should be defined.[23]

How should the economy be understood in relation to environmental matters? Environmentalists tended to believe that environmental objectives were an integral part of the economy, that they constituted new and legitimate consumer wants that were emerging in economic life. The business community, however, chose to emphasize the conflict between economic and environmental objectives. Environmental wants were extraneous factors, not central, and often not even legitimate. Here were two opposed notions, one rooted in the larger analysis of stages of evolution in the economy as a whole and the other in the more limited analysis of the immediate costs to producers. By the 1980s the political intelligentsia had accepted the second as the terms of debate.[24]

It also accepted the view that environmental policies had a detrimental effect on productivity. The business community sought to rivet public attention on labor as the crucial factor in productivity and repudiated arguments, often advanced by environmentalists, that other factors such as capital, technology, and management were equally significant productivity factors. Only in the energy sector did a major modification in thinking occur under the rubric of energy conservation or energy efficiency. But in accepting this form of analysis the political intelligentsia neither associated it with environmentalists nor placed it in the broader context of more general productivity analysis. Hence thought leaders were able to sustain in their own minds the view that environmental objectives were in some fashion inconsistent with improvements in productivity.

The business community was most successful in persuading thought leaders to accept its version of cost-benefit analysis as the central language of public discourse over environmental policy. The choice, as I have argued, involved not the fact of environmental cost-benefit analysis, which had been carried on persistently in the 1960s and 1970s, but the manner in which it would be conducted and whether it was appropriate to apply it to objectives as well as to the methods of reaching those objectives. The business community argued that only numerical analysis should be used and that costs should be an integral part of objectives analysis so that society would not adopt what it felt were unreasonable goals. The affected businesses were able to create a climate of opinion that emphasized regulatory excesses and prohibitive costs and to win adherents to their argument that numerical cost analysis should become more central in choices about the objectives as public policy.

The nation's thought leaders also accepted much of the business approach to environmental science. As the context of political issues and debate became more technical and involved increasing elements of both scientific detail and analysis, the ability to influence the direction of scientific thinking was crucial in the choice of policy. Well aware of this, business leaders expended considerable effort to shape the terms of debate over scientific issues. In so doing they were able to influence not only the way scientists thought about these matters but the way others did as well.[25]

Especially influential was the attempt to raise doubts about the scientific data on which environmental action rested and hence to generate a willingness to postpone decisions, to temporize, to wait until further scientific research had cleared up the doubts. Although the business community in the 1960s had attacked many elements of environmental science on which emerging programs rested, it had not been able to make its arguments convincing to the nation's thought leaders, who believed that even in the midst of uncertainty action should be taken. By the 1980s, however, the standards of proof for conclusions about environmental phenomena had increased considerably among scientists largely through the demands of the regulated industries for more stringent levels of evidence. Many now shifted from an emphasis on reasonable judgment in the face of uncertainty to an insistence on firm proof. Without firm proof, the argument now went, there was doubt and action was not reasonable.[26]

Thought leaders tended to accept the argument that these were issues of "good science" versus "bad science," thereby discrediting a significant sector of scientific opinion on which environmental action was based. Given such tendencies, it was difficult for the nation's thought leaders to maintain a more cautious position shaped by informed judgment rather than conclusive proof. The EPA sought to incorporate into its scientific assessments a wide range of scientific opinions, including those that rested on judgments about preliminary knowledge as well as those that demanded more extreme standards of proof. This made the agency vulnerable to attack from the "hard proof" sector of the scientific community and to being associated with "bad science."

These economic and scientific analyses were accompanied by a sociological analysis. There was a close connection, so the argument went, between individual opportunity and achievement, on the one hand, and an expanding economy, on the other, that was threatened by environmentalists. A succinct expression of this ideology appeared in the views of the National Coalition for Growth, which sought to counter the ideology of the tenth anniversary of Earth Day in 1980. "Our national wealth," the coalition affirmed in its media advertising, "isn't limited by our natural resources. If growth has any limits at all, it's our personal resources – our drive, our dedication and our desire to lead better, more fulfilling lives." And "only through the sustained growth of our economy can we keep opportunity knocking for ourselves, our children and our children's children."

False and dangerous environmental notions, it was argued,

were rooted in the new upper middle class, a relatively small group more interested in consumption than production, whose children had lost the virtues of personal achievement and had become pampered indulgers in a search for personal self-development and fulfillment. These were "elitists" rather than a cross section of American society. The nation was threatened, so the warning went, by a very small group of people with access to considerable wealth and influence, whose values were being imposed on the nation's mass of "working people."[27]

Acceptance of this analysis indicated two sets of ideas in competition. On the one hand, environmentalists sought to emphasize new goals of improved health and more attractive and pleasant surroundings and to pass those gains on to their children. In doing so they reflected one dimension of higher levels of opportunity in the nation's recent history. Their opponents, on the other hand, stressed the traditional focus on production, on personal achievement to create goods and services in the form of necessities and conveniences. Such a production analysis was especially popular among those engaged most directly in managing the nation's material resources. The response of the political intelligentsia to these competing ideas was somewhat mixed. Although they were tempted to affirm traditional views of achievement and opportunity, they also as individuals expressed new consumer values. Hence the antienvironmental sociological analysis was less rooted in the minds of the nation's thought leaders than were its economic and scientific elements.

There was also an accompanying assessment of American politics. An earlier political ideology that emphasized the need to liberate and activate subordinated political aspirations in order to make the nation's political institutions work now gave way to an argument that strong executive action was needed so as to contain the public's excessive political demands.

Because of adversary politics the courts were loaded beyond their capacity, administrative decision making was cumbersome and inordinately lengthy, and Congress was subject to so many conflicting demands that it could not act. All this, it was argued, arose from too many public demands that put too great a burden on the political system. A phrase developed by one political analyst seemed to crystallize an alternative: the "rule of reason."

Decisions, it was argued, should be made by reasoned discussion rather than by adversary political debate. The phrase seemed to focus the ideas of the political intelligentsia, both in emphasizing the undesirability of the current mode of environmental debate and in offering an alternative. It was difficult to specify what alternative was meant by the rule of reason, but it seemed to imply a reduction of litigation and an increase in compromise within a more confined context of debate among institutional and technical leaders rather than in the general public.

By the 1980s these ideas began to be linked in an argument about the general loss in effectiveness in American political life. Public affairs, so the idea went, had reached a stalemate so that inaction was common and the give-and-take of political forces made it impossible to make decisions. The system had become too open, and too many political forces had entered the fray. Political parties had declined in significance as instruments for reconciling diverse political impulses, a change reflected in declining voter turnout, reduced party control over nomination of candidates, and the conduct of campaigns; the rise of congressional subcommittes led by many aspirants for influence had eroded the power of the party to discipline the legislative process.

Amid all this, so the argument went, the most striking result was the declining ability of the president to control the bureaucracy and the excessive influence on policy of an iron triangle of experts located in the administrative agencies, the legislative committee staffs, and the interest groups. To these analysts the answer was a stronger executive, one who would bring about more central control over both the agencies and Congress and who could contain excessive demands from organized groups. From this high ground of analysis the political intelligentsia increasingly saw the environmental movement as needing constraint rather than encouragement if the American political system was to survive.

The Politics of Neutralization

These analyses were influenced by political tendencies among environmental professionals that shifted the context of environmental choice from the wider arena of public debate to the narrower and more private realm of negotiation among technical experts. Many environmental professionals felt uncomfortable in their association with popular movements and organizations. In response they sought to transfer action to areas in which popular influence was limited. These activities served to neutralize public environmental drives and enabled professionals to shape a context for decision making that was dominated by experts.

One of these activities was environmental mediation. This involved attempts to negotiate settlements to environmental disputes through neutral third parties and hence reduce controversy and conflict. Progress was hampered by excessive controversy; devices should be developed to head off incipient disputes before they emerged into hardened and irreversible political positions.[28]

Mediators sought to bring environmental and developmental groups together in many different types of situations involving general issues of potential dispute as well as specific controversies. The most visible of these efforts was Resolve, the Center for Environmental Conflict Resolution, headed by John Busterud, a former member of the federal Council for Environmental Quality. Busterud found that the nation's larger foundations were receptive to environmental mediation. Several of them had financed environmental-litigation groups in earlier years but now believed that this had gone far enough. Environmental mediation was an acceptable alternative for which they began to provide funds.[29]

Environmental professionals became interested in environmental mediation. The environmental movement had produced experts in health, ecology, engineering, law, and administration who formulated a distinctive point of view. They placed particular stress on the desirability of resolving disputes in "nonpolitical" ways, by which they meant through scientific and technical formats, under the direction of professionals rather than through more open political controversy.

In 1977 they formed the National Association of Environmental Professionals and two years later began to publish a journal, *The Environmental Professional.* They felt close to the movement for environmental mediation, shared its assumptions, rationales, and objectives, and devoted their 1980 annual conference to the subject. Although they saw themselves as pursuing nonpolitical objectives, a careful analysis would describe it as a choice of one instead of another set of political ideas and actions, an attempt to fashion political institutions that would contain what were considered to be excesses in the public environmental drive.[30]

The idea of environmental mediation was strongly supported by the business community, as well it might be. For the ideological context of mediation conveyed criticism of the citizen environmental movement. Its initial point of departure often was a focus on the litigation citizen environmentalists had generated, which was described as excessive. The atmosphere around environmental mediation continued to be one of criticism of citizen action rather than of the business community. On the whole it helped to bolster the corporate drive to discredit public environmental initiatives.

One of the most widely publicized environmental-mediation ventures was the National Coal Policy Project through which a small group of coal-industry and environmental leaders met for several years to work out common viewpoints on coal policy. On a few, but relatively minor, issues they found common ground, but on those of major importance they continued to disagree sharply. The project's initial report, *Where We Agree: Report of the National Coal Policy Project,* was widely publicized as an example of the preferable road to take in environmental disputes. But that publicity took the form of corporate public-relations strategies rather than accurate description and implied that formerly litigation-minded environmentalists had finally seen the light.[31]

Most environmental organizations concerned with coal issues such as air quality and strip mining either declined to participate in the first place or soon lost interest when the coal companies adopted a dual attitude of talking in terms of mediation at the meetings and in public while privately pursuing litigation and other conventional political tactics on the same issues. At a meeting of the project early in 1980, coal-company representatives announced that they had been instructed by their constituent firms not to discuss the scheduled topic of sulfur dioxide scrubbers and tall stacks. Thereafter the project quietly disappeared from the public scene. Despite attempts by some of its participants to tout it as a promising alternative, the project primarily emphasized the depth of disagreement on the substantive issues and heralded the continuation of vigorous political dispute.

Advocates of environmental mediation sought to bring together parties in dispute in a variety of issues. Several examples, however, illustrate the difficulties. One, an effort to resolve differences over wilderness-study proposals in Colorado, ended in stalemate; the negotiations collapsed, continued in the general political arena, and led to a congressional solution in the Colorado Wilderness Act of 1980. A more ambitious effort to tackle forest-management problems took place in the Pacific Northwest, involved leaders of environmental organizations and timber companies, and generated a series of meetings but little joint action.[32]

A third venture, concerning the Toxic Substances Control Act of 1976, was acclaimed as an alternative to open political contention. This was taken up just after the act was passed with a feeling of optimism that if the parties in dispute during the legislative debate could be brought together some hope might be entertained for agreement on implementation. Discussions ensued to find common ground. The optimism was sustained by the absence, thus far, of litigation under the act. But by early 1978 it had become clear that this restraint provided only a temporary respite. An intense climate of adversary politics soon built up involving dispute over the degree to which companies would disclose sufficient information in their applications for permits to manufacture new chemicals to enable the public to evaluate their potential harm. The companies refused to do this, and for all practical purposes this effort at mediation came to an end.

Despite these cases of unsuccessful mediation the movement maintained considerable credibility among the political intelligentsia though not among citizen environmentalists. Business leaders and environmentalists continued to work out their differences through conventional methods. Business people especially lost interest when they found support for their views from President Carter and chose to seek their fortunes there. Their hopes blossomed into full-scale triumph with the election of Ronald Reagan.

The environmental-mediation movement was less significant

as a mechanism to resolve disputes than as a reflection of major trends in thinking among the nation's thought leaders. Because that group wanted environmental mediation to replace other forms of dispute resolution they gave it support and prominence even in the face of its only modest achievements.

Whereas in earlier years the nation's thought leaders had supported measures to strengthen the role of citizen environmental action, they now came to have misgivings about what they had done and to emphasize its undesirable effects. The analysis of the political world put forward by advocates of mediation, which called for the neutralization of citizen environmental groups, struck a chord in their minds and emotions and enabled them to favor mediation as a method of resolving disputes. It was an approach whereby the political intelligentsia was transformed into opponents of citizen environmental action despite the self-image of being neutral parties who really sought the same objectives as did environmentalists but through more appropriate means.

The Conservation Foundation

The Conservation Foundation (CF) reflected this transformation in a single organizational setting. For many years the CF had been a major influence in environmental affairs. In the 1950s and 1960s it had been one of the most authoritative sources of ideas about what was then described as conservation. Some of the nation's environmental leaders, such as Russell Train and Frank Gregg, had been associated with it. By the beginning of the 1980s, however, leaders of citizen environmental organizations in the nation's capital no longer looked to the foundation for ideas and leadership. They considered it a source of useful research and publications, but somewhat peripheral to their concerns, seeking to establish a middle ground rather than to speak clearly for environmental objectives.[33]

The Conservation Foundation had been established in 1948 and over the next two decades was influenced heavily by a few leaders such as Frank Fraser Darling, whose ideas and experience had come from an ecological background. Its origin lay in the New York Zoological Society, and it continued to have its intellectual roots in natural history, wildlife biology, and efforts to deal with problems concerning the relationship between resources and population. These ideas established the CF as a source of understanding for both the older conservation and the newer environmental movements; it seemed to provide cogent explanations for what was happening to American society and what should be done about it. Much of the early environmental movement also emphasized the natural world, and with this the CF found much compatibility. It funded some of the early research on the adverse effect of pesticides on wildlife, as well as several books on the subject, such as Robert Rudd's *Pesticides and the Living Landscape.* In the late 1960s the Conservation Foundation enjoyed a commanding intellectual position within the long-standing conservation and the emerging environmental movements.

Citizen environmental activism, however, presented the CF with a considerable challenge. As citizen demands became more insistent in the late 1960s, the foundation reached out to respond to them. When Viriginia citizens, for example, believed that they were not given an opportunity to participate fully in formulating the state's clean-air program mandated by the 1967 Clean Air Act, the CF intervened with the National Air Pollution Control Administration. It established several regional centers such as the Potomac Environmental Information Center and the Florida Environmental Center, which were intended to respond to needs for information felt by active citizen groups.[34]

But the CF apparently was uncomfortable with such close connections with citizen activists, and soon these ties weakened. It continued to engage in programs to educate citizen environmentalists about new legislation and administrative programs, for example, the Water Quality Act of 1972, but in doing so it geared its education to a neutral position rather than to environmental advocacy. Although citizen environmental groups found its technical information useful, they did not find it a source of ideas that would inspire and sustain frontier citizen action.[35]

These divergent tendencies were illustrated by two separate citizen-education programs instituted in response to the 1976 Forest Management Act. One of these, under the auspices of the CF, was funded by the U.S. Forest Service, used Forest Service visual materials, focused on the technical details of legislation and planning, and attracted primarily governmental, professional, and institutional leaders. At the same time several citizen environmental groups were organizing the Forest Planning Clearinghouse, located in Eugene, Oregon, which developed a publication, *Forest Planning,* directed specifically toward citizen activists. This publication sought to give such groups arguments, information, and ideas that would enable them to turn the forest-management process more fully toward environmental objectives. In these two quite different programs the CF served as the neutral conveyor of information, and the Clearinghouse served as an advocate of environmental goals.[36]

During the late 1970s the Conservation Foundation came more and more to stress a middle ground. One of its new strategies was a special effort to steer both environmentalists and business "toward a common ground." This program, established in 1976, gave rise to a series of publications and conferences. A collection of articles was published in 1977 under the title *Business and Environment: Toward Common Ground.* In its foreword the editors laid out the "middle ground" strategy through which accommodation was to be made. It reflected the ideological transformation the CF had undergone.[37]

Business and Environment argued that environmental legislation reflected a national commitment, an agreement by all sectors of society on environmental objectives that called for an end to internal disputes. "Name-calling, agitation . . . caricature . . . and simplification of issues" should be rejected in favor of communication and "reasoned discussion" between business and environmentalists. The problem now was not to call "for reforms" but to "[make] sure that the new laws work"; the strategies of the past, geared more to open political controversy, should be discarded. The major problem now was not one of formulating and sharpening environmental concerns but that of relating "environmental concerns to economic ones" and this would require of environmentalists "a greater awareness of economic factors in public planning and regulatory processes." Although the need to "reinforce among business leaders a respect for environmental values" was also acknowledged, the emphasis was on the need for change on the part of environmentalists. In a later annual report the foundation's president, William Reilly, wrote that "the environmental rally is over" and that henceforth the focus should be on joint efforts to implement common objectives.

One could describe the significance of CF ideology not so much as an accurate portrayal of environmental history but more as an expression of change in the foundation's own perspective and intellectual position. No longer did the CF provide a clear focus on the values and objectives inherent in the environmental movement, as it had in earlier years, so as to give meaning to those who wished to develop an intellectual rationale for their belief in continuing environmental progress. One found here few attempts to elaborate on well-being as a mode of health, on natural-environment amenities in advancing the nation's standard of living, or the search for ecological integrity and permanence. Moreover, it emphasized administration and implementation as fundamentally different from legislation and thereby obscured the role of political choice in a wide range of implementation issues.[38]

In the late 1970s and early 1980s the Conservation Foundation sought to restore its leadership in environmental affairs. When in April 1980 the tenth anniversary of Earth Day provided the opportunity it held a summit meeting for state and local environmental leaders in Estes Park, Colorado, to reflect on the past and chart a road for the future. At this meeting it sought to convey a message of moderation and containment; the new decade would require a muting of environmental efforts in favor of economic practicality. But to citizen activists present this fell far short of their needs. They were interested in developing more effective tools for action: How could they hire staffs, develop publications, secure expertise, and influence elections so as to do the job more effectively? Daily they experienced vigorous developmental initiatives that blunted environmental action and vigorous antienvironmental political strategies that did not jibe with a plea for reasoning together.

Administrative Neutrality

The ultimate focus of the drive to neutralize environmental political actions was on environmental administration. In the early stages of environmental action many administrators had developed positive commitments to environmental objectives. This took a variety of forms: publications, the promotion of citizen education and action, new mechanisms for citizen involvement in administrative decision making, the selection of advisory committee members who had strong environmental interests, and the appointment of personnel favorable to shifting the weight of decision toward environmental objectives.

Developmentalists strongly objected to these innovations, arguing that administrators should be more "even handed" and not promotional. Gradually during the 1970s they were able to counter such new departures at first the state and then the federal level. This drama in state government was often little noticed. One focus was the publications of the state natural-resource departments. In the first rush of environmental advocacy magazines such as *Conservation* (New York), *Montana Outdoors,* and *Michigan Natural Resources* had become bolder in advocating environmental objectives. This was especially true of wildlife agencies, which played a key role in affirming the significance of wildlife and in objecting to developmental projects that could threaten habitat. These advocacy ventures soon ran afoul of counterpressures exercised through gubernatorial offices. Policy articles gave way to those that featured nature appreciation with an emphasis on color photography and natural history.[39]

These trends could also be observed in state administrative actions such as mechanisms for facilitating citizen participation in administrative proceedings. Here the battle took place over whether administrators, as officials of public agencies, could themselves effectively represent the public, or whether some other form of citizen representation was required. Agencies sought to reduce the significance of the latter and to assert their role as representing the public. In proceedings to revise the New York State pesticide regulations in 1980, for example, the Department of Environmental Conservation included representatives of pesticide manufacturers, farmers, and state agencies on its committee but declined to include those from citizen groups on the grounds that the department represented them effectively.

A special battleground for control was the new state advisory bodies that had been formed to advance environmental objectives more effectively in policy-making. In Montana the Environmental Quality Council, established by the legislature in 1970 as a policy-making body, flourished for four years, producing several remarkable annual reports on Montana's environment. But by the mid-1970s its personnel had shifted so heavily toward developmentalists that environmentalists considered it not to be neutral but to speak for antienvironmental objectives. In Pennsylvania the Citizens Advisory Council, established in 1970 to represent public environmental concerns, included from the start several representatives from utility and strip-mining companies. With the new Republican administration of Governor Richard Thornburg in 1978 that contingent was increased, and environmental representation and advocacy were effectively subordinated.[40]

Federal agencies constituted similar battlegrounds with similar types of controversies. Developmentalists objected that agency publications reflected advocacy rather than neutrality. It was entirely inappropriate, so they argued, for them to carry out public-awareness activities favorable to environmental objectives. They complained about personnel in advisory committees who were known in their private affairs to be supportive of environmental concerns and argued that administrators should police the contending parties in a neutral fashion rather than be advocates. These challenges worked to make the agencies more cautious in their support of environmental objectives.

The significance of these demands for neutralization could be observed by contrasting them with environmental efforts to neutralize the activities of agencies with developmental missions. That effort had taken the form of the environmental-impact statement, a strategy that focused not on transforming the personnel and practice of the agencies from within but on applying action-forcing pressure from without by requiring them to take into account the environmental consequences of their developmental activities.

Although this did lead to some modification of developmental-agency actions, it did not significantly change their basic directions; they were able to turn environmental-impact analyses to their own purposes and to use them as devices to balance environmental and developmental objectives rather than to focus on the former. Environmental agencies, on the other hand, had far less capacity to retain a strong environmental mission and to ward off external developmental pressures. They could readily fall prey to demands that they play a more neutral role in these controversies and be undermined by a direct invasion of development-minded personnel.

Both environmental managers and thought leaders developed similar and mutually reinforcing political stances that separated them from environmental advocacy and citizen groups and emphasized strategies for implementation. In so doing they chose not to work out rationales for expanding environmental objectives in American society and turned their energies, in matters such as study and research as well as in idea making, to consolidating previous gains. This meant that within the entire environmental movement, with which they sought to associate themselves in general, they played a distinctive role in which they were suspicious of environmental advocacy and environmental advocates were suspicious of them.

There was yet a larger meaning to the political role of the middle ground. It argued in terms not only of the difficulties of implementation but also of the limits to which national environmental achievement could go. Much of this kind of talk was in terms of the cost of environmental programs. But the more subtle message was just as clear, namely, that the nation's resources could not stand too much environmental progress. The public should expect only so much natural beauty, so much improvement in health, so much ecological permanence and not more. For whereas those who shaped production simply responded in terms of their own costs, it was the managers and the thought leaders who spoke of the larger limitations in the economy.

There were, of course, choices in all this. For although one might hear of the limits to environmental growth from the nation's managers and thought leaders, one did not hear equal warnings about the limits to the production of other goods and services, to the exploration of frontiers in other fields of science and technology, to the resource limitations in advancing material standards of living.

The middle ground held not a fixed political position but one in which there was considerable choice. There were varied middle grounds between environmental advocates and their opponents. In Britain, for example, Environmental Data Services, also occupied a middle ground, but its version was a belief that both sides had a common interest in expanding science and technology and that with common support of vanguard action in both fields much of the controversy between them could be reduced. In the United States, on the other hand, the middle ground took the form of direct political bargaining between parties in dispute and advice to environmentalists to tone down their demands because of the limits to environmental growth.[41]

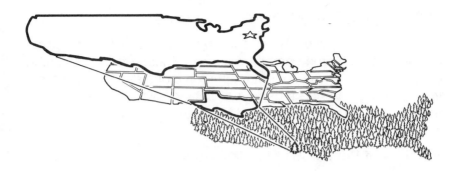

13 Environmental Politics
   in the States

The states were as significant a setting for environmental politics as was the nation. But the state level of action was often obscured by the greater emphasis on national politics and the universal context of science and technology.

Ideally it would be desirable to have a firm grasp of environmental affairs in all fifty states and to reach some generalizations about their pattern. Such would be a more than herculean task. Yet since the focus of this analysis is the interaction between interests arising from the smaller levels of social life in the community, on the one hand, and the larger world of economic and technical organization, on the other, it is appropriate to dwell more pointedly on the states.

We shall do this in two ways. First we shall examine the balance and pattern of environmental and developmental forces within the states. Much depended on the strength of environmentalists' influence in each state and the outcome of their struggle with developmental forces. We shall be especially interested in the interaction between community and state as each side of the political controversy sought to use either community autonomy or state authority in carrying out its objectives.

Second, we shall be interested in state environmental initiatives. Although national laws provided a certain minimal uniform

427

level of action, some states took up initiatives that represented considerable environmental innovation. These often constituted a threat to those who sought to limit environmental action; they, in turn, sought to use federal authority to restrain state policies that were more restrictive than federal ones.[1]

Patterns of Politics Within the States

The contending political forces in state environmental affairs were similar to those at the national level. Analysis of state legislative votes on environmental issues reveals the primary influence of urban-rural differences. Democrats scored much higher than did Republicans in each state, but this was superimposed on variations between urban and rural areas. On most issues cities provided the major initiative and support and rural areas the opposition.[2]

States, of course, differed in their degree of urbanization. At the same time, no matter what that level, there was a remarkable similarity in the balance between the highly urbanized and the less urbanized sections of each state or group of states that set the pattern for the contending environmental and developmental forces. In Michigan, for example, the one-third of the most populous counties in the southern part of the state contained 85 percent of the total population and the one-third of the least populous in the upper part contained just 2.9 percent, a marked difference that was reflected in the relative strength of the two areas in the legislature. In both Pennsylvania and New England, the most populous third of the counties contained 74 and 78 percent of the total and the least populous third 4.5 and 3.6 percent. These comparable patterns of inequality in the distribution of population identified a similar structure for environmental politics in each state and region that pitted more and less developed areas against each other.[3]

A determining factor in the emergence of environmental affairs was the timing of the rise of the city to a significant role in state politics, and this was closely connected to legislative reapportionment. For many decades rural areas had resisted urban efforts to redistrict legislative seats, and finally in 1962 the Supreme Court ruled that reapportionment was required. The censuses of 1960 and 1970 provided the new population data, and shortly thereafter state legislatures reflected more closely the distribution of population. By this time it was not so much the central city as the middle-class suburbs that were underrepresented – precisely those places where environmental attitudes were strongest. These changes added considerably to the strength of environmental objectives in state as well as national politics.[4]

Within each state the people of wildlands areas displayed vigorous opposition to environmental activities arising from urban influences in their regions. These were areas of traditional raw-material extraction; livelihoods depended on mining, lumbering, oil drilling, and gravel dredging in rivers, along the shores of lakes, and in wetlands. To environmentalists all of these rural industries were serious blights on the countryside, both because of their immediate operations and because of what was left behind in the form of tailings, land disturbance, and water pollution. But to residents these were major sources of employment and worthy historic traditions; they defended themselves tenaciously against the attempts of environmentalists to restrict raw-material extraction.[5]

In state legislatures political and economic leaders from wildlands areas constituted the most vigorous environmental opposition. Because they were outnumbered among their colleagues, and especially so after the reapportionments of the 1960s and 1970s, they concentrated their protective strategies on leadership roles and intralegislative bargaining. Urbanized people, they thought, simply did not understand rural ways or the key role of raw materials in the state and nation; they saw themselves as embattled defenders of their communities against the imperialism of the cities. Some areas – the upper peninsula of Michigan, for example – considered secession. They represented an older way of economic and political life that had held sway in many rural communities and that now was challenged by changes in the values and desires of the American people. They fought back with special vigor.[6]

The broad expanse of rural America between the cities and the wildlands where farming predominated also sustained developmental politics. There were constant thoughts here of greater things in the future – more people, more building, more income, more public services. These came not so much from farmers but from the promoters of development in the towns and smaller cities, the bankers and real estate agents, the owners of commercial property and businesses, the town chambers of commerce and governments, all of whom had a stake in rising levels of commercial activity, of buying and selling, of renting and of tax revenues.

Loans and grants for development were available from a variety of federal agencies, but two in particular played a major role in rural economic development. One consisted of programs financed through the Farmers Home Administration. Originally intended to aid farmers, this program was extended to rural "land improvement" projects for recreation, flood control, and commercial sites. This reflected a transition in many federal and state agricultural programs from an emphasis on farm production to general rural development to include business and industry.[7]

Equally significant were the federal regional economic development commissions supervised by the Department of Commerce. The first of these, the Appalachian Regional Commission, was formed in 1961; in 1965 the approach was extended to six other areas of higher than average unemployment. These provided funds for projects such as industrial parks, mineral-resource exploration, transportation, vocational training, and water and sewage works. Many rural legislators sought both kinds of federal aid.[8]

For both the wildlands and the rural countryside the promotion of tourism became an important objective. From the cities came large numbers of people who sought recreation in the countryside. Many of these looked for the natural environment setting; others preferred highly developed facilities. They stayed in motels and ate at restaurants; they rented or bought motorboats and patronized sporting goods stores.

The promotion of tourism became one of the major functions of the merchant groups in the towns of the countryside and the state departments of commerce. Each community tried to capture the tourist dollar; such areas felt that more of it would be spent in their community if only more facilities were available. After World War II their strategies were geared to the short-term visitor who came and went but did not stay long. Services for them would add to the income of the local community.

Environmentalists often came into conflict with tourism. On the one hand, they emphasized the environmental qualities that made for increased tourist activities. But the tourist trade also increased population pressures that could destroy the same values by bringing congestion and noise, development, road construction, and traffic. Did each step in greater intensity of use not degrade the recreational experience and create areas more like the cities from which one had sought to escape?

During the 1960s and 1970s new migrants came to both the wildlands and the countryside and provided support for environmental objectives in competition with long-standing developmental ones. Business enterprises arose that depended on recreational use of the forests and streams and catered to hunters, fishermen, backpackers, and tourists. More influential were those individuals who purchased property and vacationed or lived there to enjoy the natural environment and supported uses such as wildlife, the cleaner air and water, the quiet, and the forested surroundings. Tourist centers such as Aspen, Colorado, and Jackson Hole, Wyoming, vigorously supported environmental objectives within their states.[9]

In the countryside the population had been changing for more than half a century as "rural nonfarm" people moved into farming areas and engaged in rural activities different from those of older residents. Some who lived along streams and valued their natural surroundings promoted the environmental watershed; others took up an interest in nongame wildlife rather than hunting. Often they complained about farm practices. Pesticides applied by aerial spraying drifted into homes and gardens; the noise of tractors and the odors of farm animals repelled nonfarm neighbors; deer that lived in the nearby woods and were enjoyed by nonfarm residents ate farm crops. Wetlands that harbored birds were attractive to many nonfarm residents as well as urban recreationists, but farmers considered them obstructions to more productive farm enterprise. The quality of the water supply was often threatened by farm chemicals such as fertilizers and pesticides from runoff. There was an increasing incompatibility between the demands for more intensive agricultural production and the preferences of nonfarm people who lived among farmers.[10]

During the 1970s a different set of issues pertaining to the impact of large-scale development on the countryside modified the political relationships between these older and newer elements in the wildlands and the countryside. When there were proposals for siting new large-scale enterprises such as power plants, industrial facilities, mining, and especially waste-disposal landfills and hazardous-waste sites, many people in these areas reacted in opposition. Cooperation occurred between the older rural residents who now spoke in terms of "quality of life" and more typical environmentalists of urban origins. Such cooperation, however tentative, was more than fleeting and isolated.

In the 1960s and 1970s there were common actions to defend water rights in Utah and Nevada, to protect against mining in the upper Great Lakes region, to oppose energy parks in Pennsylvania, to reject nuclear-power plants in Washington, to control the impact of strip mining in the upper Plains states and to prevent the siting of synthetic-fuel plants in Kentucky and West Virginia. These issues led to some changes in the attitudes of rural legislators. Most representatives from such areas outside the South were Republican and hence predisposed to follow their party's preference for a developmental rather than an environmental stance in state legislation. But they were also directly responsive to their constituents. And this response prompted them to act, often swiftly and vigorously, on local siting proposals.

The Environmental Politics of Local Government

The expression of environmental interests usually focused on a specific place where people lived, worked, and carried on their leisure-time activities. Values were shaped by, and expressed within, the environmental quality of that place. At the same time, development, whether originating from near or afar, from local entrepreneurs or large-scale ventures in the wider society, took place on a particular site in a particular community. Local governments inevitably were at the center of such affairs.[11]

Initial action usually involved an attempt to influence local government. This might have been to improve air quality in the face of industrial emissions, to make a stream more attractive as an environmental amenity, to identify and protect open space in a congested setting, to control or eliminate billboards or junkyards, to bury unsightly overhead electrical wires, to limit the height of buildings, to move a garbage dump elsewhere, to ward off proposals to build commercial establishments in their midst, to prevent development that would bring more cars, pollution, and congestion to the community, to establish a new public park, or to beautify streets. The city council, the town government, township supervisors, and county commissioners were the initial focus of action.[12]

In many cases, however, environmentalists found local government unresponsive. Often the stumbling block was the commitment of elected officials to developmental objectives. At times action required that implementation of some of these objectives be restrained in order to benefit the community as a whole, and officials frequently hesitated to do this. And often the instincts of local government for financial survival led it to favor development, and the developers who promoted it, in order to increase tax revenues.

No matter what the source of resistance, environmentalists sought resources and authority for action from state government. Here there might be available greater technical expertise, more access to professional skills, or more funds. Here also was political authority that could overcome local tendencies toward development. If state authority was not sufficient, as appeared to be the case with air and water quality in the late 1960s, federal assistance was sought. States had not yet acted or their programs were weak and ineffective. But these efforts to enhance federal authority to secure improved environmental conditions eventually focused on the local community. The improvement of its quality of life was its intention; higher levels of authority were sought for community change when lower levels were not responsive.

Local officials constantly confronted their weakness to act effectively, both with respect to the problems at hand and to the relative power and strength of private and public institutions. Their revenues were frequently insufficient to undertake even minimally the activities they wanted to carry out. Their professional skills, expertise, and knowledge were limited in a world of decision making that required such capabilities. Local governments were continually confronted with superior resources on the part of larger institutions, both private and public, on which they could become dependent and which could compromise their autonomy and power even though they might provide needed resources for community action.[13]

Local governments came from a historic tradition that defined their major role as promoting the community's growth and development in terms of increased population, jobs, and personal income, and more intensive use of land. This role influenced a range of local decisions and led to a constant search for assistance from state and federal governments to help the community realize its objectives. Private, profit-making businesses, industry, commerce, banking, investment, raw-material extraction, and agriculture were the visible activities surrounding local government and impinging on it. Local officials, in turn, responded to these private demands as reflecting community objectives. One found in the local community a symbiotic and beneficial relationship between private and public growth and development interests.[14]

At the same time, however, the context of civic responsibility and public values that led local governments to define the community's good one way also made it susceptible to other values that could also be defined as community objectives. As an increasing number of community residents argued that there was a dimension to community life called environmental quality and that this dimension involved less intensive development, more natural-environment areas, and cleaner surroundings, local governments were constrained to respond.[15]

Often the interplay among these community values was reflected more directly and precisely in the courts than in governmental bodies that drew up ordinances and enforced them. For changing community values often appeared in the claims of one individual that personal affairs were harmed or threatened by another. Such cases were the traditional stuff of common law, the body of legal doctrine that grew not out of statutes but from the day-to-day resolution of disputes among individuals. Traditionally the courts had dealt primarily with injuries to person or property, but they had always been called on to deal with the community's less tangible values as well as its moral sensibilities. And the courts had handled demands that injury to the environmental setting of one's home and leisure be redressed. Such less tangible injuries had been spoken of as nuisances, the annoyance of one person by another with noise and odors, with interference with the enjoyment of daily life. Because courts were responsive to such claims, they were often one of the first governmental bodies to feel the impact of changing community values.

The appearance of enviromental values in a community often depended on its general character, whether it was rural, small town, suburban, or city, industrial, agricultural, commercial, or residential. A rural community that reflected the views of owners of farm property might oppose large-scale intrusions but also wish to be free to develop its own property in less intensive ways. A small town might be receptive to the desires of its property owners for more intensive development that would increase real estate values. More fully residential communities on the city fringe might well serve as special footholds for the political expression of environmental values. In almost every case, however, such values switched from a latent to an active role during some major community episode such as a land-use decision, the siting of a new commercial, industrial, or housing proposal, the proposed location of a road or a sanitary landfill. These then led to organized action to emphasize positive community enviromental amenities such as open space, parks, and nature centers that would express the newly emerging values.

State Government and Politics

Those who advanced both environmental and developmental objectives sought assistance from state government. They approached their state legislators for aid and tried to influence the policies of administrative agencies. Often governors were the major targets of their concerns. In this competition for support from state government developmentalists usually had the upper hand. More frequently than not, legislators, agencies, and governors were attuned to developmental rather than environmental goals. Only in those few states where levels of environmental interest were especially high, such as California, did the relationship between the two approach a roughly even balance. Save for a few years in the late 1960s and early 1970s state political leaders found it more advantageous to be identified with the state's developmental objectives.

In the early years of the Environmental Era some strong environmental lawmakers had been appointed to legislative committees devoted to such affairs, and in this way environmental concerns had a chance to be heard and perhaps even prevail in committee decisions. But as developmental influences increased, there were demands for balance on these committees that led to personnel changes and the neutralization and even subordination of environmental influences. There was no similar demand for balance, however, with respect to development-oriented committees, such as those dealing with mining, commerce, banking, and agriculture, where the idea that environmental representation might be desirable was rarely mentioned. At the same time administrative agencies that had been clear in their environmental advocacy in earlier years now became muted, sympathetic to developmental interests, and prone to alter advisory committees, substantive policies, and decision-making procedures so as to make the expression of environmental concerns difficult.

Developmental influences were especially dominant among those lawmakers who represented the rural areas that were so much the concern of urban-based environmentalists. The varied interests in local affairs that the legislator represented were heavily associated with development, the rising value of land that came with intensive use, and the higher tax revenues local governments would enjoy from increasing property values. Such legislators gave environmental objectives only scant attention. They were continually on the lookout for new and improved roads, state and federal funds for local schools and public works, water development and water supplies, new industry and business, and tax breaks to encourage them. The complex of people and institutions that pressed for increases in population, land development, private income, and public revenues served as the context within which the ideas and proposals of state legislators were formed.

In the face of these tendencies environmentalists could exercise little influence in areas outside the cities. At times they were able to call on state governments for action, but this was likely to occur in the more heavily urbanized states, such as New York and California, where environmental sentiment was stronger. Their successes were sporadic. Although in some states a program or two was developed, for example, to identify air, land, and water of high environmental quality and to manage it for environmental objectives, there were few cases on which this went beyond a limited action to a more comprehensive review and commitment. Environmental strength lay in the cities and statewide policies to influence action in the more environmentally valuable areas of the countryside and the wildlands.[16]

These problems raised new questions about political representation: People living in one place sought to shape policies in another under a governmental system in which legislative representation was specific to a given area and one lawmaker scrupulously declined to propose policies for another district. Urbanites who visited rural and wildlands for recreation or owned property there found that this presented a roadblock to their political influence. Local governments and their representatives were not prone to consider the rights of such people to be heard in local affairs to be as fully legitimate as those of full-time residents. Yet these people from outside the community demanded some voice. Nonresident property owners had a financial stake in the area – they paid taxes – and hence should have some say in local policies, and recreational users developed an "interest" that led them to assert legitimacy in seeking to influence decisions.

The management of the public lands also involved problems of representation. These were owned by all residents of a state, if state lands, or of the nation in the case of federal lands. And hence urban dwellers with environmental interests felt they could demand a voice in their management. It had been customary for wildlands managers to establish closer relationships with institutional leaders in the local areas rather than with the interested public elsewhere. But it was difficult for those of the environmental public who lived beyond the wildland areas to have the same degree of day-to-day personal contact and involvement with managers as people in the locality. How to bring into decision making the taxpayers and environmental users of wildlands who lived elsewhere so that local interests, more inclined toward developmental rather than environmental objectives, would not be the exclusive participants in shaping wildlands policies?

In response to demands from urban environmentalists that they be heard, wildlands managers created devices to incorporate this "citizen input" into decision making. The environmental-impact statement, as well as citizen-involvement meetings, helped to determine the degree of public interest in policies originating in metropolitan as well as wildlands areas. Yet even in such cases the managers claimed the freedom to interpret the meaning of this "representation" and frequently gave local letters and comments greater weight than those from outside the immediate area and from out of state.

To take another example, the system of representation of appointees to the New York Adirondack Park Agency included people from outside the area. Of the land in the Adirondacks, 25 percent was owned by permanent year-round residents, 35 percent by private individuals who did not live there, 38 percent by the state, and 2–3 percent by out-of-state owners. How was the interest in land management of those who did not live within the area to be represented? The law provided that the governing board of the Adirondack Park Agency should be composed of five landowners resident within the park, three nonresident landowners, and three state ex officio members. This provided some formal representation for people outside the park but gave considerable overrepresentation to resident landowners.[17]

Environmentalists sought to influence state agencies directly, but those agencies were loath to respond to such influence because they felt limited by counterpressures from the communities where the resources were located. They avoided actions that might limit the development aspirations of the local community. Urban environmentalists pressed agencies to take the initiative in such matters as wilderness and wild- and scenic-river designations, prevention of significant deterioration and water-quality degradation, for example, and found support for these in changes at the federal level, whereas state agencies dragged their feet because of the fear of local resistance.

To maneuver around this resistance on the part of state agencies, environmentalists found that planning provided a foot in the door for their views in a less immediately threatening medium. Many proposals were diverted from action to planning in order to postpone their immediate impact. Although agencies and local communities might resist environmental objectives if they involved a pending action, they were likely to be less threatened by the same proposals in a planning context that would entail discussion rather than immediate action. Environmentalists often found such a forum amenable to their objectives because they received greater positive response from planners than from legislators and administrators. Yet even in this forum the environmental-developmental tensions between rural and urban areas often were sharp; each side recognized that although planning did not mean conclusive action, it constituted the initial step, and each sought the advantage of this opening leverage.

In cases where residents of the countryside and the wildlands sought to protect themselves against intrusions from large-scale development or waste-disposal siting, the problems of representation and power were reversed. Both the affected communities and environmentalists sought to affirm the authority of local people to decide. Hence they asserted the right of self-determination through local referenda, zoning, and assent from locally elected officials. But developers shifted ground and argued that the projects were needed, that the "parochial" interests of the local community should not be allowed to prevail, and that although the community should be permitted to give its advice and opinion, the final decision on such issues should rest at a higher level of authority such as the state. In matters such as zoning, they argued, local authority had come from the state and that power should now be returned to the state. Environmentalists joined with residents of rural and wildlands areas to protest these attempts to override local authority.[18]

Attempts to shift authority from the locality to the state became commonplace in many matters of development and environmental protection. Industries faced community attempts to restrict their activities, either by establishing regulations under which they could operate or refusing to grant permission to site a project in the first place. They sought state authority to prohibit local action. In environmental-protection matters these shifts in authority came about quietly. Thus, state air-pollution laws might provide that local governments could not enact regulations more stringent than those provided by the state; similar provisions appeared in state strip-mining legislation, forest-practice acts, wetlands legislation, and pesticide-control statutes. At the insistence of developmental interests there took place a significant upward shift in political power over environmental affairs from the community to the state.[19]

Similar shifts in authority over land use and especially siting decisions came about with more controversy but with similar results. Often the issue came to a head as a community sought to use its power of zoning to prevent the siting of an industrial plant. In response the developer went to the state and demanded a new arrangement whereby siting decisions would be made at the state rather than the local level, a change the developer felt sure would make a favorable decision more likely. But local communities fought back, and few states took up a general revision of zoning authority. But they did establish a state power to override specific types of projects such as power plants or dumps for solid waste. The issue came to a head in the case of hazardous-waste laws, which many states passed in the late 1970s and early 1980s. Because of intense community opposition to hazardous-waste dumping, these laws often provided for an ultimate state authority over the opposition of local communities.[20]

State Environmental Government

During the Environmental Era the states increased their capacity for environmental government. Some environmental agencies were formed at a time when the main focus had been on the identification and exploitation of mineral, timber, and land resources. Into this context came new activities such as forestry in which state ownership of land added a new dimension to administrative jurisdiction and capabilities. In the 1920s many states added parks to this complement of tasks. Alongside all this came new wildlife-management activities. By the Environmental Era, therefore, many states had developed beginning, some much more advanced, capabilities in the management of biological resources and outdoor amenities.[21]

Environmental concerns led to new activities, especially in the realm of environmental protection, in contrast to previous functions that were usually identified as resource management. These activities emerged in a number of states in the 1950s and usually were housed in the departments of health. But as environmental-protection concerns went beyond human health to the biological environment, many states saw fit to move pollution-control affairs to natural-resource departments, which then organized separate divisions of resource management and environmental protection.[22]

The expansion of administrative capabilities arose from environmental services required by new state laws dealing with air and water pollution, solid and hazardous waste, or strip mining and wetlands protection. These functions were reflected in the agency organization in the form of divisions and bureaus. In most of the superagencies the traditional lines of distinction between resource management and environmental protection continued, but in several states, such as Michigan, new functions such as the protection of natural rivers and wetlands or natural-area management, which were not readily classified in either of these older categories, came together in new divisions. One can readily trace the extent and variety of environmental interest in each state through the extent and variety of its environmental administration.[23]

The development of new state administrative capabilities had its broader roots in the increasing urbanization of state governmental affairs that reflected the rise of cities and their increasing role in the state. The transition from a rural to an urban center of influence in state government and politics carried with it greater interest in the development of a statewide civic consciousness and a state civil service that could bring a certain disinterestedness to the management of state affairs. These changes came at different times depending on the growth of urban influence in state politics. In many northeastern and Pacific Coast states they could be observed as early as the 1960s, whereas in the South they began to take shape only in the late 1970s.[24]

Almost every federal environmental program looked to the states for implementation. Funds were provided for planning, monitoring, management, and technical studies. Although state and even local administrative capacities did not depend wholly on federal financing and expertise, the federal role was often crucial. This was especially the case in the less affluent states.

These patterns of evolution in environmental affairs were an integral part of a larger change in state government. As cities grew in the years before the 1930s they had often gone to the states for assistance. But state legislatures were then dominated by rural representatives who were none too friendly to urban aspirations. Hence cities turned to the federal government for financial aid. They organized such political-action groups as the U.S. Conference of Mayors and in the 1930s found that the federal administration was supportive of their needs. Federal aid grew to play a major role in developing the capacities of state government.

Federal statutes provided a forcing element to state environmental affairs. Most programs established national minimal standards for air, water, and solid waste that constituted both a set of goals and a floor below which environmental quality would not be allowed to fall. But states were usually permitted to exceed those standards and reach higher levels of air or water quality if they chose. Although states were not eager to take these opportunities for further action, the federal program required each state to reach farther than it had before and constantly pushed states to develop even greater administrative capacities.

It took some years for citizen environmental organizations to provide a degree of political presence in state capitals similar to that which national organizations had achieved in Washington, D.C. But by the early 1980s at least twenty states had political-action programs with paid personnel to represent environmental interests in state affairs. Their influence should not be overestimated, for they were relatively limited in contrast with their environmental opposition, but they provided an important presence for environmental interest in state politics.[25]

The initial impetus for state environmental political action was the desire to influence legislation, and hence the first steps were to encourage voluntary citizen lobbying and then later to employ paid staff during legislative sessions to make the effort more effective. But since it was clear from the beginning of these activities that success or failure was a matter of how a law was carried out, legislative action soon evolved into efforts to shape the course of administration. This required more full-time staff and the ability to bring technical studies to bear on decisions. In such ways as these citizen environmental organizations fostered greater resources and skills for environmental administration and greater support for environmental objectives in agency choices.[26]

Equally important in the development of a state's environmental governance was its available scientific and technical resources. Environmental action was begun by linking up with scientific and technical personnel to "get a handle" on the details of environmental affairs. But few states had sufficient funds to pursue desired scientific studies. California and Montana conducted their own air-pollution research, which enabled them to defend their more stringent air-quality standards against industry challenges in the courts. By the early 1980s a number of states in New England and the Middle Atlantic region provided funds to monitor and assess the effects of acid rain. Environmentalists often sought enhanced federal authority because of its superior scientific and technical capabilities. Such resources, for example, could help build a case for both state and federal action to control emissions from coal and gasoline combustion more stringently.

Federal Preemption of State Authority

The growing environmental competence of state government, and the increased authority it derived from the shift of responsibilities from local to state government, modified state policies. Slowly but persistently, and with considerable variation from state to state, there arose an environmental presence in state government that developers and those in industry found unacceptable. Whereas to prevent restrictive action at the local level they had turned to state authority to override that of the community, now they began to turn to federal authority to curb the states. Hence a new drama unfolded in the Environmental Era over the classic issue of federalism in which those who sought to restrain environmental action increasingly sought federal preemption of state authority.[27]

The evolution of the air-pollution-control program provides an example of the way such strategies proceeded. The initial drive for effective control came from local communities such as Gary, Indiana, and Steubenville, Ohio. The target was smoke, which not only was unpleasant but also, many local doctors argued, was a health hazard. Local governments sought to establish smoke-control ordinances. But industry sources of pollution demanded that local governments prove their claims about adverse health effects. Communities then turned to the U.S. Public Health Service rather than to state government, which they found somewhat lacking in sympathy and expertise, for authoritative statements about the health effects. Thus, local communities sought federal aid for leverage against the superior influence of national corporations in their midst.[28]

In response, industries turned to the states to weaken this alliance. They argued that air-quality standards should be set by the states and not by the federal government. They succeeded in sidetracking the drive for federal standards when the Clean Air Act of 1967 required that states take up the task of setting standards. But this turned out differently than industry had anticipated, for a considerable number of states, under pressure from local communities, established standards more stringent than it thought desirable. In the face of this new development industries turned to the federal government, seeking to shape a program at that level that would keep the excesses of state standard setting under control. They were not at all averse to the federal standards required in the 1970 Clean Air Act.[29]

The state of California was an instructive case. Its standards for auto emissions were stricter than industry desired. Therefore, industry sought in the 1970 act provisions that would prevent states from establishing maximum allowable auto emissions stricter than federal ones. But because of protests from California, this preemptive federal authority was not applied to that state, and it served constantly as an example of what could be accomplished in automobile air-pollution control beyond what the federal programs required. The same kind of preemptive authority was not applied to stationary sources, and the act clearly stated that states could establish air-quality standards for these that were more stringent than federal ones.[30]

Many standards initiated by the states under the 1967 law were incorporated into state plans mandated by the 1970 law. Hence in a number of states standards were stricter than federal standards. In response, industry tried to secure court rulings prohibiting this. But the courts turned down its pleas. The concerned industries then turned to the states and, in one after another, secured laws stipulating that the state could not establish standards more stringent than those at the federal level. By 1981 only a handful of states had continued to maintain their older standards. The one case of a significant industry challenge on this score that was successfully turned back occurred in Montana in the early 1980s.[31]

These maneuverings over levels of political authority in community air quality were typical of similar strategies for other environmental hazards. Noise was a case in point. Surveys during the 1970s indicated that urban residents found noise troublesome. Some of the most dramatic confrontations came over airport noise, which led to local ordinances to control noise levels. In response, the affected industries obtained a federal noise-control program by which standards would be set at the federal level, and local communities as well as states would not be permitted to establish more stringent ones. When on occasion there were efforts in Congress to change that policy, the industries involved opposed "deregulation" because they did not wish to risk direct confrontation with communities.[32]

Few of the many issues of conflicting environmental authority reached the level of constitutional debate and argument. One, however, the regulation of radioactive releases from atomic power plants, did. Minnesota established standards of radioactive release from its Monticello atomic-power plant that were more stringent than those required by the federal Atomic Energy Commission. According to the firms that manufactured the generating equipment, the more stringent levels were technically feasible, and it was on this ground that Minnesota undertook to establish them. But the AEC considered this to be a challenge to federal supremacy in matters of atomic energy and fought back. The courts decided in its favor. Minnesota could not establish stricter standards of release.[33]

Facility siting. Decisions about siting large-scale facilities such as electric-power plants produced extensive jurisdictional problems. As environmental consciousness grew in the 1970s communities raised objections to many such proposals. They sought to use local authority in their behalf, to zone areas so as to prohibit development, to require local referenda on siting decisions, to insist that local governments approve them in one way or another to enhance local power in order to restrict and even to prevent such intrusions. Developers, in turn, looked on these actions as unwarranted harassment in the pursuit of legitimate objectives. Because they could not shape the response of the community, they sought state laws under which state agencies could override local governments in siting matters.

Several states tried new devices to facilitate siting in which state authorities would have the final power to act and communities were limited to advisory roles. In Maryland the law provided that the state would identify appropriate sites for power plants, purchase them, and hold them for future development. Although the procedure may have been attractive in theory, the state found that private utilities were not prone to accept the sites as the most appropriate for their plans. Montana and Wyoming enacted industrial-siting laws that enabled the state government to review proposals for large-scale facilities and thereby to attach restrictions to them in the ensuing permitting process. Organized environmentalists often went along with such ventures, hoping to trade off some effective environmental controls for state siting authority, but they were equally constrained to respond positively to the concerns of local communities that protested against state override of their authority.[34]

These new measures often led to restrictions developers did not accept. Although the state might have established an override authority that gave it the final decision in siting, it hesitated to do so in such a way that the community response would be negative. It felt the need to compromise the desires of those proposing development and those objecting to it. As a result, developers, especially energy companies, felt that state authority was insufficient and sought federal authority to supersede it.[35]

Environmental-impact analysis was often the target of industry attack. Developers spoke most vigorously about the delay that accompanied the analysis, but they were even more concerned about the modifications of their projects such studies might require. Most of this, they argued, was unnecessary "to protect the environment." To prevent it they sought executive action by the Carter administration to speed up the process of state as well as federal decision making; moreover, they proposed that a new federal agency, the Energy Mobilization Board, be established, which would have the authority both to require speedier decisions on permit applications and to waive environmental standards.[36]

Environmentalists viewed the Energy Mobilization Board as an attempt to demolish the structure of environmental programs that had been built up over the years. But the board also met objections from state and local governments that saw it as a comprehensive displacement of their authority, thereby forcing lawmakers to confront the issue of relative state and national power it entailed. It also aroused the concern of many who called themselves conservatives, especially in the Republican party, who found it inconsistent with their ideas of states' rights.

Siting facilities for disposal of hazardous and radioactive wastes presented these issues in their sharpest form. Many communities were faced with proposals for locating hazardous-waste facilities in their midst or nearby. And in every case the community objected. The discovery of old waste sites and the controversy surrounding them only added to the intensity of the debate. But states felt under pressure to provide some method of disposing of hazardous waste because of the need to attract and retain industry and, therefore, promoted laws that would give them the right to prevail over local decisions. In cases where the controversy had become intense because of specific issues such as Love Canal in New York and Wilsonville in Illinois, authorities were open to the idea that landfills themselves were outmoded and other techniques would have to be used. But most states simply provided for landfills and state dominance in siting them.

Radioactive waste sites raised similar issues, but in this case there was far less initiative from the state level; it came more from federal authorities. In almost every case of a proposal from the federal agencies, local communities were able to arouse local legislators on their behalf and often with resulting state protective action. Michigan in 1978 banned the disposal of radioactive waste within its borders. Other states established referenda procedures through which localities could protect themselves.

Equally extensive was the reaction against the transport of radioactive waste through communities, which led to a number of city ordinances prohibiting it. But these actions were a challenge to federal authority over these matters. In the last days of the Carter administration, regulations were approved that permitted federal preemption of the control of radioactive-waste transport, and these were not disturbed by the incoming Reagan administration.[37]

Environmental cleanup. Another type of controversy over federal and state jurisdiction concerned the cost of cleaning up hazards such as oil spills or hazardous-waste dumps or more long-standing environmental blights that communities now decided should be removed. There were also cases of impending damage due to large-scale development. These cases threw environmental costs onto government, which, in a crisis was prompted to act on its own, incur costs, and then seek to recover them from the offending parties. What level of government would have the authority to do this?

People in coastal areas that catered to the tourist trade were alarmed about oil spills in coastal waters that often had dramatic onshore impacts: Beaches became unusuable, and birds and other marine life were destroyed. The environmental impact was immediate and direct; it led to public reaction and demands from local business people that the spillage be cleaned up. The U.S. Coast Guard usually took the lead in such matters, and over the years it had developed techniques for removing the worst part of a spill. It then sought to recover damages from those responsible. It was often difficult to pinpoint the specific tanker responsible, but techniques were developed to identify the specific mix of hydrocarbons in each tanker and associate it with the mix in the spill. This sharpened the issue of responsibility, but the issue of governmental jurisdiction remained.[38]

State governments often joined in cleanup action. Rarely could local governments respond, and in calling on the state to do so they set off a chain of events in which state governments incurred costs they then sought through liability suits to assign to those responsible. But this raised the possibility of double liability action from federal and state sources at the same time. Shipping firms objected to this "double jeopardy" and urged that laws providing for compensation for cleanup be relegated to the federal level and include preemption of state action. States were not enthusiastic about such demands for they argued that federal programs covered only part of the costs and this would leave states and their taxpayers with the responsibility for paying the rest.[39]

Such issues came into sharper focus with the hazardous-waste episodes of the 1970s. Once a site was discovered and believed to endanger the community citizens demanded action. At times these involved the costs of removing people from the site and buying their homes as well as containing the hazard itself. The issue became generalized in the debate over the federal Superfund that Congress approved in 1980 to clean up old sites. Who would pay, and who would be subject to liability? Industry sought to limit considerably its own responsibility and to increase the public's share of the cost. It was also concerned about the tendency of states to establish their own smaller superfunds and argued for federal preemption so that it would not be held responsible for two levels of remedial action.[40]

Environmental degradation included long-standing blight that the community now sought to remove. Who would pay the cost? One such case involved billboards, which were private property for whose removal the owners demanded compensation. Federal highway laws provided that a portion of the funds states received for highway construction would be allocated to purchase and remove billboards. Although considerable sums were spent for this, the effort was often made futile by the tendency of advertising firms simply to erect others elsewhere.

Many communities took action on their own through ordinances restricting the future erection of billboards and calling for the removal of existing ones. To survive court challenges these ordinances provided that billboards then in existence could remain until the owners had been able to recover the initial investment. Courts upheld this action as a proper exercise of municipal and state police power. In return the billboard companies took their case to Congress and in 1980 succeeded in adding a provision to the Federal Highway Act that no municipality could require removal without full compensation. Because few local governments could pay such costs, this effectively stifled local efforts to control existing billboard blight.[41]

Another type of community blight was abandoned strip mines that marred the countryside in mining areas. It was one thing to require reclamation of current and future mining sites, but the older piles of refuse from previous mining were quite another problem. Who would pay for cleanup? Pennsylvania surface-mining authorities adopted several strategies, one of which was a state bond issue, approved in 1970, that provided funds for reclamation; under it some progress was made. But the 1977 federal Surface Mining Control and Reclamation Act shifted the burden to the mining companies by requiring a severance tax on each ton of mined coal to create a reclamation fund to pay for cleanup.

The new coal-mining areas of the Upper Plains states faced considerable community impacts from mining. To pay for public services that came with mining, such as roads, schools, and fire and police protection, as well as the future costs of reclamation, these states imposed their own severance tax on each ton of coal mined. By 1980 Montana's tax was 30 percent of the value of the coal at the mine mouth and Wyoming's was 12 percent. The coal companies challenged these taxes as unwarranted interference with interstate commerce. But the federal courts upheld them as a justified attempt to meet the public costs of mining.[42]

Jurisdiction over land use. In these issues concerning the hierarchy of authority and jurisdiction between local, state, and federal governments, environmental issues shaped the direction of action toward state agencies. On the one hand, states were evolving power and authority against local municipalities. They were prone to prohibit municipalities from establishing standards of strip-mine reclamation, forest practices, dredge-and-fill controls, the use of pesticides and herbicides, or air quality with higher levels of environmental quality than the state provided. At the same time they tended to preempt the final authority of the local community in matters of siting large-scale facilities. All this led to an evolution of state environmental authority to supersede that of local government and to reverse the pattern of local action through devices such as zoning.

These innovations also often led to some sensitivity to environmental objectives at the state level, which frustrated developmentalists and prompted their search for increased federal authority to restrain the state's environmental tendencies. In these cases the states served as bastions for defense of environmental objectives, not because they were in the forefront of environmental initiatives but because they accepted as legitimate the protests from their citizens against more rapid and radical large-scale development. Although states fostered development, some were more cautious and always seemed prone to respond if a local community were united and insistent. The resultant temporizing indicated to developmental interests that they could not always count on state governments.

The issues at stake were clearly etched in the implementation of the Coastal Zone Management Act of 1972, which established a planning program for the coastal zone. From the start this involved choices between environmental and developmental objectives. The planning framework, in which the attempt to prod states to plan was facilitated by federal funds to pay for it, bore the brunt of such conflicting directions of policy. Environmentalists thought that the identification of coastal areas of high quality was proceeding much too slowly. In the 1980 amendments to the act they sought to include a provision requiring states to proceed with programs to identify areas that might or might not then require protective management. But Congress declined to establish this requirement; states could proceed if they wished but were not obligated to do so.[43]

Developers, on the other hand, had sought to turn the coastal-zone management program in their direction by using it as leverage to enchance federal authority in siting large-scale development, especially energy facilities, along the coast. Again and again the coastal states on the Atlantic and the Pacific – but not those on the Gulf – had objected to such siting, arguing both that the specific sites desired by developers were too fragile environmentally and that the manner of development did not provide sufficient environmental protection. These objections had stymied energy companies in their efforts to establish tanker terminals, oil refineries, petrochemical plants, liquefied natural gas plants, and electric-power facilities. From their point of view the problem was that states had too much authority in such matters and could slow down and even prevent development. To overcome this resistance, federal authority should be enhanced to preempt state jurisdiction.

These different interests led to a constitutional controversy over what was known as "consistency." The act provided that federal decisions on the coast must be consistent with the state coastal-management plans. But who was to determine what kinds of federal action were involved or what was meant by consistency? Would the choice be made by federal or state authority? The Coastal Zone Management agency maintained that the law anticipated a process it would supervise but that it should not force a decision one way or the other. Energy corporations and development-oriented federal agencies such as the Department of Commerce and the Department of Energy argued that federal authorities should determine the substance of consistency so that the national interest would prevail. But states objected. When they blocked several energy projects the companies filed suit in federal courts to prevent this, contending that the act was intended to facilitate and not block coastal-energy development. The courts ruled in favor of the states, and the argument continued.

Some of the most controversial issues involved offshore oil drilling. When this was in state-controlled waters within the three-mile limit, there was little debate over jurisdiction. But could the state legitimately object to the fact or the manner of drilling in federally owned waters beyond that limit? The states argued that they could. California insisted that areas scheduled for lease off the central and northern parts of the state be closed to drilling because of their value as fisheries and recreational areas. The state had worked into its program strong protection for the aesthetic quality of its coast, which it defended against energy developers. Officials under the Carter administration sought to walk a thin line by approving drilling in some cases but not in others. But those in the Reagan administration asserted federal authority against that of the states, undertook to reverse some of the earlier decisions, and set the course of coastal decisions toward federal supremacy.[44]

These controversies over the planning context of land-use decisions and of the coastal zone in particular identified the relationship between hierarchies of political authority and power on the one hand and hierarchies in the scale of institutions and organization on the other. Environmentalists sought federal authority to establish the framework of decision making in such a way as to require a focus on environmental as well as developmental values, but to use that framework they depended heavily on action at the grass roots. Developmentalists, however, although giving ideological support to local authority, increasingly found power at a higher level in the hierarchy more appropriate for their objectives.

State Environmental Initiatives

The growing interest in state environmental objectives and the equally growing capacity for state environmental government led to a significant amount of environmental initiative in the states. We are accustomed to think of the federal government as the source of innovation in these matters and the states as laggards. But the growth of citizen environmental action at the local and state levels and federal programs that helped to build state administrative capacities also tended to foster new state environmental activities. Because each state was an independent source of potential initiative and because the complex of influences leading to such action varied with each state, the results also varied. Only in the case of California did one state seem to promote a wide range of frontier actions; but many others were marked by one or two initiatives. As a whole these actions constituted a major chapter in the nation's environmental affairs.

Several aspects of the new federal programs fostered these possibilities. One was the general tenor of pollution-control programs that established minimum levels of action. Only in a few cases, such as automobile emissions and radioactive releases from atomic-power plants, did these programs actually prohibit states from going farther. In some programs, such as those for safe drinking water and the control of dredge-and-fill operations in wetlands, the states were invited to assume administration of the program, known as primacy, and in so doing were given freedom to establish more stringent controls. In matters of prevention of significant deterioration in air quality, a framework was established that called for further state decisions if the state chose to change any Class II area to either Class I or Class III. Little of this decision-making apparatus was taken up for many years, but it provided an opportunity for action once environmental interest had been aroused sufficiently to do so.[45]

This combination of influences internal and external to the state led to a number of initiatives that were distinctive among the entire fifty states. In the 1960s New England states took the lead in establishing conservation commissions to foster the acquisition of open spaces. The Pennsylvania State Bureau of Forestry developed a unique natural- and wild-areas program for the state forests that led to the classification of 10 percent of its total acreage in those categories. Delaware and California took the lead in coastal-zone management, Delaware stressing the prohibition of large-scale development and California the importance of aesthetic values. Oregon, Hawaii, and Vermont were pioneers in state land-use regulation, and even into the mid-1980s the Oregon requirement that each county develop its own land-use plan remained exemplary.[46]

The cases can be multiplied. Michigan and Florida followed the earlier lead of California in developing funds from the lease of state natural resources for the acquisition of land for environmental purposes. Illinois, Indiana, and Ohio were centers of activity for the protection of natural areas, and Illinois was the starting point for the Natural Areas Association. Forest-practice acts in California and Washington were notable for the degree to which they sought to protect environmental values as well as foster reforestation. Pennsylvania produced one of the most extensive wild- and scenic-rivers inventories in the nation, and Minnesota pioneered in establishing a new approach to the protection of undeveloped rivers that combined state, local, and federal initiatives. Montana took unusual action to appropriate in-stream water flow for environmental in contrast with commodity purposes.[47]

These kinds of actions were extended to the control of waste and pollution. A number of states – first Oregon, then Michigan, Massachusetts, New York, and others – developed returnable-bottle programs. Some states established air-quality standards under the 1970 act that were stricter than those of the federal program. Maine and Wisconsin took leading action to clean up and protect lake water quality. Pennsylvania was one of the few states to take up the federal nondegradation program for water quality, incorporating its earlier conservation-stream classification and developing a new category of outstanding resource waters for special protection. A number of states took up the acid-rain problem, funding research beyond that at the federal level; New York was the first to adopt new sulfur dioxide emission limitations to cope with the problem. In the early 1980s several states took up toxic air-pollution problems when EPA action seemed to lag.[48]

The types of state initiatives were many and varied. There were energy initiatives such as the use of funds by both Minnesota and Montana to promote alternative-energy projects and the establishment of state standards for energy efficiency. New York took the lead in restoring the bald eagle to the lower 48 by transplanting Alaskan chicks. The Ohio Biological Survey and the Illinois Natural History Survey were among the few state efforts to acquire such inventories. Some states produced innovative environmental atlases to increase public knowledge and awareness of environmental matters. The environmental-impact statement was adopted by a number of states in response to the federal program, but only California applied it to private as well as public development projects.[49]

Finally, a few states made their own assessments of health effects of pollution to undergird their own standards. In the late 1970s Montana reviewed its air-quality standards on the basis of studies about health effects, for example, impaired lung function among schoolchildren, financed partially through its own revenues. This led to a pioneering idea that air-control programs should protect people not just against major impairments but against any condition that interfered with normal daily activities. California's leadership was long-standing; an example of its continued role in such matters was its report in 1984 that the EPA had underestimated the carcinogenic effects of benzene by a hundredfold.[50]

An especially noteworthy initiative that began in the late 1970s was the so-called right-to-know law in which New Jersey took the lead, followed by several other states, which required that industries provide information about the presence of chemicals in the workplace and the community so that those affected would be able to know what they were exposed to and, if they chose, take action to protect themselves. Although there was some federal action along this line during the Carter administration, initiatives at the state level reflected a more extensive demand that persisted when the Reagan administration withdrew the federal initiatives.[51]

These state actions were accompanied by efforts to give a state's own citizens as well as others the impression that the state was in the forefront of all states in environmental matters. One could find in many state publications the claim that the particular state had long been known as an outstanding leader in environmental affairs. There were continual efforts to extend the states' natural-environment images in travel and tourist publications and by means of such license-plate slogans as "Wild, Wonderful, West Virginia." The desire to establish such images reflected the degree to which environmental quality had come to be a part of each state's civic consciousness, of what it wanted to think about itself, and what it wanted others to think of it.[52]

In years past, industries had argued that states were the place in the hierarchy of government where environmental issues should be dealt with, and had opposed new and expanded federal programs. In many cases it continued to do so. But the growth of the states' governing capacities and the increased interest in state environmental action made the federal government an attractive alternative for action. This tendency was noticeable in the Carter administration and even more so in the Reagan years. If the federal government could establish environmental standards more lenient than those emerging in the states and then impose a preemption that prevented more stringent state regulation, it would thereby provide greater protection for industry.[53]

This was the reason for the attempt by industry to secure a federal right-to-know regulation that would be weaker than those emerging in the states and preempt them; another example was the attempt by the Grocery Manufacturers Association in 1984 to establish a federal preemption of state-devised food-tolerance levels with respect to pesticides, because in the 1983 ethylene dibromide case some states had established standards stricter than those of the EPA. As the states became more vigorous in taking up environmental programs, the federal agencies and the Executive Office of the President were increasingly attractive sources of authority in protecting industry against environmental action.

14 The Politics of Legislation, Administration, and Litigation

The exercise of varied forms of public authority in American politics was carried out within the context of the separation of powers, the division of government into the legislature, the executive, and the courts. These not only constituted different governing functions but also provided active political groups with varied opportunities to implement their objectives. Each branch of government provided a different arena of political choice wherein environmentalists and their opponents strove to realize their aims.

Each arena had its distinctive set of activities and rules of the game, which in turn required different strategies. For the legislature, for example, one had to become adept at shaping the formation and passage of bills and then mobiliziing the public to influence that process. Administrative politics, on the other hand, called for technical skills with which one could comprehend the details of decisions and their environmental meaning. Critical choices often turned on fine points that only those knowledgeable about such details could understand. Litigation required still other strategies, those of selecting issues that could be made the subject of judicial choice, recruiting experts to serve as witnesses, and developing legal skills to organize and carry through the entire task. Environmentalists sought to enter each of these arenas, and each served as part of the drama of conflict over implementation of environmental objectives in public affairs.[1]

In participating in governmental decision making, environmentalists played an important role in opening up the processes of legislation, administration, and court action to environmental objectives, bringing substantive issues to each. They challenged the historic preoccupation of those institutions with developmental objectives and their close relationship with organized producers in agriculture, labor, and business.

Legislative Politics

Before the environmental decades citizen groups had engaged in political action in behalf of environmental values only sporadically. There was, for example, the unsuccessful attempt on the part of John Muir and the Sierra Club early in the twentieth century to prevent the construction of Hetch Hetchy Dam and the successful defense of Echo Park from a similar proposal in the early 1950s. During the 1960s the effort by the Sierra Club to prevent dam construction that would mar the Grand Canyon constituted still another example of these political strategies. The major political tactic was a media campaign to arouse the public. Such efforts as these, occasional lobbying by groups organized on a regional or national basis, reaching the public largely through the media, constituted the focus of this stage of citizen environmental politics.

In the 1960s lobbying became more frequent. Yet the resources of environmental groups were small and their activities still limited. They did not serve as a continuous presence for decision makers; action was restricted to crises or specific campaigns. In the late 1960s and early 1970s this changed. One could mark that change when Washington-based national organizations began to issue regular publications to their members to inform them of action and to enlist their aid. The National Wildlife Federation published the first issue of its weekly *Conservation Report* in 1964; this became the major news service about environmental legislative action in the nation's capital. By the end of the decade other organizations had established similar services for their members; the *National News Report* of the Sierra Club began publication in 1968.[2]

In the late 1960s a leap forward took place in environmental legislative activities. Established organizations such as the Audubon Society, the National Wildlife Federation, the Sierra Club, and the Wilderness Society either initiated or expanded their legislative capabilities. Often they were hampered because they were chartered as charitable organizations so as to solicit funds from the general public as nonprofit, nonpolitical organizations and hence make such contributions tax-deductible. During the 1960s, in the eyes of the Internal Revenue Service, the Sierra Club had gone too far in its nationwide campaign against damming of the Colorado River, and its nonprofit status was rescinded. The club thereby was freed to take a more vigorous political stance. It became known as more fully committed to political action than other organizations and on that score drew much support from the general public.[3]

New organizations with an active political program appeared in the late 1960s and early 1970s. Environmental Action and Zero Population Growth came directly from the campus ferment of the late 1960s, and the Environmental Policy Center was put together by several national environmental organizations in order to lobby selected subject areas. There were the new litigation organizations, the Environmental Defense Fund and the Natural Resources Defense Council; their nonprofit status prevented them from lobbying, but they were often invited by legislative committees to testify on pending bills. Each of these sought to turn the less politically minded outdoor organizations of the past into an active political force and to add to them the newer environmental interests.[4]

Three groups involved in these Washington-based activities must not be overlooked. One was the League of Women Voters, which, though much more general in the scope of its legislative activities, made major contributions to environmental affairs. The league was especially important in air- and water-pollution matters in the 1960s; environmental organizations drew heavily on its experience and example. A second comprised Ralph Nader and the public-interest organizations he formed. Although they tended to stress more the human-health hazards of pollution and the entire realm of administrative lethargy in implementing legislation to benefit the public, they contributed heavily to the weight of environmental influence in legislative affairs. Especially important were the books they sponsored, which played a critical role in bringing public opinion to bear on legislative decisions. The third group was the National Wildlife Federation, which was the first conservation or environmental organization to extend the reach of its political activities to legislation; during the 1960s it was the most important such influence on the Washington scene. It helped to carry out the transition from conservation to environment in legislative politics.[5]

These organizations took part at almost every stage of the legislative process. They participated in hearings on proposed legislation; this was a traditional part of legislative action and was fully open to citizen groups. An innovation that encouraged greater external scrutiny from the public and provided a new opportunity for action was a change in the way committees developed legislation in the initial markup sessions and the later revisions. Formerly such activities had been conducted behind closed doors, but now they were opened to the public. The National Wildlife Federation began to cover subcommittee proceedings in its *Conservation Report,* and environmental organizations began to attend these sessions, following them closely and seeking to influence the crucial committee votes.[6]

Equally important were the informal contacts with the staffs of the committees and the legislators themselves, to whom environmental groups provided useful technical information. All this required effective communications with legislative assistants and elected representatives themselves. Environmentalists hoped to establish relationships with lawmakers, which lobbyists traditionally had cultivated, and to do a better job of it by serving as more reliable sources of information and assistance.

The legislative work of environmentalists resulted in an increasing number of self-made legislative experts in the Washington environmental community. These were generally young people who had had no previous political experience or skills. They became adept at political action and demonstrated communications skills and reliability that equaled if not surpassed those of traditional developmental advocates. They established a record of dependable contributions to a growing realm of public policy that arose from disinterested concern rather than hopes for personal gain. Much of their success came from this record and reputation.[7]

The key factor in the success of environmental lobbyists in Washington was their ability with respect to information and communication in a society and politics increasingly based on technical information. Environmental organizations were able to carry out literature reviews of published studies that were of value to decision makers. They also kept abreast of research under way and made it available to legislators and their staffs. As legislative struggle hinged increasingly on the application of crucial information at strategic times, environmental activists in Washington quickly learned to cultivate these skills.[8]

Most legislators, their assistants, and their committee staffs were limited in their information resources. They could rely on such congressionally based agencies as the Library of Congress, the General Accounting Office, and the Office of Technology Assessment, but much in the wider information world escaped their limited purview. As a result they often looked to private groups to supply such information. The private corporate world, with its enormous information resources, was the major source of such aid. Environmentalists hoped to compete effectively with their opposition on this score, and they were somewhat successful in this because many of the sources were readily available.

Environmentalists often brought together scientists and technical professionals with legislators. They established contacts with technical experts in a joint effort to probe environmental problems, and they sought to give that expertise some weight on the larger political scene. Robert Alvarez of the Environmental Policy Center, interested especially in radiation exposure to workers and the general public, kept in touch with scientists investigating such matters and kept legislative staffs informed; in a series of informal meetings and formal hearings in 1977 and 1978 he brought researchers, legislators, and their staffs together in Washington to share information and ideas. On a more formal level, the Environmental Study Group, founded in 1972 by members of the House and Senate to keep them abreast of environmental affairs, regularly sponsored similar meetings, often as a result of suggestions made by environmental organizations.[9]

Legislative action inevitably turned to the record of legislators and their campaigns for reelection. Soon after the group that sponsored Earth Day in 1970 reorganized for a more permanent role as Environmental Action, it took up an election campaign program. Each year it singled out twelve legislators in both the House and the Senate who had extremely poor environmental voting records and then set out to aid in defeating them. Hence was born the biannual compilation of the "Dirty Dozen" list, which aroused considerable attention in congressional political campaigns. At times rival candidates sought the support of environmentalists to defeat incumbents on the Dirty Dozen list. Usually the approach was relatively successful; 60–70 percent of the targets of action were defeated.[10]

Electoral work was aided by the League of Conservation Voters (LCV), entirely separate from the Dirty Dozen program of Environmental Action. Each year, beginning in 1971, the LCV tallied votes in the House and Senate for the previous calendar year. This served as a guide for environmentalists around the nation who wished to provide their members and the wider public a basis for making political choices.[11]

Effective legislative politics also involved action at the grassroots. Members of Congress were responsive to the wishes of their constituents, and input from them usually was vital in determining how a legislator would vote. When environmentalists approached a legislator, they were more successful if constituents had already created a receptive ear by sending in letters and telegrams on the subject. Washington environmental lobbyists, therefore, sought to organize voters to contact their legislators so as to maximize the impact of their lobbying.[12]

Some environmental organizations had an advantage in this respect because they had developed within their own structure local groups that served as a link with national action. The Sierra Club and the Audubon Society had local units each with its own charter, officers, members, and activities. One of their main functions was to carry on outdoor activities such as hiking and birdwatching. Political education and action were now added to these activities. The Sierra Club had long maintained a dual program of outings and conservation, the latter referring to political action. The Audubon Society began to perfect such a program in the 1970s as its national political office in Washington sought to enlist additional member support for national legislation. Both the Sierra Club and the Audubon Society developed regional offices through which their national organizations hoped to stimulate political action.

Many environmental organizations on the Washington scene had no local branches. These solicited funds from the public but did not seek to organize citizens for political action. They established newsletters to keep donors informed of activities, thereby helping to sustain both interest and financial support. Most organizations, however, were wary of direct appeals to members for political action, because their tax-exempt status precluded it. This changed, however, with a new law in 1976 that permitted charitable groups to spend a certain portion of their income on direct legislative activity, including appeals for action to members.[13]

Often a looser arrangement existed between action at the national level and the grass roots. The National Clean Air Coalition, for example, which spearheaded defense of the Clean Air Act in 1975–7 when it was subject to amendment, was a loose grouping of national, state, and local organizations interested in air quality; for grass-roots support it depended on the sustained activity of its coalition members. Organizations with local groups and chapters served as local vehicles through which a number of national organizations without such a framework carried out their activities. Although during most of the 1960s and on into the 1970s the Wilderness Society did not have locally organized constituencies, it often worked through the local bodies of the Audubon Society and the Sierra Club.[14]

Local political activity became most effective, so most Washington environmental groups argued, when it involved regular liaison with legislators above and beyond letters and telegrams sent at critical times. They encouraged local environmentalists to meet with legislators and their staffs in Washington and their local staffs in the congressional districts and states. Where this could be done so that the legislator became aware of a sustained interest, a continued presence that was similar to that created by developmentalists, the grass-roots environmental support became a permanent factor to be taken into account by the legislator rather than a transitory force occasionally to be placated.

These legislative techniques reached a new plateau of effectiveness in the Alaska "national interest" lands controversy. The campaign was organized by the Alaska Coalition in Washington. An organization was formed in each congressional district with cooperative work especially on the part of the local groups and chapters of the Sierra Club and the Audubon Society. This led to many local meetings with congressional staffs, a constant flow of mail and telephone messages to Washington offices, and the most extensive coverage of congressional offices during final floor voting that had yet been seen in environmental politics. One member of Congress described it as the "most effective citizen lobbying action in Washington since the Civil Rights movement of the 1960's."

The environmental organizations on the Washington scene comprised a varied lot. There were those that had specific and limited interests, such as the Wilderness Society, Zero Population Growth, and the Defenders of Wildlife, as well as those with far broader interests, such as Friends of the Earth and the Sierra Club. Some with more circumscribed concerns, such as the National Wildlife Federation and the Izaak Walton League, had branched into new fields related to their central focus. Others began with a general environmental interest and selected issues for specialization; two such organizations were the Environmental Policy Center and Environmental Action. These groups often set up specialized sections that became active in particular policy fields, such as the American Rivers Conservation Council of the Environmental Policy Center. Finally there were the specialized older conservation groups such as the American Forestry Association and the Wildlife Management Institute.

The variety of environmental groups created a potential for considerable division of opinion. Yet a high degree of cooperative activity emerged. This was underlined when leaders of twelve such groups joined in formulating the environmental issues of 1977 in the "Environmental Agenda Project." These included the Environmental Defense Fund, Friends of the Earth, the Izaak

Walton League, the National Parks and Conservation Association, the National Wildlife Federation, the Natural Resources Defense Council, the Nature Conservancy, the Sierra Club, the Wilderness Society, and Zero Population Growth. There was a sufficient agreement to support a joint statement published in 1977 as *The Unfinished Agenda*.[15]

A specialization of responsibility soon developed among environmental groups in which one formulated an issue and others supported it. The Coal Policy Project of the Environmental Policy Institute took the lead in surface-mining legislation; the National Clean Air Coalition spearheaded the clean-air campaign; the Wilderness Society and the Sierra Club led in wilderness matters; the American Rivers Conservation Council was in the forefront of the move to establish wild and scenic rivers and slow down the rate of dam construction; the National Wildlife Federation took up channelization and ocean-dumping issues; Environmental Action organized the Highway Action Coalition to "bust the highway trust"; and Environmental Action and the Urban Environment Conference took the lead in joining with organized labor to formulate policy on workplace toxic hazards.[16]

Divisions of labor such as these were combined with coalitions to mobilize support on specific issues. One of the earliest such cases was the Emergency Coalition on Natural Resources formed to oppose the Echo Park Dam. Although few environmental organizations could be brought together in one continuing format, many could cooperate on specific proposals and problems. Hence coalition building, such as one to press for changes in national-forest policy (which led to the Forest Management Act of 1976), or to protect the Clean Water Act during the struggle over amendments in 1976 and 1977, was a major strategy of environmental groups.[17]

Environmental legislative strategists practiced much conventional political compromise. They worked closely with members of Congress to secure what was possible. Often they would retreat from one position to secure another. For example, in 1978 they backed off from earlier attempts to keep intact the 1973 Endangered Species Act when it was under attack in order to support a set of changes that would retain most of the law. Although the change weakened the law by shifting responsibility for critical conflict decisions from the Fish and Wildlife Service to a supervisory interagency body higher up the executive ladder, it did not turn sole ultimate authority over to the construction and development agencies.

One aspect of this strategy seemed to be control: If compromises were to be made with developmental influences, they should take place not at the beginning of the legislative process but at the final stage. One fought for clear-cut environmental objectives and avoided compromise at the start, and then tailored concessions to the demands of the given voting situation whether in committee or on the floor. The Washington-based environmental movement of the 1970s emphasized practical gains rather than affirmation of ideologies. The difficulty was in keeping a clear sense of direction for environmental objectives amid the constant atmosphere of compromise inherent in the process of legislative give-and-take.

The use of traditional legislative tactics reached a new phase in the 1970s in the form of log rolling. The Environmental Policy Center's water-resources project experimented with this to support wild and scenic rivers and oppose dam building. The center's American Rivers Conservation Council established contacts with a number of environmental groups fighting a dam or channelization project at one place or supporting a wild and scenic river elsewhere. The situation was ripe for organizing on the basis of cooperative action in which a legislator from one district who might be responsive to environmental objectives would trade votes with a legislator from another district. Brent Blackwelder of the center took steps to perfect this kind of action by organizing in 1976 the first of an annual series of "dam fighters' " conferences in Washington, week-long affairs that ended with groups from around the nation appearing before the relevant House and Senate committees on public works and public-works appropriations.[18]

This technique of putting together local environmental projects was extended farther in 1978 when Congressman Philip Burton of California fashioned a bill combining a wide variety of natural-environment proposals that had been languishing in Congress for years. It included national parks and monuments, wilderness areas, wild and scenic rivers, appropriations for park management, and a general authorization of funds for urban parks. The procedure was so similar to the long-standing "pork barrel" system of combining many public-works construction projects that it was described by opponents as the "parks barrel" bill. It joined projects in many congressional districts favored by many members of Congress and as a result passed the House by an overwhelming vote of 341 to 61. This indicated the degree to which the environmental political movement had succeeded in combining lobbying in Washington by national organizations with work in congressional districts to obtain maximum legislative results in a manner similar to that of groups in the past.

Several trends are reflected in this review of environmental legislative politics. First, environmentalists adopted with some success many conventional strategies that had evolved over years of lobbying. Second, they developed an ability to work within the context of technical information, which had become a major medium of legislative action. Third, they participated in shaping a more open political system in which the details of action were better known and the scheduling of committee votes was open. And fourth, they organized action by the environmental public that led to a buildup of grass-roots support that constituted a permanent rather than an occasional presence. A transition had occurred from leadership groups based in Washington, deeply involved in legislative maneuvering, to a broader and sustained public political force.

Environmental organizations were relatively slow to get involved in electoral politics. Environmental Action had developed the Dirty Dozen list, and the League of Conservation Voters had allocated some funds in the late 1970s to selected candidates in both primaries and the general elections. But the relative lack of involvement in elections stood in sharp contrast to the high degree of legislative activity. Toward the end of the 1970s, however, this began to change. Promoted by the League of Conservation Voters, door-to-door canvassing in 1978 was effective in electing to Congress Claudine Schneider, an environmental activist from Rhode Island, and reelecting Robert Edgar from a southeastern Pennsylvania district. These beginning efforts expanded rapidly in succeeding years until by 1984 environmentalists campaigned actively in one-third of the nation's congressional districts.[19]

Administrative Politics

Administrative politics was even more intense than legislative politics. For whereas the latter involved occasional input, the former involved day-to-day "watchdog" activities in relation to administrative agencies that were on the job continually and might make favorable or unfavorable environmental decisions at any time. Constant surveillance was required.

Administering a law was not merely a matter of executing the will of Congress, for in the law much was left to be decided. Frequently Congress did this intentionally because it was virtually impossible to draft wording that would translate policy into workable and detailed implementation. Hence the politics of specific choice began after a law was passed. What the agency decided could make as much difference both to the environmentalist and the developmentalist as did the legislation itself. Moreover, whereas passage of a law was only the first step to decision making, an administrative choice was more likely to be final, one from which escape was more difficult. The administrative arena was a series of moments of truth for the contending parties in which all realized the greater finality of decision.

The context of administrative choice was also more complex. Myriad specific aspects of administration, greater in range and number than in the legislation itself, were the subjects of choices that could go one way or another. Administrative issues were not difficult to comprehend, but the detail was extensive. Only those knowledgeable about that detail could successfully operate in the realm of administrative politics; a vast amount of information had to be kept in mind in order to make one's input relevant.

After a law was passed the various parties who had been active in the legislative debate transferred their interest to the agency. Each party hoped that the ensuing decisions could be shaped in accordance with its objectives. This was especially true of regulation that could lead to administrative choices that might diminish the force of implementation. The public seemed to believe that agencies merely carried out the laws Congress passed and that administrators should be thought of simply in terms of their honesty or capability in administration. But environmentalists soon learned that such was not the case. Administrators made new decisions of vast importance; the practical outcome of action would depend on the degree to which they could be persuaded that one decision was preferable to another.[20]

Administrators did not act independently of the political forces around them. On the one hand, interest groups were constantly contacting them by telephone, by mail, or in person; on the other hand, administrators often sought the public's reaction to potential choices. Although they were relatively unconcerned about the political role of individuals on whom they might impinge, administrators were seriously concerned about those who represented organizations with the ability to act politically, acquire and apply technical information, arouse the public and the media, carry through litigation, and mobilize legislators or administrative superiors on their behalf. The political world that was most important to the administrator and that was most taken into account was one of groups with significant political resources and skills.[21]

Environmentalists became influential in administrative politics by fashioning organizations with a continuing potential for effective action. A critical element was their contribution to the technical aspects of decisions. If environmentalists could convince a decision maker that important facts had been omitted or that detail was incorrect, there was a greater chance they would be heard. Environmental influence depended, then, on the degree to which generalized values and objectives of law could be translated into specific detail, which was the main language of administrative choice. By the mid-1980s half a dozen environmental organizations in the nation's capital scored high marks with administrative agencies for their effectiveness and reliability.

Public administration was heavily influenced by institutions with developmental objectives. Representatives of economic groups in agriculture, business, and labor were highly visible to administrators; equally visible were representatives of local, state and national government with similar objectives. This is not to say that all these were in agreement when it came to agency choices – far from it. But it is to say that they represented a rather distinctive point of view in administrative politics different from newer environmental and ecological objectives. That developmental organizations outweighed environmental ones in number and strength could be observed repeatedly in the administrative process in comments on proposed rules and regulations, in hearings, and in written communications.

These influences affected different kinds of administrative choices. There were those choices involving the interpretation of legislation, such as whether the Clean Air Act required a program for the prevention of significant deterioration, or whether the Coastal Zone Management Act of 1972 mandated that states should assist in the siting of large-scale development or merely establish a planning context within which contending parties could work out decisions, or whether the Organic Act of 1897 for the national forests permitted clear-cutting that included the harvest of immature trees, or whether the Wild Free-Roaming Horses and Burros Act of 1971 permitted federal control of animals on federal lands, or at what point in the course of private construction the agency could require that regulations be applied.

Administrative interpretation focused initially on the rules and regulations the agency drew up to translate the more general provisions of law into specific administrative actions. Rarely did the agency seek to expand its authority and power beyond the mandate of the law; more often it gave away some of that authority, which reduced the law's effectiveness. Developmental influences in rule making invariably worked in this direction, and on the other side environmentalists sought in their strategies to hold the line to make sure that rules and regulations carried out the full intent of the law. The stakes were high: If one did not achieve a general rule favorable to one's position, subsequent action would have to focus on specific cases, each requiring considerable time and effort and having more limited consequences.

Another arena of administrative discretion involved the formulation of specific proposals under general statutory authority. Almost every agency was asked to develop plans for legislative decision: the Corps of Engineers and the Soil Conservation Service for dams and river-modification projects, the Forest Service and other wildlands agencies for wilderness, the Bureau of Outdoor Recreation for wild and scenic rivers and hiking trails. These proposals were subject to dispute, for the contending parties well knew that a study recommendation was a major step toward final action. Often the choice was made even earlier in the chain of action in the form of an inventory from which cases for study could be chosen, such as in Roadless Area Review and Evaluation (RARE)I and II inventories of potential wilderness areas in the national forests. Inventories became intensely controversial for to include or exclude a particular site either kept the proposal alive for future action or eliminated it.

Agencies were also called on for recommendations because of their expertise, which gave them additional influence in decision making. There was a presumption of superior judgment about such advice, given either to legislative or other executive agencies. Yet that advice was often controversial, depending on the particular personal preferences or degree of knowledge of the administrator making it, or the agency's established position, which were often controlling. Judgments about the potential cost or benefit of a proposal, of the ease or difficulty in carrying it out, of cause and effect in relationships in health and ecological matters, of the kinds of data that were relevant to a decision and the ways of classifying them – a host of questions such as these, which were considered technical and professional, were often the subject of advice.

Finally, there were the choices as to whether enforcement and regulation would be less or more strict. Often these were reflected in the terms of the permits required, the variances and extensions provided for carrying out the requirements of the law, and the degree to which the conditions of the permits were supervised. If a surface-mining law required that vegetative cover be established on a site restored to contour and the rules and regulations defined the mandated standards for that cover as a "workmanlike job," an inspector had considerable leeway in determining whether the standard had been met.[22]

The details of such enforcement and regulation were carried out amid a set of unwritten understandings between the agency as regulator and the regulated private individual or firm. For each party a more intense and rigorous enforcement could present burdens and liabilities, greater cost for the private party, more time, effort, and worry for the agency. Each approached the other with some degree of flexibility and, in the course of personal contact, determined the acceptable limits of behavior. Depending on circumstances, these could fall far short of the law. But "field" or "line" agencies seemed usually to generate an atmosphere of accommodation intended to "get the job done" with as little effort as possible in the face of scarce resources.

Environmentalists challenged these arrangements only occasionally. Often the time, effort, and cost required dissuaded them from pursuing objections too far. Much depended on the political strength of the challenger. If it was an individual from the general public with little organizational backing, the agency felt free to defend its action with a perfunctory response. But if the individual represented an organization that had some capacity to influence administrative choices, more attention was paid to the complaint. All depended on the degree to which the agency felt its freedom to make choices in enforcement and regulation could be challenged successfully in the courts, in public opinion, or in the legislature where action might affect the agency adversely.

Over the years many governmental agencies had developed clientele relationships with those affected by their actions. The Corps of Engineers established close ties with private navigation lines on inland waters, the business firms that shipped goods on them, and the communities that wished to promote river navigation as a stimulus to local development or to protect themselves from flooding by means of upstream reservoirs. The Bureau of Land Management, the Forest Service, the National Park Service, and other agencies developed their particular clienteles. They did so because they knew that their actions could not be carried out in a vacuum, that most of those affected could appeal to Congress or the courts to restrain them and hence might well be headed off if the agency kept itself informed of the group's concerns.

Nor were agencies insulated from the general public. One of the major features in the evolution of administration, both public and private, had been to centralize management control so as to reduce, if not eliminate, potential claims for attention from the wider public. But after World War II citizen groups began to demand a role in making administrative decisions. This was not accepted by administrators with open arms, for they shared the management ideology that effective action depended on relative freedom from such influence. But given the general climate of interest in more citizen participation in government, they were forced to accept it. Hence the political world of the governmental agency came to be sharply different from the political world of corporate management.

Environmentalists worked hard to take part effectively in public administration so as to shape its choices. They sought to counter the heavy developmental weight in administrative politics and the similar predispositions among the professional and technical experts. The major focus was on agency procedures in decision making. The environmental-impact statement (EIS) provided a wedge for wider involvement in administrative choices. Agencies were required to include public review in this process; they were to submit a draft statement to the public for comment, permit ample notice of the availability of documents, provide them promptly without cost, allow sufficient time for review, and include in the final statement the text of comments received and the agency replies to specific points.[23]

Although the EIS did not resolve substantive questions – it served only as a procedural device – it did permit the general public to know details about proposals and to identify issues that might be controversial. It required the agency to face directly possible objections and to respond to, rather than ignore, them. In this way the issues were brought to light so that members of the public who might wish to oppose action could construct a counterargument. The EIS played an important role in opening up decision making to the environmental public.[24]

Equally significant was the expanding public role in agency studies. The 1964 Wilderness Act was the first to provide for involvement by citizen groups in the formulation of proposals, in this case recommendations for or against wilderness designation. Similar public input was obtained in a number of study proposals such as those for wild and scenic rivers and hiking trails. Often such procedures were used informally by development agencies when they were not mandated to do so, for it enabled them early in the process of formulating a proposal to identify potential opposition and thereby to forestall it. Environmentalists took advantage of opportunities to participate in these administrative actions and thereby helped to shape the results.

Environmental participation in planning came far more slowly. Planning was less project- or crisis-oriented. Hence it was more difficult for environmentalists to marshal the sustained interest it required. Planning, moreover, was far more complex; an overload of detail could successfully obscure the significant value choices. It required more careful work to ferret out issues and focus on them, a task environmentalists had not yet accomplished as fully by the 1980s as they had participation in the EIS process. Two types of planning attracted increasing interest by the end of the decade, that conducted by the Forest Service for each national forest and that undertaken by the EPA in its water-quality program. A new opportunity for participation in planning emerged in the Bureau of Land Management as a result of the Federal Land Policy and Management Act of 1976, under which the BLM now operated. Environmental participation in planning was usually on a case-by-case basis. Rarely was there an attempt to bring such efforts together in order to coordinate and improve strategy.[25]

Participation in planning provided a special opportunity for environmentalists. Planning was a comprehensive task, drawing on a wide range of specialties, and few in the administrative or even planning agencies for that matter could keep up with the evolution of professional ideas relevant to their task. Some environmentalists, on the other hand, did have time to become so informed. They were able, therefore, to bring to agency planning some expertise and knowledge the agency itself lacked and to which it was often open. Through such contributions environmentalists were able to secure an important measure of respect from agencies and acceptance of their participation.[26]

Environmentalists also sought to open up the processes of rule making, permit approvals, and enforcement. These matters were in a somewhat different realm, for they involved not so much study but action, and more formal consultations and hearings about specific agency proposals. Rule making required the agency to publish in advance of its decision the proposed rule and to invite comment. Even before this step the agency often circulated to a smaller group of interested parties a request for ideas or even draft copies for comment. Environmentalists took advantage of such opportunities, which were as open to them as to their developmental opponents under the general rules of administrative procedure.

Although agencies were content by the end of the 1970s to allow environmental involvement in rule making, they were reluctant to do the same in granting and supervising permits. It would take too much time and effort. The most extensive such participation was provided for in the 1977 federal Surface Mining Control and Reclamation Act: Notice of intent to apply for a permit had to be published in the newspapers, and the application had to be placed on file at the county seat so that citizens would know about the proposal; the agency had to provide opportunities for citizens to protest the terms of the application; citizens could object anonymously that the terms of the permit were not being fulfilled; they could accompany federal inspectors to on-site visits; the operator had to provide notice to the newspapers that a site had been reclaimed and an application for bond release was being submitted so that citizens would know and could object. At each stage there were provisions for consultations by the agency with the public and for public hearings as well.[27]

National environmental organizations early became interested in administrative proceedings and played a larger role in them. If an environmental group had worked hard to secure legislation, it almost inevitably became interested in the implementing regulations. But these organizations did not have sufficient resources to provide services to groups that wished to participate in administrative processes at the regional, state, or local level. Only if a strong environmental presence had developed within a state did such administrative involvement occur.

Advisory committees played an important role in administrative politics. These were formed to provide the agency with information from the interested public and to enable it to test proposed courses of action against the views of its constituents. Often the relationships between agency and advisory committee went beyond mere communication to committee influence in agency affairs, which set limits beyond which agency action could not go. In some cases, such as those of the grazing boards in the Bureau of Land Management, advisory committees received statutory recognition that gave them powers beyond advice.[28]

The most important feature of advisory committees was their composition. Environmentalists found them heavily loaded in favor of the groups in agriculture and business with which the agencies worked daily. Senator Lee Metcalf of Montana took a special interest in the personnel of advisory committees; he conducted hearings that identified them as a fourth branch of government that became increasingly important as the context of administrative action became more detailed and technical. By providing advice to the agency in an avowedly objective and professional manner, technical and professional experts who represented developmental groups could shape the course of agency decisions. The key factor, of course, was the choice of committee members.[29]

Metcalf's investigations led to new legislation under which the composition of advisory committees had to be broadened to include "all relevant interested groups." At first, however, the agencies were inclined to shape this requirement to exclude those with consumer, including environmental, concerns. They established membership criteria in terms of social composition such as race or sex rather than "all relevant interests." Only slowly did they admit as members those with strictly environmental interests, even though they retained those who represented regulated enterprise. Especially important to environmentalists was the degree to which appointees were selected as professional experts who, in fact, spoke for business and industry. Those agencies that sought a more balanced set of professional viewpoints tended to choose advisory committee members from academic institutions.

A closely related aspect of administrative politics was the degree to which the details of action, considered to be merely technical, often involved political choices. The ultimate outcome in management decisions was usually a set of numbers such as allowable levels of contamination. Administrators recognized the critical role of numbers both from a management and a political point of view. Hence they wished to limit influence on their formulation so as to retain freedom of action. As they became more knowledgeable about the politics of administration, however, environmentalists also realized the implications of the numbers and concentrated on them.

Thus, two tendencies were at work in administrative environmental politics. On the one hand, there were those who sought to limit the arena of influence that affected decisions, to confine the actors to a smaller circle of scientific, technical, and professional people who could establish the terms of debate and agree on the numbers. On the other hand, there were those who sought to define such decisions as political choices of consequence and to widen the arena of influence about them. Administrative agencies sought valiantly to deflect such input, giving ground often in the formalities of environmental-impact statements, studies, and planning but trying to present technical detail in such a way that the broader citizenry would have less influence than would the technical experts selected by administrators.

Relationships with environmentalists were modified on occasion when the agency considered them to be a political asset rather than a liability. The older developmental agencies such as the Forest Service usually felt environmentalists to be a hindrance rather than a help. But they could also be useful in counterbalancing the developmental side when it became too strong for the agency's liking. The EPA knew that its relative independence and and its ability to hold agricultural and industry groups at arm's length depended on its ability to develop a countervailing constituency among environmentalists. Administrators often sought to establish closer ties with them in order to keep open lines of aid and communication. EPA regional office staffs, for example, often kept in touch with environmentalists, met with them on occasion, maintained directories of environmental organizations, and produced publications describing their activities.

During the Carter administration there was a noticeable increase in the degree to which EPA officials reached out to environmental groups. Especially when the various developmental segments of the administration such as the Council on Wage and Price Stability and the Department of Energy sought to restrain environmental programs, the EPA tried to perfect its constituency. In June of 1978 it inaugurated a series of brown-bag luncheon meetings with environmental groups in Washington to inform them of pending actions. Although ostensibly the purpose of the meetings was to distribute information, they were also used to mobilize the troops more effectively for critical battles.

Agencies were less enthusiastic about environmental action that might restrain their freedom of movement such as litigation. They rarely actively encouraged environmental groups in order to pressure them to make a decision one way or another. To build a constituency that might help at critical times invited opposition as well. But when removed from the heat of battle, agencies might reflect on this as helpful to their objectives. After he resigned as administrator of the EPA late in 1976, Russell Train observed that it was essential for environmentalists to lean on administrative agencies to counter pressure from developmental advocates. The agency could then justify action on the grounds that both sides in the argument were critical of its actions and hence its position was sound.

The Politics of Litigation

In the early years of the Environmental Era many citizens found the courts to be a possible avenue for action. One who felt that the activities of another person were environmentally detrimental could seek legal redress. For centuries courts had been available to any person who felt that another was causing harm. Judges had supervised such "impacts" in innumerable instances, sorting out the effects of a wide range of acceptable and prohibited daily human activities. What these prohibited acts were changed over the years; damage to another's person was clearly to be restrained as was damage to property. Damage to one's health then came to be an acceptable cause for action. But there was also damage to one's enjoyment of life through another's annoying activities. Out of these day-to-day claims and counterclaims had evolved a body of common law that served now as precedents for citizen claims to protection against environmental harm.[30]

Courts responded positively to these overtures, not all in the same way or with the same choices, but most accepting the notions that in environmental affairs some new infringement of personal liberties and rights was involved and that this could well justify restraints. New circumstances, new social values, led to the infusion of traditional doctrines with new substance. It is impossible at this stage of environmental history to pinpoint the process by which such disputes and judicial responses worked their way through the lower courts. One suspects that there was much more of this than is readily apparent.[31]

The first well-publicized case of this kind, decided in 1965, involved a citizen protest against a proposal by Consolidated Edison in New York State to build a pumped-storage facility for generating electric power at Storm King on the Hudson River. The project would have a number of adverse effects including harm to the aesthetic quality of the river valley. The point at issue was one of the most difficult and yet most significant that could have been raised, namely, harm to aesthetic environmental values rather than to persons or property. Scenic Hudson, as the case came to be known, halted the project for many years and finally in 1980 led to a negotiated out-of-court settlement in which the project was abandoned.[32]

This case is often taken as the beginning of environmental law. It had a profound effect on both lawyers and environmentalists as to the possible role of law and the courts in achieving environmental objectives. Yet historians are often deceived by the degree to which such dramatic events are formative. Environmental litigation grew rapidly in the 1960s and 1970s as reflected in the evolution of an environmental specialization within law, new environmental law journals, new case-reporting publications, and specialized training in law schools. From the larger historical view, however, we must not overlook the need to root these changes in the evolving values of the American people to which the legal system was responding and which often revealed themselves in far less dramatic ways. The judicial response to these new values represented the larger and oft repeated process by which legal institutions found ways of incorporating into their methods of resolving disputes new substantive points at issue.[33]

In the 1970s litigation was an important realm of environmental decision making. Citizens filed lawsuits to protect themselves from environmental harm. The Environmental Defense Fund and the Natural Resources Defense Council were formed to specialize in environmental litigation; the Sierra Club established its own Legal Defense Fund, and the National Wildlife Federation added lawyers to its staff. Other organizations took up legal action by joining with one of those groups, often in combination to pool resources, or by hiring their own attorneys. This litigation received publicity and served to sharpen environmental issues for the public at large as well as to resolve disputes for the participants.[34]

Use of the courts for these purposes was facilitated by provisions in environmental statutes that citizens could bring legal action against administrators who failed to carry out the law. Laws such as the Clean Air Act and the Clean Water Act were the first to include such provisions, but they were typical elements in all the environmental legislation of the 1970s. Usually these suits were confined to cases where the administrator was required by law to carry out a nondiscretionary duty under the statutory language of "must" rather than a discretionary duty under the language of "may." A less successful venture was the proposal to provide statutory authorization for citizens generally to bring suits to protect their environmental rights. Such a statute was enacted in Michigan in 1970 under the leadership of Professor Joseph Sax of the University of Michigan Law School. These provisions were intended to extend the possibilities of citizen environmental action beyond what had already taken place.[35]

The amount of environmental litigation arising from citizen complaints was relatively limited. It had a greater media impact than would be suggested by the number of lawsuits. In 1978 and 1979 only twelve actions were brought under the citizen-suit provisions of all the federal environmental laws, and of these only seven were filed by citizen groups themselves. The Michigan Environmental Rights Act led to only 140 lawsuits in its first decade. Opponents of environmental litigation often complained about the degree to which it was "clogging the courts" and argued against further such legislation. But there was only a small amount of citizen-inspired environmental litigation in comparison with other cases. Of cases in the federal courts reported in 1979 in the *Environmental Reporter – Cases,* half were initiated by industry.[36]

The 1969 National Environmental Policy Act (NEPA) produced considerable environmental litigation as the federal courts took up the task of supervising its implementation. But they confined their role to the act's procedural requirements and declined to plunge into the substantive issues. The law, so the courts argued, called for an interdisciplinary analysis of all relevant environmental factors, including possible alternative actions that would reduce adverse environmental impacts, and struck down administrative actions that constituted a more superficial response to NEPA. As a result environmentalists found an opportunity to ensure that environmental values were considered, even if not accepted, in administrative decisions.[37]

This court action should be viewed not so much as a product of the statute itself but as an evolution of the more traditional court practice of supervising administrative procedure. Agencies should not make decisions on the basis of narrow or limited considerations that were of interest to one party alone, for to do so would be arbitrary and capricious; moreover, they should make those decisions openly and on the record so that anyone who wished to review them, Congress, the president, or the courts, as well as citizens, could fully understand their basis. Supervision of NEPA by the federal courts grew more out of the elaboration of fair administrative procedures than out of the statute itself.[38]

Courts were attractive to citizen groups partially because their basis for action lay not in numbers of people who demanded this or that or in the mobilization of opinion by means of lobbyists, which might require extensive financial resources, but in the facts of argument. It might be feasible for a legislator to tally letters or telephone calls or for an administrator to be impressed by the four-foot stack of documents submitted in rule making and hence bend in the direction of that political weight. But courts relied more on logical argument and the facts on which it was based. They sought to narrow a point at issue precisely and then weigh the evidence.

Although some cases could generate large amounts of evidence, often it was the compilation of crucial facts and selected argument about their meaning that made the difference. Hence one could have some influence in the courts by keeping fully abreast of new scientific research, bringing friendly experts to the witness stand, and presenting carefully reasoned analyses. Early in the 1970s a number of young law graduates found considerable excitement in such an opportunity. Much of the challenge was to determine precisely how to secure leverage to influence administrative agencies. Especially significant was the attempt to link legal with scientific and economic expertise, which was the hallmark of the environmental litigation organizations. At times they coaxed scientists out of the laboratory and into administrative and judicial proceedings. At other times they were able to employ scientists of high repute on their own staffs.[39]

Litigation, however, was expensive, and the resources available to citizen environmentalists were meager compared to those available to industry. The cost of bringing a lawsuit was great enough to make it unlikely that citizen-suit provisions or general citizen-suit statutes would lead to much legal action. Obtaining expert witnesses, as well as lawyers, made the cost of legal action prohibitive for most citizens, and undertaking it often depended on their ability to command volunteer or pro bono services from lawyers and technical experts. The cost of even such an elementary item as the transcript of court proceedings was often too great for a citizen environmental plaintiff.

Although environmentalists often were able to secure action more successfully in the courts than in either legislation or administration, they could not do so on a massive scale. Selective action was the rule. The relative ability of industry to bring litigation, challenge administrators through lawsuits, and thereby postpone action and neutralize administrative choice in contrast with the limited capabilities of environmentalists was striking. Often, in fact, innovations that opened the courts to citizen environmentalists led to their being used more frequently by government agencies and even industry. Litigation demonstrated the fact of political inequality between the contending parties as fully as did legislation and administration.[40]

To these demands for decisions with respect to environmental issues the courts made several responses reflective of their acceptance of changes in American society that environmental values represented. One of these concerned the question of standing, that is, the right of a person to bring an issue to the court for resolution. Traditionally the courts had been most prone to accept claims of harm to one's person or property as the major cause for action or complaint. If one could demonstrate the fact or the likelihood of such adverse effects or injuries, one had grounds for using the courts or, as it was said, had standing.

Often their developmental opponents argued that environmentalists did not have standing and hence the complaint should be dismissed at the outset.[41]

Environmentalists argued that they had environmental rights as well as the right to property ownership and freedom from physical harm that could be protected by legal action. To them, the most significant decision on this score was Sierra Club v. Morton, in which environmentalists objected to a permit application by the Disney enterprises to construct a massive ski resort in the Mineral King canyon in California. The Supreme Court affirmed that the defense of recreational rights was a legitimate cause for action. From this time on there seemed to be no doubt that courts would accept standing to defend environmental rights if those threatened sought redress.[42]

The significance of this innovation was not merely legal. In a larger sense it involved acceptance by the court of a major fact of life generated by the social changes since World War II. People valued the quality of the environment around them; they used such areas for recreation; these values were, in fact, becoming central, not remaining peripheral, in people's daily lives and in the ongoing concerns of public institutions. These changes had led to new views as to what constituted harm to the individual and to the reassessment of the effects of developmental actions that earlier had been taken for granted as necessary consequences of economic growth. Aesthetic harm could now be set alongside harm to one's person and health and property as serious personal and social values.[43]

This thinking on the part of the courts was relatively easy to maintain because it was closely related to the long-standing notion in nuisance cases that individuals should be free to enjoy daily life without unwarranted intrusion. It was often difficult to determine where the line would be drawn between others' freedom to intrude and individuals' freedom from such intrusion. But the notion of environmental intrusion as a potential adverse effect on individual rights simply elaborated, in the light of changing social values, more traditional ways in which the court had responded to similar kinds of claims.[44]

The courts also accepted an enlargement in state police powers on behalf of environmental objectives. This referred to the long-standing authority granted by state and federal constitutions of powers to protect the health, safety, and morals of citizens. This general supervisory power could well change with time and did, depending on social change itself. For as change produced new problems and new demands on government, it could well be construed as calling for a new exercise of traditional authority.

At one time, for example, it had been argued by the courts that states could not regulate wages and hours of work or work conditions. But as public views about this changed so did those of the courts, and they accepted such supervisory powers as constitutionally legitimate. In the 1950s and 1960s they extended such authority to civil rights. When storekeepers, for example, claimed a right to exclude blacks as customers on the grounds that they had a right to use their property as they wished, the courts argued that there were other rights as well, that the state could legitimately use its police power to restrain one in order to protect the other. The police power of the state, therefore, had evolved gradually over the years as the society and the economy had evolved, and the impact of the actions of one person on another, as well as those of institutions on individuals, had become more complex and intricate.

Environmental issues had implications for the police powers of the state because citizens often called on government to advance environmental objectives or to regulate to prevent harmful environmental effects. General laws would extend this protection from common law court action to general supervisory action by governmental agencies. Police powers to protect health were long established and were the most readily accepted of the new environmental concerns; those to protect amenities were less so. Yet courts now affirmed the right of a state, under the police power, to protect community aesthetic and amenity values. Other laws called for restrictions on the use of land in order to avoid adverse effects on others; these, too, the courts argued, were a legitimate use of the state's police powers. In their policies states could well recognize that they should go farther than merely protect health and property.

In the late 1960s several states amended their constitutions to affirm the "environmental rights" of their citizens, which included the right to a natural and clean environment. Such amendments reflected the widespread acceptance of environmental values. But when citizens sought to bring lawsuits on the grounds that individuals, corporations, or governmental agencies deprived them of these rights, the courts often held back. The constitutional right, they argued, was not self-enforcing and remained a mere general affirmation until turned into specific legislative statutes. Failing to secure this recognition of substantive environmental guarantees, environmentalists then sought to persuade courts that these statements of constitutional principle implied procedural safeguards on the order of an environmental-impact analysis. Some state courts were more willing to accept this.[45]

That courts would accept the role of environmental values in issues of both standing and police powers did not mean, however, that environmental rights would invariably prevail. Despite these affirmations of basic principle the courts retained considerable discretion in delineating rights, in balancing, for example, property rights and environmental rights. If two such rights were in contention, the courts might argue that although in principle the state could constitutionally use its authority to carry out environmental purposes, in specific cases action might go too far in restraining the rights of others, such as property owners. Hence litigation often appeared to be a game in which the court drew fine distinctions between competing claims, veering one way and then another, thereby retaining for itself considerable power of decision.[46]

In responding to changing social values courts often sought to grapple with fundamental aspects of modern society and the problems they generated, which were brought to the fore by environmentalists. They focused on those problems more precisely and hence more effectively than was done in either the legislative or the administrative branch of government. The courts had a way of zeroing in on the crucial point of dispute and pushing aside those aspects of argument that were more derivative and manipulative so that the nub of the controversy could be laid bare. In doing so they pinpointed the crux of broad social controversy as well as the issue immediately before them.

Three such types of controversies were involved in environmental affairs, each one involving issues arising from three major innovations in post–World War II society: new knowledge, new values, and new technologies. Judicial reasoning and argument that lay behind judicial decision highlighted these in a manner that made clear the larger meaning of environmental change.

Environmental issues and environmentalists who pressed them had stressed emerging scientific knowledge and had helped to shape controversies among scientists about the nature of scientific knowledge and the degree of proof needed to form judgments of harm. Whose view would prevail? In case after case the courts were faced with disagreement. Scientists themselves could not generate a consensus; hence their own disagreements were thrown onto political institutions for decision and ultimately onto the courts.[47]

For the most part courts did not wish to take part in the substance of these disputes; they did not have sufficient technical training. But they were willing to make judgments about whether the assessment of evidence by other governmental bodies, such as administrative agencies, constituted a reasonable conclusion and hence was an, but not necessarily *the,* acceptable alternative among possible choices. It was not enough for a plaintiff to argue that the court should not choose among claimants, because there was no scientific agreement on the issue. This strategy often stopped legislators and administrators in their tracks. But courts dismissed that response. They were established to act, to make choices, albeit difficult ones, and not to temporize. And in making this kind of choice they were quite willing to say that a decision based on frontier knowledge was sound. Although they rejected some cases of such reasoning as not demonstrable, they tended to affirm the environmental argument that emerging knowledge could constitute a basis for judgment.[48]

The courts were also willing to give legitimacy to aesthetic values; though only newly recognized in public policy, they should be allowed as much acceptance in the interplay of political objectives and alternatives as developmental ones. Social change had brought these values to the fore. Older institutions, and the scientific and technical personnel associated with them, held back; they had difficulty recognizing that such values had as much importance and legitimacy as their own, belittled them, and sought to use political strategies to restrain them.[49]

Courts on the whole would not accept their argument. As judges observed the wider social scene it seemed clear to them that aesthetic values were important to many in modern society; often the fact that they personally shared those values aided considerably in giving them greater social acceptance through their decisions. But from whatever quarter, the significance of these changes in court doctrine rested on the ability of judges to identify clearly and precisely vast and far-reaching social changes that other governmental bodies often had difficulty in emphasizing with equal sharpness and clarity.

Finally, the courts grappled with new technologies and the relationship of environmental objectives to the pace of technological change. When industrial litigants argued that an environmental regulation would be too burdensome, they sought to focus the analysis on individual firms that would be adversely affected, perhaps even forced out of business. But the courts tended to emphasize the health of the industry as a whole rather than particular firms that might be more obsolete. Was the industry capable of moving ahead with new technologies, with greater efficiencies, with greater benefit to society?[50]

The courts accepted the environmental arguments that cost-benefit analysis should not be allowed to entrench more obsolete firms by emphasizing the cost of environmental regulation to them, but that the more important question should be the degree to which modern production could move ahead. They agreed that the implication of environmental laws was to require some firms, usually the older and less efficient ones, to be replaced by more modern firms, which would enable the entire industry to progress.[51]

In these cases involving new knowledge, new values, and new technologies, environmentalists threw their weight on the side of innovation. The environmental movement constituted an expression of demand for new research in science, acceptance of new social values, and technological change. It was one among several elements in American society moving in those directions. The response of the courts to the issues stemming from these changes was to affirm their legitimacy and hence to give them the sanction of judicial approval. In this way the courts played a major role in broad social choice and decision, besides resolving more limited disputes between litigants.

As time passed, however, this larger role of the courts began to change from one of affirming new social values to one of granting agencies considerable choice in implementing environmental programs. As the agencies became more careful with respect to procedure, the court began to defer to their technical expertise. Judges did not relish the demand that they tackle complex problems such as the choice of air-quality models, substantive judgments as to health and ecological effects, or choices among alternatives in planning. Despite the obvious desire of litigants to wrest such decisions from them, the courts warned about the limitations to their jurisdiction: "Although this inquiry into the facts is to be searching and careful, the ultimate standard of review is a narrow one. The court is not empowered to substitute its judgment for that of the agency." Agency judgment was to be accepted if it constituted a "reasoned decision," a "rational conclusion based on facts" rather than the decisions preferred by one party in a dispute. As issues became more technical in the course of policy implementation judicial deference became more extensive.[52]

Environmentalists found it increasingly difficult to penetrate this deference to shape the course of implementation. Agencies sought to interpret their authority narrowly and to limit the intensity of action on behalf of environmental goals. If their decisions were "reasoned" according to judicial opinion, the courts could not serve as an effective counterweight to administrative lethargy in behalf of environmental goals. When administrative choice went in their direction and the courts deferred to it, environmentalists applauded the outcome; but the opposite happened with greater frequency over the course of time and rendered the courts less useful as a check on administrative action. If the agency argued that air-quality models were inadequate to determine the effect of automobile pollutants on ambient air, to determine "significant deterioration," or the transformation of sulfur dioxide into sulfates, the court declined to question that judgment. If an environmental-impact statement was interdisciplinary and comprehensive, a satisfactory "full disclosure" document, regardless of the substantive agency choice, it was acceptable.[53]

One might compare and contrast law and science in the response of each to changing social values represented by envi-

ronmental actions. Science reflects new realities, new circumstances for investigation and understanding, and its resources
tend to shift with the perception and comprehension of those
frontiers. Law, on the other hand, reflects new values and choices
made by individuals and institutions with respect to changing circumstances. The relationship of science to society is often indirect, mediated by those in scientific institutions who decide what
will be investigated and how research resources will be deployed. The relationship of law to society, on the other hand, is
more direct, as individuals and institutions conclude that they are
harmed by some new facet of social change, come into contention one with another, and then bring their complaints to the
courts.[54]

The environmental movement expanded the realm of science,
making greater demands on existing scientific and technical institutions than they were capable of meeting. But it also made
demands on law, which reflected social values and social change
and hence was more responsive to environmental entreaties.
Scientists tended to think of themselves as relatively independent from social context, as involved with a reality that was apart
from people, their setting, and their values. And this led to their
detachment from the public and their alignment with other scientific, technical, and managerial institutions in their strategies
for action and defense.

But courts forced scientists and technicians back into the world
of social reality to face their own particular, in contrast with their
assumed universal, values and those of society. Human aspirations and actions, even those of scientific and technical specialists, as well as in society at large, were the context of both science and law. And they were the fundamental context of
government. Courts sat squarely in the middle of those changing
desires and behaviors. Even though science and technology
sought through management to perfect institutions that would be
divorced from that setting, they could not do so fully. Not only did
courts respond directly to changing social values, but they had
the capacity to force other institutions, and especially those of
science and technology, to do so as well.

15 The Reagan Antienvironmental Revolution

The presidential administration of Ronald Reagan brought a new era in environmental affairs that helped to define their role in American history. Earlier Democratic and Republican administrations had responded to environmental objectives with some degree of favor. But the Reagan administration began with a pervasive and determined commitment to turn the environmental tide. Environmentalists were rejected as legitimate participants in the give-and-take of public affairs. The administration set out to undo the environmental work of the preceding two decades of Republican and Democratic leadership.[1]

Implicit in this radical thrust was an assumption that environmental objectives were not deeply rooted in American society and politics but were the demands of a few environmental leaders rather than of the greater public. The environmental phenomenon, it was thought, could be swept aside by vigorous presidential leadership. The resulting drama tested the strength of popular support for environmental objectives, which proved to be much greater than the administration had anticipated. Its opposition, in fact, provided an opportunity for those who shaped environmental institutions to demonstrate the breadth of concern in the broader society. In being forced to recognize that environmental affairs were not momentary, limited, and superficial, the administration,

491

in fact, more firmly rooted their legitimacy on American politics.

This drive for radical innovation was a historical experiment of sorts. For in challenging the environmental movement, Reagan tested its strength and vitality and thereby demonstrated the degree to which it had become a broad and fundamental aspect of American public life.

The Reagan Onslaught

The direction of the Reagan antienvironmental drive became clear in the last few months of 1980. During the presidential campaign Reagan had made some strong antienvironmental remarks that his campaign managers feared would alienate a substantial portion of the voting public. An advisory committee was formed of Republicans who had been prominent environmental leaders in the early 1970s, many of them officials in the Nixon administration. Among them were Russell Train, who had been head of both the Council on Environmental Quality and the Environmental Protection Agency; Nathaniel Reed, who had been assistant secretary of the interior in charge of the national parks and the U.S. Fish and Wildlife Service; and William Ruckelshaus, whom Train had succeeded as EPA administrator. This group provided the Republican campaign with a more positive environmental image. It advised the campaign managers and, after the election, started to shape an environmental program for the new administration.[2]

But the Reagan victory brought to the fore a new set of advisers, who looked forward to an opportunity to make extensive changes in public policy. They viewed these former Republican environmental leaders as "radical extremists," turned aside their recommendations, and established a new committee to redirect the future administration's policies. The new advisers cut off relationships not only with the leaders of citizen environmental organizations but with these "moderate" Republican leaders as well. Only later, after the new policies had created a vigorous backlash, did Reagan's advisers turn to them again.[3]

There were three closely related aspects of the Reagan antienvironmental revolution: ideology, the business community, and executive power. The administration spoke through an ideology intended to reduce governmental action and enhance the private economy. The most extensive expressions of this view came from the private enterprise "think tanks," the American Enterprise Institute and the Heritage Foundation. Regulatory activity and public landownership, for example, were to be sharply reduced in order to promote private enterprise as a matter of principle. It would be difficult to identify in the American past so thorough an attempt on the part of a presidential administration to apply a political ideology directly.[4]

The business community was an equally important ingredient in the administration's antienvironmental drive. For two decades it had led the opposition to environmental policies, but it had been frustrated by the persistence of environmental objectives. It had been galvanized especially by the favorable environmental attitudes of the Carter administration, so that by 1981 it was primed to carry out a counteroffensive. As the administration leaders clarified their antienvironmental attitudes, leaders of the business community rushed to take advantage of the opportunity. The haste led to actions that generated a political backlash against business. By 1984, opinion studies indicated that the public considered the business community to be less reliable than environmentalists as a source of information and public policy. Leaders in Washington ranked business groups far below environmental ones in their effectiveness.

Enhanced executive power was also central in the Reagan antienvironmental revolution. If the administration were to forge rapid and fundamental change, it would do so not through Congress or the courts but through executive action. New policymakers would bring about new policy and enhance executive authority in the face of the courts, Congress, and the agencies. One of the least observed of the changes in governance during the Reagan administration was the growth of the power of the Executive Office of the President vis-à-vis other branches of federal and state government. The key to that change was the Office of Management and Budget, which lay beyond the reach of agencies, courts, and Congress and sought to change policy by both budgetary and nonbudgetary means.[5]

The central strategy in this drive was to change policy by changing policymakers. Hence Reagan's advisers insisted that new appointees in the environmental agencies share in the administration's ideology. In this they often relied on advice, and even lists of favorable and unfavorable candidates, provided by those sympathetic to their objectives, such as the Heritage Foundation and the U.S. Chamber of Commerce. In later years "hit lists" from these groups were made public in which both science advisers and administrative personnel were identified as unacceptable.[6]

The best known of the Reagan appointees was James Watt, the new secretary of the interior, who had championed private enterprise and attacked federal regulation while he was director of the Mountain States Legal Foundation, an organization financed by business corporations to take up legal action on their behalf. The new administrator of the EPA, Anne Gorsuch, had been a leader of the Republican Right in the Colorado legislature. John Crowell, general counsel of the Louisiana-Pacific Corporation, the largest purchaser of timber from the national forests, became assistant secretary of agriculture in charge of the U.S. Forest Service. Robert Burford, a Colorado rancher and state legislator, became director of the Bureau of Land Management (BLM). Robert Harris, a leading critic of the new surface mining act and organizer of the litigation from Indiana challenging the new law, was placed in charge of the office that administered it. The director of the Occupational Safety and Health Administration (OSHA) was Thorne Auchter, head of a Florida construction firm, who had been a Republican party leader in Florida. The new assistant secretary of the interior in charge of the National Park Service and the Fish and Wildlife Service was Ray Arnett, who had been head of the California Wildlife Division during Reagan's term as governor and was openly critical of the objectives of environmental organizations.[7]

The administration did not succeed in making all the personnel changes it desired. It drew back from an attempt to abolish the Council on Environmental Quality (CEQ) when prominent Senate Republicans objected. But the CEQ's new head, Alan Hill of California, was distinguished primarily by his service as a Republican party leader. The heads of several agencies important to environmentalists were less susceptible to major change. The director of the Fish and Wildlife Service, by law, was required to be a professional expert in such matters. When the administration sought to appoint to the position Dr. Norman C. Roberts, a Los Angeles veterinarian turned investment counselor who was a friend of the president's but had no professional qualifications for the post, the International Association of Fish and Wildlife Commissioners took up cudgels, the nomination was withdrawn, and the director of the Arizona Fish and Game Commission, Robert Jantzen, was selected.[8]

Environmental regulations were of immediate concern to the administration. The agenda was set by the business community, which submitted a list of proposed changes. A temporary halt was called on pending regulations, some of which had been nearing enactment toward the end of the Carter administration. The Office of Management and Budget was given enhanced authority to grant final approval to regulatory proposals, and by 1985 it was authorized to approve initial action as well. Sometimes these moves sidetracked regulations already under way, such as the generic cancer rule OSHA had proposed. Others, such as OSHA's "right to know" rule, were modified more in accordance with the wishes of the business community. Some proposed rules that the administration favored, such as the prohibition of local restrictions on the transport of nuclear waste, were permitted to proceed.[9]

The most dramatic episodes of regulatory change occurred in the Department of the Interior, where James Watt was determined to make major innovations. Watt sought to change the "several hundred" regulations in the department so fully that no successor "would ever change them back because he won't have the determination that I do." The most controversial of Watt's actions involved surface mining and coal leasing. In these matters Watt relied on the advice of the department's solicitor, William Coldiron, former attorney for the Montana Power Company, who attempted to provide legal justifications for the changes. In both cases, however, environmentalists brought action in the courts, which later ruled that the secretary had exceeded his authority. Such restraints from the courts, and also from Congress, constantly blocked the administration's attempts to change policy.[10]

Changes in policy could also be fostered by changes in the

administration of rules already in place. Enforcement provided the most important opportunity. There were continual complaints from Congress that the EPA was more than tardy in cleaning up hazardous-waste sites, that the Office of Surface Mining (OSM) failed to enforce adequately the Surface Mining Control and Reclamation Act of 1977, or that OSHA was lax in its inspection of workplaces. Congressional investigators often uncovered evidence that lax enforcement resulted from a desire to adjust policy to the wishes of the regulated industries. In response to these circumstances environmentalists undertook a major drive to enforce the Clean Water Act of 1972 through their own litigation. They filed several hundred cases in many of which the EPA and industry had, in fact, agreed quietly that the agency would accept continued violations of the law.[11]

The assessment of scientific data as a basis for regulation was one of the most controversial issues; this, in turn, involved choosing science advisers who would make the assessments. The Reagan administration was friendly to the argument from business that present science advisers should be replaced by new ones more skeptical about the adverse effects of pollutants. Most important was the notion that the process of resolving disputes about environmental science should exclude scientists with views short of a commitment to requiring high levels of proof about the harm of chemicals. On a number of occasions the resolution of issues in the EPA involved only agency and industry personnel; those who represented the viewpoints of affected citizens or public-health advocates were not represented.[12]

The administration also sought to change policy through the budget. As it tried to increase military spending and reduce taxes it was able to exercise considerable leverage in reducing spending for domestic, including environmental, programs. Although potential opposition from Congress kept it from taking major legislative initiatives, policies could be changed by reducing funds to implement them. Major cuts were made for the EPA during 1981 and 1982, but because of congressional resistance some funds were restored in the next two years. By 1985, however, the agency's real dollar budget remained only at the 1980 level.[13]

Reaganites were less successful in revising laws. A number of statutes dealing with air and water quality and waste disposal were subject to renewal during the Reagan years. But the administration played the role largely of responding to initiatives from Congress rather than undertaking its own. It was most interested in revising the Clean Air Act, but it withheld proposals until environmentalists had gained considerable momentum in Congress, and even then sent along only some "general principles" for action rather than specific legislation. The act was not revised more because of disagreements in Congress than because of opposition from the administration.[14]

While the Reagan administration attacked on a wide front in attempting to change environmental policies, the central focus of its actions was the Office of Management and Budget. This agency had, over the years, been modified from an instrument largely to shape budget presentations to Congress into a general tool of executive authority. Presidents Nixon and Carter had extended this role, and so did Reagan. The OMB came to exercise approval over proposals to gather information, annual reports, initial recommendations for agency action, and final regulatory proposals. Although its actions were related to federal expenditure in some way, in a broader context they served primarily to provide more centralized executive control.[15]

The Reagan administration found the OMB especially useful as an agency where decision making was not subject to the scrutiny of the public, Congress, or the courts. It was able to avoid the open administrative procedures that the courts had fashioned over the years. President Carter, like Reagan, had recognized this advantage in using the OMB to make presidential decisions. An increasing number of administrative actions were removed from observation. Throughout the Reagan administration, the implication of this remarkable long-term constitutional change aroused some concern and comment in Congress and the media but did not lead to major public debate. Yet it constituted one of the most significant elements of the Reagan antienvironmental revolution.[16]

The use of the OMB to restrict access to information about policy-making was only one of many efforts to reduce the public's role in administrative decision making. Agency public-information programs established under previous administrations and often required by law were curtailed. Efforts to make information about chemical exports available to foreign countries were cut back. The administration supported industry's efforts to restrict the distribution of information about chemicals on the grounds that they were trade secrets. Citizen participation in administrative actions on such matters as transportation, water-quality planning, and hazardous-waste treatment was greatly reduced by cutbacks in appropriations. And the administration opposed funding for legal intervenors in agency actions. All these moves sharply curtailed citizen participation.[17]

Strategies to Change Policies

Policies to curtail environmental programs were instituted in almost every federal agency that dealt with such matters. The most dramatic case was the challenge to public landownership. For decades the fact that one-third of the nation's land was owned by the federal government seemed to some theorists to be inconsistent with the national self-image as a country of private enterprise. Yet public landownership had long been a part of the American tradition. Some in private-market think tanks, as well as a few in academic circles, advocated that these public resources be shifted to the private market.[18]

The national parks became a particular point of dispute because of Secretary Watt's views that the system had become too large. Acquisition of new land and park inholdings, he argued, should stop. Urban parks should be transferred to the states for management. Administrative activities such as maintenance should be contracted out to private companies. Watt urged that first priority be given to reconstruction and maintenance of park facilities. This had begun during the Carter administration as a long-term project, and Congress had increased appropriations for it each year. Now Watt urged that it proceed at an even more rapid pace and that money from the Land and Water Conservation Fund should be devoted to that purpose rather than to acquisition. Congress rejected the move, insisted that the maintenance program be financed through general revenues outside the Fund, and continued to appropriate monies from the Fund for acquisition.[19]

The most vigorous assault on public landownership came with the "Sagebrush Rebellion" and "asset management." The first, well under way before the 1980 election, was a demand, largely from livestock users of the public domain, that federally owned lands be transferred to the states. As a candidate, Reagan took up the proposal eagerly, and he later advocated it as a policy of his new administration. His advisers drew up a further plan to sell large amounts of public lands to private owners. Opposition to both proposals came primarily from the West itself. Western state-land policies, in contrast with those for federal lands, did not allow recreation or other nonincome-producing activities. Transfer to the states would replace state with federal management, and so recreational users feared that they would now be excluded from lands long open to them. The proposal to sell federal lands to private owners aroused the ire especially of livestock operators who felt that in competitive bidding with oil, gas, and mineral companies, they would be the main losers. By the end of the first Reagan term both these ventures had almost been forgotten.[20]

These proposed innovations in public-land policies caused such a widespread outcry that they were quickly abandoned in favor of policies to carry out the more pragmatic demands – from timber companies, livestock grazers, oil and gas firms, park concessionaires, tourism promoters, and motorized-vehicle firms – in the use of the public lands. A number of resources on the public lands were leased or sold – for example, grazing rights, coal, and timber. Administration policy called for more lenient terms for those who wished to purchase and less support for associated environmental concerns. Use of BLM lands had long been a subject of controversy between livestock operators, on the one hand, and environmentalists such as fish and wildlife users and recreationists, on the other. Whereas environmental uses had been expanding slowly for several decades, the administration now in a countermove took up the cause of the livestock operators and the newer mineral interests.

Grazing policy involved issues such as those of the fee charged for use and the number of grazing animals permitted. The administration continued to allow cattle and sheep owners to lease grazing rights on private or state lands for far less than the prevailing price. At the same time, the new BLM administration, under the direction of Robert Burford, abandoned attempts to reduce stocking levels to permit restoration of the quality of range as earlier policy had provided. A central issue in such matters was the membership of district, state, and national advisory committees, which in turn involved questions of who would control decisions about the use of specific areas. Would it reflect dominance by development interests or a wider range of recreational and environmental ones? Whereas the Carter administration had sought to shift the composition of the committees toward the latter, the Reagan administration now moved it back sharply toward development. Livestock interests were willing to permit wildlife interests to be represented by only one of ten members of district advisory boards, and the new BLM director supported them.[21]

Coal leasing was more controversial. During the 1970s environmentalists had sought to shape that program along several lines: Areas for leasing would be selected by federal officials rather than the coal industry so that environmental considerations would apply; leases should carry a return similar to the prevailing market value; coal under lease should be developed within a given time so that it would not be held speculatively. The Reagan administration reversed these policies. Watt sought to accelerate the leasing program to transfer coal rights more rapidly to private firms and reduce environmental safeguards that might have slowed that effort. But his eagerness to carry out these objectives proved to be his undoing. A major sale in 1983 brought only one bidder, and the return to the federal government was far less than the cost of preparing lands for bids. Events arising from the sale led directly to Watt's resignation.

In the continuing contest between commodity and environmental users of the national forests, the new assistant secretary, John Crowell, sought to accelerate timber sales and harvests. He set national harvest levels and then required each forest to adopt its share of this goal as its planning objective. This restricted the tendency of individual forest managers to respond to the growing environmental and recreational interests being brought to bear on them. Increasingly fearful of these local and regional demands, the timber industry looked to the Washington office to frustrate them. Crowell's action, in turn, stimulated local revolts throughout the nation on behalf of environmental and recreational objectives for the national forests.[22]

Forest policy also raised questions about the price for the sale of federally owned timber. Environmentalists had long objected to the practice of "residual pricing," in which prices were set not to reflect market conditions but so that purchasers would make a profit after their costs. Many contracts, consequently, involved sales far below cost. Environmentalists developed a further argument that almost all national-forest sales were "deficit sales" in that they did not cover even the administrative costs of preparing the sale for bids, let alone the costs of regenerating and growing timber. The administration was disinclined to accept either of these arguments. When firms that had agreed to purchase contracts early in the 1970s, when the lumber market had been good, now in the 1980s faced a depressed market and demanded the right to revise their original contracts, the administration finally agreed.[23]

The Reagan administration was less interested in changing the Fish and Wildlife Service. Secretary Watt desired to build a new recreational coalition that would draw hunters and fishers to his side against environmentalists. Moreover, wetlands purchases were self-financed by proceeds from duck-hunting stamps, which imposed little burden on the federal treasury. Hence Watt favored expansion of the national wetlands system. To the administration the major fault of the Fish and Wildlife Service lay in its technical resources to object to developmental projects on behalf of fish and wildlife habitats. The service had played this role from the earliest days of environmental affairs in the 1960s and had antagonized developers.[24]

Attempts to curb environmental regulation were more successful than those to privatize public lands. Although many regulatory programs were restricted, the administration adopted a persistent and often covert policy of attrition rather than frontal attack. Its greatest success came with OSHA and the Office of Surface Mining. The new OSHA administrator, Thorne Auchter, sidetracked incipient regulatory moves and adopted an enforcement strategy of limited supervision called "self-enforcement," which gave industry far greater freedom of action. Industry was pleased with the relaxation of federal influence, which enabled it, in turn, to reduce its own health and safety staffs.[25]

The OSM was restricted even more readily, because its recently established program had not yet developed a firm commitment to the law's objectives. Regulations established during the Carter administration were now revised more to reflect coal-industry desires, and enforcement capability – the heart of the program – was sharply reduced. A spate of lawsuits by environmentalists followed in which the courts ruled that the new regulations were contrary to law. OSM enforcement policies became subject to persistent congressional investigation, and by 1985 a House committee declared the program to be in a "shambles."[26]

The main target for deregulation was the Environmental Protection Agency, which housed most pollution-control activities – air, water, noise, and hazardous waste. The administration learned a lesson about the political role of regulation early on, with the noise program. Here, it thought, was a relatively useless venture that could be abolished in accord with a general theory of preference for private enterprise. But the airline and trucking industries complained, arguing that the program's primary objective was to maintain a federal preeminence in noise regulation that would prevent cities and towns from taking their own action to restrict noise levels more than industry desired. The administration beat a hasty retreat and retained the noise-regulation program to the extent of its preemptive power over state and local action, even though its role beyond that was greatly reduced.[27]

The EPA was placed under the more direct scrutiny and control of the Office of Management and Budget, which required the agency to submit markedly reduced budgets, restricted its advocacy of new programs such as those dealing with indoor air pollution, and required it to develop more detailed regulatory proposals that placed reduced emphasis on public benefits and greater emphasis on costs to industry. After the new EPA leaders initially accepted these approaches, even they soon looked on them as excessive. EPA administrator Anne Gorsuch became controversial within the administration when she resisted OMB efforts to exercise more direct control over EPA affairs. This resistance to the OMB led to her final abandonment by the administration and her resignation. In subsequent congressional investigations both she and her policy assistants criticized the pressure to which the OMB had subjected the EPA.[28]

Scientific and technical leaders reacted strongly to attempts to politicize scientific judgments. Industry representatives and EPA leaders, for example, decided in private meetings that formalde-hyde was not a carcinogen and therefore did not require regula-tion even though many scientists used quite different standards for determining carcinogenicity. Behind such changes in policy was the dramatic change in science advisers, a shift from those representing a broad cross-section of opinion within the scientific professions to those who advocated a high standard of proof and were closely affiliated with industry. Although the media high-lighted the ties between administration and industry in enforce-ment, the concern of the scientific and professional community about attempts to influence scientific judgment led to a sharp backlash within less publicized but influential circles.[29]

Two more agency variations in antienvironmental policies are instructive. By 1981 the Consumer Products Safety Commission (CPSC) was thought to be relatively weak politically – without much support in Congress, among interest groups, or in the ad-ministration – and ripe to be abolished readily as an example of antiregulatory commitments. Its funds were reduced. Yet it took up a highly controversial issue when it sought to phase out the use of urea foam formaldehyde in home insulation on the grounds that it was carcinogenic. The move was even more striking in the face of the contrary view taken by the new EPA science advisers. Evidence based on animal experiments, they argued, did not warrant action. The CPSC survived; it is not at all clear why.[30]

The Coastal Zone Management Program was more difficult for the administration to modify. Its objectives were clear enough: Change the program to facilitate development, especially energy development, in the coastal zone. Secretary Watt sought to ex-pand rapidly oil and gas drilling offshore, but nearby communities and their state governments resisted and often persuaded Con-gress to prohibit drilling in particular areas. Much of the debate depended on the outcome of court decisions, which in 1983 strengthened the hands of energy companies. Congress did not act to nullify these decisions, which left the administration free to pursue its policy of providing a climate more favorable to energy development on the coasts. In this case, after the Watt era, the administration worked its antiregulation policies more quietly and patiently, with less media drama, and hence more successfully.[31]

The Reagan administration also sought to replace the Council on Environmental Quality as a source of policy initiatives. Its personnel was reduced to a fraction of its former size, a caretaker Council was appointed, and its ability to carry out innovative studies was sharply curtailed. The CEQ hardly had sufficient resources to continue publication of its annual report, which had become over the years an extremely valuable source of information about environmental problems and trends. It finally issued one for 1981 and others for later years, but the report became simply a vehicle for rationalizing the administration's strategy to restrict environmental objectives rather than, as formerly, a firm source of ideas and action for the public to foster environmental progress. To fill the gap the Conservation Foundation published its own "state of the environment" reports in 1981 and 1983, which were of similar quality to those formerly issued by the CEQ.[32]

Leadership within the administration on environmental affairs was transferred from the CEQ to the cabinet Council on Natural Resources, headed by James Watt, who helped to establish a strongly developmental policy in environmental and resource matters throughout the administration. It was in the cabinet council that policy was made about pollution as well as land resources. Beyond this, however, an even more fundamental source of environmental leadership was the OMB under the directorship of David Stockman. Stockman did not confine himself to formal budget reviews or even cost-benefit analyses but was prone to deny the usefulness of environmental programs. When he had served formerly as a member of the House Committee on Energy and the Environment, as he said more than once, he had become convinced that pollution was no real problem; hence it could be ignored.[33]

Environmental Opportunities amid Constraints

Environmentalists were now effectively excluded from influence in both the agencies and the Executive Office of the President. The degree of that exclusion was symbolized by a meeting Secretary Watt held with environmentalists early in 1981. At its end he announced that there would be no more such meetings, because there was nothing further to discuss. Despite concerted efforts on their part, environmentalists found themselves acting almost exclusively from outside the executive branch. Their resulting strategy is a case study of the ways in which opportunities for political expression in the United States are available to those who find the administrative apparatus of the state closed to their influence.[34]

Reagan's policies actually strengthened public support for environmental organizations. Membership, resources, and organizational capabilities grew. With larger staffs they could lobby more effectively in Congress on more issues, undertake more litigation, and mobilize members more fully. They were also able to pursue new activities, such as employing technical and professional staff who brought with them a higher degree of credibility and respect in the technical and professional world. The Environmental Defense Fund, for example, hired Ellen Silbergeld, a prominent researcher on the biological effects of lead, as its toxic-chemicals specialist and Michael Oppenheimer, an established atmospheric physicist, as its expert on atmospheric chemistry and, in particular, "acid rain." The National Audubon Society hired an energy expert, and the Wilderness Society added to its staff economists who analyzed public-land policies and examined the economic analyses of the timber industry and the Forest Service.[35]

Reaction against the Reagan environmental policies also stimulated more extensive state and regional organization. Statewide coalitions to lobby in state capitals took on new significance as state environmental action was stimulated to fill the vacuum created by reduced federal activities. Federal policies to increase the allowable cut on the national forests stimulated local citizen action to participate more intensively in forest planning. State chemical right-to-know groups were organized to combat industry's attempts to use federal preemption to restrict the impact of state laws. Efforts along these lines had proceeded in earlier years, but now there were new bursts of state and local energy in reaction to the Reagan initiatives.

Environmental organizations took up electoral politics with a new intensity. During the 1980 campaign this activity, which had begun in 1978, grew rapidly, and by 1984 environmentalists played a role in one-third of the nation's congressional races, as well as gubernatorial, U.S. Senate, and state-legislative contests. Statewide political-action organizations were formed, which supported environmental candidates, raised funds for their campaigns, and provided support in getting out the vote on Election Day. Within environmental organizations there was debate whether electoral action was a desirable departure, but the majority of members approved.[36]

Increased electoral activity brought to the fore the relationship of party affiliation and environmental objectives. To environmentalists it made no difference whether the candidates they backed were Republicans or Democrats; their environmental record was the crucial test. Yet Democrats supported environmental measures far more than did Republicans. Hence environmentalists were prone to search for Republican environmental candidates and to make clear their bipartisanship. They found many such opportunities in New England, where Republicans had as strong an environmental record as did Democrats. Through their own Republican members they made special efforts to play a role in such events as the 1984 Republican National Convention. When Douglas Wheeler became the new executive director of the Sierra Club in 1985, it was emphasized that he was a Republican who had served as a deputy assistant secretary of the interior during the Nixon administration.[37]

Environmentalists found excellent opportunities for action in Congress and the courts. These had been important instruments of action in previous years, and now, in the face of opposition from the executive branch, became more vital in environmental strategies. Environmental issues played a major role in the never-ending drama of suspicion between Congress and the president, and especially now because the Executive Office of the President sought to bring the agencies more fully under its direct supervision and control. The courts were equally suspicious of "off the record" administrative action. They could be relied on by environmentalists to insist that decisions be made with full and fair participation by all interested parties. In both cases environmentalists found considerable opportunity to further their objectives when the executive branch had made clear that its resources were not available to them.

Congress objected on many occasions when the administration sought to reduce or even eliminate appropriations. Congress regularly countered proposals to eliminate funds to acquire land through the Land and Water Conservation Fund, and by 1984 the administration relented and recommended some expenditures but not at the level Congress desired. In cases of agency action to change policy on its own initiative, such as with oil and gas drilling in wilderness areas, offshore oil drilling, or accelerated sales of public lands, Congress simply enacted measures that prohibited the expenditure of public funds for such purposes. The main source of congressional resistance was the Democratic House, but the Republican environmental contingent in the Senate, led by Robert Stafford of Vermont and John Chaffee of Rhode Island, helped to create a similar role for the Senate.[38]

To environmentalists one of the most useful activities of Congress was its oversight function, its practice of reviewing executive and agency decisions. When it appeared that the administration either failed to administer effectively laws such as the Surface Mining Control and Reclamation Act of 1977 or was working too closely with industry to nullify congressional intent, Congress held hearings to publicize the matter. A House committee conducted a hearing on the formaldehyde issue in 1982 that documented the controversy over the way the administration had revised the assessment of the relevant scientific evidence. The activities of both James Watt and Anne Gorsuch were brought to public light through congressional investigations. Often such inquiries were instigated by information provided to committee staffs or to environmentalists by agency civil servants.

Congress also initiated new legislation at a time when the administration would not. Most notable was a group of wilderness bills, which it chose to consider separately for each state, all of which were products of accommodation among the interested parties carried out under the auspices of state congressional delegations. Once an agreement was worked out for one state, legislators from other states were willing to accept it without question. Several dozen wilderness bills went through Congress in 1984 and were signed by the president. Reagan approved – though reluctantly – more such acreage in the forty-eight contiguous states than had any previous chief executive.[39]

In 1982 the Endangered Species Act was renewed and strengthened, and the following year funding for the Clinch River

Breeder Reactor was finally ended. In the waning months of 1984 the Resource Conservation and Recovery Act was revised and strengthened. Small waste generators were brought under control and initial steps taken to phase out entirely the use of landfills for hazardous wastes. Renewal of other major environmental laws proceeded more slowly, but gradually new versions of the Clean Water Act, the Safe Drinking Water Act, and the Superfund moved through Congress.[40]

The courts provided an equally useful opportunity for environmentalists. Successful lawsuits required the EPA to revise its "tall stack" regulations – a task it continued to try to evade – implement emission standards for diesel automobiles and trucks, and halt efforts to weaken toxic-water quality regulations. Court decisions forced the administration to halt its efforts to limit the 1977 Surface Mining Control and Reclamation Act. The administration, however, stymied court efforts to implement "fair procedure" when it increased the authority of the OMB to make decisions and hence shifted them to an arena that provided no public disclosure. The courts were reluctant to require the president, in contrast with the agencies, to make decisions "on the record" for legislative, judicial, and public scrutiny.[41]

With respect to one major area of policy, environmentalists shared administration views: the use of federal subsidies for economic development. To the administration, subsidies were an undesirable function of government; a correct application of private-market theory required that they end. Environmentalists, however, were concerned about their harmful environmental effects. Federal funds for highways, bridges, and sewer and water lines destroyed barrier islands. Dams and channelization destroyed rivers and wetlands. Rural electric power, which since 1935 had brought electricity to farm homes through the Rural Electrification Administration, now fostered rural commercial and industrial development. Farm price supports encouraged more intensive agriculture, destroyed fencerows, increased use of pesticides and worsened water pollution, and aggravated soil erosion. Many federal programs fostered development in relatively undeveloped areas that threatened environmental values.[42]

The strategy proposed by the Reagan environmental campaign committee in 1980 had pointed up the close parallel between the president-elect's philosophy of reducing federal spending and the environmental interest in cutting funds for environmentally destructive projects. For the most part, however, environmentalists found that the administration did not wish to carry its own ideology very far. In both 1981 and 1982, environmentalists drew up an "alternative budget" that outlined proposed reductions in expenditures through cutting back subsidies and increases in revenue by charging a "fair market price" for commodities from the public lands, such as timber and grazing rights. But the administration did not take the suggestions.[43]

The most successful venture of this kind was intended to protect barrier islands by prohibiting the use of federal funds to aid in their development. Secretary Watt took up this proposition with considerable enthusiasm. Much barrier-island development was fostered by federal subsidies; hence to prohibit them would reduce federal spending and protect barrier islands. Environmentalists considered the measure to fall far short of a 1977 bill, authored by Congressman Philip Burton of California, that envisaged federal acquisition of barrier islands as a new type of unit in the national-park system. But it would be a step in the right direction. Hence they joined with the administration in a successful legislative effort. The new law provided that undeveloped barrier islands be mapped and described and established a procedure to add new units in the future.[44]

Environmental efforts to restrict water-development projects, equally significant, were far less dramatic in their impact. This drive had been under way since the early 1970s. During the Carter administration, environmentalists had persuaded the president to refuse approval of several dam projects that involved extensive federal subsidies for only a few beneficiaries. They worked in Congress to build a coalition to oppose annual bills for both authorization and appropriations for river and harbor projects. The Reagan administration bolstered their strategy of insisting that industry and local communities that benefited from the waterway traffic pay an increasing share of both construction and maintenance costs. When that idea had first been presented by the Carter administration in the form of a tax on navigation fuel, it had been stoutly resisted by the inland-waterway carriers. But during the

Reagan administration on alliance between environmentalists and the executive branch was able to insist on significant local contributions for water-development funding.[45]

More important over the long run, though less visible, were advances in scientific knowledge. The impact of such new knowledge usually was felt only slowly and was subtle and "background" in its political meaning. Yet it continually bolstered environmental strategies. The most significant opportunity of this kind under Reagan came over acid rain. The main administration response to the problem was to continue the research program initiated by President Carter. The electric-power industry took up the same line of argument and allocated large sums for research. The administration argued persistently that relatively little was known about acid rain and that no action should be instituted until the results of research both in the United States and abroad were known.[46]

Although environmentalists were frustrated by this successful use of "further research" to block control programs, the eventual results built a consistently stronger case for even more extensive action in the future. At the end of any one period of research the results corroborated and elaborated rather than contradicted what had been known earlier. Research laid out with ever greater detail the biogeochemical processes by which sulfur dioxide was transformed into sulfates and deposited in the form of acid rain, the process of dry deposition, the effects of fog and snow, and the roles of nitrogen oxides and nitrates. Rapid expansion of inquiry from the limited topic of sulfate deposition to a more extensive study of ozone, heavy metals, and toxic organics, and a detailed tracking of pollutants to distinguish between local and long-distance patterns of transmission created an increasingly extensive body of data.

This research generated the much wider knowledge about air pollution that legislation of the 1960s had contemplated but that had never been realized. The effects identified in the acid-rain debate ranged far beyond health consequences to include those affecting materials, visibility, aquatic life, forests, and agriculture, comprising the secondary effects that had been identified for action in the 1960s but with which the EPA had been little concerned in the 1970s. Through the acid-rain issue, environmentalists now broadened the base of scientific information with which these issues could be brought to the fore.

Environmental science proceeded during the Reagan years on many fronts. There was increasing knowledge about the relationship between toxic chemicals and reproductive effects. The technical ability to detect lower levels of synthetic organics in human blood improved to the extent that by 1984 a diagnostic firm in New Orleans advertised its capability to conduct a wide range of tests for those who wished to take legal action against involuntary exposures. The problem of indoor air pollution was identified with increasing detail by the EPA through research programs the administration persistently opposed and had sought to hinder, but which Congress had mandated. There were beginnings, again through congressional funding, of acquisition of scientific data about the health effects of exposures from hazardous-waste sites. And studies by the National Institute of Occupational Health and Safety continued to identify more precisely the health effects of the exposure of workers to chemicals.[47]

Still another set of environmental opportunities arose from the growing interest in world environmental affairs. The Reagan administration sought to end the nation's wider environmental involvements, a marked turnaround from the leadership of earlier administrations. There were attempts to reduce appropriations for the United Nations Environmental Program and a decision to withdraw from UNESCO. In the U.N. General Assembly the administration opposed several environmental resolutions. The actions seemed to be simply ideological, as in the case of opposition to General Assembly approval of a World Charter for Nature and to action to print a new edition of a list of chemicals various nations and international agencies had declared to be hazardous. In each of these cases the United States cast the lone dissenting vote.[48]

Even more dramatic was the reversal of the nation's role in population matters. In 1972 it had taken the lead in promoting action to reduce population growth in opposition to the views of many less developed nations, but in 1984 the Reagan administration argued at the World Population Conference in Mexico

City that population growth presented no problem and need not be a subject of international action. By this time, however, population control had become a major concern of the less developed nations, forty-seven of which had established their own programs.[49]

By 1985 the great majority of the world's nations had formed an environmental administration of some sort, and international environmental agencies had developed an increasing number of cooperative activities. One of these was the regional-seas program, which drew nations together to promote cooperative action to improve water quality. At the same time citizen environmental groups had taken steps to expand their activities on the international scene. These ranged from programs of the Natural Resource Defense Council, the Sierra Club, and the National Wildlife Federation to cooperative activity through the Global Tomorrow Coalition, which worked out policy agendas, sought action through Congress on international policies, and held a major national "Globescope" Conference in Portland, Oregon, in 1985. In a number of fields of endeavor, such as restricting pesticide exports, opposing the destruction of tropical rain forests, and designing strategies to reduce the impact of development fostered by foreign aid, citizen groups came together across national borders in "nongovernmental organizations." The World Wildlife Fund fostered the World Conservation Strategy, and the newly established World Resources Institute began useful studies of world environmental issues.[50]

These activities, reflecting an acceptance of environmental values and objectives throughout the world and growth of institutions to implement them, evolved independently of initiatives from the U.S. government. Although the administration ignored them, it could not effectively restrain private cooperative activity that emerged internationally. Moreover, it could not eradicate the implicit leadership of past U.S. conservation and environmental initiatives, which continued to inspire and often serve as models for action in other nations. Whereas the administration reduced official American support for international environmental affairs, environmental momentum in the world at large provided considerable opportunity for environmentalists in the United States to expand the range of their activities.[51]

The Limits of Antienvironmental Action

The ability of environmentalists to find openings to foster environmental progress despite the Reagan administration's opposition reflected the depth of public support on which they drew. The administration had challenged values and institutions in American society and in so doing activated deeply rooted aspirations. It is useful to identify more precisely the points of interaction at which the Reagan strategy was engaged and resisted and, therefore, to define the controlling social and political forces.

Federal public-land policies provided a useful case to examine the limits of radical action. The administration's Sagebrush Rebellion and asset-management strategies failed primarily because of opposition in the West. The area had undergone transformation from a region that emphasized timber, mineral, and livestock development to one with a more diverse economy in which consumer environmental values played an increasing role. Recreation, for example, was now far more important than wood production. Transfer of federal lands to either the states or private owners would severely restrict recreational opportunities.[52]

Most Americans rejected the idea of privatization that underlay the administration's thinking. Private-market land theorists argued with conviction that the nation was coming to agree with them because of dissatisfaction with public-land management. But the public acted in a different manner when on many occasions it sought to transfer critical land from private to public ownership in order to "save" it. This was the strategy of land "conservancies" such as the national Nature Conservancy, which purchased land and transferred it to public agencies for "protection." By 1981 more than four hundred private land trusts had been formed to protect land from development. Voters often supported bond issues or created state trust funds to purchase land for permanent public ownership. The public widely shared the view that those in the private land market could not be relied on to manage land for environmental objectives and that transfer to public agencies or private trusts was needed.

The policies Secretary Watt endorsed for the national parks met vigorous resistance from state governments, Congress, environmental organizations, and the media. They rejected his proposal to transfer urban parks to the states, and although the notion that urban national parks should be increased in number did not gain momentum, the disengagement of the federal government from the urban-park idea obtained little support. Nor did the attempt by the administration to deauthorize several recently established national parks, such as the Santa Monica Mountains Recreation Area in California, fare any better. Early in 1981 environmentalists obtained evidence that this move was under way. It created such a storm of protest that the administration denied the policy was even intended, and the proposal did not again surface. To dampen pressure for park expansion Secretary Watt sought to repeal a law passed in 1977 that required the National Park Service to draw up an annual priority list of ten additions to the national-park system. But although the bill was prepared, it was not introduced.

The most striking of Secretary Watt's proposals was to transfer the interpretive service of the national-park system to private enterprise. In this venture he threatened one of the agency's most prized endeavors. Over many years the interpretive service had been the agency's pride and the envy of those abroad who sought to develop their own national parks. Its summer interpretive program had augmented a group of individuals who had come to believe that interpretation was the heart of the work of the National Park Service. This attempt at privatization struck at the very concept and ideals of the agency. Its ready rejection identified the wide support of the "National Park idea."[53]

The gulf between the policies of Secretary Watt and the general public was reflected in his failure to build a political coalition to support his program. In various advisory committees, as well as through his own strategies, Watt sought to mobilize those who had been disaffected by the policies of previous administrations – the national-park inholders, off-road–vehicle organizations, the National Campers and Hikers Association, and some hunting and fishing groups. But the secretary found that although he could provide places of influence for those organizational leaders, they had only a small constituency on which to draw. The fate of the venture reflected a lack of public support for the administration's policies.

A similar point of engagement between the environmental public and the administration was manifested in the attempt by the Forest Service to increase timber harvests. The planning system established by the National Forest Management Act of 1976 provided an opportunity for citizens to influence management of each forest. The Forest Service drive for larger timber harvests seemed to galvanize organized efforts to achieve environmental forest objectives. Coalitions were formed to focus on individual forests, often bringing to their support citizens from out of state who used that particular forest. The Citizens Coalition for the Bighorns in Wyoming, for example, included among its twenty-six constituent groups six organized in other states, such as Texans for the Bighorns.[54]

Citizen action also restricted the administration's drive to slow down the control of hazardous-waste disposal. The initial act in 1976 had called for regulations to be in place within eighteen months, but they had not been proposed until the very end of the Carter administration. The new EPA sought to postpone them even further, but environmental lawsuits forced the agency to speed up action. With full OMB support the agency withdrew a regulation that would have prohibited the disposal of liquid hazardous wastes in landfills, but the public objected so vigorously that the president's advisers overruled both the EPA and the OMB. By 1981, organizations to protect communities against hazardous-waste sites constituted an effective check on administration action.

There was institutional as well as citizen resistance to radical change, one aspect of which was the growth of environmental science. Environmental affairs had led to a massive expansion of inquiry into a wide range of factors including human biology, the biological environment, and biogeochemical cycles. Specialized professionals took up a multitude of inquiries, which were reflected in the many new journals devoted to research. Although new knowledge was always controversial when the interested parties wished to disagree about its meaning, it also resulted in an accumulation of facts that carried considerable weight. If scientific knowledge was translated into views held by influential scientific and technical leaders, it could then retard the actions of those who sought to hamper environmental efforts.

Such restraint appeared in the administration's attempt in the spring of 1981 to reverse the timetable adopted in 1974 to reduce the level of lead in gasoline. When the proposals became subject to open hearings, scientists presented considerable recently discovered evidence about the adverse health effects of lead at low levels of exposure. Especially important was a national health survey that made it clear that blood lead levels had declined steadily at the same time that the level of lead in gasoline had been reduced. The EPA halted its efforts to end the phase-down and in 1984 went farther and took action to reduce lead in gasoline from 1.1 grams to 0.1 gram per leaded gallon by January 1, 1986.[55]

The slow accumulation of economic data played a similar role. Environmentalists sought to identify more precisely either the benefits of environmental or the costs of developmental policies. Both were important in the attempt to focus on environmental objectives and to translate them from generalized concerns to precise analysis. Although the resulting "cost-benefit" studies were always controversial, given the stakes and the intensity of the debate, the elaboration of detail provided growing support for environmental objectives that helped to restrain their opponents. Forest planners had established an accounting system that entailed efforts to quantify recreational and fish and wildlife benefits so as to compare them with commodity values over the long run, discounted into "present net value" figures. When compared, environmental values almost always considerably outweighed timber values. Timber values, in fact, often fell to less than 10 percent of present net value. Cost-benefit data established a benchmark of analysis that emphasized the environmental in contrast with the commodity values of the national forests.

The civil service was an important source of resistance to the Reagan antienvironmental revolution. In cases in which agency personnel were committed to environmental objectives, they constituted an important roadblock to change imposed from the outside on the part of the Executive Office of the President, especially if that change seemed based on ideological rather than professional considerations. The Forest Service had long had a strong esprit de corps that enabled it to sustain its organizational goals in the face of political pressures. The interdisciplinary requirements of forest planning had brought into the Forest Service a considerable number of professionals with skills beyond those related to wood production and road construction. As forest planning proceeded in the Reagan years, they protested, often in quiet and unpublicized ways, against the emphasis on wood production. A series of interviews with ex–Forest Service employees on the Tongass National Forest in Alaska publicized their criticisms.

The civil service of the EPA was a critical factor in limiting the Reagan onslaught. On more than one occasion its professional personnel either resisted major changes or provided crucial information to environmentalists and congressional leaders to expose agency policy. Even more important, however, was the way the new EPA administrator, Anne Gorsuch, who at first adopted a highly confrontational policy with agency personnel and held them under suspicion, came to respect their ability and to defend the agency against efforts by the OMB to restrain it. This brought her into sharp conflict with both the OMB and Reagan's advisers, and they, in turn, considered her disloyal and expendable. This brought about her resignation as much as did the challenges from Congress and environmentalists.[56]

Personnel in other agencies either were less committed to environmental objectives and hence were easily swayed by administration policy or were more recently hired and, therefore, had not yet developed a sufficiently influential agency esprit de corps. The U.S. Army Corps of Engineers provides an example of the first. Although it had been somewhat responsive to environmental objectives as reflected by its acceptance of the Principles and Standards of the Water Resources Council, that acceptance had not extended beyond Washington to the district offices. Hence a new set of leaders reversed the corps's limited support for environmental objectives in planning and in wetlands protection under Section 404 of the Clean Water Act.[57]

The Office of Surface Mining was a relatively new agency, and although many of its original personnel sought to implement the environmental objectives of the Surface Mining Control and Reclamation Act, these were quickly replaced by others who were of a different frame of mind. The Occupational Health and Safety Administration presented a more mixed situation. Observing the changes in leadership with the appointment of a political administrator, many professional staff left the agency and thereby reduced its potential for resistance. Whether new leadership in 1985 would revitalize its civil service remained to be seen. The agency's potential for environmental management depended not only on its own personnel but also on the work of the National Institute of Occupational Health and Safety, which provided a source of professional expertise not readily subjected to external political influence and on which OSHA could always draw.

The states often served as a source of resistance to radical environmental change. Reagan's advisers were caught in a dilemma in their relationship with the states. On the one hand, their ideology called for a transfer of power and authority to the states. On the other, their commitment to the business community led them to support the drive on the part of corporate leaders to use the federal government to override state policies to which industry objected. On some occasions the administration made it clear that whereas it might wish to override state authority, it did not wish to take a position contrary to its ideology if such action would create a media issue. But when it could assert the "national interest" against a more "limited" state interest and when it could act quietly without exposing its ideological inconsistencies, it struck out boldly. These strategies aroused states to oppose some administration anti-environmental efforts.[58]

As director of the Mountain States Legal Foundation, before his service in the Reagan administration, James Watt had brought lawsuits challenging federal authority on behalf of the states. Now as secretary of the interior he switched sides. With respect to leasing federal coal and offshore oil properties, he sought to establish national goals, much as Assistant Secretary Crowell did for the national forests. Such goals, Watt argued, served the national interest and hence should be accepted by the states. In the Carter administration a cooperative state-federal consultation process had been established to decide the amount of federal coal lands that would be submitted for lease each year. Now amid vigorous objections from the states, Watt abandoned the committee approach and on his own decision greatly increased the scheduled amounts. The governors of the Mountain states protested vigorously, and Watt backed down. The secretary's similar efforts to expand offshore oil leasing led to a different strategy on the part of the affected states. Both California and Massachusetts worked through Congress to enact legislation that prohibited the secretary from proceeding with leasing.

Many issues involving federal preemption of state authority were active during the Reagan years. For more than a decade pesticide manufacturers had sought to extend the preemption provisions of the federal pesticide law beyond its application to labeling, and when Congress began to consider revisions of the act in the early 1980s, the administration threw its weight behind that plan. The states, which had evolved elaborate and varied pesticide regulatory programs, some of which were stricter than federal law, protested and were an important force in sidetracking the move.[59]

A quieter case of state resistance involved labels on household appliances with information about their energy-consumption requirements. The Carter administration felt that such labeling would enable customers to choose appliances on the basis of their efficiency in energy use. Regulations had been under way at the advent of the Reagan administration, which now sought to change them. The revised regulations not only provided for no federal labeling requirements but also prohibited the states from adopting any. Many states, however, had already taken action on their own, and their protests caused the administration to modify its strategy.

The outcomes of these struggles over preemption varied. The states did not successfully defend in the courts their attempt to pass worker right-to-know legislation that was more stringent than federal law. By 1985 another right-to-know issue had emerged in debate over revision of the Superfund toxic-cleanup law. Should its "community right-to-know" provision preempt more stringent state laws? Another battleground of even larger consequence at the time was the industry effort, fully backed by the administration, to enact general federal liability legislation that would severely restrict consumer and environmental litigation under state liability laws. The states fought vigorously to prevent such measures.[60]

The federal fish and wildlife program involved a unique case in the ability of states to shape federal policy. Traditionally these matters had been state responsibilities, and the states had long stoutly defended their prerogatives against federal action.

National-forest managers, for example, had no authority over the number of game animals harvested each year on their lands; that was decided by the states. State fish and game officials had long been organized in a national body that often acted to defend their interests. This group had prevented the administration from appointing a candidate with no professional wildlife experience or expertise as head of the Fish and Wildlife Service. In subsequent years few major controversies arose between the administration and these state leaders, largely because they represented a political force the administration left relatively unchallenged.[61]

In a number of cases the states were able to mount an offensive against administration policy. By 1985 momentum had gathered in the states to control the effects of hazardous waste, and they played a major role in persuading the administration to shift its strategy on that issue. The states generally wished the federal government to move faster to control hazardous air emissions, to dispose of hazardous wastes, to clean up existing hazardous-waste sites under the Superfund, to protect groundwater, and to control acid rain and indoor air pollution. State resources were limited, and hence the states favored federal policies that would provide them with technical expertise and program funds. Initiatives of this kind frustrated the administration's desire to transfer programs to the states.[62]

New Administration Strategies

By the spring of 1983 the administration believed that its environmental policies had become so controversial that changes were required. Anne Gorsuch and James Watt were special targets of criticism. Watt's intensely ideological and aggressive statements made prime media copy, and private meetings between EPA agency personnel and industry management on regulatory matters had become a subject of congressional investigations. Although environmentalists were concerned about a host of substantive issues, most were not reported in the media. The media were concerned more with the personalities, and it was not until these became controversial that the administration was prompted to make concessions.[63]

Gorsuch was replaced in 1983 as head of the EPA by William

Ruckelshaus, who had been the agency's first administrator during the Nixon Presidency. Convinced that the EPA had become heavily politicized by Reaganite ideology, Ruckelshaus saw his task as one of restoring its professionalism and its credibility with the public. The agency's top personnel were replaced. Ruckelshaus insisted that personnel operate "in a fishbowl," that they keep records of all their contacts with industry and make them available to the press and the public.[64]

The administration felt that quiet action could disentangle the Department of the Interior from a wide range of controversies in which Secretary Watt had embroiled it. The new secretary, William Clark, was different in personality from Watt: Low key, inclined to make no public commitments, and devoted to negotiating the department out of as many of the Watt-generated issues as possible, Clark sought to settle many current lawsuits out of court. His job was to change an image not of agency-industry collusion but of reckless action fostered by Watt's media-lively statements.[65]

Amid these changes the administration modified considerably its highly ideological approach to environmental affairs. Strident demands for deregulation in favor of the private economy were toned down sharply. Efforts to pursue the Sagebrush Rebellion and asset management were dropped. Save in a few notable cases in which regulatory efforts by the Carter administration were sidetracked, deregulation in pollution-control matters did not proceed. The major role of the Reaganites was to retard or halt emerging action on such matters as acid rain, toxic air emissions, indoor air pollution, and hazardous waste, rather than to abandon established programs. Reaganites continued to extol the private market, but in practice they drew back from its implications because such a policy was not acceptable to the nation.[66]

There were few substantive changes in policy. Congress forced the administration to abandon its strategy of ending public land acquisition through the Land and Water Conservation Fund; in 1984 the administration recommended some expenditures but not to the extent that environmentalists and Congress desired. In the case of lead in gasoline, the administration shifted its ground markedly. It had tried to put in force regulations that allowed liquid wastes to be placed in landfills or to be burned as fuel, but these aroused such strong protests that they were quickly withdrawn. It accepted the new wilderness laws and the revised Resource Conservation and Recovery Act. By 1985, new appointments in the Department of Labor indicated that some changes were in the offing with respect to policies of the Occupational Safety and Health Administration.[67]

The most fundamental change in administration strategy came in EPA science policy. The new administrator, Ruckelshaus, rejected the previous policy of limiting science advisers to the "high proof of harm" segment of the scientific community and relied for advice on a broader range of scientists. Norton Nelson was appointed to chair the EPA Science Advisory Board, and Bernard Goldstein was made assistant administrator for science and research. Acceptable to a wide range of scientists far beyond those associated with industry, their selection indicated that the EPA was on a very different course. Scientific opinion on the EPA Science Advisory Board now became more diverse and reflected more accurately the range of views in the scientific world. These changes played a major role in "depoliticizing" the agency in the eyes of the scientific and professional community.[68]

The administration's environmental views became especially clear in opposing new legislative proposals. It stoutly resisted efforts to establish controls to reduce acid rain, argued that both groundwater protection and control of toxic air pollution were state rather than federal responsibilities, opposed efforts by Congress to expand research with respect to indoor air pollution, and rejected proposals to protect parks from development of adjacent lands. It refused to make available to factory workers studies by the National Institute of Occupational Health and Safety about the health effects of chemicals to which they had been exposed. The list of positive environmental actions opposed by the administration was long.[69]

Equally significant were innumerable undramatic agency actions. The EPA, for example, argued that models were not capable of measuring the transformation of sulfur dioxide into sulfates and that air pollution transported over long distances could be controlled only where it was the crucial, rather than a contributing, factor in damage – both of which arguments became major roadblocks impeding action to control acid rain. It turned down an Environmental Defense Fund proposal to establish a comprehensive source-reduction strategy for all dioxins and their chemically related furans and continued to confine cleanups to only a few of them. It accepted the view that chemical information was proprietary, a trade secret, and should not be made widely available to the public. The EPA argued that most chemical-pollution problems were exaggerated and blamed the media for developing scare stories that made them out to be more serious than they actually were.[70]

Forced to pull back from its efforts to convey the public lands to states and private owners, the administration turned to managing lands on behalf of developmental rather than environmental goals. Plans to increase the allowable cut on the national forests and to reduce environmental objectives went forward. In the BLM, Director Burford advanced commodity objectives. Although the administration accepted the wilderness bills for the national forests when they were presented on a state-by-state basis, it did not initiate its own and continued to seek to limit wilderness proposals for BLM lands. The appointment of William Penn Mott, Jr., as the new director of the National Park Service in 1985 was widely acclaimed by environmentalists, but little evidence appeared that Mott would be able to draw on resources or encouragement beyond his own agency in order to bring about innovations in park management.[71]

The effects of budget constraints were more difficult to observe. The administration backed off from its earlier attempts to cut EPA funding further each year, and its 1985 budget restored the dollar amount to the 1981 level; this was far below the "real" figures for that year and, so environmentalists argued, was especially low in view of the agency's expanding responsibilities. The EPA replied that it was doing a better job with less money. Congressional committees challenged this. One detailed the degree to which a high percentage of operators of hazardous-waste sites had not secured the required data about leakage and the migration of chemicals from those sites. Another reported that EPA budget requests for additional funds to clean up old sites made possible only slow progress in the task. When the EPA replied that it could not use more funds, the Sierra Club conducted a survey of EPA regional offices in which personnel argued that it was the limitation of funds that prevented progress.[72]

Environmentalists complained also about lack of enforcement and by 1983 had undertaken a more vigorous litigation strategy to supplement EPA with citizen action. Water-quality permits that established allowable levels of discharge were available to the public; so also were the periodic reports on effluents submitted by the dischargers. To identify violators, environmentalists simply took the reports and compared them with the permits. They brought more than four hundred lawsuits for violations of the permits. Dischargers complained bitterly; the EPA, they argued, had previously accepted their violations and agreed not to take legal action against them. They would be more careful in the future in agreeing to the terms of permits.[73]

Two factors played a special role in these limited but important changes in administration environmental activities. One was the influence within the Republican party of a group that supported environmental objectives and could moderate policy from within the party. The Democratic House played an important role as gadfly in exposing administration actions, but environmental Republicans, especially in the Senate, exercised a quieter but often greater influence. The continued existence of the Council on Environmental Quality, even in a severely restricted form, was a result of their influence, and much of the administration's response was shaped by its desire not to alienate an important segment of the party.

Even more important was the desire of the administration to become more respectable from a professional point of view. From its inception, technical and managerial professionals had been wary of the administration's ideological inclinations. Although they did not want to identify themselves with vigorous environmental progress, they were offended by attempts to establish ideological and political tests for scientific advisers and by the tendency of the OMB to take a cavalier attitude toward identifying environmental costs and benefits. They were more than gratified by the return to the EPA of William Ruckelshaus, with his avowed strategy of restoring professionalism to the agency.[74]

These changes were more of style than of substance – the substitution of management for ideology, and adherence to some of the accepted norms of fairness in the treatment of political demands. Although the new administrators often were willing to talk with environmentalists and listen to their views, and were eager to follow acceptable rules of administrative procedure, they did not display enthusiasm for environmental objectives. While they backed off from their intense attacks of the first two years of the administration, they now adopted a strategy of quieter action to keep them in check. This required a careful balancing of publicized interest in a minimally acceptable program with a shift of antienvironmental strategies into arenas of political choice that were more difficult to observe.

These moves and countermoves on the part of the Reagan administration and advocates of environmental objectives revealed several new balances of power between them. Within the federal government the contest produced a standoff. When the political force of public environmental desires became too great, the administration backed down, and when the administration became so zealous that it acted in disregard of established procedures or the intent of legislation, it was forced to change tactics. At the same time, however, the administration could effectively check most innovations in environmental policy that were ripe for action.

In the face of public resistance to its innovations in environmental policy, the administration perfected its major source of power – executive authority. Through a variety of devices emanating from the Executive Office of the President, it was able to exercise crucial control over environmental policy. Through the OMB it was able to bring the agencies more directly under its control and away from influence exercised by Congress and the courts. Through reduced funding and preemption of authority, it blunted the innovative actions of states. It was able to guide and direct the day-to-day choices of administrators into channels of restraint on environmental objectives in favor of developmental ones.

The larger drama of environmental affairs, however, lay in the interaction between broader environmental demands from the public and resistance to them from the Reagan executive office. The administration failed to eradicate what it considered to be ill-conceived environmental desires and wants. The public rejected the private-market ideology in environmental affairs and thereby moved the administration slightly back toward the mainstream of American politics. Administration policies aroused and mobilized the public. Yet they also served to blunt environmental efforts far more than had those of previous administrations. The Reaganites did not prevent environmentalists from making gains, but their antienvironmental revolution throttled them considerably. Once the administration had modified its confrontational style, which had been fostered by such figures as Watt and Gorsuch, its opposition became more effective.

The Reagan administration's policies demonstrate both the strength of the social changes that lay behind modern environmental affairs and the ability of the executive branch to work its will in the face of persistent political demands. Both were powerful forces in modern American politics. Two decades of environmental affairs, the 1960s and 1970s, had outlined those two sets of forces; the strategies of the Reagan administration delineated them even more sharply.

16 Environmental Society and Environmental Politics

Environmental affairs encompassed a surprisingly wide range of events and activities. The issues around which controversy swirled permeated the economy and society, science and technology, personal values and national policy, immediate preoccupations and future generations. They reflected innovations in the private market and new public responsibilities in local, state, and national governments. It was remarkable that such massive changes infused such a large sphere of life in such a short span of time. Because these events were so central and pervasive, they highlight aspects of American society and politics that are well worth exploring.

The Transformation of Values

We begin with the centrality of value change. Some have argued that environmental objectives were superficial and peripheral rather than fundamental and central in American life. The evidence argues otherwise. The importance ascribed to the quality of one's environment can be understood only by comprehending changes that came to millions of people amid their daily activities at work, home, and play.

In the previous pages we attempted to understand the broader

527

setting of these value changes, their social roots, their variation throughout the nation, and their roles in historical developments in the years after World War II. From this angle of vision the environmental interest was an expression of deeply rooted human aspirations for a better life. One cannot delve into the details of environmental action without observing the hope for personal and social achievement that lay at its roots. The casual observer might focus on negative attitudes, which could easily be found, but on a deeper level one finds a desire to reach out to create and enlarge both personal and civic life.

It is well to focus on the evolution of human aspirations – elusive, mysterious, yet powerful. Aspiration is not fully implicit in the minds and hearts of humans independent of circumstance. It grows and changes, develops and evolves. One understands much of modern history as a result of changes in human experience and vision, the twists and turns of what is thought of as achievable for oneself, one's community, and one's society. The evolution of human awareness, an expanding sense of possibilities for self and society, of one's capacity to shape the course of human affairs, constitutes a profound aspect of modern history.

These enlarged perspectives have changed with setting and time. We are struck with the differences in American society between the first and the last thirds of the twentieth century; although it is important to emphasize the social, economic, and governmental changes that took place over those years, it is equally important to stress the changes in the nature of human desire for achievement. Environmental affairs places all this on center stage.

We are especially struck by the creative role science and technology played in environmental objectives. From the beginning of our inquiry into these matters we confronted a remarkable contrast. Much writing about environmentalists identifies them as hostile to science and technology. But on almost every side we found that they reached out in positive ways to demand that environmental science be pushed forward and technological innovations be brought on line more rapidly so as to bring about greater social benefits. Environmentalists played an important role in pressing for advanced inquiry and served as an instrument in the transfer of scientific knowledge from discovery to application.

The debates over how scarce funds for research and development should be deployed were not debates over the legitimacy of technology. On the contrary, they were debates over its direction. Many technological innovations that environmentalists espoused came, in fact, to be more extensively applied: the electronically integrated internal combustion engine, energy efficiency, the photovoltaic cell, fluid-bed combustion, integrated pest management, and organic agriculture. These were cases in which environmentalists often were pioneers in advocating new technologies that, when they later became more widespread, few associated with them.

The expression of environmental aspiration was infused with a sense of place. People thought of environmental quality in terms of where they lived or worked or engaged in recreation. We have sought to focus on this vital aspect of both the roots of environmental action and the mode of its political organization by shaping the analysis of issues in terms of the city, the wildlands, the countryside, and the broader experience of the toxic environment, each a different expression of the factor of place.

It was this sense of place that undergirded not only the defense of home and community, on the one hand, and a pleasant and healthy workplace, on the other, but also the protection of natural environments at some distance from home and work that were thought of as integral to one's quality of life. The common phrase that brought together home and more remote natural environments was "backyard." Opponents of hazardous-waste sites said emphatically "not in my backyard," and urban wilderness advocates spoke of their prized wildlands as their own backyard. It was axiomatic in environmental politics that those places that inspired defenders stood a greater chance of protection than those that did not. No wonder the most bitter battles were fought over places to which people had become attached.

Several other features of environmental politics underlined the significance of the values on which it rested. One was the intensity of the opposition, which was persistent, often uncompromising, and many times successful. At the root of these controversies was not just "interest" in the conventional sense of an economic stake but values. The economic interest of producers undergirded their opposition. But at a deeper level of human response was the degree to which producers' values were offended. They could not accept the notion that what environmentalists thought was useful and valuable was, in fact, so. They were fearful of the new in American values, and that fear occasionally expressed itself in a burst of paranoia that tended to attribute change to conspiracy. But even more evenhanded opposition from producers constituted a reluctant political acceptance of something they did not seem to understand and did not share.

Equally striking was the degree to which environmental controversies over science, economics, and planning seemed to point to differences in values. Once again one can identify much here in the way of immediate economic benefits. But there was far more to it than that. Scientists of equal training and competence assessed the meaning of facts differently, drew different conclusions from the same evidence, gave different quantitative weights to factors in economic analysis and planning, all because different ways of looking at the world affected their analyses. Investigation into the roots of such controversies leads back to such intangible but powerful human factors.

A focus on environmental values and action as mainstream phenomena in American life is underlined by their persistence. Despite resistance to them, they have continued to work their influence in public life with regularity and strength. At times one can discern an ebb and flow such as the decline in interest in secondary effects of air pollution after 1970 and their revival in the acid-rain issue of the late 1970s. At other times one can identify an enduring evolution such as the wilderness movement, which seemed to become more deeply rooted, more firmly organized, and more successful with the passage of time. On still other occasions one can observe the growth of new concerns such as the drive to eliminate landfills as a means of disposing of hazardous waste, an important feature of the revised Resource Conservation and Recovery Act of 1984.

The depth of the social roots of environmental values was illustrated sharply during the Reagan administration, amid the most forceful challenge environmentalists had yet encountered. That administration was determined to reverse two decades of environmental gains across the board, from the 1965 Land and Water

Conservation Fund as a source of funds for public-land purchases to the battery of pollution-control laws to the environmental science that underpinned regulatory strategies to measures to promote energy efficiency and solar energy. The historical experiment the Reagan administration undertook, in which executive power in the presidential office was used to make radical changes in public policy, presented environmentalists with an almost unsuperable obstacle. That confrontation was a challenge to prove that environmental affairs had sufficiently deep and wide roots to constitute an effective obstacle to these strategies for sweeping change.

These administrative initiatives generated their own counterforce. They energized latent values, stimulated environmental activism, brought the support of numbers and financial resources to environmental organizations, helped environmentalists to build institutions at the state level, and activated them more aggressively to participate in electoral politics. While the environmental opposition held power in the executive branch from which it could effectively implement its efforts to turn back past gains, environmentalists worked through Congress and the courts to check the president's efforts. Even during the ensuing stalemate the administration could not halt some progress and approved congressional efforts to make significant additions to the wilderness system, as well as improve the hazardous-waste disposal program. Both the resistance and the limited gains testified to the depth of environmental affairs in American society.

The Environmental Constitution

To most Americans the nation's constitution is a written document interpreted by the courts. But the broad outline of the American constitution, like that of the British, consists of institutional arrangements that have evolved over the years, often with little reference to the document of 1787, the product of two centuries of social, economic, and political change. These changes continued amid the transformations of the decades after World War II. And to these changes environmental politics made important contributions.

One of these pertained to the mechanisms through which the public participated in governing. The environmental movement gave rise to a high degree of citizen involvement in legislative, administrative, and judicial affairs. In so doing it influenced the evolution of political representation.

The initial strategy of environmentalists was to perfect a system of group representation that had long been practiced by organizations in business, agriculture, and labor. In this they were quite successful. From the late 1960s onward they developed skills in legislative strategy, litigation, and administrative politics. They were able to attract significant segments of the public who wished to contribute personally to shaping public policy. Membership in the two litigation organizations, the Natural Resources Defense Council and the Environmental Defense Fund, for example, exceeded 40,000; yet few, if any of these members, it could be argued, had a direct stake in the outcomes of lawsuits those organizations pursued. Their support came from a more general commitment to environmental objectives as public objectives.

We should understand these actions as expanding political opportunity. When interest groups first emerged, they were looked on with fear on the ground that they restricted political expression, then conducted primarily through parties; they were a distortion of traditional practices, even alien to American politics. But those groups formed because for many people party had become a relatively ineffective instrument for expressing political concerns. Parties reflected so many demands from varied constituencies that they tended to compromise all into pale versions of what each segment of the body politic wanted. Hence those who wished to pursue clearly defined political objectives chose to organize for action with others of like mind.

At first organizations in business, agriculture, and labor dominated this process. After World War II, consumer groups, among them environmentalists, took it up. They challenged their opponents with their own strategies. These organizations enabled environmentalists to exercise some control over a governing system that often appeared to be remote and not subject to influence. They facilitated political participation despite a system in which involvement through voting by party was steadily declining.

A major aspect of changes in political participation was the changing character of its inequality. Throughout American history marked inequality in political participation and influence has persisted. In earlier times it was manifested primarily in restrictions on the right to vote. But as new kinds of participation arose, so did new political inequalities. Not all people became organized in interest groups, and those that did not had far less political influence than those that did. The rise of new groups tended to expand representation as women, environmentalists, the elderly, and consumers began to challenge formerly dominant producers. But political inequality was still commonplace, and environmental politics sharply emphasized its persistence and its detail.

There were large discrepancies in the number of lobbyists that environmentalists and developmentalists could muster, the funds they could raise for electoral as well as legislative battle, their ability to finance referendum campaigns, their public-relations activities, their development and use of attitude surveys that could be used as political weapons, and their capacity to conduct research and to bring scientific and technical expertise to bear on governmental decisions.

Environmental politics sharply etched a new stage in the history of political inequality in which the primary element lay in differences in the capacity to generate, transmit, and apply information. In the degree to which it involved technical matters, environmental politics was typical of many types of modern political controversy. The language of political debate required that one technical argument be met with another, that some way be found to confront the technical strategies of developmentalists with similar technical weapons.

But resources were limited. Environmentalists could carry out an effective strategy based on literature reviews and assessments of published research, and they often could recruit individual experts to testify on their behalf. But they could not match the resources of their opponents to generate research in the first place or employ as many experts. Often they had to rely either on pro bono work by attorneys or professional specialists or on funds derived from the awarding of court costs.

In the face of evidence about political inequality one is taken aback by environmental successes. Although some of these resulted from selective and artful application of limited resources, many also can be attributed to public support. In the eyes of the public, environmentalists were far more credible than were developmentalists. A survey by the DuPont Corporation in 1983 reported that whereas 74 percent of the public was "very or somewhat confident" of the views expressed by environmentalists, only 30 percent held a similar opinion about the views expressed by large corporations. Environmentalists continually relied on public support to help them overcome the inequality in resources they faced in struggles with developmentalists.

Another constitutional innovation in the Environmental Era took place in the relationships among the various formal institutions of government – the legislature, courts, and executive, on the one hand, and the levels of government from township and ward, through city, county, and state, to the federal government, on the other. Relationships among these governmental bodies changed over the years. As indicated so often in the preceding chapters, they continued to be shaped, in part, by environmental politics. This came about not so much because of new constitutional doctrine but because of the changing roles played by each branch of government in political controversy; decisions continually modified the respective powers and relationships of each branch.

Environmental politics involved a steady upward flow of authority from local to state governments. State law often prohibited local governments from enacting environmental standards stricter than those called for by state statutes. Most of these changes came about quietly in state laws dealing with wetlands, strip mining, and hazardous-waste disposal. Taken together these actions added up to a major change in the relative balance between local and state authority. From the standpoint of formal constitutional matters these changes were relatively unimportant because local governments were creatures of the states and had no constitutional claim to autonomy. But if one thinks of constitutional matters as institutional arrangements rather than as powers explicitly stated in documents, these shifts in authority involved major constitutional changes.

There were also innovations in the relationships between state and federal governments. Federal law often kept the door open for state action beyond minimal federal requirements. States were subject to demands from developmentalists to keep action within those minimal limits, but they also responded to environmental demands from their citizens to take more advanced action. Developmentalists, in turn, sought to enhance federal power and authority to preempt state action. This two-way set of pressures on state government, one arising from greater state authority in its power to override local government and the other from initiatives for federal preemption of state power, gave states a distinctive role in environmental constitutional development.

Equally significant changes took place in relationships among the federal legislative, judicial, and executive branches. Courts and Congress came to be receptive to environmental efforts while the executive branch sought to restrain them. Congress distrusted the agencies and, in the face of administrative temporizing, sought to force action through deadlines, mandating rules in specific cases, requiring precise standards rather than simply giving agencies general authority, and conducting oversight inquiries to determine if agencies had carried out the law. Many argued that this specificity in legislation was constitutionally undesirable, that agencies should be given freedom to make choices according to their own lights. But change was in the opposite direction as legislative oversight tended to identify agency recalcitrance and environmentalists demanded that agencies be forced to carry out the law.

Even more striking was the changing relationship between the Executive Office of the President, on the one hand, and both Congress and the agencies, on the other. Over the years presidents had sought to enhance their own authority by checking the initiatives of Congress and by bringing agencies into line by restraining their freedom to act. These tendencies greatly accelerated under the Reagan administration. The Office of Management and Budget ventured into ever tighter control of agencies by demanding power to approve not only budgets but also actions such as publication of annual reports that might make recommendations implying additional expenditures. At the same time, Reagan administrators made clear that they would use the budget to change policy, to prevent the implementation of legislation Congress approved.

The Reagan administration greatly enhanced the power of the

Executive Office of the President (EOP) in its relationship with the states, Congress, and the agencies. The EOP supported measures to extend federal preemption of state authority in a wide range of environmental policies, such as offshore oil drilling, "right to know" regulations in occupational health, energy-efficiency standards, and allowable levels of pesticide residues in food. It also severely eroded the ability of states to engage in environmental government, by reducing grants to enhance their management capabilities.

A new aspect of the age-old problem of individual liberty – access to information to enable people to act in the face of environmental hazards – was a third contribution of environmental politics to constitutional development. In some cases this came to be known as the right to know. Although that phrase pertained solely to the right to information about toxic chemicals to which one might be exposed, it was part of a wider issue of access to environmental information in general. Here was information known to some who were responsible for potential harm but kept from those who might be its victims. Some described such matters as questions of fairness; others, as ethical issues. They involved questions of personal liberty and freedom in the face of powerful institutions, both private and public.

Information played an overarching role in modern political debate; hence the concern over its availability. It was not simply a question of censorship as an infringement of freedom; rather, it concerned the need to have access to information because it played such a crucial role in public affairs. Such questions were intimately involved in environmental matters: the Freedom of Information Act enabled one to acquire information from governmental files to document a case; the use of discovery in legal proceedings gave one the right to ferret out evidence in the files of one's adversary; an open trial placed evidence on the record to be available to all parties in the case; the environmental-impact statement made hard-to-get information about developmental proposals widely available.

An increasingly important aspect of this problem was access to information in the files of private corporations that was withheld on the grounds that it was proprietary and hence could not be divulged. Did those affected have a right to this information?

Environmentalists made some inroads into this privilege to withhold information: the availability of information about industrial water-pollution discharges, which facilitated citizen action to enforce the terms of permits; the requirement that medical records of employees be made available for epidemiological studies; the provision in right-to-know laws that data sheets be available to workers and community residents so that they would know the chemicals to which they were exposed.

It is difficult to overemphasize the extent to which battles over the availability of information played a fundamental role in environmental controversy. Traditional practices in which private corporations and business groups worked out their strategies behind closed doors came under fire; over the course of the 1970s, such proceedings as in the case of the lead issue described earlier became more open. The Reagan administration once again sought to restore such closed negotiations between industry and the EPA in deciding whether certain chemicals thought to be toxic should be regulated. But the protest this evoked from environmentalists, the media, and scientists played a major role in discrediting the EPA under Anne Gorsuch. Her successor, William Ruckelshaus, restored the more open process of decision making, which had been slowly evolving in previous years.

Open decision making was fostered by the courts under the Administrative Procedures Act of 1946. Information on which regulatory action was based was to be placed in the public record so it could be subject to public scrutiny; ex parte communications with interested parties after the record was closed were prohibited. This restricted industry attempts to work out private arrangements with administrators.

But industry soon found other ways of reaching the same objectives by working through the Executive Office of the President and especially the Office of Management and Budget. Here executive privilege was asserted to prevent disclosure of negotiations between government and business, and the courts declined to extend to the presidential level their rule that proceedings be on the record.

Freedom of information and the right to know were the more prominent slogans in the struggle over the availability of information necessary for political action. The world of technical information, which was the language and the substance of environmental debate, provided a new context for the exercise or restraint of liberty. The issue was no longer simply the right to speak and be heard, but the right to have access to information that was crucial for successful public action.

The Political Legitimacy of Managerial-Technical Institutions

The preceding pages have placed considerable emphasis on the distinctive role of managers and technical professionals in environmental politics. Three decades of environmental debate, from the mid-1950s to the mid-1980s, witnessed considerable erosion of public confidence in their detachment and evenhandedness.

A continuous round of disputes over the meaning of science, economic analysis, and planning generated a sense that the outcomes of such inquiries depended as much on value commitments and cleverness at analyzing data as on technical and professional skill. Perennial confrontations with public agencies in which those agencies seemed to resist rather than facilitate action to implement environmental objectives diminished confidence in them. On all sides there seemed to be a struggle over the facts, with many on the technical and managerial side seeking to obscure details while environmentalists sought to bring them to light.

Since the mid-nineteenth century the evolution of managerial and technical institutions had constituted a major formative influence in American life. These institutions created systems of increasing scope and scale and fostered a persistent upward flow of decision making, thereby altering the source of power and authority in both private and public affairs.

This managerial order claimed political legitimacy on the ground of the benefit it bestowed on society from the material production it generated. The transforming influence of larger-scale systems of organization was detrimental to earlier ways of life. Smaller-scale institutions such as residential communities and older forms of production were swept aside in the onrushing pace of modern technology and organization. This harm was argued to be both inevitable and justifiable in the course of progress; material progress was worth the price.

In return for these benefits Americans accepted a reduction in their political influence. Most issues in public life, not the least of which concerned the appropriate arrangements of power and control, were debated in terms of popular legitimacy. But institutional development took place in the opposite direction, in which political power evolved in a more concentrated rather than a more widely distributed fashion.

Thus, in the years between 1897 and 1929, methods of representation and the powers of executive officers in municipal government became increasingly centralized, and authority over roads and schools shifted from local to state government. Under the banner of efficiency in administration, public affairs at all levels were shaped by the centralizing tendencies of modern management. So long as the benefits continued to flow in a manner acceptable to the majority of people, management claims to legitimacy had considerable force. The rising level of personal standards of living persuaded Americans to accept inequalities in the economic and political order that created the benefits they enjoyed.

After World War II, challenges to this legitimacy increased. There were persistent demands that work be made more creative and meaningful. Others became satiated with the material goods the system produced. And still others sought to advance their condition of life by emphasizing qualitative concerns – among them, the quality of their environment – many of which the managerial order did not seem able to satisfy. These concerns about substantive results were accompanied by a change in political mood in the form of a challenge to the political legitimacy of managerial leadership. In this, environmental politics played a major role.

Over the course of environmental debate a pattern of political give-and-take emerged in which managerial authorities sought to assert facts and the public was skeptical of those assertions and sought further information. There was always more than met the eye. Both environmental groups and the media engaged in a constant task of using freedom-of-information inquiries to bring facts to light, pressing Congress to undertake investigations, pursuing the legal process of discovery to obtain information from corporate files, and searching for alternative sources of data from other experts both at home and abroad. The ongoing series of episodes arising from these efforts tended to structure environmental politics as a contest between the public in its desire to unearth the facts and managerial authorities who seemed uneager to disclose them.

Political legitimacy on the part of managerial and technical leaders involved values as well as information. There were struggles not only over the availability and interpretation of facts but also over the acceptability of values. One aspect of this was the degree to which new values associated with natural environments should become legitimate human aspirations fostered by public policy. The public sought to bring to the fore the notion that natural environments were valuable and should be a central aspect of environmental progress, but those in positions of managerial leadership minimized these goals in favor of their own commitments to more traditional types of commodity development.

There was a similar reluctance of that leadership to move forward rapidly toward higher levels of personal health, toward wellness and optimum fitness, with a shift in emphasis from the acute effects of high-level exposures to the chronic effects of lower ones. Managers seemed more concerned with reducing developmental costs than with increasing environmental benefits. The focus of environmental demands lay in the expansion of health and well-being and the organization of science and technology to serve that end. But managers were slow to act, scientists demanded higher levels of proof, and those in charge of production were concerned more with the profitability of existing technologies than with the rapid deployment of new ones.

By the 1980s the managerial and technical leadership had also tended to assert that the general public would have to accept a permanent level of human and environmental contamination as a price of material progress. Whereas environmentalists continued to press for technological innovations that would constantly lower the levels of pollution of the air, land, and water, environmental managers argued that that was impossible and viewed the persistent demand for environmental progress as politically unacceptable. It was not reasonable to allocate resources to achieve higher levels of quality in the chemical environment.

These differences in values, as well as in credibility and use of information, tended to shape politics in a way that emphasized the separation between the public and the managerial and technical leadership. The two worlds had different starting points of experience from which ideas and action sprang. For the public, immediate human wants and needs, associated with the activities of daily life, were the roots of values and action. From this context came ideas about larger affairs through which one expressed the implications of personal values and aspiration for public policy. But managers were preoccupied with the organization of large-scale systems of resource production and delivery; for them it was relatively easy to argue that the decentralizing influences of elemental human aspirations should be overruled in the face of more pressing demands generated by the larger system.

In earlier years when human wants and needs had been dominated by those the production system excelled in generating, the tension implicit in those two worlds had not moved towards overt controversy. But now matters had changed. Wants and needs now evolved in a direction the system could not readily take, and this resulted in a degree of skepticism about the ability of that system to produce. What the public now wanted the system was often unprepared to supply, and at times it was extremely hostile toward those desires. Hence the managerial and technical order, admired for its ability to produce in some realms, came to be questioned in others.

Values and Limits

Throughout these twists and turns of environmental politics two broad forces were at work. One was the new values that emerged in the years after World War II, deeply rooted in changing demography, improved standards of health and living, and enhanced levels of human aspiration. Environmental politics involves the working out of these historic changes in what people sought to think, be, and do. The other was the private and public apparatus that constituted the organizational society – the managerial institutions devised to shape the social and political order according to leaders' views of what was desirable and, in so doing, to discipline the lives of others.

From the public came demands for environmental improvement and progress. From the managerial world of science, technology, economic analysis, and planning came the message that aspiration was on the point of outrunning resources. It is ironic that in erecting such doubts about environmental demands the nation's institutional leaders were insisting on the limits to growth many of them often vigorously denied. The world, they argued, simply could not be made as healthful or clean or safe or as filled with natural beauty as the environmental public seemed to want. One would have to settle for less.

It was a curious twist that environmentalists were the purveyors of optimism about the possibilities of human achievement while the administrative and technical leaders were the constant bearers of bad news. In the media the roles were reversed: Environmentalists warned of impending catastrophe, while the technical leadership exuded optimism.

But to remain on this level of media understanding seems not to fit the evidence about what people did and the values implicit in their actions. The driving forces behind environmental affairs were hope and confidence about the possibilities for a better life; there was a constant search for the very latest in science and technology to harness to that aspiration. And their opponents, who in the grand debates over limits expressed confidence about the future, were constantly warning environmentalists that their demands were outstripping resources.

Such discrepancies between what people do and the way they think and speak about what they do are not unique; they are the stock-in-trade of sensitive historical analysis that is concerned with self-images as well as actions. So we need not pause to unravel inconsistencies inherent in daily human life. It is interesting, however, that the growing mass middle class, in seeking to shape a newer world revolving around its values and conceptions about the good life, gave expression to precisely the rising standard of living the managerial and technical leadership professed to extol.

But, like Karl Marx's proletariat, the mass middle class turned out differently from what its creators sought, and it began to demand that the production system generate environmental goods and services for themselves and their children. One harks back to an observation by Adam Smith: "Consumption is the sole end and purpose of all production; and the interest of the producer ought to be attended to, only in so far as it may be necessary for promoting that of the consumer. The maxim is so perfectly self-evident, that it would be absurd to attempt to prove it." Such was the challenge of the environmental movement to the prevailing managerial institutions of America.[1]

Notes

In the notes I have occasionally used the abbreviation "AF" to indicate that the item is located in my personal file.

1. From Conservation to Environment

1. Samuel P. Hays, *Conservation and the Gospel of Efficiency* (Cambridge, Mass., 1968), and "From Conservation to Environment: Environmental Politics in the United States since World War Two," *Environmental Review,* 6(Fall 1982): 14–41.

2. William E. Smythe, *The Conquest of Arid America* (New York, 1905); Robert H. Boyle, John Graves, and T. H. Watkins, *The Water Hustlers* (San Francisco, 1971); Remi A. Nadeau, *The Water Seekers* (New York, 1950).

3. William E. Leuchtenburg, *Flood Control Politics; The Connecticut River Valley Problem, 1927–1950* (Cambridge, Mass., 1953); Arthur Maass, *Muddy Waters* (Cambridge, Mass., 1951); David E. Lilienthal, *TVA: Democracy on the March* (New York, 1944).

4. U.S. Senate, 60th Cong., 1st sess., *Preliminary Report of the Inland Waterways Commission,* Sen. Doc. 325, 19; *Newsletter,* Tennessee Citizens for Wilderness Planning (Oak Ridge, Tenn.).

5. R. Douglas S. MacDonald, "Multiple Use Forestry in Megalopolis: A Case Study of the Evolution of Forest Policies and Programs in Connecticut" (Ph.D. diss., Yale University, 1969); Ben W. Twight, *Organizational Values and Political Power* (University Park, Pa., 1983).

6. Michael Williams, "Ohio: Microcosm of Agricultural Clearing in the Mid-West" (Paper delivered at a symposium on global trade and deforestation in the nineteenth century, Oakland University, Rochester, Mich., May 1981).

7. Gifford Pinchot, *Breaking New Ground* (New York, 1947); M. Nelson McGeary, *Gifford Pinchot: Forester-Politician* (Princeton, N.J., 1960); Harold T. Pinkett, *Gifford Pinchot: Private and Public Forester* (Urbana, Ill., 1970); Harold K. Steen, *The U.S. Forest Service* (Seattle, Wash., 1976); Michael Frome, *The Forest Service* (New York, 1971).

8. Ronald F. Lockmann, *Guarding the Forests of Southern California* (Glendale, Calif., 1981); Hays, *Conservation and the Gospel of Efficiency;* G. Michael McCarthy, *Hour of Trial; The Conservation Conflict in Colorado and the West, 1891–1970* (Norman, Okla., 1977).

9. William E. Shands and Robert G. Healy, *The Lands Nobody Wanted* (Washington, D.C., 1977); Norman John Schmaltz, "Cutover Land Crusade: The Michigan Forest Conservation Movement, 1899–1931" (Ph.D. diss., University of Michigan, 1972); Vernon Carstenson, *Farms or Forests; Evolution of*

544

a *State Land Policy for Northern Wisconsin, 1850–1932* (Madison, Wis., 1958); William G. Robbins, *Lumberjacks and Legislators* (College Station, Tex., 1982), 208–10.

10. Stuart Chase, *Rich Land, Poor Land* (New York, 1936); Paul B. Sears, *Deserts on the March* (Norman, Okla., 1935).

11. U.S. Department of Agriculture, *Soils and Men* (Washington, D.C., 1938); Tom Dale and Vernon Carter, *Topsoil and Civilization* (Norman, Okla., 1955); Edward G. Cheney and Throvald Schantz-Hansen, *This Is Our Land* (St. Paul, Minn., 1946).

12. Hugh H. Bennett, *Elements of Soil Conservation* (New York, 1947); Wellington Brink, *Big Hugh: The Father of Soil Conservation* (New York, 1951).

13. R. Neil Sampson, *For Love of the Land* (League City, Tex., 1985).

14. James B. Trefethen, *An American Crusade for Wildlife* (New York, 1975).

15. John F. Reiger, *American Sportsmen and the Origins of Conservation* (New York, 1975); Michael J. Bean, *The Evolution of National Wildlife Law* (Washington, D.C., 1970).

16. James A. Tober, *Who Owns the Wildlife?* (Westport, Conn., 1981).

17. Fish and Wildlife Service, *Environmental Impact Statement; Federal Aid in Fish and Wildlife Restoration Program* (Washington, D.C., 1978).

18. *National Audubon* (New York, National Audubon Society); *National Wildlife* (Washington, D.C., National Wildlife Federation). As early as 1958 the Fish and Wildlife Service reported that of the 9,100,000 visitors to the refuges, 60 percent were appreciative users and only $3\frac{1}{2}$ percent were hunters; *National Wildlands News,* Dec. 1959, 1–6.

19. Interview with Carl Holcomb, 1934 editor of *Michigan Forests,* the student magazine of the University of Michigan School of Forestry, Blacksburg, Va., Oct. 10, 1978.

20. *Journal of Forestry* (Washington, D.C., Society of American Foresters).

21. In 1972 the statement of principles of the League of Women Voters was changed, at the request of leagues around the country. Formerly one such principle had read: "The League of Women Voters believes that responsible government should promote conservation and development of natural resources in the public interest and promote a stable and expanding economy." The words "development" and "expanding" were now dropped. This "signaled a change in emphasis from development to conservation." See statement of Ruth Clusen in *Proceedings, National Watershed Congress,* 19th National Watershed Congress (San Diego, Calif., 1972), 126.

22. William U. Chandler, *Investing in Children* (Washington, D.C.: Worldwatch Institute, 1985).

23. James Belasco, *Americans on the Road: From Autocamp to Motel, 1910–1945* (Cambridge, Mass., 1979); Joseph H. Engbeck, Jr., and Philip Hyde, *State Parks of California from 1864 to the Present* (Portland, Oreg., 1980).

24. Mary Keys Watson, "Behavorial and Environmental Aspects of Recreational Land Sales" (Ph.D. diss., Pennsylvania State University, 1975).

25. Roderick Nash, *Wilderness and the American Mind* (New Haven, Conn., 1967).

26. Division of State Planning and Community Affairs, Commonwealth of Virginia, *Preliminary Report on the Virginia Wetlands Act; The First Year* (Richmond, Va., 1973); Richard J. Angello et al., *Coastal Zone Recreational Activity and Potential Demand of Delaware Residents,* University of Delaware, College of Marine Sciences, DEL-SG-8-77 (Newark, Del., 1977); Stephen R. Kellert,

American Attitudes, Knowledge and Behaviors toward Wildlife and Natural Habitats (Washington, D.C.: U.S. Fish and Wildlife Service, 1979–81).

27. Desert Protective Council, *El Paisano* (Banning, Calif.); American Council for the Arts, *Americans and the Arts* (New York, 1981), 37; Time-Life Books, *American Wilderness Series* (New York, 1974–6); Field Research Corp., *California Public Opinion and Behavior Regarding the California Desert*, Bureau of Land Management (Riverside, Calif. 1977); the Gallup Organization, Inc., *National Opinion Concerning the California Desert Conservation Area* (Washington, D.C.: Bureau of Land Management, 1978).

28. For asbestos see Irving J. Selikoff and Douglas H. K. Lee, *Asbestos and Disease* (New York, 1978), 3–32; Paul Brodeur, *Expendable Americans* (New York, 1973).

29. Thomas H. Corbett, *Cancer and Chemicals* (Chicago, 1977); Samuel S. Epstein, *The Politics of Cancer* (San Francisco, 1978); Ralph W. Moss, *The Cancer Syndrome* (New York, 1980); Edith Efron, *The Apocalyptics* (New York, 1984).

30. Nicholas A. Ashford, *Crisis in the Workplace* (Cambridge, Mass., 1977); Daniel M. Berman, *Death on the Job* (New York, 1978).

31. Bertram W. Carnow, "The 'Urban Factor' and Lung Cancer: Cigarette Smoking or Air Pollution?" *Environmental Health Perspectives*, 22(1978): 17–21; *Art Hazards Newsletter* (New York).

32. Environmental Defense Fund and Robert H. Boyle, *Malignant Neglect* (New York, 1979), 82–101.

33. "It is out-of-date to think of health solely in negative terms – as the absence of disease and disability. The healthy individual is not merely unsick. He is strong, aware of his powers and eager to use them. . . . The truly healthful environment is not merely safe but stimulating." Dr. William H. Stewart, Surgeon General, quoted in *Environmental Science and Technology*, 2(1968): 21.

34. Kimon Valaskakis et al., *The Conserver Society* (New York, 1979).

35. The Ann Arbor Ecology Center, one of the first and one of the few still in existence, has an extensive file of its own environmental activities and those of other early ecology centers.

36. Series, "Ecology Primer," by Arnold R. Chalfant, *National Wildlife*, beginning Aug.-Sept. 1971, 38–41, and in subsequent issues. The magazine's editor cited the Kaibab deer case in his introduction to the third installment, "How Nature Keeps Its Balance," *National Wildlife*, 10(Feb.-Mar. 1972): 42–3.

37. *Nuclear Information* (St. Louis); *Science and the Citizen* (St. Louis).

38. Rachel Carson, *Silent Spring* (Boston, 1962); Thomas Dunlap, *DDT; Scientists, Citizens and Public Policy* (Princeton, N.J., 1981).

39. Arnold R. Chalfant, "Water Rules the World," Ecology Primer Part I, *National Wildlife*, 9(July-Aug. 1971): 38–41.

40. Barry Commoner, *The Closing Circle* (New York, 1971).

41. *The Interpreter* (Brookville, Ohio); *Organic Gardening; Environmental Action Bulletin* (Emmaus, Pa.); "Rodale's Food Empire Flourishes – Naturally," in *CNI Weekly Report*, May 13, 1982, 4–5 (Washington, D.C., Consumer Nutrition Institute).

42. *Whole Foods; The Natural Foods Business Journal* (Irvine, Calif.); *Whole Food Natural Foods Guide* (Berkeley, Calif., 1979), 268–74.

43. *Prevention* (Emmaus, Pa.); *Nutrition Action* (Washington, D.C., Center for Science in the Public Interest).

44. John Lobell, *The Little Green Book: A Guide to Self-reliant Living in the 80's* (Boulder, Colo.: Shambhala, 1981).

45. Robert C. Mitchell, "The Public Speaks Again: A New Environmental Survey," *Resources* (Resources for the Future), no. 60(1978): 1–6; Mitchell, "Public Opinion and Environmental Politics in the 1970s and 1980s," in Norman J. Vig and Michael E. Kraft, eds., *Environmental Policy in the 1980's: Reagan's New Agenda* (Washington, D.C., 1984), 51–74.

46. Opinion Research Corporation, *The Public's Participation in Outdoor Activities and Attitudes toward National Wilderness Areas* (Princeton, N.J., 1977).

47. R. E. Dunlap and K. D. Van Liere, "The 'New Environmental Paradigm': A Proposed Measuring Instrument and Preliminary Results," *Journal of Environmental Education,* 9(Summer 1978): 10–19.

48. Kent D. Van Liere and Riley E. Dunlap, "The Social Bases of Environmental Concern: A Review of Hypotheses, Explanations and Empirical Evidence," *Public Opinion Quarterly,* 44(1980): 181–97; Joseph Veroff, Elizabeth Douvan, and Richard A. Kulka, *The Inner American* (New York, 1981); Daniel Yankelovich, *New Rules* (New York, 1981); John Naisbett, *Megatrends* (New York, 1982).

49. Opinion Research Corporation, *Public's Participation.*

50. The Continental Group, *Toward Responsible Growth: Economic and Environmental Concern in the Balance* (Stamford, Conn., 1982).

51. U.S. Bureau of the Census, *Historical Statistics of the United States* (Washington, D.C., 1974), 396–400.

52. Advertisements for homes in the countryside and wildlands can be found in such publications as *Adirondack Life, Montana* magazine, and *Michigan Out-of-Doors.*

53. Ronald Inglehart, *The Silent Revolution* (Princeton, N.J., 1977); Lester W. Milbrath, *Environmentalists: Vanguard for a New Society* (Albany, N.Y., 1984).

54. Jane Elben Keller, *Adirondack Wilderness: A Story of Man and Nature* (Syracuse, N.Y., 1980); Philip G. Terrie, *Forever Wild: Environmental Aesthetics and the Adirondack Forest Preserve* (Philadelphia, Pa., 1985).

55. Rick Reese, *Greater Yellowstone: The National Park and Adjacent Wildlands* (Helena, Mont., 1985).

56. Rice Odell, *The Saving of San Francisco Bay* (Washington, D.C., 1972); John Capper, Garrett Power, and Frank R. Shivers, Jr., *Chesapeake Waters: Pollution, Public Health, and Public Opinion, 1607–1972* (Centerville, Md., 1983).

57. Marilyn E. Weigold, *The American Mediterranean: An Environmental, Economic and Social History of Long Island Sound* (Port Washington, N.Y., 1974).

58. Alfred Runte, *National Parks: The American Experience* (Lincoln, Nebr., 1979).

59. A. Y. Gunter, *The Big Thicket* (New York, 1971); Charles W. Boylen, ed., *The Lake George Ecosystem* (Lake George, N.Y., 1981).

60. Kevin Lynch, *Images of the City* (Cambridge, Mass., 1963).

2. Variation and Pattern in the Environmental Impulse

1. Annual summaries, in chart form, of LCV ratings (AF).

2. In the 1984 Congress, for example, Republicans in the House of Representatives had an environmental score of 36%; female members, 62%; Democrats, 68%; and Black Caucus members, 81%.

3. This state-by-state analysis rests on many types of sources besides those mentioned in subsequent notes: national and regional newspapers, popular magazine articles, scholarly journals, state agency reports, and publications of environmental groups (AF).

4. California Tomorrow, *Cry California* (San Francisco); California Air Resources Board, *Bulletin* (Sacramento); *California Journal* (Sacramento); California Coastal Commission, *Coastal News* (San Francisco); League of Women Voters of California, *Protecting the California Environment* (San Francisco, 1980).

5. New England Regional Office, EPA, *Environment News* (Boston); New England Coalition on Nuclear Pollution, *Newsletter* (Brattleboro, Vt.); Natural Resources Council of Maine, *Bulletin* (Augusto); *Maine Times* (Topsham); *New Hampshire Times* (Concord); Vermont Council on Natural Resources, *Vermont Environmental Report* (Montpelier).

6. Luther J. Carter, *The Florida Experience: Land and Water Policy in a Growth State* (Baltimore, Md., 1974); Florida Environmental Information Center, *ENFO* (Winter Park); Florida Environmental Service Center, *The Monitor* (Tallahassee).

7. *New York Environmental News* (Albany); New York Department of Environmental Conservation, *New York State Environment* (Albany); Environmental Planning Lobby, *EPL News* (Albany); The Adirondack Council, *The Adirondack Council Newsletter* (Elizabethtown, N.Y.).

8. Michigan United Conservation Clubs, *Michigan Out of Doors* (Lansing); *North Woods Call* (Charlevoix, Mich.); Department of Natural Resources, *Michigan Natural Resources* magazine (Lansing); Michigan Student Environmental Confederation, *Michigan Earth Beat* (Lansing); Michigan Environmental Council, *Michigan Environmental Report* (Lansing); Friends of the Boundary Waters Wilderness, *BWCA Wilderness News* (Minneapolis); Minnesota Public Interest Research Group, *Statewatch* (Minneapolis); Wisconsin's Environmental Decade, *Eco-Bulletin* (Madison); Wisconsin Wetlands Association, *Our Wetlands* (Madison); Department of Natural Resources, *Wisconsin Natural Resources* magazine (Madison).

9. League for Conservation Legislation (later New Jersey Environmental Lobby), *Newsletter* (Teaneck, N.J.); New Jersey Department of Environmental Protection, *The Jersey Coast* (Trenton); Barbara Eisier, *Air Pollution in New Jersey* (Union, N.J.: American Lung Association, 1979); *Delaware Conservationist* (Dover); Delaware Coastal Zone Management Program, *News* (Dover); Maryland Conservation Council, *Maryland Conservation Report* (Annapolis) and *Maryland Conservation News* (Bethesda, Md.); William Goodman newsletter, *Conservation News and Comment* (Annapolis); Committee to Preserve Assateague, *Newsletter* (Towson, Md.).

10. Washington Environmental Council, *Alert* (Seattle); Washington Wilderness Association, *Wildfire* (Seattle); Oregon Environmental Council, *Newsletter, Earthwatch Oregon* (Portland); Oregon Coastal Zone Management Association, *Oregon Coast* (Florence); 1000 Friends of Oregon, *Landmark* (Portland).

11. *High Country News* (Lander, Wyo., and Paonia, Colo.); Susan J. Harlow, "High Country News: Survival and Change" (Master's thesis, University of Wyoming, 1981); Idaho Environmental Council, *Newsletter* (Idaho Falls); Idaho Conservation League, *Newsletter* (Boise); Idaho Wildlife Federation, *Idaho Environmental Issues* (Boise, 1974); Northern Plains Resource Council, *Plains Truth* (Billings, Mont.); Montana Environmental Information Center, *Down to Earth* (Helena); Montana Wilderness Association, *Wild Montana* (Helena); Wyoming Outdoor Council, *Crossroads Monitor* (Cheyenne); *Jackson Hole News*

(Jackson, Wyo.); Colorado Open Space Coordinating Council, *Open Space Report* (Denver), *Newsletter* (Denver), *The Conservator* (Denver); Utah Wilderness Association, *Newsletter* (Salt Lake City).

12. Hawaii chapter, Sierra Club, *Malama I Ka Honua* (Honolulu); Hawaii Sea Grant/Marine Advisory Program, *Hawaii Coastal Zone News* (Honolulu).

13. Southeast Alaska Conservation Council, *Raven Call* (Juneau); Alaska Center for the Environment, *Center News* (Anchorage).

14. North Dakota Resource Council, *Dakota Counsel* (Dickinson); North Dakota chapter, Sierra Club, *Pines and Prairie* (Rapid City); South Dakota Resources Coalition, *Eco-Forum* (Brookings); Kansas chapter, Sierra Club, *The Greater Prairie Chicken* (Wichita); Oklahoma chapter, Sierra Club, *Oklahoma Sierran* (Broken Arrow).

15. Arizona chapter, Sierra Club, *Canyon Echo* (Tucson); New Mexico chapter, Sierra Club, *Rio Grande Sierran* (Albuquerque); New Mexico Conservation Coordinating Committee, *New Mexico Environmental News* (Albuquerque); New Mexico Wilderness Study Committee, *New Mexico Wilderness Newsletter* (Albuquerque); Texas chapter, Sierra Club, *Lone Star Sierran* (Austin).

16. Louisiana chapter, Sierra Club, *Delta Sierran* (New Orleans); Arkansas Ecology Center, *Newsletter* (Little Rock); Mississippi chapter, Sierra Club, *MS Sierran* (Jackson); Conservation Council of Virginia Foundation, *Virginia Environmental Legislative Reporter* (Richmond); Conservation Council of North Carolina, *Carolina Conservationist* (Chapel Hill); South Carolina Environmental Coalition, *Coalition* (Columbia); Robert H. Claxton, *The History of the Georgia Conservancy, 1967–1981* (Atlanta, 1985).

17. Tennessee Citizens for Wilderness Planning, *Newsletter* (Oak Ridge); Tennessee Environmental Council, *Tennessee Environmental Report* (Nashville); West Virginia Highlands Conservancy, *The Highlands Voice* (Webster Springs).

18. Georgia Forestry Commission, *Georgia Forestry* (Dry Branch); Society of American Foresters, *Southern Journal of Applied Forestry* (Washington, D.C.); Thomas D. Clark, *The Greening of the South* (Lexington, Ky., 1984).

19. Ohio Environmental Council, *Hotline* (Columbus); Ohio State University Earth Day Committee, *The Environmental* (Columbus); Ohio Public Interest Campaign, *Toxic Watch* (Cincinnati); Indiana Izaak Walton League, *Indiana Waltonian* (Huntertown); *Valley Environment* (Evansville, Ind.); Illinois Environmental Council, *IEC News* (Springfield); Citizens for a Better Environment, *CBE Environmental Review* (Chicago); *Illinois Times* (Springfield).

20. "Idaho's Tomorrow," special issue of Division of Tourism and Industrial Development, "Incredible Idaho: A Land for All Seasons" (Boise), Spring 1976; public-opinion study conducted in connection with the Idaho Tomorrow plan, "Idaho's Tomorrow: A Summary of the Results of the Delphi Questionnaire, the Goal Statements Generated at the Regional Conferences, and the Telephone Survey" (Boise, 1976).

21. Conclusion drawn from author's personal experience, conversations with environmental leaders in Pennsylvania, and files of news clippings, periodicals, and reports; interviews with William Eichbaum, former director of the Enforcement Division of the state Department of Environmental Resources, Washington, D.C., May 1980.

22. Rice Odell, *Environmental Awakening: The New Revolution to Protect the Earth* (Washington, D.C. 1980); Craig R. Humphrey and Frederick R. Buttell, *Environment, Energy and Society* (Belmont, Calif., 1982), 7, 122; Allan R.

Talbot, *Power along the Hudson; The Storm King Case and the Birth of Environmentalism* (New York, 1972).

23. *New York Times Index,* 1960–85 under headings, "Environment," "Environmental Pollution," "Water Pollution," "Birth Control and Planned Parenthood," "Nature," "Forests and Forestry," and similar items; Francis Sandbach, *Environment, Ideology and Policy* (Oxford, 1980), 2–10.

24. National Wildlife Federation, *Conservation Report* (Washington, D.C.); *Environmental Science and Technology* (Washington, D.C.); Richard A. Cooley and Geoffrey Wandesfode-Smith, *Congress and the Environment* (Seattle, 1970).

25. Sierra Club, *Sierra Club Bulletin,* later *Sierra;* Wilderness Society, *The Living Wilderness;* National Parks and Conservation Association, *National Parks;* National Wildlife Federation, *National Wildlife; National Wildlands News* (Washington, D.C.).

26. Stewart Udall, *The Quiet Crisis* (New York, 1963).

27. To observers in 1969 the decade of action was impressive. Some have suggested, one wrote that year, "that we are reaching the end of a long wave of significant and highly visible progress, and that the widely hailed 'environmental crisis,' has, in a certain sense, passed the peak of critical national interest and public concern." Cooley and Wandesfode-Smith, *Congress and the Environment,* xvi.

28. Marion Clawson and Carlton S. Van Doren, eds., *Statistics on Outdoor Recreation* (Washington, D.C., Resources for the Future, 1984).

29. *The Living Wilderness;* American Wilderness Alliance, *Wild America* and *Wilderness News; National Parks.*

30. William G. Wing, "The Concrete Juggernaut," and "What to Do Before the Highway Comes," *Audubon,* July–Aug. 1966, 266–72; Sept.–Oct. 1966, 360–7; *High Country News,* Jan. 8, Feb. 5, Mar. 5, Apr. 30, and May 14, 1971, for a case of the effect on fish of a proposed dam on the Upper Green River. When Russell Train of the Conservation Foundation (CF) in 1965 made one of the first proposals for an executive council on environmental affairs, he called it a "Council of Ecological Advisers"; *CF Letter,* Feb. 23, 1968. In 1966 Senator Gaylord Nelson introduced the first of a number of proposals for a broad program of ecological research; *CF Letter,* Feb. 23, 1968.

31. "What the Environmentalists Want," *National Journal,* Feb. 5, 1977, 216.

32. Charles E. Randall, "White House Conference on Conservation," *Journal of Forestry,* 60(1962): 457–8; "President's Conservation Program Stresses Recreation," *Journal of Forestry,* 60(1962): 255.

33. The National Wildlife Federation called the 1963–4 congressional session "the most outstanding conservation legislative record in history." *Conservation Report,* Oct. 6, 1964.

34. *Conservation Report,* Jan. 8, 1965, Feb. 12, 1965, Oct. 28, 1965, Oct. 26, 1966, for general summaries. One result of this interest was the Task Force on Environmental Health and Related Problems appointed by President Johnson, Nov. 1, 1966; see its report, *A Strategy for a Livable Environment* (Washington, D.C., 1967).

35. Interview with Charles Eisendrath, University of Michigan School of Journalism, a member of the press corps during the 1968 Nixon campaign, August 1979; Richard H. K. Vietor, *Environmental Politics and the Coal Coalition* (College Station, Tex., 1980), 51–5; Grahame J. C. Smith, Henry J. Steck, and Gerald Surette, *Our Ecological Crisis: Its Biological, Economic and Political Dimensions* (New York, 1974), 167–71.

36. *National Journal;* John C. Whitaker, *Striking a Balance; Environment and*

Natural Resources Policy in the Nixon-Ford Years (Washington, D.C., 1976); John Quarles, *Cleaning up America; An Insider's View of the Environmental Protection Agency* (Boston, 1976); James Rathlesburger, ed., *Nixon and the Environment* (New York, 1972).

37. *Sierra Club Bulletin,* Sept. 1976, 18–19; interview with Ted Snyder, chair, LeConte chapter, Sierra Club, Sept. 1976; Claxton, *History of the Georgia Conservancy.* The Sierra Club spoke rather mildly when it wrote that environmentalists were "generally encouraged" by Carter's win; *Sierra Club Bulletin,* Feb. 1977, 36.

38. J. Dicken Kirschten, "Environmentalists Come in from the Cold in Carter Administration," *National Journal,* Mar. 12, 1977, 382–4; Brock Evans, "The Importance of Appointments," *Sierra,* Sept.-Oct. 1980, 22–3; Dick Kirschten, "Here's the Windup and the Pitch," *National Journal,* Apr. 8, 1978, 565; "Agenda, News Conference on President Carter's Conservation Record, Dec. 20, 1978," held by leaders of ten national environmental organizations and endorsed by thirty-three prominent environmental leaders throughout the nation (AF).

39. Timothy B. Clark, "Carter's Assault on the Costs of Regulation," *National Journal,* Aug. 12, 1978, 1281–5; Timothy B. Clark, "What Will Happen When the Regulators Regulate Themselves," *National Journal,* Nov. 4, 1978, 1769–71; Timothy B. Clark, "The Year of Regulation," *National Journal* Jan. 20, 1979, 108; Timothy B. Clark, "Nordhaus: Confessions of a Former Inflation Fighter," *National Journal,* Mar. 17, 1979, 437–8.

40. Gene Coan, "The Carter Energy Plan," *Sierra Club Bulletin,* June-Aug. 1977, 22–3; Gene Coan and Carl Pope, "Energy 1979: What Happened and Why?" *Sierra,* Jan.-Feb. 1980, 11–13, 47, and "Another Crack at the EMB," *Sierra,* July-Aug. 1980, 70. For environmental endorsements of Carter in 1980 see *New York Times,* Sept. 28, 1980, and "Draft Letter of Endorsement" and the "President's Statement" in reply (AF).

41. Jonathan Lash, *A Season of Spoils; The Story of the Reagan Administration's Attack on the Environment* (New York, 1984); Joan Claybrook, *Retreat from Safety: Reagan's Attack on America's Health* (New York, 1984).

42. Some important shifts in the attitudes of such leaders can be observed in the late 1960s. For several years after its establishment in 1967 *Environmental Science and Technology* displayed a favorable attitude toward public sentiment. This had come to an end by 1971. The magazine's losing struggle to maintain a positive view of public demands was reflected in an editorial by D. H. Michael Bowen, "Depending on Your Point of View: Environmental Field Needs Open Discussion and Resolution of Opposing Points of View, Just as It Needs Hard Facts," *Environmental Science and Technology,* 4(1970): 5.

43. American Forest Institute, *Research Recap Number 10* (Washington, D.C., 1977); Continental Group, Inc., *Toward Responsible Growth; Economic and Environmental Concern in the Balance* (Stamford, Conn., 1982), 34, 36; Lester Milbrath, *Environmentalists: Vanguard for a New Society* (Albany, N.Y., 1984), 46.

44. Jamie Heard, "Washington Pressure: Friends of the Earth Give Environmental Interests an Active Voice," *National Journal,* Aug. 8, 1970, 1711–18; for a history of the Environmental Defense Fund see *Environment* magazine, Nov. 1984.

45. The range of issues can be followed in Environmental Study Conference, *Weekly Bulletin,* and varied specialized bulletins such as *Environment Reporter, Chemical Regulation Reporter, Occupational Health Letter, Environmental Health Letter,* and *Land Letter.*

46. Sierra Club, *Sierra Club Bulletin,* later *Sierra;* Wilderness Society, *The Living Wilderness;* National Parks and Conservation Association, *National Parks;* Environmental Defense Fund, *EDF Reporter;* Natural Resources Defense Council, *NRDC Reporter,* and *Amicus Journal;* Defenders of Wildlife, *Defenders;* Friends of the Earth, *Not Man Apart;* National Audubon Society, *National Audubon;* National Wildlife Federation, *National Wildlife.*

47. For one of many examples see Maggie Coon, "When Will the Trees Be 'Free to Grow'?" *Forest Planning,* Oct. 1984, 11–14.

48. *Chemical Week,* Oct. 19, 1983, 48–50, 52, 54, 56; *Environmental Forum,* Apr. 1985, 9–17; Center for Law and Social Policy and the Environmental Policy Institute, *The Strip Mine Handbook* (Washington, D.C., 1978); the Sierra Club et al. *A Conservationist's Guide to National Forest Planning,* 2d ed. (Washington, D.C., 1983).

49. For an apt expression of this view – "We all feel impotence and futility in the face of the relentless bureaucratic (whether government or corporate) onslaught" – see letter to the editor, *Alternatives,* Spring-Summer 1985, 91.

50. Sierra Club, *National News Report;* National Wildlife Federation, *Conservation Report;* annual reports, League of Conservation Voters.

51. See *Waterways Journal* (St. Louis) for reactions by navigation groups interested in river development; American Rivers Conservation Council, *American Rivers* (Washington, D.C.).

52. Henry Clepper, "The Allagash Wilderness in Controversy," *Journal of Forestry,* 60(1962): 777–81; Kenneth B. Pomeroy, "The Allagash Rehashed," *American Forests,* May 1962, 38–9, and Pomeroy, "Recreation and Landownership," *American Forests,* Aug. 1962, 385–7; Edward P. Stumm, president, American Forestry Association, "The President's Message," 87th annual meeting of the association, *American Forests,* Nov. 1962, 7, 41–3; W. G. Hagenstein, "Work or Play Forests – Or Both," *Journal of Forestry,* 60(1962): 663–4; Richard Pardo, "Tree Farmers Celebrate Forty Years and Growing," *American Forests,* Sept. 1981, 36–47.

53. Paul H. Bruns, *A New Hampshire Everlasting and Unfallen* (n.p.: Society for the Protection of New Hampshire Forests, 1969).

54. "Of Trees and Hope in the National Forests," *The Living Wilderness,* Summer 1983 issue; *Forest Planning* (Eugene Oreg.); Wilderness Society, *A Critique of the White Mountain National Forest Plan* (Washington, D.C., 1985).

55. R. Neil Sampson, *For Love of the Land* (League City, Tex., 1985), 202–32.

56. National Wildlife Federation, *National Wildlife;* Wildlife Management Institute, *Outdoor News Bulletin.*

57. "The Dream That Stamps Built," *National Wildlife,* 10(Oct./Nov. 1972): 26–33; "Your NWF At Work," *National Wildlife,* 23(Apr./May 1985): 30–6.

58. The attitudes of associate members can be followed in the annual polls conducted by the National Wildlife Federation concerning their views on a wide range of environmental issues. See *National Wildlife,* 15(Apr./May 1977); 17(June/July 1979): 18(Apr./May 1980): 19(Apr./May 1981): 20(Apr./May 1982): 21 (Apr./May 1983). For a profile of these members and their interests see *National Wildlife,* 15(Apr./May 1983).

3. The Urban Environment

1. Martin V. Melosi, *Pollution and Reform in American Cities, 1870–1930* (Austin, Tex., 1980).

2. Joel S. Hirschhorn, "Emerging Options in Waste Reduction and Treatment: A Market Incentive Approach," in Bruce Piasecki, ed., *Beyond Dumping* (Westport, Conn., 1984).

3. John C. Esposito, *Vanishing Air* (New York, 1970); Richard J. Tobin, *The Social Gamble* (Lexington, Mass., 1979); *CF Letter,* Jan. 18, 1967; July 21, 1967; Jan. 31, 1968; Nov. 1969; Oct. 1970; Sept. 1977; Feb. 1981; Mar. 1981; *Journal of the Air Pollution Control Association* (Pittsburgh, Pa.).

4. *CF Letter,* Jan. 18, 1967; Nov. 1969; statements of city mayors, Senate Subcommittee on Air and Water Pollution, *Hearings, Air Pollution – 1968,* Part I, 90th Cong. 2d sess., 1968 48–56, 72–85, 245–59 (Washington, D.C., 1968); Arthur C. Stern, "Basis for Criteria and Standards," *Journal of the Air Pollution Control Association,* 15(1965): 281–3. Industry representatives claimed that because the public was not concerned about existing levels of sulfur oxides and because no health effects had been demonstrated even at high levels of concentration, the Public Health Service was wasting its time studying the problem. See P. N. Gammelgard, American Petroleum Institute, Senate Special Subcommittee on Air and Water Pollution, *Hearings, Clean Air,* Part II, (88th Cong., 2d sess., 1964, 1326.

5. *New York Times,* Dec. 7, 1970; "Middleton Says Control Commission Should Not Have Industry Memberships," *Environment Reporter,* Jan. 8, 1971, 955–6 One industry strategy was to form interstate compacts that might ward off federal regulation; Senate Subcommittee on Air and Water Pollution, *Hearings, Air Pollution – 1968,* Part I.

6. Joel A. Tarr and William Lampres, "Changing Fuel Use Behavior: The Pittsburgh Smoke Control Movement, 1940–1950 and Energy Transitions Today – A Case Study in Historical Analogy," *Journal of Social History,* 14(Summer 1981): 561–88. Council on Economic Priorities, *The Price of Power: Electric Utilities and the Environment* (New York, 1973); *Paper Profits: Pollution in the Pulp and Paper Industry* (Cambridge, Mass., 1972); Frank P. Grad et al., *The Automobile and the Regulation of Its Impact on the Environment* (Norman, Okla., 1975).

7. John T. Middleton, "A Fresh Opportunity for Industry," *Environmental Science and Technology,* 1(1967): 206–11; Senate Committee on Public Works, *Air Quality Criteria,* staff report prepared for the Subcommittee on Air and Water Pollution, 90th Cong., 2d. sess, July 1968.

8. Benjamin G. Ferris, Jr., and Frank E. Speizer, "Criteria for Establishing Standards for Air Pollutants," *Business Roundtable Air Quality Project* (Cambridge, Mass. 1980).

9. *CF Letter,* July 21, 1967; interview with John Middleton, head of the National Air Pollution Control Administration, *Environmental Science and Technology,* 2(1968): 734–7; author interview with John Redmond secretary, Committee on Biologic Effects of Atmospheric Pollutants, National Academy of Sciences, Apr. 10, 1979; Philip Boffey, *The Brain Bank of America* (New York, 1975); David Schoenbrod, "Why Regulation of Lead Has Failed," in Herbert L. Needleman, ed., *Low Level Lead Exposure: The Clinical Implications of Current Research* (New York, 1980), 259–66.

10. *Environmental Science and Technology,* 1(1968): 731–3; *Environment and Behavior,* newsletter, Center for Science in the Public Interest (Washington, D.C.); *Washington Post,* Jan. 9, 1982; Bernard Rimland and Gerald E. Larson, "The Manpower Quality Decline: An Ecological Perspective," *Armed Forces and Society,* Fall 1981, 21–78.

11. U.S. Public Health Service, *Air Quality Criteria for Sulfur Oxides,* PHS pub. no. 1619 (Mar. 1967); "Air Quality Criteria for Sulfur Oxides Set by HEW," *Environmental Science and Technology,* 1(1967): 282–6; 1(1967): 400; *Journal of the Air Pollution Control Association,* 18(1968): 443–7; Senate Subcommittee on Air and Water Pollution, *Air Pollution – 1967,* 1456–67, 2404–5; *CF Letter,* July 21, 1967, 4; W. W. Holland et al., "Health Effects of Particulate Pollution: Reappraising the Evidence," *American Journal of Epidemiology* 110(1979): 525–659.

12. John E. Bonine, "The Evolution of 'Technology-Forcing' in the Clean Air Act," *Environment Reporter,* July 6, 1975, 1–29; "The Air Cleaning Equipment People," *Environmental Science and Technology,* 10(1976): 866–7; John P. DeKany, "Emission Control Technology for Gasoline Powered Automobiles," Manufacturers of Emission Controls Association, Washington, D.C., July 7, 1981.

13. Fredericka P. Perera and A. Karim Ahmed, *Respirable Particles: Impact of Airborne Fine Particulates on Health and the Environment* (Cambridge, Mass., 1979). James P. Lodge, American Iron and Steel Institute, for example, argued against visibility standards on the grounds that the benefits were "largely intangible." *Environment Reporter,* Nov. 27, 1981, 934–5.

14. James M. Fallows, *The Water Lords* (New York, 1971); David Zwick and Marcy Benstock, *Water Wasteland* (New York, 1971); *CF Letter,* Sept. 9, 1966; May 20, 1968; Aug. 7, 1969; Aug. 19, 1969; June 1971; July 1971; Dec. 1977; May 1980; Sept. 1981. Susan Peterson, "The Great Lakes: An Imperiled Majesty," *Environmental Action,* Jan./Feb. 1985, 16–20; newsletter, Great Lakes United.

15. EPA, Office of Water Planning and Standards, "Fish Kills Caused by Pollution; Fifteen-Year Summary, 1961–1975," EPA 440/4-78-011 (Washington, D.C., 1979).

16. *Environment Reporter,* Sept. 25, 1970, 548–9.

17. National Academy of Public Administration, "Water Quality and the Interior Department: An Aborted Experiment. A Case Study Dealing with Reorganization Plan No. 2 of 1966" (Washington, D.C., 1971); Irene L. Murphy, "The Politics of Water Pollution Control: A Bureau and Its System React to Stress" (Ph.D. diss., Columbia University, 1970).

18. House Committee on Government Operations, Subcommittee on Natural Resources and Power, *Water Pollution Control and Abatement,* 88th Cong., 1st sess. (1963), 88th Cong., 2d sess. (1964) (Washington, D.C.). Harvey Lieber, *Federalism and Clean Waters* (Lexington, Mass., 1975); Conservation Foundation, *Toward Clean Water: A Guide to Citizen Action* (Washington, D.C., 1976).

19. American Meat Institute v. EPA (8 ERC 1369); Hooker Chemicals and Plastics Corp. v. Train (8 ERC 1961); American Paper Institute v. Train (9 ERC 1065).

20. Michael G. Royston, *Pollution Prevention Pays* (Oxford, 1979); James Banks, "Dumping into Surface Waters: The Making and Demise of Toxic Discharge Regulations," in Piasecki, ed., *Beyond Dumping,* 43.

21. Martin V. Melosi, *Refuse, Reform, and the Environment, 1880–1980* (Austin, Tex., 1983).

22. *CF Letter,* Sept. 27, 1968; Apr. 1973; May 1973.

23. William Kabbert III, "Bottle Bill: Truths and Consequences" (Undergraduate research paper, Department of History, University of Pittsburgh, June 15, 1977, AF); Don Waggoner, *Oregon's Bottle Bill – One Year Later* (Portland:

Oregon Environmental Council, 1973); John F. Savage and Henry R. Richmond III, *Oregon's Bottle Bill: A Riproaring Success* (Portland: Oregon Student Public Interest Research Group, 1974).

24. New York Environmental Planning Lobby, *The Financial and Environmental Impact of Garbage Incineration* (Albany, N.Y., 1985).

25. "Many Communities around the Country Are Suffering from Growing Pains," and "Residents Jockey over New Urban Environments," *CF Letter,* Aug. 1971, July 1978.

26. "Neighborhoods Are Back in Style," *CF Letter,* Jan. 1976

27. Seymour Toll, *Zoned America* (New York, 1969).

28. Mark H. Rose, *Interstate: Express Highway Politics, 1941–1956* (Lawrence, Kans., 1979); Helen Leavitt, *Superhighway – Superhoax* (New York, 1970). "It is in the cities that our world renowned road building competence is meeting its sternest test. Our mastery of the engineering problems in moving automobiles over every conceivable terrain is unrivaled. But we have yet to reconcile it with the traditional amenities and aspirations of city life. That is the roughest terrain of all"; John W. Gardner, Chair, Urban Coalition, as quoted in *CF Letter,* June 24, 1969.

29. *CF Letter,* July 5, 1968; Aug. 30, 1968; Sept. 27, 1968; Jan. 24, 1969.

30. "An Opening Attack on the Decibel Din: New Law Seeks to Control Aircraft Noise," and "Air Transport: An Environmental Failure Story," *CF Letter,* Aug. 30, 1968, Aug. 1974.

31. George M. Raymond, "Community Revitalization and Preservation," *Amicus Journal,* 2(Spring 1981): 26–9.

32. Kenneth H. Bacon, "New Departure in Parks: New York City Begins to Put Vacant Lots to Constructive Use," *Wall Street Journal,* Sept. 6, 1966; Tom Fox, Ian Koeppel, and Susan Kellam, *Struggle for Open Space: The Greening of New York City, 1970–1984* (New York, 1985).

33. "Gregg Terms Demonstration Cities Act 'Most Promising Prospect' to Fulfill Unmet Urban Open Space and Outdoor Recreation Needs," *CF Letter,* Jan. 18, 1967, 8–11.

34. U.S. Department of Interior, Heritage Conservation and Recreation Service, *Urban Waterfront Revitalization: The Role of Recreation and Heritage* (Washington, D.C., 1979); Patrick Barry, "The Last Urban Frontier," *Environmental Action,* 15(May 1984): 14–17.

35. "Efforts to Bring Parks to the People Have Been Stymied by a Variety of Political and Financial Problems," "National Parks Are Beset by Policy Problems," "Urban Parks: Are They Successful or Unrealistic," *CF Letter,* Mar. 1972; July-Aug. 1975; July 1982.

36. Urban forestry is covered extensively in a continuing series of articles in *American Forests,* beginning with John W. Andresen, "The Greening of Urban America," Nov. 1978, 10–15, 48–50; Gene W. Grey and Frederick J. Deneke, *Urban Forestry* (New York, 1978).

37. Urban Wildlife Research Center, *Urban Wildlife News* (Elliott City, Md.).

38. "Rare is the visitor from the populous southeast corner of the state who tastes the air and senses the immediacy of nature and does not feel himself deprived"; Joe H. Stroud, *Detroit Free Press,* May 31, 1981. For a similar contrast see George Reiger, "Our Flight from Noise to Silence," *National Wildlife,* 11(Dec.-Jan. 1973): 37–9.

39. "Plant Beautification: Is It Worth the Cost?" *Chemical Week,* Apr. 9, 1960, 45–8.

40. Urban Land Institute, *Industrial Development Handbook* (Washington, D.C., 1975), 17–19.

41. "What Is the Role of the Highway in Society and the Environment?" "Very Slowly, but Steadily, Radical Changes in Urban Transportation Are Taking Place," "Automobiles Keep Posing New Dilemmas," "Should Americans Be Pried Out of their Cars"; *CF Letter,* June 1970, Nov. 1972, Mar. 1975, Apr. 1975.

42. "Congress Is Poised to Vote Another Heavy Dose of Highways as the Urban Transportation Dilemma Continues," *CF Letter,* Oct. 1972.

43. *The Costs of Sprawl,* 2 vols., prepared for the Council on Environmental Quality, the Department of Housing and Urban Development, and the Environmental Protection Agency by Real Estate Research Corp. (Washington, D.C., 1974).

44. "Enlightened Land Choices Are Very Elusive," and "Land Banking Can Ease Some Growing Pains," *CF Letter,* Apr. 1974; Dec. 1975.

45. Carolyn L. Logan, *Rebel Residents: How to Fight Developers* (Snohomish, Wash.: Western Search, 1979).

46. Charles E. Little, *Challenge of the Land: Open Space Preservation at the Local Level* (New York, 1968).

47. New England Natural Resources Center, "Case Studies in Land Conservation" (Boston, Mass., n.d.); Exploratory Project for Economic Alternatives, *Public Trusts for Environmental Protection* (Washington, D.C., 1976); Ian L. McHarg et al., *Metropolitan Open Space and Natural Process* (Philadelphia, 1970).

48. Race D. Davies, *Preserving Agricultural and Open-Space Lands: Legislative Policymaking in California,* Institute of Governmental Affairs, Environmental Quality Series, no. 10, (Davis, Calif., 1972); Margaret M. Bennett, *Transfer of Development Rights* (Philadelphia, Pa.: Pennsylvania Environmental Council, 1976).

49. "Flood Plains: No Longer up for Grabs?" *CF Letter,* May 1975.

50. Ian McHarg, *Design with Nature* (Garden City, N.Y., 1969).

51. Robert A. Baron, *The Tyranny of Noise* (New York, 1970); "Noise – Still Another Environmental Pollutant" and "Noise Control Efforts Stir Up Many Disputes," *CF Letter,* Dec. 29, 1967, June 1980.

52. Mary Cranston et al., *A Handbook for Controlling Local Growth* (Stanford, Calif.: Stanford Environmental Law Society, 1973); Richard C. Bradley, *The Costs of Urban Growth: Observations and Judgments* (Pikes Peak, Colo.: Area Council of Governments, 1973); Benny Chien, "Limitation of City Size: Whither the Initiative?" (Land-use seminar, University of San Diego Law School, 1973); *Equilibrium,* quarterly journal published by Zero Population Growth (Palo Alto, Calif. 1973–4); Potomac Institute, *Controlling Urban Growth – but for Whom?''* (Washington, D.C., 1973).

53. Eric Sloane, *For Spacious Skies* (New York, 1978); Vincent J. Schaefer and John A. Day, *A Field Guide to the Atmosphere* (Boston, 1981).

4. The Nation's Wildlands

1. The interest in the nation's wildlands can be observed in photographic books and calendars. See the Time-Life series *The American Wilderness,* twenty-seven volumes combining photography and text (New York, 1974–8).

2. Roy M. Robbins, *Our Landed Heritage* (Princeton, N.J., 1942).

3. John Ise, *The United States Forest Policy* (New Haven, Conn., 1920); Gifford Pinchot, *Breaking New Ground* (New York, 1947); Harold K. Steen, *The U.S. Forest Service* (Seattle, 1977).

4. Alfred Runte, *National Parks: The American Experience* (Lincoln, Nebr., 1979).

5. Robert Shankland, *Steve Mather of the National Parks* (New York, 1951); Donald C. Swain, *Wilderness Defender: Horace M. Albright and Conservation* (Chicago, 1970); W. C. Everhart, *The National Parks Service* (New York, 1972).

6. Carlos C. Campbell, *Birth of a National Park in the Great Smoky Mountains* (Knoxville, Tenn., 1960).

7. Nathaniel P. Reed and Dennis Drabelle, *The United States Fish And Wildlife Service* (Boulder, Colo., 1984).

8. E. Louise Peffer, *The Closing of the Public Domain* (Stanford, Calif., 1951); William Voigt, Jr., *Public Grazing Lands* (New Brunswick, N.J., 1976); Marion Clawson, *The Bureau of Land Management* (New York, 1971).

9. Desert Protective Council, *El Paisano* (Banning, Calif.); *National Wildlands News* (Washington, D.C.); Public Lands Institute, *PLI Newsletter* (Washington, D.C.); Sierra Club, *Land Letter* (Boston).

10. G. Wesley Burnett, "Montana Becomes a Landlord: A Study of State Land Selection" (Ph.D. diss., University of Oklahoma, 1976); William C. Patric, *Trust Land Administration in the Western States: A Study of the Laws, Policies and Agencies under Which State Lands Are Managed in Ten States"* (Denver, Colo.: Public Lands Institute, 1981).

11. William Shands and Robert Healy, *The Lands Nobody Wanted* (Washington, D.C., 1978).

12. Albert E. Cowdrey, *This Land, This South: An Environmental History* (Lexington, Ky., 1983).

13. Donald F. Cate, "Recreation and the U.S. Forest Service: A Study of Organizational Response to Changing Demands" (Ph.D. diss., Stanford University, 1963).

14. Susan Schrepfer, *The Fight to Save The Redwoods* (Madison, Wis., 1983); Sandra L. Keith, "Renewing Redwood Park," *American Forests,* Feb. 1983, 22–27, 58–61.

15. William Ashworth, *Hell's Canyon* (New York, 1977); Thomas J. Schoenbaum, *The New River Controversy* (Winston-Salem, N.C., 1979); A. Y. Gunter, *The Big Thicket: A Challenge for Conservation* (Austin, Tex., 1971).

16. *Appalachian Trailway News* (Harper's Ferry, W.Va.).

17. *Nature Conservancy News* (Alexandria, Va.); membership rose from 45,687 in 1977 to 239,135 in 1984.

18. For the western counterpart see Council on Environmental Quality, *Hard Rock Mining on the Public Lands* (Washington, D.C., 1977); George Riley, "The Mining Law of 1872," *Amicus Journal* 2(Spring 1981): 17–21.

19. Shands and Healy, *Lands Nobody Wanted,* title their opening chapter, "Backyard to Megalopolis."

20. Michael Berger, *The Devil Wagon in God's Country* (Hamden, Conn., 1979), 117–26. In 1926 the largest single occupation of motor-vehicle owners entering Yellowstone National Park was "agricultural pursuits."

21. Opinion Research Corporation, *The Public's Participation in Outdoor Activities and Attitudes toward National Wilderness Areas* (Princeton, N.J., 1977); Yankelovich, Skelly, and White, Inc., "Memorandum, Research on Public Attitudes Toward the Use of Wilderness Lands," Sept. 17, 1978, prepared for the Western Regional Council (n.p.).

22. James B. Trefethen, *An American Crusade for Wildlife* (New York, 1975);

John F. Reiger, *American Sportsmen and the Origins of Conservation* (New York, 1975).

23. Thomas R. Dunlap, *DDT: Scientists, Citizens and Public Policy* (Princeton, N.J., 1981)

24. U.S. Fish and Wildlife Service, *1975 National Survey of Hunting, Fishing and Wildlife-Associated Recreation* (Washington, D.C., 1977); Wildlife Management Institute, *The North American Wildlife Policy, 1973* (Washington, D.C., 1973).

25. Paul T. Ehrlich and Anne H. Ehrlich, *Extinction* (New York, 1981); U.S. Fish and Wildlife Service and Center for Action on Endangered Species, *Endangered Species Technical Bulletin* (Ayer, Mass., 1976–).

26. Robert Cahn, "The God Committee," *Audubon,* May 1979, 10, 13; Bruce Hamilton, "The Whooping Crane: A Success Story," *Sierra,* May-June 1979, 56–61; Ross Sandler, "Tellico Dam," *Amicus Journal,* 1(Fall 1979): 4–5.

27. Lee M. Talbot, "New Principles for Management of Wild Living Resources," *Western Wildlands,* Winter 1976, 28–32.

28. James A. Tober, *Who Owns the Wildlife?* (Westport, Conn., 1981).

29. Marion Clawson and Carlton S. Van Doren, eds., *Statistics on Outdoor Recreation* (Washington, D.C.: Resources for the Future, 1984).

30. Stephen R. Kellert, *American Attitudes, Knowledge and Behaviors toward Wildlife and Natural Habitats* (Washington, D.C., 1978–80).

31. *PATC Bulletin* (Washington, D.C.), published continuously since 1932, provides an opportunity to observe changes in values and activities over a long period of time.

32. John C. Hendee, George H. Stankey, and Robert C. Lucas, *Wilderness Management,* U.S. Forest Service Misc. Publ. no. 1365 (Washington, D.C., 1978), 281–310.

33. Environmental Defense Fund, *ORV Monitor* (Berkeley, Calif., 1974–9).

34. Conrad L. Wirth, *Parks, Politics and the People* (Norman, Okla., 1980).

35. Craig Allin, *The Politics of Wilderness Preservation* (Westport, Conn., 1982); Michael Frome, *Battle for the Wilderness* (New York, 1974).

36. Roderick Nash, *Wilderness and the American Mind* (New Haven, Conn., 1967); Susan L. Flader, *Thinking Like a Mountain* (Columbia, Mo., 1974).

37. James P. Gilligan, "The Development of Policy and Administration of Forest Service Primitive and Wilderness Areas in the Western United States," 2 vols. (Ph.D. diss., University of Michigan, 1953).

38. *Living Wilderness* and *Sierra Club Bulletin.*

39. Frome, *Battle for the Wilderness,* 159–61; Parker v. U.S. (1 ERC 1163) was crucial in this development.

40. Senate Subcommittee on Public Lands, *Eastern Wilderness Areas,* 93d Cong., 1st sess., 1973.

41. American Wilderness Alliance, *Wild America, On the Wild Side,* and *Proceedings, 1980 Western Wilderness and Rivers Conference* (Denver, Colo., 1980); newsletters of state wilderness groups (AF).

42. Bureau of Land Management, *Wilderness Management Policy* (Washington, D.C., 1981).

43. "Interview: Director Gregg on BLM Wilderness," *Living Wilderness,* Apr.-June 1978, 22–3; John Hart, "Deciding the Future of BLM Wilderness," *Sierra,* Nov.-Dec. 1979, 16–19.

44. Richard G. Walsh, Richard A. Gillman, and John B. Loomis, *Wilderness Resource Economics* (Denver, Colo.: American Wilderness Alliance, 1982).

45. Rick Fletcher, *Endangered: Mountain Air,* Rocky Mountain Forest and Range Experiment Station, Ft. Collins, Colo., FTS #323–5211.

46. EPA, Office of Air Quality Planning and Standards, *Protecting Visibility: An EPA Report to Congress,* EPA-450/5-79-008 (Research Triangle Park, N.C., 1979).

47. Thomas M. Disselhorst, "Sierra Club v. Ruckelshaus: On A Clear Day," *Ecology Law Quarterly,* 4(1975): 739–80; Marc Bramer Mihaly, "The Clean Air Act and the Concept of Non-Degradation: Sierra Club v. Ruckelshaus," *Ecology Law Quarterly,* 2(1972): 801–36.

48. National Research Council, *On Prevention of Significant Deterioration of Air Quality* (Washington, D.C., 1981).

49. "Preserving Our Visibility Heritage," *Environmental Science and Technology,* Mar. 1979, 266–8; "Parks Versus Power Plants?" *National Parks and Conservation* Oct. 1979, 25–6.

50. Robert H. Boyle and R. Alexander Boyle, *Acid Rain* (New York, 1983); Ellis B. Cowling, "Acid Precipitation in Historical Perspective." *Environmental Science and Technology,* 16(1982): 110A–23A.

51. ASAP Coordination Committee, *Proceedings of the Action Seminar on Acid Precipitation, Nov. 1st to 3rd 1979* (n.p., n.d.).

52. Carolyn Curtis, ed., *Before the Rainbow: What We Know About Acid Rain* (Washington, D.C.: Edison Electric Institute, 1980); Alan W. Katzenstein, *An Updated Perspective on Acid Rain* (Washington, D.C.: Edison Electric Institute, n.d.).

53. Herbert Kaufman, *The Forest Ranger* (Baltimore, Md., 1960); Glen O. Robinson, *The Forest Service* (Baltimore, Md., 1975).

54. Gordon L. Bultena and John C. Hendee, "Foresters' Views of Interest Group Positions on Forest Policy," *Journal of Forestry,* 70(1972): 337–42; Southeast Alaska Conservation Council, "Transcripts of Tongass Accountability Project Interviews" (Eugene, Oreg.: Hot Type Publishers, 1984).

55. Leon Minckler, "Ecological Bookkeeping," *American Forests,* Aug. 1973, 22–3 argued that environmental and ecological values should be given greater emphasis in forestry; Samuel T. Dana, "On Environmental Redundancy," *American Forests,* Nov. 1973, 7, replied that the term "environmental forestry" was redundant: "All forestry is 'environmental' and 'ecological.' "

56. Opinion Research Corporation, *The Public's Participation in Outdoor Activities.*

57. Jack Sheperd, *The Forest Killers* (New York, 1975); Eleanor C. J. Horwitz, *Clearcutting: A View from the Top* (Washington, D.C., 1974); Senate Subcommittee on Public Lands, *Clear-cutting Practices on National Timberlands,* 3 parts, 92d Cong., 1st sess., Apr.-June 1971.

58. Benjamin W. H. Jahn, J. Douglas Post, and Charles B. White, *National Forest Resource Management* (Stanford, Calif.: Stanford Environmental Law Society, 1978); *Forest Planning* (Eugene, Oreg.).

59. Clawson, *Bureau of Land Management;* Paul J. Culhane, *Public Lands Politics* (Baltimore, Md., 1981); Public Lands Institute, *PLI Newsletter."*

60. Philip O. Foss, *Politics and Grass* (New York, 1960); William Voigt, Jr., *Public Grazing Lands* (New Brunswick, N.J., 1976).

61. Stanford Environmental Law Society, *Public Land Management: A Time for Change?* (Stanford, Calif.; Stanford Law School, 1971).

62. *High Country News* (Lander, Wyo., and Paonia, Colo.).

63. Senate Subcommittee on Environment and Land Resources, *Manage-*

ment of National Resource Lands, 94th Cong., 1st sess., Mar. 7 and May 15, 1975.

64. Culhane, *Public Lands Politics;* Philip L. Fradkin, "The Eating of the West," *Audubon,* Jan. 1979, 94–7, 102–6, 110–15, 119–21.

65. Joseph L. Sax, *Mountains without Handrails* (Ann Arbor, Mich., 1980); Reed and Drabelle, *Fish and Wildlife Service.*

66. The Conservation Foundation, *National Parks for the Future* (Washington, D.C., 1972), and *National Parks for a New Generation* (Washington, D.C., 1985).

67. Department of the Interior, National Park Service, *State of the Parks – 1980: A Report to the Congress,* May 1980.

68. Reed and Drabelle, *Fish and Wildlife Service.*

69. U.S. Fish and Wildlife Service, *Operation of the National Wildlife Refuge System* (Washington, D.C., 1976).

70. Forest Service planning can be followed in the magazine, *Forest Planning* (Eugene, Oreg.).

71. Richard M. Alston, *Forest – Goals and Decisionmaking in the Forest Service* USDA Forest Service Research Paper INT-128, Intermountain Forest and Range Experiment Station (Ogden, Utah, 1972).

5. The Countryside: A Land Rediscovered, yet Threatened

1. James Belasco, *America on the Road: From Autocamp to Motel, 1910– 1945* (Cambridge, Mass., 1979); Michael Berger, *The Devil Wagon in God's Country* (Hamden, Conn., 1979); Ronald Briggs, "Amenity Rich, Amenity Poor," *American Demographics,* 3(July-Aug. 1981): 9.

2. J. E. deSteiguer, "Forestland Market Values," *Journal of Forestry,* 80(1982): 214–16; "Leisure: Where No Recession Is in Sight," *U.S. News and World Report,* Jan. 15, 1979, 41.

3. Jack Doyle, *Lines Across the Land* (Washington D.C., 1979).

4. Files of American Rivers Conservation Council (ARCC) (Washington, D.C.).

5. William Ashworth, *Hells Canyon* (New York, 1977); interview with Brock Evans, then with the Sierra Club, Washington, D.C., May 1980.

6. Material in files of ARCC; *Newslettter,* Tennessee Citizens for Wilderness Planning; Coalition on American Rivers, *The Wabash Canal and Related Projects* (Champaign, Ill., 1976).

7. Ohio was a major center of opposition to PL 566 projects; see *Rivers Unlimited* publication of Rivers Unlimited (Cincinnati).

8. Council on Environmental Quality, *Report on Channel Modifications,* 2 vols. (Washington, D.C., 1973); House Committee on Government Operations, *Stream Channelization,* 4 parts. 92d Cong., 1st sess., 1971; *Proceedings, Symposium on Stream Channel Modification* (Grottoes, Va., 1975).

9. American Rivers Conservation Council, *American Rivers* (Washington, D.C., 1974–).

10. Miscellaneous material, "Dam Fighter Conferences" (AF).

11. American Rivers Conservation Council, *Disasters in Water Development I* (Washington, D.C., 1973); *Disasters in Water Development II* (Washington, D.C., 1977).

12. *California Environment Report,* Jan. 1977, 5; Feb. 1977, 1–2; Senate Subcommittee on Air and Water Pollution, Hearing, *The Relationship of Economic Development to Environmental Growth* (the Machiasport, Maine, oil refinery), 91st Cong., 2d sess., Sept. 8–9, 1970; J. Douglas Peters, "Durham, New Hampshire: A Victory for Home Rule?" *Ecology Law Quarterly,* 5(1975): 53–68; Raymond L. Gold, *Ranching, Mining and the Human Impact of Natural Resources Development* (New Brunswick, N.J., 1985).

13. Clippings, *Los Angeles Times* (AF) (Caltex pipeline); Lee Niedringhaus David, *Frozen Fire* (San Francisco, 1979); clippings, *Missoulian* (Missoula, Mont.) (AF) (Northern Tier pipeline).

14. For one proposal to site an "energy park" in Pennsylvania, see news clippings and reports (AF). Of 1,274 letters written to the Pennsylvania Energy Council concerning the proposals, 1,247 were opposed, 17 in favor, 8 neutral, and 2 mixed. Margaret E. Cawley and Matthew Hastings, "Pennsylvania Citizens Respond to Rural Energy Park Proposal," *Small Town,* 9(Sept. 1978).

15. Louise B. Young, *Power over People* (New York, 1973); Barry M. Caspar and Paul David Wellstone, *Powerline* (Amherst, Mass., 1981); *Hold That Line,* newsletter published by a Minnesota organization, GASP; "The Power Line Battle: The Fight May Shift to the South," *New Hampshire Times,* Jan. 10, 1982.

16. For Bodega Bay, *Sierra Club Bulletin,* Apr. 1962, 9; June 1962, 9; Nov. 1964, 14; Apr.-May 1963; Ross Sandler, "Settlement on the Hudson," *Amicus Journal,* 2(Spring 1981): 42–5; David Lambert, "Line of Fire: Montana's Transmission Corridor Controversy," *Montana* magazine, Sept. 1981, 35.

17. *A Land Policy Program for Pennsylvania: An Interim Policy Report* (Prepared for the Governor's Office of State Planning and Development, Harrisburg, Pa., 1976). For western mining interference with wildlife routes and habitat, see *High Country News* and *Ketchum Tomorrow* (Ketchum, Idaho).

18. John F. Stacks, *Stripping: The Surface Mining of America* (San Francisco, 1972).

19. Michael Parfit, *Last Stand at Rosebud Creek: Coal, Power and People* (New York, 1981); *The Plains Truth,* newsletter, Northern Plains Resource Council (Billings, Mont.); author interview with William Eichbaum, Washington, D.C., May 1979.

20. Author interview with Louise Dunlap, Washington, D.C., May 1979.

21. *Environment Reporter* for details about the strip-mining regulation program; author interview with William Eichbaum, Washington, D.C., 1979.

22. *Environment Reporter* for details about the Reagan program.

23. Center for Law and Social Policy and Environmental Policy Center, *The Strip Mine Hand Book* (Washington, D.C., 1978).

24. Rachel Carson, *The Edge of the Sea* (New York, 1955); John McPhee, *The Pine Barrens* (New York, 1967); William H. Amos, *The Infinite River* (New York, 1970); John and Margaret Teal, *Life and Death of the Salt Marsh* (New York, 1971); John Janovy, Jr., *Keith Country Journal* (New York, 1980).

25. University of Rhode Island, Marine Experiment Station, *Coastal and Offshore Environmental Inventory* (Kingston, R.I., 1973); Paul L. Ringold and John Clark, *The Coastal Almanac* (Washington, D.C., 1980); Denis M. Anderson and Charles C. King, *Environmental Analysis of Central Ohio,* 3 vols. (Huntington, W.Va.: U.S. Army Corps of Engineers, 1976).

26. National Audubon Society, *Directory of Nature Centers* (New York, 1975).

27. Council on Environmental Quality, *The Delaware River Basin: An Environmental Assessment of Three Centuries of Change* (Washington, D.C., 1975). Clair Patterson, *Natural Levels of Lead in Humans,* Carolina Environmental Essay Series III, Institute for Environmental Studies (Chapel Hill, N.C., 1982).

For a compilation of historical baseline data, see Monitoring and Assessment Research Center, *Historical Monitoring,* MARC Report No. 31 (London, 1985).

28. Joseph V. Siry, *Marshes of the Ocean Shore* (College Station, Tex., 1984); U.S. Congress, Office of Technology Assessment, *Wetlands: Their Use and Regulation* (Washington, D.C., 1984); *National Wetlands Newsletter* (Washington, D.C.).

29. Luther J. Carter, *The Florida Experience* (Washington, D.C., 1974).

30. Lance D. Wood and John R. Hill, Jr., "Wetlands Protection: The Regulatory Role of the U.S. Army Corps of Engineers," *Coastal Zone Management Journal,* 4(1978): 378–80.

31. Richard J. Angello et al., *Coastal Zone Recreational Activity and Potential Demand of Delaware Residents,* University of Delaware, College of Marine Sciences, DEL-SG-8-77 (Newark, Del., 1977).

32. Rice Odell, *The Saving of San Francisco Bay* (Washington, D.C., 1972).

33. *Wisconsin Wetlands,* newsletter, Wisconsin Wetlands Association (Madison); *The Riparian,* newsletter, Michigan Lakes and Streams Association (Three Rivers).

34. NRDC v. Calloway, 392 F. Supp. 685 (DDC 2975).

35. Thomas J. Schoenbaum, *The New River Controversy* (Winston-Salem, N.C., 1972).

36. *Tennessee Scenic Rivers, A Progress Report* (n.p., n.d.); Wayne D. Oliver, *Pathways and Paddleways: A Trails and Scenic Waters Feasibility Study* (Austin, Tex., 1971); Gladney Gene Davison, *Streams and Stream Preservation* (Baton Rouge, La., 1971).

37. Pamphlet published by eight national conservation organizations, National Wildlife Foundation, *Federal Flood Control Programs Are Failing to Prevent Flood Losses. Federal Flood Control Projects Can Increase Flood Losses* (Washington, D.C., n.d.).

38. U.S. Army Corps of Engineers, Memphis District, *Final Environmental Impact Statement: Cache River Basin Project, Arkansas* (Memphis Tenn., 1984).

39. University of Michigan Biological Station, *Lakeland Report* (Pellston, Mich., 1974–).

40. Environmental Protection Agency, *Restoration of Lakes and Inland Waters,* EPA 440/5-81-010 (Washington, D.C., 1980); Office of Water Regulations and Standards, *Report of an International Symposium on Inland Waters and Lake Restoration, Sept. 8–12, 1980, Portland, Maine* (Washington, D.C., 1980); North American Lake Management Society (Merrifield, Va.), *Lake Line* (1981–).

41. For the Views of Trout Unlimited see its publication, *Trout* magazine (Vienna, Va.).

42. Wallace Kaufman and Orrin Pilkey, *The Beachers Are Moving: The Drowning of America's Shoreline* (New York, 1979); Orrin H. Pilkey, Jr., William J. Neal, and Orrin H. Pilkey, Sr., *From Currituck to Calabash: Living with North Carolina's Barrier Islands* (Research Triangle Park, N.C., 1978).

43. John Clark, *Coastal Ecosystems: Ecological Considerations for Management of the Coastal Zone* (Washington, D.C., 1974); Clark, *The Sanibel Report* (Washington, D.C., 1976).

44. *Barrier Islands Newsletter,* National Wildlife Federation (Washington, D.C.); *Barrier Islands and Beaches,* newsletter, Barrier Islands Workshop (Washington, D.C.).

45. *Newsletter.* Association for the Preservation of Assateague (Towson, Md.).

46. *Nature Conservancy News* (Washington, D.C.); *Natural Areas Journal* (Rockford, Ill.)

47. *Michigan Natural Areas,* newsletter, Michigan Natural Areas Association (East Lansing); Jerry F. Franklin et al., *Federal Research in Natural Areas in Oregon and Washington,* Pacific Northwest Forest and Range Experiment Station, U.S. Forest Service (Portland, Oreg., 1972).

48. "Ecology Forum," a regular series in *Nature Conservancy News.*

49. Philip M. Hoose, *Building an Ark* (Covelo, Calif., 1981).

50. A. A. Lindsey, D. V. Schmeltz, and S. A. Nicholas, *Natural Areas in Indiana and Their Preservation* (Lafayette, Ind., 1969).

51. Samuel P. Hays, "Human Choice in the Great Lakes Wildlands," in Susan Flader, ed., *Environmental Change in the Great Lakes Forest* (Minneapolis, Minn., 1982).

52. Aubrey P. Altshuller, "Atmospheric Sulfur Dioxide and Sulfate: Distribution of Concentration at Urban and Nonurban Sites in the United States," *Environmental Science and Technology,* 7(1973): 709–12; National Research Council, *Sulfur Oxides* (Washington, D.C., 1978); Environmental Protection Agency, *Position Paper on Regulation of Atmospheric Sulfates,* EPA-450/2-75-007 (Research Triangle Park, N.C., 1975); for an atmospheric tracking program, "Project DaVinci," see *Environmental Science and Technology,* 10(1976): 730; "Smog: Both a Rural and Urban Headache," *Environmental Science and Technology,* 10(1976): 1084–5; William S. Cleveland and T. E. Graedel, "Photochemical Air Pollution in the Northeast United States," *Science,* June 22, 1979, 1273–8.

53. Bruce Hamilton, "Indians, Ranchers and Environmentalists Fight for Clean Air," *Sierra,* Nov.-Dec. 1977, 35–6.

54. Environment Canada, *Downwind: The Acid Rain Story* (Ottawa, 1981); "Acid Rain Bills Reflect Regional Dispute," *Science,* Nov. 13, 1981, 770–1.

55. Journal of the *Air Pollution Control Association,* 17(1967): 179; A. E. Mercker, executive secretary, Vegetable Growers Association of America, Senate Committee on Public Works, Hearings, *Air Pollution,* Part 3, 90th Cong., 1st sess., 1967, 2227; John T. Middleton, "Air Quality Criteria and Standards for Agriculture," *Journal of the Air Pollution Control Association,* 15(1967): 476–80; Alex Hershaft, "Air Pollution Damage Functions," *Environmental Science and Technology,* 10(1976): 995.

56. LRE, "Preserving Our Visibility Heritage," *Environmental Science and Technology,* 13(1979): 266–8; *Protecting Visibility: An EPA Report to Congress,* EPA-450/5-79-008 (Research Triangle Park, N.C., 1979); John Trojonis and Kung Yuan, *Visibility in the Southwest: An Exploration of the Historical Data Base,* EPA-600/3-78-039 (Research Triangle Park, N.C., 1978); *Visibility in the Northeast: Long-term Visibility Trends and Visibility/Pollutant Relationships,* EPA-600/3-78-975 (Research Triangle Park, N.C., 1978).

57. David E. Burnmaster, "The New Pollution: Groundwater Contamination," *Environment,* 24(Mar. 1982): 6–13, 33–6; Amy Horne, "Groundwater Policy: A Patchwork of Protection," *Environment,* 24(Apr. 1982): 6–11, 35; Well Water Publishing, *Alert* (Worthington, Ohio, 1982).

58. William K. Reilly, ed., *The Use of Land* (New York, 1973).

59. David Callies, *The Quiet Revolution in Land Use Control* (Washington, D.C., 1971).

60. *Coastal Zone Management Newsletter* (Washington, D.C., 1969); *Coastal Zone Management Journal* (New York, 1974); Robert G. Healy, ed., *Protecting the Golden Shore* (Washington, D.C., 1974).

61. House Subcommittee on Fisheries and Wildlife Conservation, Hearings, *Estuarine Areas,* 90th Cong., 1st sess., 1967; Senate Committee on Commerce, *Estuaries and Their Natural Resources,* 90th Cong., 2d sess., 1968; Commission on Marine Science, *Our Nation and the Sea* (Washington, D.C., 1969); House Subcommittee on Rivers and Harbors, *Coastal Zone Management,* 91st Cong., 1st sess., 1969; Anne W. Simon, *The Thin Edge* (New York, 1978); The Coast Alliance and Friends of the Earth, *Coast Alert; Scientists Speak Out* (n.p., 1981); Jenning C. Myers, *America's Coasts in the 1980's: Policies and Issues* (Washington, D.C., 1981).

62. State coastal zone management plans and newsletters issued by the state authorities (AF).

63. Lorraine M. Fleming, *Delaware's Outstanding Natural Areas and Their Preservation* (Hockeissen, Del., 1978).

64. Marc Hershman et al., *Under New Management: Port Growth and Emerging Coastal Management Programs* (Seattle, Wash., 1978).

65. *Environmental Quality,* 8th Annual Report of the Council on Environmental Quality (Washington, D.C., 1977), 109–110; Robert L. Bish et al., *Coastal Resource Use: Decisions on Puget Sound* (Seattle, Wash., 1975).

66. *Coastal Zone Management: Today and Tomorrow – The Necessity for Multiple Use,* conference proceedings, Gleneden Beach, Oreg., Feb. 20–23, 1979, Oregon Coastal Zone Management Association and the Association of Oregon Counties.

6. The Toxic Environment

1. *Chemical Regulation Reporter; Nucleonics Week; Exposure; Chemical Week; Toxic Substances Journal.*

2. Ralph H. Lutts, "Chemical Fallout: Rachel Carson's *Silent Spring,* Radioactive Fallout, and the Environmental Movement," *Environmental Review,* 9(Fall 1985): 210–25.

3. "Food Chains of the North," *Nuclear Information,* Sept.-Oct. 1963, 15; W. O. Pruitt, Jr., "A New Caribou Problem," *The Beaver,* Winter 1962; *Environmental Health Letter,* Jan. 1, 1982, 7–8.

4. Robert H. Wirtz, "War and the Living Environment," *Nuclear Information,* Sept.-Oct. 1963, 10–11; Robert L. Rudd, *Pesticides and the Living Landscape* (Madison, Wis., 1964), 250–4.

5. Paul Langner, "Hazardous Wastes: Ghosts of a Prodigal Past," *Technology Review,* Aug.-Sept. 1980, 10–11.

6. D. R. Greenwood et al., *A Handbook of Key Federal Regulations and Criteria for Multimedia Environmental Control,* EPA-600/7-79-175 (Washington, D.C., 1979).

7. Adeline Gordon Levine, *Love Canal* (Lexington, Mass., 1982).

8. *Nuclear Information; Science and the Citizen; Environment.* Rae Goodell, *The Visible Scientists* (Boston, 1975), 60–9. Barry Commoner, "Fallout and Water Pollution – Parallel Cases," *Science and the Citizen,* Dec. 1964, esp. 4–5; Louise Zibold Reiss, "Strontium-90 Absorption by Deciduous Teeth," *Science,* Nov. 24, 1961, 1669–73.

9. Rudd, *Pesticides and the Living Landscape;* articles on pesticides in *Science and Citizen,* May 1964, Apr. 1965, Oct. 1965, Oct. 1966.

10. The *New York Times Index* did not carry a separate pesticide heading until 1959; coverage increased steadily thereafter. For evolution of the issue see items in the *New York Times;* editorials urged caution in applying pesticides, which brought forth criticism from the National Agricultural Chemicals

Association and support from the National Wildlife Federation. *New York Times,* July 31, 1961, Aug. 16, 1961, Aug. 30, 1961. Aerial spraying to control the fire ant in the South and the gypsy moth in the Northeast led to protests from the New York Zoological Society, the Audubon Society, the Wildlife Management Institute, the National Wildlife Federation, and the Nature Conservancy and to federal funds for research on the problem. *Living Wilderness,* Summer-Fall 1958, 20–2.

11. Thomas R. Dunlap, *DDT: Scientists, Citizens and Public Policy* (Princeton, N.J., 1981). A little-publicized impact of pesticides involved the destruction of bees; for protests from bee farmers and the establishment of a federal indemnification project based on pesticide-caused loss, see *American Bee Journal,* 1958–77; *Michigan Farmer,* 1967–9.

12. Thomas Whiteside, *The Pendulum and the Toxic Cloud: The Course of Dioxin Contamination* (New Haven, Conn., 1979).

13. Robert Van Den Bosch, *The Pesticide Conspiracy* (New York, 1978); Samuel S. Epstein, *The Politics of Cancer* (San Francisco, 1978).

14. Charles O. Jackson, *Food and Drug Legislation in the New Deal* (Princeton, N.J., 1970); James S. Turner, *The Chemical Feast* (New York, 1970).

15. Ralph Nader and John Abbotts, *The Menace of Atomic Energy* (New York, 1977); Harvey Wasserman and Norman Solomon, *Killing Our Own* (New York, 1982); Bernard L. Cohen, *Before It's Too Late* (New York, 1983); *Nucleonics Week,* newsletter of the Atomic Industrial Forum; *Critical Mass,* newsletter, Critical Mass Project (Washington, D.C.).

16. Earth Day events on college campuses in 1970 dealt with atomic energy primarily in terms of its thermal effects as did most early licensing issues before the Atomic Safety and Licensing Board. They can be followed in *Nucleonics Week.*

17. John W. Gofman and Arthur R. Tamplin, *Poisoned Power* (Emmaus, Pa., 1971); debates over the Gofman-Tamplin arguments can be followed in *Nucleonics Week.*

18. Richard Curtis and Elizabeth Hogan, *Perils of the Peaceful Atom* (New York, 1969); Petr Beckmann, *The Health Hazards of Not Going Nuclear* (New York, 1976).

19. *Nucleus,* newsletter, Union of Concerned Scientists (Cambridge, Mass.); Daniel Ford, *The Cult of the Atom* (New York, 1982).

20. Daniel Martin, *Three Mile Island* (Cambridge, Mass., 1980); Bill Keisling, *Three Mile Island* (Seattle, Wash., 1980); news clippings during the three months following the accident, from the *Washington Post, Washington Star, Baltimore Sun, Philadelphia Inquirer, New York Times,* and *New York Daily Herald* in (AF).

21. Ernest Sternglass, *Low Level Radiation,* rev. ed. (New York, 1982); Charles W. Huver et al., *Methodologies for the Study of Low-Level Radiation in the Midwest* (Millville, Minn., 1979).

22. Union of Concerned Scientists, *The Nuclear Fuel Cycle: A Survey of the Public Health, Environmental and National Security Effects of Nuclear Power* (Cambridge, Mass., 1974).

23. Ronnie D. Lipschutz, *Radioactive Waste* (Cambridge, Mass., 1980); Terry Lash, "Radioactive Waste: Nuclear Energy's Dilemma," *Amicus Journal,* 1(Fall 1979): 24–34.

24. *Groundswell,* newsletter, Nuclear Information and Research Service (Washington, D.C.); *Critical Mass* (Washington, D.C.).

25. Richard Pollock, "Congress Charts Pro-Nuclear Course," *Critical Mass,* 6(June-July 1980): 6–7.

26. Daniel M. Berman, *Death on the Job* (New York, 1978); Nicholas A. Ashford, *Crisis in the Workplace: Occupational Disease and Injury* (Cambridge, Mass., 1976); John Mendeloff, *Regulating Safety: An Economic and Political Analysis of Occupational Safety and Health Policy* (Cambridge, Mass., 1979).

27. *Lifelines: OCAW Health and Safety News,* newsletter, Oil, Chemical and Atomic Workers Union (Denver, Colo.).

28. See items from the *New York Times, Washington Post, Wall Street Journal, Pittsburgh Post-Gazette,* and *Pittsburgh Press* (AF).

29. John Mendeloff, "Reducing Occupational Health Risks: Uncertain Effects and Unstated Benefits," *Technology Review,* May 1980, 66–68, 73–8.

30. Paul Brodeur, *Expendable Americans* (New York, 1973); *Occupational Health and Safety Letter; Occupational Health and Safety Reporter.*

31. *Chemical and Engineering News,* July 3, 1978; *Environment Reporter,* June 23, 1978, 448–9, and June 30, 1978, 478–9; "OSHA's War on Cancer: What It Means to Plastics," *Plastics World* (Society of the Plastics Industry), 4 parts, June-Sept. 1978.

32. National Research Council, *Epidemiology and Air Pollution* (Washington, D.C., 1985).

33. Sir Richard Doll and Dr. Richard Peto, *The Causes of Cancer: Quantitative Estimates of Avoidable Risks of Cancer in the United States Today* (Oxford, 1981); the issue can be followed in *Environmental Health Letter,* e.g., Feb. 22, 1982, 5, reporting recent German research indicating that 25 percent of workers' cancer in ten industrial plants, 1950–68, was caused by "influences at work."

34. Michael Stuart Brown, *Acceptable Risks: Occupational Health in the Nuclear Industry,* Department of City and Regional Planning (Ithaca, N.Y., 1980); Wasserman and Soloman, *Killing Our Own,* 140–62.

35. John G. Fuller, *The Day We Bombed Utah* (New York, 1984).

36. *OSHA/Environmental Watch,* newsletter, OSHA/Environmental Network (Washington, D.C.).

37. Robert H. Boyle, *Malignant Neglect* (New York, 1979); Ralph Nader, Ronald Brownstein, and John Richard, *Who's Poisoning America* (San Francisco, 1981); Christopher Norwood, *At Highest Risk* (New York, 1979).

38. One such case involved action of the Food and Drug Administration that had established a "zero tolerance" level in food for the pesticide heptachlor but, because heptachlor was an "unavoidable contaminant," with an "enforcement level" of 0.3 ppm at which it would be withdrawn from the market. "Heptachlor," *Pesticides and You,* May 1982, 6; Gerald Rimland and Gerland E. Larson, "The Manpower Quality Decline: An Ecological Perspective," *Armed Forces and Society,* Fall 1981, 21–78.

39. National Academy of Sciences, Commission on Natural Resources, *Analytical Studies for the U.S. Environmental Protection Agency,* vol. I, "Decision Making in the Environmental Protection Agency," and IIa, "Case Studies" (Washington, D.C., 1977).

40. Council on Agricultural Science and Technology (CAST), *The Environmental Protection Agency's Nine "Principles" of Carcinogenesis,* CAST Report no. 54 (Ames, Iowa, 1976).

41. Thomas Whiteside, *The Withering Rain* (New York, 1971) and *The Pendulum and the Toxic Cloud* (New Haven, Conn., 1979); Michael Uhl and Tod

Ensign, *GI Guinea Pigs* (n.p. 1980), 109–225; Bureau of Land Management, *Vegetation Management with Herbicides: Western Oregon: Final Environmental Impact Statement,* 2 vols. (Portland, Oreg., 1978).

42. Ronald Brownstein and Larry Lack, "Trees vs. People," *Amicus Journal,* 2(Summer 1980): 24–30; for the Maine case see *Maine Times;* for Montana see clippings from *Missoulian* (AF); Northwest Coalition for Alternatives to Pesticides, *NCAP News* (Eugene, Oreg.); Jan M. Newton, *An Economic Analysis of Herbicide Use for Intensive Forest Management* (Eugene, Oreg., 1979)

43. *Down to Earth,* quarterly publication of the Dow Chemical Company (Midland, Mich.), contains a running defense of its point of view; see also a series of articles by reporter Paul Rau in *Midland News,* Sept. 2–Sept. 12, 1980.

44. The issue can be followed in *Chemical Week,* 1980–1.

45. See also issues of *Chemical Regulation Reporter* and *NCAP News,* both of which follow the proceedings.

46. Department of Agriculture, Food Safety and Quality Service, *Report on the PCB Incident in the Western United States* (Washington, D.C., 1980).

47. National Research Council, *Polychorinated Biphenyls* (Washington, D.C., 1979); EDF v. EPA, Nov. 3, 1978 (12 ERC 1353), esp. 1354–9 for a capsule history of the issue up to 1978.

48. Arthur B. Ferguson, "Direct Federal Controls: New Source Performance Standards and Hazardous Emissions," *Ecology Law Quarterly,* 4(1975): 645–59.

49. David D. Doniger, "Federal Regulation of Vinyl Chloride: A Short Course in the Law and Policy of Toxic Substances Control," *Ecology Law Quarterly,* 7(1978): 497–677.

50. National Research Council, *Lead: Airborne Lead in Perspective* (Washington, D.C., 1972); National Research Council, *Lead in the Human Environment* (Washington, D.C., 1980); Herbert L. Needleman, *Low Level Lead Exposure* (New York, 1980); Donald Lynam, Lillian G. Piantanida, and Jerome F. Cole, *Environmental Lead* (New York, 1981); Michael Rutter and Robin Russell Jones, eds., *Lead versus Health* (London, 1983).

51. Gregory S. Wetstone and Jan Goldman, *Chronology of Events Surrounding the Ethyl Decision,* and Gregory S. Wetstone, ed., *Meeting Record from Resolution of Scientific Issues and the Judicial Process: Ethyl Corporation v. EPA, Oct. 21, 1977* (Washington, D.C.: Environmental Law Institute, 1981).

52. Gordon J. Stopps, paper read before the Air Quality Criteria Symposium, New York, June 4–5, 1968, as published in Senate Public Works Committee, *Air Pollution – 1968,* vol. 3, 90th Cong., 2d sess., pp. 1054–68; views of Jerome F. Cole, Lead Industries Association, *Environment Reporter,* Jan. 13, 1978, 1392–3; views of Francis X. McCardle, commissioner, Department of Environmental Health, New York City, *Environment Reporter,* July 7, 1978, 427–8.

53. Herbert L. Needleman et al., "Deficits in Psychologic and Classroom Performance of Children with Elevated Dentine Lead Levels," *New England Journal of Medicine,* Mar. 29, 1978, 689–95; testimony of Dr. Jerome Cole of the International Lead-Zinc Association: "Drs. Sergio Piomelli and Herbert Needleman . . . represent what is at best a minority view that adverse health effects occur at blood-levels below 40 μg/dl." House Subcommittee on Health and the Environment, Hearing, *Oversight – Clean Air Act Amendments of 1977,* 95th Cong., 2d sess., 1978, 344.

54. Environmental Defense Fund, *Petition for the Initiation of Rulemaking Proceedings to Establish a Policy Governing the Classification and Regulation* *of Carcinogenic Air Pollutants under the Clean Air Act* (Washington, D.C., 1977); *Environment Reporter,* Nov. 11, 1977, 1028; Mar. 31, 1978, 1871.

55. *Environment Reporter,* Apr. 6, 1979; Sept. 20, 1979; Sept. 18, 1979; Oct. 11, 1979; Nov. 2, 1979. R. E. Albert, R. E. Train, and E. Anderson, "Rationale Developed by the Environmental Protection Agency for the Assessment of Carcinogenic Risks," *Journal of the National Cancer Institute,* May 1977, 1537–41.

56. Environmental Defense Fund and Robert Boyle, *Malignant Neglect;* Paul Moskowitz et al., *Troubled Waters: Toxic Chemicals in the Hudson River* (New York, 1977); Robert V. Bartlett, *The Reserve Mining Controversy* (Bloomington, Ind., 1980).

57. James Banks, "Dumping into Surface Waters," in Bruce Piasecki, ed., *Beyond Dumping* (Westport, Conn., 1984), 37–52.

58. Patricia A. D'Itri and Frank M. D'Itri, *Mercury Contamination* (New York, 1977).

59. William R. Ginsberg, "Land Pollution: Where Do We Go From Here?" *Amicus Journal,* 1(Winter 1980): 3–37.

60. Newspaper clippings, Hardeman County, Tenn. (AF).

61. Samuel S. Epstein, Lester O. Brown, and Carl Pope, *Hazardous Waste in America* (San Francisco, 1982); Levine, *Love Canal.*

62. Michael H. Brown, "Portrait of a Polluter: Hooker Chemical Company," *Amicus Journal,* 1(Winter 1980): 20–9.

63. Ronald Brownstein, "Resource Conservation and Recovery Art: Four Years Old and Still Not Off the Ground," *Amicus Journal,* 1(Spring 1980): 13–15.

64. Gary N. Dietrich, "Information Burdens and Difficulties in Conceptualizing the Crisis: A Reappraisal," in Piasecki, ed., *Beyond Dumping,* 19–26.

65. Council on Environmental Quality, *Chemical Hazards to Human Reproduction* (Washington, D.C., 1981).

66. Water Well Publishing *Alert* (Worthington, Ohio, 1982); Council on Environmental Quality, *Contamination of Ground Water by Toxic Organic Chemicals* (Washington, D.C., 1981); EPA, *Proposed Ground Water Protection Strategy* (Washington, D.C., 1980).

67. *Ecological Illness Law Report* (Chicago, Ill.)

68. *Risk in a Complex Society,* a Marsh and McLennon Public Opinion Survey conducted by Louis Harris and Associates, Inc. (n.p., 1980), 7–10.

69. Council on Environmental Quality, *Toxic Chemicals and Public Protection* (Washington, D.C., 1980).

70. *Risk in a Complex Society;* Lois Gibbs, *Love Canal: My Story* (Albany, N.Y., 1982).

7. Population, Resources, and the Limits to Growth

1. Francis R. Thibodeau and Hermann H. Field, *Sustaining Tomorrow* (Hanover, N.H., 1984); Lester R. Brown et al., *State of the World,* 1984 (Washington, D.C., 1984).

2. "Suburbs Are Getting Crowded," *Pittsburgh Post-Gazette,* Sept. 17, 1984.

3. Samuel P. Hays, "The Limits to Growth Issue: An Historical Perspective," in Chester L. Cooper, ed., *Growth in America* (Westport, Conn., 1976).

4. Edwin R. Squires, ed., *The Environmental Crisis: The Ethical Dilemma* (Macedonia, Mich., 1982); Eleventh Commandment Fellowship, *Eleventh Commandment Newsletter* (San Francisco); Mark Harwell, *Nuclear Winter* (New York, 1984).

5. International Union for the Conservation of Nature and World Wildlife Fund, *World Conservation Strategy* (n.p., 1980).

6. Statements about the relative lack of interest by grass-roots environmental groups come from discussions with environmental leaders in Washington, D.C.

7. Catherine Caufield, *In the Rainforest* (New York, 1984); Norman Myers, *The Primary Source: Tropical Forests and Our Future* (New York, 1984).

8. Paul R. Ehrlich, Anne H. Ehrlich, and John P. Holdren, *Ecoscience: Population, Resources and Environment* (San Francisco, 1970); Noel Hinrichs, *Population, Environment, and People* (New York, 1971).

9. Mark Perlman, "The Role of Population Projects for the Year 2000," in Julian Simon and Herman Kahn, eds., *The Resourceful Earth: A Response to "Global 2000"* (Oxford, 1984).

10. Charles F. Westoff and others, *Toward the End of Growth* (Englewood Cliffs, N.J., 1973).

11. Barry Commoner, *The Closing Circle* (New York, 1971).

12. Lester R. Brown, *The Twenty-ninth Day* (New York, 1978).

13. Donella H. Meadows et al., *The Limits to Growth* (New York, 1972).

14. Commoner, *Closing Circle.*

15. Barry Commoner, Michael Carr, and Paul J. Stamler, "The Causes of Pollution," *Environment,* 13(Apr. 1971): 2–19.

16. Council on Environmental Quality, *The Global 2000 Report to the President,* 3 vols. (Washington, D.C., 1981); Simon and Kahn, eds., *Resourceful Earth;* Julian L. Simon, *The Ultimate Resource* (Princeton, N.J., 1981).

17. Commission on Population Growth and the American Future, *Population and the American Future* (New York, 1972); Edward Pohlman, ed., *Population: A Clash of Prophets* (New York, 1973).

18. Charles F. Westoff, "The Decline of Unplanned Births in the United States," *Science,* Jan. 9, 1976, 38–41.

19. Zero Population Growth, *National Reporter* (Washington, D.C.).

20. William U. Chandler, *Investing in Children,* Worldwatch paper no. 64 (Washington, D.C., 1985); William M. Chamberlain, "Population Control: The Legal Approach to a Biological Imperative," *Ecology Law Quarterly,* 1(1971): 143–72.

21. Rebecca J. Cook, *State Population Legislation: A Report Prepared for the New England Regional Conference on Population* (New York: Population Council, 1972).

22. National Wildlife Federation surveys of its associate members' interests ranked population quite high, in 1977 fifth among ten issues and in 1982 second among six; see *National Wildlife,* Apr.-May 1977, and Apr.-May 1982; see also Sierra Club leaflet, "The Need for Zero Population Growth" (1984).

23. The Population Fund newsletter, *The Other Side* (Washington, D.C.), follows the issue; Richard D. Lamm and Gerry Imhoff, *The Immigration Time Bomb* (New York, 1985).

24. Lester R. Brown, "The World Food Prospect," *Science,* Dec. 12, 1975, 1053–9; David Pimentel and Carl W. Hall, *Food and Energy Resources* (Orlando, Fla., 1984).

25. See articles in the *New York Times* on the "world food situation," Aug.-Nov. 1974, and a summary, Boyce Remsberger, "World Food Crises: Basic Ways of Life Face Upheaval," *New York Times,* Nov. 5, 1974.

26. Articles on the World Food Congress, *New York Times,* Nov. 5–19, 1974.

27. Georg Borgstrom, *The Hungry Planet* (New York, 1965); Borgstrom, *Too Many* (New York, 1969).

28. S. H. Wittwer, "Maximum Production Capacity of Food Crops," *Bioscience,* 24(1974): 216–23.

29. Jane Brody, "Search for Protein Crucial in Struggle against Hunger," *New York Times,* Oct. 11, 1974.

30. Boyce Remsberger, "Curb on U.S. Waste Urged to Help World's Hungry," *New York Times,* Oct. 25, 1974.

31. Neil Sampson, *Farmland or Wasteland* (Emmaus, Pa., 1981); W. Wendell Fletcher and Charles E. Little, *The American Cropland Crisis* (Bethesda, Md., 1982).

32. Jay W. Forrester, *World Dynamics* (Cambridge, Mass., 1971); Donella H. Meadows et al., *The Limits to Growth;* H. S. D. Cole et al., eds., *Models of Doom* (New York, 1973); Cy A. Adler, *Ecological Fantasies* (New York, 1973); J. Peter Vajk, *Doomsday Has Been Cancelled* (Culver City, Calif. 1978).

33. Hays, "The Limits to Growth Issue."

34. Sam H. Schurr, ed., *Energy, Economic Growth, and the Environment* (Baltimore, 1972); John Holdren and Philip Herrera, *Energy* (San Francisco, 1971); Barry Commoner, *The Poverty of Power* (New York, 1976).

35. Barry Commoner, Howard Boksenbaum, and Michael Corr, *The Social Costs of Power Production* (New York, 1975); The Georgia Conservancy, *The Wolfcreek Statement* (Atlanta, Ga., 1976).

36. Amory B. Lovins and John H. Price, *Non-Nuclear Futures* (New York, 1975).

37. Wilson Clark, *Energy for Survival* (New York, 1975); Barry Commoner, Howard Boksenbaum, and Michael Corr, *Alternative Technologies for Power Production* (New York, 1975).

38. David Roe, *Dynamos and Virgins* (New York, 1984).

39. Gerald O. Barney, ed., *The Unfinished Agenda* (New York, 1977), 50–68; Keith Roberts, ed., *Toward an Energy Policy* (San Francisco, 1973).

40. Energy Policy Project of the Ford Foundation, *A Time to Choose* (Cambridge, Mass., 1974); Solar Energy Research Institute, *A New Prosperity* (Andover, Mass., 1981).

41. Ralph Cavanagh, "The Pacific Northwest Is Praying for Rain: A Cautionary Tale for Utility Executives," *Amicus Journal,* 2(Summer 1980): 31–8; Laura B. King, *Moving California toward a Renewable Energy Future: An Alternative Scenario for the Next Fifteen Years* (San Francisco: Natural Resources Defense Council, 1982).

42. Letter, Charles Komanoff to editor, *Science,* Sept. 13, 1985, 1038.

43. Richard Morgan and Sandra Jerabeck, *How to Challenge Your Local Electric Utility* (Washington, D.C.: Environmental Action Foundation, 1974).

44. Richard A. Kerr, "Another Oil Resource Warning," *Science,* Jan. 27, 1984, 382.

45. U.S. Congress, Office of Technology Assessment, *The Direct Use of Coal: Prospects and Problems of Production and Combustion* (Washington, D.C., 1979).

46. Daniel Behrman, *Solar Energy* (Boston, 1976); Denis Hayes, *Rays of Hope* (New York, 1977); John Keyes, *The Solar Conspiracy* (Dobbs Ferry, N.Y., 1975); Stephen Lyons, ed., *Sun! A Handbook for the Solar Decade* (San Francisco, 1978).

47. *Solar Age; Solar Intelligence Digest; Renewable Energy News.*

48. Allen L. Hammond, "Photovoltaics: The Semiconductor Revolution Comes to Solar," *Science,* July 29, 1977, 445–7; U.S. Congress, Office of Technology Assessment, *Application of Solar Technology to Today's Energy Needs* (Washington, D.C., 1977); Jeffrey L. Smith, "Photovoltaics," *Science,* June 26, 1981, 1472–8.

49. See story about a case of personal ingenuity in the development of solar energy in Conrad, Montana, *Montana Eagle,* Apr. 7, 1982, 7–9.

50. For cost implications of hard energy see Bartle Bull, "Voodoo Energy," *Amicus Journal,* 3(Spring 1982): 4–6; Ralph Cavanagh, "Recycling Our Electric Utilities: Can the Industry Be Saved from Itself and the Department of Energy," *Amicus Journal,* 6(Summer 1984): 28–33.

51. Roger W. Sant and Steven C. Carhart, *Eight Great Energy Myths: The Least-Cost Energy Strategy – 1978–2000* (Arlington, Va.: Energy Productivity Center, Mellon Institute, 1981).

52. Letter, Amory Lovins to editor, *Science,* Sept. 6, 1985, 914; chapter entitled "Scale," in Amory B. Lovins, *Soft Energy Paths* (San Francisco, 1977), 85–103.

53. For the decentralist stance see the publications of the Institute for Local Self-Reliance (Washington, D.C.), such as *Self-Reliant Cities* (1981); *Waste to Wealth* (1984); *Be Your Own Power Company* (1984).

54. James Bishop, Jr., "Oil Shale: Bonanza or Bust for the Rockies," *National Wildlife,* 12(June-July 1974): 11; *CF Letter,* Oct. 1975, "Net Energy Analysis Can be Illuminating"; Charles A. S. Hall and Cutler J. Cleveland, "Petroleum Drilling and Production in the United States: Yield Per Effort and Net Energy Analysis," *Science,* Feb. 6, 1981, 576–9.

55. Amory Lovins, "Energy Strategy: The Road Not Taken," *Foreign Affairs,* 55(Oct. 1976): 65–96.

56. See "Energy Quality," in Lovins, *Soft Energy Paths,* 73–83.

57. Barry Commoner, Howard Boksenbaum, and Michael Corr, *Human Welfare: The End Use of Power* (New York, 1975).

58. Lovins, *Soft Energy Paths,* 105–44.

59. Hugh Nash, ed., *The Energy Controversy: Soft Path Questions and Answers by Amory Lovins and His Critics* (San Francisco, 1979); Charles Yulish Associates, Inc., *Soft vs. Hard Energy Paths: Ten Critical Essays on Amory Lovins' "Energy Strategy: The Road Not Taken"* (New York, 1977).

60. Publications of the Rocky Mountain Institute, formed by Lovins in 1982 at Old Snowmass, Colorado; see varied institute publications (AF); Lovins, "Saving Gigabucks with Negawatts," *Public Utilities Fortnightly,* March 21, 1985, 19, and April 4, 1985, 12.

8. Environmental Inquiry and Ideas

1. *Environmental Ethics* (Athens, Ga.); Ian G. Barbour, *Technology, Environment and Human Values* (New York, 1980); Albert J. Fritsch, *Environmental Ethics: Choices for Concerned Citizens* (New York, 1980); Bill Devall and George Sessions, *Deep Ecology* (Salt Lake City, Utah, 1985).

2. Theodore Roszak, *Where the Wasteland Ends* (New York, 1973); Allen Schnaiberg, *The Environment: From Surplus to Scarcity* (Oxford, 1980); Craig R. Humphrey and Frederick R. Buttel, *Environment, Energy and Society* (Belmont, Calif., 1982).

3. Robert Harris, contribution to debate, *Environmental Forum,* 1(July 1982): 14–16; Edith Efron, *The Apocalyptics* (New York, 1984).

4. Jack Doyle, *Lines Across the Land* (Washington, D.C., 1979); *Radical*

America, 17(1983) entire issue, especially Jim O'Brien, "Environmentalism as a Mass Movement: Historical Notes," 2–28; Malcolm Forbes Baldwin, "A Conservative's Program for the Environment," *Environment* (23 Apr. 1981): 25, 29.

5. Publications of Florida Defenders of the Environment (AF) reflect the heavy participation of technical experts in its affairs; Gov. Reubin Askew stated that "Florida Defenders of the Environment is an organization that has a tradition of going to the experts in seeking solutions to environmental problems," in *Florida: Paradise Regained* (Conference report, Florida Defenders of the Environment, Gainesville, Fla., 1985).

6. Gene E. Likens, "A Priority for Ecological Research," *Bulletin of the Ecological Society of America,* Dec. 1983, 234–43; Daniel B. Tunstall, "Developing Indicators of Environmental Quality," *Social Indicators Research,* 6(1979): 301–47; Monitoring and Assessment Research Center, *Historical Monitoring,* MARC Report no. 31 (London, 1985); articles in *Western Wildlands,* 11(Fall 1985): 2–19, concerning the use of honeybees, microinvertebrates, and lichens for pollution monitoring.

7. See *Birth Defect Prevention News,* National Network to Prevent Birth Defects (Washington, D.C.); *Indoor Air News,* Consumer Federation of America (Washington, D.C.); Frederica P. Perera and A. Karim Ahmed, *Respirable Particles: Impact of Airborne Fine Particulates on Health and the Environment* (Cambridge, Mass., 1979).

8. "The Air Cleaning Equipment People," *Environmental Science and Technology,* 10(1976): 866–7; Bruce Piasecki, "Struggling to Be Born: A New Industry Takes on Toxic Wastes and the EPA," *Amicus Journal,* 4(Spring 1983): 9–11; *Biocycle* (Emmaus, Pa.).

9. Michael G. Royston, *Pollution Prevention Pays* (Oxford, 1979); Donald Huisingh and Vicki Bailey, eds., *Making Pollution Prevention Pay* (New York, 1982); Dr. Robert P. Bringer, 3M Corporation, "Making Pollution Prevention Pay," *EPA Journal,* Dec. 1984, 28–9.

10. John E. Bonine, "The Evolution of 'Technology-Forcing' in the Clean Air Act," *Environment Reporter,* monograph no. 21, July 25, 1975; D. Bruce LaPierre, "Technology Forcing and Federal Environmental Protection Statutes," *Iowa Law Review,* 62(1977): 771–838; "Firms Curb Hazardous Wastes to Avoid Expensive Disposal," *Wall Street Journal,* May 31, 1985.

11. David Doniger, *The Law and Policy of Toxic Substances Control* (Baltimore, 1979).

12. "1970, a Year of Environmental Concern, Ends on a Sobering Note," *CF Letter,* Dec. 1970, 3–4; American Paper Institute v. Train, Aug. 6, 1976 (9 ERC 1065); American Frozen Food Institute v. Train, May 11, 1976 (8 ERC 993).

13. Charles Xintaras, "Behavioral Toxicology Looks at Air Pollutants," *Environmental Science and Technology,* 2(1968): 731–3.

14. Laura Tangley, "A National Biological Survey," *BioScience,* 35(1985): 686–90.

15. Acid-rain monitoring was an exception; see, e.g., James A. Lynch, Edward S. Corbett, and Gregg B. Rishel, "Atmospheric Deposition: Spatial and Temporal Variation in Pennsylvania, 1982," and similar reports for 1983 and 1984 (University Park, Pa., 1982, 1983, 1984).

16. Lester Breslow, "Trends in Health-Ecological Consequences for the Human Population," in "Science as a Way of Knowing II – Human Ecology," *American Zoology,* 25(1985): 433–9.

17. Virginia Brodine, "Running In Place," *Environment,* 14(Jan.-Feb. 1972): 2–11.

18. Stephen Croall and William Rankin, *Ecology for Beginners* (New York, 1981); Thomas C. Emmel, *An Introduction to Ecology and Population Biology* (New York, 1973).

19. John R. Sheaffer, "Circular vs. Linear Water Systems: Going Back to Nature's Way," *Environment,* 26(Oct. 1984): 10, 12–15, 42–4; *Environmental Action Bulletin* (Emmaus, Pa.).

20. Likens, "A Priority for Ecological Research."

21. Gary W. Barrett, George M. Van Dyne, and Eugene P. Odum, "Stress Ecology," *BioScience,* 26(1976): 192–4; G. M. Woodwell, "Effects of Pollution on the Structure and Physiology of Ecosystems," *Science,* Apr. 24, 1970, 429–33.

22. Robert VanDen Bosch, *The Pesticide Conspiracy* (New York, 1978); William R. Lambert, ed., *A Decade of Extension Cotton Integrated Pest Management* (Athens, Ga., 1983); *The IPM Practitioner* (Berkeley, Calif., Bio-Integral Resource Center); *Journal of Pesticide Reform* (formerly *NCAP News*) (Eugene, Oreg.).

23. William M. Harlow and Ellwood S. Harrar, *Textbook of Dendrology Covering the Important Forest Trees of the United States and Canada* (New York, 1937); Wilderness Society et al., *National Forest Planning: A Conservationist's Handbook* (Washington, D.C., 1983); Bruce Boccard, "How Much Old Growth and Where?" *Newsletter,* Idaho Conservation League, 8(Aug. 1982): 6–7; Edward C. Fritz, *Sterile Forest: The Case against Clearcutting* (Austin, Tex., 1983).

24. *Prevention* magazine (Emmaus, Pa.); *Organic Gardening* (Emmaus, Pa.); *Mother Earth News* (Hendersonville, N.C.); *New Age* (Brighton, Mass.); *New Roots* (Greenfield, Mass.).

25. Jurgen Schmandt, Rose Ann Shorey, and Lilas Kinch, *Nutrition Policy in Transition* (Lexington, Mass., 1980); New England Conference on Food, Nutrition, and Health, *Final Report,* 2 vols. (Boston, 1979); *Nutrition Action,* Center for Science in the Public Interest (Washington, D.C.); *Nutrition Week,* Community Nutrition Institute (Washington, D.C.); U.S. Department of Health, Education, and Welfare, Public Health Service, *Healthy People* (Washington, D.C., 1979).

26. U.S. Congress, Office of Technology Assessment, Health Program Staff, *Smoke-Related Deaths and Financial Costs* (Washington, D.C., 1985; draft).

27. Adelle Davis, *Let's Eat Right to Keep Fit* (New York, 1954); Laurel Robertson, Carol Flinders, and Bronwen Godfrey, *Laurel's Kitchen* (Berkeley, Calif., 1976); Senate Select Committee on Nutrition and Human Needs, *Dietary Goals for the United States,* 95th Cong., 1st sess., 1977; Eliot Marshall, "The Academy Kills a Nutrition Report," *Science,* Oct. 25, 1985, 420–1.

28. Michael LaFavore, "Unseen Additives," *Organic Gardening,* July 1984, 68; Donald Scherer, *Personal Values and Environmental Issues* (New York, 1978), preface; Arthur J. Vander, *Nutrition, Stress and Toxic Chemicals* (Ann Arbor, Mich., 1981).

29. Richard C. Dorf and Yvonne L. Hunter, eds., *Appropriate Visions: Technology and the Individual* (San Francisco, 1978); *Rain* (Portland, Oreg.); *Alternative Sources of Energy* (Waseca, Minn.); the editors of "Rain," *Rainbook: Resources for Appropriate Technology* (New York, 1977).

30. *New Farm* (Emmaus, Pa.); *New Shelter* (Emmaus, Pa.); Institute for Alternative Agriculture, *Alternative Agriculture News* (Greenbelt, Md.); Dick Russell, "The Prairie Perspectives: Setting Agriculture Back on Its Biological Feet," *Amicus Journal,* 6(Winter 1985): 34–40.

31. Jim Leckie et al., *Other Homes and Garbage: Designs for Self-Sufficient Living* (San Francisco, 1975).

32. Gary Snyder, *Turtle Island* (New York, 1974), *The Old Ways* (San Francisco, 1977), *The Real Work* (New York, 1980); Albert J. Fritsch, ed, *99 Ways to a Simple Lifestyle* (New York, 1977).

33. Kimon Valaskakis et al., *The Conserver Society* (New York, 1979).

34. James A. Tober, *Who Owns the Wildlife?* (Westport, Conn., 1981), 49, 131.

35. Jonathan H. Turner and Charles E. Starnes, *Inequality: Privilege and Poverty in America* (Pacific Palisades, Calif.: Goodyear, 1976); Jeffrey G. Williamson and Peter H. Lindert, *American Inequality: A Macroeconomic History* (New York, 1980).

36. *Islands* (Santa Barbara, Calif.).

37. Matthew Roush, "Platte River Canoe Trip Creates Sense of Peace," *Traverse City* (Mich.) *Record Eagle,* Aug. 17, 1985, 7.

38. Most wilderness use was by day, rather than overnight, users and by people who lived nearby. Users were slightly above average in incomes, but with a significant proportion, between one-third and one-half, below the median income, varying with the area. In 1970–2 most spent less than twenty dollars a day, besides travel, in wilderness recreation. See Robert C. Lucas, "Use Patterns and Visitor Characteristics, Attitudes and Preferences in Nine Wilderness and Other Roadless Areas," USDA, Forest Service, Research Paper INT-253.

39. Brownie Carson, "Who Owns the Coast?" *Maine Environment,* Oct. 1985, 1–2.

40. Steve Griffiths, "Inner City Outings; Recruiting Allies for the Environment," *Sierra,* 70(Nov.-Dec. 1985): 110–13.

41. Bernard J. Frieden, *The Environmental Protection Hustle* (Cambridge, Mass., 1979); Susan Mulloy, "Housing Price Inflation: Whose Responsibility? A Report to the Sierra Club Conservation Department" (April 1978) (AF).

42. Paul P. Craig and Edward Berlin, "The Air of Poverty," *Environment,* 13(June 1971): 2–9.

43. See, for example, the economic analysis of "bequest value" of natural-environment areas in Richard G. Walsh, Larry D. Sanders, and John B. Loomis, *Wild and Scenic River Economics: Recreation Use and Preservation Value* (Englewood, Colo.: American Wilderness Alliance, 1985).

44. Herman Daly, *Steady State Economics* (San Francisco, 1977); H. V. Hodson, *The Diseconomies of Growth* (London, 1972); Warren Johnson, *Muddling Toward Frugality* (San Francisco, 1978).

45. Fred Hirsch, *Social Limits to Growth* (Cambridge, Mass., 1976); "The New Wealth," editorial, *Amicus Journal,* 3(Winter 1982); 2–3.

46. Barbara Everitt Bryant, "Marketing Newspapers With Lifestyle Research," *American Demographics,* Jan. 1981, 20, 22–5; Georgia Dulles, "Why Do We Buy? The Answer is Symbol," *New York Times,* May 20, 1980.

47. Michael S. Baram, "Cost-Benefit Analysis: An Inadequate Basis for Health, Safety, and Environmental Regulatory Decisionmaking," *Ecology Law Quarterly,* 8(1980): 473–532.

48. Charles Warren, chairman, Council on Environmental Quality, "In Search of a Better Thermometer: Economic Growth and Environmental Health" (Remarks at Pennsylvania Environmental Conference, Harrisburg, Pa., Mar. 3, 1978) (AF).

49. For cost-benefit strategies in forest management see *Forest Planning* (Eugene, Oreg.).

50. Richard N. L. Andrews and Mary Jo Waits, *Environmental Values in Public Decisions* (Ann Arbor, Mich.: School of Natural Resources, University of Michigan, 1978).

51. John V. Krutilla, *Natural Environments: Studies in Theoretical and Applied Analysis* (Baltimore, Md., 1972).

52. Hugh M. Pitcher, *Comments on Issues Raised in the Analysis of the Neuropsychological Effects of Low Level Lead Exposure* (Office of Policy Analysis, U.S. Environmental Protection Agency, 1984).

53. John H. Dickerson, "Limited Liability for Nuclear Accidents: Duke Power Co. v. Carolina Environmental Study Group, Inc." *Ecology Law Quarterly,* 8(1979): 163–86.

54. Talbot Page, "A Generic View of Toxic Chemicals and Similar Risks," *Ecology Law Quarterly,* 7(1978): 207–44.

55. Neil Orloff, *The Environmental Impact Statement Process* (Washington, D.C., 1978); Joan Willey and Jerome Kohl, *A North Carolina Citizen's Guide to Commenting on Environmental Impact Statements* (Raleigh, N.C., 1973).

56. Luther J. Carter, *The Florida Experience* (Baltimore, Md., 1974), 54, 168; *Water Resources Newsletter,* Dec. 5–6, 1970, 4; *CF Letter,* Apr. 1970, Dec. 1970, May 1972.

57. Frederick R. Anderson, *NEPA and the Courts* (Baltimore, 1973); Richard A. Liroff, *A National Policy for the Environment* (Bloomington, Ind., 1976); Stuart L. Hart and Gordon A. Enk, *Green Goals and Greenbacks* (Rensselaerville, N.Y.: Institute of Man and Science, 1978).

58. Water Resources Council, "Principles and Standards for Planning Water and Related Land Resources," *Federal Register,* Sept. 10, 1973, vol. 38, no. 174.

59. "Do Future Projects Have a Future?" Interview with Clement Bezold, *State Legislatures,* 6(May 1980): 18–21.

60. James P. Jackson, *Passages of a Stream: A Chronicle of the Meramec* (Columbia, Mo., 1984).

61. U.S. Fish and Wildlife Service et al., *Cache River Basin, Arkansas: A Task Force Report* (Jackson, Miss., 1978); Coastal Environments, Inc., *Cache River Basin: A Study in Floodplain Management* (Baton Rouge, La., 1977).

62. Hazel Henderson, *Creating Alternative Futures: The End of Economics* (New York, 1978).

63. George W. Pring and Karen A. Tomb, "License to Waste: Legal Barriers to Conservation and Efficient Use of Water in the West," *Proceedings, Twenty-fifth Annual Rocky Mountain Mineral Law Institute* (New York, 1979), 1–65.

64. Avraham Shawa and Ken Jacobs, *Social Values and Social Energy Policy,* Solar Energy Research Institute, SERI/RR-51-329 (Golden, Colo., 1979).

9. The Environmental Opposition

1. William Tucker, *Progress and Privilege* (New York, 1982); Edith Efron, *The Apocalyptics* (New York, 1984); Julian Simon, "This juggernaut [environmentalism], fueled by false information and special interest values, must be stopped before the world is led too far along the road to disaster." *Interaction,* 3(Fall 1983): 5; Luke Popovitch, "Environmentalism and the New Conservatives," *American Forests,* Mar. 1983, 18–20, 50–1.

2. Samuel P. Hays, "Political Choice in Regulatory Administration," in Thomas K. McCraw, ed., *Regulation in Perspective* (Cambridge, Mass., 1981), 124–54.

3. House Subcommittee on Natural Resources and Environment and Subcommittee on Conservation and Credit, Report, *Agricultural and Environmental Relationships: Issues and Priorities,* 96th Cong., 1st sess., 1979.

4. Carrol L. Henderson, "A Summary of Donation Rates to Minnesota's Nongame Wildlife Checkoff for 1982, by Occupation and County," *Nongame Newsletter,* 3(Sept. 1984): 6–7.

5. Farmers often demanded compensation for crop losses from deer, bear, and elk; "Farmers Bidding for Cash for Wildlife Crop Losses," *North Woods Call,* Aug. 28, 1985, 3.

6. Donald G. Schueler, *Incident at Eagle Ranch: Man and Predator in the American West* (San Francisco, 1980).

7. Farmers were among the first opponents of throwaway bottles; see *Business Week,* Sept. 1939, 32; flier showing farm membership of coalition to support a bottle bill in Pennsylvania, 1985 (AF).

8. *Appalachian Trailway News,* newsletter of the Appalachian Trail Conference (Harper's Ferry, W.Va.); *Bulletin of the Potomac Appalachian Trail Club* (Washington, D.C.).

9. *Our Wetlands,* newsletter, Wisconsin Wetlands Association (Madison).

10. James P. Jackson, *Passages of a Stream: A Chronicle of the Meramec* (Columbia, Mo., 1984); John Madson and Len Lahman, "The River They Couldn't Kill," *Audubon,* 88(Jan. 1986): 70–86.

11. *Dakota Council,* newsletter, Dakota Resource Council (Dickinson, N.D.); *The Plains Truth* newsletter, Northern Plains Resource Council (Billings, Mont.); *Eco-Forum* newsletter, South Dakota Resources Coalition (Brookings, S.D.).

12. Publications of the Illinois South Project, Herrin, Ill. (AF); see, e.g., *The Lost Harvest: A Study of the Surface Mining Act's Failure to Reclaim Prime Farmland in the Midwest* (July 1984).

13. Jack Doyle, *Lines across the Land* (Washington, D.C., 1979); *Hold That Line: Powerline Protest Newsletter of Central Minnesota* (Lowry, Minn.).

14. Philip V. Petersen, "An Interview With Sierra Club Executive Director J. Michael McCloskey," *Journal of Forestry,* 80(1982): 176.

15. *Farm Chemicals,* July 1971, 28; Aug. 1971, 35; Sept. 1971, 28, 69; Jan. 1972, 21, 23; Aug. 1972, 42.

16. Material about these issues is derived from *Farm Chemicals,* a publication of the farm-chemical industry, and farm journals such as *Agricultural Age* (San Francisco), *California Farmer,* and *Michigan Farmer,* especially issues during 1969–72.

17. For attempts by the farm-chemical industry to shape scientific assessments of the effects of farm chemicals see *News from CAST,* newsletter of the Council on Agricultural Science and Technology, an organization that brought together funding from the agricultural-chemical industry and scientists from major universities, primarily the agricultural colleges.

18. For rural-urban differences in state-legislative voting see Chapter 13, note 2.

19. For a general treatment of the relationship between labor and environment see Richard Kazis and Richard L. Grossman, *Fear at Work: Job Blackmail, Labor and the Environment* (New York, 1982).

20. United Steelworkers of America and the National Air Pollution Control Administration, *Poison in Our Air* (Washington, D.C., 1969); John G. Fuller, *We Almost Lost Detroit* (New York, 1975).

21. For an account of one labor-industry conference involving construction and the Clean Air Act see *Environment Reporter,* Jan. 19, 1979, 1729–30.

22. *NCAP News,* later *Journal of Pesticide Reform* (Eugene, Oreg.); *Pesticides and You,* newsletter, National Coalition against the Misuse of Pesticides (Washington, D.C.).

23. *Lifelines,* newsletter, Oil, Chemical and Atomic Workers Union (Denver, Colo.).

24. Harvey Wasserman and Norman Solomon, *Killing Our Own* (New York, 1982), 125–62; Christopher Norwood, *At Highest Risk* (New York, 1979), 156–88.

25. Richard Rashke, *The Killing of Karen Silkwood: The Story Behind the Kerr-McGee Plutonium Case* (Boston, 1981).

26. For activities of NEDA and its proposals see articles in *Environment Reporter,* Dec. 7, 1979, 1599–1600; June 20, 1980, 268; Nov. 7, 1980, 990–1; Nov. 14, 1980, 1018; Jan. 16, 1981, 1623; June 26, 1981, 278. Quarles worked for other industry groups; see his report, "Federal Regulation of New Industrial Plants," produced under corporate sponsorship including the National Association of Manufacturers. *Environment Reporter,* Feb. 9, 1979, 1914.

27. For a Nader-related state organization see *State Watch,* newsletter, Minnesota Public Interest Group (Minneapolis).

28. Kazis and Grossman, *Fear at Work,* 250ff.

29. Steve Griffiths, "Inner City Outings: Recruiting Allies for the Environment," *Sierra,* 70(Nov.-Dec. 1985): 110–13.

30. *Regional Workshops of Labor, Minorities, and Environmentalists,* Final Report on EPA Training Grant Number T 900 643 010 (Washington, D.C.: Urban Environment Conference, 1978); miscellaneous documents and personal observations of the author from the Philadelphia workshop in 1977.

31. A number of business organizations were formed specifically to counter environmental objectives, for example, the American Industrial Health Council. For businesses with a stake in environmental objectives see activities of the Industrial Gas Cleaning Institute in the early pages of each issue of the *Journal of the Air Pollution Control Association;* for outdoor recreation see advertisements in *Backpacker, National Audubon,* and *Sierra.*

32. For more strident business views after the 1980 election see *Chemical Week,* Nov. 26, 1980, 16; Dec. 3, 1980, 16; Dec. 10, 1980, 16; Dec. 17, 1980, 5. The phrase "maximum feasible resistance and minimum feasible retreat" is suggested by occasional statements in the record; see, for example, James E. Krier and Edmund Ursin, *Pollution and Policy* (Berkeley, 1977).

33. "When the Japanese historians one day set about chronicling the rise and fall of the late and great American empire, they'll surely turn to the tumultuous post-Vietnam era and note the ascendence of the environmental movement in our social and political life." Luke Popovitch, "Environmentalism and the New Conservatives," *American Forests,* Mar. 1983, 18–20, 50–1.

34. For the history of pulp- and paper-industry activities see testimony of Richard M. Billings, Paul C. Baldwin, and William H. Chisholm in House Committee on Government Operations, Hearing, *Pollution Control and Abatement,* Part IA, *National Survey,* 679–736, 88th Cong., 1st sess., 1963. Timber-industry opposition can be followed in *Lumber Letter* of the National Lumber Manufacturers Association; in its issue for Jan. 29, 1960, it complained about the "threat to the forest industries" from the Nature Conservancy, whose purpose was to help local citizens establish "natural areas blocked off from commercial development and improvement." For river navigation see issues of *Waterways Journal* (St. Louis, Mo.), 1968–74.

35. Richard H. K. Vietor, *Environmental Politics and the Coal Coalition* (College Station, Tex., 1980). The range of opposition can be observed in the industries represented on the committee to revise the sulfur oxides criteria document in 1967: Crown Zellerbach (paper), the Bituminous Coal Research Association (coal), Esso Research (petroleum), and Ford Motor Co. (automobiles).

36. *Waterways Journal;* National Water Resources Association; Water Resources Congress.

37. The best source for industry views on nuclear power is *Nucleonics Week* (Washington, D.C.).

38. For the chemical industry see *Chemical Week* (New York); *Chemical and Engineering News* (Washington, D.C.). See also *Chemecology,* published by the Manufacturing Chemists Association, which in the late 1970s changed its name to the Chemical Manufacturers Association and became much more aggressive in public affairs; see Chris Murray, "CMA Charges Ahead under New Mandate," *Chemical and Engineering News,* Aug. 13, 1979, 17.

39. Material in AF from such groups as the American Forest Institute and the American Petroleum Institute; see especially the publication of the Tobacco Institute, *Tobacco Observer* (Washington, D.C.)

40. *Ecolibrium* (Houston, Tex., Shell Oil Co.); *Exxon USA* (Houston, Tex., Exxon Co., U.S.A.); *Down to Earth* (Midland, Mich., Dow Chemical Co.); *Chemecology* (Washington, D.C., Chemical Manufacturers Association). For the Widener incident see *Los Angeles Times,* Jan. 9, 1979, announcing the settlement of the suit.

41. *New York Times,* Sept. 28, 1979.

42. "Single interest environmental groups [among others] have a proper place, but their role should be one of a 'watchdog' to observe and comment on the regulatory product, not to inject themselves into the 'nuts and bolts' of the process." Monte E. Throdahl, group vice-president of the environmental policy staff at Monsanto Co., in a speech to the American Institute of Chemical Engineers; *Chemical Regulation Reporter,* Nov. 17, 1978, 1415. In 1984 Norman Alpert, vice-president for environmental affairs at Occidental Company, objected to a proposal that the public be allowed to take part in the preliminary planning and discussion of remediation strategies for inactive hazardous-waste sites. Public participation, instead, should begin after the decisions have been made. See *New York Environmental News* 11(Dec. 31, 1984): 2–3.

43. See opposition to the concept of a Greater Yellowstone ecosystem by the oil, gas, mining, and lumber industries at congressional hearings, Oct. 24, 1985. *PLI Newsletter* (Public Lands Institute, Washington, D.C.) Nov. 1985, 8–11.

44. For industry attempts to shape the criteria process see testimony of George D. Clayton, executive secretary, the American Industrial Hygiene Association, in Senate Committee on Public Works, Hearings, *Air Pollution – 1968,* 90th Cong., 2d sess., 1968, 906–7. Included in this testimony is a list of members of the Committee on Criteria for Community Air Quality, which was headed by Allen D. Brandt, environmental control officer of the Bethlehem Steel Corporation. For an industry-sponsored symposium on air-quality criteria, held in June 1968, see *Environmental Science and Technology,* 2(1968): 584–5.

45. The farm-chemical industry objected to the "open book" administration the EPA instituted in 1972 that would allow "legitimate third parties . . . a voice in the proceedings for the first time." *Farm Chemicals,* Feb. 1972, 10.

46. *Risk in a Complex Society,* a Marsh and McLennon Public Opinion Survey (n.p., 1980); *Research on Public Attitudes toward the Use of Wilderness Lands,* Yankelovich, Skelly, and White for the Western Regional Council, Sept. 27, 1978; Union Carbide, *The Vital Consensus: American Attitudes on Economic Growth* (New York, n.d.).

47. For the California case see James E. Krier and Edmund Ursin, *Pollution and Policy* (Berkeley, 1977); for the Pennsylvania case see clippings, I/M problem (AF).

48. *Chemical Regulation Reporter,* Dec. 8, 15, 22, 29, 1978.

49. Measures to provide tax credits for air-pollution control were reported regularly in the 1960s in the *Journal of the Air Pollution Control Association;* see issues for May 1965, 238; Aug. 1967, 548.

50. For one example of industry resistance to the development of data see its objection to action by the National Institute for Occupational Safety and Health to develop maps to portray both the incidence of occupational diseases and their possible related industrial causes "because of the undue alarm" that would result among people living in high-risk areas; see Cathy Trost, "Agency's Maps Help Researchers Prevent Occupational Injuries, Disease, Death," *Wall Street Journal,* Dec. 9, 1985.

51. See *Chemical Week,* May 12, 1982, 24, 27, for a California dispute over a permit for a new Chevron lubricating-oil unit in which environmentalists challenged the company's claim as to future emissions but the company would not release data to substantiate the claim. Montana authorities were unable to warn citizens about eating game possibly tainted with endrin because the State Department of Agriculture yielded to company pressure not to release data about location and timing of spraying claiming it was a trade secret. Bill Schneider, "Endrin: The Politics of Poison," *Montana* magazine, Apr.-May, 1982, 58–64; Jim Robbins, "The Deadly Irony of Endrin," *Sierra,* Nov.-Dec. 1981, 30–2, and a letter in response from Gail M. Anderson, *Sierra,* Mar.-Apr. 1982, 8.

52. For extensive use of freedom of information by newspaper reporters see the case of the effect of radioactive fallout in Utah from atomic tests in Nevada in John G. Fuller, *The Day We Bombed Utah* (New York, 1984).

53. See material on the Pennsylvania Environmental Council in AF.

54. *Upper Peninsula Environmental Coalition Bulletin* (Houghton, Mich.).

55. *Enviro South* (Montgomery, Ala.).

56. For an account of the activities of a state branch of KAB, Keep Michigan Beautiful, Inc., see column by Hugh McDiarmid, *Detroit Free Press,* July 18, 1978.

57. Miscellaneous material concerning Americans for Energy Independence and its Pittsburgh program, Project Pacesetter, in AF.

58. Vietor, *Environmental Politics and the Coal Coalition,* 168–78.

59. R. Laurie, "The Diversion of Investment due to Environmental Regulation" (Ph.D. diss., Yale University, 1982).

60. Joseph Ling, in foreword to Michael G. Boyston, *Pollution Prevention Pays* (New York, 1979), ix–xv.

61. Annual reports, Chemical Industry Institute of Toxicology; *Lead Research Digest* and *Cadmium Research Digest,* International Lead Zinc Research Organization, Inc. (New York).

62. The Continental Group Report, *Toward Responsible Growth: Economic and Environmental Concern in the Balance* (Stamford, Conn., 1982).

63. Letter to the editor, *Environmental Forum,* 3(Aug. 1984): 40, from Terry

L. Thoem, Conoco, Inc., Houston, reporting on a DuPont Corporation opinion survey of January 1984 concerning the public credibility of various groups, ranging from "very or somewhat confident" as to their credibility to "not very or not at all confident." As to the first, high levels of confidence, environmental groups scored 74%, regulators, 57% and large corporations, 30%. In the second or low levels of confidence group, environmental groups scored 20%, regulators 35%, and large corporations 64%, respectively.

10. The Politics of Science

1. Scientific issues and controversies can be followed at an introductory level in *Journal of Air Pollution Control, Journal of the Water Pollution Control Federation, Journal of Forestry, Environmental Science and Technology, Chemical and Engineering News, Scienctist, American Scientist,* and *BioScience.* More detailed information can be secured through specific controversies such as disputes over EPA criteria documents or agency regulatory proposals with associated documents from participants. Articles about the social analysis of values in science can be found in *Science, Technology and Human Values* (Cambridge, Mass.).

2. Scientists continually called for more research on environmental problems, and numerous journals were started in the 1960s and 1970s to publish environmental research.

3. Philip Boffey, *The Brain Bank of America* (New York, 1975); Mary E. Ames, *Science and the Political Process* (Washington, D.C., 1978); Joel Primack and Frank von Hippel, *Advice and Dissent: Scientists in the Political Arena* (New York, 1974); Allan Mazur, *The Dynamics of Technical Controversy* (Washington, D.C., 1981).

4. For a discussion of the membership of the Committee on the Biological Effects of Ionizing Radiation, III, which assessed the health effects of low-level radiation, see Edward P. Radford, "Cancer Risks from Ionizing Radiation," *Technology Review,* Nov.-Dec. 1981, 66–78.

5. For a celebrated case, the first NAS lead study, see Robert Gillette, "Lead in the Air: Industry Weight on Academy Panel Challenged," *Science,* Nov. 19, 1971, 800–2; Boffey, *Brain Bank of America,* 228–44; author interview with Wallace Bowman, former secretary of the Board of Environmental Health, National Academy of Sciences, June 28, 1984.

6. Rae Goodell, *The Visible Scientists* (Boston, 1975); an important vehicle for the expression of scientists who took more advanced positions in environmental health was the Society of Environmental and Occupational Health. See its publication, *SEOH Letter.*

7. For a typical example, involving the allocation of funds for cancer research, see Daryl Chubin, "Research Mission and the Public: Over-Selling and Buying the U.S. War on Cancer," in James C. Petersen, ed., *Citizen Participation in Science Policy* (Amherst, Mass., 1984), 109–29.

8. For a recent episode see Eliot Marshall, "The Academy Kills a Nutrition Report," *Science,* Oct. 25, 1985, 420–1; letters to the editor, *Science,* Dec. 20, 1985, 1324, 1326, 1410. For the debate over cancer strategies see Ralph W. Moss, *The Cancer Syndrome* (New York, 1980); Christopher Norwood, *At Highest Risk* (New York, 1980).

9. For an affirmation of the value of epidemiology see National Research Council, *Epidemiology and Air Pollution* (Washington, D.C., 1985).

10. An important medium through which forest research was interpreted for the general public was *Western Wildlands,* published by the School of Forestry, University of Montana, Missoula.

11. *Environmental Science and Technology,* 1(1967): 386–8, 400–3; 1(1967); Federal Council for Science and Technology, Committee on Water Resource Research, *A Ten-Year Program of Federal Water Resources Research* (Washington, D.C., 1966); annual reports, Office of Water Resources Research; see also newsletters of the state water-research institutes in AF.

12. Newsletters of university sea grant research centers in AF.

13. For one study of private, nonindustrial, forest owners see Paul V. Ellefson, Sally L. Palm, and David C. Lothner, "From Public Land to Nonindustrial Private Forest: A Minnesota Case Study," *Journal of Forestry,* 80(1982): 219–22, 234; the article defined the "problem" as the 25 percent of land acquired by seventy-four individuals and families for "nonindustrial" purposes rather than the 72 percent of land purchased by seven corporations for wood production. For a more general treatment see Jack P. Royer and Christopher D. Risbrudt, eds., *Nonindustrial Private Forests: A Review of Economic and Policy Studies* (Durham, N.C., 1983).

14. A variant on this question was that of the "burden of proof." See, e.g., Martin H. Belsky, "Environmental Policy Law in the 1980's; Shifting Back the Burden of Proof," *Ecology Law Quarterly,* 12(1984): 1–88.

15. Environmental issues pushed science to new frontiers in a variety of fields, e.g., the health effects of lead; see Herbert L. Needleman, *Low Level Lead Exposure: The Clinical Implications of Current Research* (New York, 1980).

16. The course of acid-precipitation science and debate can be followed most readily by material in Center for Environmental Information, Inc., *Acid Precipitation Digest* (Rochester, N.Y.).

17. Ocean dumping was a significant case of demand by environmentalists for more knowledge before action. See Donald F. Squire, *The Ocean Dumping Quandry* (Albany, N.Y., 1983).

18. W. W. Holland et al., "Health Effects of Particulate Pollution: Reappraising the Evidence," *American Journal of Epidemiology,* 110(1979): 525–659; this assessment was commissioned by lawyers for the American Iron and Steel Institute, as reported by David Olds to Walter Goldburg, chair, Group Against Smog and Pollution, Pittsburgh, July 18, 1979. See also Carl M. Shy, "Epidemiologic Evidence and the United States Air Quality Standards," *American Journal of Epidemiology,* 110(1979): 661–71.

19. For the controversy over chromosome studies of Love Canal residents see Ruth Gordon Levine, *Love Canal: Science, Politics, and People* (Lexington, Mass., 1982), esp. 71–174. See also *Science,* June 13, 1980, 1239–42; Aug. 15, 1980, 741–56; Aug. 19, 1980, 1002–3; Lois R. Ember, "Uncertain Science Pushes Love Canal Solutions to Political, Legal Arenas," *Chemical and Engineering News,* Aug. 11, 1980, 22–9; *New York Times,* May 27, 1980, June 9, 1980, June 14, 1980, and June 18, 1980; David Dickson, "Love Canal Continues to Fester as Scientists Bicker over the Evidence," *Ambio,* 9(1980): 257–9. The *New York Times* (June 18, 1980) reported: "People in the field of genetics pointed out that everyone has some chromosome damage . . . and that the examination of cells for such damage was extremely subjective."

20. Benjamin Ferris and Frank E. Speizer, "Criteria for Establishing Standards for Air Pollutants," *The Business Roundtable Air Quality Project* (Boston, 1980).

21. See also Kay H. Jones, "The Science Backs a 2-Gram Standard," *Environmental Forum,* May 1982, 21–3, which defines the debate over automobile pollution standards as a distinction between "sound scientific reasoning" and "irrational political decisions."

22. George M. Woodwell "The Scientist's Testimony," *BioScience,* 28(1978): 427.

23. The criteria document process led to extensive assessments of health effects. It can be followed in brief in *Environment Reporter* and in greater depth in the administrative documents, many of which are in AF.

24. Philip Boffey observed that the first NAS lead committee in 1971 contained no member who was an expert in inhalation, in contrast with ingestion. See Boffey, *Brain Bank of America,* 228–44. There was a tendency to define such issues as controversies over personal integrity rather than matters of limited perspectives. The secretary of the board under which the first NAS lead committee was conducted objected that the attack on Gordon Stopps, who had been criticized because he was employed by the DuPont Corporation, was unwarranted because Stopps "was as honest as the day is long" (author interview with John Redmond, Apr. 10, 1979).

25. A set of forest categories with an environmental perspective, based on "multistory" and "continuous cover" forest characteristics is Rt. Hon. the Earl of Bradford, "An Experiment in Sustainable Forestry," *Ecologist,* 10(1980): 165–6.

26. *Report, President's Advisory Panel on Timber and the Environment,* appendix O, "Forest Recreation: An Analysis with Special Reference to the East" (Washington, D.C., 1973), 490–516.

27. For a discussion of the distinction between maturity of individual trees versus maturity of the forest as an ecosystem see Alaska Fish and Game Commission, *Report to the Board of Game on Wildlife and Forest Practices in Southeast Alaska* (Juneau, 1980).

28. Robert F. Pfister et al., *Forest Habitat Types of Montana,* Department of Agriculture, Intermountain Forest and Range Experiment Station, General Technical Report, INT-34 (Ogden, Utah, 1977).

29. For the British case, in which a broader range of ecological indicators was used, see Nature Conservancy Council, *Focus on Conservation,* no. 7, G. L. A. Fry and A. S. Cooke, "Acid Deposition and Its Implication for Nature Conservation in Britain" (Shrewsbury, 1984).

30. David Rosner and Gerald Markowitz, "A 'Gift of God'?: The Public Health Controversy over Leaded Gasoline during the 1920's," *American Journal of Public Health,* 75(1985): 344–52.

31. Needleman, *Low Level Lead Exposure;* Clair C. Patterson, *Natural Levels of Lead in Humans,* Carolina Environmental Essay Series, III, Institute of Environmental Studies (Chapel Hill, N.C., 1982).

32. Gregory S. Wetstone and Jan Goldman, *Chronology of Events Surrounding the Ethyl Decision* (Washington, D.C., Environmental Law Institute, 1981).

33. "Health and Lead Phasedown," an interview with Bernard Goldstein, *EPA Journal,* 11(May 1985): 9–12.

34. Rosalie Bertell, *No Immediate Danger* (Toronto, 1985), 135–98; Charles W. Huver et al., *Methodologies for the Study of Low-Level Radiation in the Midwest* (Millville, Minn., 1979).

35. Harvey Wasserman and Norman Solomon, *Killing Our Own* (New York, 1982), 207–22; Ernest Sternglass, *Secret Fallout* (New York, 1982), 139–76;

Bertell, *No Immediate Danger,* 206–10; *Radiation Standards and Public Health,* Proceedings of a Second Congressional Session on Low-Level Ionizing Radiation (Washington, D.C., 1978).

36. Ellis B. Cowling, "Acid Precipitation in Historical Perspective," *Environmental Science and Technology,* 16(1982): 110A–123A; Ernest Y. Yanarella and Randal H. Ihara, eds., *The Acid Rain Debate* (Boulder, Colo., 1985).

37. EPA, *Addendum to "The Health Consequences of Sulfur Oxides: A Report from Chess, 1970–1971,"* May 1974, EPA-600/1-80-021 (Washington, D.C., 1980).

38. Center for Environmental Information, Inc., *Acid Precipitation Digest* (Rochester, N.Y.).

39. Lois R. Ember, "U.S., Canada Set Up Separate Acid Rain Panels," *Chemical and Engineering News,* June 21, 1982, 22; Ember, "U.S. Accused of Hindering Progress in Acid Rain Control," *Chemical and Engineering News,* Apr. 11, 1983, 20–22; Executive Office of the President, Office of Science and Technology Policy, "Interim Report from OSTP's Acid Rain Peer Review Panel" (Washington, D.C., June 28, 1983, press advisory mimeo); Copper Smelter Information Committee, *Western Smelters and Acid Rain: Setting the Record Straight* (Phoenix, Ariz., 1985).

40. Daryl Chubin, "Research Missions and the Public: Over-Selling and Buying the U.S. War on Cancer," in James C. Peterson, ed., *Citizen Participation in Science Policy* (Amherst, Mass., 1984), 109–29; Keith Schneider, "The Data Gap: What We Don't Know about Chemicals," *Amicus Journal,* 6(Winter 1985): 15–24; "Dr. David P. Rall: Director, National Toxicology Program," *Amicus Journal,* 6(Winter 1985): 25. David J. Hansen, "Cooperation Key to EPA's Disaster Plan," *Chemical and Engineering News,* Jan. 6, 1986, 20–2.

41. Nicholas A. Ashford, C. William Ryan, and Charles C. Caldart, "A Hard Look at Federal Regulation of Formaldehyde: A Departure from Reasoned Decision-making," *Harvard Environmental Law Review,* 7(1983): 297–370; Mark E. Rushefsky, "The Misuse of Science and Governmental Decision-making," *Science, Technology and Human Values,* 9(Summer 1984): 47–59.

42. *Chemical Regulation Reporter,* May 25, 1984, 237; 49 *Federal Register,* 21594, May 22, 1984; the draft proposal read: "Agents found carcinogenic in animal studies . . . are considered suspect human carcinogens."

43. There were continual suggestions that research on the health effects of radiation be shifted from the Department of Energy, which conducted more than 60 percent of it, to the National Institutes of Health. *Chemical and Engineering News,* Apr. 30, 1979, 20; Dr. Edward Radford, "Scientific Controversy in the Public Domain," *Technology Review,* Nov.-Dec. 1981, 74–5.

44. Paul Brodeur, *Expendable Americans* (New York, 1973).

45. For observations about disagreement among specialists see Jeffrey L. Fox, review of *Malignant Neglect* in *Chemical and Engineering News,* May 28, 1979, 44: "There's a great deal of thundering about at prestigious international meetings when epidemiologists, radiologists, cell biologists, and others compare uncomparable data. They often reach contradictory conclusions, and the uproar can continue for years."

46. Much of the attack on John Gofman and Arthur Tamplin after their AEC-sponsored report on the health effects of the then-allowable exposures to radiation came from scientists associated with federal atomic agencies. For lead see the brief account of the Lead Liaison Committee in Gregory S. Wetstone and Jan Goldman, *Chronology of Events Surrounding the Ethyl Decision.*

47. The change was described by Terry Yosie, acting director of the EPA's Science Advisory Board: "Within the scientific community itself, the standards for scrutiny of scientific evidence have gotten a lot more rigorous. Approximately ten years ago, EPA promulgated standards for such pollutants as sulfur dioxide, particulate matter, and nitrogen dioxide. When you talk to some of the participants in those decisions of ten years ago, you get a sense that the process of coming up with specific estimates was altogether different from the current revision of those standards." See Peter S. Gold, ed., *Acid Rain* (Buffalo, N.Y.: Canadian-American Center, State University of New York, 1982), 47–9.

48. For peer review see "Peer Review Plan Muddies Acid Rain Talks," *Chemical and Engineering News,* May 10, 1982, 12.

49. For proposals to establish review procedures beyond the National Academy of Sciences see Congressman William Wampler's proposal for a national science council, *Environmental Health Letter,* July 1, 1981, 6–7. For the science-court proposal see Arthur Kantrowitz, "Controlling Technology Democratically," *American Scientist,* 63(1975): 505–9; "The Science Court Experiment," *Bulletin of Atomic Scientists,* Apr. 1977, 43–53.

50. For concerns about the impartiality of judges see Sheldon Krimsky, "Beyond Technocracy: New Routes for Citizen Involvement in Social Risk Assessment," in Peterson, ed., *Citizen Participation in Science Policy,* 43–61. For a variant see Milton R. Wessel, "Arriving at a Scientific Consensus," *Chemical Week,* May 12, 1982, 5.

51. Of all the methods of arriving at a workable consensus, the EPA's practice of drawing on a wide range of scientific opinion in formulating criteria documents was the most successful. The lead issue, a case in point, can be followed in documents in AF.

11. The Politics of Economic Analysis and Planning

1. Peter Self, *Econocrats and the Policy Process* (Boulder, Colo., 1975).

2. Laurence H. Tribe, Corinne S. Schelling, and John Voss, eds., *When Values Conflict* (Cambridge, Mass., 1976); Harold A. Feiverson, Frank W. Sinden, and Robert H. Socolow, *Boundaries of Analysis: An Inquiry into the Tocks Island Dam Controversy* (Cambridge, Mass., 1976); "Has Environmental Regulation Gone Too Far? A Debate on the Costs versus the Benefits," *Chemical and Engineering News,* Apr. 23, 1979, 24–53.

3. Henry M. Peskin, Paul R. Portney, and Allen V. Kneese, *Environmental Regulation and the U.S. Economy* (Baltimore, 1981).

4. A. C. Fischer and F. M. Peterson, "The Environment in Economics: A Survey," *Journal of Economic Literature,* 14(1976): 1–33; John V. Krutilla and Anthony C. Fisher, *The Economics of Natural Environments* (Baltimore, 1975); Richard G. Walsh, Richard A. Gillman, and John B. Loomis, *Wilderness Resource Economics: Recreation Use and Preservation Values* (Denver, 1982); Allen R. Ferguson and E. Phillip LeVeen, *The Benefits of Health and Safety Regulation* (Cambridge, Mass., 1981).

5. "Cost-Benefit Analysis: A Tricky Game," *CF Letter,* Dec. 1980; Nicholas A. Ashford, "The Limits of Cost-Benefit Analysis in Regulatory Decisions," *Technology Review,* May 1980, 70–2; John Mendeloff, "Reducing Occupational Health Risks: Uncertain Effects and Unstated Benefits," *Technology Review,* May 1980, 66–9, 73–8; Richard Liroff, "Cost-Benefit Analysis and Environmental Regulation: Does It Clear the Air or Muddy the Water?" *Environmental Forum,* 1(1982): 11–13. The role of economic analysis in environmental affairs is reflected in *Journal of Environmental Economics and Management,* first issued in May 1974, which was heavily oriented toward emphasizing the costs of managing residuals.

6. David Gordon Wilson, "Building in Environmental Costs," *Technology Review,* Nov.-Dec. 1981, 10–11; Allen V. Kneese and Charles L. Schultze, *Pollution, Prices and Public Policy* (Washington, D.C., 1975); Frederick B. Anderson and Allen V. Kneese et al., *Environmental Improvement through Economic Incentives* (Washington, D.C., 1977).

7. "EPA Begins Implementation of Noncompliance Penalty Regulations, Fights Rearguard Action in D.C. Circuit," *Environmental Law Reporter,* Feb. 1982, 10012–18; for an account of the Connecticut case see EPA, *Connecticut Enforcement Project Report* (Washington, D.C., 1977).

8. Robert H. Haveman, *Water Resource Investment and the Public Interest* (Nashville, 1965); Charles Garrison, "A Case Study of the Local Economic Impact of Reservoir Recreation," *Journal of Leisure Research,* 6(Winter 1974); 7–19; Bruce Hannon and Roger Bezek, "Job Impact of Alternatives to Corps of Engineers Projects," *Engineering Issues* (Oct. 1973).

9. The Wilderness Society et al., *National Forest Planning,* 2d ed. (Washington, D.C., 1983); Marion Clawson, *Forests for Whom and for What* (Baltimore, 1975); William Hyde, *Timber Supply, Land Allocation, and Economic Efficiency* (Baltimore, 1980); Thomas J. Barlow et al., *Giving Away the National Forests: An Analysis of U.S. Forest Service Timber Sales Below Cost* (Washington, D.C.: Natural Resources Defense Council, 1980).

10. Douglas M. Costle, "The Decision Maker's Dilemma," *Technology Review,* July 1981, 10–11; James Hamilton and Suzanne Scotchmer, "Assessing the Economic Effects of Implementing Air Quality Management Plans in California," *Public Interest Economics – West,* June 1979, 134; W. Curtiss Priest, "The Cost-Benefit Charade," *Wall Street Journal,* June 18, 1979; Steven Phillips and Marc Moller, "Putting a Price on Death," *Psychology Today,* May 1972, 70–3; Devra Lee Davis, "Multiple Risk Assessment and Public Health," *Toxic Substances Journal,* 1(1979–80): 205–55.

11. National Research Council, "Economic Benefits of Reducing Human Exposure to Toxic Substances," in *Nonfluoridated Halomethanes in the Environment* (Washington, D.C., 1978), 228–33.

12. "Economists Jump into Pollution Control Scraps," *CF Letter,* Aug. 1978; Richard E. Ayres, "Trading Health for Dollars," *Amicus Journal,* 3(Winter 1980): 5–6.

13. William W. Lowrance, *Of Acceptable Risk* (Los Angeles, 1976); R. W. Kates, *Risk Assessment of Environmental Hazard* (New York, 1978); Chauncy Starr, "Social Benefit vs. Technological Risk," *Science,* Sept. 19, 1969, 1232–8; Paolo F. Ricci and Lawrence S. Molton, "Risk and Benefit in Environmental Law," *Science,* Dec. 4, 1981, 1096–1100.

14. Richard Liroff, paper presented at Conference on Cost-Benefit Analysis, sponsored by the Conservation Foundation and the Illinois Institute of Natural Resources, Chicago, Oct. 15–16, 1980, as reported in "Cost-Benefit Analysis: A Tricky Game," *CF Letter,* Dec. 1980.

15. A. Myrich Freeman III, "The Benefits of Air and Water Pollution Control: A Review and Synthesis of Recent Estimates," prepared for the Council on Environmental Quality, 1979; Mark Green and Norman Waitzman, *Business War on the Law: An Analysis of the Benefits of Federal Health/Safety Enforcement* (Washington, D.C., 1979).

16. *Toxic Substances Journal* (New York).

17. "Economic Dislocation Early Warning System; Region II Meeting," Sept. 22, 1976 (AF); quarterly reports, EPA to secretary of labor, concerning the "Economic Dislocation Early Warning System" (AF).

18. The steps by which this took place were outlined by the federal court in Hercules, Inc., v. EPA, Nov. 3, 1978 (12 ERC 1376), 1392.

19. Bruce Piasecki, "The Politics of Toxic Wastes: Why the OMB Weakens EPA Programs," in Piasecki, ed., *Beyond Dumping: New Strategies for Controlling Toxic Contamination* (Westport, Conn., 1984), 53–68; see *Summary and Proceedings* from a congressional workshop on "Research Needed to Improve the Quality of Socioeconomic Data Used in Regulatory Decision Making," 1980; U.S. General Accounting Office, *Cost-Benefit Analysis Can Be Useful in Assessing Environmental Regulations, Despite Limitations,* GAO-RCED 84-62, Apr. 6, 1984 (Washington, D.C., 1984).

20. See reports of the Council on Wage and Price Stability, e.g., "Environmental Protection Agency's Proposed Revisions to the National Ambient Air Quality Standard for Photochemical Oxidants," Oct. 16, 1978 (CWPS 291) (AF).

21. In the report cited in note 20, the CWPS objected to protection against "discomfort" that "is reversible and apparently has no long-term debilitating effects" (p. 2).

22. Douglas Costle, "Cost-Benefit Analysis," *Environmental Science and Technology,* Dec. 1980, 1416; Costle, "Decision Maker's Dilemma," 10–11; for the beryllium case see *Washington Post,* Sept. 18, 1978; for vinyl chloride see *New York Times,* "Did Industry Cry Wolf?" Dec. 28, 1975.

23. Costle, "Cost-Benefit Analysis," 1416; Costle, "Dollars and Sense: Putting a Price Tag on Pollution," *Environment,* 21(Oct. 1979): 25–7.

24. Lester C. Thurow, "The Productivity Problem," *Technology Review,* Nov.-Dec. 1980, 40–51.

25. William J. Abernathy, *The Productivity Dilemma: Roadblock to Innovation in the Automobile Industry* (Baltimore, 1978).

26. Nicholas A. Ashford and George R. Heaton, "The Effects of Health and Environmental Regulation on Technological Change in the Chemical Industry: Theory and Evidence," in Christopher T. Hill, ed., *Federal Regulation and Chemical Innovation* (Washington, D.C., 1979).

27. Wil Lepkowski, "Jordan Baruch Making His Mark on Innovation," and "White House Awaits Huge Innovation Report," *Chemical and Engineering News,* Jan. 1, 1979, 13, and Feb. 11, 1979, 14–16.

28. Richard Liroff, note 14; Cyril L. Comer, "SO_2 Regulation Ignores Costs, Poor Science Base," *Chemical and Engineering News,* April 23, 1979, 42–6, 48–9.

29. Robert M. Wolcott and Adam Z. Rose, *The Economic Effects of the Clean Air Act,* prepared for the Natural Resource Defense Council by the Public Interest Economics Foundation (Washington, D.C., 1982); William Drayton, letter to *Amicus Journal,* 3(Summer 1981): 47; Chase Econometric Associates, Inc., *The Macroeconomic Impacts of Federal Pollution Control Programs,* undertaken for the Council on Environmental Quality and the Environmental Protection Agency (n.p., Jan. 1975).

30. Steve Kelman, *What Price Incentives: Economists and the Environment* (Boston, 1981).

31. Department of Environmental Resources, Commonwealth of Pennsylvania, *Programs and Planning for the Management of the Water Resources of Pennsylvania* (Harrisburg, Pa., 1971); *Clean Water, Comprehensive Water Quality Management Plan, Ohio Valley Study Area,* prepared for the Department of

Environmental Resources, Commonwealth of Pennsylvania by Green International, Inc. (Sewickly, Pa., 1979); James Ragan Associates, *The Water Pollution Control Act of 1972 – Public Participation: Institutional Assessment* (Washington, D.C.: National Commission on Water Quality, 1975). For a coastal management plan see State of New Jersey, *Coastal Management Program: Bay and Shore Segment* (Trenton, N.J.: Department of Environmental Protection, 1978). Many of these state coastal plans are in AF.

32. Fred Bosselman and David Callies, *The Quiet Revolution in Land Use Control* (Washington, D.C.: Council on Environmental Quality, 1971).

33. Samuel P. Hays, "Value Premises for Planning and Public Policy – The Historical Context," in Richard N. L. Andrews, ed., *Land in America* (Lexington, Mass., 1979), 149–66.

34. Idaho Conservation League, "Conservationists' Alternatives – Part One" and "Part Two," *Newsletter,* Oct. 1981, 1–9; Nov. 1981, 5–11.

35. U.S. Fish and Wildlife Service, *Operation of the National Wildlife Refuge System,* Final Environmental Impact Statement (Washington, D.C., 1976); Upper Mississippi River Development Commission, *Comprehensive Master Plan for the Management of the Upper Mississippi River System,* technical report volume, *Review Comments* (Minneapolis, 1982).

36. Ian L. McHarg, *Design with Nature* (New York, 1969).

37. Michael Beck et al., "The Laurel Hill Study: An Application of the Public Trust Doctrine to Pennsylvania Land-Use Planning in an Area of Critical State and Local Concern" (master's thesis, University of Pennsylvania, Department of Landscape Architecture and Regional Planning, May 1975).

38. U.S. Water Resources Council, *Water and Related Land Resources: Establishment of Principles and Standards for Planning* (Washington, D.C., 1973).

39. Samuel P. Hays, "The Changing Political Structure of the City in Industrial America," *Journal of Urban History,* 1(1974): 6–38; National Academy of Sciences, *Toward an Understanding of Metropolitan America* (Washington, D.C., 1974); Basil G. Zimmer and Amos H. Hawley, *Metropolitan Area Schools: Resistance to District Reorganization* (Beverly Hills, Calif., 1968).

40. Judith Kunofsky, "The Use of Population Projections by the Federal Government for Programs at the Local Level," House Select Committee on Population, Hearings, *The Capacity of the Federal Government to Plan for Population Change and Its Consequences: Local Needs and the Federal Response,* 95 Cong., 2d sess., June 8, 1978; Elizabeth W. Moen, "Voodoo Forecasting: Technical, Political and Ethical Issues Regarding the Projection of Local Population Growth," *Population Research and Policy Review,* 3(1984): 1–25.

41. Harland L. Menkin, *Population Projections and Their Use as a Fund Allocation and Policy Tool,* a project presented to the California Council for Environmental and Economic Balance, Building Industry Association of Northern California, and the Coalition of Labor and Business (n.p., Feb. 1980).

42. U.S. Forest Service, Southwest Region, *Gila Wilderness* (Albuquerque, N.Mex., 1974); U.S. Department of the Interior, *New Mexico Statewide Wilderness Study,* 3 vols. (Santa Fe, N.Mex., 1985).

43. *Forest Planning,* journal of the Nationwide Forest Planning Clearinghouse (Eugene, Oreg.,); Ken Fletcher, Cynthia Williams, and Randal O'Toole, "Forest Planning Bibliography," Cascade Holistic Economic Consultants, CHEC Research Paper no. 15 (Eugene, Oreg., 1985).

44. Philip V. Petersen, "An Interview with Sierra Club Executive Director J. Michael McCloskey," *Journal of Forestry,* May 1932, 179.

45. Sierra Club et al., *A Conservationist's Guide to National Forest Planning,*

2d ed. (n.p., 1983); U.S. Forest Service, *RPA: A Recommended Renewable Resources Plan, as Required by the Forest and Rangeland Renewable Resources Planning Act of 1974* (Washington, D.C., 1976); U.S. Forest Service, *An Assessment of the Forest and Range Land Situation in the United States* (Washington, D.C., 1980); Southeast Alaska Conservation Council, *The Tongass Timber Problem: The Full Report of The Tongass Accountability Project* (Juneau, 1985); Washington Environmental Council, *Review of Proposed Forest Land Management Program* (Seattle, 1983).

46. National Park Service, *Final Environmental Impact Statement: General Management Plan – Yosemite National Park, California* (Washington, D.C., 1980).

47. The Conservation Foundation, *National Parks for a New Generation* (Washington, D.C., 1985), 171–218, 347–8.

48. Bureau of Land Management (BLM), *Draft EIS: Proposed Domestic Livestock Grazing Program for the Challis Planning Unit* (Boise, Idaho, 1976); BLM, *The California Desert Conservation Area Plan* (Sacramento, 1980); *Snake River Birds of Prey, Environmental Statement* (Boise, Idaho, 1979); Committee for Idaho's High Desert, newsletter, *Desert Notes* (Boise).

49. U.S. Fish and Wildlife Service, *Final EIS: Acquisition of Lands for the Canaan Valley National Wildlife Refuge* (Washington, D.C., 1979).

50. Office of the Governor, Budget and Program Planning, *Montana Futures: A Survey of Citizen Choices* (Helena, Mont., 1977); Richard Vandiver and Stefani Forster, *Montana Futures, Update 1984* (Missoula, Department of Sociology, University of Montana, Mar. 1984); "Special Issue: Idaho's Tomorrow," *Incredible Idaho, A Land for All Seasons* 7(Spring 1976): 1–39.

51. Philip H. Abelson, "Of Mice and Men," *Resources* (Washington, D.C., Resources for the Future), 81(Summer-Fall 1985): 5; Philip H. Abelson, *Enough of Pessimism* (Washington, D.C., 1985).

52. Rachelle Hollander, "Institutionalizing Public Service Science: Its Perils and Promise," in James C. Peterson, ed., *Citizen Participation in Science Policy* (Amherst, Mass., 1984), 75–95.

53. Richard N. L. Andrews and Mary Jo Waits, *Environmental Values in Public Decisions: A Research Agenda* (Ann Arbor, Mich.: School of Natural Resources, University of Michigan, 1978); David D. DeWalle, "Acidic Deposition," *Journal of Forestry*, 83(1985): 614.

12. The Middle Ground: Management of Environmental Restraint

1. *Environmental Science and Technology* (Washington, D.C., American Chemical Society); *Journal of the Air Pollution Control Association* (Pittsburgh, Pa.); *Journal of the Water Pollution Control Federation* (Washington, D.C.); *Science* (Washington, D.C., American Association for the Advancement of Science); *Journal of Environmental Economics and Management* (New York); *Journal of Environmental Management* (New York); National Association of Environmental Professionals, *Environmental Professional* (New York).

2. The concept of "thought leaders" has been derived from pubic-attitude studies commissioned by industry groups. I have defined it operationally by a set of publications political leaders in the nation's capital appear to read and refer to consistently. They include the *New York Times*, the *Washington Post*, the *Wall Street Journal*, the *National Journal, Business Week, Time, News-*

week, and, more peripherally, the *Los Angeles Times, Regulation,* and *Public Interest.*

3. Marion Clawson, "Politicizing the Environment," *Environmental Professional* 2(1980): 223; Arthur E. Kauders, president of the National Association of Environmental Professionals, "What Is the Prognosis for the Environmental Professional and the Environmental Movement?" *Environmental Professional,* 1(1979): 167. For a "middle ground" perspective see *Environmental Forum* (Washington, D.C., Environmental Law Institute).

4. Environmental-management issue can best be followed in the specialized newsletters, *Environment Reporter, Chemical Regulation Reporter, Air/Water Pollution Report, Occupational Health and Safety Letter, Environmental Health Letter, Inside EPA, Coastal Zone Management News, Land Letter;* the *Federal Register* is a major source of information concerning rule making.

5. For self-images of neutrality see *Environmental Professional.*

6. For the attempt to portray forest-management issues in environmental terms on periodical covers and in illustrations while maintaining a developmentally oriented text see National Conference of State Legislatures, *A Legislator's Guide to Forest Resource Management* (Denver, Colo., 1982).

7. Benjamin A. Roach, *Selection Cutting and Group Selection,* State University of New York College of Environmental Science and Forestry, Applied Forestry Research Institute Miscellaneous Report no. 5 (Syracuse, N.Y., 1974); James C. Nelson et al., "Timber Management," in Pennsylvania State University, School of Forest Resources, *Clearcutting in Pennsylvania* (University Park, Pa., 1975), 33–49.

8. Lawrence W. Dietz, "A Layman Looks at Evenaged Management of Mixed Hardwoods in Eastern National Forests" (AF); Edward C. Fritz, *Sterile Forest: The Case Against Clearcutting* (Austin, Tex., 1983). One poll on timber harvest revealed the views of different groups. While the public was divided 21% in favor and 39% against clear-cutting, the Forest Service divided 75% in favor and 0% against; 54% of the public favored individual tree selection (10% were opposed), 25% of the Forest Service favored it, and 31% were opposed. See U.S. Forest Service, Hoosier National Forest, *Midlands Area: Situation and Issues: Summary of Public's Comments* (Milwaukee, Wis., n.d.), 17–18.

9. Gordon L. Bultena and John C. Hendee, "Forester's Views of Interest Group Positions on Forest Policy," *Journal of Forestry,* 70(1972): 337–42; William M. Harlow and Ellwood S. Harrar, *Forest Dendrology* (New York, 1937).

10. Leon Minckler, "Ecological Forestry," *National Parks and Conservation,* 54(Apr. 1980): 2, 31; Minckler, *Woodland Ecology: Environmental Forestry for the Small Owner* (Syracuse, N.Y., 1975).

11. Hercules Incorporated v. EPA, Nov. 3, 1978 (12 ERC 1376), 1393–4, provides an example of dispute over dilution factors that determined the extent of the mixing zone. Kristine Hall, "The Control of Toxic Pollutants under the Federal Water Pollution Control Act Amendments of 1972," *Iowa Law Review,* 63(1978): 609–48, at 618 and n. 109, argues that the 1972 act "probably does not allow mixing zones at all." The EPA, in turn, argued that mixing zones may not be appropriate for toxics; see *EPA Memorandum on Water Quality Standards Guidelines* (1976), chapter 5, 16.

12. Hercules Incorporated v. EPA.

13. For an argument over three-hour versus thirty-day averaging see *Inside EPA,* Jan. 17, 1984, 7–8; in 1981–2 the auto industry proposed in H.R. 5252 that measurement of auto emissions be changed from "maximums to "averages," which some argued might well have doubled total emissions. For a related issue, the number of permitted exceedances in the carbon monoxide standard, see *Science News,* May 15, 1982, 327; *Environment Reporter,* May 14, 1982, 15.

14. In the regulation of benzene the EPA proposed that the results of different scientific studies be averaged to determine risk estimates; see *Inside EPA,* Aug. 9, 1985, 7. For controversies over models see Phyllis Austin, "Keeping the Air Clean: In a New Period of Regulatory Accommodation the Emphasis Is on Granting Licenses Quickly," *Maine Times,* Nov. 11, 1983, 2–5; Dave Shearer, "Air Quality in Billings: A Dirty Story Continues." *The Plains Truth,* 16(Dec. 1985): 1–2, 7; L. W. Barnthouse et al., "Population Biology in the Courtroom: The Hudson River Controversy," *Bio-Science* 34(1984): 14–19.

15. *Natural Areas Journal,* Natural Areas Association (Rockford, Ill.); *Lake Line,* newsletter, North American Lake Management Association (Merrifield, Va.); *Nongame Wildlife,* newsletter, Nongame Wildlife Association of North America (Springfield, Ill.)

16. Research reports and histories of individual U.S. Forest Service experiment stations can be obtained from each one. See collection in AF.

17. The *Journal of the Air Pollution Control Association* contains reports of related industry groups such as the Electric Power Research Institute and the Industrial Gas Cleaning Institute. For regular reports of the activities of the former see *EPRI Journal* (Palo Alto, Calif.).

18. See, e.g., *Journal of Forestry* (Society of American Foresters, Washington, D.C.); *North American Journal of Fisheries Management* (American Fisheries Society, Bethesda, Md.); *Journal of Range Management* (Society for Range Management, Denver, Colo.); *Journal of Wildlife Management* (The Wildlife Society, Bethesda, Md.).

19. See activities of the American Industrial Hygiene Association; the American Conference of Governmental and Industrial Hygienists; the National Council on Radiation Protection.

20. See, for example, the decision of Secretary of the Interior Donald Hodel not to identify integral vistas in high-quality environmental areas such as national parks; *National News Report,* Sierra Club, Nov. 15, 1985; or the EPA decision not to enforce the law prohibiting the use of landfills for hazardous waste; "EPA's Standards for Toxic Wastes Termed Deficient," *Wall Street Journal,* Jan. 10, 1986.

21. In public-land matters the American Forestry Association considered itself a "middle ground" organization. "Where does the American Forestry Association stand in all this controversy between user and non-user groups? Right in the middle!" Statement of William E. Towell, executive vice-president, in *American Forests,* Jan. 1972, 23. See also *American Forests,* Mar. 1985, 25–34. Other middle-ground environmental organizations were Resources for the Future, the Conservation Foundation, and the Environmental Law Institute.

22. Middle-ground publications often shaped their articles around forums for debate in which all sides were presented. See, for example, "Point . . . and Counterpoint," a regular feature of *Environmental Forum,* and "At issue" in *American Forests.*

23. By the 1980s the interpretation of recent environmental history had come to be an important element in political debate. Opponents argued that an earlier, somewhat emotional and juvenile, environmental movement had now been forced by cost considerations to become more realistic; the view was accepted by many writers. For one case see James D. Range and James A. Miller, "The Greening – and Graying – of Environmental Politics," *Environmental Forum,* 1(Oct. 1982): 28–9, 37.

24. The problem of "the environment and the economy" came to be a standard way of introducing environmental issues. The Conservation Foundation and Resources for the Future wrote in these terms.

25. One such issue involved the CHESS studies, epidemiological studies in which the EPA sought to establish relationships between sulfur oxide exposures and adverse health effects. See EPA, *Health Consequences of Sulfur Oxides: A Report from CHESS, 1970–1971,* EPA-650/1-74-004 (Research Triangle Park, N.C., 1974). For the debate over the report see Environment Reporter, 1974–6; see also House Subcommittee on the Environment and the Atmosphere, *The Environmental Protection Agency's Research Program with Primary Emphasis on the Community Health and Environmental Survelliance System (CHESS): An Investigative Report,* 94th Cong., 2d sess., 1976); and EPA, *Addendum to "The Health Consequences of Sulfur Oxides: A Report from CHESS, 1970–1971, May 1974,"* EPA-600/1-80-021 (Washington, D.C., 1980).

26. The high levels of proof industry demanded in the acid-rain dispute were reflected in the way federal managers of the National Acid Precipitation Assessment Program identified problems that required research and assessed the results of that research. See National Acid Precipitation Assessment Program, *Annual Report, 1984, to the President and Congress* (Washington, D.C., 1985).

27. Herman Kahn and Ernest Schneider, "Globaloney 2000," *Policy Review,* Spring 1981, 129–47.

28. *Environmental Mediation: An Effective Alternative?* A report of a conference held in Reston, Va., Jan. 11–13, 1978, sponsored by the Center for Environmental Conflict Resolution, the Aspen Institute for Humanistic Studies, and the Sierra Club Foundation.

29. *Environmental Consensus,* newsletter of Resolve, the Center for Environmental Conflict Resolution, later published by the Conservation Foundation and titled, *A Quarterly Newsletter on Environmental Dispute Resolution.* Since many cases of so-called environmental-dispute resolution came to involve controversies among business groups rather than between business and environmentalists, a new phrase arose that was more general in its meaning, "alternative dispute resolution" (ADR). See, for example, "Alternative Dispute Resolution Gaining Prominence as a Way of Solving Environmental Issues, Avoiding Rising Litigation Costs," *Environment Reporter,* Sept. 20, 1985, 908–14.

30. Norman Arnold, "NAEP: Past, Present, and Future," *Environmental Professional,* 1(1979): 3–5; "Environmental Mediation and Conflict Management," *Environmental Professional,* 2(1980), entire issue.

31. Francis X. Murray, ed., *Where We Agree: Report of the National Coal Policy Project,* 2 vols. (Boulder, Colo., 1978).

32. Richard Livermore, Projects Director, *Resolve,* "RARE II Consensus-Building Project in Colorado," *Environmental Consensus,* Dec. 1978, 1–2; materials on the same project from participants in AF; interview with William Shands, the Conservation Foundation, Nov. 8, 1978.

33. The work of the Conservation Foundation can be traced through its annual reports, beginning in 1949. See, for example, the first, *In View of the Future* (New York, 1949).

34. The role of the Conservation Foundation in promoting citizen action can be traced in *CF Letter;* see issues of Jan. 18, 1967; Jan. 31, 1968; Jan. 1970; Apr. 1970; Aug. 1970; July 1971; Apr. 1972; May 1972; Dec. 1972; and Mar. 1973.

35. After March 1973, *CF Letter* ceased to publish information oriented toward citizen action. This seemed to reflect a change in policy that came when the foundation's president, Sydney Howe, was fired early in 1973. Howe had come to the foundation in 1965 as director of conservation activities and had succeeded Russell Train as president in 1967. After an interview with Howe, reporter Philip Shabecoff wrote in the *New York Times,* Oct. 20, 1984: "He sought to make the Conservation Foundation a national service center for the growing environmental movement of the late 1960's. In so doing he incurred the displeasure of the more conservative businessmen on its board of directors, as well as that of some of the staff members who thought he was not moving fast enough."

36. William E. Shands, Perry R. Hagenstein, and Marissa T. Roche, *An Issue Report: National Forest Policy from Conflict toward Consensus* (Washington, D.C., 1979). For documents from the citizen national-forest sector that present a contrasting approach, see Randal O'Toole, *The Citizen's Guide to Forplan* (Eugene, Oreg., 1983), and the magazine, *Forest Planning,* published by Cascade Holistic Economic Consultants (Eugene, Oreg.).

37. H. Jeffrey Leonard, J. Clarence Davies III, and Gordon Binder, *Business and Environment: Toward Common Ground* (Washington, D.C., 1977).

38. William K. Reilly, "After the Environmental Rally," *The Conservation Foundation: A Report for the Year 1977* (Washington, D.C., 1977).

39. Author interpretation from reading state publications from New York, Michigan, Montana, Maine, Tennessee, Delaware, and other states.

40. For the early work of the Montana Environmental Quality Council, see its annual reports, 1972–6, which provide an extensive analysis of the state's environmental problems. For debate over new personnel who changed the council's policy direction and led to suggestions by environmentalists that it be abolished see *Down to Earth,* newsletter of the Montana Environmental Information Center, and news articles in the *Missoulian* (Missoula, Mont.) in AF.

41. Environmental Data Services, *Ends Report* (London).

13. Environmental Politics in the States

1. Elizabeth Haskell, *Managing the Environment: Nine States Look for New Answers* (Washington, D.C., 1971); Robert C. Hoffman and Keith Fletcher, *America's Rivers: An Assessment of State River Conservation Programs* (Washington, D.C., 1984).

2. Calculations of rural-urban voting patterns and party voting patterns in state legislatures are based on voting scores prepared by state citizen-environmental groups (AF).

3. Regional urbanization calculations are based on the U.S. Population Census.

4. Frank Trippett, *The States, United They Fell* (Cleveland, Ohio, 1967).

5. *Jackson Hole News* (Jackson, Wyo.); *Leelanau Enterprise* (Leland, Mich.); *North Woods Call* (Charlevoix, Mich.).

6. Anthony N. D'Elia, *The Adirondack Rebellion* (Loon Lake, N.Y., 1979).

7. U.S. Department of Agriculture, Farmers Home Administration, *A Brief History of FmHA* (Washington, D.C., 1980).

8. *Appalachia,* magazine published by the Appalachian Regional Commission (Charleston, W.Va.); annual reports of the various regional commissions (AF).

9. *Jackson Hole News; Maine Times* (Topsham); *New Hampshire Times* (Concord); *Illinois Times* (Springfield).

10. *Pittsburgh Press,* Nov. 24, 1985, concerning the role of retired people in a community organization that objected to a proposed nuclear-waste incineration facility.

11. Philip Shabecoff, "The Acre-by-Acre Effort to Save the Environment," *New York Times,* Dec. 30, 1984; Alan H. Magazine, *Environmental Management in Local Government* (New York, 1977).

12. National Association of Counties, "Community Action Guide for Air Pollution Control," in Senate Committee on Public Works, Hearings, *Air Pollution, 1967,* 90th Cong., 1st sess., 1363–1434. Local ordinance restricting radioactive emissions in section, "Legal Notices," *News-Citizen,* Vandergrift, Pa., Sept. 6, 1985.

13. *Michigan Environmental Report,* Nov. 4, 1985, 1–4.

14. Statement by Paul McCloskey at the Conservation Foundation Conference on Environmental Law, as reported in *CF Letter,* Sept. 30, 1969.

15. "Community Action Guide," 1267–1377, 1394ff.

16. The division in environmental attitudes in Montana is a case in point. Whereas the more urbanized western part of the state expressed relatively strong environmental interest in both the state legislature and through its congressional representatives, the eastern portion of the state did the opposite. See events in *Down to Earth,* newsletter of the Montana Environmental Information Center, *Montana* magazine, and the *Missoulian* (Missoula, Mont.).

17. *Newsletter,* the Adirondack Council, 2(1978): 1.

18. *Detroit Free Press,* July 29, 1978, editorial.

19. *Nucleonics Week,* Feb. 26, 1970; *Illinois Times,* Sept. 5–11, 1980, 81; *Environmental Science and Technology,* Aug. 1980, 894; *Our Wetlands* (Wisconsin Wetlands Association, Madison), Aug-Sept. 1980; Town of Glocester v. Rhode Island Solid Waste, Supreme Court of Rhode Island, Aug. 9, 1978 (12 ERC 1334); Simpson Timber Co. v. Olympia Air Pollution Control Authority, Washington Supreme Court Apr. 22, 1976 (9 ERC 1619); Tobe F. Arvola, *Regulation of Logging in California, 1945–1975* (Sacramento, Calif., 1976), 62–5; *New York Times,* Dec. 28, 1983; *New Hampshire Times,* Dec. 30, 1981; "States Mount Attack on Local Restrictions," *Pesticides and You,* May 1982, 5.

20. Pennsylvania Office of State Planning and Development, *A Land Use Strategy for Pennsylvania* (Harrisburg, Pa., 1976), 114–20.

21. Haskell, *Managing the Environment;* Richard W. Jones, "Forest Policy in Georgia's Changing Socio-Political Environment" (Ph.D. diss., University of Georgia, 1968); R. Douglas S. MacDonald, "Multiple Use Forestry in Megalopolis: A Case Study of the Evolution of Forest Policies and Programs in Connecticut" (Ph.D. diss., Yale University, 1969).

22. Gerson Fishbein, editor of the *Environmental Health Letter* (Washington, D.C.), expressed this view on numerous occasions; author interview with Prof. Maurice Shapiro, School of Public Health, University of Pittsburgh, Mar. 3, 1981.

23. The changing structure of the Michigan Department of Natural Resources, which reflected these new interests, can be followed in its biennial reports, 1965–78.

24. For a brief but comprehensive account see Denis P. Doyle and Terry W.

Hartle, "A Funny Thing Happened on the Way to New Federalism . . ." *Washington Post National Weekly Edition,* Dec. 2, 1985, 23–4.

25. State activities are drawn from material in Chapter 2, notes 3–21.

26. A variety of reports of state investigations in the health effects of air pollution, for example, in AF, reflect California's vigorous role in environmental science and technology. The state, to cite one case, published the first comprehensive survey of indoor air pollution.

27. "The States, Playing a Crucial Role in Environmental Management, Try a Variety of Innovations in 1970," *CF Letter,* Nov. 1970.

28. See testimony of city officials from East Chicago, Indiana, Steubenville, Ohio, and Marietta, Ohio, concerning the problem in Senate Subcommittee on Air and Water Pollution, Hearings, *Air Pollution – 1968,* 90th Cong., 2d sess.

29. For material on interstate compacts see ibid., part I.

30. James E. Krier and Edmund Ursin, *Pollution and Policy* (Berkeley, Calif., 1977).

31. *Environmental Science and Technology,* May 1970, 4–5; *CF Letter,* Nov. 1969; *Air and Water News,* Oct. 17, 1969; "1970, A Year of Environmental Concern, Ends on a Sobering Note," *CF Letter,* Dec. 1970; Exxon Corporation v City of New York, Jan. 17, 1976 (9 ERC 1670).

32. "Federal-State Clashes Hamper Many Programs," "Noise Control Efforts Stir Up Many Disputes," *CF Letter,* Oct., June 1980; *Wall Street Journal,* Sept. 8, 1981.

33. *Groundswell,* newsletter of the Nuclear Information and Research Service, Sept.-Oct. 1981, 1–3, 5–11.

34. David Lambert, "Line of Fire: Montana's Transmission Corridor Controversy," part 2, *Montana* magazine, Dec. 1981, 31–7.

35. *NRDC Newsline,* Oct.-Nov. 1985, 3–4; *Coastal Zone Management,* Sept. 5, 1985.

36. Environmental Study Conference, *Weekly Bulletin,* and *Environment Reporter,* 1979–80.

37. *Environment Reporter,* 1980–1.

38. Peter N. Swan, "Challenges to Federalism: State Legislation Concerning Marine Oil Pollution," *Ecology Law Quarterly,* 2(1972): 437–70; Lee S. Weinberg, "Askew v. American Waterways Operators, Inc.; The Emerging New Federalism," *Publius, The Journal of Federalism,* 8(Fall 1978): 37–53.

39. For objections from navigation firms see *Waterways Journal* (St. Louis, Mo.).

40. For state action in New Jersey see *Environment Reporter,* 18(Aug. 28, 1981): 543; *Exposure,* 18(May-June 1982): 1.

41. *CF Letter,* Oct. 1980; *U.S. News and World Report,* Sept. 11, 1980.

42. Newspaper clippings, *Missoulian* (AF).

43. *Coastal Zone Management,* 1979–80.

44. The issue can be followed in *Coastal Zone Management;* early in 1979 Senator Stevens of Alaska introduced a bill to go beyond preemption and to increase federal authority vis-à-vis the states. According to *Coastal Zone Management,* May 9, 1985, the bill was aimed at California and the main force behind it was Exxon.

45. David J. Lennett and Linda E. Greer, "State Regulation of Hazardous Wastes," *Ecology Law Quarterly,* 12(1985): 163–89; Sarah E. Redfield, *Report to the Maine Pesticide Board. Pesticide Drift: The State of the Law* (Franklin Pierce Law Center, June 1984); National Academy of Sciences, *On Prevention of Significant Deterioration of Air Quality* (Washington, D.C., 1981).

46. Andrew J. W. Sheffey, *Conservation Commissions in Massachusetts* (Washington, D.C., 1969); Robert G. Healy, *Land Use and the States* (Washington, D.C., 1976); Robert G. Healy, ed., *Protecting the Golden Shore* (Washington, D.C., 1978).

47. The federal Land and Water Conservation Fund was modeled after a 1946 California law that provided financing for state parkland acquisition with the tidelands oil revenues. *CF Letter,* Mar. 15, 1967.

48. Missouri took steps in 1985 to establish a statewide nondegradation standard for groundwater; *Environment Reporter,* Nov. 8, 1985, 1244–7.

49. Peter G. Truitt, *Maryland Air and Water Quality Atlas* (Annapolis: Office of Environmental Programs, 1984); William L. Kahrl, *The California Water Atlas* (Sacramento, 1978).

50. Montana Department of Health and Environmental Sciences, Air Quality Bureau, *Montana Ambient Air Quality Standards Study, Final Environmental Impact Statement,* Feb. 14, 1980 (Helena, Mont.).

51. *Chemical Week,* June 17, 1981, editorial, and 54–8; May 26, 1982, 13–14.

52. *Alert,* newsletter, Washington Environmental Council (Seattle), Nov. 1984, 7.

53. "Noise Control Efforts Stir up Many Disputes," *CF Letter,* June 1980.

14. The Politics of Legislation, Administration, and Litigation

1. George Alderson and Everett Sentman, *How You Can Influence Congress* (New York, 1979); William Ashworth, *Under the Influence: Congress, Lobbies and the American Pork-Barrel System* (New York, 1981).

2. *National Parks* (Washington, D.C., National Park and Conservation Association); *Living Wilderness* (Washington, D.C., Wilderness Society); *Sierra Club Bulletin* (San Francisco, Sierra Club); *Conservation Report* (Washington, D.C., National Wildlife Federation); *CF Letter* (Washington, D.C., Conservation Foundation).

3. *CF Letter,* Sept. 1969; Dec. 1969.

4. For these groups see *National Reporter* (Zero Population Growth, Washington, D.C.); *Environmental Action* (Environmental Action, Washington, D.C.); *EDF Letter* (Environmental Defense Fund, New York, N.Y.); *NRDC Newsletter* (Natural Resources Defense Council, New York, N.Y.).

5. For the League of Women Voters see miscellaneous items concerning its political positions in AF.

6. National Wildlife Federation, *Conservation News* and *Conservation Report.*

7. Such experts include Louise Dunlap (Environmental Policy Center), Richard Morgan (Environmental Action Foundation), Erik Janssen (Friends of the Earth), Tim Mahoney (Sierra Club), Debby Sease (Wilderness Society, Sierra Club), Destry Jarvis (National Parks and Conservation Association), Richard Ayers (Natural Resources Defense Council), Michael Bean (Environmental Defense Fund), and Maureen Hinkle (Environmental Defense Fund, Audubon Society).

8. National Clean Air Coalition, *Legislative Handbook* (Washington, D.C., 1983, 1985); National Coalition for Reproductive Effects, *Newsletter* (Washington, D.C., 1984–).

9. *Radiation Standards and Public Health: Proceedings of a Second Congressional Seminar on Low-Level Ionizing Radiation,* sponsored by the

Congressional Environmental Study Conference, the Environmental Policy Institute, and the Atomic Industrial Forum, Feb. 10, 1978 (Washington, D.C., 1978).

10. The various "Dirty Dozen" campaigns can be followed in *Environmental Action,* magazine of Environmental Action (Washington, D.C.).

11. Annual compilations of congressional votes, in chart form, by the League of Conservation Voters in AF.

12. *Grassroots Sierra,* publication of the Sierra Club; miscellaneous material from Sierra Club Washington seminars to promote grass-roots participation in legislative action.

13. Washington groups with no local chapters, but regular or occasional newsletters or other publications, include the Natural Resources Defense Council, the Environmental Defense Fund, the Environmental Policy Center, and Environmental Action.

14. "Environmental Coalitions: Here to Stay?" *CF Letter,* Oct. 1974; publications of the Greater Yellowstone Coalition, the Clean Air Coalition, the Coalition to Prevent the Misuse of Pesticides, and the National Network to Prevent Birth Defects (AF).

15. Gerald O. Barney, ed., *The Unfinished Agenda* (New York, 1977); *Environmental Agenda for the Future* (Washington, D.C., 1985).

16. The Environmental Policy Institute, for example, took the lead on surface-mining legislation and administration through its Coal Policy Project; the Natural Resources Defense Council did so for air quality through the National Clean Air Coalition.

17. Material from the environmental coalition that worked to secure the National Forest Management Act of 1976 (AF).

18. Material from several dam-fighter conferences (AF).

19. Miscellaneous material concerning the 1978 campaigns (AF).

20. For a classic case see Natural Resources Defense Council, *Tall Stacks – A Decade of Illegal Use; A Decade of Damage Downwind* (Washington, D.C., 1985).

21. Paul J. Culhane, *Public Lands Politics* (Baltimore, Md.: Resources for the Future, 1981), focuses on the "capture and control" theory.

22. For issues pertaining to quality of forage on the public range see Samuel P. Hays, "Public Values and Management Response," in *Developing Strategies for Rangeland Management.* A report prepared by the Committee on Developing Strategies for Rangeland Management of the National Research Council/National Academy of Sciences (Boulder, Colo., 1984), 1811–44.

23. For changes toward a role for the public in the EIS see *CF Letter,* Mar. 1973.

24. The EIS provided for a limited interagency role, confined to comments on another agency's proposed actions, and the Council on Environmental Quality, which supervised the EIS program, refused to become involved in substantive issues between agencies. A notable case of quite a different relationship, in which the EPA took action to check the Tennessee Valley Authority, is described in Robert F. Durant, *When Government Regulates Itself* (Knoxville, Tenn., 1985).

25. The Clean Water Act of 1972 provided that the EPA should encourage public participation, and the most extensive citizen participation in planning came with water quality under section 208 of the act; see Conservation Foundation, *Toward Clean Water: A Guide to Citizen Action* (Washington, D.C., 1976), financed partly by the EPA.

26. The role of planning as an opportunity through which environmentalists became more knowledgeable about forest management can be observed in their critiques of forest plans. See, for example, Robert B. Smythe and John M. Pye, *A Review and Critique of the Proposed Land and Resource Management Plan and the Draft Environmental Impact Statement for the Nantahala and Pisgah National Forest,* submitted on behalf of the Sierra Club, North Carolina Chapter, and the North Carolina Wildlife Federation (Chapel Hill, N.C., 1985).

27. Center for Law and Social Policy and Environmental Policy Institute, *The Strip Mine Handbook* (Washington, D.C., 1978); Sierra Club et al., *A Conservationist's Guide to National Forest Planning* 2d ed. (n.p., 1983); Concern, Inc., *Pesticides: A Community Action Guide* (Washington, D.C., 1985).

28. Nicholas Ashford, "Advisory Committees in OSHA and EPA: Their Use in Regulatory Decision Making" *Science, Technology and Human Values,* 9(Winter 1984): 72–82; the changing composition of the Science Advisory Board, the major such committee in the EPA, can be followed in the pages of *Environment Reporter;* see also " 'Good Science' Gets a Hearing at EPA," *Chemical Week,* Feb. 1, 1984, 23–4. For the grazing advisory boards see Philip O. Foss, *Politics and Grass* (New York, 1960), 99–139; *High Country News,* Jan. 13, 1978, 7.

29. Senate Committee on Government Operations, Subcommittee on Intergovernmental Relations, Hearings, *Advisory Committees,* 3 parts, 91st Cong., 2d Sess., 1970; Hearings, *Advisory Committees,* 3 parts, 92d Cong., 1st sess., 1971.

30. John C. Bryson and Angus Macbeth, "Public Nuisance, the Restatement (Second) of Torts, as Environmental Law," *Ecology Law Quarterly,* 2(1972): 241–82.

31. In the mid-1950s the Sierra Club had tried to gain access to the courts to protect Rainbow Bridge National Monument but was told that it lacked standing; Sierra Club, *National News Report,* Feb. 20, 1970.

32. Alan R. Talbot, *Power along the Hudson: The Storm King Case and the Birth of Environmentalism* (New York, 1972); Ross Sandler, "Settlement on the Hudson," *Amicus Journal,* 2(Spring 1981): 42–5.

33. Malcolm F. Baldwin and James K. Page, Jr., *Law and the Environment* (New York, 1970); *Environmental Law Reporter* (Washington, D.C.); Environmental Law Institute, *The First Decade* (Washington, D.C., 1980); *Environment Reporter – Cases* (Washington, D.C.).

34. James B. MacDonald and John E. Conway, *Environmental Litigation* (Madison, Wis., 1972); Joseph L. Sax, *Defending the Environment* (New York, 1971).

35. Environmental Law Institute, *Citizen Suits: An Analysis of Citizen Environment Actions under EPA-Administered Statutes* (Washington, D.C., 1984); Roger C. Cranston and Barry B. Boyer, "Citizen Suits in the Environmental Field: Peril or Promise?" *Ecology Law Quarterly,* 2(1972): 407–36; Daniel K. Sloan, "The Michigan Environmental Protection Act: Bringing Citizen-Instituted Environmental Suits into the 1980's," *Ecology Law Quarterly,* 12(1985): 271–362.

36. Jethro K. Lieberman, *The Litigious Society* (New York, 1981).

37. Frederick R. Anderson, *NEPA and the Courts* (Baltimore, 1973); Richard a. Liroff, *A National Policy for the Environment: NEPA and Its Aftermath* (Bloomington, Ind., 1976); Lettie M. Wenner, *The Environmental Decade in Court* (Bloomington, Ind., 1982).

38. Citizen Committee v. Volpe, Apr. 16, 1970 (1 ERC 1237); EDF v. Blum, Sept. 27, 1978 (12 ERC 1088).

39. David Schoenbrod, "Why Regulation of Lead Has Failed," in Herbert Needleman, ed., *Low Level Lead Exposure: The Clinical Implications of Current Research* (New York, 1980), 259–66; Herbert L. Needleman and Sergio Piomelli, *The Effects of Low Level Lead Exposure* (New York, 1978); Bud Ward and Jan Floyd, "Washington's Lobbying Groups . . . How They Rate," *Environmental Forum,* Apr. 1985, 9–17.

40. Ross Sandler, "Citizen Suit Litigation," *Environment,* March 1981, 38–9; Ross Sandler, "Equal Time in the Courts," *Amicus Journal,* 3(Winter 1980): 3–4.

41. Mark Hardin, "Conservationists Standing to Challenge the Actions of Federal Agencies," *Ecology Law Quarterly,* 1(1971): 305–29.

42. Arthur B. Ferguson, Jr., and William P. Bryson, "Mineral King: A Case Study in Forest Service Decision Making," *Ecology Law Quarterly,* 2(1972): 493–532; comments of Louis L. Jaffe, Harvard Law School in *CF Letter,* Sept. 30, 1969.

43. Metromedia Inc. v. City of San Diego, California Supreme Court, Mar. 21, 1979 (12 ERC 2089).

44. Anonymous, "Aesthetic Nuisance: An Emerging Cause of Action," *New York University Law Review,* 45(1970): 1075–97.

45. Robert Broughton, "The Proposed Pennsylvania Declaration of Environmental Rights, Analysis of HB 958," *Pennsylvania Bar Association Quarterly,* 41(1970): 421–38; Delano M. Loutz, "An Analysis of Pennsylvania's New Environmental Rights Amendment and the Gettysburg Power Case," *Dickinson Law Review,* 78(1973): 331–64; *CF Letter,* Apr. 1970, 3.

46. Denis Binder, "Taking Versus Reasonable Regulation: A Reappraisal in Light of Regional Planning and Wetlands," *Florida Law Review,* 25(1972): 1–48.

47. Reserve Mining Co. v. EPA, Mar. 14, 1975 (7 ERC 1619) (asbestos fibers in drinking water); Industrial Union Department, AFL-CIO v. Hodgson, Apr. 15, 1974 (4 ELR 10415) (occupational asbestos exposure); EDF v. EPA, Apr. 4, 1975 (7 ERC 1689) (aldrin/dieldrin); EDF v. EPA, Nov. 20, 1975 (9 ERC 1433) (chlordane and heptachlor); Ethyl Corp. v. EPA, Mar. 19, 1976 (8 ERC 1785) and Lead Industries Association, Inc., v. EPA, June 27, 1980 (14 ERC 1906) (lead); Society of the Plastic Industry, Inc., v. OSHA, Jan. 31, 1975 (5 ELR 20157) (vinyl chloride); EDF v. EPA, Nov. 3, 1978 (12 ERC 1353) (polychlorinated biphenyls). See also Harold P. Green, "The Risk-Benefit Calculus in Safety Determination," *George Washington Law Review,* 43(1975): 791–807.

48. EDF v. EPA, Nov. 3, 1978 (12 ERC 1353), fn. 76: "We cannot accept the proposition . . . that the Administrator's findings [are] insufficient because controverted by respectable scientific authority. It [is] enough at this stage that the administrative record contain[s] respectable scientific authority supporting the Administrator."

49. B. Riley McClelland, "The Courts and the Conservation of Natural Beauty," *Western Wildlands,* Spring 1974, 20–6.

50. International Harvester v. Ruckelshaus, Feb. 10, 1973 (4 ERC 2041) (extension of automobile standards); NRDC v. EPA, Apr. 22, 1981 (15 ERC 2057) (diesel exhaust standards); Department of Environmental Resources v. Pennsylvania Power Co., Pennsylvania Supreme Court, Western District, July 3, 1980 (14 ERC 1796) (sulfur dioxide scrubbers); John E. Bonine, "The Evolution of 'Technology-Forcing' in the Clean Air Act," *Environmental Reporter,* 6(July 1975): 1–29.

51. American Textile Manufacturers Institute v. Donovan, June 17, 1981 (11 ELR 20736–20751).

52. Environmental Defense Fund v. Hoffman, Mar. 22, 1976 (9 ERC 1706); Save the Dunes Council v. Alexander, Aug. 21, 1978 (12 ERC 1026); R. Shep Melnick, *Regulation and the Courts: The Case of the Clean Air Act* (Washington, D.C., 1983); Harold Leventhal, "Environmental Decisionmaking and the Role of the Courts," *University of Pennsylvania Law Review,* 122(1974): 509–55.

53. James S. Kumin, "Substantive Review under the National Environmental Policy Act: EDF v. Corps of Engineers," *Ecology Law Quarterly,* 3(1973): 173–208; Lynton B. Caldwell, "NEPA's Unfulfilled Potential," *Environmental Forum,* Jan. 1985, 38, 40–1.

54. David L. Bazelon, "Coping With Technology through the Legal Process," *Cornell Law Review,* 62(1977): 817–32; Bazelon, "Risk and Responsibility," *Science,* July 20, 1979, 277–80.

15. The Reagan Antienvironmental Revolution

1. Jonathan Lash, *A Season of Spoils* (New York, 1984); Joan Claybrook, *Retreat from Safety: Reagan's Attack on America's Health* (New York, 1984).

2. "Reagan Criticizes Clean Air Act, EPA, Announces New Environmental Task Force," *Environment Reporter,* Oct. 17, 1980, 811–12; report of the campaign task force, "Protecting the Environment: A Statement of Principles" (AF).

3. "Seven-Member Team Appointed to Manage Change to Reagan Administration at EPA," *Environment Reporter,* Dec. 12, 1980, 1226; *Wilderness Report,* Dec. 1980; Morris K. Udall, "No Republican Rivers; No Democratic Mountains," *Environmental Forum,* Nov. 1982, 37–8.

4. Heritage Foundation, *Mandate for Leadership* (Washington, D.C., 1981); Blaine Fielding, "The Environmental Interregnum – It's Over," *Environmental Forum,* June 1983, 10–15.

5. Bartle Bull, "Acid Rain from OMB," *Amicus Journal,* 2(Spring 1981): 7–8; James Banks, "Dumping into Surface Waters: The Making and Demise of Toxic Discharge Regulations," in Bruce Piasecki, ed., *Beyond Dumping: New Strategies for Controlling Toxic Contamination* (Westport, Conn., 1984); House Committee on Energy and Commerce, Subcommittee on Oversight and Investigations, *Report on a Case Study on OMB Interference in Agency Rulemaking,* 99th Cong., 1st sess., 1985.

6. " 'Hit List' Is Uncovered at EPA," *Environmental Health Letter,* Mar. 15, 1983, 3; Letter to editor, Janet D. Rowley et al., *Science,* Jan. 20, 1984, 236; Keith Schneider, "Hard Times: Government Scientists Fall Victim to the Administration's Policy to Silence Debate," *Amicus Journal,* 4(Fall 1982): 22–31.

7. *Environmental Health Letter,* Jan.-July 1981; Peter Borelli, "The New Beginning," *Amicus Journal,* 2(Spring 1981), 2–6; Peter Borelli, "Knight of the Business Roundtable," *Amicus Journal,* 3(Summer 1981), 8–9.

8. Environmental Health Letter, Mar. 1, 1985; Ernest O. Ferguson, "Departing Conservation Staff Holds Wake for a Crusade Foundering under Reagan," *Baltimore Sun,* May 5, 1981; Malcolm Baldwin, "The Environment in the Eighties," May 4, 1981, speech (AF); *Outdoor News Bulletin* (Wildlife Management Institute), July 24, Sept. 5, Sept. 18, and Oct. 16, 1981.

9. Morton Rosenberg, *Presidential Control of Agency Rulemaking: An Analysis of Constitutional Issues That May Be Raised by Executive Order 12291* (Report prepared by the Library of Congress for the House Committee on Commerce, 97th Cong., 1st sess., 1981); Erik Olson, "The Quiet Shift of Power: Office of Management and Budget Supervision of Environmental Protection Agency Rulemaking under Executive Order 12291," *Virginia Journal of Natural Resources,* 4(1984): 1–80b; symposium on Executive Order no. 12291 by Edwin H. Seeger, Frances Dubrowski, and Richard D. Morgenstern, *Environmental Forum,* 2(1983): 30–4.

10. Ron Arnold, *At the Eye of the Storm: James Watt and the Environmentalists* (Chicago, 1982); Leilani Watt, *Caught in the Conflict* (Eugene, Oreg., 1984); James Watt, *The Courage of a Conservative* (New York, 1985); statement by Watt, May 7, 1981, at an evening dialogue, "Relation between Environmental Conservation and Economic Development in Recent American History," Woodrow Wilson International Center for Scholars.

11. National Wildlife Federation, *Failed Oversight – a Report on the Failure of the Office of Surface Mining to Enforce the Federal Surface Mining Control and Reclamation Act* (Washington, D.C., 1985); Environmental Law Institute, *Citizen Suits: An Analysis of Citizen Enforcement Actions under EPA-Administered Statutes* (Washington, D.C., 1984).

12. Robert Nelson, *A World of Preference: Business Access to Reagan's Regulators,* Democracy Project Reports, no. 5 (n.p., Oct. 1983); House Committee on Science and Technology, Subcommittee on Investigations and Oversight, Hearing, *Formaldehyde: Review of Scientific Bases of EPA's Carcinogenic Risk Assessment,* 97th Cong., 2d sess., 1983.

13. *CF Letter,* May 1981, Mar. 1982, Feb. 1983; William Drayton, "Can Half Do Twice as Much?" *Amicus Journal,* 3(Winter 1982): 21–4; *Land Letter,* July 1983, Oct. 1983, Feb. 1984, June 1984, July 15, 1984, Oct. 15, 1984, Feb. 15, 1985.

14. *Environmental Health Letter,* Dec. 15, 1981; Bud Ward, "Clean Air Act Amendments . . . Why They Bombed," *Environmental Forum,* 1(Feb. 1983): 14–16; (Mar. 1983): 31–4; (Apr. 1983): 45–9.

15. *Inside EPA,* Aug. 9, 1985; Kenneth B. Noble, "U.S. Agency Threatens to Delay Rules Protecting Textile Workers," *New York Times,* Nov. 5, 1985.

16. Bruce Piasecki, "The Politics of Toxic Wastes," in Piasecki, ed., *Beyond Dumping;* "Compilation of Conversations and Correspondence on the Permanent Regulatory Program Implementing Section 501 (b) of the Surface Mining Control and Reclamation Act of 1977" (AF); "5 House Chairmen Back Suit on Ethylene Oxide," *Occupational Health and Safety Letter,* July 8, 1985, 1–2; "Environmentalists' Suit Seeks Limit to OMB Reg. Review Powers," *Inside EPA,* June 7, 1985, 1; "EDF Charges Justice Is Using EPA as Scapegoat to Curtail Probe of OMB," *Inside EPA,* Aug. 1, 1985, 3.

17. *CF Letter,* Nov. 1981, "Agencies Curtail Access to Data and Decisions"; Peter Ajemian, *Grasping for Information at Reagan's EPA* (Washington, D.C., 1984).

18. Richard L. Stroup and John A. Baden, *Natural Resources: Bureaucratic Myths and Environmental Management* (Cambridge, Mass., 1983).

19. The Wilderness Society, *The Watt Record: The National Park System* (Washington, D.C.), and *Bureau of Land Management Lands* (Washington, D.C., 1983); "Bureau of Livestock and Mining," *Amicus Journal,* 6(Summer 1984): 16–18.

20. LaVarr Webb, "The Sagebrush Rebellion: Coming on Strong," *State Leg-

islatures, 6(1980): 18–21; Luke Popovich, "Privatization: An Idea Whose Time Must Wait," *American Forests,* Sept. 1982, 36–8, 44–5; debate, James Watt and Daniel A. Poole, "Sale of Public Lands: Common Sense or Con Job?" *American Forests,* Apr. 1983, 12–13, 54–8; debate on the issue, Gaylord Nelson and Steve Hanke, *Environmental Forum,* 2(May 1983): 32–3; *Outdoor News Bulletin,* issues of 1980 and 1981; Bil Gilbert and Robert Sullivan, "Inside Interior: An Abrupt Turn" and "Alone in the Wilderness," *Sports Illustrated,* Sept. 26, 1983, 66–78, and Oct. 3, 1983, 96–111.

21. *Land Letter,* Apr. 1980; July 1, 1984; June 15, 1985; Charles H. Callison, "Public Lands Report: Partisan Advice Strictly Preferred," *Amicus Journal,* 7(Fall 1985): 9–11.

22. *Land Letter,* Feb. 1, 1985; Aug. 15, 1985.

23. Thomas J. Barlow et al., "Giving Away the National Forests: An Analysis of U.S. Forest Service Timber Sales Below Cost" (Washington, D.C., 1980); debate over "Below Cost Timber Sales," between Mark Rasmussen and Anthony T. Stout, *American Forests,* Jan. 1985, 10–11, 44, 62, 64.

24. U.S. Fish and Wildlife Service, *Biological Services Program* (fiscal year 1975ff.).

25. *Occupational Health and Safety Letter,* May 8, 1982.

26. Land Letter, Feb. 1, 1985; May 15, 1984; General Accounting Office, *Surface Mining Operations in Two Oklahoma Counties Raise Question about Prime Farmland and Bond Adequacy* (Washington, D.C., Aug. 8, 1985).

27. *Pittsburgh Press,* Dec. 8, 1980, article by Ann McFeatters; Environmental Study Conference, *Weekly Bulletin,* Feb. 23, 1981, C7.

28. Mark Green and Norman Waitzman, *Business War on the Law* (Washington, D.C., 1981).

29. Earon S. Davis and Valerie Wilk, *Toxic Chemicals: The Interface Between Law and Science* (n.p., Farmworkers Justice Fund, 1982); "Examining the Role of Science in the Regulatory Process: A Roundtable Discussion about Science at EPA," *Environment,* 25(June 1983): 6–14, 33–41; *Letter,* Society for Occupational and Environmental Health (Washington, D.C., 1975).

30. Claybrook, *Retreat from Safety,* "Product Safety," 58–70.

31. *Land Letter,* June 1, 1984; Sept. 15, 1985.

32. Council on Environmental Quality, *Environmental Quality,* 1981–4; Conservation Foundation, *State of the Environment, 1982* (Washington, D.C., 1982); Conservation Foundation, *State of the Environment: An Assessment at Mid Decade* (Washington, D.C., 1984).

33. "Profile – OMB's Jim Tozzi," *Environmental Forum,* 1(1982), 11–12.

34. "The New Beginning," *Amicus Journal,* 2(Spring 1981): 2–6; Borelli, "Knight of the Business Roundtable," 8–9; Bartle Bull, "Barbarians at the Gate," *Amicus Journal,* 1(Fall 1981): 10–11.

35. David Hawkins, head of the Clean Air Coalition argued, "There was more interest in the Air Act among groups in the environmental community than at any time in the previous 12 years." See Bud Ward, "Clean Air Act Amendments . . . Why They Bombed," *Environmental Forum,* Apr. 1983, 45–9.

36. League of Conservation Voters, *Election Report, 1984* (Washington, D.C., 1985), covers 1984 races for the U.S. House and Senate.

37. "A Call for Tougher – Not Weaker – Antipollution Laws," *Business Week,* Jan. 24, 1983, 85–6, reported a poll that indicated that 13 percent of Republicans and 10 percent of Democrats claimed membership in at least one environmental group.

38. *Land Letter,* Sept. 1983; William H. MacLeish, *Oil and Water: The Strug-*

gle for Georges Bank (New York, 1985); Peter Borelli and Kirk Scharfenberg, "Senators Stafford and Chaffee; Messrs. Clean," *Amicus Journal,* 2(Spring 1981): 9–12.

39. *Land Letter,* Nov. 1983; June 1, 1984; May 1, 1984; debate, John B. Crowell, Jr., and M. Rupert Cutler, "Roadless Lands in Limbo," *American Forests,* Mar. 1983, 12–13, 60–3; House Subcommittee on Public Lands, *Additions to the National Wilderness Preservation System,* Hearings on USDA RARE II Review and Recommendations, 96th Cong., 1st sess., Feb. 14, Mar. 6, 8, and June 25, 1979, parts I–X; and *Additions to the National Wilderness Preservation System,* 98th Cong., 2d sess., Feb. 1983-Apr. 1984, parts I–XI.

40. "Endangered Species Act Reauthorization Bulletin"; "New Endangered Species Law Takes Effect: Substantial Changes Made in Program," *Land Letter,* Dec. 1982; "Endless Energy or Endless Risk? Clinch River Breeder Reactor," *Amicus Journal,* 2(Summer 1982): 10–12.

41. NRDC v. EPA (17 ERC 1721), 1982; NRDC v. *Gorsuch* (17 ERC 2013), 1982; Gregory S. Wetstone, ed., Meeting Record from Resolution of Scientific Issues and the Judicial Process: Ethyl Corporation v. EPA, Oct. 21, 1977, held under the auspices of the Environmental Law Institute, Washington, D.C., 1981), discussion on 84ff. and especially between Judges Skelly Wright and Harold Leventhal of the D.C. Court of Appeals (AF).

42. H. Richard Heede and Amory B. Lovins, "Hiding the True Costs of Energy Sources," *Wall Street Journal,* Sept. 17, 1985.

43. "Protecting the Environment: A Statement of the Principles" (AF); "Alternative Budget Proposals for the Environment: Fiscal Years 1981–1982," prepared by nine environmental groups, dated Mar. 15, 1981 (AF); "Alternative Budget Proposals for the Environment: Fiscal Year 1983," prepared by eleven environmental groups, Mar. 1, 1982 (AF).

44. Tom Horton, "Relief from Disaster Relief," *Amicus Journal,* 1(Summer 1981): 22–25; Laurance Rockefeller, "Chaffee-Evans: A Bill to Save Islands, Lives and Taxes," *Amicus Journal,* 3(Winter 1982): 31–3; Robert R. Kuehn, "The Coastal Barrier Resources Act and the Expenditures Limitation Approach to Natural Resources Conservation," *Ecological Law Quarterly,* 11(1984): 583–670.

45. *Land Letter,* Mar. 15, 1984.

46. *Acid Precipitation Digest,* Center for Environmental Information, Inc. (Rochester, N.Y.).

47. "Detecting Toxic Microdose Exposures," *Science News,* Nov. 24, 1984, 329; *Environmental Health Letter,* Nov. 1, 1981; Marjorie Sun, "EPA Said to Bar Official from Meeting," *Science,* Nov. 6, 1981, 639; *Inside EPA,* Aug. 9, 1985; *Indoor Air News,* Consumer Federation of America (Washington, D.C.); "Indoor Air: The Problem Looms Large," *CF Letter,* Sept.-Oct. 1985.

48. "Let Them Eat Cake," *Amicus Journal,* 4(Winter 1983): 3; Coordinating Committee on Toxics and Drugs, "A Life Saving Directory: Turning the Tide on Trade in Hazardous Products" (AF).

49. Robert Repetto, "Population Policy after Mexico City," *Journal '85,* World Resources Institute (Washington, D.C., 1985), 5–16.

50. The Global Tomorrow Coalition, *Interaction* (Washington, D.C.); Environmental and Energy Study Institute, *A Congressional Agenda for Improved Resource and Environmental Management in the Third World* (Washington, D.C., 1985); World Wildlife Fund, *World Conservation Strategy* (n.p., 1980); World Resources Institute, *Journal '84, Journal '85* (Washington, D.C., 1984, 1985).

51. *World Environment Report* and *Europe Environment.*

52. Ken Robison, "Sagebrush Rebellion Could Mean 'This Land Was Your Land,' " *Idaho Citizen,* 3(Feb. 1980): 4, 7.

53. "A-76 Dispute Simmers," *Land Letter,* July 1, 1984.

54. *Forest Management* (Eugene, Oreg., 1980–); R. H. Ring, "Taming the Forests," *Arizona Star,* Feb. 5 to Feb. 12, 1984; Sierra Club, *National News Report,* May 14, 1985, 7; *Land Letter,* Feb. 1, 1985; Aug. 15, 1985.

55. Devra Lee Davis, "Lead: Ancient Metal, New Concerns," *Environmental Forum,* 1(May 1982): 24–6, 35; "Phasing Down Lead in Gasoline," *Amicus Journal,* 6(Summer 1984): 2–3; "Phasing Down Lead in Gasoline," *EPA Journal,* 11(May 1985): 2–18.

56. "Maverick EPA Official Criticizes Agency's Land Disposal Regs. as Unworkable," *Environmental Health Letter,* Dec. 1, 1982, 3–4; "The Case of Hugh Kaufman – Cutting on the Bias," *Environmental Health Letter,* Dec. 15, 1982, 3; Keith Schneider, "Hard Times," 26–7; Bruce Piasecki, "The Politics of Toxic Wastes: Why OMB Weakens EPA Programs," in Piasecki, ed., *Beyond Dumping,* 53–6.

57. Daniel A. Mazmanian and Jeanne Nienaber, *Can Organizations Change?* (Washington, D.C., 1979).

58. Andrea Cailo, "Federal Pre-emption of State Law Is Alive and All Too Well," *State Legislatures,* 8(1982): 15–18, 29; Judy Jeffner, "New Federalism Seedlings Sprouts Pre-emption Thorns," *State Legislatures,* 10(1984): 21–6.

59. Environmental Study Conference, *Weekly Bulletin,* 1981 and 1982, Kenneth W. Weinstein, "Amending FIFRA – an Industry View,"*Environmental Law Reporter,* May 1985, 10130–1; statement by David Morris before National Association of Counties, County Energy Action Conference, *Energy Information and Energy Planning Report,* vol. 1, May 25, 1981, 1, 5.

60. "Workers' Right-to-Know Moves into Town," *Chemical Week,* May 26, 1982, 13–14; "Right-to-Know Debate May Delay Energy and Commerce Superfund Action," *Inside EPA,* July 12, 1985, 4–50; "Congress to Face Product Liability Bill in 1985," *Congressional Quarterly,* Dec. 8, 1984, 3067–71.

61. Debate, Robert A. Jantzen and Robert L. Herbst, "Federal Fisheries Management: Headed Upstream or Out to Sea," *American Forests,* July 1983, 12–13, 53–4, 58–9.

62. *State Legislatures,* Apr. 1980, 22–4; July-Aug. 1980, 13–19; Oct. 1980, 16–21; Nov.-Dec. 1980, 2–8; Apr. 1981, 6–11; May 1982, 15–19; Nov.-Dec. 1982, 21–7; Stephen W. Sawyer and John R. Armstrong, eds., *State Energy Policy* (Boulder, Colo., 1985).

63. Clippings, *New York Times, Wall Street Journal, Washington Post, Newsweek, Time* (AF); LaVarr Webb, "Half of Utahns Say Watt Should Go," *Deseret News,* Oct. 7, 1983.

64. Editorial, "Enter 'Ruck,' " *Amicus Journal,* 4(Spring 1983): 2–3.

65. *Land Letter,* Dec. 1983.

66. Richard N. L. Andrews, "Deregulation: The Failure at EPA," in Norman Vig and Michael Draft, eds., *Environmental Policy in the 1980's* (Washington, D.C., 1984).

67. Kristine L. Hall, "Keeping the EPA Vigilant: The Role of Private Watchdog Agencies," in Bruce Piasecki, ed., *Beyond Dumping,* 27–35; *Environmental Health Letter, Occupational Health and Safety Letter.*

68. " 'Good Science' Gets a Hearing at EPA," *Chemical Week,* Feb. 1, 1984, 23–4; *Environmental Health Letter.*

69. *Land Letter,* Sept. 1983; Sept. 15, 1984; Oct. 1, 1984; Consumer Federation of America, *Indoor Air News* (Washington, D.C.); *Land Letter,* May 1983, Apr. 15, 1984.

70. "Internal EPA Report Says Press Turns Chemical Incidents into 'Crises,' " *Inside EPA,* Jan. 13, 1984, 1, 12–14.

71. Dieter Mahlein, "Take Another Walk on the Wild Side," *Forest Planning,* 4(July 1985): 11–14; "House Scrutinizes BLM Wilderness Review Process," *Land Letter,* July 1, 1984; letter to editor, Joyce M. Kelley, former BLM national wilderness coordinator, *Idaho Statesman,* Sept. 24, 1985; Ray Wheeler, "Last Stand for the Colorado Plateau," *High Country News,* Oct. 14, Oct. 28, 1985.

72. William Drayton, *America's Toxic Protection Gap* (Washington, D.C., Environmental Safety, 1984); Sierra Club, "Superfund or Superstall? The EPA and Toxic Waste Cleanup" (San Francisco, June 1985).

73. Environmental Law Institute, *Citizen Suits.*

74. *Environmental Health Letter* and *Occupational Health and Safety Letter.*

16. Environmental Society and Environmental Politics

1. Adam Smith, *The Wealth of Nations* (New York, 1937), p. 625.

Index